Communalism from Indian Perspective

By the Same Author

- Communalism and Constitution*
- Disintegration and Constitution*
- Panchayti Raj and Views of the Founding Fathers*
- Governor's Role in Indian Constitution*
- The Scheduled Castes in India (four volumes)
- Educational Development of Scheduled Castes: Looking Ahead
- North-East India: Dispersion and Discontent (two volumes)
- SCs, STs and OBCs in the Indian Polity

(* in the penname of Anirban Kashyap)

About the Author

For more than two and a half decades, **Sarajit Kumar Chatterjee**, a former member of the Indian Police Service, has been consistently engaged in in-depth studies of policies that continue to have an impact on all Indians. His earlier books include *Communalism and Constitution, Disintegration and Constitution, Panchayti Raj and Views of the Founding Fathers, Governor's Role in Indian Constitution, The Scheduled Castes in India, Educational Development of Scheduled Castes: Looking Ahead, North-East India: Dispersion and Discontent* and *SCs, STs and OBCs in the Indian Polity.*

COMMUNALISM FROM INDIAN PERSPECTIVE

Sarajit Kumar Chatterjee

CONCEPT PUBLISHING COMPANY PVT. LTD.
NEW DELHI-110059

ISBN-13: 978-93-5125-199-6

First Published 2016

Published and Printed by:

Since 1974

Concept Publishing Company Pvt. Ltd.
A/15-16, Commercial Block, Mohan Garden,
New Delhi-110059 (INDIA)
Phones : 25351460, 25351794, *Fax* : 091-11-25357109
E-mail : publishing@conceptpub.com
Website: www.conceptpub.com

Editorial Office: H-13, Bali Nagar, New Delhi-110 015, India.

Cataloging in Publication Data—DK Courtesy: D.K. Agencies (P) Ltd. <docinfo@dkagencies.com>

Chatterjee, S. K. (Sarajit Kumar), author.
Communalism from Indian perspective / Sarajit Kumar Chatterjee.
pages cm
Includes bibliographical references and index.
ISBN 9789351251996

1. Communalism—India. 2. Communalism—Religious aspects. I. Title.

DS422.C64C43 2016 DDC 302.140954 23

The book is
dedicated to
Ranajit Kumar Chatterjee
my younger brother

Preface

Communalism and communal cleavage became part of the Indian life since the advent of foreign rule in the mediaeval period. This cleavage was nurtured by the British rulers as a policy in furtherance of prolongation of its rule in India. They projected themselves as the true protector of religious minorities and in all their plans and programmes in the administrative, economic, educational, cultural and political fields they assiduously followed this policy so much so that, they took it to the level of an art. After the partition of the country into three parts on the basis of religion, it was the general hope and belief that with no foreign power to use the communal cleavages, the truncated India will at least be not subject to communal politics any more. But that did not happen. Why the religious divisions continued to torment the country even after independence is a million dollar question. The ghost of communal politics still hunts the Indians. The polity is so much embroiled in communal conflicts that an India devoid of communal cleavages and communal politics has become a distant dream. Communalism has grown like a cancer which is spreading its tentacles in every nook and corner of the country.

Deliberations and discussions at various forums and at different levels are going on to diagnose the nature, character and contour of the problem. Some scholars describe communal violence as the direct result of mounting religious tension, some state that it is caused mostly by political and economic factors, and some claim it results from a confluence of factors—ideological, religious, political and material.

A comprehensive review of the literature on communalism by Surya Prakash Upadhyaya and Rowena Robinson in Volume XLVII, No. 36 of September 8, 2012 issue of the *Economic and Political Weekly* indicates that communalism is an outcome of the competitive aspirations of domination and counter-domination that began in colonial times. Cynical distortions of the democratic process and the politicisation of religion in the early decades of independence intensified it. In recent years, economic liberalisation, the growth of opportunities and a multiplying middle class have further aggravated it. More alarmingly, since the 1980s, Hindu communalism has morphed into fundamentalism, with the *Sangh parivar* and its cultural politics of *Hindutva* playing ominous roles. The object of this book is to look at the problem from an altogether different angle—the constitutional angle.

Though the word "secular" was added to the Preamble of the Constitution by the Constitution (forty-second) Amendment Act, which became effective from January 3, 1977, the Framers of the Constitution always thought that they were framing a 'secular' Constitution. Though their interpretation of the term 'secular' differed, but they always harped on the secular nature of the Constitution. But what we see in the field? Unfortunately, even after the partition of the country on the basis of religion and putting into place a secular Constitution, we are confronted with the problem of communalism. As a matter of fact the communal forces have gained in stature and strength with the passage of time during the last 68 years of independence.

Molestation or inter-community love affairs had caused social tension in the areas leading to conflagrations in a big way. Even seemingly trivial incidents are leading to communal riots. Playing loud music during a religious procession, a petty quarrel in a roadside eatery, or even dumping of garbage had led to incidents of violence—looting, arson and killing—between two communities. In an article titled "Hindu-Muslim Tension: Cause and Cure" published in *Young India* in June 1924, Mahatma Gandhi wrote that cow slaughter and music outside a mosque were two of the several reasons behind communal tension. That both these issues raise temperatures even today only emphasizes the fact that nothing has changed in the last 90 years. Moreover, communal riots which were essentially an urban phenomenon have now spread to rural areas. There is a tendency to polarisation on communal lines. Political parties bring that frenzy to the fore as and when they find it advantageous—during elections or on other occasions. The same type of madness that one saw ahead of Partition continues to simmer just below the surface. Communalism is gaining legitimacy. More and more people are turning fanatical. There are even allegations that the police and other security forces have not been able to remain free from contamination. But why this happened?

The object of this study is to draw attention to the presence or absence of certain provisions in the Constitution which directly or indirectly have contributed to the growth and sustenance of communalism in free India. The Constituent Assembly debated extensively on these provisions before accepting or rejecting them. As the readers have a right to know what were the exact views of the Framers of the Constitution on these crucial issues I thought it proper to place the unedited versions by quoting them *in extenso*. The judicial pronouncements of the High Courts and the Supreme Court interpreting the different provisions of the Constitution, the findings and recommendations of different Commissions and Committees, the various news items on these issues and the published materials have been drawn upon extensively to enrich the discussions on these topics. The communal profile in pre-independence and post-independence periods, discussed in details, may help in understanding the problem in its true perspective.

My son Arijit went through the draft and offered his critical comments and suggestions. I am immensely benefited by them. This book would not have seen the light of the day, but for his encouragement, tenacity and help.

I am indebted to all those academicians, writers and columnists whose views and observations I have drawn upon liberally in this book.

I am grateful to Shri Ashok Kumar Mittal of Concept Publishing Company Pvt. Ltd., New Delhi, for bringing out this book within a very short time.

Sarajit Kumar Chatterjee

Contents

1
Introduction

I

India boasts of framing the bulkiest written Constitution of any sovereign country in the world. Though the word "secular" was formally incorporated in the Preamble of the Constitution only in 1976, the secular intention of the Framers is embodied in many of its articles. Yet, India is a happy hunting ground of communal forces. Its political parties never miss any opportunity to blame one another for giving a fillip to these forces. In the years before independence, India had witnessed the worst manifestation of communalism in the vivisection of the country on the basis of religion. In those days, a common assumption was that in free truncated India communalism would not have a hey-day. But it did not happen. Communalism has become the proverbial Gordian Knot belying any solution.

Several theories have been put forward to explain communalism in post-independence India. Some have argued that the long history of communal hatred and animosity between Hindus and Muslims – the two major religious groups in India – has continued unabated and the partition of the country has not been able to contain this antagonism and hostility.[1] Some are of the opinion that slow economic growth, scarce opportunities and rising unemployment in independent India have contributed to the spread of communalism. From this perspective, economic disparity and lack of educational development of the Muslims are the main culprits.[2] Some others have identified exogenous forces such as remittances and the inflow of "Arab money" as key stimuli for constructing mosques and madrasahs, hardening of religious beliefs, and financing of terrorism.[3] Finally, many are of the belief that widespread politicisation of religion in India has intensified communalism in independent India. Political mobilisation on religious lines and relying on "vote-banks" to win elections are the primary bases on which communalism has grown in independent India. Perhaps, this is the most common cause of communalism identified by common people, journalists, as well as scholars.[4]

All of these explanations might be true but they also gloss over the most significant inflection point in the history of independent India: the framing of the Constitution of India, the nation's imprint. In this book, I argue that the presence or absence of certain provisions in the Constitution, the mother of all laws, can help us understand why communalism thrives in independent India. After years of slavery and subjugation, both indigenous and foreign, the people of India for the first time had got the right to frame the Constitution for themselves. The Framers had the experience of knowing very intimately the different factors which were responsible for the growth and perpetuation of communalism in India. Moreover, they got about two and a half years to have a feel of the events in free India as well, to supplement their personal and political experience. The Framers of the Constitution were playing a historic role because in their hands lay the destiny of future India. The role played by them in that great and historic task of nation building has got to be put through searching scrutiny because it is ascribed in many quarters that failure to contain the communal forces in independent India is due to lacunae in some of the constitutional provisions. In this day and age of 24/7 news reporting of immediate causes, we must occasionally take a long view and look at the causes of causes.

It is very difficult to give a precise definition of communalism. Communalism is derived from the word "community". "Communalism", Anirban Kasyap notes, "broadly speaking, is the manifestation of that philosophy which stands for the promotion of the interests of a particular community based on religion, race, caste or language. It is, perhaps, one of those virtues or vices, whatever it is called, which is prevalent in society since the early days of civilization. No human being can live in seclusion. He has to live in community. The community is his identity, his prop, his means of sustenance. It is quite natural that he is also drawn to his community which gives him his identity, his character, his mode and manner of living, his outlook and so on. His affinity towards his own community is an inherent weakness. This cannot be avoided. But when this attachment assumes bigotry, when he becomes obsessed with matters pertaining to his own community only, he is said to be communal in approach. He cannot see anything beyond his own community. Rightly or wrongly the interests of his own community are uppermost in his mind and the activities of other communities are always looked upon with suspicion as if their activities are directed against the interests of his own community. Due to such approach and way of thinking, not only the persons belonging to other communities suffer but people belonging to his own community also suffer in the process. Imaginary and illusive grievances are put forward, unreasonable demands are projected, an artificial barrier is raised and an inferiority psyche is foisted. Communalism sets in. It becomes a means of exploitation, of furthering one's own objectives, of capturing power—political, religious, social or otherwise, of perpetuating obscurantism and of projecting one's own image."[5]

Initially the colonial rulers, and later, nationalist leaders, used the term 'communalism' in the pejorative sense of sectarian strife in the political sphere.[6] In European vocabulary, communalism meant something quite different: it would refer, in the dictionary sense of the term, to the theory of government by local autonomy. As late as 1938, the *Concise Oxford Dictionary of Current English* ignored the peculiar Indian sense of the term: it defined 'communal' "as 'of a commune; of the Paris Commune; of the commonalty, of or for the community; for the common use (esp. c. kitchens in the great war)'". During the Second World War, the dictionary dropped the reference to communal kitchens in the First World War, but added to the rest an interesting new clause: "(India) of the antagonistic religious and racial communities in a district (voting, elections, disturbances, etc)".[7]

Communalism in any form and colour assumes notoriety. It thrives whenever there is a difference between community and community over religion, culture, language, race, caste, or region. Of all of them, communalism which is sustained due to difference over religion is most powerful. The religious communalism is the most dominant amongst all other forms of communalism. Religious communalism in one form or the other is present everywhere because the division on religious basis is more pronounced, the hold and impact of religion on one's life is astounding and people can easily be mustered and swayed in the name of religion. It is even said that religious communalism is synonymous with communalism. Bipan Chandra notes: "Simply put, communalism is the belief that because a group of people follow a particular religion they have, as a result, common social, political and economic interests".[8] It is the religion round which communalism is riveted. In popular parlance, whenever communalism is talked about, it is the religious communalism which is hinted at. And in the Indian context communalism has become synonymous with Hindu-Muslim communalism, though the end of the last century widened its boundary to include all religions, castes, races and even regions. It is essentially the Hindu-Muslim relationship that forms the core of the debate on communalism in India.

Who are the Hindus and the Muslims? How to define them? The Hindu community is rather difficult to define given the diverse natures of belief and worship. The historical and etymological genesis of the word 'Hindu' has given rise to a controversy amongst indologists; but the view generally accepted by scholars appears to be that the word "Hindu" is derived from the river Sindhu otherwise known as Indus which flows through the Punjab. That part of the great Aryan race which immigrated from Central Asia, through the mountain passes into India, settled first in the areas near the river Sindhu (now called the Indus). The Persian pronounced this word Hindu and named their Aryan brothers Hindus.

The *Encyclopaedia of Religion and Ethics*, Vol. VI, at page 686 has described 'Hinduism' as the title applied to that form of religion which prevails among the vast majority of the present population of the Indian Empire. As Dr. Radhakrishan has observed: "The Hindu civilization is so called, since its original founders or earliest followers occupied the territory drained by the Sindhu (the Indus) river system corresponding to the North-West Frontier Province and the Punjab. This is recorded in the *Rig Veda*, the oldest of the *Vedas*, the Hindu scriptures which give their name to this period of the Indian history. The people on the Indian side of the Sindhu were called Hindu by the Persian and the later Western invaders."[9] That is the genesis of the word 'Hindu'.

When we think of the Hindu religion, we find it difficult, if not impossible, to define Hindu religion or even adequately describe it. Unlike other religions in the world, the Hindu religion does not claim anyone prophet; it does not worship anyone God; it does not subscribe to anyone dogma; it does not believe in anyone philosophic concept; it does not follow anyone set of religious rites or performances; in fact, it does not appear to satisfy the narrow traditional features of any religion or creed. It may broadly be described as a way of life and nothing more.

Confronted by this difficulty, Dr. Radhakrishnan realized that "to many Hinduism seems to be a name without any content. Is it a museum of beliefs, a medley of rites, or a mere map, a geographical expression?"[10] Having posed these questions which disturbed foreigners when they think of Hinduism, Dr. Radhakrishnan has explained how Hinduism has steadily absorbed the customs and ideas of peoples with whom it has come into contact and has thus been able to maintain its supremacy and its youth. The term 'Hindu', according to Dr. Radhakrishnan, had originally a territorial and not a credal significance. It implied residence in a well defined geographical area. Aboriginal tribes, savage and half-civilized people, the cultured Dravidians and the Vedic Aryans were all Hindus as they were the sons of the same mother. The Hindu thinker reckoned with the striking fact that the men and women dwelling in India belonged to different communities, worshipped different gods, and practiced different rites.[11]

Monier Williams has observed that "the Hindu religion is a reflection of the composite character of the Hindus, who are not one people but many. It is based on the idea of universal receptivity. It has ever aimed at accommodating itself to circumstances, and has carried on the process of adaptation through more than three thousand years. It has first borne with and then, so to speak, swallowed, digested, and assimilated something from all creeds.[12] Unlike other religions and religious creeds, Hindu religion is not tied to any definite set of philosophic concepts as such.

Though philosophic concepts and principles evolved by different Hindu thinkers and philosophers varied in many ways and even appeared to conflict with each other in some particulars, they all had reverence for the past and accepted the *Vedas* as sole foundation of the Hindu philosophy. It was realized by Hindu religion from the very beginning of its career that truth was many-sided and different views contained different aspects of truth which no one could fully express. This knowledge inevitably bred a spirit of tolerance and willingness to understand and appreciate the opponent's point of view. That is how "the several views set forth in India are considered to be the branches of the self-same tree. The short cuts and blind alleys are somehow reconciled with the main road of advance to the truth".[13] When we consider this broad sweep of the Hindu philosophic concepts, it would be realized that under Hindu philosophy, there is no scope for ex-communicating any notion or principle as heretical and rejecting it as such.

The development of Hindu religion and philosophy shows that from time to time saints and religious reformers attempted to remove from the Hindu thought and practices elements of corruption and superstition and that led to the formation of different sects. If we study the teachings of these saints and religious reformers, we would notice an amount of divergence in their respective views; but underneath that divergence, there is a kind of subtle indescribable unity which keeps them within the sweep of the broad and progressive Hindu religion.

The notion of a Hindu community evolves from a geographic and ethnic description gradually giving way to religious association. The crystallization of this perception occurs when erstwhile Vaishnavas, Shaivas, Lingayats and others begin to refer to themselves as Hindus, rather than by their earlier separate labels—which in most cases is a late occurrence. Hinduism in its various ramifications was derived from a common stock. As the great scholar Dr. Suniti Kumar Chatterji says, "it is not at all a single religion with a creed to which everybody must subscribe. It is rather a federation of different kinds of approach to the Reality that is behind life. That is the unique character of Hinduism".[14] Hindu is an equivocal term, something used with reference to adherents of more or less "orthodox" Vedic and Brahmanical communions and at other times used to embrace the full array of "heterodox" sects. Hindu religion is a conglomeration of different sects and religious denominations whose mode and manner of worship, ways of living and of thinking and even food habits differ. It is all-inclusive; one can be a believer and a Hindu or a non-believer and a Hindu. The uniqueness of Hinduism is that it transcends the cultural and generational time barrier.

After citing the relevant Rulings of the Court, Marc Galanter says:

> the legal definition of Hinduism, developed for the purpose of applying appropriate personal law, was neither a measure of religious belief nor a description of social behaviour as much as a civil status

> describing everyone subjected to the application of "Hindu law" in the areas reserved for personal law. Heterodox practice, lack of belief, active support of non-Hindu religious groups, expulsion by a group within Hinduism—none of these removed one from the Hindu category, which included all who did not openly renounce it or explicitly accept a hostile religion. The individual could venture as far as he wished over any doctrinal or behavioural borders; the gates would not shut behind him if he did not explicitly adhere to another communion. The same negative definition remains today for purposes of application of personal law. In the post-constitutional cases involving preferences the same latitudinarian conception of Hinduism has been carried over from the area of personal law... To "profess" Hinduism merely means to be a Hindu by birth or conversion. Unorthodox practice or lack of personal belief in its tenets does not mean lack of profession for this purpose—one may eat beef and deny the authority of the *Vedas*. In effect the test seems to amount to a willingness to refrain from calling oneself something else.[15]

In one word, a modern Hindu of the twenty first century has travelled a long way from the strict orthodox Hinduism of the sixteenth century.

By contrast, the definition of the Muslim community extends to all those who claim adherence to Islam and the adherence is said to be demonstrated by a clearly stated belief and form of worship. A practising Muslim believes in "salutation, submission, sacrifice". The other obligatory ordinances of Islam are known as the Five Pillars of Islam:

(1) *Shahda*, or Confession of faith. There is no God, but God, and Mohammed is the Prophet of God.
(2) *Salat*, or prayers offered five times daily.
(3) Alms-giving, or *Zakat.*
(4) Fasting during *Ramadan,* the ninth lunar month, dedicated to month-long daytime fasting and observing *eid al-fitr* (lesser 'id: festival celebrating the end of *Ramadan).*
(5) *Haji*, or the pilgrimage to Mecca*, eid al-adha* (greater 'id: celebration and animal sacrifice to mark the end of the pilgrimage).

One may add other optional festivals.

Professor Hossainur Rahman observes: "Religion is like oxygen to a Mussalman. He needs it all the time. The glorification of Allah is a continuous process and essentially beyond question. So, Islam is a faith that lives by the unity of the God-head, the efficacy of his Prophet, the sovereignty of His law, the certainty of His will and the finality of His Power. Therefore, a Mussalman is he who gathers all the resources of religion to confirm and affirm the strict monotheism."[16] Islam, like Christianity, allows or even encourages conversion to its own faith while discouraging and opposing conversion of its own members to other faiths. The apostate is regarded as more reprehensible than the infidel in many countries till this day.

Generally, it is held that adherence to some minimum of beliefs (the unity of God, the mission of Mohammed as His Prophet, and the authority of the *Quran*) is necessary and sufficient to make one a Muslim. Repudiation of these beliefs, even without conversion to another religion, makes one not a Muslim.[17]

Of the major immigrant religions, Islam was the last to arrive in India. The ethnic mix and sectarian diversity of the population reflected the early immigration of self-contained groups. The Jews, who had come to Cochin as early as the first century of the Christian era, were found by Ibn Battuta to have their own chief at Quilon. The Syrian Christians followed. They traced their origin to Saint Thomas who was said to have been martyred and buried at San Thome. His sepulcher was held in "devout estimation, both of the Moors, Gentiles, Christians, each pretending the right of his own Religion to the Church, where this Saint lieth interred". We are informed by Samuel Purchas that a Moor had the keeping of the church where a light was kept continually burning. The sixteenth century Portuguese traveller Tome Pires noted 15,000 Christians of Saint Thomas in Malabar and distinguished these early Christians, who were 'privileged' and were allowed to touch the Nayar, from "those who are now being converted everyday, and who are numerous". One other group, "who were made free denizens by the *Indians* before the *Moors* were Masters", was the fire-worshipping sect of the Parsees. They were mentioned by Fryer as having escaped in boats from the Muslim conquerors of Iran. Entertained and allowed to live among the Hindus on the condition that they were not to kill cows, they conformed to 'many of the Gentue Ceremonies' and enjoyed the same rights.[18]

In the early age of Islam, Indians were known as Hindus in both Arab (Arabic-speaking lands) and Ajam (non-Arabic lands of Islam), the term being derived from Sapta Sindhu (the seven Indus rivers) *via* the Iranian equivalent Hapta Hindu. The warriors of Ajam, belonging to both Iran (Iranian-speaking lands) and Turan (Turkic-speaking lands), knew of Hindustan (yet another Iranian term) as a land of infidel Hindus. The Turks of Khurasan (situated at the junction of Iran and Turan), having risen to military and political prominence in both Iran and Turan, extended their hold over Hindustan in the thirteenth century. The people of Hindustan, whom they called Hindus, knew them as Turashkas, Turaks, Turks. The Turkish conquerors themselves, however, preferred the term Muslim, instead of Turk, in their chronicles. Meanwhile, a similar transition from an ethnic to a religious category began to take place in their use of the term Hindu. Originally, this meant, to the incoming 'Muslims' the indigenous Indian people over whom they had imposed their domination. Such Hindus might also include Indians of the Buddhist faith. Hindus were Indians irrespective of their religious affiliation. However, through gradual shift, the confrontations between the warriors of the two lands, Khurasan and Hindustan, transmuted within Hindustan into a religious contradistinction between the Muslims and the Hindus. Whether of Brahmanical or Buddhist persuasion, the Hindus were all infidels in the eyes of the Muslim. Gradually, a community of Indian-born Muslims sprang up in the town of northern India, mainly through conversion. They could not be called Hindus, though they were Indians, for the term Hindu was used in opposition to Muslim. Therefore, a new term was invented to describe Indians, as distinct from foreigners. This was 'Hindi', or alternately, 'Hindustani'. A 'Hindi' then meant an Indian, a native of Hind. At that stage the term Hindu, by the implied exclusion of the Indian-born Muslim, became a religious category, indicating a particular community of faith.[19]

It is evident from the Sanskrit inscription dated 1328 AD that the natives of India at this time referred to the invaders who had displaced the indigenous dynasty as Mlechchhas and Turashkas. The equation of Hindu with native, and of Muslim with newcomers, is implicit in the early Muslim literature in Arabic and Persian. Only gradually the distinction between native and alien shifted to the recognition of two separate religious communities living in India. Although the Muslim geographers of the Arab world had, so to speak, 'created' the Hindus by identifying them as the ethnic population of India as early as the ninth century, it was only from around the last quarter of the fourteenth century, to judge by the evidence of the Hindi literature of the period, that the Hindus began, for the first time, to refer to themselves as 'Hindu'. Hitherto lacking a name the Hindus at long last denominate themselves by adopting the name given to them by the Muslims.[20] The non-Muslim writers adopted the designation Hindu which began to figure in Andhra inscriptions from 1352 AD onward, in the title Sultan assumed by several kings of the Vijayanagara empire. This is the earliest dated usage of the term Hindu in any Indian language source.[21] Without the Muslims, there would be no 'Hindus'; at any rate not ones who would have come to profess themselves as such. The formation of a Muslim community imparted, therefore, a new shape and denomination to the Hindu social structure.[22]

The arrival of Islam in India—a process which may be reckoned to stretch from the first Arab settlement on the west coast in the time of Hajjaj bin Yusuf (c. 661-714) to the campaigns of Malik Kafur to the far south (1310-11)—coincided with the emergence of what the Muslims called Hinduism. What the Muslims came to define as the Hindu religion, and which its own adherents knew as the nameless, eternal law (*Sanatana Dharma*), was but the third and last phase of a proto-historic cult. The cult evolved from Vedic to Brahmanical, and from Brahmanical to Hindu. A millennium (1500-500 BC) elapsed before the original Vedic cult of the sacrificial fire evolved into the orthodox Brahmanical rituals against which the Buddha organized his sect (*Sangha)* in protest. It took another millennium and a half for this Brahmanical orthodoxy to assume, through the missions of Shankara (c. 788-820) and Ramanuja (eleventh century), the shape of religion which Al Biruni (1030) defined as Hindu. The *Sanatana Dharma* gradually assuming the new form of Hinduism was again remoulded as the religion of the *sants* by interaction with Islam. Only then did it assume the contours which the enlightened Parsi author of *Dabistan-i-Mazahib* found in the seventeenth century, and which the well-known orientalist H.H. Wilson delineated at the beginning of the nineteenth century.[23]

II

Hindu-Muslim Détente

The encounter between the two world civilizations—Brahmanical and Islamic— differed from one part of the subcontinent to the other, depending on the manner in which Islam came to India. In particular, the way in which Islam interacted with Hindu society at the tip of the subcontinent on both sides of the peninsula, that is to say, Malabar and the Coromandel coasts, differed radically from the encounter that occurred on the Indo-Gangetic plains and the Deccan plateau. This was so because Islam came to India entirely by two different modes: by sea and by land; in the former instance, on the basis of quiet, peaceful settlement on the coastal stretches of the deep south facing the Arabian Sea and the Bay of Bengal; and in the latter instance, by sudden, purposeful expansion in Hindustan and the Deccan. In consequence, the Mappila Muslims of Malabar and the Marakkaiyar Muslims of Coromandel were peacefully absorbed into the Indian social system in much the same way as the Jews and Syrian Christians had been accommodated earlier in Kerala, and the Parsis in Gujarat. However, in Hindustan, Bengal, and the Deccan by contrast, the system of self-contained communities, unable to accommodate the power and influence of the Sultans and Sufis in quite the same manner, experienced violent disjuncture.[24]

The Mappilas were placed, along with the Syrian Christians and Jews, below the Nambudri Brahmans and Nayars, and well above the 'untouchable' groups. On the opposite side of the peninsula, Tamil-speaking Muslim traders and ship-owners claiming Arab descent won recognition as the Maraikkayar caste, the rest of the Muslim population—native fishermen, pearl divers, weavers, artisans, petty traders, leather-sellers, and other occupational groups engaged in 'polluting' activities—formed the lower-ranking Labbai caste.[25] The Mappilas and Maraikkayar of the deep South belong to the Shafi School of Islamic law which was once popular in Arabia; the Urdu, Bengali, and Dakhni speaking Muslims to the north belong to the Hanafi school of law which had prevailed in the Perso-Turkic area of Khurasan at one time.[26] The division coincides with the Arab-Ajam divide in the central lands of Islam. Arab immigration to the tip of the Indian peninsula began as early as the eighth and ninth centuries.[27] Turkish campaigns to the Gangetic basin from the Khurasan area of Ajam got underway not earlier than the eleventh and twelfth centuries. Subsequently, the two colonizations proceeded along divergent paths, and with differential consequences. Arab-Shafi colonization at the tip of the peninsula saw the emergence of a unique Hindu-Muslim symbiosis. A complex interweaving of clashes and reconciliations was the hallmark of the Ajam-Hanafi colonization in the other parts of India.

At the very first encounter between Mahmud of Ghazni and his Hindu opponents, before the Turks settled in the country, Al Biruni was moved to explain:

> ...the Hindus entirely differ from us in every respect...they totally differ from us in religion, as we believe in nothing in which they believe, and *vice versa*...in all manners and usages they differ from us to such a degree as to frighten their children with us, with our dress, and our ways and customs, and as to declare us to be devil's breed, and our doings as the very opposite of all that is good and proper.[28]

The clash, he saw, was inherent in the fundamentals of the two religions: Hindu religious practice was based on the worship of idols, whereas Muslim tenets uncompromisingly prohibited even the making of a picture of the prophet.[29] The Hindus discriminated among themselves on the basis of caste, and did not sit, eat, or drink with the Muslims because they thought they would be polluted thereby.[30] "We Muslims, of course", Al Biruni took care to point out, "stand entirely on the other side of the question, considering all men as equal".[31]

The symbols were so contrary in the two religions, and the sensibilities were so opposed, that a clash of fundamentals could not be avoided. The Muslims of India prayed facing west, in the direction of Mecca; Hindus prayed facing east, in the direction of the rising sun. Muslims buried their dead; Hindus burned theirs. The two communities also differed on what happened after death: Muslims did not accept the Hindu notion of reincarnation, insisting that, under divine judgement, one either rose up to heaven or sank down to hell. Touch was, however, a more sensitive matter.

Afanasy Nikitin drew a vivid picture of the Hindus from his experience during his travels in the Deccan in the latter part of the fifteenth century, setting them off against the Muslims as 'Indians':

> The Indians eat no flesh at all—no beef, mutton, fowl, fish, or pork, although they have a great many pigs...They do not eat or drink with Moslems. Their food is poor and they do not eat or drink with one another, not even with their wives...And they eat everything with their right hand, never touching any food with the left; they never use a knife, and have no spoons. When journeying, each carries a pot to boil food in. And they hide from the Moslems lest they should look into the pot or at the food. And should a Moslem look at the food, the Indian will not eat it. When eating, some cover themselves with a shawl, so that no one may see them.
>
> And they pray facing eastwards, in the Russian manner; they raise high both hands and put them on their crown, and lie face downwards on the ground and stretch out on it—that is how they worship. And when they sit down to take a meal, some wash their hands and feet, and also rinse their mouths. Their *butkhanahs* [temples] have no doors, and face eastwards; the *buts* [idols], too, stand facing eastwards, and when someone dies, they burn him and scatter the ashes over water....The Indians call the ox 'father' and the cow 'mother'; they use the dung as fuel to bake and cook food and smear their faces, foreheads, and bodies with the ashes.[32]

Titus indicates that Indian religious thought influenced Muslims before Islam became established in India. In fact, Buddhist thought and 'wandering Indian monks' too, could have significantly influenced the development of *tasawwuf* (Islamic mysticism) which occurred mainly in Persia.[33] The Sufi (the name derives from the word *tasawwuf*) sub-variant of Islam, in particular, found a fertile ground in India where asceticism and mystical activities already had widespread acceptance.

In the hands of the Sufis, Islam gradually assumed a local shape which made it attractive to the native population. Shaikh Nizamuddin Auliya had been a vegetarian. Shaikh Azizullah, the medieval Sufi, too, was an adherent of non-violence. They not only practised, but sincerely believed in non-violence. It was out of such strong convictions that the Sufis affected, after the initial clash, the reconciliation between Islam and India; so much so that the community of Muslims and their saints became an integral part of Indian civilization by the time Emperor Akbar adopted Sulh-i-Kul, or peace with everyone, as the spiritual objective of his regime. By then, the Khurasani Turks, who in their first rush had turned the temples of the country upside down from Delhi to Benaras, were assimilated within its population. As

Akbar and his band of Turki-speaking people Mughal soldiers drove the Pathans before them as far as Orissa, the original Turks were nowhere in sight.

A sure sign of the process of acculturation which resulted in the absorption of the Khurasani immigrants was the replacement of Turki by Urdu as the spoken language of the camp, and the penetration of the new mixed Indo-Muslim language to the south in the form of Dakhni. The spread of this common Indian language was an index of the gradual disappearance of the Turushka conquerors amidst the population of India. The process was at work silently from the thirteenth to the fifteenth century.[34]

Conversion to Islam, notwithstanding the tenacity of the indigenous culture and the loss of contact with the homeland of Islam, led to the emergence of several syncretic forms among Muslims in India. In south India, for example, magical practices were combined with Muslim rituals. Thurston[35] reports that in Madras tribal rituals were incorporated into Muslim marriages. *Quranic* verses were assumed to possess special powers of healing and warding off evil, and hence were written on pieces of article and stuck above doors and widows. With reference to north India, Herklots[36] observed that the Rajputs and Jats "often supplement the orthodox ritual of Islam by Hindu marriage and death rites, follow Hindu rules of succession to real and personal property and particularly in times of trouble revere the local village deities".

There was also a widespread belief that God can be better reached through some physical medium, and hence a system of saint and tomb worship evolved. Individuals with outstanding knowledge or allegedly superior powers came to be treated with awe and reverence by the masses. These 'saints' were perceived as being able to "avert calamity, cure disease and procure children for the childless".[37] Upon the death of these saints, their tombs were often worshipped by subsequent generations.

In attempting to illustrate the close relationship between Hindus and Muslims, Herklots reports that Hindus were involved in the procession of *taziyas* or *tabuts*, reminiscent of the martyrs Hassan and Hussein in the battle of Karbala, during the festival of Muharram. Samaroo[38] also documents the influence of Hindu religious rituals upon the form this festival assumes in India.

The binary opposition between Hindu-Muslim impeded the development of political commonality in India, until the rule of Akbar and his successors fostered the notion of a legitimate *badshahi* in which these distinctions were effectively combined to create a new and inclusive sovereignty over Hindustan. The Portuguese, who captured Goa by a series of raids in and around 1510, were certainly a lot less tolerant of non-Christians than the Muslim powers were of other faiths. The Archbishop of Goa forbade Hindus, Muslims, Jews, and Armenians open performance of their religious ceremonies, such as cremation, marriage, and "other superstitions and devilish institutions" so as to "avoid all occasions of dislike that might be given to Christians". By contrast, the freedom of worship prevailed at the time throughout Mughal India. In Akbar's capital, the *Ibadat Khana* accommodated free debates between learned men of every belief on Friday nights. Sufis, Ulama, Sunnis, Shias, Brahmans, Jains, Buddhists, Christians, Jews, Zoroastrians, and even the materialist followers of Charvak's atheist creed gathered together in the royal assembly, and the arguments and counter-arguments were long and heated. The fact that the Shias and Sunnis were accommodated along with members of every other faith made the Mughal empire a uniquely tolerant realm at a time when Christian Europe was torn by wars of religion and contending Catholic and Protestant persecutions and burnings. This intellectual trend towards synthesis led Akbar's great-grandson Prince Dara Shikoh to demonstrate that the doctrines of the Hindus of antiquity and the Sufis of the Islamic world were the very same as regards the godhead.[39]

The soil of the country was sacred, and not just to the Hindus, but, as time passed, to adherents of exogenous religions as well. The sepulchre of the martyr St. Thomas was sacred to Indian Christians during the reign of Jahangir. Those who went on pilgrimage there on the first day of July, carried back with them a little of that earth for a great relic. A *Mahua* tree by the bathing *ghat* at Bahraich, where the shrine of the martyr Salar Masud was established, provided in Muslim legend the first holy spot of Islam in India. Next in line were the Chishtiyya shrines, stretching down from the *dargah* of Shaikh Muin-ud-Din Chishti at Ajmer all the way to the grave of Bandanawaz Gisudaraz in the Deccan. The shrines of Muinuddin and Gisudaraz attracted Hindu pilgrims too. The growth of tomb-worship at various spots so disturbed the theologian Shah Waliullah that he denounced pilgrimages to the shrines of Mainuddin Chishti, Salar Masud, and Shah Madar as a sin worse than murder or adultery. Islam had assumed an Indian shape for some purists by the mid-eighteenth century. On the eve of Nadir Shah's invasion, Muslim social life in Delhi included a well established weekly round of *dargahs* around the capital. The soil was by now sacred to the Muslims and the water too.[40]

Under the influence of the common imperial patriotism, even the Marathas who had rebelled against the Mughal sovereign rallied to the throne when Nadir Shah of Iran invaded India in 1739. When the Mughal army gave way, the people of Delhi, both Hindu and Muslim, rose in a body against the Iranian troopers in a popular insurrection. Even as the central Mughal power decayed after the sack of Delhi by Nadir Shah, the common Hindustani patriotism of the Hindus and Muslims, on the one hand, and the imperial Mughal legitimism of the officers and troopers, on the other, fused into a political commonality which provided the only all-India basis for resistance to the colonial encroachments of the English. In the First War of Independence in 1857, the

Hindus and Muslims fought unitedly under Muslim/Hindu leaders and the expression "Hindus and Mussalmans of Hindustan" occurred in all correspondences and pronouncements by the mutineers.

The collapse of the Mughals had been one of the most conspicuous catastrophes afflicting Islam in India. After the deposition of the Nawab-Wazir in 1856, Hyderabad alone remained as a centre of Muslim supremacy. In the reactions of Indian Islam there were echoes of Islamic movements elsewhere—those who called for resistance, and those who preached the need for reconciliation and adaptation, the harsh militancy of Waliullah and Syed Ahmed of Bareilly, the Farazis of Bengal and the Deoband school of north India and the suaver moderation of the Aligarh school. The efforts of the Wahhabi reformers to purge Islam of the faithless led them to try purging India of infidel and their resistance which extended over Bengal, Bihar, the Punjab and the North-West Frontier, was not quelled until 1871.[41] The programme elaborated by the Wahhabis and by the theorists of Deoband, was of higher generality, founded on the common duties of all true believers in the Dar-ul-Harb, i.e. "the land of war", a territory in which it was a religious duty to fight for the faith. In 1870 Mayo induced a group of ulemas to issue a fatwa proclaiming that India was now a Dar-ul-Islam, or a land of Islam.[42] The seminary at Deoband was a centre of Muslim fundamentalism, hostile both to the British and to the modernizing movements in Islam. In a later age, when the options had changed, it was to support the Congress against the demand for Pakistan.

III

Hindu-Muslim Relations in Pre-colonial Period

The communal consciousness, however, got a fillip as a result of the transformation of Indian society under the impact of the colonial rule and the need to struggle against it. It gradually dawned on a section of the Indian people that they can act socially and politically and protect their collective or corporate or non-individual interests only as members of the religion-based communities. It is also believed that the secular interests, that is, the social, cultural, economic and political interests, of the followers of one religion are not only dissimilar and divergent from, but also are opposed to, the interests of the followers of another religion. When the interests of the followers of different religions or of different 'communities' are seen to be mutually incompatible, antagonistic and hostile, communalism in its extreme form sets in.[43]

Religion was used as a mobilizing factor by the communalists. Communalism could become a popular movement only when it adopted inflammable cry of religion in danger. Moreover, differing religious practices were the immediate cause of situations of communal tension and riots. While religion was not responsible for communalism, religiosity was a major contributory factor. Religiosity which has been defined as intense emotional commitment to matters of religion and the tendency to let religion and religious emotions intrude into non-religious and non-spiritual areas of life and beyond the individual's private and moral world was not communalism, but it opened a person to the appeal of communalism in the name of religion. Secularization did not, therefore, mean removing religion, but it did mean reducing religiosity or increasingly narrowing down the sphere of religion to the private life of the individual.[44]

British rule and its policy of Divide and Rule bore special responsibility for the growth of communalism in modern India, though it is also true that it could succeed only because of internal social and political conditions. The colonial state used communalism to counter and weaken the growing national movement and the welding of the Indian people into a nation. Communalism was presented by the colonial rulers as the problem of the defence of religious minorities. Hindu-Muslim disunity and the need to protect the minorities from domination and suppression by the majority were increasingly offered as the main justification for the maintenance of British rule.[45]

Communalism was, of course, not the only constituent of the policy of Divide and Rule. Every existing division of Indian society was encouraged to prevent the emerging unity of the Indian people. An effort was made to set region against region, province against province, caste against caste, language against language, reformers against the orthodox, the moderate against the militant, leftist against rightist, and even class against class. It was, of course, the communal and the caste divisions which survived to the end and proved the most serviceable. In fact, near the end, they were to become the main prop of colonialism, and colonial authorities were to stake their all on them. On the other hand, communalism could not have developed to such an extent as to divide the country permanently into two halves solely on the basis of religion, if it did not have the powerful support of the colonial state. In fact, communalism was the route through which colonialism was able to extend its narrow social base to sections of workers, peasants, the middle classes and the bourgeoisie whose interests were otherwise in contradiction with colonialism.

While a communalist talked of, or believed in, defending his 'community's' interests, in real life no such interests existed outside the field of religion. The economic and political interests of Hindus, Muslims, and others were the same. In that sense they did not even constitute separate communities. As Hindus or Muslims they did not even have a separate political-economic life or interests on an all-India or even regional basis. They were divided from fellow Hindus or Muslims by region, language, culture, class, caste, social status, social practices, food and dress habits, etc., and united on these aspects with followers of other religions. An upper class Muslim had far more in common, even culturally, with an upper class Hindu than with a lower class Muslim. Similarly, a Punjabi Hindu stood closer culturally to a Punjabi Muslim than to a Bengali Hindu; and of course, the same was true of a Bengali Muslim in relation to a Bengali Hindu and a Punjabi Muslim. The real division, thus, obscured the real division of the Indian people into linguistic-cultural regions and social classes as well as their real, emerging and growing unity into a nation. While communalism uses, and is based on, many elements of ancient and medieval ideologies, basically, it is a modern technology and political trend that expresses the social urges and serves the political needs of modern social groups, classes and forces. Its social roots as also its social, political and economic objectives lie very much in the modern period of Indian history. It was brought into existence and sustained by contemporary socio-economic structure.[46] This was recognised by many perceptive Indians. Jawaharlal Nehru, for example, noted in 1936: "One must not forget that communalism in India is a latter-day phenomenon which has grown up before our eyes".[47]

Muslim and Hindu sentiments were forces to reckon within pre-colonial Indian politics not least of all in the eighteenth and early nineteenth centuries which witnessed a series of riots: in Ahmedabad, between Banias and Muslims in 1713, in Delhi, Agra, and Kashmir, during the festivals of Holi, Muharram and Id in the 1720s; in Surat, by Muslim weavers against Parsee and Bania contractors in 1788 and 1795; in Delhi, by Muslim crowds against Hindu bankers in 1807; and in Benaras, between Hindus and Muslims over a disputed shrine in 1809.[48] Recent research suggests that a pre-existing religious tension dating back to the later Mughals was linked up with the disturbance of the economic and political balance between Bania capital and Muslim crowds during the ascendancy of the East India Company at the turn of the nineteenth century. The specificity of the confrontations between the Bania allies of the Company and its Muslim opponents combined, according to Lakshmi Subramanian, with the pre-existing tension to produce the Surat riot of 1795 and that in Delhi in 1807.[49]

According to Chattopadhyaya, there were at least two spheres of conflict in the pre-colonial period—(i) conflict over political supremacy; and (ii) conflicts over assertion of doctrinal and sectarian supremacy.[50] Wherever possible, communities fought over available resources; for example, the land wars during the Mughal period. Bayly notes that in the Punjab there were cases of the obliteration of the old Muslim towns and their replacement by totally new semi-urban settlements under the complete control of the local Sikh warrior lineages. He asserts that these land wars were the result of the

Mughal policy of land grant, *madad-i-maash*, to Muslims or Islamised Hindus and these groups were locally competed against by Hindu agricultural castes such as Jats, Bhumihars or Rajputs. He further argues that communal conflict, though mediated by religious symbols, was rooted in contestations around land or over political authority.[51]

Another form of violence that left a deep and bitter deposit in folk memory was the desecration of temples and mosques. In a cultural context, where the affirmation of authority following upon a conquest required the performance of certain symbolic religious actions, the enemy's religious symbols were obvious targets. But as Rajat Kanta Ray very rightly points out:

> Mutual violence was *not* the established pattern of Hindu-Muslim interactions. The outrages occurred during war. Such transgression as occurred were the work of the powers, not of the population at large, and only during hostilities were the soldiery urged to commit such excesses. Even the most intolerant of rulers, whether Hindu or Muslim, allowed subjects of all persuasions to practise their faith, subject to certain understood laws: no cow might be sacrificed in Hindu territory, and no new and unauthorized temples might be built in Muslim territory. The Vijaynagar soldiers might show disrespect to the *Quran* and destroy mosques in enemy territory, but the king erected a mosque in the capital for his Muslim subjects and showed marked respect to their holy book. Similarly, even in the orthodox reign of Aurangzeb, who ordered demolition of all new and unauthorized temples, the Hindu population was allowed, according to Bernier, "free exercise of its religion". The contemporary observations of Manucci and Tavernier made it evident that the *Kumbh Mela* at Allahabad and the pilgrimages to Mathura, Banaras, Puri, and Tirupati were not interrupted by the Emperor.[52]

This fact of Indian life was perhaps known to the East India Company officials. That is the reason why in the worst days of the Uprising of 1857, Mangles, the Chairman of the Board of Directors of the East India Company suggested to Canning, the Governor-General of India, that 'something' might be done to 'separate' the Hindus and the Muslims from each other by distributing proclamations and posting 'placards' in provinces like Rohilkhand, where 'actual strife' had commenced between the two communities. He wondered whether measures might not be taken to impress upon the 'more intelligent' Hindus, through their 'natural leaders' throughout India, the 'perils' to their interests which would 'certainly' follow the establishment of Muslim ascendancy and 'domination'. It is not clear if Canning took up the suggestion. But, as a future policy, he outlined that as the British were a 'handful' ruling

150 million people they must do so in the manner 'best calculated' to leave the two communities 'divided'. The germs of separatist politics were probably being sown, concludes a researcher.[53] The renowned historian R.C. Majumdar, however, traces the 'Divide and Rule' policy as far back as 1821 and notices a positive adoption of that policy during the mutiny and in post-mutiny army reorganisation.[54]

Leaving aside the question whether the "Divide and Rule" policy was first introduced in 1821 or in 1857, it is a fact that the British viewed India more as an economic possession than as a political entity. Indian society was looked upon as pre-capitalist entities largely constituting primordial communities. Their attention to India's social divisions was unapologetic, partly because they never really envisioned India as a single community, but as a hotchpotch of disparate groups, communities and regions that had stitched together into a colony. The Empire's governors and census officers emphasized country's social divisions in its imperial surveys and district gazetteers used caste and religious identities to classify Indian populations. As pointed out, "it turned out that instead of the occupiers transforming Indian attitudes, it was the British officers who absorbed the caste, religious and regional distinctions within Indian society, and they tended to stereotype Indians accordingly—into the 'bigoted julaha', the 'brave Sikh' and so on".[55]

IV

Census and Communalism

The colonial census which began in 1872 introduced the question on religion, caste and race and religion was used as a fundamental category in census tabulations and data on this published without any restraint. While numerous communities existed in India, these communities in terms of castes, religions, and groups have existed as 'fuzzy' communities from time immemorial, but their congealing into distinct, discrete and mutually antagonistic communities was certainly aided to a great extent by the counting of heads. The 'fuzzy' communities were indistinct groups with neither internal cohesion nor well known externalities and as such, were communities without overt communication. The group did not know how far it extended and what was its strength in numbers and, therefore, had less accurate and less aggressive self-awareness. The 'fuzzy' communities also did not require any developed theory of 'otherness'.[56]

Colonialism changed this blissful state of social ignorance through census. The colonial enterprise of population enumeration had a far-reaching impact on the development of communal ideologies. In fact, census data is crucial to the construction of communalism. As Bhagat says, "A census is not a passive account of statistical tables, but also engages in re-shaping the world through categories and their definitions".[57] It had far-reaching impact on the creation of various imaginations—communal, national, caste, gender—as well as several stereotypes about Muslims. Census data has not been an instrument just for enumeration, but also for comparison. "From the 1870s the decennial census operations reinforced existing social divisions by creating a countable Hindu majority and Muslim minority".[58]

Numbers became a political tool as Hindus were told that they constituted a majority and an effort was made to persuade them to act as a uniform community regardless of sect, caste or class affiliation. Before head counts of people were announced, it was neither possible nor necessary for communities across the land to identify themselves with any degree of preciseness and to seek similarities or differences with others outside their immediate kin. There was, thus no general 'Hindu' community and people defined themselves with reference to their specific modes of worship as localized Shaivites (worshippers of Shiva), or Shakts (worshippers of the Goddess Kali) or Vaishnavas (worshippers of Vishnu) and the like.

Indeed, in the pre-modern periods, it is doubtful if even the Muslim 'ummah' (global community) had any more than a symbolic meaning. The censuses, however, not only counted people, but also pigeon-holed them and made it possible for them to seek self-definition in terms that were set for them by external enumerations.

There is little historical evidence of sustained communal hatred operating at the popular level prior to colonial rule.[59] The 'fuzzy' communities have been turned into enumerated communities and further into political communities by the instruments and mechanism of colonial policy of divide and rule. The census counts first tried out in 1872 aided in the articulation of the cleavages of majority and minority, a handmaiden in creating communal consciousness in the early twentieth century.[60]

The Census Commissioner of 1931 Census was aware about the role of census statistics on religion flaring up communal divisions in the country. Thus, he wrote:

> It has been argued that the census statistics of religion tend to perpetuate communal divisions: the census cannot, however, hide its head in the sand like the proverbial ostrich but must record as accurately as possible facts as they exist and there is no question of the existence of communal differences which are reflected at present in political constituencies.[61]

The above justification, however, did not conform to the social reality of India that existed during colonial time. The comments of the Census

Commissioner of 1911 Census are very pertinent:

> In India the line of cleavage is social rather than religious, and tendency of the people themselves is to classify their neighbours, not according to their beliefs, but according to their social status and manner of living. No one is interested in what his neighbour believes, but he is very much interested in knowing whether he can eat with or take water from his hands.[62]

The census data on religion not only brought to the fore the majority-minority cleavage, but also sparked off a communal debate on the size and growth of population of different religious communities. Since, the early twentieth century, census data have been immensely politicised. The idea of the demographic decline of Hindus and demographic rise of Muslims is an extremely powerful device employed in communal discourses.

In the wake of the fear of a declining Hindu population, a variety of literature was produced around census data in the early twentieth century in the form of pamphlets, booklets and newspaper articles. *Hinduon ke Saath Viswasghat* (Treachery with Hindus), *Hinduon ka Bhayankar Haas* (Terrible Mockery of Hindus); *Humara Bhishan Haas* (Our Terrible Mockery) dealt with the declining Hindu population.[63] These literatures provided materials that fed the construction of a single Hindu identity.

In 1909, U.N. Mukherjee of Calcutta published a series of articles in the 'Bengalee', which was later published as a pamphlet, *Hindus: A Dying Race*. On the basis of census figures of 1901 Census, Mukherjee drew attention towards the declining proportion of Hindus in the total population. In 1912 he also raised the phobia of Hindus being swallowed up in next 420 years in a personal meeting with Swami Shraddhananda who became convinced enough to begin the work of re-conversion of Hindus from Mohammedan and Christian communities. Swami Shraddhananda wrote an influential book entitled *Hindu Sangsthan: Saviour of Dying Race* in 1926. As such, the idea of demographic decline became entrenched as a core feature of Hindu communalism and the demographic divide was brought to the centre stage of communal politics.

The census also allowed the creation of a range of other stereotypes such as dress, food habits, living style, family relationship and bodies. In the images produced on communal harmony, communities are shown in typical dress such as Muslims in lungi with a cap and fine cut beard, Sikhs with turbans, Christians with neck-ties and Hindu males in *dhoti-kurta*.[64]

The census figures also provided the geographical distribution of religious communities. Both size of religious communities and their distribution was used to widen the rift between religious communities particularly between Hindus and Muslims. Numerous such examples are found with intent to perpetuate divisions in Indian society along caste, religion and linguistic lines.[65] The division of Bengal based on religion in 1905 was the most glaring example of fomenting communalism by the British policy of divide and rule. A new province of East Bengal and Assam was created with predominance of Muslims in 1905. In Dacca in February, 1904, Curzon spoke of offering the East Bengal Muslims the prospect of unity which they have not enjoyed since the days of the old Mussalman viceroys and kings.[66] Though the partition of Bengal was annulled in 1912 due to sustained movements it was the prelude to what was going to happen within the next 45 years.

Not only Bengal was partitioned, at the suggestion of the British Rulers the first communal political set-up in India, the Muslim League, was founded in December, 1906 under the leadership of the Nawab of Dacca. This political organisation was created to safeguard the interests of the Muslims who were smarting under the fear of being dominated by the Hindus, of falling behind the Hindus in modern callings and opportunities and of being reduced to a subordinate position.

The use of religion was found in other areas of discourse as well. This is evident from the periodisation of Indian history in terms of Hindu and Muslim periods unlike European history—ancient, medieval and modern.[67] A communal and distorted unscientific view of Indian history, especially of its ancient and medieval periods, was a major instrument for the spread of communal consciousness as also a basic constituent of communal ideology. A beginning was made in the early nineteenth century by the British historian, James Mill, who described the ancient period of Indian history as the Hindu period and the medieval period as the Muslim period.[68] Other British and Indian historians followed him in this respect. The teaching of Indian history in schools and colleges from a basically communal point of view made a major contribution to the rise and growth of communalism. For generations, almost from the beginning of the modern school system, communal interpretations of history of varying degrees of virulence were propagated, first by imperialist writers and then by others, although an unbiased review of history would show that Hindus and Muslims enjoyed centuries of harmonious co-existence. Over and above the textbooks which are rife with negative comments regarding the relations between two major religious communities, the communal view of history was spread widely through poetry, drama, historical novels and short stories, newspapers and popular magazines, pamphlets, and above all, orally through the public platform, classroom teaching, socialization through the family, and private discussion and conversation.[69] It seems that the projection of cleavages within colonial society was essential for sustaining colonial rule which used variety of texts, forms and methods to continue and promote their rule even at the cost of strained communal relationships in India.[70]

V

Trendsetters in Early Twentieth Century

The first decade of the twentieth century is marked as the trend-setter of the future course of events of Indian history. It legitimized the birth of two powerful forces—communalism and casteism—all in pursuance of the 'divide and rule' policy, which in course of time changed the entire complexion of Indian polity. As nationalism grew and the movement towards greater Indian participation in the governance gathered momentum in the late nineteenth century, the British Government was forced to revaluate its policy of giving more representation to the Indians in the Administration. Lord Minto (18 November, 1905 to 23 November, 1910), the new Viceroy, took a new approach to give representation to the Indian people in legislatures. He hit upon a novel idea which introduced communalism for the first time in the polity of the Indian state after the advent of the British rule and adopted a clever ploy of exacerbating the open rivalry between the two dominant religious communities—Hindus and Muslims. Colonel Dunlop Smith, Private Secretary to the Viceroy wrote a letter to Archibald, the Principal of the Aligarh Muslim College, that the Viceroy would be happy to receive a Muslim deputation. A 35-member deputation called the All India Mohammedan Deputation met the Viceroy on 1 October, 1906 in Simla. Its leader was His Highness the Agha Khan of Bombay. Nawab Khwaja Salimulla, Nawab of Dacca, under whose leadership the Muslim League was founded in December, 1906 could not, however, join the Deputation due to illness. This deputation made the demand for separate electorates for Muslims in any scheme of political reform and said that the representation of the Muslims should be more than what was warranted by their numerical strength in the country. They further demanded that only Muslims should be allowed to choose the Muslim members of the Council, and also a "due share in the gazetted and the subordinate and ministerial services". Lord Minto went a step further than what was demanded or claimed. He said in his reply: "I am grateful to you for the opportunity you are affording me of expressing my appreciation of the just aims of the followers of Islam and their determination to share in the political history of our Empire... You justly claim that your numerical strength both in respect to the political importance of your community and the service it has rendered to the Empire entitle you to consideration". While the claim of the Deputationists was only related to the Imperial Legislative Council's election or nomination, the Viceroy went further to say: "The pith of your address is a claim that in any system of representation, whether it affects a Municipality, a District Board or a Legislative Council in which it is proposed to introduce or increase an electoral organization, the Mohammedan community should be represented as a community". He further added that he was firmly convinced that "any electoral representation in India would be doomed to mischievous failure which aimed at granting a personal enfranchisement regardless of the beliefs and traditions of the communities composing the population of this continent".[71]

The address by the Deputationists and Lord Minto's reply thereto has a great importance and significance in the history of India. It marked the beginning of the British Government's policy of giving favourable treatment to the Muslims in the administration of India, which was intended to wean them away from the Congress and to create a breach and disunity between the Hindus and the Muslims. It has also acquired a certain amount of notoriety in the minds of the Indians in view of the fact that the address was arranged by the British Government. The Address presented to Lord Minto and his reply thereto is reproduced at Appendix A.

Lord Minto's assurance was reflected in the Morley-Minto Reforms of 1909 which introduced for the first time separate communal electorate with weightage to the Muslims that became a permanent feature of Indian political system since then. Commenting on this provision for separate electorate Eleanor Zelliot observes:

> The granting of an electorate for Muslims in which they alone would vote brought the idea of communal electorate for minorities to the forefront in the minds of all communities which feared their submersion in a government run by the dominant caste Hindu community. The granting of special electorates to the Muslim community also made numbers important.[72]

Mushirul Hasan believes that the roots of communal competition can be traced to the Morley-Minto Reforms which, by creating communal electorates, exacerbated Hindu-Muslim divisions and fostered the spirit of political exclusivism. Their impact was particularly marked on Muslims who saw the advantage of pressing for special safeguards and concessions in accordance with the numerical strength, social status, local influence and social requirements of their community.[73]

As the reforms of 1909 conceded to the Muslims practically all that they had demanded, some political leaders regarded the time as favourable for bringing about a rapprochement between the Hindus and the Muslims. Accordingly, a conference was held at Allahabad on January 1, 1911, which was attended by about 60 Hindus and 40 Muslims. G.K. Gokhale took the leading part. The Conference dispersed after appointing a Committee which, of course, did nothing. But in spite of its failure, R.C. Majumdar, the noted historian, commented that

> the Conference is of great historical importance. For, it marks the beginning of that policy of appeasement which the Congress henceforth adopted towards the Muslim community. However laudable its object might be, in practice it led to two undesirable consequences. Though it did not reconcile the Muslims, it irritated the Hindus and increased the importance of the Hindu Mahasabha, counterpart of the Muslim League. Secondly, it encouraged, almost incited, the Muslims always to pitch their demands too high.[74]

The Muslim League had been founded with the sole object of preventing the Muslims from joining the Congress. In 1912 there occurred a change in the Muslim League's attitude towards the Government and the Congress. Turkey was considered to be the only living temporal power of Islam. Indian Muslims owed their allegiance to the Turkish Khalifa. During the Turko-Italian War of 1911, England did not help the Turkish Sultan. The Balkan Wars of 1912-13 also convinced the Muslims that all the Christian powers were conspiring against Turkey. They interpreted the campaign against Turkey as a struggle between the "Cross and Crescent". Indian Muslims began to nurse a grudge against the British Government for its cold indifference towards and treachery against Turkey. The annulment of the Partition of Bengal further irritated and disappointed them. Capping it all, the decision of Turkey to enter into war on the side of Germany finally decided the course of the Muslim League's actions. All these brought about a rupture in the unholy alliance between the League and the Government. Nationalist Muslim leaders and even Jinnah began to exhort their co-religionists to throw aside their distrust of the Hindus and join them in the struggle for freedom.

As a result of the hard work of Jinnah, both the Muslim League and the Congress met for their annual sessions at Bombay in December, 1915. The principal leaders of the two political parties assembled at one place for the first time in the history of these organizations. The speeches made from the platform of the two groups were similar in tone and theme. Prominent Congress leaders, namely Gandhi, Pandit Madan Mohan Malaviya and Sarojini Naidu spoke from the League platform. Within a few months of the Bombay meetings, 19 Muslim and Hindu elected members of the Imperial Legislative Council addressed a memorandum to the Viceroy on the subject of reforms in October, 1916. Their suggestions did not become news in the British circle, but were discussed, amended and accepted at a subsequent meeting of the Congress and the Muslim League leaders at Calcutta in November, 1916. This meeting settled the details of an agreement about the composition of the legislatures and the quantum of representation to be allowed to the two communities. The agreement was confirmed by the annual sessions of the Congress and the

League in their annual sessions held at Lucknow on December 29 and December 31, 1916 respectively.

The main features of the Lucknow Pact[75], amongst others, are:

(1) Provincial Legislative Councils shall consist of four-fifths elected and of one-fifth nominated members.
(2) The membership of the Legislatures in big Provinces should be raised to 125 and in the smaller ones between 50 and 75.
(3) The members of Councils should be elected directly by the people on as broad a franchise as possible.
(4) The minorities should be given adequate separate representation in the elected bodies. The Muslims may be entitled to a share in the elective seats to the extent of 50 per cent in the Punjab, 30 per cent in U.P., 40 per cent in Bengal, 25 per cent in Bihar, 15 per cent in C.P., and in Madras, and one-third in Bombay. The Muslims would be debarred from contesting the elective seats in excess of the number allotted to them.
(5) That no Bill would be introduced by a non-official member if it affected the interests of any other community, and such a Bill would not be passed if three-fourths of the members of that community opposed it.
(6) The strength of the Imperial Legislative Council shall be one hundred and fifty. Four-fifths of the members shall be elected. The franchise for the Imperial Legislative Council should be widened as far as possible on the lines of the Mohammedan electorates, and the elected members of the Provincial Legislative Councils should also form an electorate for the return of members to the Imperial Legislative Council.

This entente, however, did not find support among those Hindus who placed their religion before politics, and it was condemned at a meeting of the All-India Hindu Mahasabha which was held at Lucknow at the same time. It was alleged that the Muslim League at this period had become little more than an adjunct to the Congress. It disaffiliated the old Punjab Provincial Branch of the League of which, Mian Muhammad Shafi was President and which incidentally was then the only section on revolt against the current policy of the main body.[76]

Sarojini Naidu gave Jinnah, the chief architect of the Lucknow Pact, the title of "the Ambassador of Hindu-Muslim Unity". The Congress-Muslim League Lucknow Pact of 1916 can easily be considered an important landmark during the nationalist movement in India. But in fact the Congress in its bid to win Muslim support committed blunders. A diplomatic blunder of high magnitude was committed in conceding the right to separate Muslim representation through members of the community themselves. It was an evidence of the bankruptcy of the Congress leaders and their helpless lack of shrewdness. They ought to have understood that this concession to the Mussalmans would tear the nation for ever in two sharply divided communities and the breach shall be widened by the foreign ruling power. Besides perpetuating the system of communal electorate and separate electorate it is surprising why the Congress agreed to give the Muslims unfair representation much in excess of their numerical strength. The compromise demanded more sacrifice on the part of Hindus and abject yielding to League's demands. According to many political thinkers the Lucknow Pact marked the beginning of the appeasement policy of the Congress towards the Muslim community. Acceptance of the basis of separate electorate led inevitably to the division of the country. The second defect of the Pact was that it did not advance its demand for self-government in an emphatic manner.[77]

In view of the political situation created by the First World War, the Congress leaders were led to believe that Britain would be forced to grant a substantial measure of self-government to India if there was a united political front to bring pressure upon her. With a view to achieving such political unity they had amended the Constitution of the Congress in 1915 in order to bring back within its fold the Nationalists or Extremists who had seceded from it in 1907. To complete this unity they were determined to win over the Muslim League at any cost. They succeeded, but at a very heavy price. For, no one can doubt in the light of subsequent events that the Congress action in 1916 well and truly laid the foundation on which Pakistan was built up thirty years later. A compromise on the fundamental basis of Indian nationality, once begun, was bound to lead to further and further compromises till the whole foundation gave way.[78]

As to the reactions of the Press on the Lucknow Pact, Bamford, a Deputy Director of the Intelligence Bureau, Government of India comments thus:

> During the first half of 1917 it became apparent from the tone of the Indian Press that the agreement arrived at between the leaders of extremist Mohammedan and extremist Hindu opinion did not find a counterpart among the two communities generally. Some of the Hindu organs blamed their leaders for consenting to confer so generous a representation upon Mohammedan; but their attitude was far less strongly marked than that of the conservative Mohammedan press which continued to voice distrust of the intention of the Hindus and denied that the Mohammedan political leaders, in assenting to the Lucknow compromise, had any claim to represent Mohammedan opinion throughout the country at large. Doubts were also thrown on the power of the Indian National Congress to commit Hindus in

> general to such liberal recognition of Mohammedan claims, while the Muslim League was accused of betraying the interests of Islam into the hands of the Hindus who would subordinate these interests to their Home Rule Movement.[79]

Lord Chelmsford, the Viceroy (4 April, 1916 to 2 April, 1921), in his opening address to the Delhi session of the Legislative Council on 7th February, 1917 brushed aside the Lucknow Pact whose acceptance would have cemented the Congress-League entente.[80] An analyst has pointed out that the Congress leaders agreed to the Pact in the expectation that the executive-legislature relationship in the package of constitutional reforms would essentially be a continuation of the Morley-Minto reforms. But the Montagu-Chelmsford reforms, when announced, revealed that the nature of this relationship would be significantly different, leading the Congress leaders to oppose the Pact and to the acceptance of communal electorates for the Muslims that it entailed, before the Southborough Committee. The pact also contained significant omissions and ambiguities which led to divergent interpretations on crucial provisions.[81]

The Montagu-Chelmsford Reforms of 1919 initiated several significant changes in the structure of politics. On the legislative side, they increased the number of voters, and established enlarged central and provincial legislatures with a majority of elected and non-official members. On the administrative side, the reforms divided the functions of government between 'reserved' and 'transferred' departments. The 'reserved' departments were administered by the Governor-in-Council, but the control of such important departments as education, agriculture and local self-government in the 'transferred' departments was handed over to ministers responsible to the legislature. This was the principle of dyarchy. In the local self-government bodies, too, the electoral qualifications were reduced, the official and nominated element was curtailed and the principle of election was widely extended.

Recent studies on the impact of the changes introduced by the Montford Reforms have clearly demonstrated that the enlargement of legislative councils, the broadening of the franchise and the extension of the scope and activities of the local bodies contributed to the growth of communal awareness, sharpened existing cleavages and encouraged communal alignments.[82] These developments which were clearly evident from 1921 to 1926, were the consequences of several factors. The first was, undoubtedly, the retention of communal electorates in the Montford Reforms and their gradual extension to local bodies. The implications of this measure were not realised during the Khilafat and non-co-operation movements when the anti-government spirit reigned supreme, and the majority of Congress and Muslim League leaders boycotted the 1920 provincial elections.

Minto's regime had sown the seeds of Muslim separatism. Chelmsford's viceroyalty had given a new dimension to the policy of divide and rule because while Muslim separatism could take care of the situation in the Indo-Gangetic plain, the regions below the Vindhyas had to be tackled differently. Here a beginning was made with the sponsoring of a non-Brahmin movement. The final bid to split the Hindu community was even more ingenious; the untouchables were encouraged to claim they were a sub-nation entitled to separate electorates. An attempt has been made to deal with this subject at length in the third part of this trilogy.

VI

Khilafat Movement and its Impact

Right from Gandhi's time secularism[83] in India has meant pandering to the most fundamentalist elements of Islam. The abolition of Khilafat by Kamal Ataturk was at the volition of the Turkish people, symbolically realizing the segregation of religion from politics in the Islamic world. It was a rational and forward-looking move by Turkey, but failed to vibe with Indian Muslims, the majority of whom remained steeped in literatim religiosity and backwardness. Fanaticism over the Khilafat reached such a pitch that thousands of Indian Muslims began to migrate to Afghanistan. But King Amanulla persuaded their leaders to give up the movement and the majority returned to India disillusioned and penniless.[84] By the way, Gandhi had gone all out to support the demand of Indian Muslims for restoration of Khilafat.

Jinnah criticised Gandhi's Khilafat advocacy, which he saw as an endorsement of religious zealotry. In a letter to Gandhi, Jinnah said that the movement was bound to lead to disaster. He said that this kind of a plan has appealed only to the illiterate and the inexperienced youth of the country. He said that though he had no power to remove the cause, he wished to advise his countrymen against the dire consequences of such an extreme act.[85]

Jinnah was the only mainstream Muslim politician who vehemently opposed it labelling Maulana Muhammad Ali Johar and his brother Maulana Shaukat Ali as 'religious fanatics'. Jinnah opposed the Khilafat movement for a couple of reasons including its non-secular nature, Khilafat in itself being no more than a symbolic position more corrupted than any other institution and its ties to the Hijrat movement which was devastating to the families that took part in it.

Commentators see in Jinnah's criticism of the Khilafat movement his principled opposition to both unconstitutional political forms and any articulation of Islam with politics. Thus, Jinnah's secularism emerges in the wake of his commitment to constitutionality and his unemotional, detached personality, in contrast to the rabble-rousing antics of the leaders of the Khilafat movement. For example, S. Mahmud Ali writes:

> In 1919, Gandhi had aroused Jinnah's constitutionalist ire by offering the support of Congress to the Khilafat movement. This meant that, instead of remaining a well-mannered debate in the well-appointed homes of well-bred natives, the nationalist campaign would become a mass movement in which English-educated lawyers and professionals might lose control. The prospect of mass violence forced Jinnah to abandon politics and return to London.[86]

Similarly, adds A.C. Neimeijer, Jinnah viewed the Khilafat movement as a 'false religious frenzy'.[87] For Ayesha Jalal, Jinnah "derided the false and dangerous religious frenzy which had confused Indian politics and the zealots ... who were harming the national cause".[88] All these readings share a view of Jinnah as being, by nature, an emotionless character who thus would oppose any political movement that was based on emotional frenzy. In other words, it is the personality of Jinnah that determines his disdain for the Khilafat movement. On the other hand, Mujahid argues:

> Jinnah was sympathetic to the Khilafat cause: see, for instance, his 1916 address on India's Claim for Home Rule (Madras, 1917), pp. 277-78; his presidential address at the Calcutta Special League session (September 1920) wherein he makes some very trenchant criticism and caustic comments on British attitude towards the Turks ... Jinnah not only led a League delegation to the British Prime Minister in the summer of 1919 and handed him a memorial on behalf of Muslims; he also telegraphed full support to the demands of the Khilafat deputation waiting to see the Viceroy in January 1920 since he could not join it.[89]

S. Sayyid and I.D. Tyrer also point out that Jinnah never publicly attacked the Khilafat movement or the ideal of Khilafat. Rather, he focused his concern especially on the Khilafat movement's alliance with non-cooperation under Gandhi, and directed his opposition especially at Mohammad Ali.[90] Jinnah after the Nagpur Congress of December 1920 even criticised Muhammad Ali not as an advocate of an Islamic order, but as pseudo-religious.[91]

The special session of the Congress at Calcutta in September 1920 passed the resolution adopting non-cooperation with the Government to right the wrong done to the Ottoman Empire, which represented the Khilafat, the Papacy of the Muslim world, and as a protest against the terrorist regime in the Punjab. Though many Hindu leaders participated in the Khilafat movement, all of them did not wholeheartedly participate in this movement. In a surcharged atmosphere Pandit Madan Mohan Malaviya and Dr. Munje raised a dissenting voice. Even Lala Lajpat Rai, the President of the Calcutta Congress session privately expressed his diffidence about the Gandhian programme.[92]

Dr. B.R. Ambedkar's views on the issue were:

> The Mohammedans started the Khilafat movement in 1919. The objective of the movement was two-fold; to preserve the Khilafat and to maintain the integrity of the Turkish Empire. Both these objectives were unsupportable. The Khilafat could not be saved simply because the Turks, in whose interest this agitation was carried on, did not want the Sultan. They wanted a republic and it was quite unjustifiable to compel the Turks to keep Turkey a monarchy when they wanted to convert it into a republic. It was not open to insist upon the integrity of the Turkish Empire because it meant the perpetual subjection of the different nationalities to the Turkish rule and particularly of the Arabs, especially when it was agreed on all hands that the doctrine of self-determination should be made the basis of the peace settlement.[93]

Gandhi not only agreed with the Muslims in the Khilafat cause, but acted as their guide and their friend. He toured the country between 1st August and 1st September, 1920 in the company of the Ali Brothers impressing upon the people the necessity of non-co-operation. People could notice the disharmony in the tune of Gandhi and the Ali Brothers. The *Modern Review* pointed out: "Reading between the lines of their speeches, it is not difficult to see that with one of them the sad plight of the Khilafat in distant Turkey is the central fact, while with the other attainment of *Swaraj* here in India is the object in view."

Dealing with this criticism of the *Modern Review* in his article for 20th October, 1921 Gandhi said:

> I claim that with us both the Khilafat is the central fact, with Maulana Mahomed Ali because it is his religion, with me because, in laying down my life for the Khilafat, I ensure safety of the cow, that is my religion, from the Musalman knife.[94]

Gandhi's approach to Khilafat was quite unrealistic. He tried to be too idealistic in political matters. He espoused the Khilafat with a view to forging Hindu-Muslim unity but the results obtained were disappointing. Why it happened? A plausible answer was perhaps given by Nehru in *An Autobiography* thus: "the oft-repeated appeal for Hindu-Muslim unity, useful as it no doubt is, seemed to me singularly inane, unless some effort was made to understand the causes of the disunity".[95] Both Jinnah and Tilak had strong reservations about Gandhi's decision to lend support to the Khilafat movement. The argument was that Muslims should be brought within the fold of the Congress on the basis of *swaraj* and not on sectarian grounds on an issue that was foreign.

Another point that Gandhi overlooked at the time of joining hands with the League over Khilafat issue was that Khilafat was a religious issue in which not to speak of all non-Muslims, even the Mussalmans of Turkey, had no interest. As soon as Kamal Pasha came to power in Turkey, he called off the Khilafat movement and even turned the Khalifa out of Turkey. Interestingly, Nehru points out, the word 'Khilafat' bore a strange meaning in most of the rural areas. People thought it came from *khilaf*, an Urdu word meaning 'against' or 'opposed to'. And so they took it to mean: opposed to Government![96] By confusing a religious issue with national struggle, Gandhi earned nothing, but disaffection and criticism and in the process "helped in spreading the atmosphere of revivalism".[97]

Subhas Chandra Bose did not think one could find fault with the Mahatma for his intimate association with the Khilafat movement. The real mistake in his opinion

> did not lie in connecting the Khilafat issue with the other national issues, but in allowing the Khilafat Committee to be set up as an independent organization throughout the country, quite apart from the Indian National Congress. The result of this was that when later on Ghazi Mustafa Kemal Pasha, as the leader of the New Turkey, forced the Sultan to abdicate and abolished the office of Khalifa altogether, the Khilafat question lost all meaning and significance and the majority of the members of the Khilafat organization were absorbed by sectarian, reactionary and pro-British Moslem organizations. If no separate Khilafat Committees had been organized and all Khilafatist Moslems had been persuaded to join the ranks of the Indian National Congress, they would probably have been absorbed by the later when the Khilafat issue became a dead one.[98]

Gandhi's effort to promote Hindu-Muslim unity by appeasing the Muslims also bore bitter fruits in the years that followed. His effort was, however, in consonance with the formula laid down by him for solving the communal problem. According to him, it could only be solved by goodwill and the generosity of the majority group, and so he was prepared to agree to everything that the Muslims might demand. He wanted to win them over, not to bargain with them.[99] As a true follower of Gandhi his heir-apparent, Jawaharlal Nehru said in the All-India Congress Session at Lucknow in 1935 that the majority community must show generosity in the matter (of communal question) to allay the fears of the minority.[100] This was and has remained to be the declared

Congress policy since then. How far it has succeeded in achieving the desired objective is a matter to be seriously pondered over. Apparently, the implications and fall-out of this policy were not realized either by Gandhi or by his die-herd followers, as the later-day events suggest.

On the pitfalls of the Khilafat Movement the renowned historian R.C. Majumdar commented:

> Gandhi's attitude towards the Khilafat question was criticized even by his friends; he justified himself in the name of Hindu-Muslim unity, and on grounds of expediency. But Gandhi failed to realize that the pan-Islamic idea which inspired the Khilaft question cut at the very root of Indian nationality. If the real sympathy and "vital interests" of a large section of Indians were bound up with a State and society which lay far outside the boundaries of India and had no political connection with it, they could never form a unit of Indian nationality. Howsoever opinions might differ on the basic requirements of nationality, it is generally agreed that different groups of people cannot constitute a nation unless they have common sympathy, agreement, and interest to such an extent as does not subsist between any of them and any external group. If a hundred million Muslims are more vitally interested in the fate of Turkey and other Muslim States outside India, than they are in the fate of India, they can hardly be regarded as a unit of Indian nation. By his own admission that the Khilaft question was a vital one for Indian Muslims, Gandhi himself admitted in a way that they formed a separate nation; they were in India, but not of India.
>
> That 'expediency' had also a share in the formulation of Gandhi's views is fully proved by his oft-quoted statement that such an opportunity of winning over the Muslims and forging the unity of Indian people to fight the British would not come in a hundred years. It is really this feeling that was uppermost in the minds of the Hindu leaders. But they did not realize the true significance of the Khilafat Movement and the danger to Indian nationality lurking behind it.[101]

The semblance of communal harmony which appeared during the year 1920-21 disappeared for ever. "During 1920 and 1924, the Moslem League was eclipsed by the All-India Khilafat Committee. But after the abolition of the Khalifaet in 1924, the Khilafat movement in India collapsed, and the Moslem League regained its former importance."[102] The Muslim League revived its ignominious activities. The Ali Brothers who at one time used to be called the two arms of Gandhi began to preach the gospel of communalism. In 1923 Mohammad Ali presided over the session of the Indian National Congress. In his address he spoke highly of Gandhi. A year after, he speaking at Aligarh and Ajmere said: "However pure Mr. Gandhi's character may be, he must appear to me from the point of view of religion inferior to any Musalman, even though he be without character". And he repeated it at Aminabad Park in Lucknow: "Yes, according to my religion and creed, I do hold an adulterous and a fallen Musalman to be better than Mr. Gandhi."[103]

Pandit Jawaharlal Nehru commented in his *Autobiography*:

> Owing to the prominence given to the Khilafat movement in 1921 a large number of Moulvies and Muslim religious leaders took a prominent part in the political struggle. They gave a definite religious tinge to the movement, and Muslims generally were greatly influenced by it. Many a Westernised Muslim, who was not of a particularly religious turn of mind, began to grow a beard and otherwise conform to the tenets of orthodoxy. The influence and prestige of the Moulvies, which had been gradually declining owing to new ideas and a progressive Westernisation, began to grow again and dominate the Muslim community. The Ali brothers, themselves of a religious turn of mind, helped in this process, and so did Gandhiji, who paid the greatest regard to the Moulvies and the Maulanas.[104]

The incorporation of the *ulema* and the open use of religious symbols instilled religious sentiments among the Muslim masses. The discord between the two communities—Hindus and Muslims— became wider than it was ever before. The Moplah rebellion broke out in August 1921 after Khilafat agitators, including Abul Kalam Azad, who was described by Rajaji as "The Great Akbar of Today", and Hakim Ajmal Khan, had been making violent speeches in that area. The principal feature of this rebellion was its religious aspect and the forcible conversion of Hindus to Islam in complete disregard of the much-vaunted Hindu-Muslim unity.[105]

By the end of 1921, besides the Moplah rebellion, there were a number of communal riots at various places within the country and by 1922-23 the Hindu-Muslim alliance was practically over. In 1923, "a movement was started among Indian Moslems in opposition to the Indian National Congress—called 'Tanzeem' and 'Tabligh'—which aimed at organising the Moslem as strong and virile community. This movement gained adherents for some time, but before long it fell into disfavour and was replaced by communal or sectarian organisations of a different kind. While the above movement was going on among the Moslems, the Hindus were not altogether idle. Their communal organization—called the *Hindu Mahasabha*—sought to strengthen itself by deciding at its annual meeting in August to admit the depressed classes to all the rights and privileges enjoyed by high-caste Hindus. Corresponding to 'Tanzeem' and 'Tabligh' movement among the Moslems, a 'Sangathan' movement was started among the Hindus. Further, in order to reclaim those

Hindus who for some reason or other had left the Hindu fold in the past, the '*Shuddhi*' (or purification) movement was started. By performing the *Shuddhi* ceremony, it was made possible for a non-Hindu to become a Hindu. The apostle of this movement was Swami Shraddhananda, a highly respected leader of the *Hindu Mahasabha*, through whose influence thousands of non-Hindus, including Moslems and Christians, were converted to Hinduism."[106] Swami Shraddhananda was subsequently murdered by a Muslim fanatic probably out of his resentment at the *Shuddhi* movement.

The abolition of the Khalifate in March 1924 by Mustapha Kemal Pahsa "struck at the root of the Khilafat Committees in India and indirectly helped the revival of the All-India Muslim League. In December 1924, when the All-India Moslem League met once again, the Khilafatists were defeated for the first time since 1920. The newly-revived All-India Moslem League became more sectarian and reactionary that it had been prior to 1920."[107] The religious fervour articulated by a segment of Muslims to Indian nationalism was matched by the consolidation of militant Hindu chauvinism exemplified by the metamorphosis of a revolutionary Veer Savarkar to a Hindu fundamentalist and the establishment of the Rashtriya Swayamsevak Sangh in 1925.

Namboodiripad describes the situation thus:

> Many of the non-cooperators of the 1921 period became champions of the sectional claims of this or that community. Communal organizations in general, and those of Hindus and Muslims in particular, began to grow and make tall claims for their respective communities. What was worse, these sectional claims of particular communities found their champions even among well-known leaders of the Congress, some of whom helped Hindu communal organizations while others helped their Muslim counterparts.
>
> Communalism, however, did not confine itself to the making of claims and counter-claims at the top level alone; it enveloped the whole public life of the country. Issues like cow slaughter, music before mosques, conversion and reconversion of individuals from one religion to another—all these assumed serious proportions, and in several instances, led to clashes and even murders. The atmosphere of communal unity, which had been generated in the days of non-cooperation and Khilafat and which gave a national, democratic character to the movement gave place to one of acute tension.
>
> Gandhi's reaction to this situation was characteristic. The sensitive soul in him revolted at the internecine quarrel that had destroyed the exhilarating atmosphere of the glorious days of non-cooperation. His heart bled at the inhuman deeds perpetrated by people who spoke in the name of God, but acted as agents of Satan. Against the indescribable horrors that had been perpetrated in the name of

religion, he entered his first public protest by undertaking a fast for bringing peace and harmony.

This had, of course, a temporary effect. Leaders of different communities came together and promised Gandhi that they would do their utmost to preserve communal peace. But it had no lasting effect on the public life of the country. On the contrary, further the Congress under Gandhi's leadership advanced in the direction of successful struggle for *swaraj*, the worse became the communal situation. At every subsequent phase in the struggle against imperialism, the communal situation became the biggest stumbling block in Gandhi's way. In the end, it led to a distorted type of *swaraj* which was a blow against all that Gandhi stood for—the partition of India into the Hindu-majority Indian Union and the Muslim-majority Pakistan—and his own tragic end at the hands of an assassin risen from the ranks of the Hindu communalists.[108]

VII

Fall-out of the 1923 Bengal Pact and the 1935 Government of India Act

By the end of 1922, the Civil Disobedience Enquiry Committee appointed by the Congress found that "the country is not prepared at present to embark upon general Mass Civil Disobedience... (but) recommend that provincial committees be authorized to sanction such limited Mass Civil Disobedience on their responsibility of the conditions laid down by the All-India Congress Committee in that behalf are fulfilled."[109] But this failed to settle the controversy between those who favoured the continued boycott of the new Councils and those who urged the reversal of Gandhi's ban on Council entry. At the Gaya Congress in December 1922, in his presidential address C.R. Das made a vigorous plea for Council entry. This was turned down by the 'no-changers'. The dissidents then constituted themselves into the Swaraj Party with C.R. Das as leader, and Motilal Nehru, with three others, as secretaries. Throughout the summer of 1923, the *Swarajists* steadily gained ground. The tide finally turned in their favour in September 1923. The Congress approved the modification of the boycott in favour of Council entry, and made it possible for them to breach the 'citadel of bureaucracy' both from inside and outside the Councils. In the elections the *Swarajists* won a clear majority in the Central Provinces. In Bengal, where Das had privately concluded a pact with Muslims as an electioneering device, they represented the strongest individual group. In the UP and Bombay, though the *Swarajists* were returned in considerable numbers, they did not have the majority of votes. In Punjab, Madras, Bihar and Orissa they were very weak.

Das concluded a pact with Bengali Muslim politicians between September and early December, 1923. This Pact was more favourable to the Muslims than the Lucknow Pact of 1916. Its main features were:

(1) For the provincial Council—representation on a population basis with separate electorates for Muslims.
(2) For the local bodies—representation in district boards and municipalities in the proportion of 60 to 40 in every district; 60 to the majority community and 40 to the minority community. The question of separate electorates was kept open.
(3) For government appointments—55 per cent seats were fixed for Muslims and the remaining 45 per cent were for other communities.
(4) To ensure religious tolerance and communal harmony, music was to be prohibited before the mosques and Muslims were to enjoy the freedom to perform cow-killing for religious purposes (*Korbani*).

The Montegu-Chelmsford Reforms had started the process by which Muslims could wrest control of local patronage from the *zamindars* and their clients; the Bengal Pact went a step further in the same direction.

Most of the Bengali Hindus regarded the pact as a one-sided bargain and launched a massive agitation against it. In December 1923, the Congress at Coconada in Madras Presidency rejected the Bengal Pact under pressure from Malaviya and Lajpat Rai who deprecated the attempt to solve what they regarded as an all-India question on provincial lines. It was alleged that it showed partiality for the Muslims and violated the principles of nationalism. Another pact which had been drawn up by Lala Lajpat Rai and Dr. M.A. Ansari for the settlement of the communal question was referred by the Coconada Congress to the All-India Congress Committee for consideration. These pacts indicated, points out Subhas Chandra Bose, that the better minds among the Congress leaders had began to realise the possibility of a communal rift and the necessity for making some sort of settlement before the breach widened. But sufficiently speedy or sufficiently drastic action was not taken, with the result that the differences did become more acute and grave and the country had to face a communal storm as soon as the political tension created by the Swaraj Party subsided after the death of Deshbandhu Das in June, 1925.[110]

C.R. Das warded off the attacks against him by prevailing upon the Bengal Provincial Conference to ratify the Pact in May 1924. The 'Bengal Pact' had served to convince the Muslims that Das was their real friend. That such a man was at the head of the *Swaraj* Party helped to rally Muslim support for that Party and as a matter of fact, the *Swaraj* Party in the Bengal Legislative

Council had a large number of Muslim members who had been elected on the basis of separate electorate. However, soon after his death the Congress leadership in Bengal was divided over the pact and the Swaraj Party even repudiated the Bengal pact under the exigency of elections.[111]

It did not need any great degree of perception to understand that if the *Swarajists* were to maintain their ascendancy in Bengal politics, they had to abandon their policy of pandering to the Muslims. Any further attempt to enforce the Bengal Pact in the spirit of Das was bound to drive the new mass of Hindu electorate into communal organisation, the most important being the *Hindu Mahasabha.*

The non-co-operation movement having spent its force, the breach between Indian politicians began to widen. In the Councils, communalism raised its ugly head, and on questions such as the slaughter of cows, the representation of Muslims on local bodies and in public services, there was a marked tendency towards communal groupings. Muslims were committed to communal representation and reservation of seats for their community; Hindus, on the other hand, were against these demands, and were particularly opposed to separate electorates for Muslims. Many UP Hindus resigned from or boycotted the municipal boards against the Jhangirabad amendment of March, 1916 and in 1922 many Punjabi Hindus did the same. In both the cases, the protest was against the concession of separate representation. Similarly, when Surendranath Banerjea, the first minister for local self-government in Bengal, agreed to concede separate electorates in the Calcutta Municipal Bill of 1923, a massive agitation was launched against him by the Hindu commercial and professional classes.[112]

Another important factor which deepened communal rivalries was the devolution of power to Indian hands which led to a struggle for power and patronage. The desire to obtain office or to prevent others from obtaining office became the mainspring of political activity, and politicians who had worked together for reforms became competitors in a struggle for power.[113]

The separatist system of representation by religious communities and other groups was retained in the Government of India Act, 1935. This Act went another step forward in perpetuating communal cleavage between the Muslim and the non-Muslim communities by prescribing separate electorates on the basis of the 'Communal Award' of the British Prime Minister on August 4, 1932. From now onwards, the agreement between the two religious communities was continuously foisted as a condition precedent for any further political advance. This system of communal electorate cut into the growth of a national feeling. In the constitutional set up under this Act, certain Provinces had legislatures with the largest number of seats ensured for the Muslims. Those were Bengal, the Punjab, the N.W.F.P. and Sind. Excepting the N.W.F.P., other Provinces were under the control of Muslim parties. Thus, from 1937,

India came to be divided, as it were, into two Zones—Muslim and Non-Muslim. Enough spade work was, therefore, done for the future demand for Pakistan.

Besides the Muslims, there were separate constituencies for General, European, Anglo-Indian, Indian Christian and Sikh communities. The electoral provisions of the Act of 1935 were governed by the communal decision of the British Government as modified by the Poona Pact of September 25, 1932. The communal decision of the British Government accentuated the communal dissension in the country, which paved the way for the partition of the country.

There were also separate constituencies for Labour, Land-holders, Commerce and Industry etc. The division of the constituencies into so many fragments helped in the polarisation of sectional interests. Whereas the growth of a party or parties having commanding influences in all the Provinces should have checked the disintegrating tendencies, the set up envisaged in the Act, as it were, were against the growth of such parties having a fully national character.

It was also during this period that party dissensions reached a point at which nationalism itself was at stake. The Act of 1935 conferred on the Governor-General and the Governors special responsibilities for the protection of the rights of minorities. The Muslim League was pledged to protect religious rights of the Muslims and to protect and promote the Urdu language and Persian script. The Muslim League often complained that the Governors and Governor-General had failed to protect the interests of the Muslims. Similarly, the Hindus of the Muslim-majority provinces were feeling bitterly about the administration there, and on some occasions, the Hindu leaders demanded the intervention of Governors.

The traits of disintegration and division of the country, given a constitutional and legal validity in the 1935 Act continued to be a prominent feature in the subsequent decisions of the British Government. The Cripps Proposal propounded the right of any province not to accede to India. If any province was not satisfied with the Constitution, then that province could go out and remain out of it with complete self-government by simple majority vote in the Legislative Assembly. The acceptance beforehand of the novel principle of non-accession for a province was a severe blow to the conception of Indian unity and an apple of discord likely to generate growing trouble in the provinces, and which might well lead to further difficulties in the way of the Indian States merging themselves in the Indian Union. The draft declaration encouraged and led to attempts at separation at the very inception of the Union and created friction just when utmost cooperation and goodwill were needed. The hint of a possible partition of the country encouraged fissiparous tendencies and this stirred into consciousness many a sleeping ambitions of having separate enclaves or *sthans* for them that would reduce the country to a non-entity.[114]

Apart from these constitutional, legal and administrative measures, the Colonial rulers also took other measures to exacerbate communalism. The different ways and policies, or acts of omission or commission, through which the British encouraged and nurtured communalism have been enumerated by Bipan Chandra *et al.,* thus:

> First, by consistently treating Hindus, Muslims and Sikhs as separate communities and socio-political entities which had little in common, India, it was said, was neither a nation nor a nation-in-the-making, nor did it consist of nationalities or local societies, but consisted of structured, mutually exclusive and antagonistic religion-based communities.
>
> Second, official favour and patronage were extended to the communalists.
>
> Third, the communal Press and persons and agitations were shown extraordinary tolerance.
>
> Fourth, communal demands were readily accepted, thus politically strengthening communal organizations and their hold over the people. For example, while the Congress could get none of its demands accepted from 1885-1905, the Muslim communal demands were accepted in 1906 as soon as they were presented to the Viceroy. Similarly, in 1932, the Communal Award accepted all the major communal demands of the time. During Second World War, the Muslim communalists were given complete veto on any political advance.
>
> Fifth, the British readily accepted communal organizations and leaders as the real spokesperson for their 'communities', while the nationalist leaders were treated as representing a microscopic minority—the elite.
>
> Lastly, the colonial government encouraged communalism through a policy of non-action against it. Certain positive measures which the state alone could undertake were needed to check the growth of communalism. The failure to undertake them served as an indirect encouragement to communalism. The Government refused to take action against the propagation of virulent communal ideas and communal hatred through the Press, pamphlets leaflets, literature, public platform and rumours. This was in sharp contrast with the frequent suppression of the nationalist Press, literature, civil servants, propaganda, and so on. On the contrary, the government freely rewarded communal leaders, intellectuals and government servants

with titles, positions of profit, high salaries, and so on. The British administrators also followed a policy of relative inactivity and irresponsibility in dealing with communal riots. When they occurred, they were not crushed energetically. The administration also seldom made proper preparations or took preventive measures to meet situations of communal tension, as they did in case of nationalist and other popular protest movements.[115]

VIII

Reification

The polarization of Muslims and Hindus under communal banner became the hallmark of the 1930s and 1940s. Though people professing different religions, including Hindus and Muslims, were living in India for centuries together, there was no vertical division of Indians on account of religion till the Muslim League ascribed separate nationhood to the Muslims in its struggle for carving out a separate state out of India, only for the Muslims. The famous Lahore Resolution of the Muslim League of 23rd March, 1940, demanded separation of Muslim-majority areas (of India) from India and their formation into independent States. The resolution ran as follows:

1. While approving and endorsing the action taken by the Council and the Working Committee of the All-India Muslim League as indicated in their resolutions dated the 27th of August, 17th and 18th of September and 22nd of October, 1939 and 3rd of February, 1940 on the constitutional issue, this session of the All-India Muslim League emphatically reiterates that the Scheme of Federation embodied in the Government of India Act, 1935, is totally unsuited to, and unworkable in, the peculiar conditions of this country, and is altogether unacceptable to Muslim India;
2. It further records its emphatic view that while the declaration dated the 18th of October, 1939 made by the Viceroy on behalf of His Majesty's Government is reassuring in as far as it declares that the policy and plan on which the Government of India Act, 1935, is based will be reconsidered in consultation with the various parties, interests and communities in India, Muslim India will not be satisfied unless the whole constitutional plan is reconsidered *de novo*, and that no revised plan would be acceptable to the Muslims unless it is framed with their approval and consent;
3. Resolved that it is the considered view of this Session of the All-India Muslim League that no constitutional plan would be workable

> in this country or acceptable to the Muslims unless it is designated on the following basic principles, *viz.* that geographically contiguous units are demarcated into regions which should be so constituted with such territorial readjustments as may be necessary, that the areas, in which the Muslims are numerically in a majority, as in the North-Western and Eastern Zones of India, should be grouped to constitute 'Independent States' in which the constituent units shall be autonomous and sovereign;
>
> 4. That adequate, effective and mandatory safeguards should be specifically provided in the constitution for minorities in these units and in the regions for the protection of their religious, cultural, economic, political, administrative, and other rights and interests in consultation with them; and in other parts of India where the Musalmans are in a majority, adequate, effective and mandatory safeguards shall be specifically provided in the constitution for them and other minorities for the protection of their religious, cultural, economic, political, administrative, and other rights and interests in consultation with them; and
> 5. The Session further authorizes the Working Committee to frame a Scheme of Constitution in accordance with these basic principles, providing for the assumption finally by the respective regions of all powers such as defence, external affairs, communication, customs and such other matters as may be necessary.[116]

With the announcement of the demand for Pakistan, the Muslim League and Jinnah set about stoking communal frenzy, telling Muslims that they couldn't co-exist with Hindus. Congress couldn't handle the upsurge of hatred and soon riots rocked the country, forcing the British to panic over the settlement of the independence and partition question.

The Lahore resolution was based on the idea that the Muslims were a nation as distinct from the Hindus who formed the bulk of the population of India, and as such, the Muslims must have a separate state of their own so that they might have an opportunity of developing their spiritual, cultural, economic and political life in accordance with their genius.

According to Jinnah, Islam and Hinduism

> are not religions in the strict sense of the word, but are different and distinct social orders. The Hindus and the Muslims have different religions. The Hindus and Muslims belong to different religious philosophies, social customs and literatures. They neither intermarry nor interdine together, and indeed, they belong to two different civilizations which are based mainly on conflicting ideas and conceptions. Their aspects on life and of life are different. It is

> quiet clear that Hindus and Muslims derive their inspiration from different sources of history. They have different epics, different heroes, and different episodes. Very often, the hero of one is a foe of the other and, likewise, their victories and defeats overlap. To yoke together two such nations under a single state, one as a numerical minority and the other as a majority, must lead to growing discontent and final destruction of any fabric that may be so built up for the government of such a state... Mussalmans are not a minority as is commonly known and ùnderstood...Mussalmans are a nation...and they must have their homeland, their territory, their state.[117]

As very rightly pointed out by A. Chatterjee:

> The claim to nationhood, it must be admitted, was not based strictly on logic. The difference between the Hindus and the Muslims were not much more glaring than the differences among the Muslims themselves. Religion was practically the sole criterion for determining the Muslim nationhood. No doubt, there were some divergences between the courses of development of the Hindus and the Muslims under British rule. But these were only historical accidents and not certainly germane to nationhood. The generally accepted criteria of nationality, other than religion, hardly distinguished the Muslims from the non-Muslims of India.[118]

Once it was recognized that British rule could not survive on the old basis for long, a graceful withdrawal from India became the overarching aim of British policy-makers. The British had three contingency plans, and were willing to give each a try. They would like to transfer power to the duly constituted government of a united India; they would, if necessary, devolve authority to two successor governments in Hindustan and Pakistan; and they might, at a pinch, proceed under 'Plan Balkan' to hand over power to a separate government in each province. While Gandhi pleaded for a united India, and Nehru and Patel maneuvered to hand Jinnah a 'moth-eaten Pakistan', there were takers for bits of Plan Balkan, too: H.S. Suhrawardy and Sarat Chandra Bose set a move afoot for United Bengal, and Khan Abdul Gaffar Khan pleaded desperately that if the country were to be divided after all, then the North-West Frontier Province should be allowed to go its own free and separate way as Pathanistan.[119]

The Cabinet Mission Plan of 16th May, 1946 was a sort of compromise between union and division of British India. It repudiated the scheme of Pakistan and instead brought the provisions for the grouping of Provinces. The compulsory grouping of the six Muslim Provinces of the 'Pakistan Group' in Sections B and C and the right of secession of Provinces or Groups from the Union provided for the basis of Pakistan by implication. The Cabinet Mission hoped that by the grouping provision, the Muslims would secure the advantages of Pakistan without its disadvantage. Subsequent interpretation of the Cabinet Mission Plan embodied in the Statement of 6th December made the grouping of Provinces compulsory. Moreover, there was an encouragement to an unwilling part to demonstrate its unwillingness by refusing to attend the Constituent Assembly, so that the Constitution framed by the Assembly would not apply to it. The expression 'parts of the country' might be rightly taken to mean even parts of the Provinces. This interpretation prompted the non-Muslims to start agitation for partition of the Muslim-majority areas, whereas a direct bid for Pakistan seemed to be the card Jinnah now sought to play.

With the battle cry, *Lekar rahenge Pakistan, Larke lenge Pakistan,* Muslim communal groups provoked communal frenzy in Calcutta on August 16, 1946. Hindu communal groups retaliated in equal measure and the cost was 5000 lives lost. The British authorities were worried that they had lost control over the 'Frankenstein monster' they had helped to create, but felt it was too late to tame it. They were frightened into appeasing the League by Jinnah's ability to unleash civil war. Wavel quietly brought the League into the Interim Government on October 26, 1946 though it had not accepted either the short or long term provisions of the Cabinet Mission Plan and had not given up its policy of Direct Action. Jinnah had succeeded in keeping the British in his grip.[120]

The demand for Pakistan, first mooted on March 23, 1940, became a reality on August 14, 1947, i.e. within 8 years. The demand for separation was ascribed in certain quarters to the annoyance caused to the Muslim League by the Congress in its refusal (a) to recognise the Muslim League as the only representative body of the Muslims in India and (b) to form coalition Ministries in the Congress Provinces when the Provincial part of the Government of India Act, 1935, was introduced in 1937.[121] In his book, "*Partition: The Real Story*", Prof. Mushtaq Naqvi says that Partition "was a surgical operation by an amateur butcher performed in the dark on a pavement...Partition was uncalled for, unnatural, not at all inevitable and a negation of all that India stood for throughout her long and chequered history spanning 50 centuries".[122] Prof. Stanley Wolpert, author of *Jinnah of Pakistan*, feels Nehru's intransigence was as responsible for the cataclysmic fall-out in both the key issues of Partition and Kashmir as was Jinnah's cussedness.[123]

India was partitioned as the Muslim League, the dominant political party of the Muslims of undivided India, had no faith in the secular credentials of the Congress. Jinnah used to call the organization the "Hindu Congress Party". According to Ayesha Jalal, the Pakistani-American historian and author of *The Sole Spokesman; Jinnah*, it was the inability of the Congress and the

Muslim League to arrive at a power sharing arrangement that led to the partition of India. Instead of the purported unities of religion that were supposed to be the driving force in the making of Pakistan, it was regional, class and ideological differences among Muslims and Congress's emphatic opposition to what it saw as Jinnah's unreasonable demands that led to partition.[124] According to Liaquat Ali Khan, the First Prime Minister of Pakistan: "Pakistan was founded by the indomitable will of a hundred million Muslims who felt they were a nation too numerous and too distinct to be relegated for ever to the unalterable position of a political minority, especially when in the vast subcontinent which was their homeland, there was enough room for two great nations".[125]

While historian Sumit Sarkar thought that in the context of the riots, both the Congress and Muslim League felt a parting of ways was inevitable, historian Mushirul Hasan was of the view that Pakistan became unavoidable after Second World War "simply because Jinnah had raised the expectations of his Muslim constituency. In other words, the pressures from below were too strong for reversing attitudes and strategies. Jinnah could ill-afford to backtrack. For him, achieving 'Pakistan' became a matter of life and death." Ram Chandra Guha felt that "after the start of Second World War and the 1946 elections—where the Muslim League swept the Muslim vote and the Congress the Hindu vote—it certainly became unavoidable". The Pakistani historian Mubarak Ali pointed out that "some historians believe that Jinnah used Pakistan only as a card to get political rights for Muslims and he never wanted separation. This argument was validated when he accepted the Cabinet Mission Plan in 1946; it was Nehru and the Congress who rejected it. In the end, Partition was actually thrust upon him by Mountbatten. Jinnah was not in favour of the partition of Punjab and Bengal. He had also not expected mass migration. However, on his departure from India he did ask Indian Muslims to be loyal to their country and later asked the same of non-Muslims in Pakistan".[126] While the Indian leaders did not also enforce mass migration, a corollary of the acceptance of the Two Nation Theory, and thereby kept the rancour of communalism for ever, Jinnah's plan of non-division of Punjab and Bengal was scuttled mainly by the efforts of Hindu nationalists like Dr. Shyama Prasad Mookherjee. If Jinnah's plan had succeeded there would have been no place to live in for the Bengali Hindus and the Punjabi Hindus and Punjabi Sikhs in independent India.

Whatever might be the immediate cause(s), the fact remains that the Congress could not win over the Muslim masses and prevent partition on the basis of Muslim-majority areas. Jinnah was obdurate that the Muslims would settle for nothing less than a sovereign state. The British could keep India united only if they gave up their role as mediators trying to effect an agreed solution. Unity needed positive intervention in its favour, including putting down communal elements with a firm hand. This they chose not to do. Ultimately the country was partitioned on the basis of Muslim-majority areas according to the June 3, 1947 Statement of the British Government which later formed the basis of the Independence Act, 1947, the legal document formalising the creation of two Dominions—India and Pakistan. It was the culmination of the communal politics so assiduously pursued by the British since the First War of Independence.

The logical inference of partition solely on the basis of religion should have been that communalism would be completely eradicated from the body polity in independent India. The factors which paved the way for creation of Pakistan like separate electorates, special and additional seats in the legislatures, reservation in elective posts, quota in service, separate identity of the Muslims and so on and so forth were all known to our national leaders. The Independent truncated India should have been free of the virus of communalism. But that did not happen. While Pakistan declared itself a theocratic Muslim State, India chose to remain secular. But even after witnessing the consequences of religious fundamentalism and communal carnage India did not take effective steps to enforce secularism in the real sense of the term.

The narrow political demands which often created barriers in the way of national unity and progress,[127] the forces which were spreading communalism, the persons who were fomenting communalism, the issues which were supposed to be the causes for generating communalism, should not have found a congenial atmosphere to sustain themselves in this country specially after its vivisection on the basis of religion. But it did not. "The socio-political context of communalism, however, underwent basic structural changes after partition".[128] Colonial State which was a major prop of communalism was succeeded by a secular State. A secular Constitution has also been framed with the very idea of de-linking religion from state affairs. The social, class character and base of communalism have also undergone major changes after 1947.[129] The colonial outlook, imperialistic hegemony, capitalist interest, bourgeoisie exploitation which nurtured and sustained communalism during the British rule had no longer any role to play. Even then communalism could not be eradicated from the society. Bipan Chandra notes:

> Indian society continues to provide objective social, economic and political bases as also ideological and cultural soil for the rise and growth of communalism.[130]

There are issues which still create a congenial atmosphere for the growth and sustenance of communalism in free India. We propose to undertake an in-depth study on some of them which are causing a hiatus between the major religious communities and directly or indirectly are creating conducive atmosphere for the continuance of communal cleavages in our body politic. These are:

1. Separate teaching—minority schools and religious teaching at government expense;
2. Propagation of religion and conversion from one religion to another;
3. Hurting the religious susceptibilities—slaughter of cow; and
4. Separate laws—uniform civil code.

Appendix A

Address presented to Lord Minto, Viceroy and Governor-General of India by a Deputation of the Muslim Community of India on 1st October, 1906 at Simla

ADDRESS

May it please your Excellency,—Availing ourselves of the permission accorded to us, we, the undersigned nobles, *jagirdars*, *taluqdars*, lawyers, *zamindars*, merchants and others representing a large body of the Mohammedan subjects of His Majesty the King-Emperor in different parts of India, beg most respectfully to approach your Excellency with the following address for your favourable consideration.

We fully realize and appreciate the incalculable benefits conferred by British rule on the teeming millions belonging to diverse races and professing diverse religions who form the population of the vast continent of India, and have every reason to be grateful for the peace, security, personal freedom and liberty of worship that we now enjoy. Further, from the wise and enlightened character of the Government, we have every reasonable ground for anticipating that these benefits will be progressive, and that India will in future occupy an increasingly important position in the comity of nations.

One of the most important characteristics of British policy in India is the increasing deference that has so far as possible been paid from the first to the views and wishes of the people of the country in matters affecting their interests, with due regard always to the diversity of race and religion which forms such an important feature of all Indian progress.

Claims of the Community

Beginning with the confidential and unobtrusive method of consulting influential members of important communities in different parts of the country, this principle was gradually extended by the recognition of the right of recognized political or commercial organisations to communicate to the authorities their criticisms and views on measures of public importance, and finally by the nomination and election of direct representatives of the people in Municipalities, District Boards, and above all in the Legislative Chambers of the country. This last element is, we understand, about to be dealt with by the Committee appointed by your Excellency with the view of giving it further extension, and it is with reference mainly to our claim to a fair share in such extended representation and some other matters of importance affecting the interests of our community, that we have ventured to approach your Excellency on the present occasion.

Past Traditions

The Mohammedans of India number, according to the census taken in the year 1901, over sixty-two millions or between one-fifth and one-fourth of the total population of His Majesty's Indian dominions, and if a reduction be made for the uncivilized portions of the community enumerated under the heads of animist and other minor religions, as well as for those classes who are ordinarily classified as Hindus, but properly speaking are not Hindus at all, the proportion of Mohammedans to the Hindu majority becomes much larger. We, therefore, desire to submit that under any system of representation extended or limited a community in itself more numerous than the entire population of any first class European power except Russia may justly lay claim to adequate recognition as an important factor in the State.

We venture, indeed, with your Excellency's permission to go a step further, and urge that the position accorded to the Mohammedan community in any kind of representation, direct or indirect, and in all other ways affecting their status and influence should be commensurate, not merely with their numerical strength, but also with their political importance and the value of the contribution which they make to the defence of the empire, and also hope that your Excellency will in this connection be pleased to give due consideration to the position which they occupied in India a little more than hundred years ago and of which the traditions have naturally not faded from their minds.

The Mohammedans of India have always placed implicit reliance on the sense of justice and love of fair dealing that have characterised their rulers, and have in consequence abstained from pressing their claims by methods that might prove at all embarrassing, but earnestly as we desire that the Mohammedans of India should not in the future depart from that excellent and time-honoured tradition, recent events have stirred up feelings, especially among the younger generation of Mohammedans, which might, in certain circumstances and under certain contingencies easily pass beyond the control of temperate counsel and sober guidance.

We, therefore, pray that the representations we herewith venture to submit, after a careful consideration of the views and wishes of a large number of our co-religionists in all parts of India, may be favoured with your Excellency's earnest attention.

European Representative Institutions

We hope your Excellency will pardon our stating at the outset that representative institutions of the European type are new to the Indian people; many of the most thoughtful members of our community in fact consider that the greatest care, forethought and caution will be necessary if they are to be successfully adapted to the social, religious and political conditions obtaining in India, and that in the absence of such care and caution their adoption is likely, among other evils, to place our national interests at the mercy of the unsympathetic majority. Since, however, our rulers have, in pursuance of the immemorial instincts and traditions, found it expedient to give these institutions an increasingly important place in the Government of the country, we Mohammedans, cannot any longer in justice to our own national interests hold aloof from participating in the conditions to which their policy has given rise. While, therefore, we are bound to acknowledge with gratitude that such representation as the Mohammedans of India have hitherto enjoyed has been due to a sense of justice and fairness on the part of your Excellency and your illustrious predecessor in office and the heads of Local Governments by whom the Mohammedan members of Legislative Chambers have almost without exception been nominated, we cannot help observing that the representation thus accorded to us has necessarily been inadequate to our requirements, and has not always carried with it the approval of those whom the nominees were selected to represent. This state of things was probably under existing circumstances unavoidable, for a while on the one hand the number of nominations reserved to the Viceroy and Local Governments has necessarily been strictly limited, the selection on the other hand of really representative men has, in the absence of any reliable method of ascertaining the direction of popular choice, been far from easy.

The Results of Election

As for the results of election, it is most unlikely that the name of any Mohammedan candidate will ever be submitted for the approval of Government by the electoral bodies as now constituted unless he is in sympathy with the majority in all matters of importance. Nor can we in fairness find fault with desire of our Non-Muslim fellow-subjects to take full advantage of their strength and vote only for members of their own community, or for persons who, if not Hindus, are expected to vote with the Hindu majority on whose goodwill they would have to depend for their future re-election. It is true that we have many and important interests in common with our Hindu fellow-countrymen and it will always be a matter of the utmost satisfaction to us to see these interests safeguarded by the pressure in our Legislative Chambers of able supporters of these interests, irrespective of their nationality.

A Distinct Community

Still, it cannot be denied that we Mohammedans are a distinct community with additional interests of our own which are not shared by other communities, and these have hitherto suffered from the fact that they have not been adequately represented. Even in the provinces in which the Mohammedans constitute a distinct majority of the population, they have too often been treated as though they were inappreciably small political factors that might without unfairness be neglected. This has been the case, to some extent, in the Punjab, but in a more marked degree in Sind and in Eastern Bengal.

Before formulating our views with regard to the election of representatives, we beg to observe that the political importance of a community to a considerable extent gains strength or suffers detriment according to the position that the members of that community occupy in the service of the State. If, as is unfortunately the case with the Mohammedans, they are not adequately represented in this manner, they lose in the prestige and influence which are justly their due.

Employment in Government Service

We therefore pray that Government will be graciously pleased to provide that both in the gazetted and the subordinate and ministerial services of all Indian provinces a due proportion of Mohammedans shall always find place. Orders of like import have at times been issued by Local Governments in some provinces, but have not, unfortunately, in all cases been strictly observed on the ground that qualified Mohammedans were not forthcoming. This allegation however, well founded it may have been at one time, is, we submit, no longer tenable now, and wherever the will to employ them is not wanting the supply of qualified Mohammedans, we are happy to be able to assure your Excellency, is equal to the demand.

The Competitive Element

Since, however, the number of qualified Mohammedans has increased, a tendency is unfortunately perceptible to reject them on the ground of relatively superior qualifications having to be given preference. This introduces something like the competitive element in its worst form, and we may be permitted to draw your Excellency's attention to the political significance of the monopoly of all official influence by one class. We may also point out in this connection that the efforts of Mohammedan educationists have from the very outset of the educational movement among them been strenuously directed towards the development of character, and this we venture to think is of greater importance than mere mental alertness in the making of good public servants.

Mohammedans on the Bench

We venture to submit that the generality of Mohammedans in all parts of India feel aggrieved that Mohammedan Judges are not more frequently appointed to the High Courts and Chief Courts of Judicature. Since the creation of these Courts only three Mohammedans lawyers have held these honourable appointments, all of whom have fully justified their elevation to the Bench. At the present moment there is not a single Mohammedans Judge sitting on the Bench of any of these Courts, while there are three Hindu Judges in the Calcutta High Court, where the proportion of Mohammedans in the population is very large, and two in the Chief Court of Punjab, where the Mohammedans form the majority of the population. It is not, therefore, an extravagant request on our part that a Mohammedan should be given a seat on the Bench of each of the High Courts and Chief Courts. Qualified Mohammedan lawyers eligible for these appointments can always be found, if not in one province then in another. We beg permission further to submit that the presence on the Bench of these Courts of a Judge learned in the Mohammedan Law will be a source of considerable strength to the administration of justice.

Municipal Representation

As Municipal and District Boards have to deal with important local interests affecting to a great extent the health, comfort, educational needs and even the religious concerns of the inhabitants, we shall, we hope, be pardoned if we solicit for a moment your Excellency's attention to the position of Mohammedans thereon before passing to higher concerns. These institutions form, as it were, the initial rungs in the ladder of self-government, and it is here that the principle of representation is brought home intimately to the intelligence of the people, yet the position of Mohammedans on these Boards is not at present regulated by any guiding principle capable of general application, and practice varies in different localities. The Aligarh Municipality, for example, is divided into six wards and each ward returns one Hindu and one Mohammedans Commissioner, and the same principle we understand is adopted in a number of Municipalities in the Punjab and elsewhere, but in a good many places the Mohammedan tax-payers are not adequately represented. We would, therefore, respectfully suggest that the local authority should in every case be required to declare the number of Hindus and Mohammedan entitled to seats on Municipal and District Boards, such proportion to be determined in accordance with the numerical strength, social status, local influence and special requirements of either community. Once their relative proportion is authoritatively determined, we would suggest that either community should be allowed severally to return their own representatives as is the practice in many towns in the Punjab.

Fellows of Universities

We would also suggest that the Senates and Syndicates of Indian Universities might be similarly dealt with, that is to say, there should, so far as possible, be an authoritative declaration of the proportion in which Mohammedans are entitled to be represented in either body.

Nomination to Provincial Councils

We now proceed to the consideration of the question of our representation in the Legislative Chambers of the country. Beginning with the Provincial Councils, we would most respectfully suggest that as in the case of Municipalities and District Boards the proportion of Mohammedan representatives entitled to seats should be determined and declared with due regard to the important considerations which we have ventured to point out in paragraph 5 of this address, and that the important Mohammedan landowners, lawyers, merchants and representatives of other important interests, the Mohammedan members of District Boards and Municipalities and the Mohammedan graduates of universities of a certain standing, say five years, should be formed into Electoral Colleges and be authorized, in accordance with such rules of procedures as your Excellency's Government may be pleased to prescribe in that behalf, to return the number of members that may be declared to be eligible.

The Viceroy's Council

With regard to the Imperial Legislative Council whereon the due representation of Mohammedan interests is a matter of vital importance, we crave leave to suggest (1) that in the cadre of the Council the proportion of Mohammedan representatives should not be determined on the basis of the numerical strength of the community, and that in any case the Mohammedan representatives should never be an ineffective minority; (2) that as far as possible, appointment by election should be given preference over nominations; (3) that for the purposes of choosing Mohammedan members, Mohammedan landowners, lawyers, merchants and representatives of other important interests of a status to be subsequently determined by your Excellency's Government, Mohammedan members of the Provincial Councils and Mohammedan fellows of universities should be invested with electoral powers to be exercised in accordance with such procedure as may be prescribed by your Excellency's Government in that behalf.

The Executive Council

An impression has lately been gaining ground that one or more Indian Members may be appointed on the Executive Council of the Viceroy. In the event of such appointment being made we beg that the claims of Mohammedans in that connection may not be overlooked. More than one Mohammedan, we venture to say, will be found in the country fit to serve with distinction in that august chamber.

A Mohammedan University

We beg to approach your Excellency on a subject which must closely affect our national welfare. We are convinced that our aspirations as a community and our future progress are largely dependent on the foundation of a Mohammedan University which will be the centre of our religious and intellectual life. We, therefore, most respectfully pray that your Excellency will take steps to help us in an undertaking in which our community is so deeply interested.

In conclusion, we beg to assure your Excellency that in assisting the Mohammedan subjects of His Majesty at this stage in the development of Indian affairs in the directions indicated in the present address, your Excellency will be strengthening the basis of their unswerving loyalty to the Throne and laying the foundation of their political advancement and national prosperity, and your Excellency's name wall be remembered with gratitude by their posterity for generations to come, and we feel confident that your Excellency will be gracious enough to give due consideration to our prayers. We have the honour to subscribe ourselves, Your Excellency's most obedient and humble servants.

LORD MINTO'S REPLY

Your Highness and Gentlemen, Allow me before I attempt to reply to the many considerations your address embodies, to welcome you heartily to Simla. Your presence here today is very full of meaning. To the document which you have presented to me are attached the signatures of nobles, of Ministers of various States, of great landowners, of lawyers, of merchants and of many others of His Majesty's subjects. I welcome the representative character of your deputation as expressing the views and aspirations of the enlightened Muslim community of India. I feel that all you have said emanates from a representative body basing its opinions on a matured consideration of the existing political conditions of India, totally apart from the small personal or political sympathies and antipathies of scattered localities, and I am grateful to you for the opportunity you are affording me of expressing my appreciation of the just aims of the followers of Islam and their determination to share in the political history of our Empire.

As your Viceroy, I am proud of the recognition you express of the benefits conferred by British rule on the diverse races of many creeds who go to form the population of this huge continent. You yourselves, the descendants of a conquering and ruling race, have told me to-day of your gratitude for the personal freedom, the liberty of worship, the general peace and the hopeful future which British administration has secured for India.

Help in the Past

It is interesting to look back on early British efforts to assist the Mohammedan population to qualify themselves for the public service. In 1782 Warren Hastings founded the Calcutta Madrasah with the intention of enabling its students to compete on more equal terms with the Hindus for employment under Government. In 1811 my ancestor, Lord Minto, advocated improvements in the Madrasah and the establishment of Mohammedan Colleges at other places throughout India. In later years the efforts of the Mohammedan Association led to the Government resolution of 1885 dealing with the educational position of the Mohammedan community and their employment in the public service, whilst Mohammedan educational effort has culminated in the College of Aligarh that great institution which the noble and broad-minded devotion of Sir Syed Ahmed Khan has dedicated to his co-religionists.

The Aligarh College

It was in July 1877 that Lord Lytton laid the foundation stone of Aligarh, when Sir Syed Ahmed Khan addressed these memorable words to the Viceroy: "The personal honour which you have done me assures me of a great fact and fills me with feelings of a much higher nature than mere personal gratitude. I am assured that you, who upon this occasion represent the British rule, have sympathies with our labours and this assurance is very valuable and a source of great happiness. At my time of life it is a comfort to me to feel that the undertaking which has been for many years, and is now the sole object of my life has roused on the one hand the energies of my own country-men and on the other has won the sympathy of our British fellow-subjects and the support of our rulers, so that, when the few years I may still be spared are over, and when I shall be no longer amongst you, the College will still prosper and succeed in educating my countrymen to have the same affection for their country, the same feelings of loyalty for the British rule, the same appreciation of its blessings, the same sincerity of friendship with our British fellow-subjects as have been the ruling feelings of my life."

Sir Syed's Influence

Aligarh has won its laurels. Its students have gone forth to fight the battle of life strong in the tenets of their own religion, strong in the precepts of loyalty and patriotism, and now when there is much that is critical in the political future of India the inspiration of Sir Syed Ahmed Khan and the teachings of Aligarh shine forth brilliantly in the pride of Mohammedan history, in the loyalty, commonsense and sound reasoning so eloquently expressed in your address. But, gentlemen, you go on to tell me that sincere as your belief is in the justice and fair dealings of your rulers, you cannot but be aware that "recent events" have stirred up feelings amongst the younger generation of Mohammedans which might "pass beyond the control of temperate counsel and sober guidance."

Policy in Eastern Bengal

Now, I have no intention of entering into any discussion upon the affairs of Eastern Bengal and Assam, yet I hope that without offence to anyone I may thank the Mohammedan community of the new Province for the moderation and self-restraint they have shown under conditions which were new to them, and as to which there has been inevitably much misunderstanding, and that I may at the same time sympathise with all that is sincere in Bengalee sentiments. But above all, what I would ask you to believe is that the course the Viceroy and the Government of India have pursued in connection with the affairs of the new Province, the future of which is now I hope assured, has been dictated solely by a regard for what has appeared best for its present and future populations as a whole, irrespective of race or creed and that the Mohammedan community of Eastern Bengal and Assam can rely as firmly as ever on British justice and fairplay for the appreciation of its loyalty and the safeguarding of its interests.

The Unrest in India

You have addressed me, gantlemen, at a time when the political atmosphere is full of change. We all feel it would be foolish to attempt to deny its existence, hopes and ambitions new to India are making themselves felt. We cannot ignore them—we should be wrong to wish to do so—but to what is all this unrest due? Not to the discontent of misgoverned millions—I defy anyone honestly to assert that—not to say uprising of a disaffected people.

Fruits of Western Education

It is due to that educational growth in which only a very small portion of the population has as yet shared, of which British rule first sowed the seed and the fruits of which British rule is now doing its best to foster and to direct. There may be many tares in the harvest we are now reaping. The Western gain which we have sown may not be entirely suitable to the requirements of the people of India, but the educational harvest will increase as years go on, and the healthiness of the nourishment it gives will depend on the careful administration and distribution of its products. You need not ask my pardon, gentlemen, for telling me that "Representative institutions of the European type are entirely new to the people of India" or that their introduction here requires the most earnest thought and care. I should be very far from welcoming all the political machinery of the Western world amongst the hereditary instincts and traditions of Eastern races. Western breadth of thought, the teachings of Western civilization, the freedom of British individuality can do much for the people of India, but I recognise with you that they must not carry with them an impracticable insistence of the acceptance of political methods.

Political Future of Mohammedan

And now, gentlemen, I come to your own position in respect to the political future; the position of the Mohammedan community for whom you speak. You will, I feel sure, recognise that it is impossible for me to follow you through any detailed consideration of the conditions and the share that the community has a right to claim in the administration of public affairs. I can at present only deal with generalities. The points which you have raised are before the Committee, which, as you know, I have lately appointed to consider the question of representation, and I will take care that your address is submitted to them, but at the same time I hope I may be able to reply to the general tenor of your remarks without in any way forestalling the Committee's report.

The Question of Representation

The pith of your address, as I understand it, is a claim that in any system of representation whether it affects a Municipality, a District Board or a

Legislative Council, in which it is proposed to introduce or increase an electoral organisation, the Mohammedan community should be represented as a community. You point out that in many cases electoral bodies, as now constituted, cannot be expected to return a Mohammedan candidate, and that if by chance they did so it could only be at the sacrifice of such a candidate's view to those of a majority opposed to his own community whom he would in no way represent, and you justly claim that your numerical strength both in respect to the political importance of your community and the service it has rendered to the Empire entitle you to consideration. I am entirely in accord with you; please do not misunderstand me. I make no attempt to indicate by what means the representation of communities can be obtained, but I am as firmly convinced as I believe you to be that any electoral representation in India would be doomed to mischievous failure which aimed at granting a personal enfranchisement regardless of the beliefs and traditions of the communities composing the population of this continent. The great mass of the people of India have no knowledge of representative institutions. I agree with you, gentlemen, that the initial rungs in the ladder of self-government are to be found in the Municipal and District Boards and that it is in that direction that we must look for the gradual political education of the people.

An Assurance

In the meantime I can only say to you that the Mohammedan community may rest assured that their political rights and interests as a community will be safeguarded in any administrative reorganisation with which I am concerned and that you and the people of India may rely upon the British Raj to respect, as it has been its pride to do, the religious beliefs and the national traditions of the myriads composing the population of His Majesty's Indian Empire.

Your Highness and gentlemen, I sincerely thank you for the unique opportunity your deputation has given me of meeting so many distinguished and representative Mohammedans. I deeply appreciate the energy and interest in public affairs which have brought you here from great distances, and I only regret that your visit to Simla is necessarily so short.

[*Source*: Dr. Babasaheb Ambedkar: *Writings and Speeches*, Vol. 8, Pakistan or the Partition, 1990, Education Department, Government of Maharashtra, pp. 430-445.]

Appendix B

Lucknow Pact, December 1916

Scheme of Reforms passed at the 31st session of the Indian National Congress held at Lucknow on 29 December, 1916 and adopted by the All-India Moslem League at its Meeting on 31 December, 1916.

I. PROVINCIAL LEGISLATIVE COUNCILS

1. PROVINCIAL Legislative Councils shall consist of four-fifths elected and of one-fifth nominated members.

2. Their strength shall be not less than one hundred and twenty-five members in the Major Provinces, and from fifty to seventy-five in the Minor Provinces.

3. The members of Councils should be elected directly by the people on as broad a franchise as possible.

4. Adequate provision should be made for the representation of important minorities by election, and that the Mohammedans should be represented through special electorates on the Provincial Legislative Council.

Punjab	—One half of the elected Indian members.
United Provinces	—30 per cent.
Bengal	—40 per cent.
Behar	—25 per cent.
Central Provinces	—15 per cent.
Madras	—15 per cent.
Bombay	—One-third

Provided that Mohammedans shall not participate in any of the other elections to the Legislative Councils:

Provided further that no Bill, nor any clause thereof, nor a resolution introduced by a non-official member affecting one or the other community, which question is to be determined by the members of that community in the Legislative Council concerned, shall be proceeded with, if three-fourths of the members of that community in the particular Council, Imperial or Provincial, oppose the bill or any clause thereof or the resolution.

5. The head of the Provincial Government should not be the President of the Legislative Council, but the Council should have the right of electing its President.

6. The right of asking supplementary questions should not be restricted

to the member putting the original question, but should be allowed to be exercised by any other member.

7. (a) Except customs, post, telegraph, mint, salt, opium, railways, army and navy, and tributes from Indian States, all other sources of revenue should be provincial.

(b) There should be no divided heads of revenue. The Government of India should be provided with fixed contributions from the Provincial Governments, such fixed contributions being liable to revision when extraordinary and unforeseen contingencies render such revision necessary.

(c) The Provincial Council should have full authority to deal with all matters affecting the internal administration of the province, including the power to raise loans, to impose and alter taxation and to vote on the Budget. All items of expenditure and all proposals concerning ways and means for raising the necessary revenue should be embodied in Bills and submitted to the Provincial Council for adoption.

(d) Resolutions on all matters within the purview of the Provincial Government should be allowed for discussion in accordance with rules made in that behalf by the Council itself.

(e) A resolution passed by the Legislative Council shall be binding on the Executive Government, unless vetoed by the Governor in Council, provided however that if the resolution is again passed by the Council after an interval of not less than one year, it must be given effect to.

(f) A motion for adjournment may be brought forward for the discussion of a definite matter of urgent public importance if supported by not less than one-eighth of the members present.

8. Any special meeting of the Council may be summoned on a requisition by not less than one-eighth of the members.

9. A Bill, other than a Money Bill, may be introduced in Council in accordance with the rules made in that behalf by the Council itself, and the consent of the Government should not be required therefor.

10. All Bills passed by Provincial Legislatures shall have to receive the assent of the Governor before they become law, but may be vetoed by the Governor-General.

11. The terms of office of the members shall be five years.

II. PROVINCIAL GOVERNMENTS

1. The head of every Provincial Government shall be a Governor who shall not ordinarily belong to the Indian Civil Service or any of the permanent services.

2. There shall be in every Province an Executive Council which, with the Governor, shall constitute the Executive Government of the Province.

3. Members of the Indian Civil Service shall not ordinarily be appointed to the Executive Councils.

4. Not less than one-half of the members of Executive Council shall consist of Indians to be elected by the elected members of the Provincial Legislative Council.

5. The term of office of the members shall be five years.

III. IMPERIAL LEGISLATIVE COUNCIL

1. The strength of the Imperial Legislative Council shall be one hundred and fifty.

2. Four-fifths of the members shall be elected.

3. The franchise for the Imperial Legislative Council should be widened as far as possible on the lines of the Mohammedan electorates, and the elected members of the Provincial Legislative Councils should also form an electorate for the return of members to the Imperial Legislative Council.

4. The President of the Council shall be elected by the Council itself.

5. The right of asking supplementary questions shall not be restricted to the member putting the original question but should be allowed to be exercised by any other member.

6. Any special meeting of the Council may be summoned on a requisition by not less than one-eighth of the members.

7. A Bill, other than a Money Bill, may be introduced in Council in accordance with rules made in that behalf by the Council itself, and the consent of the Executive Government should not be required therefor.

8. All Bills passed by the Council shall have to receive the assent of the Governor-General before they become law.

9. All financial proposals relating to sources of income and items of expenditure shall be embodied in Bills. Every such Bill and the Budget as a whole shall be submitted for the vote of the Imperial Legislative Council.

10. The term of office of members shall be five years.

11. The matters mentioned herein below shall be exclusively under the control of the Imperial Legislative Council:

(a) Matters in regard to which uniform legislation for the whole of India is desirable.

(b) Provincial legislation in so far as it may affect inter-provincial fiscal relations.

(c) Questions affecting purely Imperial revenue, excepting tributes from Indian States.

(d) Questions affecting purely Imperial expenditure, except that no resolution of the Imperial Legislative Council shall be binding on the Governor-General in Council in respect of military charges for the defence of the country.

(e) The right of revising Indian tariffs and customs duties, of imposing, altering, or removing any tax or cess, modifying the existing system of currency and banking, and granting any aids or bounties to any or all deserving and nascent industries of the country.

(f) Resolutions on all matters relating to the administration of the country as a whole.

12. A resolution passed by the Legislative Council should be binding on the Executive Government, unless vetoed by the Governor-General in Council: provided, however, that, if the resolution is again passed by the Council after an interval of not less than one year, it must be given effect to.

13. A motion for adjournment may be brought forward for the discussion of a definite matter of urgent public importance, if supported by not less than one-eighth of the members present.

14. The Crown may exercise its power of veto in regard to a Bill passed by a Provincial Legislative Council or by the Imperial Legislative Council within twelve months from the date on which it is passed, and the Bill shall cease to have effect as from the date on which the fact of such veto is made known to the Legislative Council concerned.

15. The Imperial Legislative Council shall have no power to interfere with the Government of India's direction of the military affairs and the foreign and political relations of India, including the declaration of war, the making of peace and the entering into treaties.

IV. THE GOVERNMENT OF INDIA

1. The Governor-General of India will be the head of the Government of India.

2. He will have an Executive Council, half of whom shall be Indians.

3. The Indian members should be elected by the elected members of the Imperial Legislative Council.

4. Members of the Indian Civil Service shall not ordinarily be appointed to the Executive Council of the Governor-General.

5. The power of making all appointments in the Imperial Civil Services shall vest in the Government of India as constituted under this scheme, and subject to any laws that may be made by the Imperial Legislative Council.

6. The Government of India shall not ordinarily interfere in the local affairs of a province, and powers not specifically given to a Provincial Government shall be deemed to be vested in the former. The authority of the

Government of India will ordinarily be limited to general supervision and superintendence over the Provincial Governments.

7. In legislative and administrative matters, the Government of India, as constituted under this scheme, shall, as far as possible, be independent of the Secretary of State.

8. A system of independent audit of the accounts of the Government of India should be instituted.

V. THE SECRETARY OF STATE IN COUNCIL

1. The Council of the Secretary of State for India should be abolished.

2. The salary of the Secretary of State should be placed on the British Estimates.

3. The Secretary of State should, as far as possible, occupy the same position in relation to the Government of India as the Secretary of State for the Colonies in relation to the Governments of the self-governing Dominions.

4. The Secretary of State should be assisted by two under-secretaries, one of whom should always be an Indian.

VI. MILITARY AND OTHER MATTERS OF POLICY

1. The military and naval services of His Majesty, both in their commissioned and non-commissioned ranks, should be thrown open to Indians and adequate provision should be made for their selection, training and instruction in India.

2. Indians should be allowed to enlist as volunteers.

3. Indians should be placed on a footing of equality in respect of status and rights of citizenship with other subjects of His Majesty the King throughout the Empire.

4. The Executive Officers in India shall have no judicial powers entrusted to them, and the judiciary in every province shall be placed under the highest Court of that province.

[*Source*: A. Berriedale Keith, ed. *Speeches and Documents on Indian Policy, 1750-1921.* Vol. III. London: Humphrey Milford, Oxford University Press, 1922, 116-131.]

Notes and References

1. Bayly, C.A., "The Pre-History of Communalism: Religious Conflict in India, 1700-1869", *Modern Asian Studies*, 1985, 19(2), pp. 177-203.
Chhachhi, Amrita *et al.*, "Concern on Communalism", *Economic and Political Weekly,* 1993, No. 28(17), p. 778.
Chakrabarti, D., "Modernity and Ethnicity in India", *South Asia*, 1994, No. 17, pp. 143-155.

Embree, A., *Utopias in Conflict: Religion and Nationalism in Modern India*, 1992, Oxford University Press, Delhi.
Kakar, Sudhir, *The Colours of Violence: Cultural Identities, Religion and Conflict*, 1996, University of Chicago Press, Chicago.
Khilani, Sunil, *The Idea of India*, 1997, Penguin, Delhi.
Krishna, Gopal, "Communal Violence in India: A Study of Communal Disturbance on Delhi", *Economic and Political Weekly*, 1985, 20(3), pp. 117-131.
Pandey, Geetanjali, "North Indian Intelligentsia and Hindu-Muslim Question: A Study of Premhand's Writings", *Economic and Political Weekly,* 1984, 19(38), pp. 1664-70.
Thapar, Romila, "Communalism and the Historical Legacy: Some Facets", 1990, *Social Scientist*, 1990, 18(6/7), pp. 4-20.

2. Dutta, Ratna, "Social and Economic Compulsions behind Communalism", *Economic and Political Weekly*, 1972, No. 7(5/7), pp. 255-57, 261, 263-264.
   Heehs, Peter, "Indian Communalism: A Survey of Historical and Social Scientific Approaches", *Journal of South Asian Studies,* 1997, No. 20(1), p. 101.
   Bharadwaj, Krishna, "Economic Development and Communalism: A Note", *Social Scientist*, 1990, 18(8/9), pp. 66-70.
3. Ahmad, Imtiaz, "Political Economy of Communalism in Contemporary India", *Economic and Political Weekly*, 1984, No. 19 (22/23), pp. 903-06.
   Thapar, Romesh, "Muslim Communalism", *Economic and Political Weekly*, 1980, 15(35), p. 1463.
   Bakshi, Rajni, "Changing Dimensions of Communalism", *Economic and Political Weekly*, 1984, 19(51/52), pp. 2152-53.
4. Wantoo, Pran *et al*., "Separate Religion from Politics", *Economic and Political Weekly,* 2002, No. 37(20), p. 1854, p. 1949.
   Lieten, GK. "On Caste and Communalism in Uttar Pradesh", *Economic and Political Weekly*, 1994, No. 29(14), pp. 777-781.
   Ahmad, Imtiaz, "Secularism and Communalism", *Economic and Political Weekly,* 1969, No. 4(28/30), pp. 1139-45, 1147- 52, 1155-58.
   Wilkinson, Steven, "Putting Gujarat in Perspective", *Economic and Political Weekly,* 2002, No. 38(17), pp. 1579-83.
   Desai, A.R., "Congress(I), Communist Parties and Communalism,", *Economic and Political Weekly*, 1984, No. 19(30), pp. 1196-97.
   Kharkhate, Deena, "Congress(I) and Communalism", *Economic and Political Weekly,* 1990, No. 25(2), p. 62.
   Oomen, John, "Politics of Communalism in Kerala", *Economic and Political Weekly,* 1995, No. 30(11), pp. 544-47.
   Hasan, Mushirul, *Nationalism and Communal Violence in India*, 1979, Manohar, Delhi.
5. Kashyap, Anirban, *Communalism and Constitution*, 1988, Lancers Books, New Delhi, pp. 9-10.
6. Pandey, Gyanendra, *The Construction of Communalism in Colonial North India*, 1990, Oxford University Press, Delhi, pp. 1-22.
7. *The Shorter Oxford Dictionary*, 1994.
8. Chandra, Bipan, *Communalism in Modern India*, 1984, Vikas, New Delhi, p. 1.

9. Dr. Radhakrishann, S., *The Hindu View of Life*, 1926, Oxford University Press, p. 12.
10. *Ibid.*, p. 12.
11. *Ibid.*
12. Monier, Williams, *Religious Thought and Life in India*, 1883, J. Murray, London, p. 57.
13. *Ibid.*, p. 48.
14. Chatterji, Suniti Kumar, Preface, *The Cultural Heritage of India*, Volume IV, Calcutta, 1983 reprint, The Ramakrishna Mission Institute of Culture, p. xix.
15. Galanter, Marc, *Competing Equalities*, 1984, Oxford University Press, Delhi, pp. 305-307.
16. Rahman, Prof. Hossainur, "The two Faces of Islam", *The Statesman*, April 17, 1991, p. 6.
17. *Jiwan Khan v. Habid*, I.L.R. 14 Lah. 518 [1933].
    Resham Bibi v. Khuda Bakhsh, I.L.R. 19 Lah. 277 [1938].
18. Ray, Rajat Kanta, *The Felt Community*, 2003, Oxford University Press, New Delhi, pp. 126-127.
19. *Ibid.*, pp. 538-539.
20. *Ibid.*, pp. 85-88.
21. Tablot, Cynthia, "Inscribing the Other, Inscribing the Self: Hindu-Muslim Identities in Pre-Colonial India", *Comparative Studies in Society and History*, Vol. 37, 4 October 1995, p. 703 quoted by Ray, Rajat Kanta, *Ibid.*, p. 30.
22. Ray, Rajat Kanta, *Ibid.*, p. 90.
23. *Ray, Rajat Kanta, Ibid.*, pp. 104-105.
24. *Ray, Rajat Kanta, Ibid.*, p. 109.
25. Bayly, Susan, *Saints, Goddesses and Kings: Muslims and Christians in South Indian Society 1700-1900*, 1992, Cambridge University Press, pp. 79-80.
26. *Ibid.*, p. 80.
27. Dale, Stephen Frederic, *The Mappilas of Malabar, 1498-1922: Islamic Society in the South Asian Frontier*, 1980, Oxford University Press, p. 24.
28. *Alberuni's India*, (ed.) Edward C. Sachau, New Delhi, 1983, pp. 17-20.
29. *Ibid.*, p. 111.
30. *Ibid.*, pp. 19-20.
31. *Ibid.*, p. 100.
32. Nikitin, Afanasy, *Voyage Beyond Seas 1466-1472*, translated by Stepan Apresyan, 1985, Moscow, pp. 28-34.
33. Titmus, M.T., *Islam in India and Pakistan*, 1930, Madras, Christian Literature Society, pp. 11-12, quoted by Mustapha, Nasser, *op. cit.*, p. 130.
34. Ray, Rajat Kanta, *op. cit*, pp. 122-123.
35. Thurston, M., *Castes and Tribes of Southern India* (in 7 Volumes), 1909, Madras, Christian Literature Society, p. 231, quoted by Mustapha, Nasser, *op. cit.*, p. 130.
36. Harklots, G.A., *Islam in India*, 1921, London, Kurzon Press, p. 7, quoted by Mustapha, Nasser, *op. cit.*, p. 130.
37. Herklots, *Ibid.*, pp. 7-8.
38. Samaroo, B., "Early African and East Indian Muslims in Trinidad and Tobago", paper presented at a Conference on Indo-Caribbean History and Culture, University of Warwick, May 1988, quoted by Mustapha, Nasser, *Ibid.*, p. 131.

39. Ray, Rajat Kanta, *op. cit.*, pp. 132-133.
40. *Ibid.*, pp. 157-158.
41. Ahmad, A., *Studies in Islamic Culture in the Indian Environment*, 1964, Claredon Press, London, pp. 209-217.
42. Seal, Anil, *The Emergence of Indian Nationalism*, 1968, Cambridge University Press, Cambridge, pp. 13-14.
43. Chandra, Bipan, Mridula Mukherjee, Aditya Mukherjee, K.N. Panikkar, and Sucheta Mahajan, *India's Struggle for Independence*, 1989, Penguin Books, New Delhi, pp. 398-399.
44. *Ibid.*, p. 413.
45. *Ibid.*, p. 408.
46. *Ibid.*, pp. 400-401.
47. Gopal, Sarvepalli (ed.), *Selected Works of Jawaharlal Nehru*, Vol. 7, Oxford University Press, New Delhi, p. 69.
48. Ray, Rajat Kanta, *op. cit.*, p. 29.
49. Subramanian, Lakshmi, *Indigenous Capital and Imperial Expansion: Bombay, Surat and the West Coast*, 1996, Oxford University Press, Delhi, pp. 206-308.
50. Chattopadhyaya, B.D., *Studying Early India: Archaeology, Texts and Historical Issues*, 2005, Permanent Black, Delhi, pp. 198-199.
51. Bayly, C.A., "The Pre-History of Communalism Religious Conflict in India, 1700-1860", in *Modern Asian Studies*, 19(2), 1985, pp. 192-193.
52. Ray, Rajat Kanta, *op. cit.*, p. 102.
53. Chatterji, Prashanto K., *The Making of India Policy 1853-65*, 1975, Orient Longman Limited, Calcutta, p. 110.
54. Majumdar, R.C., Majumdar A.K., and Ghose, D.K. (eds.) *British Paramountcy and Indian Renaissance*, Part II, 1965, p. 321, Bombay.
55. Joshi, Sashi and Josh, Bhagwan, *Struggle for Hegemony in India, 1920-1947*, 1994, Sage Publications, quoted by Nandan Nilekani, *Imagining India 2008*, Penguin, Allen Lane, p. 152.
56. Bhagat, R.B., "Census and the Construction of Communalism in India", *Economic and Political Weekly*, November 24, 2001, p. 4353.
57. *Ibid.*, p. 4352.
58. Kooiman, Dick, "Communalism and Indian Princely States: A Comparison with British India", *Economic and Political Weekly*, 1995, No. 30(34), p. 2123.
59. *Ibid.*, p. 117.
60. *Ibid.*, pp. 114-117.
61. *Census of India*, 1931, Vol. I, India, Report (with complete survey of tribal life and system) by J.H. Hutton, (reprinted by Gian Publishing House, Delhi, 1989), p. 379.
62. *Census of India*, 1911, Vol. I, India, Report by E.A., Gait, Superintendent, Government Printing Press, Calcutta, (reprinted by Usha, Delhi, 1987). p. 117.
63. For a more detailed discussion on the census, see Gupta "Censuses, Communalism, Gender and Identity: A Historical Perspective", *Economic and Political Weekly*, 2004, No. 39(39), pp. 4302-04. Datta, P.K., "Dying Hindus' Production of Hindu Communal Common Sense in Early Twentieth Century Bengal", *Economic and Political Weekly*, 1993, No. 19(30), pp. 1305-19.

64. Amin, Shahid, "Representing the Musalman: Then and Now, Now and Then", in Shail Mayaram. MSS Pandian and Ajay Skaria (ed.), *Muslims, Dalits and Fabrications of History*, Subaltern Studies, Vol. 12, 2005, Permanent Black and Ravi Dayal, New Delhi, pp. 1-35.
65. Sarkar, Sumit, *The Swadeshi Movement in Bengal 1903-1908*, 1973, Peoples Publishing House, New Delhi, pp. 15-20.
66. Sarkar, Sumit, *Modern India 1885-1947*, 1983, MacMillan India, New Delhi, p. 106.
67. Pandey, G., "The Colonial Construction of Communalism: British Writings on Benaras in the nineteenth Century", In *Subaltern Studies VI: Writings on South Asian History and Society* (ed.) Ranjit Guha, 1989, Oxford University Press, Delhi, p. 132.
68. Mill, James, *The History of British India*, 1826, London. Since then the work has been reprinted several times.
69. Chandra, Bipan, *et al.*, *op. cit.*, p. 411.
70. Datta, P.K., "Dying Hindus: Production of Hindu Communal Common Sense in Early Twentieth Century Bengal", *Economic and Political Weekly*, June 19, 1993, pp. 1305-19.
71. Appendix A.
72. Zelliot, Eleanor, *Dr. Ambedkar and the Mahar Movement*, Ph.D. dissertation, 1969, University of Pennsylvania, p. 141.
73. Hasan, Mushirul, "Communalism in the Provinces: A Case Study of Bengal and Punjab, 1922-26, *Economic and Political Weekly*, August 16, 1980, pp. 1395-96.
74. Majumdar, R.C., *Struggle for Freedom*, 1978, Bharatiya Vidaya Bhavan, Bombay, p. 239.
75. Appendix B.
76. Bamford, P.C., *Histories of the Non-Co-operation and Khilafat Movements*, 1974, Delhi, Deep Publications (originally published by the Government of India Press in 1925), p. 128.
77. Agarwal, R.C., *Constitutional Development and National Movement of India*, 1988, S. Chand & Company (Pvt.) Ltd., New Delhi, pp. 171-172.
78. Majumdar, R.C., *Struggle for Freedom*, *op. cit.*, p. 248.
79. Bamford, P.C, *op. cit.*, pp. 127-128.
80. Das, Durga, *India: From Curzon to Nehru and After*, 1974, Rupa & Co., Calcutta, p. 58.
81. Datar, Abhay, "The Lucknow Pact of 1916", *Economic and Political Weekly*, vol. xlvii no. 10, March 10, 2012, pp. 65-69.
82. Page, D.J.H., "Prelude to Partition: All India Muslim Politics, 1909-1930", unpublished D.Phil. thesis, Oxford, 1973, quoted by Hasan, Mushirul, *op. cit.*, p. 1397.
83. The term 'secularism' is used throughout this book in a very restricted sense to denote that generally accepted concept of an ideology which is opposed to anything connected with religious communalism, irrespective of majoritarian or minoritarian communalism. As an ideology and practice it upholds the spirit of secular values. The term secular refers innocuously and indiscriminately to all things that are "worldly" and "mundane" in the sense of being outside the reach of religious institutions and concerns. Strictly speaking, in the Indian context,

the Western idea of separation of Church and State does not make ready sense because unlike the Catholic Church, there is no structured, hierarchical clergy with institutionalised control of the State in most religious traditions prevalent in India. Religion is a private affair and should not have anything to do with the formulation and execution of State policy. Our concept of the secular, however, cannot operate outside our understanding of the idea of religion, or *vice versa*, and that this relationship is an ongoing, dialectical one.

There is no apparent contradiction between a truly religious man and a secular man. One can be deeply religious and at the same time be a believer of secular ideas. Take for instance, Gandhi. He was a deeply religious man but he was for a secular India. For Gandhi, religion was clearly a place for peace and there was absolutely no room in his thinking for religious differences turning violent. He wrote way back in 1934: "I believe in the fundamental truth of all great religions of the world. I believe that they are all God-given, and I believe that they were necessary for the people to whom these religions were revealed. And I believe that, if only we could all of us read the scriptures of different faiths from the standpoint of the followers of those faiths we should find that they were at bottom all one and were all helpful to one another" (*Harijan,* February 16, 1934, pp. 5-6). One is prone to agree with Fatima Bhutto when she says that secularism in South Asia, especially in the Indian subcontinent, means tolerance. It is the inclusivity of the really syncretic ideas (*The Hindu,* November 5, 2013, p. 7). In that sense, India is the most secular country in the world because it gave shelter to all those who were persecuted for their religious belief in their homeland.

84. Das, Durga, *op. cit.*, pp. 72-73.
85. http://www.pakistan.gov.pk/Quaid/politician6.htm
86. Mahmud Ali, S., *The Fearful State: Power, People And Internal War in South Asia*, London, 1993, Zed, 1993, pp. 6-7.
87. Niemeijer, A.C., *The Khilafat Movement in India 1919-1924*, The Hague, 1972 Martinus Nijhoff, p. 90.
88. Jalal, Ayesha, *The Sole Spokesman: Jinnah, the Muslim League and the Demand for Pakistan*, Cambridge, 1985, Cambridge University Press, p. 8.
89. Mujahid, Sharif al, *Quaid-I-Azzam Jinnah: Studies in Interpretation*, Karachi, 1981, South Asia Books: Ref. 74, 15n.
90. Sayyid. S., and Tyrer, L.D., "Ancestor worship and the irony of the 'Islamic Republic' of Pakistan", In *Contemporary South Asia* II(1), 2002, p. 63.
91. Pirzada, S.S., *The Collected Works of Quaid-E-Azam Mohammad Ali Jinnah: Volume 2, 1921-1926*, Karachi, 1986, East-West, Ref. 19, p. 402.
92. Das, Durga, *op. cit.*, p. 77.
93. *Dr. Babasaheb Ambedkar: Writings and Speeches*, Vol 8, "Pakistan or The Partition of India", 1990, Government of Maharashtra, pp. 146-147.
94. *Ibid.*, p. 151.
95. Nehru, Jawaharlal, *An Autobiography*, 1962, New Delhi, Allied Publishers, (first published in 1936 by John Lane, the Bodley Head Limited, London), p. 460.
96. *Ibid.*, p. 69.
97. *Ibid.*, p. 71.
98. Bose, Subhas Chandra, *The Indian Struggle*. (1920-1942), Revised Second Edition 2005, Natyachinta Foundation, Kolkata, p. 84.

99. Nehru, Jawaharlal, *op. cit.*, p. 136.
100. Biswas, Kalipada, *Yukta Banglar shesh adhaya* [the last phase of united Bengal], 1966, Calcutta, Orient Book Company, p. 335.
101. Majumdar, R.C., *Struggle for Freedom*, *op. cit.*, pp. 318-319.
102. Bose, Subhas Chandra, *op. cit.*, p. 45.
103. *Dr. Babasaheb Ambedkar: Writings and Speeches*, Vol. 8, "Reprint of Pakistan or The Partition of India, *op. cit.*, p. 302.
104. Nehru, Jawaharlal, *An Autobiography, op. cit.*, pp. 71-72.
105. Bamford, P.C., *op. cit.*, p. 174.
106. Bose, Subhas Chandra, *op. cit.*, p. 121.
107. *Ibid.*, pp. 135-136.
108. Namboodiripad, E.M.S., *The Mahatma and the Ism*, 1981, Calcutta, National Book Agency (P) Ltd., pp. 41-42.
109. Bamford, P.C., *op. cit.*, pp. 78-79.
110. Bose, Subhas Chandra, *op. cit.*, p. 122.
111. Hasan, Mushirul, "Communalism in the Provinces: A Case Study of Bengal and the Punjab 1922-26", *Economic and Political Weekly,* August 16, 1980, pp. 1397-99.
112. *Ibid.*, p. 1397.
113. Page, D.J.H., "Prelude to Partition: All India Muslim Politics, 1909-1930, unpublished D.Phil. thesis, Oxford, 1973, Chapter one, quoted by Hasan, Mushirul, *ibid.*, p. 1397.
114. Kashyap, Anirban, *Communalism and Constitution*, *op. cit.*, pp. 22-24.
115. Chandra, Bipan *et al.*, *op. cit.,* pp. 409-410.
116. *Indian Annual Register*, 1940-41, pp. 311-12.
117. Speech of M.A. Jinnah in the Lahore Session of the Indian Muslim League reported in the *IAR*, 1940-41, pp. 309-310.
118. Chatterjee, A., *Constitutional Development of India* 1937-47, 1985, Calcutta, Firma K.L. Mukhopadhyay, pp. 53-54.
119. Ray, Rajat Kanta, *op. cit.*, p. 557.
120. Chandra, Bipan *et al.*, *op. cit.*, p. 494.
121. *Dr. Babasaheb Ambedkar: Writings and Speeches*, Vol. 8, "Pakistan or The Partition of India", *op. cit.*, p. 43.
122. Naqvi, Mushtaq, *Partition: The Real Story*, 2006, Renaissance Publishing House, 2006.
123. Chowdhury, Prasenjit, "Jinnah's Secularism-I", *The Statesman*, July 11, 2005, p. 8.
124. *The Hindu*, July 23, 2013, p. 12.
125. Liaquat Ali Khan's address to the United States Senate in May 1950 on why Pakistan became a separate state, quoted by Walter Bennett Evans in his book *The Genesis of the Pakistan Idea*, 2013, Oxford University Press, New Delhi.
126. *The Sunday Times of India*, June 12, 2005, p. 13.
127. Nehru, Jawaharlal, *An Autobiography, op. cit.,* p. 138.
128. Chandra Bipan, *Communalism in Modern India, op. cit.*, p. 310.
129. Nehru, Jawaharlal, *Constituent Assembly Debates* henceforth *CAD*, Vol. VII, dated 5-11-48, p. 318.
130. Chandra Bipan, *Communalism in Modern India, op. cit.*, p. 310.

2
Imparting of Religious Instruction in Educational Institutions

I

The Article which was debated in the Constituent Assembly for a long time over a number of days was Article 28. The members were in a fix as to what should be their stand so far as imparting of religious instruction in educational institution was concerned. Should they ban it completely or not? What about state-aided institutions? Should the state educational institutions allow such religious instructions or not? What would be the role of a secular state? What about imparting of religious instruction outside the school hours? Many such pertinent questions were considered by them and the more they tried to go deep into the matter, the more they landed in the quagmire of problems. They solved the puzzle no doubt by evolving a policy which is apparently secular, but in actuality it is not so. They did not separate the church from the state as obtains in the USSR and the USA and prohibit religious instruction in educational institutions. They adopted a *via* media policy neither sponsoring religious education, nor banning it altogether.[1] As a result, points out Anirban Kashyap, the very purpose for which this article was brought in lost much of its relevancy and significance and the article, its teeth and utility. On the other hand, it has become a tool in the hands of the communalist and fundamentalist forces. It has a retrograde effect on the secular character of the Indian polity.[2]

The Constituent Assembly, on January 24, 1947, on a motion by Pandit Gobind Ballabh Pant, adopted a resolution setting up an Advisory Committee to determine the fundamental rights of citizens, minorities etc. At the first meeting of the Advisory Committee on Fundamental Rights, Minorities, etc., held[3] on February 27, 1947, Sardar Vallabhbhai Patel was unanimously elected Chairman and five Sub-Committees—including one on Fundamental Rights and another on Minorities—were appointed. The Fundamental Rights Sub-Committee consisted[4] of—(1) Acharya J.B. Kripalani, (2) M.R. Masani, (3) Prof. K.T. Shah, (4) Rajkumari Amrit Kaur, (5) Alladi Krishnaswamy Ayyar, (6) K.M. Munshi, (7) Sardar Harnam Singh, (8) Maulana Abul Kalam Azad,

(9) Dr. B.R. Ambedkar, (10) Jairamdas Daulatram. Sardar K.M. Panikkar was nominated[5] on April 10, 1947 and joined the deliberations only on April 14. The Fundamental Rights Sub-Committee held three sittings. At the first sitting, which took place on February 27 itself, J.B. Kripalani was elected Chairman and the general procedure and order of business for the Sub-Committee was settled. The Sub-Committee held its second sitting from March 24-31 and the third sitting from April 14-16 and submitted its final report[6] to the Advisory Committee on April 16, 1947. The Sub-Committee had the benefit of (1) the notes[7] prepared by the Constitutional Adviser, B.N. Rau, on September 2, 1946, (2) a comprehensive note[8] on fundamental rights prepared and sent to the President of the Assembly by Prof. K.T. Shah on December 23, 1946, (3) the note[9] submitted by Alladi Krishnaswamy Ayyar on March 14, 1947, (4) the note and draft articles on the fundamental rights submitted[10] by K.M. Munshi on March 17, 1947, (5) Sardar Harnam Singh's draft[11] on fundamental rights submitted on March 18, 1947, and (6) the memorandum and draft articles on the rights of States and Minorities submitted[12] by Dr. Ambedkar on March 24, 1947. The Sub-Committee in its meeting held on March 24, 1947 decided to take up Munshi's draft and examine it in conjunction with other drafts.[13] Clause (5) of Article VI of Munshi's draft had the following provision:

> Religious instruction shall not be compulsory for a member of a community which does not profess such religion.[14]

In the meeting of the Fundamental Rights Sub-Committee of March 26, 1947 it was, however, decided to adopt the following draft of B.N. Rau in place of that clause:

> No person attending any school maintained or receiving aid out of public funds shall be compelled to attend the religious instruction that may be given in the school.[15]

Rau's draft was based on one of the recommendations of the All Parties Conference, 1928 which was included under 'Fundamental Rights'. It was as follows:

> (xii) No person attending any school receiving state aid or other public money shall be compelled to attend the religious instruction that may be given in the school.[16]

In its draft report of April 3, 1947 prepared for the Advisory Committee the Sub-Committee incorporated the above provision as Clause 20 which read as follows:

> No person attending any school maintained or receiving aid out of

> public funds shall be compelled to take part in the religious instruction that may be given in the school.[17]

It may be noted that a slight modification in the wording of this clause was effected in that the word "attend" was substituted by the words "take part in".

Again in the meeting of the Fundamental Rights Sub-Committee of April 15, 1947, a further change in the clause was introduced. It was decided to add the words "or to attend religious worship".[18]

The Sub-Committee in its report of April 16, 1947 to the Advisory Committee recommended the following provision in Clause 19 under the broad head "Rights relating to religion".

> "No person attending any school maintained or receiving aid out of public funds shall be compelled to take part in the religious instruction that may be given in the school or to attend religious worship held in the school or in premises attached thereto".[19]

K.M. Panikkar in his minute of dissent, however, observed that the right enumerated in Clause 19 should be enforceable by the machinery of the units and not by the Supreme Court and recommended that the relevant Article should be suitably amended.[20]

The Sub-Committee on Minorities thereafter examined the draft clauses recommended by the Fundamental Rights Sub-Committee in order to see whether any of them was required to be amplified or amended for the specific purpose of protecting minority rights. The discussion lasted three days, viz. April 17, 18 and 19, 1947. In the meeting of April 17, the Sub-Committee examined and accepted the above clause without any comments.[21] The Minorities Sub-Committee in its report of April 19, 1947 to the Advisory Committee did not suggest any change in this clause.[22]

The Advisory Committee on Fundamental Rights, Minorities, etc., met for two days during April 1947, viz. on April 21 and 22 and discussed the recommendations made by the Fundamental Rights Sub-Committee together with the report of Minorities Sub-Committee thereon.[23] The Advisory Committee discussed this clause on April 21. C. Rajagopalachari suggested that since there was a similar clause, this clause would be unnecessary. Many members, however, demanded that the clause should be retained and the clause was accepted.[24]

The Advisory Committee in its report to the President of the Constituent Assembly on April 23, 1947 incorporated this clause as clause 16.[25]

Clause 16 was discussed in the Constituent Assembly on May 1, 1947 and it was decided to refer it back to the Advisory Committee for reconsideration.[26] The Advisory Committee in its report[27] submitted on August 25, 1947 recommended retention of the clause in its original form.

Clause 16 came up for discussion in the Constituent Assembly on August 30, 1947.

Srimati Purnima Banerjee wanted to add the following new paragraph to Clause 16 as an explanation:

> All religious education given in educational institutions receiving state-aid will be in the nature of elementary philosophy of comparative religion calculated to broaden the pupils' mind rather than such as will foster sectarian exclusiveness.

Giving reasons for introducing this additional clause, Srimati Banerjee said that she was in perfect agreement with the object of the clause that the students attending these schools should be prevented from being forced to attend the religious classes, if they did not wish to do so. She continued: "But I know there are a large number of institutions which are run on religious lines and which came into the field of education much before the state came in. There are in my province '*Maktabs*' and '*Pathshalas*' which perform the function of imparting education to children of school going age. But we have seen that the religious instructions given here are of such a nature that, instead of broadening the mind of the child, they mis-educate the mind and sometimes breed a certain type of fanaticism and religious bigotry as a result of receiving education in these '*Maktabs*' and '*Pathshalas*'. It is a controversial point, as to whether we should give any aid to denominational schools at all—I do not wish to open that subject at all because there are experts appointed for this purpose and their report is awaited and I am sure after that the legislature will enter into that subject in fuller detail. My object in moving the amendment is that the education imparted in these institutions should be restricted or controlled by the Government without any fear of interfering with anybody's religion. The curriculum should be in the control of the Government and should be of such a nature that it broadens the mind rather than creates an exclusiveness. When we were discussing the Minority Rights Report, we said that our aim should be to form a united nation and we have done away with separate electorates and agreed on Fundamental Rights and give each the right to follow his own religion. But I do believe that, however secular a state you wish to build up unless one member of it appreciates the religion of the other member of the state, it would be impossible for us to build a united India. Therefore, without interfering with the religion of anybody, the state should be perfectly entitled to see that in the formative stage of the child, when he is of the school-going age, the religious instruction is controlled and that the syllabus is of such a nature that the child will develop into a healthy citizen of India, capable of appreciating each other's point of view. We may be united by political parties—but if we do not appreciate each others' religions, we shall find that instead of having really men of religion in our midst we shall be breeding a type of exclusiveness which will be most harmful and on that type of mind, I am afraid, the future of the nation cannot be built up".[28]

None supported this amendment. On the other hand, this amendment was opposed by B. Pocker Sahib, Mahboob Ali Baig and K.M. Munshi.

B. Pocker Sahib spoke against the amendment of Smt. Purnima Banerjee. "The object of this amendment seems to be to unify all the people of this country towards one religion or something tending towards it. If that is the object, then I certainly oppose it. I must say that in some previous speech in Hindustani on the general discussion, some similar suggestion was made. Of course, I have not been able to follow that and I am not proficient to deal with that. But generally, I would say that any attempt towards the unification of all religions or towards giving instructions in public schools which is intended to unify religion is fundamentally opposed to the other classes of Fundamental Rights which we have passed"[29], he said.

Mahboob Ali Baig Sahib Bahadur also opposed the amendment of Smt. Banerjee because it was "somewhat controversial. What should be the fundamental education that should be given to the child would be a matter of opinion and it might lead to controversy. For, this elementary philosophy of comparative religion is very difficult to define."[30]

K.M. Munshi also opposed this amendment of Smt. Banerjee. His argument was that "however laudable the object, the House will remember that this is a justifiable right and therefore every word of it will have to be discussed, considered and decided upon by the different High Courts and the Supreme Court in the end. Now, if Mrs. Banerjee's amendment becomes law as a justifiable right, this will be the position. There is a school in which religious education is given. The first question raised by some friends or enterprising men will be "Is it in the nature of elementary philosophy of comparative religions?" So, the matter will have to be taken to the Supreme Court and eleven worthy judges will have to decide whether the kind of education given is of a particular religion, or in the nature of elementary philosophy of comparative religion. Thus after having decided that the second point which the learned judges will have to direct their attention to will be whether this elementary philosophy is calculated to broaden the minds of the pupils or to narrow their minds. Then they will have to decide upon the scope of every word, this being a justifiable right which has to be adjudicated upon by them. If this amendment is accepted it will work great hardship and will remain a dead letter.

"...Now, with regard to the words 'educational institutions' I submit it enlarges the meaning of the word 'school' to a very large extent. It would create grave difficulties if it is allowed to be used. Their may be '*Pathshalas*' or '*Maktabs*' giving religious instruction. Their express object is to give religious instruction and everywhere today these are aided by the state. Any such rigid Fundamental Right would have the effect that all those thousands of educational institutions will have to go out of existence",[31] he concluded.

The amendment of Smt. Banerjee was negatived by the Assembly.

Srimati Renuka Ray moved another amendment against imparting of religious instruction. Her amendment was as follows:

> No denominational religious instructions shall be provided in schools maintained by the State. No person attending any School or educational institution recognised or aided by the state shall be compelled to attend any such religious instruction.

While elucidating her amendment she stated that no "instruction given in the schools maintained by the state or out of the public funds may be of a denominational character. Surely denominational schools cannot be run by a democratic secular state. Such schools may be recognised or even aided, but as the state we envisage under the new constitution will be secular having no state religion as such, it cannot set up denominational religious institutions as state schools".[32]

While supporting the amendment of Smt. Renuka Ray, K. Santhanam pointed out that "in our country, even in the same religion there are any number of denominations. We want the village Panchayats to control education, we want the local boards to control education. In a particular village or a particular area, a particular Hindu denomination may be in a majority. We do not want Shaivites give Shaivite instructions, the Vaishnavites to give Vaishnavite education; the Lingayats to give Laingayat instruction. We do not want to give even the slightest loophole for such controversies. Therefore, it is essential that all schools maintained by the state should have no religious instruction whatsoever. Let other agencies provide the instruction, if they so choose, in 'out of class' hours. That is a different thing altogether. I am not objecting to religious instruction as such, nor I am objecting even to denominational character of religious instruction, but our public instructions should be absolutely secular. They should be beyond the reach of all religious controversies".[33]

B. Pocker Sahib had no objection to this amendment but, "I would point out that even though no denominational religious instruction may be provided in schools maintained by the state, what we find in all the text books which are prescribed for the various classes in the schools we find so many religious topics are introduced particularly topics which deal with Hindu religion or some other religion. I would like to say that a subject which deals with the moral aspects only without having any religious idea introduced may find a place, but if it does find a place in the text books it may be from all religions alike and not from any particular religion. But I would only add there are so many educational institutions which are intended to promote some particular minorities or religious minorities because of their backwardness in the matter of education. I submit that such institutions should not be affected by this clause",[34] he said.

Dr. S. Radhakrishnan wanted to know whether the term 'recognised or receiving aid from' included or excluded institutions wholly maintained, administered and financed by the state to which Sardar Patel replied in the affirmative.

When the amendment of Smt. Ray was being read out in the Assembly with a view to obtaining the members' vote on it, Munshi wanted to know whether the mover of the amendment had accepted word 'recognised' in place of 'maintained'.

Pandit Hriday Nath Kunzru emphasised that "if it is the intention of the Government that denominational religious instruction might be given by the state in the state schools, then that should be stated clearly so that we make up our minds and decide how we should vote on this clause".[35]

Dr. S. Radhakrishnan pointed out that "if the institutions which are maintained by the state are to impart denominational religious instruction then what happens to our declarations that the state is a secular institution which will not impart any instruction of any denominational kind? That is the real question. We have adhered to the first principle that the state as such shall not be associated with any kind of religion and shall be a secular institution. In other words we are a multi-religious state and therefore, we have to be impartial and give uniform treatment to the different religions, but if institutions maintained by the state, that is, administered, controlled and financed by the state, are permitted to impart religious instruction of a denominational kind, we are violating the first principle of our constitution. on the other hand, if we say aided institutions may impart religious instruction, we protect the interests of the people against the violation of their religious conscience by saying that they shall not be compelled against their will to join classes on religion. So, a distinction will have to be made between institutions maintained by the state and those institutions which are merely aided from state funds. So far as the former are concerned we cannot allow any religious instruction of a denominational character. So far as the latter is concerned, you may allow, provided you protect the rights of the minorities concerned. We have to make ourselves absolutely clear on this matter".[36]

Sardar Vallabhbhai Patel's reply was that "there is some confusion. So far as any school that is entirely maintained by the state is concerned, we cannot do anything by way of introducing Fundamental Rights for which the remedy of taking it to the court is given. Because, this is not restricted to the British-Indian portion alone; it covers the whole of India; that is the Indian Union. Therefore, if a unit which is a state, take the case of Hyderabad, wants to maintain wholly its own school in which it wants to introduce religious education, it may compel; but we cannot give a remedy by which anybody can go to the court and say, "you will not impart religious education here". I do not think this is proper at this stage. Therefore, the wording "recognised by or receiving aid from the State funds' is introduced".[37]

K.M. Munshi pointed out that "the object of this clause is not to fetter the state from putting up religious schools but from insisting that every student shall be compelled to undergo religious instruction. The matter came up again and again and the committee always held that it was not necessary to put down in Fundamental Rights the converse proposition."[38]

Dr. Mohan Sinha Mehta made a plea for referring the clause to the committee again for reconsideration because "from the explanation that has been given, it is quite obvious that what we understand was not really intended. Now, we are told that an institution maintained by the State may have religious instruction compulsory. Well, Sir, that is a position about which some of us in this House have very strong feelings, and since the matter is not clear, I would strongly submit for your consideration that it be referred back to the Committee."[39]

Alladi Krishnaswami Ayyar also favoured the idea of referring it back to the Committee.

Sardar Vallabhabhai Patel suggested that "instead of referring this small matter to the whole Advisory Committee, it should be referred to a small Committee and if they make any suggestions, they can be brought forward at the next session. I do not think it advisable to refer it back a third time to the committee."[40] After some deliberations the proposal of Sardar Patel was accepted. Accordingly, the President of the Constituent Assembly appointed on August 30, 1947 a Sub-Committee consisting of

1. Dr. Mohan Sinha Mehta,
2. Pandit Hriday Nath Kunzru,
3. Mr. Hussain Imam,
4. Dr. S. Radhakrishnan,
5. Smt. Renuka Ray,
6. Mr. K.M. Munshi.

The Sub-Committee was empowered to submit the report, not to the House, but to the Drafting Committee which would consider the report.[41]

II

With a few minor changes and drafting adjustments the provisions were reproduced in the Constitutional Adviser's Draft Constitution as clause 23.[42] He in his note raised the question whether this clause should be confined to schools or extended to all educational institutions. As worded, it was confined to schools.[43]

The Drafting Committee on November 1, 1947, held over the consideration of this clause pending the report of the sub-committee appointed by the President of the Constituent Assembly for the consideration of the clause.[44] This committee recommended to the Drafting Committee that a specific provision should be included to the effect that religious instruction should not be permitted in schools run by the State.[45] The Drafting Committee accepted the recommendation of the *ad hoc* committee. Accordingly, Article 22 of the Draft Constitution which followed the recommendation of the *ad hoc* committee, read:

> 22(1) No religious instruction shall be provided by the State in any educational institution wholly maintained out of State funds.
> Provided that nothing in this clause shall apply to an educational institution which is administered by the State but has been established under any endowment or trust which requires that religious instruction shall be imparted in such institution.
> (2) No person attending any educational institution recognised by the State or receiving aid out of State funds shall be required to take part in any religious instruction that may be imparted in such institution or to attend any religious worship that may be conducted in such institution or in any premises attached thereto unless such person or, if such person is a minor, his guardian has given his consent thereto.
> (3) Nothing in this article shall prevent any community or denomination from providing religious instruction for pupils of that community or denomination in an educational institution outside its working hours.[46]

Original clause 16 was included in clause (2) whereas the first clause of the amendment of Smt. Renuka Ray found a place in Clause (1) of Article 22. Proviso to Clause (1) and Clause (3) of Article 22 were new additions.

When the Draft Constitution was circulated for eliciting opinion, a number of amendments were received from the members—two from R.K. Sidhva, two from T.A. Ramalingam Chettiar and one from Tejamul Hussain.

R.K. Sidhva suggested for insertion of the words 'or partly' after the word wholly' in clause (1) of draft Article 22. B.N. Rau's remark was that it involved a question of policy.

R.K. Sidhva and S.V. Krishnamoorthy Rao suggested for the deletion of the Proviso to Clause (1). B.N. Rau remarked that the article followed the recommendations of the *ad hoc* committee, appointed by the Constituent Assembly. The question whether this amendment should be accepted or not should, therefore, be left to the decision of the Constituent Assembly. He added that as a matter of drafting, this proviso seemed unnecessary, because the main clause applied only to educational institutions wholly maintained out of State funds, while the proviso applied to educational institutions maintained out of private endowments or trust funds. If, however, the main clause was amended by substituting 'wholly or partly' for 'wholly', the proviso might not be redundant.

T.A. Ramalingam Chettiar suggested for insertion of the following at the end of the Proviso to Clause (1):

> nor to an institution administered by the State to which an endowment or trust is attached to provide religious instruction.

B.N. Rau commented that if it was considered necessary or desirable to meet the point raised in the amendment then the words 'is subject to' might be substituted for the words 'has been established under' in the proviso to clause (1) of Article 22.

T.A. Ramalingam Chettiar also suggested that clause (2) of Article 22 be substituted by the following:

> No educational institution recognized by the State or receiving aid from State funds shall make it obligatory on its pupils to take part in any religious instruction that may be imparted in such institution or to attend any religious worship that may be conducted in such institution or any premises attached thereto.

This amendment, B.N. Rau remarked, involved a question of policy because under the draft article attendance at religious instruction etc., could be made obligatory on a minor pupil if his guardian consented, whereas under the amendment it could not be made obligatory.

Tejamul Hussain suggested that the words "by the State" and the words "wholly maintained out of State funds" in clause (1) of Article 22 be deleted. B.N. Rau commented that the Drafting Committee had recommended the omission of the words "by the State" from this clause as being redundant. The second part of the amendment, if accepted, would prevent the imparting of religious instruction in any educational institution. Clauses (2) and (3) of the Article would then also become unnecessary. This involved a question of policy.

The Drafting Committee, however, decided to sponsor no other amendment except the one for omission of the words 'by the State' in Clause (1) of draft Article 22.[47]

At the time of general discussion on the motion of consideration of the Draft Constitution only Mohammed Ismail Sahib and M. Thirumala Rao touched upon this subject.

Mohammad Ismail Sahib's view on this was that "one important fundamental thing I want to refer to and that is regarding religious instruction. The Constitution says that religious instruction shall not be provided in any of the State schools. Taking this provision with the compulsory elementary education which is being introduced in almost all the provinces, it means that the Government is against religious instruction, it is against people getting instruction in their own religion even if they wanted it. Therefore, until 15 years of age up to which age the children have to be sent to these elementary schools they shall not have an opportunity in these schools of having any instruction in religion. But it is the right of the people to have instructions in their respective religion. That right is not derogatory to the neutrality or secular nature of this State. The State would not impose any religious instruction upon people who do not like it. They only give facilities for the people, if they want to give instruction to their children in their own religion."[48]

M. Thirumala Rao was for the protection of the ancient traditions and culture of the country. "We have been talking too much of a secular State. What is meant by a secular State? I understand that a secular State may not allow religion to play a very important part to the exclusion of other activities of the State. But we must make it clear that the ancient traditions and culture of this country will be fully protected and developed by the Constitution and through the Constitution." He continued: "Wherever you go, to the Mother of Parliaments or to other British Institutions, you find invariably the Church is associated with them, with their universities, with their Parliament, with their Courts of Law and so on. Although I do not want to impose our religion in our institutions to that extent, I do plead that we should protect our culture, our peculiar national characteristics and traditions. These should be protected by the Constitution. We should not forget, wherever we go, that we are not a hybrid nation or a disproportioned mixture of several cultures, but that we have a culture and a Government and a civilization of our own. This should be reflected in our Constitution."[49]

This article was debated on December 7, 1948 at the time of clause-wise discussion of the articles. As many as 14 Members participated in the discussion. Two sets of amendments were moved. One required that no obstacle should be placed to the imparting of religious instructions in educational institutions. Another set of amendments wanted that stringent provisions should be made so that religious instructions were not imparted even in those educational institutions which are not exclusively or wholly maintained, aided or recognised by or dependent on the state. To the first group come Mohammad Ismail Sahib and Shibban Lal Saksena whereas Prof. K.T. Shah, Sardar Hukum Singh, Sardar Bhopindar Singh Mann and Tejamul Hussain belong to the second group. But none of their amendments were adopted. Only two amendments were accepted—one moved by Dr. Ambedkar for deletion of the words 'by the State' occurring in clause (1) of Article 22 and the other for deletion of clause (3) of the Article.

Dr. Ambedkar moved an amendment for omission of the words "by the State" occurring in clause (1) of Article 22. His contention was: "The object of this amendment is to remove a possibility of doubt that might arise. If the words 'by the State' remain in the draft as it now stands, it might be construed that this article permits institutions other than the State to give religious instruction. The underlying principle of this article is that no institution which is maintained wholly out of State funds shall be used for the purpose of religious instruction irrespective of the question whether the religious instruction is given by the State or by any other body."[50]

Tejamul Hussain[51] also moved an amendment for deletion of the words 'by the State' in clause (1) of Article 22.

M. Ananthasayanam Ayyangar supported the amendment of Dr. Ambedkar.[52] Without much deliberation the House adopted this amendment of Dr. Ambedkar.

There were three distinct lines of arguments on clause (3) of Article 22. Md. Ismail Sahib wanted to broaden the scope of Article 22(3) while Prof. K.T. Shah wanted to make this provision more stringent. The third line of argument advanced mainly by Prof. Shibban Lal Saksena and Jaspat Roy Kapoor was for deletion of Article 22(3).

Mohammad Ismail Sahib brought an amendment to Article 22(3) which materially broadens its scope. He wanted to substitute the word 'providing' by the words 'being permitted to provide' and to insert the words 'in or' after the words 'educational institution'. This clause after this amendment would read as follows:

> "Nothing in this article shall prevent any community or denomination from being permitted to provide religious instruction for pupils of that community or denomination in an educational institution in or outside its working hours".[53]

Prof. K.T. Shah in consonance with his avowed policy of making the imparting of religious education in educational institutions more stringent moved an amendment for substituting the words 'outside its working hours' by the following:

> maintained by that community from its own funds provided that no educational institutions, nor any education or training imparted therein shall be recognised unless it provides instruction or training in courses laid down for public instruction in the regular system of education for the country and complies in all other respects with methods, standards, equipment and other requirements of the national system of education.[54]

Prof. Shibban Lal Saksena wanted that at least clause (3), if not both the clauses (1) and (3), of Article 22 should be deleted, so that, the State could impart religious instructions in educational institutions. His point of view as elaborated by him was: "what is really intended is this, that no minority community shall be compelled to have religious instruction in a religion not his own. That is the real purpose. But although I fully appreciate the purpose, I find that this clause is worded in too general terms and it will preclude the majority community from even imparting any religious instruction to their children because of the minorities. While minorities should not be compelled to have religious instructions against their wishes, they should be provided facilities for having their religious education if the number of their children is sufficient. It should not be forbidden to provide religious education by the State. Now, after partition of this country, about 30 to 33 crores will be the majority community and if these people want that their children should have education in their religion, they will not be able to have it if this article is passed. This is not fair. What I want is that they should be enabled to have instruction in their religion provided the same facilities they are prepared to afford to children of other denominations if the number is sufficiently large... This clause as it stands will really preclude the majority from giving religious education to their children. For example the District Board in Gorakhpur will not be able to teach *Gita* to children in the schools. I think this should not be so. These big scriptures of the world are really meant to develop the morality and tolerance and they should be taught and I do not wish that anything in the Fundamental Rights should forbid this. I discussed this with Dr. Ambedkar and I have said that clauses (1) and (3) should be deleted, so that this would prevent anybody from forcing any instructions against their wishes, but it would not have precluded the State from imparting instruction in religion to the children of various denominations if the number was sufficient. But, I want that clause (1) also should be deleted because in that case it will be possible for the State to impart instruction in religion, in *Gita*, in Sermon on the Mount, etc., to the children in the schools, but not force this instruction on anybody against his wishes. It should be permissible to the State to give instruction in religion to children according to their desire and choice and if their guardians permit. This is what I wish but if it is not acceptable, I am not insisting on the deletion of the first part. But clause (3) should be deleted. But I would request Dr. Ambedkar to see that the clause does not forbid the institutions in the State from giving religious instruction. This clause is too wide and should be redrafted to include this".[55]

Jaspat Roy Kapoor moved an amendment for deletion of clause (3) of Article 22. He contended: "My reasons are four. Firstly, this clause is in conflict with clause (1) of Article 22 which reads: "No religious instruction shall be provided in any educational institution wholly maintained out of State funds". I am of course reading clause (1) as it will stand after the amendment moved by Dr. Ambedkar is incorporated. So that, while clause (1) lays down that no religious instruction shall be imparted in any institution which is maintained wholly by the State, clause (3) lays down that such religious instruction can be imparted out of working hours. Obviously, therefore, these two are in conflict with each other. If clause (1) is to remain, clause (3) must go. Clause (3) cannot stand in the face of clause (1)."

"My second reason is that the retention of clause (3) is likely to lead to conflict between the different religious denominations because different religious denominations may claim the right to impart religious instruction to their pupils in any institution at the same time and in the same premises. That will certainly lead to a good deal of conflict. The convenient time for imparting religious instruction, after working hours, is very limited and several religious denominations may like to impart religious instruction to their pupils in the same premises and at the same convenient hour. This will place the head of the educational institution concerned in a very embarrassing position. He may be in a dilemma as to whom he should grant permission and to whom not. If a particular denomination is refused permission it might make a very serious grievance of it and, even may, in order to exercise the fundamental right granted to that community, seek forcible entry into that institution. This is likely to lead to communal and religious riots. The retention of the clause being full of mischievous potentialities, it must be deleted."

He continued : "my third reason is that the management of a denominational institution may not like that religious instruction in a different religion from its own should be imparted there. A Muslim school which may perhaps be run within the precincts of a mosque would surely not like religious instruction to Hindus being imparted there in Vedic Dharma. So also an educational institution run by Arya Samajists would surely not like religious instruction in *Quran* being imparted in the premises of that institution. For this reason also this clause must go.

"My fourth reason is that it is absolutely unnecessary in view of clause (2). Clause (2) already provides that religious instruction can be imparted by the management of an educational institution provided of course the students agree to it or if they are minors their guardians agree to it. Such instruction can be provided not only during working hours, but even outside working hours. So it is unnecessary in view of clause (2). For these reasons I submit that clause (3) should be deleted",[56] he concluded.

Smt. Renuka Roy also supported this amendment of Kapoor "because as he has pointed out there is no doubt that if this clause remains, there is likelihood that in a certain area where there may be a small number of schools or only one school, a fight between the various denominations as to which particular type of religious instruction should be given out of school hours may ensue. Therefore, it is much better that clause (3) be deleted from this article".[57]

Kazi Syed Karimuddin also objected to clause (3) because "what has been given in clauses (l) and (2) has been taken away in clause (3). But who would be responsible for imparting the religious education in such institutions? Any outside agencies who would be giving religious instructions to the boys may not be acceptable to the authorities and moreover much mischief will be done if this religious education is given in outside hours by people who are irresponsible and by people who will be recklessly teaching boys that may be to the detriment of the nation",[58] he said.

V.S. Sarwate[59] and M. Ananthasayanam Ayyangar[60] were also in favour of deletion of Article 22(3).

Dr. B.R. Ambedkar accepted this proposal because "clause (3) is really unnecessary. It relates to a school maintained by a community. After school hours, the community may be free to make use of it as it likes. There ought to be no provision at all in the Constitution"[61] and this clause was deleted.

III

But the amendments that were not accepted were not few. Let us look into those amendments one by one and see what were the arguments advanced in support of or against these amendments.

Mohammad Ismail Sahib moved an amendment for substitution of Article 22 by the following:

> No person attending an educational institution maintained, aided or recognised by the State shall be required to take part in any religious instruction in such institution without consent of such persons if he or she is a major or without the consent of the respective parent or guardian if he or she is a minor.

Giving reasons for introduction of this amendment, he said: "Article 22 in the Draft Constitution, as it stands, puts a taboo on all religious instructions being given in State-aided schools or State educational instructions. It is not necessary for a Secular State to ban religious education in State institutions. Sir, it will not be in contravention of the neutrality or the secular nature of the State to impart religious instructions. It will be going against the spirit of the Secular State if the State compels the students or pupils to study a religion to which they do not belong. But, if the pupils or their parents want that religious instruction should be given in the institutions in their own religion, then, it is not going against the secular nature of the State and the State will not be violating the neutrality which it has avowedly taken in the matter of religion. My amendment purports to make leeway in case religious instruction is required to be given in the schools; it puts the matter in a negative form. It does not say that the religious instruction must be imparted at all costs in educational institutions; it only says, no compulsion shall be put upon anybody to study in any school a religion to which he or she does not belong. Therefore, my amendment is quite harmless and it does not go in anyway against the spirit of the Constitution. Sir, the necessity of imparting religious instruction has been recognised in many countries, which are non-religious in nature. They have made religious instruction even compulsory, that is, compulsory with regard to those people who want such instruction to be given to the children in the religion to which they belong. They have not thought it fit to bar religion altogether from their secular State. Therefore, I hold that we shall not be doing anything in violation of the secular nature of our State if we do not ban religious instruction altogether. As my amendment proposes, we shall leave the matter to the future, to the Parliament. According to my amendment, we are not saying anything now positively about religious instructions; we are only saying, nobody shall be compelled to have religious instructions in a religion to which he does not belong. Whether to give religious instructions or not may be left to Parliament. According to my amendment, that is my proposal."[62]

None supported this stand of Ismail Sahib. On the other hand, Kazi Syed Karimuddin criticised him. "In my opinion the provisions of Article 22 except clause (3) are very salutary and I really do not understand how these provisions have been opposed by Mr. Ismail from Madras. In the state of things as they stand today, in my opinion, it is much better for the minorities to avoid religious controversies, conflicts and religious dogmas to be taught in the schools and we have seen in the past, as several speakers the other day have said, that in Missionary schools people were persuaded to have conversion from one faith to the other because of the undue influence or monetary gains. Now in a Secular State, where religion will be a personal matter, my submission is that in educational institutions wholly managed or wholly aided by the Government or State, religious education should not be provided. It is said that unless religious education is given in the schools financed by the State it would not be possible for the minorities to be educated in their religion. My submission is that if the communities want that their children should be educated or should be given religious education, then it will be their duty to educate their children in pathsalas or schools",[63] he said.

Dr. B.R. Ambedkar gave reasons as to why Ismail's amendment could not be accepted. "There are three reasons in my judgement, which militate against the acceptance of the view advocated by my friend Mr. Ismail, namely that there ought to be no ban on religious instructions rather that religious instructions should be provided and I shall state those reasons very briefly.

"The first reason is this. We have accepted the proposition which is embodied in Article 21, that public funds raised by taxes shall not be utilised for the benefit of any particular community. For instance, if we permitted any particular religious instruction, say, if a school established by a District or Local Board gives religious instruction on the ground that the majority of the students studying in that school are Hindus, the effect would be that such action would militate against the provisions contained in Article 21. The District Board would be making a levy on every person residing within the area of that District Board. It would have a general tax and if religious instructions given in the District or Local Board was confined to the children of the majority community, it would be an abuse of Article 21, because the Muslim community children or the children of any other community who do not care to attend these religious instructions given in the schools would be none-the-less compelled by the action of the District Local Board to contribute to the District Local Board funds."

"The second difficulty", he continued, "is much more real than the first, namely the multiplicity of the religions we have in this country. For instance, take a city like Bombay which contains a heterogeneous population believing in different creeds. Suppose, for instance, there was a school in the city of Bombay maintained by the Municipality. Obviously, such a school would contain children of the Hindus believing in the Hindu religion, there will be pupils belonging to the Christian community, Zoroastrian community, or to the Jewish community. If one went further and I think it would be desirable to go further than this, the Hindus again would be divided into several varieties, there would be the *Sanatani Hindus*, Vedic Hindus believing in the Vedic religion, there would be the Buddhists, there would be the Jains, even among Hindus there would be the Shaivites, there would be the Vaishnavites. Is the educational institution to be required to treat all these children on a footing of equality and to provide religious instruction to all the denominations? It seems to me that to assign such a task to the State would be to ask it to do the impossible.

"The third thing which I would like to mention in this connection is that unfortunately the religions which prevail in this country are not merely non-social, so far as their mutual relations are concerned, they are anti-social, one religion claiming that its teachings constitute the only right path for salvation, that all other religions are wrong. The Muslims believing that anyone who does not believe in the dogma of lslam is a Kafir not entitled to brotherly treatment with the Muslims. The Christians have a similar belief. In view of this it seems to me that we should be considerably disturbing the peaceful atmosphere of an institution if these controversies with regard to the truthful character of any particular religion and the erroneous character of the other were brought into juxtaposition in the school itself. I, therefore, say that in laying down in Article 22(1) that in State institutions there shall be no religious instruction, we have in my judgement travelled the path of complete safety",[64] he concluded.

There was no further discussion on this amendment and it was negatived by the House.

Sardar Hukum Singh, Sardar Bhopindar Singh Mann and Tejamul Hussain wanted to make clause (1) of Article 22 more stringent against religious instructions being imparted in educational institutions.

Sardar Hukum Singh moved an amendment for insertion of the words 'or permitted' after the words 'shall be provided' in clause (1) of Article 22. His point of view was: "I am conscious that the definition of the words 'the State' as given in Article 7 is very comprehensive and it includes all authorities whether of the Centre or of the States, and it does include local bodies as well. Even then, I feel that the object would not be fulfilled, if we do not add these words 'or permitted' as I have proposed. We are going to build a Secular State. The object of this article, so far as I have understood it, is to prohibit all religious instructions in those institutions which are maintained by the State. If the article were to stand as it is, then it would mean that the State would not provide or I might say, any authority would not provide any religious instruction in such institutions. I presume the object is not economic; we are not safeguarding against the State spending funds on imparting religions but we are providing, rather, against imparting religious education in these institutions. And, in that case, our object cannot be served unless we definitely prohibit that in these institutions. Even if no provision is made for the imparting of such religious education, it should also not be permitted. I may say that the staff might take into its head though the State has not made any provision, the imparting of such instruction, and might start imparting such religious instructions; or a particular teacher, say, might begin in his class the imparting of such instructions. Then, so far as the article stands it would not be offended against by the action of the teacher or the staff. That object can only be achieved if we definitely ban the imparting of such instructions, when we are making the State a secular one. Therefore, I move that after the words 'shall be provided', the words 'or permitted' should be added, so that there would be no chance for such religious instruction being imparted in any case, in institutions that are to be controlled and subsidised by the State."[65]

Sardar Mann wanted to drop the word 'education' from Article 22(1) to make it more wide and "thus keep up the strict neutrality of the State so far as religious matters are concerned, and to maintain the secular character of the State". He said: "Sir, I, a member of the minority community, wholeheartedly welcome it and I believe that the State should function along that principle laid down in this Article, and that in all spheres of State activity, the members of the minority community shall be left no cause of apprehension or fear and that it will happen very soon. However, Sir, I wonder why this article is permitted to remain so incomplete, because only educational institutions are mentioned here. Probably educational institutions were mentioned because in the popular opinion they are the only places where religious instructions are given. But I may point out that there are other places or institutions which are completely and wholly maintained by State funds and which in modern times can be used as vehicle for religious or communal propaganda very effectively. To mention one such vehicle, there is the radio. We all know how effectively it can be used as a platform for religious propaganda day after day. I want that this article should conform to its own logical conclusion and that it should be made complete, and that religious or communal propaganda should be prohibited in all state-owned institutions. Otherwise, to me it looks useless that you should prohibit communal or religious propaganda in one institution but allow it to go full blast in other spheres of activity. For example, take the Army itself; religious and communal propaganda can very easily be imparted there. I want that religious instruction should expressly be prohibited not only in educational institutions but in all institutions which are maintained by the State."[66]

Tejamul Hussain wanted deletion of the words 'by the State' and 'wholly maintained out of State funds' from this article. Clause 22(1), as it read then "means that religious instruction can be provided in any educational institution which is partly maintained out of State funds or are not maintained out of State funds at all. The result would be that all private and aided schools and colleges and *pathshalas* and maktabs will impart religious instructions to boys and girls. I submit that this should not be allowed in a secular State. What is the use of calling India a secular State if you allow religious instruction to be imparted to young boys and girls? By this article you do not prevent if parents want to give religious instruction to their children—they are at liberty to do so at home, and nobody will object to it. In fact, every parent gives his child education well before he goes to school; generally what happens in this country is that all religious instruction is given to a boy before he attends the schools; and that should be done, it is the duty of the parents to educate their children according to their own ways. But I object to a public institution, whether maintained by Government or partly maintained by Government, imparting religious training",[57] he argued.

Commenting on the amendments of Sardar Mann and Tejamul Hussain, Kazi Syed Karimuddin said: "It has also been stated that the word 'educational' should be removed from clause (1) and it is stated that Radios may be used to propagate and teach a particular religion. This is a State which has been declared to be secular and if a secular State decides to propagate a particular religion through radios, it will not be worth the name that it is a secular State. In my opinion, it is more a question of administrative policy and the word 'educational' need not be taken away from clause (1). Sir, it has been stated that religious education should be given at home. I also oppose this. In aided schools run by communities religious education can be given and the amendment of Mr. Tejamul Hussain cannot be accepted that religious education should be given at home. I contemplate a position that if parents are atheists, in that case, there will be no religious education in their houses; and if people are only to be known by numbers and not by names, then it will be very difficult for them to be educated or instructed in religious theology. Therefore, my submission is that Article 22 as it stands is not to the disadvantage or detriment of the minorities".[68]

None other spoke on these amendments and all the three amendments were negatived by the House.

The amendment, which drew a measure of support from some members who elicited proper interpretation of the clause from the Mover of the Article, i.e. Dr. Ambedkar, was the one moved by Prof. K.T. Shah. Prof. Shah wanted that the words "or partly" be added after the word 'wholly' in clause 22(1). He pointed out that "all institutions or most of them are maintained wholly or partly out of public revenues, whether they are in the form of the entire bill footed by the State, or in the shape of some grants, or in the shape of fees, etc. received from the public by regular charge; and, as such, no public institutions would be free from an incursion of any particular religious instruction of a denomination—and even, may I say of a controversial character. If you permit one, you will make it impossible to refuse admission to another. That means that in a public institution, any number or any section of people who are being educated there, if only one donor can be found for each to endow a particular scholarship, or to provide for some particular item of expenditure, let us say, library grant, or some item of laboratory equipment, or some small donation for general purposes, and couple it with the condition that Religious Instruction shall be provided therein for that particular sect to which the donor belongs, then I am afraid, your educational institutions will be converted into a menagerie of faiths. There will be unexpected conflicts and controversies; and the very evil which you are out to stop by the opening words would be all the more encouraged and supported, so to say, by public countenance. I would like entirely to dissociate the State in India from any such interpretation as you desire to exclude. Religious Instruction from public institutions maintained from common funds, whether they be the entire expenditure of such institution, or whether they be a part only by way of a grant or by way of fees, or scholarships, or endowments of any kind met by the State out of public revenues, then it would be absurd—I think it would be inconsistent with the basic principle of this constitution, to permit Religious Instruction on the excuse that part of the expenditure is met by other than State funds."[69]

Srimati Renuka Ray, author of this clause, also wanted that the position arising out of the word "wholly" be cleared up. She observed: "Part (I) of this article says: "No religious instruction shall be provided in any educational institution wholly maintained out of State funds". There is likelihood of this being misinterpreted in the future, so as to nullify its very object. As he (Prof. K.T. Shah) has pointed out even if a small donation is paid to a public school, it can be held that such a school is not wholly maintained out of State funds, and therefore, denominational religious instruction may be given. I hope that when Dr. Ambedkar speaks, he will clear up this point because it is a very important one. If such interpretation can be given then it is necessary to have safeguards against it. In this country we have seen the exploitation, and the prostitution of what we call religion and we have seen to our bitter cost what is done in the name of denominational religion. It has not only led to the dismemberment and division of our country, but it has also led to the worst horrors that could be perpetrated in the name of religion. Now, when we are building for the future, we must build in such a manner that we are able to do so untrammeled by the legacy of the past. The only real way in which this could be done is to see that the next generation is educated in such a manner that they are not actuated by motives that divide and disintegrate man from man, but that the religion of humanity is much greater to them than religious dissensions on a denominational religious basis. If that is to be so, we must be very careful, now that we are building up the Constitution for the future, that there shall not be in the fundamental rights any kind of confusion as to the kind of instruction that is to be given at least in those institutions that are maintained out of public funds. If we use this word 'wholly', there is likely to be this confusion that has been already pointed out and I would like to hear from Dr. Ambedkar if it is possible for him either to accept this amendment or at least to assure the House that no such interpretation will be possible in the future."[70]

Commenting on this clause of the article M. Ananthasayanam Ayyangar said that he was neither for imparting of religious instructions in the educational institutions nor for imposing total ban on such instructions. He was, however, "very much pained that religious instruction is not to be taught in any school in a country which is full of religion. Inside our schools, we may refuse to teach religion to the children. But outside the schools we cannot forget our denominations. Religion, according to me, is the basic foundation of any society; all morality, and all good principles have to be traced to religion. But situated as we are, it is unfortunate that we are not able to come to any arrangement regarding the teaching of religion to our children in our schools. ...We are pledged to make the State a secular one. I do not, by the word 'secular', mean that we do not believe in any religion, and that we have nothing to do with it in our day-to-day life. It only means that the State or the Government cannot aid one religion or give preference to one religion as against another. Therefore, it is obliged to be absolutely secular in character, not that it has lost faith in all religions. Not even members in charge of the

Government have lost faith in religion. I am sure none of us to that extent an iconoclast or non-believer. We all do believe in some religion or other, including those who have spoken and taken part in the deliberations about this article in the Constitution. But it is regrettable that we have not been able to evolve a universal religion, a religion where the religious practices need not cloud the issues. We all believe in the existence of one God, in prayer, in meditation and so on. We all believe in the ultimate surrender to Him and that by sacrifice and service alone can we hope to realise Godhead. These are common to all religions. The *Bhagavad Gita* lays down that by sacrifice and service we have to see Godhead in humanity, that service to humanity is the essence of God. I will not go into all the details; suffice it to say that I regret that in the circumstances in which we are, we are not able to teach religion to our children. If we introduce the teaching of one religion, even if there is only one boy belonging to another religion in that school, we have to make provision for the teaching of his religion also. And we know very well that even under one religion there are sects and sub-sects. There are Hindus of various sects. And then there is Jainism, Buddhism, Christianity, and there are the Muslims, the Parsis and so on. Therefore, it is not possible, it is physically impossible for the State to make provisions for the teaching of all the religions. The only thing under the circumstances that we can do is to avoid religious instructions in State-aided schools. If a small contribution is made by some agency and religious instruction is provided, it will all the same, be controlled by the local authority, and if the teaching is rabid, and if hatred is being taught in the school, certainly the grant can be withheld and other measures adopted to stop that kind of thing. It is not obligatory upon the State to give its grants irrespective of the way in which the educational institution is being run. So we need not think that religious instruction will be given in an institution where the major portion is contributed by the State and a small contribution—may be a farthing—is contributed by some other agency. We need not make it part and parcel of the Constitution here. I am sure no government would contribute 99 per cent and allow an educational institution to impart religious education because 1 per cent comes from some other source",[71] he observed.

V.S. Sarwate and Kazi Syed Karimuddin did not like any alteration in this clause. V.S. Sarwate said that "as I see from the word 'wholly' I do think that if the State wants to partially aid any school which is imparting religious instructions, it is enabled to do so and I think it is right. If any community does maintain a school and imparts particular religious education and it deserves help from the State, the State should be in a position to give such aid. Therefore, the word 'wholly' is necessary and I oppose the other amendment which has been moved inserting the words 'or partially'."[72]

Syed Karimuddin also opposed this amendment of Prof. Shah, "The amendment moved by Professor Shah in my opinion cannot be acceptable at the present stage. His amendment is that no religious instruction should be provided by the State in any educational institution wholly or partly maintained out of public funds. Today as things stand in India there is Aligarh University, there is Banaras University and there are several colleges run by the Christian Missionaries which are aided by the Government. If his amendment is accepted today there will be hundreds and thousands of institutions which will be closed down immediately. Let us proceed very cautiously. For that the provision in clause (2) is very salutary. In aided schools or institutions in which there will be no compulsion on the students to take a particular religious education. I think the opposite point of view can be partially met by clause (2)",[73] he said.

Dr. Ambedkar did not clarify the points raised by Prof. K.T. Shah, Renuka Ray or Ananthasayanam Ayyangar in his closing address and this amendment of Prof. Shah was negatived.

Prof. K.T. Shah moved another amendment for addition of the following words at the end of the proviso to clause (1) of Article 22:

> "and the income from which trust or endowment is sufficient to defray the entire expenditure of such institution."

His argument was more or less on the same line as advanced in the earlier amendment to Article 22(1) over the word 'wholly'.

He argued: "It would be a simple proposition, as I understand this proviso to the clause as it stands, for anybody to make a Trust or Endowment, sufficient, let us say, to meet part of the cost, e.g. building and furniture; then divest himself of the care and responsibility of managing that institution, hand it over to the State, earn cheap immortality and the title of being a munificent donor, and then ask the State to carry on the institution and also to provide Religious Instruction therein, negativing the principle on which the clause to which this is a proviso was founded.

"The idea, as I have understood this clause, would be defeated and the clause turned into grotesqueness I think, if such should be the result. Perhaps, it was not intended to be so twisted out of the intention. My amendment, therefore, only seeks to make it clear and explicit.

"Even so, I am, for my part, not entirely satisfied that any excuse should be left to provide Religious Instruction of a particular character in any public institution managed by the State, and of which only a part, or even the whole of the expenditure is coming from the grant, Trust fund or Endowment that a donor has made.

"This will be the negation, I repeat, of the basic principle on which this clause is based. The omission of the words 'by the State' under an amendment just moved by the Chairman of the Drafting Committee would if adopted-- and I suppose it will be adopted—make the position still more complicated, unless it be that by a consequential amendment the authorities themselves would see that the words 'by the State' here are also omitted—I do not know that they be omitted here. I am just suggesting a possibility of conveying a hint which may reconcile to some extent the main clause with the proviso", he continued.

"Whether or not these words are deleted from the main clause, and whether or not these words are retained in the proviso, the objection I am urging will apply all the same. I hold that it should not be open to anybody to make a trust for an educational institution in the first instance and then handover its management to the State and demand that in that institution simply on the ground that the founder has been providing the capital or recurring cost of the institution, there shall be religious instruction of the type favoured by him or professed by him.

"I still believe that it could not be really the intention of the authors of this clause; and this proviso which permits any such irregularity or exception should be made explicit in the way I am trying by amendment to do. I trust that common sense, if not legal sense, will assert itself; and the substance, if not the actual form, of my amendment will be accepted",[74] he concluded.

Only Dr. Ambedkar mentioned about this point in his reply. He said, "I do not think really that there is much substance in the point raised by Prof. Shah. I think he will realise that there have been cases where institutions in the early part of the history of this country have been established with the object of giving religious instructions and for some reason they were unable to have people to manage them and they were taken over by the State as a trustee for them. Now, it is obvious that when you accept a trust you must fulfil that trust in all respects. If the State has already taken over these institutions and placed itself in the position of trustee, then obviously you cannot say to the Government that notwithstanding the fact that you were giving religious instruction in these institutions, hereafter you shall not give such instruction. I think that would be not only permitting the State but forcing it to commit a breach of trust. In order therefore to have the situation clear, we thought it was desirable and necessary to introduce the proviso, which to some extent undoubtedly is not in consonance with the original proposition contained in sub-clause (1) of Article 20".[75] After this reply, the amendment of Prof. Shah was negatived by the House.

H.V. Kamath moved an amendment for deletion of the words 'recognised by the State or' in clause (2) of Article 22. He stated: "I move this amendment with a view to obtaining some clarification on certain dark corners of these two articles—Articles 22 and 23. I hope my learned friend Dr. Ambedkar will not, in his reply, merely toe the line of least resistance and say, 'I oppose this amendment', but will be good enough to give some reasons why he opposes or rejects my amendment, and I hope he will try his best to throw some light on the obscure corners of this article. If we scan the various clauses of this article carefully and turn a sidelong glance at the next articles too, we will find that there are some inconsistencies or at least an inconsistency. Clause (1) of Article 22 imposes an absolute ban on religious instruction in institutions which are wholly maintained out of State funds. The proviso, however, excludes such institutions as are administered by the State which have been established under an endowment or trust—that is, under the proviso those institutions which have been established under an endowment or trust and which require, under the conditions of the trust, that religious instruction must be provided in those institutions, about those, when the State administers them, there will not be any objection to religious instruction. Clause (2) lays down that no person attending an institution recognised by the State or receiving aid out of State funds shall be required to take part in religious instruction. That means, it would not be compulsory. I am afraid I will have to turn to Article 23, sub-clauses (3)(a) where it is said that all minorities, whether based on religion, community or language, shall have the right to establish and administer educational institutions of their choice. Now, it is intended that the institutions referred to in the subsequent clause which minorities may establish and conduct and administer according to their own choice, is it intended that in these institutions the minorities would not be allowed to provide religious instruction? There may be institutions established by minorities which insist on students' attendance at religious classes in those institutions and which are otherwise unobjectionable. There is no point about State aid, but I cannot certainly understand why the State should refuse recognition to those institutions established by minorities where they insist on compulsory attendance at religious classes. Such interference by the State I feel is unjustified and unnecessary. Besides, this conflicts with the next article to a certain extent. If minorities have the right to establish and administer educational institutions of their own choice, is it contended by the Honourable Dr. Ambedkar that the State will say: "You can have institutions, but you should not have religious instructions in them if you want our recognition". Really, it beats me how you can reconcile these two points of view in Articles 22 and 23. The minority, as I have already said, may establish such a school for its own pupils and make religious instruction compulsory in that school. If you do not recognise that institution, then certainly that school will not prosper and it will fail to attract pupils. Moreover, we have guaranteed certain rights to the minorities and, it may be in a Christian School, they may teach the pupils the Bible and in a Muslim School the *Quran*. If the minorities, Christians and Muslims, can administer those institutions according to their choice and manner, does the House mean to suggest that the State shall not recognise such institutions? Sir, to my mind, if you pursue such a course, the promises we have made to the minorities in our country, the promises we have made to the ear we shall have broken to the heart. Therefore, I do not see any point why, in institutions that are maintained and conducted and administered by the minorities for pupils of their own community the State should refuse to grant recognition, in case religious instruction is compulsory. When once you have allowed them to establish schools according to their choice, it is inconsistent that you should refuse recognition to them on that ground. I hope something will be done to rectify this inconsistency."[76]

V.I. Muniswami Pillai, however, welcomed the second clause in Article 22 as a very important one. He said: "It will be in the knowledge of this sovereign body that certain institutions in the past, due to the aid that was given by the former Government, under the garb of imparting education to the masses, have taken a different stand. This has led to masses of the unfortunate communities embracing a religion that was not their own. This article makes it clear that any educational institution receiving aid from the State should not indulge in matters of religious education. This mostly helps those unfortunate communities that have fallen a prey in this respect. Sir, further it goes to say that in the case of a minor, unless the parent has given his consent, he should not be given religious instruction or required to attend any religious worship. I feel, Sir, it is not always possible for the parents to give this consent and the institutions that are working in the rural areas and outskirts of towns will not get the genuine consent of the parents in this respect. This important duty of seeing whether the consent given is genuine and true, falls upon the local authorities who will have to verify and create agencies so that the students or pupils that are attending any institutions of certain denominations are not converted to other religions. This is my emphatic plea and I am hopeful that the local Governments will take care about what is said about consent. I entirely welcome the provisions of this Article 22 of the Constitution."[77]

V.S. Sarwate also supported Article 22(2). He commented: "One need not be obsessed by what happened in the past. I know and I have read in schools and colleges where certain religious education was imparted. I am grateful for the teachings which I received there, but there were certain objectionable features. In one educational institution there was a religious instruction imparted in the first hour and if we did not attend in that hour, we were marked absent for the rest of the periods. In another college where I learnt, it was necessary that we attended a religious worship and if we did not attend it, we were subjected to certain fines. These were objectionable features and these are to be removed. They are removed by clause (2). Nobody is required to attend such religious worship or to attend such classes where religious education is given. But it does not prohibit the State from giving aid to such institutions; what is only meant is nobody against his will be required or forced and compelled to receive such education or attend such religious worship, and I think, this is a very salutary provision and also the permission which is given to the State to aid such institutions is necessary. Otherwise I believe certain very good institutions in the country would suffer."[78]

In reply to the criticism of H.V. Kamath on Article 22(2), Dr Ambedkar highlighted the salient features of Article 22(2) in the following words: "Now, with regard to the second clause I think it has not been sufficiently well-understood. We have tried to reconcile the claim of a community which has started educational institutions for the advancement of its own children either in education or in cultural matters, to permit to give religious instruction in such institutions, notwithstanding the fact that it receives certain aid from the State. The State, of course, is free to give aid, is free not to give aid; the only limitation we have placed is this, that the State shall not debar the institution from claiming aid under its grant-in-aid code merely on the ground that it is run and maintained by the community and not maintained by a public body. We have there provided also a further qualification, that while it is free to give religious instruction in the institution and the grant made by the State shall not be a bar to the giving of such instruction, it shall not give instruction to, or make it compulsory upon, the children belonging to other communities unless and until they obtain the consent of the parents of those children. That, I think, is a salutary provision. Therefore, by clause (2) we are really achieving two purposes. One is that we are permitting a community which has established its institutions for the advancement of its religious or its cultural life, to give such instruction in the school. We have also provided that children of other communities who attend that school shall not be compelled to attend such religious instructions which undoubtedly and obviously must be the instruction in the religion of that particular community, unless the parents consent to it. As I say, we have achieved this double purpose and those who want religious instruction to be given are free to establish their institutions and claim aid from the State, give religious instruction, but shall not be in a position to force that religious instruction on other communities. It is, therefore, not proper to say that by this article we have altogether barred religious instruction. Religious instruction has been left free to be taught and given by such community according to its aims and objects subject to certain conditions. All that is barred is this, that the State in the institutions maintained by it wholly out of public funds shall not be free to give religious instruction."[79]

A piquant situation arose as to the interpretation of the words 'religious instruction'. Pandit Lakshmi Kanta Maitra wanted to know whether the teaching of the *Vedas*, or *Smritis,* or *Shastras* or the *Upanishads* in the Sanskrit College, Calcutta, which was wholly maintained out of State funds should be interpreted as coming within the meaning of religious instruction.[80] Dr. Ambedkar wanted to explain away the issue by saying that in his own view "religious instruction is to be distinguished from research or study. Those are quite different things. Religious instruction means this. For instance, so far as the Islam religion is concerned, it means that you believe in one God, that you believe that *Pagambar* the Prophet is the last Prophet and so on, in others words, what we call 'dogma'. A dogma is quite different from study."[81] Dr. H.C. Mukherjee, Vice-President of the Constituent Assembly, who was then on the chair interposed at this point. "As Inspector of Colleges for the Calcutta University, I used to inspect the Sanskrit College, where-as Pandit Maitra is aware, students have to study not only the University course but books outside it in Sanskrit literature and in fact Sanskrit sacred books, but this was never regarded as religious instruction; it was regarded as a course in culture",[82] he commented. But Pandit Maitra insisted an answer to his question. Ultimately Dr. Ambedkar had to retreat saying[83] that the courts would decide when the matter was brought before them.

Thus Article 22 in the amended form (since renumbered as 28) was adopted in the Constituent Assembly on December 7, 1948.

During the third reading of the Draft Constitution Bill, two members, namely Prof. Shibban Lal Saksena and Algu Rai Shastri criticised the provisions of Article 28. Prof. Shibban Lal Saksena said: "Another Article on Fundamental Rights which I consider to be most unfair to the people is Article 28, where it has been said that no religious instruction shall be provided in any educational institution wholly maintained out of State Funds. I consider religious instruction, by which I mean instruction in true religion and its eternal principles, to be the most important of a child's education. Ban on religious instruction in State schools may result in the prohibition even of the teaching of books like the *Gita* and the *Ramayana* in schools. I am sure peoples' representatives will not tolerate this ban and this article will soon have to be amended. This is an instance where secularity has gone too far."[84]

Algu Rai Shastri also referred to this issue in the following words: "Further, Sir, we have prohibited the religious education being imparted in schools particularly in schools which are being run by Government aid. I feel, Sir, that this has not been wisely done. Mahatma Gandhi used to study *Gita* and *Ramayana* practically everyday. If these and other religious books would not be read I fail to see how proper citizenship would be developed in our country. The fact is, Sir, that if we banish religion, I do not understand how we will be able to maintain a normal code. My feeling is that our fundamental rights have this fundamental defect."[85]

Article 28, thus framed, reads as follows:

Freedom as to attendance at religious instruction or religious worship in certain educational institutions—(1) No religious instruction shall be provided in any educational institution wholly maintained out of State funds.

(2) Nothing in Clause (1) shall apply to an educational institution which is administered by the State but has been established under any endowment or trust which requires that religious instruction shall be imparted in such institution.

(3) No person attending any educational institution recognized by the State or receiving aid out of State funds shall be required to take part in any religious instruction that may be imparted in such institution or to attend any religious worship that may be conducted in such institution or in any premises attached thereto unless such person or, if such person is a minor, his guardian has given his consent thereto.

IV

The institution of the *Madrasah*, *Maktab*, *Gurukul*, *Pathshala* and *Tol* was a part of the age-old education system much before the commencement of the British rule in India. These are religion-based institutions. The *Gurukul* system of education is one of the earliest forms of education. *Gurukulam* have existed since the Vedic age. *Upanishads* mention many *gurukulas*, including that of Yajnavalkya, Varuni. A *gurukul* is a type of school in India, residential in nature, with *shishyas* (students) living in proximity to the *guru* (teacher), often within the same house. While living in a *gurukul* the students had to be away from his house and family. In *gurukul*, *shishyas* reside together as equals, irrespective of their social standing, learn from the *guru* and help the *guru* in his day-to-day life, including the carrying out of mundane chores such as washing clothes, cooking, etc. The *gurus* didn't take any fees. The *gurukuls* were supported by public donation. The *guru-shishya parampara* (tradition) is a hallowed one in Hinduism and appears in other religious groups in India, such as Jainism, Buddhism and Sikhism. By the colonial era the *gurukul* system was declining in India except in a few regions, such as Kerala. Recently several *gurukulas* have begun, such as Sree Swaminaryan *gurukul*, ISKCON *gurukul*.[86]

Then there were the village *pathshalas*. The village *pathshalas* were often housed in shabby dwellings and taught by ill-qualified teachers. Instruction was limited mainly to the three R's and the native *mahajani-zamindari* accounts. Printed books were not used, and most writing was done on palm leaf, plantain leaf, or on sand. There was no fixed class routine, timetable, or school calendar. There was no annual examination, pupils being promoted whenever the *guru* was satisfied of the scholar's attainments. There were no desks, benches, blackboards, or fixed seating arrangements. By the colonial-era both these systems of education were declining. The decline in this form of institution probably started in the mid-1700s.[87]

Another variant of *Gurukulam* system of education was the *Tol* or *Chatuspathi; Chatuspathi* means the centre for study of the *Shastras* and the *Vedas.* Most of them were free residential educational institutions maintained either by the landed gentry or by the teacher himself. Sanskrit was the medium of instruction. In the Muslim era such institutions flourished in Kashi, and Mithila, apart from Nabadwip. From the end of the Eighteenth century, the *tol* system of education faced crisis due to the increasing demand for the Western system of education. It was Raja Rammohun Roy who first realized that these systems of education were totally inadequate to meet the requirements of a society which had any expectation to measure up to the standards of the enlightened countries of his days. The existing 'Sanskrit' system of education could, at best, load the minds of youth with grammatical niceties and metaphysical distinctions of little or no practical use to the society. Besides, the Sanskrit language itself—the vehicle of this education—was very difficult for the common people to learn. This alone, in no small measure, had checked the spread of knowledge and learning in India for ages. The Sanskrit system of education, Rammohun felt, was best calculated to keep his countrymen in ignorance and darkness.

In 1781 the Calcutta Madrasah was set-up with the primary intention to promote the study of the Arabic and Persian languages, and a deeper understanding of Mohammedan law. In 1792 was set up the Benares Sanskrit College. The objective behind its establishment was the preservation and cultivation of laws, literature and scriptures of the Hindus—particularly their laws. Both these institutions were formed with the basic objective of producing scholars who could help European judges in understanding and appreciating traditional law and dispensing justice. Oriental learning as such did not receive any appreciable patronage until 1811, when Lord Minto, the then Governor-General, seized with the apprehension that the revival of oriental learning had little chance of success, took the initiative to recommend the long-felt need of reform of the Sanskrit College of Benares to ensure greater diffusion of knowledge among the people. He proposed the establishment of two similar institutions in Tirhut and Nuddea. It was ultimately decided in 1821, to establish, in Calcutta, an institution similar to the one at Benares. H.H. Wilson, the great orientalist, first mooted this idea, and his proposal was readily accepted by the Government. Himself a profound oriental scholar Rammohun, on the other hand, advocated the need for the spread of education in a direction entirely different from the one followed by the authorities. He urged the desirability of imparting instruction in useful branches of knowledge, instead of exclusively promoting Sanskrit learning.

Rammohun's approach towards the nature of the educational system was clearly stated in his famous letter of December11, 1823, to Lord Amherst, in which Rammohun wrote:

> We now find that the Government are establishing a Sanskrit school under Hindu Pandits to impart knowledge as is already current in India. This seminary (similar in character to those which existed in Europe before the time of Lord Bacon) can only be expected to load the minds of youth with grammatical niceties and metaphysical distinctions of little or no practical use to the society. The pupils there acquire what was known two thousand years ago, with the addition of vain and empty subtleties since produced by speculative men such as is already commonly taught in all parts of India. If it had been intended to keep the British nation in ignorance of knowledge, the Baconian philosophy would not have been allowed to displace the system of schoolmen, which was best calculated to perpetuate ignorance. In the same manner, the Sanskrit system of education would be best calculated to keep this country in darkness, if such has been the policy of the British legislature.
>
> But as the improvement of the British native population is the object of the Government, it will consequently promote a more liberal and enlightened system of instruction, embracing mathematics, natural philosophy, chemistry and anatomy with other useful sciences which may be accomplished with the sum proposed by employing a few gentlemen of talent and learning educated in Europe, and providing a college furnished with the necessary books, instruments and other apparatus.[88]

It may be noted in passing that appeals to the Government for the introduction of the teaching of Mathematics, Natural Science, Chemistry, and other allied subjects, as envisaged in his letter to Lord Amherst in 1823, were made 37 years before the Faculty of Science was created in the University of London, and 46 years before the course in Science were established in the Oxford and Cambridge Universities.[89] Rammohun's proposals on the system of education were ultimately adopted by the Government, though after a considerable delay. In 1835 was passed the famous Education Decree inaugurating the present system of English education. The 1882 Education Commission's Report stated: "It took twelve years of controversy, the advocacy of Macaulay, and the decisive action of a new Governor-General, before the Committee could, as a body, acquiesce in the policy urged by him (Rammohun).[90]

Like Rammohun, Vidyasagar also wanted to remodel the traditional way of imparting Sanskrit education. The educational scheme submitted by him in 1850 and 1852 to the higher authority sought to bring harmony between the English and the Sanskrit education.

However, with the introduction of the English education, the traditional *tol* system of education through the medium of Sanskrit lost much of its pride and relevancy. Moreover, the students of the *tol* after passing out could not get any gainful employment. As a result, people in general lost interest in the *tol* system of education.

Madrasah/maktab system of education, which came up primarily during the Muslim regime to impart religious education to members of the community, still continues. The institution of *Madrasah* and the *ulema* as a class of religious specialists emerged with the spread of Islam outside the Arabian Peninsula in the years after the death of the Prophet. By the eighth century, large parts of West and Central Asia, in addition to almost the whole of North Africa, had been brought under Muslim rule. A *de facto* division between political and religious power, foreign to pristine Islam, now came into being. *Madrasahs* played a very significant role to the spread and development of Islamic civilization and culture.

The word *Madrasah* is an Arabic word, which has originated from another Arabic word *Madaris*, and this comes from another Arabic word *Dars*. *Dars* means "to tell something" or "to teach something". So, the word *Madaris* means the "one who tells *Dars*", i.e. the one who tells or teaches something. Therefore, the word *Madrasah* means "the place where something is taught." The word school in English also carries the similar meaning. So, the word *Madrasah* actually means "school". The *Madrasah* is similar to the church school. In both places religious education is taught and people go there for prayers and for studying religion. *Madrasahs* can also be referred to as *Deeni madaris* (religious schools). The other variants of *madrasah* are *ma-dras-sah* or *ma-dra-sah*, also *ma-dras-sa*; or *ma-dra-sa*.[91]

Madrasahs were usually attached to a large mosque. Examples include al-Azhar University in Cairo, Egypt (founded in 970) and al-Karaouine in Fes, Morocco (founded in 859). Later, numerous *madrasahs* were established across the Muslim world by the great Seljuk vizier, Nizam al-Mulk. At a *madrasah*, students would be educated further in religious sciences, Arabic, and secular studies such as medicine, mathematics, astronomy, history, and geography, among many other topics. In the 1100s, there were 75 *madrasahs* in Cairo, 51 in Damascus, and 44 in Aleppo. There were hundreds more in Muslim Spain at this time as well.

These *madrasahs* can be considered the first modern universities. They had separate faculties for different subjects, with resident scholars that had expertise in their fields. Students would pick a concentration of study and spend a number of years studying under numerous professors. When a student completed their course of study, they would be granted an *ijaza*, or a licence certifying that they have completed that programme and are qualified to teach it as well. *Ijazas* could be given by an individual teacher who can personally attest to his/her student's knowledge, or by an institution such as a *madrasah*, in recognition of a student finishing their course of study. *Ijazas* today can be most closely compared to diplomas granted from higher educational institutions.

Institutions known as Madrasah may be divided into three categories: (a) *Maktab*, (b) *Madrasah*, and (c) *Jamia*. *Maktabs* provide instruction in religious as well as some secular subjects up to primary stage. They function from a masjid or a small modest building. *Madarsahs* are institutions imparting education generally up to senior secondary level. *Jamias* are institutions of higher learning providing instruction up to post-graduation and specialization level.

According to Dr. Salamatullah, there was no government control on the education system during the rule of Muslim kings in India. Education was free of government controls. However, sometimes rulers and members of the rich class donated grants to educational institutions. The credit for governmental interest in education goes to Akbar in whose reign the government took some steps in the realm of education for the first time. A department of education was established which provided education to the masses without discrimination between the communities. Both Hindus and Muslims studied in the same institution, albeit their syllabi were different save for common subjects such as mathematics and sciences.[92]

Signs of change emerged in the late seventeenth century, when the Mughal Emperor Aurangzeb Alamgir (1658-1707) commissioned a team of *ulamas* to prepare a compendium of Islamic law, named after him as the Fatwa-i-Alamgiri. Aurangzeb granted one of the *ulamas* associated with this project, Mulla Nizamuddin, an old mansion owned by a French trader, the Firangi Mahal, in Lucknow, where the latter set-up a *Madrasah*, which soon emerged as the leading centre of Islamic studies in north India. Mulla Nizamuddin prepared a fresh curriculum for study here, which came to be known after him as the Dars-i-Nizami or the 'Syllabus of Nizami'. For its age, it was a revolutionary system. It laid emphasis on the natural sciences like mathematics, algebra, astronomy, physics, and physiology. The contemporariness of the Dars-i-Nizami can be gauged from the fact that Mullah Nizamuddin included a book by Mullah Zahid, which had been completed and published just as the curriculum was designed. Unfortunately, in the last three hundred years, the Dars-i-Nizami (Deoband Hanafi school) has remained almost unchanged, though it continues to be the syllabus of most *Madrasahs* in South Asia today. In fact, one of the reasons why *Madrasahs* in India have come under attack is because this curriculum is also followed by the hundreds of *madrasahs* on the Pakistan-Afganistan border, which churned out the Talibs (students) who made up the leadership and rank and file of the Taliban.

Syed Ahmad Khan found the *madrasah* syllabus "unsuited to the present age and to the spirit of the time". He criticised it for encouraging memorising rather than real understanding.[93] With a view to establishing an institution which considered the best of both the orient and the occident religious teaching combined with scientific education, he founded the Madrasatul Uloom in 1875 which grew to be the Aligarh Muslim University in 1920.

Maulana Shibli Naumani was another person to raise a voice against the anachronistic tendency of the Nizami Syllabus. Because of his different views on the modernization of the *Madrasah* syllabus, Nadvatul Ulama came into being in Lucknow in 1894. The *ulama* were now convinced that the Islamic curricula need revolutionary change.

While in Mughal times the *Madrasahs* served the purpose of training intellectual and bureaucratic elite, leaving the poorer classes largely out of their purview, things began to change with the onset of British rule. The British rule brought about a new administrative and educational set up which changed various aspect of Indian life. Before the introduction of the Anglo-Saxon juridical system in India, the Company's magistrates and judges had to depend on Hindu pandits and Muslim quazis for the administration of justice. Thus in spite of the general disinclination of the Company's board of directors to introduce any system of education, the local government had to introduce both the Hindu and Mohammedan systems of education to perform the basic duty of administering law and justice. In 1780, Warren Hastings established the Calcutta Madrasah College to promote the study of Arabic and Persian languages and Islamic law with the aim of producing competent officers for the courts of justice. It became Aliah University—Aliah meaning supreme—with the enactment of the Aliah University Act (Act XXVII), 2007. It started its academic session from the year 2008-09.

The Chancellor is called Amir-I-Jamia and the Vice-Chancellor is known as Shaikh-Ul-Jamia. The Registrar is Musajjil and the Controller of Examinations is Mudir-Ul-Imtihanat. Why an institution set up in West Bengal should flaunt alien names may be questioned. Is the State Government demonstrating that it cares for Non-Bengali people as well?

In 1837, Persian was replaced by English as the language of the courts. Lawyers trained in English law replaced the Muslim qazis and muftis. The eclipse of Muslim political power in the region following the Uprisings of 1857 and the subsequent transfer of authority of governance of India from the East India Company to the British Crown meant that the *ulama* and their *Madrasahs* were now bereft of sources of political support and patronage. In many cases, the British revoked the vast grants that Muslim rulers had provided the *Madrasahs*. While the *Madrasahs* were left largely untouched, the effective delinking of *Madrasahs* education from the job market led to the declining popularity of traditional Islamic schools. The Muslims had to face many formidable changes along with general animosity of the British rulers. They had to counter the proselytizing activities of the Christian missionaries. In this rapidly changing context, the *ulama* now began to turn to the Muslim society for support. The *ulama* and the masses rose to the occasion and started a series of *Madrasahs* in the country. A large member of *Madrasahs* was set-up in the latter half of the nineteenth century. Most important and famous among them were:[94]

(1) Darul-uloom, Deoband, 1866.
(2) Mazaheral-uloom, Saharanpur, 1866.
(3) Madrasah Baqyatris Salehat, Vellore, Tamil Nadu, 1883.
(4) Jamia Mazharul-uloom, Benares, 1893.
(5) Darul Uloom Nadwat-ul-lema, Lucknow, 1894.
(6) Madrasah Ameenia, Delhi, 1897.
(7) Darul-uloom Khalilia Nizamia, Tonk, 1899.
(8) Jamia Arabia Hayatul-uloom, Mubarakpur, 1899.
(9) Madrasatul-Islah, Sarai Mir, Azamgarh, 1909.
(10) Jamia Darus Salam, Umnabad, 1924.

For the thousands of *Madrasahs* that operate in India, there are three kinds of funding available to them: 1. charity, 2. Government grants, and 3. overseas charity. All *Madrasahs* are charitable institutions. Almost all of them depend on the support of charity. Most *Madrasahs* have their designated "Safeels" (charity collectors) who go door to door to the Muslim masses to collect money. Sometimes, an individual chooses to give a *Madarsah* a big grant. People donate their *zakat* and *fitra* to these seminaries. During Id-ul-Azha, Muslims often donate the *charm-e qurbani* (the skin of the slaughtered animal) to the *Madrasahs*. Some *Madrasahs* have permanent sources of income, such as land, buildings and other property that produce regular returns. In some States, such as Bihar, West Bengal, and U.P., there are *Madarsah* boards, just like the school boards. The government in these States allocates some funds to those *Madarsahs* that are registered with the *Madrasah* Board[95]. The number of such *Madrasahs*, however, is very few. Most *Madrasahs* choose to survive without government grants because of two basic reasons: one, they feel government funding would lead to governmental intervention in their work, jeopardizing their independence; and two, the teachers of such government supported *Madrasahs* start behaving like government employees (having the assurance that whether they work sincerely or not, they will get their salaries). Well-known *Madrasahs* including the three at Deoband, Lucknow and Saharanpur have refused to accept government aid since 1947, though they had played a major role in mobilizing Muslims for anti-British freedom struggle. There are really a very limited number of *Madrasahs* that fall in the third category of funding.[96]

Since *Madrasahs* run on charity, they are often looked down upon by the Muslim elite. Affluent Muslims do not send their children to *Madrasahs*. As a result *Madrasahs* have become veritable orphanages. As Syed Shahabuddin says: "Hunger for education is increasing and even poor families are investing in education. In Muslim areas, one sees private schools sprouting as also private *Madrasahs*. They compete with each other. Naturally, the well-to-do go to schools; *Madrasahs* care for the poor".[97]

Today, *Madrasahs* across the country provide free education to the poor Muslims. According to a Study,[98] around 36 per cent of all school age children in the age group of 6-18 years have been found to be studying in *Madrasahs* in India. During initial years of schooling, more than half of the Muslim children are sent to *Madrasahs*. Moreover, of those who seek enrolment in *Madrasahs*, only 22 per cent of boys and 17 per cent of girls and 20 per cent of total students manage to reach up to Class VIII.

Among the Sunnis, who now account for nearly ninety per cent of the world's Muslim population, four schools of jurisprudence developed—the Hanafi, Hanbali, Maliki and Slafi. Each of these schools had its chain of *madrasahs* wherein its own system of jurisprudence was taught. That is the reason why every *Madrasah* follows its own pattern in the matter of study structure. There is no uniformity with regard to subjects, books or emphasis. Secondly, there is no uniformity in the number of years for preparing students for various degrees. Let us take the example of the Bihar Madrasah Education Board which is government funded and has a semblance of organization. It entails 17 years of study for graduating as a Fazil which is equivalent to M.A. The pattern is a bit different in U.P. In West Bengal, who go for higher theological studies take the Fazil (Plus 2), Kamil (graduation) and Mumtazul Muhaddathin (Master's degree) courses.[99] However, the standard syllabi of *kharizi* or any religious *madrasah* of the world include learning the *Quran* by heart, *tajweed* (correct pronunciation of *Quran* verses), *tafseer* (interpretation of holy scriptures), *fiqah* (Islamic jurisprudence), *Shariah* (Islamic law), *ahadis* (life and decisions of the Prophet on various issues brought before him by the faithful), *mantiq* (philosophy), *riazi* (mathematics), *falakiat* (astronomy) and *tabligh* (spreading the word of God).[100]

At the moment, it is difficult to make any generalized statement about the *Madrasah* curriculum. Every *Madrasah* follows its own pattern in the matter of curriculum. There is no uniformity with regard to subjects, books or emphasis. Secondly, there is no uniformity in the number of years for preparing students for various degrees.

After examining the curricula of the 14 well-known *Madrasahs*, Manzoor Ahmed[101] observes that the subjects taught in these *Madrasahs* can be divided in four categories:

1. Languages and Literature
2. Contemporary Learning
3. Commentary and Discourse
4. Law and Jurisprudence.

In the language section, Urdu, Persian, Arabic language and literature, and at places Hindi and English and regional languages in south India are taught in various *Madrasahs*. In contemporary learning, Mathematics, General Sciences, Hygiene, Geography, History, Economics, Political Science, and Philosophy are taught. In the third category, *Sarf-o-Naho*, *Mantiq, Falsafa, Balaghat, Hayyat, Tafseer-e Quran*, and the art of *manazirah* are taught. The fourth category consists of *Fiqh*, *Usool-e Fiqh*, *Hadith*, *Usool-e Hadith*, *Aqeeda*, etc.

Some of the major problems of curricula in *Madrasahs* are:

1. The curriculum puts undue emphasis on memorization drill and repetition. It fails to create the width of vision, a scholarly objectivity and freedom of thought that are essential for missionary work.
2. There is difference in emphasis laid on the study of subjects taught in various *Madrasahs*.
3. There is not much emphasis on the study of the Holy *Quran*. The syllabus of Arabic literature is old and archaic, and modern writers hardly find any place in it. *Fiqh* (Jurisprudence) is taught in a partisan manner, creating *Maslaki* (schools of thought) differences.
4. The contemporary subjects are taught in a slip-shod manner. As a result, students are not able to get an insight into the problems.

For a long time now, there has been a debate on the need for reforms in *Madrasah* syllabus. At the root of the inertia with regard to a change in syllabus is the fear of change. Many Muslim scholars apprehend that in the name of modernization of *Madrasahs*, the government may have been trying to deprive them of their independence and autonomy. Some Islamic scholars and educational bodies are, however, trying to update the syllabus. One of the most interesting efforts has come from the U.P. Arabi Farsi Board. Commissioned by this board, Dr. Ghulam Yahya Anjum of Jamia Hamdard, New Delhi, has come up with a revised syllabus.[102] This syllabus has been implemented across all those *Madrasahs* in U.P. that are supported by the government. Dr. Anjum claims that the revised syllabus can make a student of the Madrasah system at par with the student of a modern secular institution.

According to Syed Shahabuddin[103], the community should provide basic Islamic instruction to all boys and girls in maktabs as in Kerala and rationalize the *Madrasah* system for quality education and for producing the Islamic scholars it needs; this it can do on its own. The government should, on the other hand:

- Establish primary, middle and secondary government schools in villages, Blocks, Mohallas of Muslim concentration in accordance with national norms.
- Modify its policy on medium of instruction (in Urdu-speaking States) and on languages, the contents of the textbooks and the school culture, so that an orthodox Muslim does not apprehend any distortion of or threat to his ward's religious identity in government schools.
- And allow continued freedom to the community to establish and run its *Madrasahs*.

Dr. Syed Hamid, the former Vice Chancellor of Aligarh Muslim University and a renowned Muslim educationist, has come up with the following suggestions:[104]

- *Madrasahs* need to revise and update their syllabi; they need to integrate contemporary knowledge with religious education.
- The emphasis should be on intellectual learning, not on learning by cramming.
- *Madrasahs* need to streamline and organize their poor funding structures; teachers should not be underpaid.
- *Madrasahs* should be able to attract the best of talents; and not just the residue among the students.
- Well-educated and trained teachers should be employed.
- Industrial, technical, and professional training should also be provided.
- *Madrasahs* should aim to have three streams: stream of pure religious education; stream of religious and contemporary education; and stream of religious education and technical training. Students should be free to choose anyone of these streams.

The Ministry of Human Resource Development, Government of India, had a series of meetings with representatives of the *Madrasahs* discussing the desirability of their modernization and clarifying that it would not entail either compulsion or interference by government. After being satisfied with the result of these discussions, the Ministry formulated the scheme of modernization of *Madrasahs*. The main features of the scheme, launched in 1993-94, are as follows:[105]

1. The objective of the scheme is to encourage traditional institutions

like *maktabs* and *Madrasahs* to introduce teaching of science mathematics, social studies, Hindi and English in order to provide opportunities to students to acquire education comparable to the national system of education.

2. The process of modernization is entirely voluntary.
3. In the first phase, primary classes of middle and secondary level *Madrasahs* were to be covered. In the second phase (during the 9th Plan), the coverage was to be extended to institutions providing education equivalent to secondary stage.
4. The scheme covered the following items in the first phase:
   (a) 100 per cent assistance for appointment of qualified teachers,
   (b) assistance for book bank and strengthening of libraries,
   (c) provision of science, mathematics kits and essential equipment.
5. Only registered voluntary organizations, which have been in existence for three years, were considered for assistance.
6. The performance of the scheme was to be reviewed after three years of its operation.

The scheme has been criticized by many Muslim intellectuals for its hidden agenda. The ostensible purpose of the Scheme administered by the Ministry of Human Resource was to prevail on the *Madrasahs* to revise their conventional curriculum to add modern subjects—English, Hindi, Science, Mathematics and Social Science including History and Geography. Certainly, there should be no objection to the idea of reforming the *Madrasah* curriculum.

The National Commission for Minorities wanted to review the syllabi of the *Madrasahs* but its efforts failed due to strong opposition by the *Madrasah* bodies and others on the ground that the statutory panel has no right to go through the syllabi of the minority educational institutions.[106]

The BJP in its 2014 election manifesto under the heading Minorities—Equal opportunity has promised to "strengthen and modernize minority education systems and institutions; dovetailing them with modern requirements". It also said that the "National *Madrasahs* Modernization programme would be implemented".[107] If the modernization programme is implemented in the right direction, it may put the *Madrasahs* on an even keel.

However, *Madrasahs* in India have been undergoing vigorous reforms in the recent decades to enable their graduates to keep pace with the fast changing world and meet the requirements of the community at all stages. For instance, Darul-uloom Deobond teaches in the eight years of total duration of study modern disciplines like Modern Indian History, Islamic History, Civics, Geography, General Sciences including some information on Zoology, Botany, principles for health care, some chapters of the Indian Constitution, principles of economics, philosophical theories, life history of modern philosophers and computer application.

Darul-uloom Nadwat-ul-ulema at Lucknow in its total 16 years of study lays emphasis on English Language and Literature at par with other Islamic disciplines. From the primary level, it teaches various modern disciplines, especially English, Hindi, Science, Indian History and Economics, almost up to the graduation level.

Madrasatul-Ishah provides knowledge of modern disciplines. It includes in its curriculum English language and literature, history of classical and modern philosophy almost up to the graduation level.

Jamiatul-hidaya at Jaipur in Rajasthan teaches not only the afore-mentioned disciplines but Business Management, Commerce and Agriculture as well. And the most surprising aspect of the modernization is that Jamia Mohammadia Mansura at Malegaon in Maharashtra produces medical practitioners, as medical science is one of the distinguishing features of this *madrasah*.[108]

V

The *Madrasah* system of education and its continuity in India has been a topic for hot discussion since the colonial regime. The relevance of this system has also been debated and discussed at various forums of intellectuals inside and outside the country. It has been often alleged that the *madrasahs* are the breeding ground of conservatism and obscurantism and they create fundamentalist minds. They have also allegedly been places where anti-national elements are being produced. It has been conclusively proved that on the Pakistan-Afghanistan border the *madrasahs* contributed to the growth of fundamentalism and provided the bulk of the manpower for the Taliban. Unquestionably there has been a rise in the number of religious schools in the Islamic world and particularly of schools dominated by the more fundamentalist Deoband, Wahhabi and Salafi strains of Islam. Pakistan reported that between Independence in 1947 and 2001, the number of religion-based *madrasahs* increased from 245 to 6,870. A few schools have produced militants, especially in Pakistan, where the government in the 1980s actively supported the formation of Islamic militias to fight in Kashmir and Afghanistan.[109]

With rising unemployment and increasing pauperization of the society, Pakistan has become a fertile land for the recruitment of Islamists and *jehadis*, Most of the outfits concentrate on the poorest regions to recruit their cadre. This is particularly true of the organisations which recruit their cadre from *madrasahs*. Such groups include the three factions of Jamiat Ulema-e-Islam, the Sipah-e-Sahaba Pakistan, the Harkat-ul-Mujahideen, the Harkat Al-Jihad

Al-Islami, the Jaish-e-Mohammad and the Jamat Ahle Sunnat. With the exceptions of a few Islamist parties—the Jamat-e-Islami (JeI), the Jamiat Ulema-e-Islam (JUI) and the Jamiat Ulema-e-Pakistan (JUP)—most Pakistani Islamist and *jehadi* organizations trace their origins to the Zia era and flourished with the assistance from around three dozen countries, particularly the US and Saudi Arabia. Tariq Ali in *On the Abyss* says that "the dragon seeds sown in 2,500 *madrasahs* produced a crop of 225,000 fanatics ready to kill and ready to die for their faith when ordered to do so by their religious leaders".[110]

Soon after 9/11 (September 11, 2001), the US placed a list of demands before General Musharraf; one of those was the 'reform' of the *madrasah* system of education with particular emphasis on syllabus and the source of funding. Washington believed these institutions imparting "Islamic education" were producing radicalised graduates ready to be hired by Al Qaeda. President Musharraf obediently decreed on June 19, 2002[111] the registration of all *madrasahs* in Pakistan; the introduction of a mixed curriculum to teach subjects such as modern mathematics, science, and information technology along with Islamic subjects; and an audit of *madrasah* accounts. However, he quickly retreated from enforcement, evidently because these 'reforms' generated a tremendous backlash from the seminaries and religious political parties. After a period of negotiations with the institutions that ended in mid-2002, the government decided to do nothing much about them.[112] Religious schools in Pakistan with an estimated enrolment of 10 lakh students, once again became the focus of attention of the international community after the 7/7 London blasts in 2005 in the wake of the reports that at least two of those involved were products of Pakistan's religious schools. This time the General expelled about 1400 foreign students enrolled in Islamic religious schools.[113]

In 2007, he ordered Operation Sunrise, i.e. the siege of the Lal Masjid Complex in Islamabad which included the Jamia Hafsa Madrasah, world's largest *madrasah* for women, both established by Maulana Qari Abdullah in 1965 and 1992, respectively, for flushing out the militants. The complex was besieged for eight days from July 3 to 11. The operation resulted in 154 deaths, capture of 50 militants and seizure of a huge cache of arms and ammunition. At least 1,096 people—628 men, 465 women, and 3 children—either left or were rescued from the complex. The Lal Masjid Commission in March 2013 held Musaraf, the then Prime Minister Shaukat Aziz and others responsible for the operation and recommended institution of murder cases against them.[114] Musaraf was arrested on October 10, 2013 for ordering the crackdown on the Lal Masjid.[115]

In the UK a post-7/7 report indicates that virtually every mosque across Britain has a *madrasah* attached to it. With close to a thousand *madrasahs* effectively across Britain, Muslim leaders say the overwhelming majority of Muslim children in Britain are receiving a strong education within the *madrasah* system, mainly in the evening after the regular school hours. Besides, there are more than a hundred Muslim schools where the national curriculum is taught alongside Islamic studies. Most *madrasahs* have a mix of Pakistanis, Indians, Bangladeshis, Somalis and others. The *madrasahs* follow the philosophy of the Khilafat movement that sought to present a single Muslim Ummah (community) around the world, with no national barriers. And that is how Islamic history is taught, with a clearly strong 'hate India' syllabus. None of the suicide bombers in London's 7/7 had achieved much by way of regular education. But they were regulars at the Masjid-e-Umar on Stratford Street in Beeston, Leeds, and the *madrasah* attached to it. There is little doubt that it is among the *madrasah* products that terrorist groups are likely to search for recruits, given their religious and political grounding.[116]

Peter Clarke, a retired police officer who was earlier the national counterterrorism coordinator was commissioned to look into the complaints of increasing control of state schools in Birmingham by aggressively Islamic elements. Although he has not found any evidence of attempts to teach students the value of violent *jihad*, this particular paragraph from his report is particularly damning: "Essentially the ideology revealed by this investigation is an intolerant and politicized extreme social conservatism that claims to represent and ultimately seeks to control all Muslims...The all-male discussions include homophobia, highly offensive comments about British service personnel, stated ambition to increase segregation at the school, disparagement of Muslims in sectors other than their own, scepticism about the truth in the reports on the murder of Lee Rigby (the British sailor brutally murdered in broad daylight before witnesses by two Muslims in 2013) and the Boston bombings, and constant undercurrent of anti-Western, anti-American and anti-Israeli sentiment."[117]

It is no secret that the Islamic schools are often funded by Saudi Arabia. Most of these are the ones who are charged, mainly by other *madrasahs*, for propagating the Wahabi brand of Islam in the country. The Centre for Islamic Pluralism (www.islamicpluralusm.org), a web site that bills itself as a voice of moderate Islam, quotes David D. Aufhauser, a former Treasury Department general counsel, who told a Senate Committee some years ago that estimates of Saudi spending on the schools worldwide are of the order "of $75 billion". The Centre says that the money finances construction of thousands of mosque schools and Islamic centres, the employment of at least 9,000 proselytizers and the printing of millions of books of religious instruction. The Centre for Islamic Pluralism says Saudi Arabia has a "pervasive influence on Islamic education in the United States that has led to the development of a new breed of American: the Jihadist".[118]

With the growing militancy in Kashmir as elsewhere in India and in the South Asian region as a whole, especially in the wake of the 9/11, *madrasah* system of education has come to the centre-stage of discussions. According to an estimate, in 2002 there were 31,850 *madrasahs* in India and 11,453 were in the border areas.[119] By this time the number must have exceeded forty thousands. Besides the approved *madrasahs* conducting stipulated academic courses, there are a few thousand unrecognized ones whose particulars are not on record. The growing number of Khareji (non-affiliated) *madrasahs* in the country, especially in the bordering States has been a cause for concern. Many State Governments have, therefore, decided to grant recognition to them. For instance, in West Bengal the Minority Welfare Department announced on January 28, 2013 its decision to give recognition to the 10,000 private *madrasahs* on a first come, first serve basis.[120]

In some States like West Bengal, Bihar and U.P. Madrasah Boards also function just like the school boards. The Uttar Pradesh Madrasah Vocational Training Scheme was launched on January 31, 2004 to establish Mini ITIs in the State.[121] Some State Governments have set-up separate Department/ Directorate for looking after the *Madrasah* education. For instance, in West Bengal, the Directorate of Madrasah Education functions under the Minority Affairs and Madrasah Department. There is even the West Bengal Madrasah School Service Commission constituted under an Act of 2008 to recruit a range of teachers along with headmasters and headmistresses who can handle recognised non-Governmental aided Junior High, Higher Secondary and Senior Madrasahs. Besides, the Commission also recruits non-teaching staff like librarian and others who are part of the teaching process. A single judge bench of the Calcutta High Court, however, struck down this Act on March 12, 2014 declaring the above Act "ultra vires" to the Constitution as it "is contrary to the provisions laid down in Article 30 of the Constitution."[122]

The *Madrasah* education in West Bengal is three-tiered. Out of the 601 recoognised *Madrasahs* as on May 20, 2011, 105 are Junior High Madrasahs for classes V to VIII, 394 are High Madrasahs from Classes V to X including Higher Secondary and 102 are Senior Madrasahas from Classes I to X. It is only at the senior *madrasahs* that Arabic and theology are accorded primacy. The Madrasah Board conducts the Alim examination for Class X students of senior *madrasahs*, and a regular school-leaving exam for Class X students of high *madrasahs*. Both these are equivalent to the *Madhymika* examinations conducted by the West Bengal Board of Secondary Education. Nearly 85 per cent of those who take the Alim exams from senior *madrasahs* switch to the regular stream, the rest go for higher theological studies and take the *Fazil* (Plus 2), *Kamil* (graduation) and *Mumtazul Muhaddathin* (master's degree) conducted by the Board. These are pure theological courses.[123]

Indeed, the *Madrasahs* in West Bengal are quite unlike those elsewhere in the country and the world. Around 12 per cent of the total students are Hindus and there are Hindu teachers as well. *Madrasah* teachers enjoy the same pay scales and perks as their counterparts in regular schools. There is little difference between the *madrasah* and other schools in West Bengal. Save for a compulsory paper in either Arabic or Islamic studies, the *madrasahs* have the same syllabi as any secondary school, and their Class X certificates are equivalent to those given out by other school boards. The West Bengal Board of Madrasah Education is the only *madrasah* board in the country that is a member of the Council of Boards of School Education in India and is recognised by the NCERT. The West Bengal's *madrasahs* are indeed modern and unique.[124] The State Government has also decided to give stress on science subjects and English in the curriculum of the *Madrasahs* from Class eight onwards from the academic year 2013-14 so that the students can compete with other students on equal terms.[125] It is said that the lure of free cycles that are being distributed among the girl students of higher *madrashs* is drawing a sizeable section of Hindu girls from the *Madhyamik* and Higher Madhyamik schools of rural areas to the *Madrashs*.[126]

But today what is generally imparted in *Madrasahs* elsewhere is purely Islamic knowledge. Some institutions have, however, realized the need to introduce modern disciplines like economics, political science, education, etc. Unfortunately, this change is too slow to bring about any worthwhile result. Availability of competent teachers to teach these subjects is also a problem. Unfortunately, most of the *Madrasah* teachers are untrained and there is no provision of training, pre-service or in-service. Therefore, *Madrasah* teachers are unaware of the techniques of teaching. As a result of untrained teachers, the educational objectives of the *Madrasahs* remain unfulfilled. Students study aimlessly and teachers teach arbitrarily, without any enthusiasm. Only a few after their pass-outs get admission in universities for higher studies. Some of them go in for professional courses such as Bachelor in Unani Medicine and Surgery (BUMS), Arabic-Urdu translations, etc. Some go into teaching and most of them go back home with no definite aim. One of the major reasons for this unimpressive performance is the lack of educational infrastructure. Both teachers and students live in cramped quarters, without proper lighting, fans, beds, desks and chairs, and toilets. Most of them neither have playgrounds nor any library. Salaries are low and stagnant. Since most of the teachers are untrained, capital punishment is generally practised. Students of different ages study in the same class. There is hardly any motivation to excel. Learning by rote is the norm. Very few teachers use blackboards and other teaching aids. All these issues make the learning poor and tardy.[127]

The Indian Muslim minority is quite backward in science education and its representation and participation in the scientific activity of the country is woefully low. The situation, if allowed to persist for long would certainly hinder the progress of the country. In these days of fast expanding frontier of scientific knowledge and its multiplying technological spin-offs, no nation can afford to have a sizeable chunk of its population illiterate in science, and no community can hope for a respected place in the national stream without equipping itself with science education.[128] "For this to happen, the secular and religious leadership has to amend the curriculum in order to make it responsive to the requirements of this millennium. The principles of intellectual integrity, I repeat, necessitate a fundamental reconstruction of Muslim educational thought",[129] says Prof. Mushirul Hasan, a former Vice Chancellor of Jamia Millia Islamia (2004-2009). It is good that many teachers as well as students of *Madrasahs* increasingly realize the datedness and irrelevance of their curriculum and methods of teaching. However, things are changing now, albeit a little slowly.

In the last sixty-five years since Independence, the abject failure of the education system in particular and the skewed nature of economic development in general have left the Indian Muslim disgruntled. Most Muslim scholars allege that after Independence, the curriculum was given a communal texture in the Hindi belt. As a result, Muslim children kept away from government schools. Also, Urdu language was banished from the government educational set-up, which consequently led to the growth of religious institutions.[130]

Part of the reason why they flourish is because the State has not done enough to promote 'secular' education in mofussil towns and the rural hinterland. Hence, children of poor Muslim families flock to religious schools. Given the limited access to state-run or state-aided schools, religious schools provide space for education and cultural-religious survival for the depressed who suffer from poverty, conflict and oppression.

It has also been argued that the growth in number of *madrasahs* is because of the growing poverty among the Muslims. If poverty is removed the number of *madrasahs* will atomically decline. But if one does not bother to address the problem of Muslim poverty and go ahead and close the *madrasahs* the poor children who now study in them would be denied food and education. They would become beggars, dacoits and criminals and might even take to terrorism, asserts Yoginder Sikhand.[131]

Muslim intellectual A.N. Khusro says: "*Madrasah* education is inward-looking but often it is the only education available to Muslims who now face discrimination along with poverty and illiteracy".[132] Shahabuddin's assertion that most of the children who are studying or are forced to study in *madrasah* would make a beeline for modern education, provided the contents of the text books and the culture of the school are secular[133] seems to be to the point. Would our "truly secular" academic guardians pay heed to this?

Some of the fundamentalist outfits like the Student Islamic Movement of India (SIMI), the Indian Muzaheeds (IM) are in the forefront in creating subversive activities in different parts of the country. They have found happy hunting ground in the religious schools for recruiting their cadres and forming sleeper cells in Muslim dominated areas to be activated when required for the purpose. The spotlight on madrashas and talk of "modernization" of religious schools is making the Muslim community uncomfortable. The overwhelming opinion among the Muslim leaders, intellectuals and political activists is that "reforms, modernization and change" should come from within the community instead of "State-sponsored measures".[134]

The 'accidental' blast in Khagragarh of Burdwan town in West Bengal on October 2, 2014, the arrest of Bangladeshi nationals from across the state and the arrest of a Myanmar militant from Hyderabad has turned the spotlight on unauthorized madrasas as a breeding ground for terrorists. The investigation into the Khagragarh blast has revealed that a part of the operational wing of the Jamaat-ul-Mujahideen Bangladesh (JuMB) crossed the international border in 2009 and found safe havens in the unauthorized madrasahs which mushroomed in different parts of West Bengal including the interior areas of Burdwan and Birbhum districts.

Far from masquerading as purported centres of learning, many *madrasahs* have been converted to hubs for indoctrination and then training the potential terrorists. The phenomenon is not confined to the border districts; it has spread further. *Madrasahs* have come to symbolize the sinister underbelly of what now passes for education in West Bengal. The administration appears to have little or no control over their mushroom growth. The government has advanced figures that are awesome enough—while there are 614 recognised and government-aided *madrasahs*, there have been an exponential growth of the unaffiliated variety—a staggering 5,000 across the state.[135] Burdwan illustrates that location is not the only major determinant of terrorist training academies and the training is not confined to males only; women are as much part of this indoctrination as males are.

A discreet survey of the country's *madrasahs* undertaken in October 2014 by the Modi government has reportedly found the foreigners teaching there, largely Bangladeshi instructors who have managed to acquire Indian identity documents, to be a key source of indoctrination among young Indian Muslims. The report has flagged the mushrooming of unaided and unregulated *madrasahs* along the Indo-Bangladesh and Indo-Nepal border in West Bengal, Assam and Terai region. Many of these seminaries have foreign teachers, mostly Bangladeshis who have worked closely with elements associated with outfits such as Jamaat-ul-Mujahideen Bangladesh. They digress from the normal religious teachings and 'correct' interpretation of Islam by the *madrasahs* having Indian teachers, and highlight the alleged atrocities on Indian Muslims through videos and other provocative materials. The aim is to exploit the feeling of alienation or discontent among young impressionable Muslims, with the larger purpose of radicalizng them to take up *jihadi* terror.[136]

The Home Ministry has called for a report on the *madrasahs* in the state. It has set certain critical parameters for the survey—specifically, the location, the names and profession of the organizing committee members, and the number of teachers and students in each of them.[137] The course contents of each of the *madrasahs* should have been part of the report. It would have revealed how many of these *madrasahs* have switched over to updated syllabi in step with the times. Since many *madrasahs* are reportedly engaged in fundamentalist instruction and now as it turns out in training *jihadis* as well, a manifestation of which is found in other parts the world also, such reports should be collected from all the States, not only from West Bengal. Very recently, in March 2015, five *madrasahs* across Uganda had been shut down over allegations that those were training students to become extremists.[138]

Just as all 'Hindu' or Arya Samaj schools do not spew venom against Islam and Christianity, the *maktabs* and *madrasahs* do not necessarily nurture fundamentalist ideas. Overwhelmingly, the *madrasahs* are apolitical and provide instruction and boarding to the poorest segment of society—segments generally neglected by the State. But the negative connotation of the word "*madrasah*" as it has come to be understood in the English-speaking world—as referring to a place where fundamentalist Islamic instruction is combined with anti-Western vocations, or in the extreme, as a place where terrorists are formed ideologically—is largely an American and English conceit. It is for the most part, but not entirely, inaccurate.

The Indian *ulamas* are second to none in condemning the terrorism perpetrated by some misguided Muslim youths. It also devolves on them to restore the public confidence by ensuring that the *madrasahs* do not become the grooming ground for terrorists. It has to be ensured that the organizations and persons who are out to defame Islam by their terrorist activities should not get any chance to use the *madrasahs* as a platform for their nefarious activities. One method could be to get as many of the unauthorized *madrasahs* converted into authorized ones as possible by adhering to the government-stipulated yardstick. The time has come when the community at large, especially its saner elements including the *ulamas*, should come forward to take a decision in this respect by shaking off its past antipathy to government interference. The State Governments have an equal responsibility in opening as many government institutions as possible in rural areas, especially dominated by the minority population.

According to the findings of a *Public Report* based on a fairly large survey of over 97,000 households in West Bengal, 3 per cent of the 325 surveyed villages having a population of more than 1,000 people had no educational institution at all. An analysis of the District Information System of Education Report for 2011-12 brings this situation up even more clearly; while blocks with Muslim population beyond 50 per cent had 5.6 primary schools per 10,000 people, the corresponding figure for blocks with less than 15 per cent Muslim population was 8.6, the state average being 7.2. Again, the pupil-teacher ratio for primary schools in the blocks having a 50 per cent plus share of Muslim population was nearly 37:1, while the same was 23:1 for the blocks with the corresponding share of 15 per cent or less, with the state average of 27.[139] This study calls for positive action from the state government to take effective measures not only for opening new primary schools but also for improving the quality of education by increasing the teacher-student ratio in the schools in Muslim-dominated areas.

VI

For hundred of years, religious schools like the *Madrasahs*, *Gurukuls* and the Christian schools have performed a valuable social service without much help from Government or other agencies in spreading education. But that does not mean that the State in order to prove its secular credentials should spend public funds in setting up new religious schools and in the financing of such institutions with antiquated syllabi in the name of their modernization.

A real progressive measure would be to set-up good secular schools throughout the country, even in far-flung areas, where children of all religious background could receive good, secular education. Moreover, spending of public money for the cause of religious education, be it *Madrasah*, *Gurukul*, Christian school or Buddhist seminary or any other such institutions would be violative of the spirit of clause (1) of Article 28 of the Constitution of India.

There are no two opinions that public fund should not be spent in religious education. Indeed such expenditure, applying equally to all religious communities, is against the letter and spirit of the Constitution. Both Central and State governments have an abiding obligation to observe the "letter and spirit" of the Constitution and uphold the plural character of Indian society. Political parties championing, openly or otherwise, religious lines within any community, major or minor, might have been successful in achieving their hidden agenda for some time initially, but they are, in the ultimate analysis, doing more harm than good not only to that particular community but to the nation also. The atmosphere is becoming increasingly surcharged with communal overtones. An atmosphere of growing mistrust is being perpetuated; a malignant mindset is being fostered to accept even violent outbursts. Indian society in general must stand against such vested interests.

The taboo against religion in State Schools is merely to indicate that the State holds the balance equal as between all religions and would not sponsor one at the cost of another religion.[140] But instead of holding the balance and acting as a referee, it should have been ensured that the State does really maintain its neutrality towards religion by not holding the balance between different religions but by not associating itself with any kind of religion, because once the State associates itself with any matter pertaining to religion, it compromises its secular approach, the very basis of our Constitution. Willy nilly it becomes very much involved in matters connected with religion, as it has developed today.

In Russia the State is completely severed from the church and no religious instruction is given in schools. In secular India, the ideal condition would have been to impose a complete ban on religious instruction in educational institutions, recognised or aided or maintained, or administered, wholly or partly, by the State. Even if it was not possible to impose a total ban on religious instruction in educational institutions in free India, it could have been enforced at least in those educational institutions which are aided or maintained by the State, wholly or partly. In that case, the State would not have been accused of involvement in religious matters and could have dissociated itself completely from such practice. If there were some constraints to enforce it at a time, this could have been enforced gradually within a time frame, as was done in respect of providing grants to the Anglo-Indian Schools. This becomes all the more relevant in the backdrop of the insertion of new Article 21A in the Fundamental Rights chapter of the Constitution enjoining upon the State to provide free and compulsory education to all children of the age of six to fourteen years and the Directive enunciated in Article 45 of providing early childhood care and education for all children until they complete the age of six years and also casting a duty on the parent to provide opportunities for education to his child between the age of six and fourteen years as in Article 51A(k). Free and compulsory education can be provided only when the expenses of running the educational institutions are borne or shared by the State. When there is already such a provision of providing compulsory and free education, ample care should have been taken to ensure that educational institutions are not 'converted into a menagerie of faiths', as warned by Prof. Shah. It has got to be remembered that a secular State cannot run a denominational educational institutions. The State educational institutions have got to be not only absolutely secular but should be beyond the reach of religious controversies. But actually the Framers did the opposite. They failed to create "a wall of separation between Church and State in India as obtained in the USA".[141] The result is for all to see. In the name of secularism, communalism is perpetrated everywhere with impunity.

Article 28 forbids religious instruction only in those educational institutions which are wholly maintained out of State funds. It however does not forbid religious instruction in those educational institutions which are not wholly maintained by the State, i.e. if a part of the cost may be even one per cent, is borne by any person or a body of persons or a society then those educational institutions do not attract the provisions of this Article. Similarly, the educational institutions established under an endowment or trust, even if administered by the State, are allowed to impart religious instruction. This Article however prohibits only compulsory religious instruction, i.e. no pupil or student should be compelled to attend such religious instruction against his choice or will.

Article 28 clearly manifests the dilemma of the Framers as to their approach towards religion. Even members like Dr. Radhakrishnan vehemently objected to the imparting of religious instruction in educational institutions maintained by the State because that would violate the very principle of secularity in our Constitution. As a matter of fact, Dr. Ambedkar could not give any answer when he was asked as to why he was allowing religious instruction in educational institutions partly maintained by the State. He thought silence was the golden means. It is contended that "the prohibition in Article 28 is to ensure that the State is neutral in the matter of religion." But this neutrality perhaps could not touch even the fringe of the problem, rather this neutrality is further compromised by Article 28(2) which allows religious instruction in educational instructions established under an endowment or trust, even if these institutions are administered by the State. Dr. Ambedkar himself admitted that clause 2 of Article 28 to some extent undoubtedly is not in consonance with the original proposition contained in sub-clause (1). He had no argument to offer except that it would be forcing the State to commit a breach of trust. But who has asked the State to commit a breach of trust which is sought to be thrust on it by some persons in the name of endowment or trust? The fact is not that there exists a trust. The point is: should the State be a party to the imparting of religious instruction? Whereas the State should have no say in the matter of religion, it is the other way round. It got mixed up or rather became a willing partner in dispensing religious instruction. Did it not compromise its position as a secular State or violate the principle of the secular Constitution, as pointed out by Dr. Radhakrishnan and other members?

And to cap it all, even the Framers did not know as to what religious instruction denotes. They themselves were a confused lot. Dr. Ambedkar thought that the teaching of *Vedas*, the *Upanishads* and other sacred Sanskrit books was not religious instruction but a 'study and research' and Dr. H.C. Mookherjee termed it as a 'course in culture'. So what is a religious instruction and what is not is a matter of opinion and can be explained away as one likes or left to the judiciary for a decision. When such was the attitude of the Framers why such a provision was incorporated in the Constitution at all?

Incidentally, the Madhya Pradesh State Government decided to introduce the *Bhagavad Gita* in the public school curriculum in the State. This decision was challenged in the State High Court. A Bench of the Madhya Pradesh High Court comprising Justices Ajit Singh and Sanjay Yadav on January 27,

2012 rejected the plea against inclusion of *Gita* in school syllabus. The Bench noted that the *Bhagavad Gita* is not a text of Indian religion, but that of Indian philosophy.[142] But in the face of outrage that swept across the Muslim community, the Chief Minister had to recall on August 6, 2013 the State Government's order that *Bhagavad Gita* be taught in *madrasahas*.[143]

In the backdrop of inter-religion rivalry and conflicts some ideas currently discussed in the increasingly multi-cultural, multi-religious and multi-ethnic societies of Europe was pointed out by Dileep Padgaonkar. For example, efforts are now mooted in France to offer no religious instruction but instruction in the fundamentals of major religions at all levels of education. The emphasis would partly be on how religions have evolved in history but more importantly on their ethical, moral and spiritual content. The study of the aesthetic expressions of this content would be especially encouraged. The first part of these efforts has met with some resistance on the grounds that even instruction about religions can quickly degenerate into a wishy-washy ecumenism. But there seem to be many takers for the second part of the efforts to promote secularism along different lines. Padgaonkar thinks that these should appeal to us as well.[144]

Padgaonkar's suggestion is akin to what Srimati Purnima Banerjee proposed in the Constituent Assembly on August 30, 1947. She proposed that the religious education given in educational institutions receiving state-aid would be in the nature of elementary philosophy of comparative religion calculated to broaden the pupils' mind rather than such as will foster sectarian exclusiveness,[145] but her proposal was turned down.

There is much truth in what Anirban Kashyap has observed way back in 1990:

> If the Framers were a little bold and less compromising they could have created an atmosphere conducive enough to ensure that the boys and girls born in free India were insulated from the virus of communalism and religious dogma, at least at that impressionable age of their childhood so as to make them true citizens of free and secular India.[146]

In their pursuit to effect a compromise this policy was evolved by the Framers which surely did not enhance the secularity of the Constitution, and like many other compromise formula effected by them, this is responsible for many ills and maladies confronting free India even after 68 years of Independence. Obviously, our rulers are concerned only with the vote bank politics. They have little respect for the discharge of their constitutional obligations.

Notes and References

1. Ramachandran, V.G., *Fundamental Rights and Constitutional Remedies,* Vol. II, Lucknow, 1982, p. 393.
2. Kashyap, Anirban, *Disintegration and Constitution, op. cit.*, p. 141.
3. Rao, B. Shiva, *The Framing of India's Constitution*, Vol. II, 1967, New Delhi, The Indian Institute of Public Administration, p. 64.
4. *Ibid.*, p. 65.
5. *Ibid.*, p. 171.
6. *Ibid.*, pp. 169-198.
7. *Ibid.*, pp. 21-36.
8. *Ibid.*, pp. 36-55.
9. *Ibid.*, pp. 67-69.
10. *Ibid.*, pp. 69-80.
11. *Ibid.*, pp. 81-84.
12. *Ibid.*, pp. 84-114.
13. *Ibid.*, p. 116.
14. *Ibid.*, p. 76.
15. *Ibid.*, p. 123.
16. *Ibid.*, Vol. I, p. 60.
17. *Ibid.*, Vol. II, p. 140.
18. *Ibid.*, p. 166.
19. *Ibid.*, p. 174.
20. *Ibid.*, p. 190.
21. *Ibid.*, p. 202.
22. *Ibid.*, pp. 207-209.
23. *Ibid.*, p. 210.
24. *Ibid.*, p. 270.
25. *CAD*, Vol. III, dated 29-4-47, p. 427.
26. *Ibid.*, dated 1-5-47, p. 480.
27. *CAD*, Vol. V, dated 30-8-47, pp. 404-405.
28. *Ibid.*, dated 30-8-47, pp. 379-380.
29. *Ibid.*, p. 382.
30. *Ibid.*, pp. 382-383.
31. *Ibid.*, pp. 383-385.
32. *Ibid.*, pp. 379-380.
33. *Ibid.*, p. 381.
34. *Ibid.*, p. 382.
35. *Ibid.*, p. 387.
36. *Ibid.*
37. *Ibid.*, p. 388.
38. *Ibid.*, p. 391.
39. *Ibid.*, p. 389.
40. *Ibid.*, p. 392.
41. *Ibid.*, pp. 393, 402.
42. Rao, Vol. III, *op. cit.*, p. 11.
43. *Ibid.*, pp. 190-200.

44. *Ibid.*, p. 330.
45. *Ibid.*, Vol. V, p. 264.
46. *Ibid.*, Vol. III, p. 525.
47. *Ibid.*, Vol. IV, pp. 43-44.
48. *CAD*, Vol. VII, dated 8-11-48, p. 331.
49. *Ibid.*, p. 348.
50. *Ibid.*, dated 7-12-48, p. 871.
51. *Ibid.*
52. *Ibid.*, p. 882.
53. *Ibid.*, p. 875.
54. *Ibid.*, p. 876.
55. *Ibid.*, pp. 867-868.
56. *Ibid.*, pp. 874-875.
57. *Ibid.*, pp. 878-879.
58. *Ibid.*, p. 881.
59. *Ibid.*, p. 879.
60. *Ibid.*, p. 881.
61. *Ibid.*, p. 885.
62. *Ibid.*, pp. 866-867.
63. *Ibid.*, p. 880.
64. *Ibid.*, pp. 883-884.
65. *Ibid.*, p. 870.
66. *Ibid.*, pp. 870-871.
67. *Ibid.*, pp. 871-872.
68. *Ibid.*, pp. 880-881.
69. *Ibid.*, p. 869.
70. *Ibid.*, p. 878.
71. *Ibid.*, pp. 881-882.
72. *Ibid.*, pp. 879-880.
73. *Ibid.*
74. *Ibid.*, pp. 872-873.
75. *Ibid.*, p. 886.
76. *Ibid.*, pp. 873-874.
77. *Ibid.*, p. 879.
78. *Ibid.*, p. 880.
79. *Ibid.*, p. 884.
80. *Ibid.*, p. 885.
81. *Ibid.*
82. *Ibid.*
83. *Ibid.*
84. *CAD*, Vol. XI, dated 9-11-49, p. 706.
85. *Ibid.*, dated 21-11-49, p. 765.
86. *en-wikepedia.org/wiki/gurukul*
87. *www.amaidi.org/pdf/History of Indian Education.pdf*
88. Tagore, Saumyendranath, *Rammahun Roy; His Role in Indian Renaissance*, 1975, Calcutta, The Asiatic Society, p. 16.
89. *Ibid.*, p. 17.

90. *Ibid.*, p. 16.
91. *www.merriam-webster.com/dictionary/madrasa*
92. Salamatullah, Dr., *Hindustan me Musalman ki Taleem*, 1990, Maktaba Jamia, New Delhi.
93. Hasan, Mushirul, "The *madrasahs* in India", *The Hindu*, May 21, 2003, p. 10.
94. *Muslim India*, October 21, 2001.
95. In West Bengal up to 1977 there were 238 recognised *Madrasahs* which increased to 601 as on 20-5-11.
96. Khan, Amir Ullah, Saqib, Mohammad and Anjum, Zafar H., To Kill the Mockingbird, Madrasah System in India: Past, Present, and Future, *www.idfresearch.org/ipnservice/pdfs/madarsas.pdf.*
97. *Muslim India*, October 21, 2001.
98. Dr. Fahimuddin, Globalization and Growth of Madrasahs in India, seminar paper, *http://www.bsos.umd.edu/socy/conference/newpapers/uddin.txt*
99. Mazumdar, Jaideep, "The Bengal Alifate', *Outlook*, 30, January 2006, p. 63.
100. Ahmed, Samim, "Secular dilemma", *The Telegraph*, May 6, 2008, p. 11.
101. Please see the chapter "An Appraisal of Islamic Curricula in India," in *Islamic Education*, New Delhi, Genuine Publications, 1990, pp. 47-48.
102. Anjum, Dr. Ghulam Yahya, *Nisab-e Taleem*, 2001, Jamia Hamdard, New Delhi.
103. "Throttling the Madrasha in the name of security", Milli Gazette, New Delhi, *http.//www.milligzette.com./archives/01072001/ib.htm.*
104. Syed Hamid, "Deeni Madaris aur Asri Uloom," in *Deeni Madaris aur unke masayal*, Seminar papers, February 1988, Idara-e Ilmia, Jamiat ul Falah, Azamgarh.
105. *Evaluation Report on Madrasah Education Scheme*, 2003, Hamdard Education Society, New Delhi.
106. *The Telegraph*, June 16, 2003, p. 10.
107. *www.bjp.org/images/pdf-2014/full-manifesto-english-07.04.2014.pdf*, p. 17.
108. Alam, Muzaffar, "Modernisation of *madrasahs* in India", *The Hindu*, April 23, 2002, p. 16.
109. *middleeast.about.com/od/glossary/g/me071201b.htm*
110. Quoted by Arif Jamal in "Clotted Streams", *Outlook*, July 23, 2001, p. 40.
111. *The Hindu*, June 21, 2002, p. 1.
112. Editorial entitled "Pakistan's *madrasahs* in perspective", *The Hindu*, August 5, 2005, p. 10.
113. *The Hindu*, December 3, 2005, p. 16.
114. *The Hindu*, September 3, 2013, p. 9.
115. *The Statesman*, October 11, 2013, p. 10.
116. Suri, Sanjay, "ILM by rote", *Outlook*, August 15, 2005, 40-42.
117. Husain, Irfan, "Brainwashing Muslim kids in Birmingham", *The Statesman*, July 22, 2014, p. 7.
118. *www.merriam-webster.com/dictionary/madrasa*
119. *The Telegraph*, March 20, 2002, p. 7.
120. *The Statesman*, January 29, 2013, p. 1.
121. Bhaumik, Saba Naqvi, "*Madrasah* kids need zero-terror seal", *Outlook*, October 25, 2004, p. 40.
122. *The Telegraph*, March 13, 2014, p. 7.

123. Mazumdar, Jaideep, "The Bengal Alifate', *Outlook*, 30, January 2006, p. 63.
124. *Ibid.*
125. *Dainik Statesman,* January 8, 2013, p. 1.
126. *Dainik Statesman*, March 22, 2013, p. 6.
127. Khan, Amir Ullah, Saqib, Mohammad and Anjum, Zafar H., To Kill the Mockingbird, Madarsah System in India: Past, Present, and Future, *www.idfresearch.org/ipnservice/pdfs/madarsas.pdf.*
128. *ops.amu.org/reorient.htm*
129. Hasan, Mushirul, "The *madrasah* in India", *The Hindu*, May 21, 2003, p. 10.
130. Dr. Rahat Abrar and Dr. M. Qamar Ishaque, "Introduction," in *Directory of Muslim Educational Institutions in India,* New Delhi, Institute of Objective Studies, 2002.
131. Sikand, Yoginder, *Bastion of Believers*, 2006, Delhi, Penguin, p. 280.
132. Bhaumik, Saba Naqvi, "Old-school ties", *Outlook*, December 31, 2001, p. 19.
133. *The Statesman*, May 9, 2002., p. 5.
134. *The Telegraph*, February 14, 2002, p. 7.
135. Editorial entitled Data on *madrasahs*, *The Statesman*, October 23, 2014, p. 6.
136. *The Times of India*, November 13, 2014, p. 6.
137. Editorial entitled Data on *madrasahs*, *The Statesman*, October 23, 2014, p. 6.
138. *The Statesman*, March 25, 2015, p. 10.
139. "Preliminary Public Report on the Status of Muslims of West Bengal", Association SNAP and Guidance Guild 2014, Kolkata, quoted by Kumar Rana and Manabi Majumdar, "Cultivating Communal Hatred in Bengal", *Economic and Political Weekly*, Vol. XLIX, No. 46, pp. 70-71.
140. Ramachandran, *op. cit.*, p. 395.
141. *Ibid.*, p. 394.
142. *The Hindu*, January 28, 2012, p. 3.
143. *The Times of India*, August 7, 2013, p. 10.
144. Padgaonkar, Dileep, "India Injured", in *Communalism Condemned Gujarat Genocide 2002,* 2002, Kolkata, Progressive Publishers, p. 63.
145. *CAD*, Vol. V, dated 30-8-47, pp. 379-380.
146. Kashyap, Anirban, *Disintegration and Constitution*, Lancers Books, New Delhi, p. 175.

3

Right of Religious Minorities to Establish and Administer Educational Institutions

I

Another Article of the Constitution which calls for a closer and in-depth study is Article 30. As stated in the earlier chapter, the Advisory Committee on Fundamental Rights, Minorities, etc., at its first meeting on February 23, 1947, appointed five sub-committees including one on Minorities and another on Fundamental Rights. The Minorities Sub-Committee consisted[1] of (1) The Hon'ble Shri Jagjivan Ram, (2) The Hon'ble Maulana Abul Kalam Azad, (3) Dr. B.R. Ambedkar, (4) Sardar Jogendra Singh, (5) Dr. S.P. Mukherjee, (6) Sardar Ujjal Singh, (7) Sardar Harnam Singh, (8) Bakshi Sir Tek Chand, (9) Dr. Gopi Chand Bhargava, (10) Shri H.J. Khandekar, (11) Mr. P.R. Thakur, (12) Sir Homi Mody, (13) Dr. H.C. Mookherjee, (14) Shri P.K. Salve, (15) Mr. S.H. Prater, (16) Mr. F.R. Anthony, (17) The Hon'ble Shri C. Rajagopalachari, (18) Rajkumari Amrit Kaur, (19) Shri Jairamdas Daulatram, (20) Mr. R.K. Sidhwa, (21) Shri Rup Nath Brahma, (22) Mr. M. Ruthnaswamy, (23) Mr. M.V.H. Collins, (24) Dr. Alban D'Souza, (25) Shri K.M. Munshi, and (26) The Hon'ble Govind Ballabh Pant.

The Fundamental Rights Sub-Committee while considering Munshi's draft for preparation of its recommendations, found on March 27, 1947 that clauses (2), (3), (8) and (9) of Article VI of Munshi's draft were outside the scope of the Fundamental Rights Sub-Committee, but they might come within the scope of the Minorities Sub-Committee.[2] Clauses (3) and (9) of Munshi's draft were as follows:

> (3) Citizens belonging to national minorities in a State whether based on religion or language have equal rights with other citizens in forming, controlling and administering at their own expense, charitable, religious and social institutions, schools and other educational establishments with the free use of their language and practice of their religion.

> (9) No legislation providing State-aid for schools shall discriminate against schools under the management of minorities whether based on religion or language.[3]

Harnam Singh's draft had a provision, similar to clause (9) of Munshi's draft, in Article 19, reproduced below:

> Legislative or administrative measures providing state aid for schools shall not discriminate between schools under the management under different religious denominations.[4]

The Minorities Sub-Committee while examining the draft clauses recommended by the Fundamental Rights Sub-Committee in order to see whether any of them required to be amplified or amended for the specific purpose of protecting minority rights, also considered these 4 clauses of Munshi's draft and the letter from K.M. Munshi circulated to the members of the Minorities Sub-Committee on April 16, 1947.[5] The Sub-Committee decided on April 19, 1947 that some provisions relating to the educational and cultural rights of minorities should be incorporated in the Fundamental Rights at the appropriate places.[6]

The interim report of the Minorities Sub-Committee to the Advisory Committee on April 19, 1947, contained a separate part—Part III—Cultural and Educational Fundamental Rights of Minorities. Clause (iv) of this Part had the following provision:

> All minorities whether of religion, community or language shall be free in any unit to establish and administer educational institutions of their choice, and they shall be entitled to State aid in the same manner and measure as is given to similar State-aided institutions.[7]

The Advisory Committee considered this clause on April 21, 1947. Alladi Krishnaswamy Ayyar wondered what was "the meaning of minorities of religion". Rajkumari Amrit Kaur felt that they were perpetuating communal institutions. Her belief was that State aid should not be forthcoming to communal institutions. That way they would be perpetuating communal institutions for ever. She was against any communal schools of any form. Alladi Krishnaswamy Ayyar also supported her move for dropping this clause. Frank Anthony wanted to put the words "And they shall be entitled to State aid as determined by the State" in place of "in the same manner and measure". Ujjal Singh however objected to that amendment of Anthony as that would defeat the very object of the clause. The Chairman took votes on the question of the retention of this clause in some form. The majority was for the retention of this clause. The clause was then split up in two parts and adopted as follows:

(a) All minorities whether based on religion, community or language shall be free in any unit to establish and administer educational institutions of their choice.

The State shall not while providing State aid to schools discriminate against schools under the management of minorities whether based on religion, community or language.[8]

The Advisory Committee on Fundamental Rights, Minorities, etc., in its report[9] dated April 23, 1947 to the President of the Constituent Assembly incorporated the above clause as clause 18(3) (a) and (b).

On May 1, 1947, Sardar Vallabhbhai Patel moved[10] the entire clause 18 for the acceptance of the Constituent Assembly. Mohanlal Saksena moved an amendment that the clause should be referred back to the Advisory Committee for reconsideration.[11] K.M. Munshi moved another amendment for referring back only sub-clause (2) of clause 18 to the Advisory Committee.[12]

Supporting the amendment of Mohanlal Saksena, Mahavir Tyagi said: "I think, Sir, we are taking this document lightly. It may be that in matters like these, i.e. cultural and educational rights, they could be defined only as far as they appertain to individuals and the question of minorities had better be left for the future Governments. I think we are binding the hands of our future Governments too much. We should leave them free to do according to the times and the situations they face.

"Now, the question of guaranteeing the rights of minorities with regard to culture and education privileges, I would suggest that in future occasions may arise when the Governments belonging to the Union may have to negotiate with other units and may have to know from them as to what is happening to the minorities that reside in the areas which have not chosen to join the Union. Now, supposing the Governments of the Units which belong to the Union are committed by means of this clause 18 to a certain policy towards the minorities, the people here may feel the necessity of knowing as to what is happening to the minorities who reside in those units which have refused to join the Union and belong to Pakistan or any other parts of India which may organise themselves separately. My suggestion is that on the question of minorities we may not be committed here and this question be left over for the time when we may definitely know as to whether the whole of India is going to be one Unit or is going to be partitioned into two. If there is to be a partition, we must know what is happening to the minorities on the other side, in the other units. Therefore, the question is not so easy to solve just now. I submit that the whole House will support me when I say that this question had better be hanging fire till we definitely know as to what is going to be the final shape of India and how the Units are going to treat the minorities. I therefore support the motion of Mr. Mohanlal Saksena that the consideration of this clause be put off."[13]

Rohini Kumar Chaudhury also supported the amendment of Mohanlal Saksena. Regarding sub-clause 3(b) he said: "Then turning to sub-clause 3(b), if the clause stands as it is, it will seriously interfere with proper distribution of grants. So, on the whole, I think, instead of remitting sub-clauses piece-meal, it will be wise to refer the whole clause 18 to the Advisory Committee."[14]

Opposing the amendment of Mohanlal Saksena and the contention of Mahavir Tyagi, Seth Govind Das observed: "I think the motion before us contains no such clause which can be considered controversial. Mr. Mahavir Tyagi has said that we do not know till now whether India is to remain one or is to be partitioned. For reasons which lead him to think that this should be sent to the Advisory Committee, I feel that it should be passed by us today. Whether there is one Hindustan or Pakistan, undivided or divided India—the phantom of this thought sticks to us and we look at all problems when they come up, obsessed with that view.

"While supporting the resolution of Pandit Jawaharlal Nehru I said that we should not care whether our Muslim League brothers enter the assembly or not. On the same grounds I again wish to say that we should not care whether India is to remain undivided or is to be divided. We want one India. We want that India should remain one. We are not to stop any of our efforts. I am even against Mr. Munshi's amendment, for I cannot see anything in this whole clause against any caste or community. As I have said that without looking to what is going to happen to India in future, we should pass this resolution keeping in view as to what our duties are and what should be done in this Assembly."[15]

Rajkrishna Bose supported the amendment of Munshi and was for retention of clause 3(a) and (b). His views were: "...Then sub-clause (3) (a) reads

> All minorities whether based on religion, community or language, shall be free in any Unit to establish and administer educational institutions of their choice."

"This is a right, Sir, which I think no country can take away and ought to take away and all constitutions should concede this right to the minorities. It is such a simple thing that it needs no reference back to the Advisory Committee again. Now, sub-clause (3) (b) reads

> The State shall not, while providing State aid to schools, discriminate against schools under the management of minorities whether based on religion, community or language.

"This again is such a simple question. If any minority wants to start a school of its own in any part of the Union, certainly you are not going to forbid them from doing so, or pass laws whereby they cannot have this ordinary right. If you are going to do that, all your claim to give protection to the minorities will be reduced to a farce. Therefore, I do not see why this simple clause, namely, clause 18, with all its sub-clauses should be referred back to the Advisory Committee. Of course, a point has been raised by one of the members that the consideration of matters relating to minorities should be put off till we know the mind of the Pakistanis in the matter and the rights they are going to concede to the minorities in their areas. Well, Sir, if, knowing fully well that those who oppose India's independence today like the Muslim League are adopting dilatory tactics to delay our freedom, we put off our business till Doomsday or wait till they have made some decisions, we shall have to wait indefinitely. If, say for instance, they go beyond June 1948 to reach a decision with regard to these matters, are we to postpone our decisions on matters so simple and ordinary? I think, Sir, that it will be foolish on our part to delay decisions on matters like these, and therefore clause 18 as moved by Sardar Patel and amended by Mr. Munshi should be adopted by the House."[16]

Dr. B.R. Ambedkar did not agree to refer back the entire clause to the Advisory Committee. He had however no objection to clause (2) being referred to the Advisory Committee. This is what he had stated: "I confess that I am considerably surprised at these amendments—both by Mr. Munshi as well as Mr. Tyagi. They have, I submit, given reason why this clause 18 should be referred back to the Committee. The only reason in support of this proposal—one can sense—is that the rights of minorities should be relative, that is to say, we must wait and see what rights the minorities are given by the Pakistan Assembly before we determine the rights we want to give to the minorities in the Hindustan area. Now, Sir, with all deference I must deprecate such idea. Rights of minorities should be absolute rights. They should not be subject to any consideration as to what another party may like to do to minorities within its jurisdiction. If we find that certain minorities in which we are interested and which are within the jurisdiction of another State have not got the same rights which we have given to minorities in our territory, it would be open for the State to take up the matter in a diplomatic manner and see that the wrongs are rectified. But no matter what others do, I think we ought to do what is right in our own judgment, and personally I think that the rights which are indicated in clause 18 are rights which every minority, irrespective of any other consideration is entitled to claim. The first right that we have given is the right to use their language, their script and their culture. We have stated that "there shall be no discrimination on the ground of religion, language, etc." in the matter of admission into State educational institutions. We have said that "no minority shall be precluded from establishing any educational institution which such minority may wish to establish." It is also stated there that whenever a State decides to provide aid to schools or other educational institutions maintained by the minority, they shall not discriminate in the matter of giving grant on the basis of religion, community or language. Sir, I cannot understand how there can be any objection to these rights which have been indicated in clause 18. At any rate nobody who has supported the motion that this may be referred back to the Committee has advanced any argument that either these rights are in excess of what a minority ought to have or are such that a minority ought not to have them. Therefore, it seems to me a great pity that the labours of three Committees which have evolved these provisions should be so brusquely set aside simply because for some reasons people want that this matter should be referred back to the Committee. I do not know what objection my friend Mr. Munshi has to sub-clause (2) as it stands, but if it is necessary that this sub-clause may be referred back to the Committee I certainly would raise no objection. That sub-clause may be referred back because I understand that we have limited this matter to State educational institutions and we have said nothing about those which are only State-aided. If that point needs to be further clarified the matter may be referred back, but because there may be something to be said in favour of the reference back of sub-clause (2) I do not see that the same logic could be extended to the whole of the clause. I submit therefore that the clause as it stands should be passed, barring sub-clause (2) which may, if necessary, be referred back to the Committee for consideration."[17]

Mohanlal Saksena withdrew his amendment and Munshi's amendment of referring back sub-clause (2) to the Advisory Committee was accepted. The rest of the clause was adopted.[18] Incidentally, sub-clauses (1) and (2) of Clause 18 latter became Article 29.

Clause 18(1), (2), (3) and (4) as adopted by the Assembly was incorporated by the Constitutional Adviser in his draft constitution as clause 24 (1), (2), (3) and (4) with some drafting changes.[19] Commenting on the use of the term "minorities" in the provision, he pointed out:

> The term 'minorities' is not defined in the Constitution and indeed having regard to the fact that under sub-clause (2) of this clause minorities may be based on religion, community or language, it would be difficult to frame a comprehensive definition. At the same time to leave a vague justiciable right to undefined minorities is unsatisfactory. The provision is vague because even the declaration of a particular language as the national language might be said to prejudice the interests of the "minorities" whose mother tongue is different. In view of these difficulties it should be considered whether the right conferred by this clause should be made justiciable at all.[20]

D.P. Khaitan, a member of the Drafting Committee, suggested that Clause 24(3) should be 'subject to public order, health and morality'.[21]

The Drafting Committee deliberated on clause 24 on November 1 and 3, 1947, and again on January 20, 1948, and revised its text thrice.[22] Ultimately, it appeared as Draft Article 23 under the heading Cultural and Educational Rights with a marginal note "Protection of interests of minorities" in the Draft Constitution prepared by the Drafting Committee and circulated on February 21, 1948. Sub-clause (a) and (b) of Clause 3 of Article 23 of the Draft Constitution read as follows:

> (3) (a) All minorities whether based on religion, community or language shall have the right to establish and administer educational institutions of their choice.
> (b) The State shall not, in granting aid to educational institutions, discriminate against any educational institution on the ground that it is under the management of a minority, whether based on religion, community or language.[23]

A number of amendments and comments were received from members and others in respect of this draft article. B. Pattabhi Sitaramayya and six others suggested that in sub-clauses (a) and (b) of clause (3) of article 23, after the word "religion', the words "caste, creed" be inserted. The Constitutional Adviser noted that the term "community" would seem wide enough to include "caste"; and "creed" would seem to be covered by "religion". The amendment would therefore seem to be unnecessary.

Commenting on the draft article Jaya Prakash Narayan said that the secularization of general education was necessary for the growth of a national outlook and unity. With this object in view he suggested that sub-clause (a) of clause (3) of Article 23 should be substituted by the following:

> (a) Linguistic minorities shall have the right to establish, manage and control educational institutions and cultural associations for the promotion of the study and knowledge of their language and literature, as well as for imparting general education to their children at primary and pre-primary stages through the medium of their languages.

Jaya Prakash Narayan also suggested the addition of the following sub-clause to clause (3) of Article 23

> "(c) Denominational and communal educational institutions are forbidden except for the purposes of the study of religion and oriental learning."

Both the amendments, B.N. Rau remarked, involved questions of policy. If the second amendment was accepted, then educational institutions established for the promotion of education among the Anglo-Indian community under special endowments or trusts, such as La Martiniere College, St. Thomas School, St. Xavier's College, etc., would be hit by this provision, and in addition would conflict with draft Article 298 (corresponding provision in the Constitution is Article 337) under which special safeguards were provided for such institutions.[24]

The Drafting Committee however did not sponsor any of these two amendments of Jaya Prakash Narayan.

Draft Article 23 (3) (a) and (b) came up before the Constituent Assembly for consideration on December 8, 1947.

Damodar Swarup Seth moved an amendment on lines similar to those favoured by Jaya Prakash Narayan for substitution of sub-clause (a) of clause (3) of Article 23 by the following:

> (a) Linguistic minorities shall have the right to establish, manage and control educational institutions for the promotion of the study and knowledge of their language and literature, as well as for imparting general education to their children at primary and pre-primary stage through the medium of their own languages.

Elaborating on his amendment he said: "While in sub-clause (a) of clause (3) of Article 23, obviously minorities based on religion and community have been recognised, my amendment recognises only minorities based on language. I feel, Sir, that in a secular state minorities based on religion or community should not be recognised. If they are given recognition then I submit that we cannot claim that ours is a secular state. Recognition of minorities based on religion or community is the very negation of secularism. Besides, Sir, if these minorities are recognised and granted the right to establish and administer educational institutions of their own, it will not only block the way of national unity, so essential for a country of different faiths, as India is, but will also promote communalism, and narrow antinational outlook as was the case hitherto, with disastrous results. I, therefore, submit that only minorities based on language should be recognised and be granted the right to establish and administer educational institutions and that too for the purpose of promotion of their language and literature and for imparting primary and pre-primary education in their own language. Higher studies are to be conducted in the national language of the State. I, therefore, submit, Sir, that this amendment is most harmless and innocent and hope that it will be accepted by the House quite unreservedly."[25]

None else spoke on this amendment of Damodar Swarup Seth and the amendment was negatived.

Prof. K.T. Shah wanted the following to be added after sub-clause (a) of clause (3) of Article 23:

> Provided that no part of the expenditure in connection with such institutions shall fall upon or be defrayed from the public purse; and provided further that no such institution, nor the education and

training given therein shall be recognised, unless it complies with the courses of instruction, standards of attainment, methods of education and training, equipment and other conditions laid down in the national system of education.

Prof. Shah commented that this amendment of his was the same amendment or similar amendment moved a day or two earlier. (That is amendment to clause 22(3) which was discussed on December 7, 1948 and deleted in pursuance of an amendment of Jaspat Roy Kapoor). "Only, there it was in a more positive form", he continued, "and here it is in a negative form, making it more clear that whatever be the foundation or endowment, in the first instance, of any such national institutions, no part of the expenditure should fall upon the public purse—neither partly or wholly. This I consider is necessary to provide specifically in view of the possibility of any party taking advantage of the positive provision made above. I should not like to waste the time of the House beyond just pointing out that this in reality is not identical, but that in substance it is the same. I am afraid I have not much hope of making the House change its viewpoint within 48 hours, and therefore, I do not wish to take any more time of the House by speaking on it".[26]

There was no comment from other members on this amendment and the amendment was ultimately negatived.

Pandit Thakur Das Bhargava moved an amendment for deletion of the word 'community' from clause (3) of Article 23 because "the word 'community'", he contended, "has no meaning. No common characteristics can differentiate one community from another which is not covered by the words 'religion or language'. These words sufficiently cover the field that is sought to be covered by the word 'community'. Therefore, the word 'community' has no meaning in that provision and therefore it should be deleted".[27] This amendment was adopted[28] by the Constituent Assembly without any debate and the word 'community' was deleted from Article 23(3).

Commenting generally on this clause R.K. Sidhwa observed: "Regarding this article on education based on religion or otherwise, I would have certainly preferred a very clear and unambiguous provision. Sir, some of the provisions of this article are contradictory. While the Constitution has recognised that all communities have a right to give education on religion, Article 22 states that where State aid is given, there shall be no religious education provided. Again, here is a proviso that communities which do not expect any State aid shall have a right to give education on religion according to their choice and custom. Personally, Sir, I feel that as far as religious education is concerned, it should have been mentioned in unambiguous terms that wherever an educational institution receives State aid, there shall be no religious education taught in those institutions. My objection is not because I am averse to religion, I believe in religion, Sir, I believe in the existence of God. But, I do feel to-day that the religious books of the various communities are translated by various authors in a manner which has really brought disgrace to several religions. The authors have translated some of the very beautiful original phrases in their own language to suit their own political ends, with the result that today on religious grounds we know the country has broken into various pieces. I therefore desire, Sir, that in the matter of education, which is the fundamental basis of our future, it should have been clearly stated that under the existing circumstances, there shall be no religious education provided in any institution which receives State aid. As I have stated, Sir, while the State has not recognised any religion, they have allowed those institutions which do not receive State aid to impart religious education in their institutions. I do not want to go into the various phases of the religious scriptures which are being taught in the various schools. I know of instances where in the name of religion communal hatred has been taught. I do not know whether in this new era when we will be functioning under this Constitution the same type of religious education would be taught. There is no restriction regarding that kind of religious instructions that are being given in various schools. I can quote them; but I do not want to create any kind of ill-feeling between community and community. I only wish that in this matter the Constitution should have made it clear as to what education means as far as religious education is concerned. On that matter, this chapter is silent; not only silent, but I apprehend that in the name of religion, there will be the same type of religious education taught in the institutions. I have been reading and re-reading these two chapters and I feel that there is no kind of control over such kind of schools and colleges. On the contrary, it will be stated that the Constitution has given them freedom to teach religion in any manner they like. Knowing fully well, as we do, what religion in this country means to various communities, this chapter, I feel, Sir, should have been more clear."[29]

There was practically no discussion in the Constituent Assembly on the provisions of Article 23(3)(a) and 23(3)(b) and the Article finds place in the Constitution as Article 30(1) and 30(2). [Another clause, namely clause 1A, was added to this Article by the Constitution (Forty-fourth Amendment) Act, 1978 making acquisition of property of an educational institution established and administered by a minority more stringent]. The full attention of the members was lent to the discussion of the provisions of Article 23(1) and 23(2) [renumbered as Article 29(1) and 29(2)]. We are, therefore, denied of knowing the minds of the Framers as well as their logic for clubbing together the religious minorities and the linguistic minorities in the matter of establishment of and administering educational institutions. Educational institutions are meant for imparting education and not religion. The linguistic minorities have a stake in that because of the medium of instruction. If the medium of instruction is a language which is not understood by them, they are deprived of the facility of education. So, the right has got to be given to the linguistic minorities to establish and administer educational institutions of their choice. But the same facility was extended to the religious minorities as well.

II

In the earlier chapter we have seen that Article 28 allows imparting of religious instruction in such educational institutions which have been established under any endowment or trust which requires that religious instructions shall be imparted in such institution, even if the same institution is administered by the State. The avowed objective of imparting religious instruction in such institutions should be clearly laid down in the endowment or trust under which it has been established. Other educational institutions recognized by the State or receiving aid out of State funds or not wholly maintained out of State funds may impart religious instructions. They have not been debarred from doing it. And, to be fair, Article 28 does not discriminate between one religion and another, or to be precise, between minority religions and majority religions, though the very idea of imparting religious instruction in educational institutions whether by the majority groups or minority groups, militate against the very secular character of the Constitution. But it has gone one step further in Article 30.

Anirban Kashyap has very rightly pointed out about 25 years ago:

> The most unfortunate part is that Article 30 did not evidently receive that much of attention from the Framers as it should have. This is the only Article in the entire Constitution which recognizes the separate existence of religious minorities and extends a specific right to them. In no other Article of the Constitution the words 'minorities based on religion' do find any place. What is meant by religious minorities has not, however been spelt out anywhere. This was left to the judiciary to decide. Under the provisions of this Article, religious minorities not only have been allowed to run their own educational institutions but are also entitled to receive grants from the Government for such educational institutions. This is a right given only to the religious minorities and not to the religious majority. It is a discriminatory provision against the religious majority in the sense that they cannot run any educational institution in the same lines as the religious minorities have been permitted to. Secondly, it is a provision which allows the Government to patronise even religious educational institutions, and thirdly, it divides the citizens on the basis of religion, which perhaps negates the very basis of secularity of the Constitution.[30]

This Article has given rise to a large number of litigations in the highest courts of the country. The aggrieved parties, in most cases the religious minorities, had gone to the High Courts and the Supreme Court for protection of the right guaranteed under this Article. Hardly any case worth mentioning was instituted by the linguistic minorities. V.G. Ramchandran in his book *Fundamental Rights and Constitutional Remedies* discussed this provision of the Constitution from a legal angle. He also quoted in his book the judgments and the interpretations of the various High Courts and the Supreme Court on this Article. For instance, this right cannot be restricted by reference to Article 29(2) and the protection narrowed down only to such institutions as are established by the religious minority for conserving the languages, script or culture of its own.[31] It can promote its religion, language or culture or merely give a thorough good secular education to the children.[32] Even if the educational institution is meant primarily for the propagation of a particular religion and secondarily for rendering humanitarian services it is well within the bounds of this Article.[33] The State cannot dictate to a minority what the nature of its educational institution should be.[34] So, this Article confers the right to any religious minority to establish and administer educational institution of their choice for teaching either their language or their religion.[35] These institutions however cannot impose any condition which would offend public order, morality or health. Nor can there be any compulsion on anyone to practise or profess any religion.

Under this Article, a religious minority has two rights: (a) to establish an educational institution of its choice; and (b) to administer it.[36] In order to bring a case under this Article, the minority community has got to establish its character first either as a religious[37] or linguistic community.[38] Then it has further to prove that the institution was established by it.[39] Without satisfying these two conditions, it cannot claim the guaranteed right to administer it.[40] If these two conditions are satisfied, then and only then there can be a claim to administer the educational institution. The right under Article 30 extends to the institutions established prior to the commencement of the Constitution as well as to those established after its commencement.[41]

The right to administer may be said to consist of the following rights—

(a) to choose its managing or governing body;
(b) to choose its teachers;
(c) not to be compelled to refuse admission to students;
(d) to use its properties and assets for the benefit of the institution;
(e) to select its own medium of instruction; hence, a legislation which would penalise by disaffiliation from the University any institution which uses a language as the medium of instruction other than the one prescribed by it, offends Article 30(1).[42]
(f) to enjoy total freedom to admit students.[43]

There are however limits to the right to administer. D.D. Basu, after going through the different judgements on the subject, listed them as follows:

1. Though Article 30 itself does not lay down any limitations upon the right of a minority to administer its educational institutions, this right is not absolute, but must be subject to reasonable regulations for the benefit of the institution as the vehicle of education for the minority community consistent with the national interest such as—
   (a) to maintain the educational character and standard of such institutions, e.g. to lay down qualifications or conditions of service, to secure appointment of good teachers, to ensure interests of students, to maintain a fair standard of teaching;
   (b) to ensure orderly, efficient and sound administration and to prevent maladministration, and to secure its proper functioning as an educational institution, to ensure that its funds are spent for the betterment of education and not for extraneous purposes;
   (c) to prevent anti-national activity;
   (d) to enforce the general laws of the land, applicable to all persons, e.g. taxation, sanitation, social welfare, economic regulations, public order, morality.
2. Such regulations may be made either by legislation or by executive order.
3. Since the right to 'administer' confers upon the minority institutions the right to manage the institution, and the right conferred by Clause (1) is absolute, no 'restriction' can be imposed by the State on the right of the minority community to manage the institution. On the other hand, the right to 'administer' cannot include the right to 'mal-administer'. Hence, under the guise of exclusive right of management, a minority institution cannot be allowed to fall below the standards of excellence expected of 'educational institutions' or to resist regulations which are conducive to maintain that standard; such regulations do not bear directly upon the management though they may indirectly affect it.
4. It will cease to be a 'regulation' where the condition imposed is not related to any of the legitimate interest for which the State may intervene, such as efficiency, health, morality or the like. Thus, where there is no question of maintenance of discipline or morality, the State educational authorities cannot debar a minority educational institution to admit girls merely on the ground that the school was being run as a boys' school for a number of years, since its establishment.
5. It will also cease to be a regulation where the power conferred upon

an extraneous authority, whether the State or the University, is uncanalised or unreasonable in extent.

6. Such regulations are, however, permissible only in so far as they do not restrict the right of administration of minority community, but facilitate and ensure better and more effective exercise of that right for the benefit of the institution. They must allow the institution to retain its minority character.
7. It follows that no such regulation would be valid if it has the effect of displacing the minority administration or to completely take away its autonomy, e.g.—
   (i) enabling the Government to take over the management of the institution;
   (ii) providing that appointments and dismissals by the Governing body were to be subject to absolute veto or prior approval of the State or the University;

   While the Government or the University may frame rules and regulations relating to the conditions of service and tenure of teachers under the employ of minority institutions to ensure that they are not arbitrarily treated, e.g. to insist that they must be given an opportunity to be heard before being punished, such regulation becomes a 'restriction' and therefore, violative of the right of the minority to administer the institution, if the power given to the State or University authority to interfere is uncanalised, or unlimited and takes away the right of the minority to administer the institution as a minority institution, even though such restriction may be in the interests of the general public; in short, although disciplinary control over teachers is with the management, regulations can be made by the State for ensuring proper conditions of service for teachers as well as ensuring a fair procedure in disciplinary action against them;

   (iii) enabling the State to constitute a Managing Committee according to its order, or to interfere with the minority's choice of a governing body, by including persons other than members of that community; but it would not be unconstitutional to direct that the Principal and senior teacher appointed by the Governing Body itself must be taken into that Body;
   (iv) enabling the State to place the management in a body corporate which is not answerable to the Founders of the institution;
   (v) enabling the State to require the institutions to reserve seats under orders of the Government;
   (vi) imposing any language (not even the official language, Hindi) as the compulsory medium of instruction in a minority institution;

(vii) compelling the institution to refer to a Government nominated arbitrator all disputes between the governing body and its staff;

(viii) requiring that all teaching in under-graduate classes of such institution must be within the University area and only by University teachers.

8. In short, in order to be consonant with Article 30(1), a regulation imposed by the State upon a minority institution must be (a) reasonable and must also be (b) regulative of the educational character of the institution and conducive to making the institution an effective vehicle of education for the minority community or other persons who resort to it.
9. The right conferred by Clause (1) of Article 30 is also subject to the condition imposed by Clause (2) of that Article, in case the minority institution received aid from the State.[44]

It has just been explained that the right conferred by Article 30(1) upon a minority community is not absolute, but is subject to reasonable regulations. The scope for State regulation by way of recognition or aid has been explained by D.D. Basu, thus:

1. It is evident that neither Article 30(1) nor any other provision in the Constitution confers any right upon the minority to obtain recognition or aid from the State. It follows that in consideration for granting aid or recognition to an institution coming under Article 30(1), the State may impose reasonable regulations for the purpose of ensuring sanitation, competence of teachers, maintenance of discipline, conditions of service and the like. In case of aid, the State may also make regulations to ensure that the aid is utilised for the purpose for which it is granted.
2. But the regulation cannot go to the extent of virtually annihilating the right guaranteed by Article 30(1), by introducing regulations which are not related to the interests of the institution as an educational institution even though they may be in the interests of the general public.
3. Hence, even though there is no constitutional right to receive State aid outside Article 337 (special provision with respect to educational grants for the benefit of Anglo-Indian community), if the State does in fact grant aid to educational institutions, it cannot impose such conditions upon the right to receive such aid as would virtually deprive the members of a religious or linguistic community of their right under Article 30(1). It cannot be held that the right under Article 30(1) is available only so long as the community is in a position to

run the institution with its own resources and that if they seek State aid, they must submit to any terms which the State may impose. While the State has the right to impose reasonable conditions, it cannot impose such conditions as will substantially deprive the minority community of its rights guaranteed by Article 30(1). Surrender of fundamental rights cannot be exacted as the price of aid doled out by the State. Thus, the State cannot prescribe that if an institution, including one entitled to protection of Article 30(1), seeks to receive State aid, it must submit to the condition that the State may take over the management of the institution or acquire it, under certain contingencies—for such condition would completely destroy the right of the community to administer the institution.

4. Similarly, in the matter of the right to establish in relation to recognition of an institution by the State, though there is no constitutional or other right for an institution to receive State recognition, and though the State is entitled to impose reasonable conditions for receiving State recognition, e.g. as to the qualifications of teachers to be employed by the institution, the State cannot impose conditions the acceptance of which would virtually deprive a minority community of their right guaranteed by Article 30(1), e.g. a condition that a certain percentage of seats must be reserved for students or teachers nominated by the Government.
5. Where, therefore, the State regulations debar scholars of uncognised educational institutions from receiving higher education or for entering into the public services, the right to establish an institution under Article 30(1) cannot be effectively exercised without obtaining State recognition. In such circumstances, the State cannot impose it as a condition precedent to State recognition that the institution must not receive any fees for tuition in the primary classes. For, if there is no provision in the State law or regulation as to how this financial loss is to be recouped, institutions solely or primarily dependent upon the fees charged in the primary classes cannot exist at all. Such a condition would thus be void for contravention of Article 30(1).
6. In short, in order to be consonant with Article 30(1), a regulation imposed by the State upon a minority institution must be (a) reasonable and must also be (b) regulative of the educational character of the institution and conducive to making the institution an effective vehicle of education for the minority community or other persons who resort to it. A regulation would be reasonable if it reconciles or secures a reasonable balance between the two objectives of ensuring a standard of excellence of the institution and of preserving the right of the minority to administer the institution as a

minority institution. If the regulations are not relevant to these objectives, a regulation would not be consistent with the minority right under Article 30(1) even though it may otherwise be conducive to the interests of the general public or otherwise salutary.

7. A minority institution may seek relief under Article 32 or 226 if the State threatens to withdraw recognition or aid on the failure of the institution to comply with unconstitutional conditions.[45]

III

A three-member National Commission for Minority Educational Institutions (NCMEI) was established in November, 2004 by an Act of Parliament to advise the Central or any State Government on any question relating to the education of minorities that may be referred to it. It will also look into specific complaints regarding deprivation or violation of rights of minorities to establish and administer educational institutions of their choice, any dispute regarding affiliation to a scheduled university and report its findings to the Centre for its implementation.

The National Commission for Minority Educational Institutions Act, 2004 (2 of 2005) was amended by the National Commission for Minority Educational Institutions (Amendment) Act, 2006 (18 of 2006) to give the NCMEI the power to decide all questions of minority status and cancel such recognition if the situation so warrants. It was clarified that this amendment would facilitate the implementation of Article 15(5) to reserve seats for socially and educationally backward classes of citizens, besides the Scheduled Castes and Scheduled Tribes, in educational institutions including private aided or unaided educational institutions, other than those run by the minorities. The amendment also seeks to give appellate jurisdiction to the Commission in matters of refusal of issuing No Objection Certificate for establishing a minority institution.[46] This Act was further amended by the National Commission for Minority Educational Institutions (Amendment) Act, 2010 (20 of 2010). The Commission now has three members, apart from the chairman.

The origin of the National Commission for Minority Educational Institutions dates back to the manifesto of the UPA I Government, namely 'National Common Minimum Programme'. The NCMP said that a Commission should be established for "minority educational institutions" which would provide affiliation to "minority professional institutions" to Central Universities. The NCMEI Act was the result of detailed meeting at New Delhi on Minority Welfare and Education which was followed by discussions at "National Monitoring Committee on Minority Education".

The three-member (increased to four from 1-9-2010) Commission comprises a chairman, who would be a judge of a High Court, and two members. All the members should, as far as possible, be chosen from among the minority communities. It is a "quasi-judicial" commission which is bestowed with the powers and responsibilities of a Civil Court.

The Commission plays three kinds of roles, namely adjudicatory function, recommendatory powers, and advisory function. The commission takes the decision of the affiliation of any minority educational body. It also has the powers to suggest and recommend to the Central Government or the State Government regarding minority education or deprivation of the rights of the minorities in matters pertaining to education. In case of any kind of dispute between a University and a minority academic institution, the National Commission for Minority Educational Institutions has the power to take the final decision.

The National Commission for Minority Educational Institutions can recommend to the State or Central Government on matters related to the education of the minorities. It can intervene in proceedings that involve the violation and deprivation of the minority's educational rights, undertake measures for the promotion and preservation of the status of the minority, decide on all the questions pertaining to the position of minority educational institution, and recommend to the Government for implementation of various programmes associated with the educational institutions of the minorities.[47]

In the *P.A. Inamdar* vs. *State of Maharashtra*, (2005) 6 SCC 537, the Supreme Court had stated that the minority educational institution is primarily for the benefit of minority. Sprinkling of the non-minority students in the student population of minority educational institution is expected to be only peripheral either for generating additional financial source or for cultural courtesy. Thus, a substantive section of student population in minority educational institution should belong to the minority. But the judgement did not define "substantial" and did not lay down any minimum percentage of students from such communities that institutions need to claim for the status.

In March 2011 the NCMEI issued an order fixing 30 per cent as the yardstick for preferring such a claim. The NCMEI order fuelled resentment among the missionaries who felt that if it was implemented, the educational institutions they run would not be able to fill the 30 per cent quota and thus lose the minority status. The missionaries apprehended that once the institutions they run lose their minority status, those would be converted into general category institutions raising the fear that the state Governments would impose its education policies on them. Once the minority educational institutions lose their minority status, the government-aided missionary schools may be asked to recruit teachers through the State School Service Commissions. The government may also take away their right to appoint their own principals. As of now, unaided as well as state-aided minority schools enjoy the freedom to appoint their own teachers and principals, select their students and follow their own admission and educational policies.

In West Bengal, Christians comprise only 1 per cent of the total population. Therefore, it is not possible to enroll 30 per cent of their students from the Christian community in the 5,000 missionary educational institutions in the country[48] and 700 in the State of West Bengal. Such may be the case with minority schools run by the Buddhists, Sikhs and Jains. A delegation comprising representatives of all minority schools met the NCMEI authorities in Delhi on April 5, 2010 and submitted a memorandum demanding the scrapping of the order.[49] The Christian community also petitioned the Prime Minister, the Human Resource Development Minister and even the Vatican expressed concern.

Under pressure from the Christian groups and the government, the NCMEI backtracked and declared on April 7, 2010, that the full Commission would debate and discuss how to determine what constitutes a "substantial" population as required by the Supreme Court judgement.[50]

The NCMEI has finally done away with the criterion of fixation of percentage of minority students in a Minority Educational Institution (MEI), as the determining factor of its minority status. The Commission said that imposing a criterion which mandates a minority-run educational institution to admit a fixed percentage of students from their own community will impinge on the rights of minorities to establish and run minority educational institutions as enshrined in Article 30(1) of the Constitution.

In the past, there had been some instances where a number of States had denied minority status to many educational institutions, on the ground that they didn't have the required percentage of students from their community. It was this practice which was challenged before the Commission by Buckley Primary School, Cuttack. In its order on July 6, 2010, the Commission comprising its Chairman Justice M.S.A. Siddiqui and Members, Dr. Mohinder Singh and Dr. Cyriac Thomas, said that neither a fixed percentage formula for admissions can be binding on such institutes nor can it be made a criterion to deny them minority status.[51] The NCMEI order will bring relief for hundreds of minority educational institutes, particularly the Christian-run ones, many of which have been denied minority status by State Governments on that basis.

As regards the prescription of a percentage governing admissions in a minority educational institution, it would be useful to excerpt the following observations of their lordships of the Supreme Court in *T.M.A. Pai Foundation* vs. *State of Karnataka*, (2002) 8 SCC 481:

> "...The situation would vary according to the type of institution and the nature of education that is being imparted in the institution. Usually, at the school level, although it may be possible to fill up all the seats with the students of the minority group, at the higher level, either in colleges or in technical institutions, it may not be possible

> to fill up all the seats with the students of the minority group. However, even if it is possible to fill up all the seats with students of the minority group, the moment the institution is granted aid, the institution will have to admit students of the non-minority group to a reasonable extent, whereby the character of the institution is not annihilated, and at the same time, the rights of the citizen engrafted under Article 29(2) are not subverted."

The State Government can prescribe percentage of the minority community to be admitted in a minority educational institution taking into account the population and educational needs of the area in which the institution is located. There cannot be a common rule or regulation or order in respect of types of educational institutions from primary to college level and for the entire State fixing the uniform ceiling in the matter of admission of students in minority educational institutions. Thus a balance has to be kept between two objectives—preserving the right of the minorities to admit students of their own community and that of admitting "sprinkling of outsiders" in their institutions subject to the condition that the manner and number of such admissions should not be violative of the minority character of the institution. It is significant to mention here that Section 12C (b) of the NCMEI Act, 2004 also empowers the State Government to prescribe percentage governing admissions in a minority educational institution. Thus, the State Government has to prescribe percentage governing admissions of students in the minority educational institutions in accordance with the aforesaid principles of law enunciated by their Lordships of the Supreme Court in the cases of T.M.A. Pai Foundation and P.A. Inamdar.[52]

The Minority Affairs and Madrasah Education Department of the Government of West Bengal has drawn up new rules for granting minority status to educational institutions in the State. From 2012, new educational institutions seeking minority status would be required to reserve 50 per cent seats for students of the particular community. Apart from reserving half the seats, the managing committee of the institution should be constituted with members of the community. Again, such institutions should have requisite infrastructure and faculty strength. This rule has been prepared keeping in mind the provisions of the Right of Children to Free and Compulsory Education Act, or Right to Education (RTE) Act, 2009.[53]

On a reading of Article 30(1) of the Constitution read with several authoritative pronouncements of the Supreme Court and the definitions of Minority Educational Institution in Section 2(g) of the NCMEI and Section 2(f) of the Central Educational Institutions (Reservation in Admission) Act, 2006, the NCMEI concluded that following facts should be proved for grant of minority status to an educational institution on religious basis:

(i) that the educational institution was established by a member/members of the religious minority community;
(ii) that the educational institution was established for the benefit of the minority community; and
(iii) that the educational institution is being administered by the minority community.

The aforesaid facts may be proved either by direct or circumstantial evidence. There must be some positive index to enable the educational institution to be identified with religious minorities. There should be nexus between the means employed and the ends desired. If the minority educational institution concerned is being run by a trust or a registered society, then majority of the trustees of the trust or members of the society, as the case may be, must be from the minority community and the trust deed/Articles of Association or any other document duly executed in this regard must reflect the objective of subserving the interest of the minority community. In the absence of any documentary evidence some clear or cogent evidence must be produced to prove the aforesaid facts. There is no bar to the members of other communities to extend their help to the members of a minority community to establish an educational institution of its choice.[54]

It needs to be highlighted that Sec. 2(f) of the Central Educational Institutions (Reservation in Admission) Act, 2006, defines a minority educational institution as under:

> "Minority Educational Institution" means an institution established and administered by the minorities under clause (1) of Article 30 of the Constitution and so declared by an Act of Parliament or by the Central Government or declared as a minority educational institution under the National Commission for Minority Educational Institutions Act, 2004."

It has to be borne in mind that the right guaranteed under Article 30(1) is a right not conferred on individuals but on religious denomination or section of such denomination. It is also universally recognised that it is the parental right to have education of their children in the educational institutions of their choice. It has been held by a Full Bench of the Karnataka High Court in *Associated Managements of Primary and Secondary Schools in Karnataka* vs. *State of Karnataka and Ors.*, 2008 K.L.J 1 (Full Bench) that the words of "their choice" which qualify "educational institutions" shows the vast discretion and option which minorities have in selecting the type of the institution which they want to establish.

Needless to add here that an educational institution is established to subserve or advance the purpose for its establishment. Whereas the minorities have the right to establish and administer educational institutions of their choice with the desire that their children should be brought up properly and be eligible for higher education and go all over the world fully equipped with such intellectual attainments as it will make them fit for entering the public service, surely then there must be implicit in such a fundamental right the corresponding duty to cater to the needs of the children of their own community. The beneficiary of such a fundamental right should be allowed to enjoy it in the fullest measure. Therefore, the educational institutions of their choice will necessarily cater to the needs of the minority community which had established the institution.

A minority educational institution continues to be so whether the Government declares it as such or not. When the Government declares an educational institution as a minority institution, it merely recognizes a factual position that the institution was established and is being administered by a minority community. The declaration is merely an open acceptance of the legal character of the institution which must necessarily have existed antecedent to such declaration.[55]

It may be mentioned that it has been held by the Madras High Court in *T.K.V.T.S.S. Medical Educational & Charitable Trust* vs. *State of Tamil Nadu*, AIR 2002 Madras 42 that a minority status can not be conferred on a minority educational institution for a particular period to be renewed periodically like a driving license. It is not open for the State Government to review its earlier order conferring minority status on a minority educational institution unless it is shown that the institution concerned has suppressed any material fact while passing the order of conferral of minority status or there is fundamental change of circumstances or suppression of facts warranting cancellation of the earlier order.

It is now well settled that any administrative order involving civil consequences has to be passed strictly in conformity with the principles of natural justice.[56] If any order relating to cancellation of minority status granted to a minority educational institution has been passed without affording an opportunity of being heard to such educational institution, it gets vitiated. If a minority status certificate has been obtained by practising fraud or if there is any suppression of any material fact or any fundamental change of circumstances warranting cancellation of the earlier order, the authority concerned would be within its powers to cancel the minority status certificate after affording an opportunity of being heard to the management of the institution concerned, in conformity with the principles of natural justice.

It is also relevant to note that the minority status certificate granted by the NCMEI or by any authority can be cancelled under Section 12C of the National Commission for Minority Educational Institutions Act for violation of any of the conditions enumerated therein. Section 12C is as under:

"12C. **Power to cancel.**—The Commission may, after giving a reasonable opportunity of being heard to the Minority Educational Institution to which minority status has been granted by an authority or Commission, as the case may be, cancel such status under the following circumstances, namely:

(a) if the constitution, aims and objects of the educational institution, which has enabled it to obtain minority status has subsequently been amended in such a way that it no longer reflects the purpose, or character of a Minority Educational Institution;

(b) if, on verification of the records during the inspection or investigation, it is found that the Minority Educational Institution has failed to admit students belonging to the minority community in the institution as per rules and prescribed percentage governing admissions during any academic year."

The right of the minorities to establish educational institutions of their choice will be without any meaning if affiliation or recognition is denied. It has been held by a Constitutional Bench of the Supreme Court in *St. Xavier's College, Ahmedabad* vs. *State of Gujarat,* 1974(1) SCC 717 that "affiliation must be a real and meaningful exercise of right for minority institutions in the matter of imparting general secular education. Any law which provides for affiliation on terms which will involve abridgment of the right of linguistic and religious minorities to administer and establish educational institutions of their choice will offend Article 30(1). The educational institutions set-up by minorities will be robbed of their utility if boys and girls cannot be trained in such institutions for university degrees. Minorities will virtually lose their right to equip their children for ordinary careers if affiliation be on terms which would make them surrender and lose their rights to establish and administer educational institutions of their choice under Article 30. The primary purpose of affiliation is that the students reading in the minority institutions will have qualifications in the shape of degrees necessary for a useful career in life. The establishment of a minority institution is not only ineffective but also unreal unless such institution is affiliated to a University for the purpose of conferment of degrees on students." It has been held in *T.M.A. Pai Foundation* that affiliation and recognition has to be available to every institution that fulfills the conditions for grant of such affiliation and recognition.

IV

Article 30(1) of the Constitution postulates that members of religious or linguistic minority have the right to establish and administer educational institutions of their choice. A Society or Trust consisting of members of a minority community, or even a single member of a minority community, may establish an institution. "It matters not if a single philanthropic individual with his own means, institution or the community at large founds the institution or the community at large contributes the funds. The position in law is the same and the intention in either case must be to found an institution for the benefit of a minority community by a member of that community. It is equally irrelevant to this right that in addition to the minority community, others from other minority communities or even from the majority community can take advantage of these institutions."[57] The key factor in deciding whether a trust or foundation can legitimately claim minority status is the intention with which it was founded. A trust has to be "both by and for" a minority community, as intended by the founder, to qualify as a minority institution, the Supreme Court bench of Justices R.V. Raveendran and H.L. Gokhale said on October, 2011 while holding that the T. Thomas Educational Trust, Perambur, was a secular trust.[58]

It is a matter of proof through production of satisfactory evidence that the institution in question was established by the minority community claiming to administer it. The proof of the fact of the establishment of the institution is a condition precedent for claiming the right to administer the institution. The onus lies on one who asserts that an institution is a minority institution. It has been held by a Division Bench of the Madras High Court in *T.K. V.T.S.S. Medical Educational and Charitable Trust* vs. *State of Tamil Nadu*, AIR 2002 Madras 42 that "once it is established that the institution has been established by a linguistic minority, and is administered by that minority, that would be sufficient for claiming the fundamental right guaranteed under Article 30(1) of the Constitution." The same principle applies to religious minority also. In *Andhra Pradesh Christian Medical Association* vs. *Government of Andhra Pradesh*, AIR 1986 SC 1490, the Supreme Court has held that the Government, the University and ultimately the Court can go behind the claim that the institution in question is a minority institution and "to investigate and satisfy itself whether the claim is well founded or ill founded." A minority educational institution continues to be so whether the Government declares it as such or not. When the Government declares an educational institution as a minority institution, it merely recognizes a factual position that the institution was established and is being administered by a minority community. The declaration is merely an open acceptance of the legal character of the institution which must necessarily have existed antecedent to such declaration.[59]

In 1968, the Supreme Court in *Azeez Basha* case[60] held that a university created by an Act of Parliament cannot be considered a minority institution. The Aligarh University which came into existence in 1920 was not established by the minority as such and so they cannot claim to administer it.[61] It is of no relevance that it was partly or wholly due to the effort of the Muslims that the Act became law. This verdict had then cost the Aligarh Muslim University (AMU) its minority status. This denial to the Muslims to administer the Aligarh Muslim University has very often given rise to acrimonious situations. This University is considered to be the epicenter of Muslim fundamentalist forces. They are bent on restoring the minority character of this institution. The Muslim community being a national minority, the demand for the restoration of the minority character was based on the assertion that in a special sense AMU belongs to the Muslim community, that the latter should have a controlling interest in its affairs, that it should respect the Muslim ethos and that its facilities should be largely utilized for promoting the educational and cultural advancement of the Muslim community.

In 1981 in accordance with the Congress election manifesto of 1979 largely to undo the "secular and modern" innovation introduced by the amendment of 1965 and 1972 and to meet, to the extent politically feasible, the unanimous Muslim demand for the restoration of what was euphemistically called the "minority character" of the university, the Indira Gandhi government conferred the minority status on it by amending the AMU Act of 1920. The 1981 Amendment did not bring AMU explicitly within the definition of a minority educational institution under Article 30(1) of the Constitution. In introducing the 1981 Amendment Bill the then Minister of State for Education carefully avoided the phrase "minority character", but referred to its "historical character". It can, however, be validly argued, says Syed Shahabuddin, that historically, the institution has always been a Muslim institution. Therefore, the line drawn between its historical and its minority character is rather thin and almost invisible.[62]

The amended Act has defined the term 'university' as "the educational institution of their choice established by the Muslims of India, which originated as the Mohammedan Anglo-Oriental College and which was subsequently incorporated as the Aligarh Muslim University". Since the Aligarh Muslim University Amendment Act has virtually lifted the words 'educational institution of their choice' from Article 30, it is being made out that Aligarh Muslim University could claim minority status.

Though AMU gets all its funds from the Central Government some powerful people have deliberately used the Aligarh Muslim University Amendment Act, 1981, to plead that it has given the university the status of a minority educational institution and, therefore, the university could go ahead and reserve seats for Muslims or make changes in its admission policy to give preferential treatment to the community.

Despite the fact that the provisions of Article 29(2) of the Constitution and Section 8 of the AMU Act prohibit discrimination in university admissions, in almost all the meetings of the court a motion seeking 75 per cent reservation for Muslim students in different courses is tabled. This is accompanied by considerable mud slinging and hurling of the choicest abuses on those who oppose it. The Vice-Chancellor is often accused of following a 'transparently unjust admission policy' and 'alienating the Muslim community'. The Vice-Chancellor was however of the opinion that the demand for reserving seats for Muslims or giving them preferential treatment was similar to the demand for Pakistan by the Muslims of Uttar Pradesh. They suffered most from the partition. The situation was the same. If this lobby had its way then it was the local AMU boys who would get left in the cold. The Government of India cannot also possibly allow any preferential admission policy in any Central University as it may open a Pandora's box. The innate weaknesses of the provisions of the AMU (Amendment) Act of 1981 and their constant misinterpretation and violation are likely to sap the vitality of the Institution.[63]

As the noted historian Professor Irfan Habib, who has long taught at AMU, has noted, at no time did "the founder [Sir Syed Ahmad Khan] and his successors...see any conflict in the university keeping its doors open to all, while promoting the spread of modern education among Muslims".[64]

In October 2005 a single-judge Bench of the Allahabad High Court held that the AMU Amendment Act of 1981 giving it a minority status was unconstitutional. On January 5, 2006, the Division Bench of Chief Justice A.N. Ray and Justice Ashok Bhusan of the Allahabad High Court upheld the judgement of the single bench. Striking down two sections of the Aligarh Muslim University (Amendment) Act, 1981, that purportedly gave the university a minority status, the High Court echoed the 11-judge Bench of the Supreme Court's 1968 judgement in *Azeez Basha* case that held that AMU was not a minority institution.[65]

The Aligarh Muslim University as well as the Centre moved the Supreme Court challenging the Allahabad High Court's verdict. The Supreme Court of India on April 26, 2006, while admitting the appeal ordered that "*status quo*" on the minority status of Aligarh Muslim University be maintained but refused to stay, till the pendency of the matter, the Allahabad High Court's verdict striking down the provision of the Aligarh Muslim University Amendment Act, 1981. The Court also asked the AMU not to enforce 50 per cent reservation for Muslims in admissions to M.D. and M.S. courses during the pendency of appeals. The Court, while issuing notice to the respondent students, referred the matter to a five-judge Constitution Bench. The Aligarh Muslim University hailed the SC's interim order on the institution's minority character as a 'major victory' and said the issue of granting 50 per cent reservation to Muslims would be held in abeyance till a final verdict.[66]

Though AMU is a Central university, what is its image? "Two images of Aligarh, one as a bastion of Islam in a Hindu world of India, the other as a focal point of communalism and a recruiting ground for Pakistan are generally held even by enlightened persons ...both the views are not only wrong but a deliberate distortion of the original purposes and spirit of Aligarh and latter of Jamia", said A. Rahaman in the Foreword to the book *Aligarh and Jamia Fight for National Education System* written by S.M. Tonki. But in course of time AMU acquired a communal and sectarian outlook which was admitted by A. Rahaman when he himself raised this question in the following words: "The question naturally arises as how an institution with such lofty ideals and objectives which was started as a joint endeavour of Hindus and Muslims, became sectarian appealing to narrow loyalties?"[67] Without delving deep into the causes, it may safely be said that AMU has acquired this image mainly due to the failure of the authority to keep its secular image. The pressure to restore its communal character is mounting daily. The movement is on and in the process it throws up such issues as should have no place in a secular country. But this cannot be avoided at this stage because secularity has already been sacrificed at the altar of communality. Secularism, as practised in India today, is circumscribed by communalism.

The AMU plans to establish full-fledged centres (in effect, regional campuses) in Malappuram district in Kerala, Murshidabad district in West Bengal, Kishanganj in Bihar, Pune and Bhopal under Section 12(2) of the AMU Act.[68] But the Aligarh Muslim University Old Boys' Association articulated its objection to the establishment of such centres of the University in different parts of the country on the ground that it violated the residential and historic character of AMU. The establishment of the special education centres is restricted by Section 5(9A) of the AMU Act which states that the setting up of such centres should be within the radius of 25 km of university campus. These new centres are for day scholars which violates the residential character of AMU. Further, the new centres will not have any reservations for the Muslim community. This will damage the traditionally minority character of AMU, said former AMU Students' Union president and Rajya Sabha Member Mohammad Adeeb.[69]

Former Rajya Sabha member Wasim Ahmed, who is the Visitor's nominee to the Executive Council of the University, even alleged that what had "actually been" cleared at the meeting of the Council in 2009 was the proposal to establish "centres for advanced studies and research" with the permission of the Visitor. He alleged that University officials were "playing" with the word "centre" and "what is now being set up is *de facto* affiliated institutions of routine graduate studies".[70]

The AMU Malappuram Centre in Kerala and the AMU Murshidabad Centre in West Bengal were launched in 2010 after lots of hues and cries. But both the Centres faced trouble because of insufficient funds. The Ministry for Human Resource Development, Government of India has, however, sanctioned about Rs. 105 crore for AMU Malappuram Centre in Kerala and Rs. 108 crore for

Murshidabad Centre in West Bengal in May 2013. It was decided that school level education will be started in both Centres. Initially teaching for Class IX will commence with an intake of 90 students at both the Centres. Further, a B.Ed. Course will also be introduced at both the Centres with an intake of 60 students. Presently, both these Centres are conducting BA, LLB and MBA courses.[71] The Aligarh Muslim University has written to the Union minority affairs minister to turn the AMU Centre at Murshidabad into a Central university. If the proposal is accepted, around Rs. 250 crore allocated in the 12th Five-Year Plan will go up 10 to 15 times. This will give tremendous impetus to education in Bengal. Both Maharashtra and Rajasthan have expressed interest and requested AMU to set-up centres, which may be next in the pipeline.[72]

Another institution which attracted a lot of attention for obtaining the minority tag was Jamia Millia Islamia. Jamia was founded by Maulana Mahmud Ali, Hakim Ajmal Khan, M.A. Ansari, Abdul Majid Khwaja and Zakir Hussain in 1920 in response to Mahatma Gandhi's call for boycott of British sponsored educational institutions. It was registered as a society in 1939 and was declared a deemed university in 1962. It became a central university through the Jamia Millia Islamia Act, 1988.

The Jamia Millia Islamia University used to reserve 15 per cent of seats for the SCs, 7.5 per cent for the STs and 25 per cent for those from its own intermediate colleges. The HRD Ministry was goading the Jamia to implement the quota rule, but the Jamia, caught in an internal debate over whether to seek minority status, has not even started implementing the OBC quota rule and instead sought time. In the meantime, Jamia Students' Union, Jamia Old Boys' Association and Jamia Teachers' Association submitted petitions to the National Commission for Minority Educational Institutions (NCMEI) in 2006 to grant minority status to the Jamia.

Sections of the "secular" intelligentsia are opposed to the granting of minority status to Jamia, an institution with a history of closely linked to India's Independence movement. It was a product of the Gandhian revolution, the national liberation struggle and the anti-colonial scheme, spreading liberal and nationalist education. It fought relentlessly the creation of Islamic Pakistan and the irrational two-nation theory. Many within the Jamia establishment today are also opposed to minority status for the university.[73]

On February 22, 2011, the Commission's three-judge bench headed by Justice M.S.A. Siddique declared the JMI a minority institution, the first Central university to be accorded such a status. The Commission said: "On a conjoined reading of Sections 2(O) and 4 of the Jamia Millia Islamia Act along with the history and facts and events which led to the establishment of Jamia, we have no hesitation in holding that Jamia was founded by the Muslims for the benefit of the Muslims and it never lost its identity as a Muslim minority educational institution".[74]

This Order will enable Jamia to reserve up to 50 per cent seats for Muslims. It will be exempted from SC, ST and OBC quotas followed by the general category institutions. Though the National Commission for Scheduled Castes[75] and the National Commission for Scheduled Tribes[76] have appealed to the HRD Ministry to ensure that reservations for the SC/ST communities are not done away with, the HRD Ministry can hardly do anything in this regard in view of Article 15(5) which exempts minority educational institutions from the purview of such reservations.

Clause (5) was added to Article 15 by the Constitution (Ninety-third) Amendment Act, 2005, which became effective from January 20, 2006. The Clause reads as follows:

> (5) Nothing in this article or in sub-clause (g) of clause (1) of Article 19 shall prevent the State from making any special provision, by law, for the advancement of any socially and educationally backward classes of citizens or for the Scheduled Castes or the Scheduled Tribes in so far as such special provision relate to their admission to educational institutions including private educational institutions, whether aided or unaided by the State, other than the minority educational institutions referred to in clause (1) of Article 30.

After the insertion of this Clause in Article 15, the Central Government enacted the Central Educational Institutions (Reservation in Admission) Act, 2006 which stipulated reservation of 27 per cent, 15 per cent and 7.5 per cent of seats respectively for the SEBCs, SCs and STs in all centrally funded educational institutions to be enforced from the 2008-09 academic year. However, minority institutions are exempt because they can reserve up to 50 per cent of seats for students from their own community. Ironically, the insertion of Article 15(5) in the Constitution is compelling many institutions like that of the Jamia Millia Islamia to go for the minority tag in order to avoid the reservation provisions of the 2006 Act.

As a matter of fact, since its inception the Commission has accorded minority status to as many as 7727 institutions so far (1180 in 2005-07, 2477 in 2008-2010, 3620 in 2011-12 and 450 up to March 19, 2013).[77]

V

Clause (1) of Article 30 implies the right of a minority community to impart instruction to the children of its own community in institutions run by it and in its own language and if such right is infringed, an institution run by the community may seek relief for violation of the fundamental right.[78] This Article protects minorities based on religion or culture. It guarantees two distinct rights under the Constitution to the minority, i.e. to establish and to administer educational institutions of their choice.

In 1952, the Anglo-Indians, who ran many reputed schools in Bombay, were adversely affected by an order passed by the Government of Bombay. It forbade state-aided schools using English as a medium of instruction to admit pupils other than Anglo-Indians or citizens of non-Asiatic descent. Anglo-Indians could maintain and administer their schools and teach in English, but only to Anglo-Indians. If they admitted other Indians, they forfeited state aid, unless, of course, they switched over to Hindi as the medium of instruction. The effort was to encourage the use of Hindi. Although the object was laudable, the order was struck down by the Supreme Court, because under the Constitution the Anglo-Indians had a distinct language (which was English), and has a fundamental right to conserve it, and because the direct effect of the order was to prevent Indians from entering Anglo-Indian schools on grounds of race and language.[79]

Seven years later, in 1959, the Supreme Court thwarted an attempt by the Communist Party of India-controlled Government of Kerala to take over the management of Christian schools contrary to Article 30. In an advisory opinion given by a bench of seven judges of the Supreme Court, rendered in a presidential reference, large parts of the Kerala Education Bill were declared unconstitutional.[80] Chief Justice S.R. Das at the same time gave a peroration, which he wrote for himself and for five of his colleagues on the bench. This is how it read:

> There can be no manner of doubt that our Constitution has guaranteed certain cherished rights of the minorities concerning their language, culture and religion. These concessions must have been made to them for good and valid reasons. Article 45, no doubt, requires the State to provide for free and compulsory education for all children, but there is nothing to prevent the State from discharging that solemn obligation through government and government-aided schools and Article 45 does not require that obligation to be discharged at the expense of the minority communities. So long as the Constitution stands as it is and is not altered, it is, we conceive, the duty of this court to uphold the fundamental rights and thereby honour our sacred obligation to the minority communities who are of our own.

Even the judge who did not entirely agree with the views of Chief Justice and his five companion justices in the *Kerala Education Bill* case, Justice Venkatarama Aiyar said:

> But what is the policy behind Article 30(1)? As I conceive it, it is that it should not be in the power of the majority in a State to destroy or to impair the rights of the minorities, religious or linguistic. That is a policy which permeates all modern constitutions, and its purpose

is to encourage individuals to preserve and develop their own distinct culture.

After the *Kerala Education Bill* case, some State Governments said they found it increasingly difficult to regulate educational standards, and so, the highest court in 1974 was requested to constitute a larger Constitution Bench to reconsider its previous decisions. It did.

Certain provisions of the Gujarat University Act, 1949 laid down statutory conditions for the affiliation of colleges in Gujarat to the Gujarat University. They applied to all educational institutions, including those run by minorities, and they provided that teaching and training in all colleges affiliated to the university would be conducted and imparted by teachers appointed only by it. Since the provisions interfered with the minorities' right to administer and run educational institutions "of their choice"—a fundamental right guaranteed under Article 30—these provisions were challenged by St. Xavier's College, Ahmedabad (managed by Jesuits).

The Court heard the case, this time sitting in a larger bench of nine judges to reconsider the decision in the *Kerala Education Bill* case. This bench re-affirmed what was said by the bench of seven judges in the *Kerala Education Bill* case. It struck down the offending provisions as inapplicable to minority-run colleges.[81]

The difficulty the Apex Court confronted was how to reconcile the provisions of Article 30(1) with the seemingly contrary provisions in Article 29(2). Article 30(1) provided, "(1) All minorities, whether based on religion or language, shall have the right to establish and administer educational institutions of their choice". But Article 29(2) provided, "(2) No citizen shall be denied admission into any educational institution maintained by the State or receiving aid out of State funds on grounds only of religion, race, caste, language or any of them". In the *Kerala Education Bill* case, an attempt had been made at a reconciliation. This is what the Court said: "Articles 29(2) and 30(1), read together, clearly contemplate a minority institution with a 'sprinkling' of outsiders admitted in it. By admitting a member of non-minority into the minority institution it does not shed its character and cease to be a minority institution". The expression "sprinkling of outsiders" was later explained in *Inamdar.*

It has been held in *Inamdar* that "the minority institutions are free to admit students of their own choice including students of non-minority community and also members of their own community from other States, both to a limited extent only and not in a manner and to such an extent that their minority educational status is lost. If they do so, they loose the protection of Article 30(1) of the Constitution".

In *Andhra Pradesh Christian Medical Association* vs. *Government of Andhra Pradesh,* AIR 1986 SC 1490, the Supreme Court has also held that "what is important and what is imperative is that there must exist some real positive index to enable the institution to be identified as an educational institution of the minorities." Needless to add here that the right enshrined in Article 30(1) of the Constitution is meant to benefit the minority by protecting and promoting its interests. There should be a nexus between the institution and the particular minority to which it claims to belong. The right claimed by a minority community to administer the educational institutions depends upon the proof of establishment of the institution.

The right of administering such institutions has four integral parts according to the Constitutional Bench of the Supreme Court as ruled by it in *St. Xavier's College, Ahmedabad* vs. *State of Gujarat,* 1974 (1) SCC 717. They have the right to constitute their own governing body, the right to admit students of their choice subject to reasonable restrictions imposed by the State, the right to choose teachers and the right to use the assets of the institution for its own development.

Mere receipt of state aid does not annihilate the right guaranteed under Article 30(1). It has been held in *P.A. Inamdar* that "a minority institution does not cease to be so the moment grants-in-aid is received by the institution. An aided minority educational institution, therefore, would be entitled to have the right of admission of students belonging to the minority group and at the same time, would be required to admit a reasonable extent of non-minority students, so that the rights under Article 30(1) are not substantially impaired and further the citizens' rights under Article 29(2) are not infringed. What would be a reasonable extent, would vary from the types of institution, the courses of education for which admission is being sought and other factors like educational needs. The State Government concerned has to notify the percentage of the minority students to be admitted in the light of the above observations." Their Lordships of the Supreme Court has further observed in *P.A. Inamdar* that "the object underlying Article 30(1) is to see the desire of minorities being fulfilled that their children should be brought up properly and efficiently and acquire eligibility for higher university education and go out in the world fully equipped with such intellectual attainments as will make them fit for entering public services, educational institutions imparting higher instructions including general secular education. Thus the twin objects sought to be achieved by Article 30(1) in the interest of minorities are: (i) to enable such a minority to conserve its religion and language, and (ii) to give a thorough good general education to the children belonging to such minority. So long as the institution retains its minority character by achieving and continuing to achieve the aforesaid two objectives, the institution would remain a minority institution."

In *St. Stephen's College* vs. *University of Delhi,* (1992) SCC 558, the Supreme Court had ruled that Article 30(1) is a protective measure only for the benefit of the religious and linguistic minorities and "no ill fit or camouflaged institution can get away with a constitutional protection."

Emphasising the need for preserving its minority character so as to enjoy the privilege of protection under Article 30(1), it is necessary that the objective of establishing the institution was not defeated. The management of a minority institution cannot resort to the device of admitting the minority students of the adjoining state in which they are in majority to preserve minority status of the institution. Reference may, in this connection be made to the following observations made in *T.M.A. Pai*:

> "...If so, such an institution is under an obligation to admit the bulk of the students fitting into the description of the minority community. Therefore, the students of that group residing in the State in which the institution is located have to be necessarily admitted in a larger measure because they constitute the linguistic minority group as far as that State is concerned. In other words the pre-dominance of linguistic minority students hailing from the State in which the minority educational institution is established should be present. The Management bodies of such institutions cannot resort to the device of admitting the linguistic students of the adjoining states in which they are in a majority, under the facade of the protection given under Article 30(1)."

In *Inamdar* the said proposition of law has been applied to religious minority. According to their Lordships, "if any other view was to be taken the very objective of conferring the preferential right of admission by harmoniously construing Articles 30(1) and 29(2) may be distorted". It was further observed in *Inamdar* that "it necessarily follows from the law laid down in *T.M.A. Pai Foundation* that to establish a minority institution the institution must primarily cater to the requirements of that minority of that State else its character of minority institution is lost. However, to borrow the words of Chief Justice S.R. Dass in *Kerala Education Bill*, "a sprinkling of that majority from the other States on the same footing as a sprinkling of non-minority students would be permissible and would not deprive the institution of its essential character of being a minority institution, determined by reference to that State as a unit."

The emphatic point in the *P.A. Inamdar* reasoning is that the minority educational institution is primarily for the benefit of minority. Sprinkling of the non-minority students in the student population of minority educational institution is expected to be only peripheral either for generating additional financial source or for cultural courtesy. Thus, a substantive section of student population in minority educational institution should belong to the minority. In the context of commercialisation of education, an enquiry about composition of student population of minority educational institution will reveal whether the substantive peripheral formula that can be gathered from *P.A. Inamdar* is adequately complied with or whether minority educational institution is only a façade for money making.

The law laid down with regard to the admission procedure and fee structure of unaided educational institutions including minority institutions in *Pai Foundation* was further clarified in *P.A. Inamdar*. It was clarified that *Pai Foundation* has held that minority unaided institutions can legitimately claim unfettered fundamental right to choose the students to be allowed admission and the procedure therefore subject to it being fair, transparent and non-exploitative. The Court has further held that there may be a single institution imparting a particular type of education which is not being imparted by any other institution and having its own admission procedure fulfilling the tests of being fair, transparent and non-exploitative. All the institutions imparting the same or similar professional education can join together for holding a common entrance test satisfying the triple tests of being fair, transparent and non-exploitative. The Court further observed that the State can also provide for a procedure of holding a common entrance test in the interest of securing fair and merit-based admissions and preventing mal-administration.[82]

In view of this judgement, Tamil Nadu, Andhra Pradesh and Karnataka already have a separate engineering entrance test for minority institutions. In West Bengal too separate test is being organized by Association for Minority Academic Professional Institute (AMAPI) from the academic year 2014-15. Anyone—not necessarily from a minority community—can appear in the entrance test, but preference will be given to minority students in such colleges. If seats remain vacant, they will be open to other candidates and if some seats are still left over, they will be allotted through e-counselling.[83]

In *St. Stephen's College* vs. *University of Delhi,* (1992) SCC 558, the Supreme Court had ruled that Article 30(1) is a protective measure only for the benefit of the religious and linguistic minorities. But who constitutes a minority needing the protection of the State? The courts have to constantly confront such questions as whether Ramkrishanites or Jains or some other sects are a minority.

The most obvious definition of minorities and majorities is in terms of numbers. A minority is a group that is numerically smaller than the majority in society. But the Constitution does not define the term "minority". In the absence of any special decision it may be held that any community—religious or linguistic—which is numerically less than fifty per cent of the population of the State is entitled to claim the protection of the guarantee in Article 30.[84] It has been held by the Eleven Judge Bench of the Supreme Court in *T.M.A.*

Pai Foundation vs. *State of Karnataka,* (2002) 8 SCC 481 that a minority, whether linguistic or religious, is determinable only by reference to demography of the State and not by taking into consideration the population of the country as a whole. According to this interpretation, non-Christians have a minority status in Nagaland, Mizoram and Meghalaya, the Christian majority States, non-Muslims in Jammu & Kashmir, the Muslim majority State and non-Sikhs in Punjab, the Sikh majority State. So any Act which infringes their rights guaranteed under this Article is bad in law and cannot be enforced.

According to Explanation II of Article 25, "the reference to Hindus shall be construed as including a reference to persons professing the Sikh, Jain or Buddhist religion". These religions though very much close and akin to Hinduism, having been originated from it, even then, for statistical and census purposes, are classified as separate religions. Truly speaking, Hindu religion is a conglomeration of different sects and religious denominations whose mode and manner of worship, ways of living and of thinking and, even food habits differ. They are variously called as Vaishnavites, Lingayats, Shaivites, Shaktas, Advaitavadis, Arya Samajists, Brahmo Samajists etc. and again these sects are sub-divided into various sub-sects. Now, all these sects and sub-sects want to establish their separate entity and identity. Extension of the protection of Article 30 to the Ramkrishna Mission by the Calcutta High Court was reversed by the three-judge Bench of the Supreme Court consisting of Justices Kuldip Singh, N. Venkatachala and S. Saghir Ahmad on July 2, 1995. This Bench, however, held that persons belonging to or owing their allegiance to Ramakrishna Mission or Ramakrishna Math belong to a religious denomination within Hindu religion or a section thereof as would entitle them to claim the fundamental rights conferred on either of them under Article 26 of the Constitution of India.[85]

Earlier, in *Acharya Jagdishwaranand Avadhuta etc.* vs. *Commissioner of Police, Calcutta & Anr.,* (1984) 1 SCR 447, Ranganath Misra, J. (as he then was) speaking for a three-Judge Bench of the Supreme Court has held that *Anand Margis* being a collection of individuals who have a system of beliefs with regard to their conducive spiritual well-being, a common organization and a definitive name, would be a religious denomination within the Hindu religion, in as much that satisfy the tests laid down by the Constitution Bench of the Supreme Court in that regard in the *Commissioner, Hindu Religious Endowments, Madras* vs. *Sri Lakshmindra Thirtha Swamiar of Sri Shirur Mutt,* (1954) SCR 1005.

In view of the said pronouncements of the Supreme Court, persons who claim to belong to religious denomination envisaged under Article 26 of the Constitution can succeed in such claim only when they fulfil or satisfy the tests laid down therein, to wit,

(i) a collection of individuals who have a system of beliefs with regard to their conducive spiritual well-being;

(ii) a common organization; and
(iii) a definite name.

These judgements have virtually opened a pandora's box for the society and the Government. Now, that the Apex Court of the land has accepted the plea of the followers of Anand Margi and Ramakrishna Mission that they have a system of beliefs with regard to their conducive spiritual well-being, and therefore enjoy the status of religious denominations, though within the Hindu religion, only future will tell whether their claim for the status of a minority religion would ever be conceded. There is a belief in certain quarters that other Hindu sects and sub-sects may be forced to seek minority status for their own security although such a development may be sad and shocking. And if each of these sects is going to have the right to establish and administer its own educational institutions, there will be more educational institutions run by the minorities than by the State or the majority community.

By getting involved with religion, the State actually creates religious identities. The courts have constantly put themselves in the awkward position of defining which groups belong to which religion.[86] If a particular sect, thus far treated as Hindus, is going to be given the minority status, it would be difficult to deny the same to others, argues S. Sahay.[87]

In a pluralistic society like India, there ought to be no dispute over the fact that a wide range of minority institutions should flourish and be cherished. The minorities are as much the citizen of India as the majority and the approach has been to ensure that nothing should be done as might deprive the minorities of a sense of belonging, of a feeling of security, of a consciousness of equality and of the awareness that the conservation of their religion, culture, language and script as also the protection of their educational institutions is a fundamental right enshrined in the Constitution.

Justice H.R. Khanna in *St. Xavier's College, Ahmedabad* vs. *State of Gujarat*, 1974(1) SCC 717 gave reasons why minority interests are so zealously protected in every society, especially in India:

> The safeguard of the interest of the minorities amongst section of the population is as important as the protection of the interest among individuals or persons who are below the age of majority or are otherwise suffering from some kind of infirmity. The Constitution and the laws made by civilised nations, therefore, generally contain provisions for the protection of those interests. It can, indeed, be said to be an index of the level of civilization and catholicity of a nation as to how far their minorities feel secure and are not subject to any discrimination or suppression.

The State has constitutional obligations to ensure that the rights of minorities to freely create and administer their institutions are protected. Articles 25, 26 and 27 provide sufficient safeguards for minorities to establish and maintain institutions for religious and charitable purposes. But freedom of religion is a highly restricted fundamental right in our scheme of civil liberties. It is not only "subject to public order, morality and health", but also all other fundamental rights. Thus, the right to religion is subservient to other fundamental rights. A question may be raised whether religion can be a criterion for making only one Article, i.e. Article 30, absolute. Can just one Fundamental Right be 'absolute'? Are Fundamental Rights prioritised? As warned by Anirban Kashyap:

> Will it not be a very bad day for India when people professing different faiths will vie with each other for their pound of flesh, will organize and regroup themselves on religious basis for enjoying the constitutional rights being enjoyed by other religious groups and sub-groups? It is no doubt a portrayal of a grim future but is not this sign already visible in the horizon? If the seed of dividing and sub-dividing the people on religious basis is already there, whose fault is it if it develops into a big poisonous tree with its roots firmly entrenched in the soil? Is it not proper to look at things as they are and then find out what can be done to stem the rot?[88]

According to Article 30, the religious minority has the right to establish and administer educational institutions of their choice for teaching their religion and the State will have to give grants-in-aid for the running of those institutions so that the teaching of religion can go on unhampered in those institutions. Educational institutions are to be run on non-communal line to promote national unity and integrity. Minorities based on language may ask for safeguards, so that, the educational institutions can be run by them for those speaking the particular language. But why extend this facility to minorities based on religion? What religion has got to do with imparting of education? But if people of different faiths are granted right to establish and administer educational institutions of their choice and that too for teaching religion at State cost, it will promote communalism, narrow sectarian outlook and disunity, as warned by members like Damodar Swarup Seth (a Congress Socialist) in the Constituent Assembly way back in 1948. And the result is very much manifest today in our body polity. Now, there is a mad race to anyhow come under the protective umbrella of this constitutional provision. Once the right guaranteed under this Article is secured, the institution becomes an entity by itself and can charter its own course in the cause of religion. It is an 'absolute' Fundamental Right. Absolute power corrupts absolutely; hence checks and safeguards need to be provided especially when the likely victims of this absolute power are going to be the most vulnerable sections of the population.

Alladi Krishnaswamy Ayyar and Rajkumari Amrit Kaur tried in vain in the Advisory Committee meeting to get this clause dropped. B.N. Rau questioned the prudence for making this provision a justiciable right. Jaya Prakash Narayan pleaded for modification of this article for secularisation of education for the growth of national outlook and unity. Damodar Swarup Seth and Prof. K.T. Shah made a valiant effort in the Constituent Assembly to alter the course of this article. But none could succeed. Again, demands have been raised to suitably amend the provision of the Constitution which not only discriminates between religious groups but also divides the people on religious basis for obtaining certain extra rights and benefits. Conferring such constitutional guarantee on religious basis breeds a sense of disunity, discord and exclusiveness and fosters communalism and sectarianism. It makes people more conscious about their religious grouping and rights, contrary to democratic rights and privileges obtainable in a democracy. Though enough precaution has been taken to dilute the religious character of this guarantee in including a religious right under heading "Cultural and Educational Rights" under which Articles 29 and 30 have been placed, its effect is very much felt in every nook and corner of the society.

The management of Hindu educational institutions have criticised the 'step-motherly' treatment being meted out to non-minority groups in the sphere of education and sought restoration of the rights of these managements to administer their institutions without intervention from the Government.[89] "It is imperative then," argues Hilda Raja, "to make the rights guaranteed by Article 30 an affirmative one and prevent the danger of it becoming a tool of exploitation—this calls for reasonable checks and the curbing of the 'Absoluteness' theory of Article 30."[90] Educational institutions "should be centres of secular and modern education, not religious institutions", asserts Faizan Mustafa, Vice-Chancellor, National Law University, Orissa.[91] It perhaps calls for a national debate whether such a provision in the Constitution is compatible with the secular character of our Constitution and society.

Notes and References

1. Rao, B. Shiva, *The Framing of India's Constitution*, Vol. II, 1967, New Delhi, The Indian Institute of Public Administration, pp. 65-66.
2. *Ibid.*, p. 125.
3. *Ibid.*, p. 76.
4. *Ibid.*, p. 82.
5. *Ibid.*, p. 202.
6. *Ibid.*, pp. 206-207.

7. *Ibid.*, p. 209.
8. *Ibid.*, pp. 280-282.
9. *CAD*, Vol. III, dated 29-4-47, p. 443.
10. *Ibid.*, dated 1-5-47, p. 503.
11. *Ibid.*
12. *Ibid.*, p. 504.
13. *Ibid.*, p. 505.
14. *Ibid.*, p. 506.
15. *Ibid.*, p. 505.
16. *Ibid.*, p. 507.
17. *Ibid.*, pp. 507-8.
18. *Ibid.*, p. 509.
19. Rao, B. Shiva, Vol. III, *op. cit.*, p. 11.
20. *Ibid.*, p. 200.
21. *Ibid.*, p. 215.
22. *Ibid.*, pp. 332, 335, 410.
23. *Ibid.*, pp. 525-526.
24. Rao, Vol. IV, *op. cit.*, pp. 45-46.
25. *CAD*, Vol. VII, dated 8-12-48, pp. 899-900.
26. *Ibid.*, p. 900.
27. *Ibid.*, p. 899.
28. *Ibid.*, p. 925.
29. *Ibid.*, pp. 905-06.
30. Kashyap, Anirban, *Disintegration and Constitution*, 1990, Lancers Books, New Delhi, p. 177.
31. Ramchandran, V.G., *Fundamental Rights and Constitutional Remedies*, Volume II, Second edition, p. 400.
32. *Ibid.*, p. 407.
33. *Ibid.*, p. 410.
34. *Ibid.*, p. 411.
35. *Ibid.*, p. 412.
36. *Kerala Education Bill, A. 1958 SC 956; Rev. Father* vs. *State of Bihar*, A 1969 SC 465.
37. *D.A.V. College* vs. *State of Punjab*, (1) A 1971 SC 1731.
38. *Mittal* vs. *Union of India*, A. 1983 SC 1 (paras 138, 143).
39. *Azeez* vs. *Union of India*, A 1968 SC 662 (670).
40. *D.A.V. College* vs. *State of Punjab*, (II) A 1971 SC 1737.
41. *Kerala Education Bill*, A. 1958 SC 956; *Rev. Father* vs. *State of Bihar*, A 1969 SC 465.
42. Basu, D.D., *Shorter Constitution of India*, tenth edition, 1988, Prentice Hall of India Private Limited, New Delhi, p. 213.
42. *Ibid.*, pp. 215-216.
43. *T.M. Pai Foundation* v. *State of Karnataka*, 2002 (8) SCC 481.
P.A. Inamdar v. *State of Maharashtra*, (2005) 6 SCC 537.
44. *Basu, op. cit.*, pp. 213-215.
45. *Ibid.*, pp. 215-216.
46. *The Hindu*, January 7, 2006, p. 1.

47. *education.mapsofindia.com/universities/national commission for minority educational institutions.*
48. *The Times of India*, February 9, 2010, p. 14.
49. *The Telegraph*, March 25, 2010, p. 7.
50. *Ibid.*, April 8, 2010, p. 5.
51. *The Indian Express*, July 7, 2010, p. 1.
52. *http://ncmei.gov.in/writereaddata/filelinks/c296efcb_Guidelines.pdf*
53. *The Statesman*, January 24, 2012, p. 1.
54. *http://ncmei.gov.in/writereaddata/filelinks/c296efcb_Guidelines.pdf*
55. *N. Ammad* vs. *Emjay High School*, (1998) 6 SCC 674.
56. AIR 1978 S.C. 851.
57. *State of Kerala* vs. *Mother Provincial,* AIR 1970 SC 2079.
58. *The Telegraph*, October 17, 2011, p. 4.
59. *N. Ammad* vs. *Emjay High School,* (1998) 6 SCC 674.
60. *Azeez* v. *Union of India A. 1968 SC 662.*
61. Ramchandran, *op. cit.*, p. 408.
62. Syed, Shahabuddin, "AMU seems to have developed a siege mentality", *The Times of India*, May 13, 1988, p. 3.
63. Vyas, Neena, "Communalist lobby targets AMU admission", *The Statesman*, March 2, 1988, p. 1. Hamid, Saiyid, "The Court and the Community", *The Times of India*, February 29, 1988, p. 6.
    Haider, Syed Najaf, "AMU Affairs", Letters to the editor, *The Times of India*, March 23, 1988, p. 6.
64. Editorial entitled "Religious reservation and AMU", *The Hindu,* January 9, 2006, p. 6.
65. *The Telegraph*, January 6, 2006, p. 1.
66. *The Hindu*, April 27, 2006, p. 1.
67. Rahman, A. in the Foreword to *Aligarh and Jamia Fight for National Education System* by S.M. Tonki, 1983 People's Publishing House, New Delhi.
68. *The Hindu*, July 14, 2010, p. 22.
69. *Ibid.*, July 11, 2010, p. 4.
70. *Ibid.*, June 16, 2010, p. 7.
71. *The Indian Express*, May 10, 2013, p. 1.
72. *The Sunday Times of India*, February 23, 2014, p. 5.
73. *The Telegraph*, April, 29, 2010, p. 4.
74. *The Hindu*, February 23, 2011, p. 1.
75. *The Telegraph*, March 17, 2011, p. 6.
76. *The Hindu*, April 19, 2011, p. 9.
77. *http://ncmei.gov.in/writereaddata/filelinks/cbb33e58_MSC-2013.pdf*
78. *State of Bombay* vs. *Education Society,* (1955) 1 SCR 568.
79. *State of Bombay* vs *Bombay Education Society,* AIR 1954 SC 561.
80. *Kerala Education Bill,* 1957: AIR 1958 SC 956.
81. *St. Xavier's College, Ahmedabad* vs. *State of Gujarat,* 1974(1) SCC 717.
82. *P.A. Inamdar* vs. *State of Maharashtra*, (2005) 6 SCC 537 (para 140).
83. *The Times of India*, April 5, 2014, p. 1.
84. Ramchandran, *op. cit.*, p. 408.

85. *Brahmachari Sidheswar Shai* vs. *State of West Benal,* (1995) 4 SCC 646; AIR 1995 SC 2089.
86. Mehta. Pratap Bhanu, "Minority institutions and the state", *The Hindu*, August 10, 2002, p. 10.
87. Sahaya, S. *The Statesman*, May 15, 1986.
88. Kashyap, Anirban, *Disintegration and Constitution, op. cit.*, p. 192.
89. *The Hindu*, August 6, 1995, p. 3.
90. Raja, Hilda, "Minority institutions", *The Hindu*, August 27, 2002, p. 14.
91. Mustafa, Faizan, "Religious policing-I", *The Statesman*, June 12, 2009, p. 6.

4
Propagation of Religion and Conversion

Clause (1) of Article VI of the Note and Draft Articles on Fundamental Rights submitted by K.M. Munshi to the Fundamental Rights Sub-Committee on March 17, 1947 read as follows:

> All citizens are equally entitled to freedom of conscience and to the right freely to profess and practise religion in a manner compatible with public order, morality or health:
> Provided that the economic, financial or political activities associated with religious worship shall not be deemed to be included in the right to profess or practice religion.[1]

Sardar Harnam Singh's Draft on Fundamental Rights submitted on March 18, 1947 quoted the Sapru Conciliation Committee Report in which at page 10 it was stated that "in India there is freedom of religion and conscience" and at page 241 it was stated that "all communities shall be free to preach their religion so far as they do not violate the law or public order and morality, or offend the sentiment of other communities".[2]

Clause 14 of Section I of Article II of Dr. Ambedkar's Memorandum and Draft Articles on the Rights of States and Minorities submitted on March 24, 1947 to the Fundamental Rights Sub-Committee stipulated:

> The State shall guarantee to every Indian citizen liberty of conscience and the free exercise of his religion including the right to profess, to preach and to convert within limits compatible with public order and mortality.[3]

The Fundamental Rights Sub-Committee in its meeting held on March 26, 1947 decided to adopt Article VI (1) of Munshi's draft in the following form:

> All persons are equally entitled to freedom of conscience and the right feely to profess and practise religion in a manner compatible with public order, mortality or health. The right to profess and practise religion shall not include economic, financial or political activities associated with religious worship.

Rajkumari Amrit Kaur wanted it to be recorded that the clause is defective inasmuch as it might invalidate legislation against anti-social customs which have the sanction of religion.

Sardar Harnam Singh raised the question of the right of Sikhs to wear and carry *kirpans.* It was decided to provide in sub-clause (1) of Article VI, an explanation to the effect that the practice of religion includes in the case of Sikhs the right to wear and carry *kirpans*. It was also decided that it would be provided in the clause dealing with the right to assemble peaceably and without arms that this does not prohibit the Sikhs from wearing and carrying *kirpans.*[4]

This clause as revised appeared as follows:

> All persons are equally entitled to freedom of conscience and the right freely to profess and practise religion in a manner compatible with public order, morality or health.
> *Explanation I*—The wearing and carrying of *kirpans* shall be deemed to be included in the practice of Sikh religion.
> *Explanation II*—The right to profess and practise religion shall not include economic, financial, political or other secular activities associated with religious worship.[5]

This clause was amended on March 29, 1947 so as to include at the end the following words "and with the other rights guaranteed by this Constitution".[6]

The Draft report of the Sub-Committee as prepared on April 3, 1947 contained the following as clause 16:

> All persons are equally entitled to freedom of conscience and the right freely to profess and practise religion subject to public order, morality or health and to the other provisions of this chapter.
> *Explanation I*—The wearing and carrying of *kirpans* shall be deemed to be included in the practice of Sikh religion.
> *Explanation II*—The right to profess and practise religion shall not include any economic, financial, political or other secular activities that may be associated with religious worship.
> *Explanation III*—No person shall refuse the performance of civil obligation or duties on the ground that his religion so requires.[7]

Rajkumari Amrit Kaur in a letter dated March 31, 1947 to B.N. Rau, the Constitutional Adviser, informed that

> We still feel considerable hesitation in accepting clause 16 as worded, even with explanation II. As we are all aware there are several customs practiced in the name of religion, e.g. *pardah*, child marriage, polygamy, unequal laws of inheritance, prevention of inter-caste marriages, dedication of girls to temples. We are naturally anxious

> that no clause in any fundamental right shall make impossible future legislation for the purpose of wiping out these evils. As worded, clause 16 may even contradict or conflict with the provision abolishing the practice of untouchability in clause 6.
> Indeed we have a further fear that validity of existing laws such as the Sarda Act, and the Widow Remarriage Act may even be questioned.

In the light of the above objections we would like to amend the said clause as follows:

> Freedom of conscience, freedom of religious worship and the free profession of religion subject to public order, morality or health and to the other provisions of this chapter are guaranteed to every citizen. In other words, we would like "freedom of religious worship" to replace "free practice of religion".[8]

B.N. Rau's notes dated April 8, 1947 on the Draft Report circulated for the benefit of the Members stated that clause 16 was adapted from the Irish Constitution, section 44(2)1. Explanation I was based on the recommendations of the All Parties Conference, 1928. Explanation III was adapted from the Yugoslavian Constitution, Article 12, paragraph 2, but omitting reference to military obligations.[9]

Alladi Krishnaswami Ayyar's comments dated April 14, 1947 on clause 16 of the Draft Report were:

> On further consideration and with due regard to the innumerable acts from the beginning of Anglo-Indian history bearing upon social rights and obligations which are inter-mixed with Hindu religion and the danger of such legislation being upset in the peculiar conditions of this country by force of this clause I am for some clause being inserted on the lines suggested by the lady members of the committee. To meet the point an explanation or proviso to the following effect may be added: "The right to profess and practise religion shall not preclude the legislature from enacting laws for the social betterment of the people."[10]

The Fundamental Rights Sub-Committee meeting on April 14, 1947 decided to redraft Clause 16 as follows:

> All persons are equally entitled to freedom of conscience, to freedom of religious worship and to freedom to profess religion subject to public order, morality or health and to the other provisions of this chapter.

> *Explanation I*—The wearing and carrying of *kirpans* shall be deemed to be included in the profession of the Sikh religion.
> *Explanation II*—The above rights shall not include any economic, financial, political or other secular activities that may be associated with religious worship.
> *Explanation III*—No change.[11]

The Fundamental Rights Sub-Committee in its report to the Advisory Committee on April 16, 1947 included this provision in clause 16 as follows:

> All persons are equally entitled to freedom of conscience, to freedom of religious worship and to freedom to profess religion subject to public order, morality or health and to the other provisions of this chapter.
> *Explanation I*— The wearing and carrying of *kirpans* shall be deemed to be included in the profession of the Sikh religion.
> *Explanation II*—The above rights shall not include any economic, financial, political or other secular activities that may be associated with religious worship.
> *Explanation III*—No person shall refuse the performance of civil obligations or duties on the ground that his religion so requires.[12]

In his lengthy minute of dissent to this report K.M. Panikkar noted, amongst others:

> In Article 16, Explanation III provides that "No person shall refuse the performance of civil obligations or duties on the ground that his religion so requires". To call this a fundamental right is to my mind to strain the plain meaning of words. In a country like India where *Sanyasa* is a part of the accepted tradition of life and is considered a fundamental element of religion in many sects, this provision is both impracticable and unwise. Where religion provides that a *Sannyasi* shall have no attachment to the world, to ask that he shall perform civil duties is in fact to ask him to give up his religion. In the case of certain sects of Jains the severance from civil life is so complete that their *Sadhus* refuse to give evidence in courts of law, and even to use the ordinary machinery of posts, telegraphs and railways. To compel them to perform civil obligations is to ask for disobedience on large scale on the basis of unalterable moral convictions. However much, we may consider such doctrines unsocial we have to face existing facts and any attempt to change the doctrine of renunciation of worldly attachment will not only be contrary to what is accepted by large sections of the community as a higher moral law, but an invitation to resistance at all costs by the more orthodox sections of the people as

> being a challenge to their conscience. I would also venture to add that to seek to bring in religious reforms by back door cannot be considered as being within the legitimate sphere of the declaration of fundamental rights.[13]

K.T. Shah in his minute of dissent on Explanation III of Article 16 stated that

> If a civil obligation is imposed to kill rats as plague carriers, or commit any similar *Himsa* for similar reasons, a conscientious Jain would refuse to shoulder such an obligation, or perform such a duty. The right of the genuine conscientious objector, in such cases, should, I think, be safeguarded.[14]

It may be recalled that only on April 3, 1947 Explanation III was appended to Clause 16 by the Fundamental Rights Sub-Committee.[15]

In the Minorities Sub-Committee meeting held on April 17, 1947, Ruthnaswamy pointed out that certain religions, such as Christianity and Islam, were essentially proselytizing religions, and provision should be made in Clause 16 to permit them to propagate their faith in accordance with their tenets.[16]

Accordingly, the Minorities Sub-Committee in its report dated April 19, 1947 to the Advisory Committee recommended that Clause 16 should be redrafted as follows:

> All persons are equally entitled to freedom of conscience and the right freely to profess, practise and propagate religion subject to public order, morality or health and to the other provisions of the chapter; and that in Explanation II for the words "religious worship", "religious practice" should be substituted.[17]

The Advisory Committee met on April 21 and 22, 1947 to discuss the recommendations of the Fundamental Rights Sub-Committee and the Minorities Sub-Committee. Before the committee met, Rajkumari Amrit Kaur intimated her opposition to the changes made in Clause 16 by the Minorities Sub-Committee. This is what she stated:

> I beg to submit my emphatic opposition to the revision by the Minorities Committee of clause 16 of the report of the Fundamental Rights Committee. The matter was thoroughly discussed in the latter committee and the words "free practice of religion" were deliberately omitted. It was felt that they would not only be a bar to future social legislation, but would even invalidate past legislation such as the Widow Remarriage Act, the Sarda Act or even the law abolishing *sati*. Everyone is aware how many evil practices, which one would

> like to abolish, are carried on in the name of religion, e.g. *pardah*, polygamy, caste disabilities, animal sacrifice, dedication of girls to temples, to mention a few.
>
> The propagation is amply assured in clause 10 dealing with freedom of speech and expression.
>
> Since conversion by force or undue influence only is to be banned, it follows that conversion of an adult to any religion by reason of conviction will be permissible.
>
> Freedom of religious worship, freedom of conscience and free profession of religion should really give to the individual; and community all he or it needs.
>
> The clause, as revised, is also going to make it extremely difficult for the State to ban religious meetings or professions that may be adjudged to lead to communal strife or public disorder. Such bans may be defied on the plea that they are an encroachment on fundamental rights and endless litigation may ensue. I am informed that the right to religious processions has in fact been the subject of litigation in courts right up to the Privy Council.
>
> To make the "free practice of religion" a justiciable right is, I submit, an error and will defeat not only social progress but will keep alive communal strife.[18]

In the meetings of the Advisory Committee on April 21-22, 1947, clause 16, as revised by the Minorities Sub-Committee, was considered by the members. Jagjivan Ram proposed for the retention of the original clause and Rajkumari Amrit Kaur supported him. There was considerable debate whether the words "religious worship" or the words "religious practice", as suggested by the Minorities Sub-Committee, are to be retained in Explanation II. The Chairman put the matter to vote and the decision to insert the words "religious practice" in Explanation II was taken by a majority of 2 votes.

C. Rajagopalachari then pointed out that having accepted the enlargement of practice of worship, social reforms in the particular community and conflicts and mutual difficulties would have to be provided in a comprehensive clause. The Chairman then suggested that Messers C. Rajagopalachari and Dr. Shyama Prasad Mookherjee should submit a draft proviso to the main clause permitting social legislation which may affect religious practice.

The word 'propagate' also raised some controversy. Munshi was against it as the word might be brought to cover even forced conversion. Alladi Krishnaswamy Ayyar said that he personally did not recognize the right of propagation. Even in the American continent such practices were not there. The word "propagate" was, however, retained by a majority of votes. On a protest by K.T. Shah and K.M. Panikkar, Explanation III was omitted with the concurrence of the Members.[19]

Clause 16, as settled by the Advisory Committee,[20] was incorporated as clause 13 of the report of the Advisory Committee to the President of the Constituent Assembly on April 23, 1947:

> All persons are equally entitled to freedom of conscience and the right freely to profess, practise and propagate religion subject to public order, morality or health and to the other provisions of the chapter.
> *Explanation I*—The wearing and carrying of *kirpans* shall be deemed to be included in the profession of the Sikh religion.
> *Explanation II*—The above rights shall not include any economic, financial, political or other secular activities that may be associated with religious worship.
> *Explanation III*—The freedom of religious practice guaranteed in this clause shall not debar the State from enacting laws for the purpose of social welfare and reform.[21]

Clause 13 was discussed by the Constituent Assembly on May 1, 1947 and was adopted the same day. There were only two speakers K.M. Munshi and H.J. Khandekar. Munshi moved an amendment for adding "and for throwing open Hindu religious institutions of a public character to any class or section of Hindus" to the last part of Explanation III. Khandekar wanted to know the definition of 'religious institutions of a public character', but the same was not furnished. The amendment of Munshi was accepted by Sardar Patel who congratulated "the House on agreeing to pass this very controversial matter which has taken several days in the Committees and gone through several Committees. There might be differences of opinion, but on the whole we have tried our best to accommodate all sections of the people."[22]

II

The Draft Constitution prepared by the Constitutional Adviser in October 1947 for the benefit of the Drafting Committee incorporated the above decision of the Constituent Assembly in Clause 20 which read as follows:

> 20(1) Subject to public order, morality and health and to the other provisions of this Part, all persons are equally entitled to freedom of conscience and the right freely to profess, practise and propagate religion.
> *Explanation I*: The wearing and carrying of *kirpans* shall be deemed to be included in the profession of the Sikh religion.
> *Explanation II*: The rights conferred by this sub-section shall not include any economic, financial, political or other secular activities

> which may be associated with religious practice.
> (2) Nothing in this section shall preclude the State from making laws for social welfare and reform and for throwing open Hindu religious institutions of a public character to any class or section of Hindus.[23]

The Drafting Committee in its meeting on November 1, 1947[24], November 3, 1947[25] and January 29, 1948[26] considered and revised this clause and included it as Article 19 in the Draft Constitution which was submitted to the President of the Constituent Assembly on February 21, 1948, and published in the Gazette on February 26, eliciting comments, etc. It read as follows:

> 19(1) Subject to public order, morality and health and to the other provisions of this Part, all persons are equally entitled to freedom of conscience and the right freely to profess, practise and propagate religion.
> *Explanation I.* The wearing and carrying of *kirpans* shall be deemed to be included in the profession of the Sikh religion.
> (2) Nothing in this article shall affect the operation of any existing law or preclude the State from making any law—
> (a) regulating or restricting any economic, financial, political or other secular activity which may be associated with religious practice; and
> (b) for social welfare and reform or for throwing open Hindu religious institutions of a public character to any class or section of Hindus.[27]

R.R. Diwakar and S.V. Krishnamoorthy Rao commented that in clause (1) of Article 19 after the words "freely to profess" the word "and" be inserted and for the words "and propagate religion" the words "what one believes to be his religion" be substituted. On this suggestion, the Constitutional Adviser noted that this amendment sought to omit the reference to the propagation of religion from clause (1) of Article 19. This involved a question of policy. The expression "what one believes to be his religion" used in the amendment appeared to draw an unnecessary distinction between a person's religion and what he believed to be his religion.

B. Pattabhi Sitaramayya commented that in clause (2) (b) of Article 19 for the words "any class or section" the words "all classes and sections" be substituted. To this suggestion the Constitutional Adviser noted that the expression "any class or section of Hindus" used in sub-clause (b) of clause (2) of Article 19 would not prevent the making of any law for throwing open Hindu religious institutions of a public character to *all classes and sections* of Hindus. There was, however, no objection to this amendment: discrimination on the ground of caste etc. was already forbidden by Article 9.

Tejamul Husain suggested that in clause (1) of article 19 the words "and the right freely to profess, practise and propagate religion" be deleted. Or alternatively, in clause (1) of Article 19, for the words "practise and propagate religion" the words "and practise religion privately" be substituted. On this suggestion the Constitutional Adviser's comments were that this amendment which sought to omit the reference to the right of freely professing, practising and propagating religion, or in the alternative to omit the reference to the propagation of religion and to restrict the right to profess and practise religion to the professing and practising religion privately, involved a question of policy.

Tejamul Husain proposed that the Explanation to clause (1) of Article 19 be deleted and the following be inserted in its place: "No person shall have any visible sign or mark or name, and no person shall wear any dress whereby his religion may be recognized". The Constitutional Adviser noted that this involved a question of policy.

Tejamul Husain suggested that in sub-clause (b) of clause (2) of Article 19, the words "of Hindus" be deleted. The Constitutional Adviser commented that if this amendment was given effect to, then sub-clause (b) of clause (2) of Article 19 would not prevent the making of any law throwing open Hindu religious institutions of a public character to members of any other religious community, such as Muslims or Christians.

The Editor of the Indian Law Review and some other members of the Calcutta Bar had suggested that in sub-clause (b) of clause (2) of Article 19 (a) the word "Hindu" should be omitted and (b) for the words "of Hindus" the words "of persons professing that religion" should be substituted. To this suggestions, the Constitutional Adviser noted that clause (2) of Article 19 was based on the decision of the Advisory Committee on Fundamental Rights as adopted by the Constituent Assembly.

Asthika Sabha, Nungambakkam (Madras) had sent a representation for the amendment of Article 19(2) on the ground that it would seriously interfere with the religious rights of the citizens. Several similar representations were received from the South. The Constitutional Adviser commented that these criticisms expressed the orthodox point of view which was fully considered by the sub-committees of the Constituent Assembly. Article 19(2) was essential in the interests of social reform.

The Drafting Committee decided in October 1948 that for the word "preclude" in clause (2) of Article 19 the word "prevent" be substituted.[28]

Discussion on this article took place in the Constituent Assembly on December 3 and 6, 1948. There were objections mainly for the word 'propagate' in this article. Tejamul Husain, Lok Nath Mishra and Rohini Kumar Choudhury spoke against this provision in this article while Mohammad Ismail Sahib, Lakshmi Kanta Maitra, L. Krishnaswami Bharathi, K. Santhanam, T.T.

Krishnamachari and K.M. Munshi pleaded for retention of this provision in the article.

Tejamul Husain moved an amendment for substituting the words 'practise and propagate religion' by the words 'and practise religion privately'. His contention was: "religion is a private affair between oneself and his Creator. It has nothing to do with others. My religion is my own belief, and your religion, Sir, is your own belief. Why should you interfere with my religion and why should I interfere with your religion? Religion is only a means for the attainment of one's salvation. Supposing I honestly believe that I will attain salvation according to my way of thinking, and according to my religion, and you, Sir, honestly believe that you will attain salvation according to your way, then why should I ask you to attain salvation in my way, or why should you ask me to attain salvation according to your way? If you accept this proposition, then, why propagate religion? As I said, religion is between oneself and his God. Then, honestly profess religion and practise it at home. Do not demonstrate it for the sake of propagating. Do not show to the people that this is your religion for the sake of showing. If you start propagating religion in this country, you will become a nuisance to others. So far, it has become a nuisance.

"I submit, Sir, that this is a secular State, and a secular State should not have anything to do with religion. So, I would request you to leave me alone, to practise and profess religion privately".[29]

Lok Nath Misra vehemently opposed this clause specially the propagation part of it. He stated: "To my mind, if Article 13 of this Draft Constitution is a Charter for liberty, Article 19 is a Charter for Hindu enslavement. I do really feel that this is the most disgraceful Article, the blackest part of the Draft Constitution. I beg to submit that I have considered and studied all the constitutional precedents and have not found anywhere any mention of the word 'propaganda' as a Fundamental Right, relating to religion.

"Sir, we have declared the State to be a Secular State. For obvious and for good reasons we have so declared. Does it not mean that we have nothing to do with any religion? You know that propagation of religion brought India into this unfortunate State and India had to be divided into Pakistan and India. If Islam had not come to impose its will on this land, India would have been a perfectly secular State and a homogenous state. There would have been no question of Partition. Therefore, we have rightly tabooed religion. And now to say that as a fundamental right everybody has a right to propagate his religion is not right. Do we want to say that we want one religion other than Hinduism and that religion has not yet taken sufficient root in the soil of India and do we taboo all religions? Why do you make it a Secular State? The reason may be that religion is not necessary or it may be that religion is necessary but as India has many religions, Hinduism, Christianity, Islam and Sikhism, we cannot decide which one to accept. Therefore, let us have no religion. No. That cannot be. If you accept religion, you must accept Hinduism as it is practised by an overwhelming majority of the people of India.

"Sir, it has been repeated to our ears that ours is a secular State. I accepted this secularism in the sense that our State shall remain unconcerned with religion, and I thought that the secular State of partitioned India was the maximum of generosity of a Hindu-dominated territory for its non-Hindu population. I did not of course know what exactly this secularism meant and how far the State intends to cover the life and manners of our people. To my mind life cannot be compartmentalised and yet I reconciled myself to the new cry.

"Gradually, it seems to me that our 'secular State' is a slippery phrase, a device to by-pass the ancient culture of the land.

"The absurdity of this position is now manifest in Articles 19 to 22 of the Draft Constitution. Do we really believe that religion can be divorced from life or is it our belief that in the midst of many religions we cannot decide which one to accept? If religion is beyond the ken of our State, let us clearly say so and delete all references to rights relating to religion. If we find it necessary, let us be brave enough and say what it should be.

"But this unjust generosity of tabooing religion and yet making propagation of religion a fundamental right is somewhat uncanny and dangerous. Justice demands that the ancient faith and culture of the land should be given a fair deal, if not restored to its legitimate place after a thousand years of suppression.

"We have no quarrel with Christ or Mohammad or what they say and said. We have all respect for them. To my mind, Vedic culture excludes nothing. Every philosophy and culture has its place but now the cry of religion is a dangerous cry. It dominates, it divides and encamps people to warring ways. In the present context what can this word 'propagation' in Article 19 mean? It can only mean paving the way for the complete annihilation of Hindu culture, the Hindu way of life and manners. Islam has declared its hostility to Hindu thought. Christianity has worked out the policy of peaceful penetration by the back-door on the outskirts of our social life. This is because Hinduism did not accept barricades for its protection. Hinduism is just an integrated vision and a philosophy of life and cosmos, expressed in organised society to live that philosophy in peace and amity. But Hindu generosity has been misused and politics has over-run Hindu culture. To-day religion in India serves no higher purpose than collecting ignorance, poverty and ambition under a banner that flies for fanaticism. The aim is political, for in the modern world all is power-politics, and the inner man is lost in the dust. Let everybody live as he thinks best but let him not try to swell his number to demand the spoils of political warfare. Let us not raise the question of communal minorities any more. It is a device to swallow the majority in the long run. This is intolerable and unjust.

"Indeed in no constitution of the world right to propagate religion is a fundamental right and justiciable. The Irish Free State Constitution recognises the special position of the faith professed by the great majority of the citizens. We in India are shy of such recognition. U.S.S.R. gives freedom of religious worship and freedom of anti-religious propaganda. Our Constitution gives the right even to propagate religion, but does not give the right to any anti-religious propaganda.

"If people should propagate their religion, let them do so. Only I crave, let not the Constitution put it as a fundamental right and encourage it. Fundamental rights are inalienable and once they are admitted, it will create bad blood. I therefore say, let us say nothing about rights relating to religion. Religion will take care of itself. Drop the word 'propagate' in Article 19 at least. Civilisation is going headlong to the melting pot. Let us beware and try to survive."[30]

Rohini Kumar Chaudhury was not against propagation as such, but against vilification of a religion by another during propagation. He said: "I have no objection to the propagation of any religion. If anyone thinks that his religion is something ennobling and that it is his duty to ask others to follow that religion, he is welcome to do so. But what I would object to is that there is no provision in this Constitution to prevent the so-called propagandist of his religion from throwing mud at some other religion. For instance, Sir, in the past we remember how missionaries went round the country and described Sri Krishna in most abominable terms. They would bring up particular activities of Sri Krishna and say, "Look here, this is your Lord Krishna and this is his conduct". We also remember with great pain how they used to decry the worship of the idols and call them names. Sir, in the new Constitution we must make it perfectly clear that no such thing will be tolerated. It is not necessary in the course of propagating any particular religion to throw mud at other religions, to decry them and bring out their unsatisfactory features according to the particular supporters of a particular religion. There should be a provision in the law, in the Constitution itself that such conduct will be met with exemplary punishment."[31]

Earlier on November 9, 1948 at the time of discussion on motion for consideration of the Draft Constitution S.V. Krishnamurthi Rao had also pleaded for omission of the provision for freedom to propagate religion. "This right which has been claimed by some has been the bane of our political life in this country. Probably it might have been thought proper to include it in the old set-up of things. In a secular State, such a provision, especially with the guarantee for the free exercise of religion and freedom of thought, is out of place in our Constitution and I submit to this House that that provision should be omitted."[32]

None else raised any voice of dissent during discussion but from the manner the protagonists of the 'propagation' clause aired their views it appeared that there were strong resentments against opposition to this word 'propagate'. Mohammad Ismail Sahib, in course of discussion of an amendment of his, commented: "the question of professing, practising and propagating one's faith is a right which the human being had from the very beginning of time and that has been recognised as an inalienable right of every human being, not only in this land but the whole world over and I think that nothing should be done to affect that right of man as a human being. That part of the article as it stands is properly worded and it should stand as it is. That is my view.

"Another honourable Member spoke about the troubles that had arisen as a result of the propagation of religion. I would say that the troubles were not the result of the propagation of religion or the professing or practising of religion. They arose as a result of the misunderstanding of religion. My point of view, and I say that that is the correct point of view, is that if only people understand their respective religions aright and if they practise them aright in the proper manner there would be no trouble whatever; and because there was some trouble due to some cause it does not stand to reason that the fundamental right of a human being to practise and propagate his religion should be abrogated in anyway".[33]

Pandit Lakshmi Kanta Maitra argued in favour of retention of the word 'propagate' in the clause. He said, "It has been further argued that by conferring the additional right to propagate a particular faith or religion the door is opened for all manner of troubles and conflicts which would eventually paralyse the normal life of the State.... It has been objected to and it has been said that the right to propagate should be taken away. One honourable Member suggested that if we conceded the right, the bloody upheaval which this country has witnessed of late would again recur with full vehemence in the near future.... It has also been said. that the Christian community in its proselytising zeal has sometimes transgressed its limits and has done acts which can never be justified.... The Indian Christian Community happens to be the most inoffensive community in the whole of India.... This Indian Christian community, so far as I am aware, spend to the tune of nearly Rs. 2 crores every year for educational uplift, medical relief and for sanitation, public health and the rest of it. Look at the numerous educational institutions, dispensaries and hospitals they have been running so effectively and efficiently, catering to all classes and communities. If this vast amount of Rs. 2 crores were utilised by this Christian community for purposes of seeking converts, then the Indian Christian Community...would have gone up to 70 millions .... The Christian community in India has not done that proselytising work with that amount of zeal and frenzy with which some of our friends have associated it. I am anxious to remove that misconception. Sir, I feel that every single community in India should be given this right to propagate its own religion.... Propagation does not necessarily mean seeking converts by force or arms, by the sword, or by coercion. But, why should obstacles stand in the way if by exposition, illustration and persuasion you could convey your own religious faith to others? I do not see any harm in it. And I do feel that this would be the very essence of our fundamental right, the right to profess and practise any particular religion. Therefore this right should not be taken away, in my opinion. If in this country the different religious faiths would go on expounding their religious tenets and doctrines, then probably a good deal of misconception prevailing in the minds of the people about different religions would be removed, and probably a stage would be reached when by mutual understanding we could avoid in future all manner of conflicts that arise in the name of religion. From that point of view I am convinced that the word 'propagate' should be there and should not be deleted. In this connection I think I may remind the House that the whole matter was discussed in the Advisory Council (Committee?) and it was passed there".[34]

L. Krishnaswami Bharathi was also in favour of keeping this propagation clause in the Article. He wanted that "the word 'propagate' ought to be there. After all, it should not be understood that it is only for any sectarian religion. It is generally understood that the word 'propagate' is intended only for the Christian community. But I think it is absolutely necessary, in the present context of circumstances, that we must educate our people on religious tenets and doctrines. So far as my experience goes, the Christian community have not transgressed their limits of legitimate propagation of religious view, and on the whole they have done very well indeed. It is for other communities to emulate them and propagate their own religions as well.... The different communities may well carry on propaganda or propagate their religion and what it stands for. It is not to be understood that when one propagates his religion he should cry down other religion. It is not the spirit of any religion to cry down another religion. Therefore, it is absolutely necessary and essential.

"Again, it is not at all inconsistent with the secular nature of the State. After all, the State does not interfere with it. Religion will be there. It is a personal affair and the State as such does not side with one religion or another. It tolerates all religions. It is very necessary that we should show tolerance. That is the spirit of all religions. To say that some religious people should not do propaganda or propagate their views is to show intolerance on our part.

"Let me also, in this connection, remind the House that the matter was thoroughly discussed at all stages in the Minorities Committee, and they came to the conclusion that this great Christian community which is willing and ready to assimilate itself with the general community, which does not want reservation or other special privileges should be allowed to propagate its religion along with other religious communities in India. Therefore, in good grace, the majority community should allow this privilege for the minority communities and have it for themselves as well. I think I can speak on this point with a certain amount of assurance that the majority community is perfectly willing to allow this right. I am therefore strongly in favour of the retention of the word 'propagate' in this clause".[35]

K. Santhanam however found a difference between propagation and conversion. He said: "Some discussion has taken place on the word 'propagate'. After all, propagation is merely freedom of expression. I would like to point out that the word 'convert' is not there. Mass conversion was a part of activities of the Christian Missionaries in this country and great objection has been taken by the people to that. Those who drafted this Constitution have taken care to see that no unlimited right of conversion has been given. People have freedom of conscience and, if any man is converted voluntarily owing to freedom of conscience, then well and good. No restrictions can be placed against it. But if any attempt is made by one religious community or another to have mass conversions through undue influence either by money or by pressure or by other means, the State has every right to regulate such activity. Therefore, I submit to you that this article, as it is, is not so much an article ensuring freedom, but toleration—toleration for all, irrespective of the religious practice or profession. And this toleration is subject to public order, morality and health".[36]

T.T. Krishnamachari not only supported the retention of propagation clause but also pleaded for the right of conversion. He stated: "Objection has been taken to the inclusion of the word 'propagate' along with the words 'profess and practise' in the matter of religion. Sir, it does not mean that this right to propagate one's religion is given to any particular community or to people who follow any particular religion. It is perfectly open to the Hindus and the Arya Samajists to carry on their *Suddhi* propaganda, as it is open to the Christians, the Muslims, the Jains and the Buddhists and to every other religionist, so long as he does it subject to public order, morality and the other conditions that have to be observed in any civilized government. So, it is not a question of taking away anybody's rights. It is a question of conferring these rights on all the citizens and seeing that these rights are exercised in a manner which will not upset the economy of the country; which will not create disorder and which will not create undue conflict in the minds of the people. That, I feel, is the point that has to be stressed in regard to this particular article. Sir, I know as a person who has studied for about fourteen years in Christian institutions that no attempt had been made to convert me from my own faith and to practise Christianity. I am very well aware of the influences that Christianity has brought to bear upon our own ideals and our own outlook, and I am not prepared to say here that they should be prevented from propagating their religion. I would ask the House to look at the facts so far as the history of this type of conversion is concerned. It depends upon the way in which certain religionists and certain communities treat their less fortunate brethren. The fact that many people in this country have embraced Christianity is due partly to the status that it gave to them. Why should we forget that particular fact? An untouchable who became a Christian became an equal in every matter along with the high-caste Hindu, and if we remove the need to obtain that particular advantage that he might probably get— it is undoubtedly a very important advantage, apart from the fact that he has faith in the religion itself—well, the incentive for anybody to become a Christian will not probably exist. I have no doubt, Sir, we have come to a stage when it does not matter to what religion a man belongs, it does not matter to what sub-sect or community in a particular religion a man belongs, he will be equal in the eyes of law and in society and in regard to the exercise of all rights that are given to those who are more fortunately placed. So, I feel that any undue influence that might be brought to bear on people to change their religion or any other extraneous consideration for discarding their own faith in any particular religion and accepting another faith will no longer exist, and in the circumstances, I think it is only fair that we should take the *status quo* as it is in regard to religion and put it into our Fundamental Rights, giving the same right to every religionist, as I said before, to propagate his religion and to convert people, if he felt that it is a thing that he has to do and that is a thing for which he has been born and that is his duty towards his God and Community.

"Subject to the overriding considerations of the maintenance of the integrity of the State and the well-being of the people,—these conditions are satisfied by this article—I feel that if the followers of any religion want to substract from the concessions given herein in anyway, they are not only doing injustice to the possibility of integration of all communities into one nation in the future but also doing injustice to their own religion and to their own community".[37]

K.M. Munshi, a member of the Advisory Committee and of the Drafting Committee, gave reasons for incorporation of the word 'propagate' in this article and emphasised the need for its acceptance. He said: "I have only a few words to say with regard to the objections taken to the word 'propagate'. Many honourable Members have spoken before me placing the point of view that they need not be afraid of the word 'propagate' in this particular article. When we object to this word, we think in terms of the old regime. In the old regime, the Christian Missionaries, particularly those who were British were at an advantage. But since 1938, I know, in my part of Bombay, the influence which was derived from their political influence and power has disappeared…In the present set up that we are now creating under this Constitution, there is a secular State. There is no particular advantage to a member of one community over another; nor is there any political advantage by increasing one's fold. In those circumstances, the word 'propagate' cannot possibly have dangerous implications, which some of the Members think that it has.

"Moreover, I was a party from the very beginning to the compromise with the minorities which ultimately led to many of these clauses being inserted in the Constitution and I know it was on this word that the Indian Christian community laid the greatest emphasis, not because they wanted to convert people aggressively, because the word 'propagate' was a fundamental part of their tenet. Even if the word were not there, I am sure, under the freedom of speech which the Constitution guarantees it will be open to any religious community to persuade other people to join their faith. So long as religion is religion, conversion by free exercise of the conscience has to be recognised. The word 'propagate' in this clause is nothing very much out of the way as some people think, nor it is fraught with dangerous consequences.

"Speaking frankly, whatever its results we ought to respect the compromise. The Minorities Committee the year before the last-performed a great achievement by having a unanimous vote on almost every provision of its report.

"This unanimity created an atmosphere of harmony and confidence in the majority community. Therefore, the word 'propagate' should be maintained in this article in order that the compromise so laudably achieved by the Minority Committee should not be disturbed".[38]

There was no further discussion on this Article and the same was adopted on December 6, 1948. At the revision stage this Article was renumbered as Article 25.

III

While Dr. Ambedkar proposed the right to convert, it was M. Ruthnaswamy, a Roman Catholic leader and Vice-Chancellor of Annamalai University who first pointed out in the Minorities Sub-Committee meeting on April 19, 1947 about the desirability of the right to propagate religion as a fundamental right and it was accordingly suggested by the Minorities Sub-Committee. Jagjivan Ram and Rajkumari Amrit Kaur did not support the revised clause in the Advisory Committee meeting. K.M. Munshi was against it and Alladi Krishnaswamy Ayyar also did not like this clause, but it was retained by the Advisory Committee by a majority vote. R.R. Diwkar and S.V. Krishnamoorthy Rao as well as Tejamul Husain, a Shia Muslim leader from Bihar, suggested its deletion after the publication of the Draft Constitution. In the Constituent Assembly Tejamul Husain, Lok Nath Misra and Rohini Kumar Chaudhury pleaded in vain for the deletion of the 'propagation clause', though for different reasons. While Tejamul Hussian contended that it would be a nuisance to others, Rohini Kumar Chaudhury wanted that the vilification of

Gods, specially the Hindu Gods, should not be resorted to at the time of propagation. The most severe criticism was however put forth by Lok Nath Misra. While exposing the political angle, he wanted that "the cry of religion is a dangerous cry. It dominates, it divides and encamps people to 'warring ways... Hinduism did not accept barricades for its protection.... But. Hindu generosity has been misused and politics has overrun Hindu culture. Today religion in India serves no higher purpose than collecting ignorances, poverty and ambition under a banner that flies for fanaticism. The aim is political, for in the modern world all is power-politics and the inner-man is lost in the dust. Let everybody live as he thinks best, but let him not try to swell his number to demand the spoils of political warfare. Let us not raise the question of communal minorities anymore. It is a device to swallow the majority in the long-run. This is intolerable and unjust."

Mohammed Ismail Sahib, Pandit Lakshmi Kanta Maitra, L. Krishnaswami Bharathi, K. Santhanam, T.T. Krishnamachari and K.M. Munshi argued for the retention of this provision in the Constitution. Curiously enough, no Christian member spoke in the Constituent Assembly in support of this provision.

It may be recalled that on October 30, 1945 representatives of the Catholic Union of India and the All-India Council of Indian Christians formed a joint Committee with M. Ruthnaswami, Vice-Chancellor of the Annamalai University, as its Chairman. The Committee adopted a resolution suggesting that

> in the future Constitution of India the free profession, practice and propagation of religion should be guaranteed and that a change of religion should not involve any civil or political disability.[39]

The Committee also appointed a sub-committee "to formulate proposals for a future constitution to be placed before the Constituent Assembly".[40]

The Christians were quite clear in their mind as well as pronouncements that the "right to propagate religion" entitled them to (1) receive massive financial help from foreign sources; (2) maintain and multiply churches and missions; (3) train and mobilize an ever expanding army of missionaries, native and foreign; (4) enlarge the mission infrastructure of seminaries, social service institutions and mass media; and (5) convert an increasing number of Hindus to Christianity by every means including fraud and material inducements. They had been holding meetings and passing resolutions on all these points even before the Constituent Assembly was mentioned in the negotiations between the Congress leaders and the British Cabinet Mission.

The Hindu participants, on the other hand, did not grasp the full meaning of the "right to propagate religion". They did understand that the word "propagate" was only a substitute for the word "convert", and tried to hedge in the provision with various restrictions. But they did not realize or think it important that "propagation of religion" had employed and would employ a formidable organisational weapon forged almost entirely with the help of foreign money and controlled completely by foreign establishments including intelligence networks. Therefore, the points they raised in the course of the dialogue did not go to the heart of the matter.[41]

Pandit Lakshmi Kanta Maitra did not think that the Indian Christian community had taken up the proselytising work with that amount of zeal and frenzy with which this community was associated with. L. Krishnaswami Bharathi opined that the Christian community had not trangressed their limits of legitimate propagation of religious view. T.T. Krishnamachari's experience was that no attempt was ever made to convert him to Christianity even though he was a student in Christian Institutions. K.M. Munshi felt that the Christian Missionaries had already lost much of their clout after the change in administration of the country. All these Members were narrating from their personal experience. The Christian Missionaries, specially the Indian Christians, were not as bad as they were painted, they thought. That the position was otherwise was brought out by the Neogy Committee.

K.M. Munshi, a member of the Advisory Committee on Minorities, etc., and of the Drafting Committee pointed out that he was a party from the very beginning to the compromise with the minorities, which ultimately led to many of these clauses being inserted in the Constitution and that the Indian Christian community laid the greatest emphasis on this right to propagate, not because they wanted to convert people aggressively, but because the word 'propagate' was a fundamental part of their tenet. He asserted that whatever its results, the compromise had to be respected. L. Krishnaswami Bharathi was also very explicit when he reminded the House that this great Christian community which was willing and ready to assimilate itself with the general community, which did not want reservation or other special privileges should be allowed to propagate its religion along with other religious communities in India.

So, it was a deal between the Indian Christian community and the Advisory Committee on Minorities etc. Since the Indian Christians gave up their demand for reservation of seats for themselves, the Advisory Committee, it appears, was duty-bound to give them the right to propagate religion.

It is a fact that propagation does not mean forcible conversion. Pandit Maitra thought that "propagation does not necessarily mean seeking converts by force of arms, by the sword or by coercion." What he visualised might have been the ideal concept of propagation. Conversion by coercion or undue influence might not be the idea behind propagation. But, if taking advantage of this propagation clause some preachers propagate religion solely for the purpose of converting others by any means, would it be allowed or would certain restrictions be put on such activities? He did not touch on that issue and simply left it to the goodwill of the religious communities.

K. Santhanam admitted that mass conversion was a part of the activities of the Christian Missionaries in this country and great objection had been taken by the people to that and thought that if any attempt was made by one religious community or another to have mass conversions through undue influence either by money or by pressure or by other means, the State has every right to regulate such activity. He however did not elaborate how the State would regulate such activity. He did not state whether any Act would be enacted for this purpose or a provision was to be inserted in the Constitution itself. As it appears, he felt the necessity of regulating such activities by the State.

T.T. Krishnamachari envisaged a '*Ram Rajya*' on the promulgation of Fundamental Rights when it would not matter to what religion a man belonged, it would not matter to what sub-sect or community in a particular religion a man belonged, he would be equal in the eyes of law and in society and in regard to the exercise of all rights that are given to those who are more fortunately placed. So he felt that any undue influence that might be brought to bear on people to change their religion or any other extraneous consideration for discarding their own faith in any particular religion and accepting another faith would no longer exist. What a pious wish! He however visualised that integrity of the State might suffer due to conversion and thought that ample provision had been made in the Article against that eventuality. His warning that if this right was not given at the instance of one religious group, thereby meaning Hindus, they would be doing injustice to the possibility of integration of all communities into one nation in the future! Subsequent developments have proved that the integration of all communities had suffered due to this provision in the Constitution.

In the larger and broader canvas of life this attitude of the protagonists of 'propagation' clause might be correct but in our very limited objective, when the vision is blurred by communal passion, it has to be ensured that the privileges enshrined in the Constitution are not misused or do not lead to acrimonious situation. The fact remains that this particular provision in the Constitution has done more harm than good to the process of integration, unification and assimilation of different communities in this country. It has made the different communities aware of the necessity of protecting their folk from the preying eyes of other communities at any cost, and has, in the process, further embittered the relationship between different communities.

K.M. Munshi's assertion that in a secular State there would be no particular advantage to a member of one community over another nor there would be any political advantage by increasing one's fold does not appear to have withstood the test of time. One is prone to believe that Munshi would have modified his stand if he were alive today.

But one thing the Framers perhaps did not consider very seriously. This right was given not to the Christian community only but to all religionists. This right was to be enjoyed by all. There would not have been much objection if they merely confined their activities to propagation of religion only but this provision also conferred the right to convert people. It is true that the right to propagate one's religion means the right to communicate a person's beliefs to another person or to expose the tenets of that faith, but would *not* include the right to 'convert' another person to the former's faith,[42] because the latter person is "equally entitled to freedom of conscience"[43] which words precede the word 'propagate'. But it is not possible always to remember the niceties of the legal interpretations. Taking advantage of this provision some might start converting people. Some sort of safeguards against conversion should have been incorporated in the Constitution. It is worthwhile to find out why safeguards against conversion do not find any place in our Secular Constitution.

IV

Munshi's Note and Draft Articles on Fundamental Rights submitted on March 17, 1947 to the Sub-Committee on Fundamental Rights included the following two clauses in Article VI:

> (6) No person under the age of eighteen shall be free to change his religious persuasion without the permission of his parent or guardian.
>
> (7) Conversion from one religion to another brought about by coercion, undue influence or the offering of material inducement is prohibited and is punishable by the law of the Union.[44]

Ambedkar's Memorandum and Draft Articles on the Rights of States and Minorities, submitted on March 24, 1947, included the following clause in Article II-Section I:

> 15. No person shall be compelled to become a member of any religious association, submit to any religious instruction or perform any act of religion. Subject to the foregoing provision, parents and guardians shall be entitled to determine the religious education of children up to the age of sixteen years.[45]

The Fundamental Rights Sub-Committee in its meeting on March 27, 1947 decided to drop clause (6) of the Munshi's Draft Article.[46]

Draft Report of the Sub-Committee prepared and circulated on April 3, 1947 contained the following two clauses:

22. No person under the age of 18 shall be converted to any religion other than the one in which he was born or be initiated into any religious order involving a loss of civil status.
23. Conversion from one religion to another brought about by coercion or undue influence shall not be recognized by law and the exercise of such coercion or undue influence shall be an offence.[47]

The Constitutional Adviser in his note on the Draft report dated April 8, 1947 informed that Clauses 22 and 23 "are meant to stop certain practices which, it is feared, are becoming increasingly common".[48]

The Fundamental Rights Sub-Committee in its meeting on April 15, 1947 decided to substitute the words "made to join or profess" for the words "converted to" in Clause 22 and omit the words "or undue influence" in the third line of Clause 23. Ambedkar's proposal that the clause should end with the words "recognised by law" was not accepted by the Sub-Committee.[49]

In its report to the Advisory Committee on April 16, 1947, the Sub-Committee included the following two clauses:

21. No person under the age of 18 shall be made to join or profess any religion other than the one in which he was born or be initiated into any religious order involving a loss of civil status.
22. Conversion from one religion to another brought about by coercion or undue influence shall not be recognized by law and the exercise of such coercion shall be an offence.[50]

In the Sub-Committee on Minorities' meeting held on April 18, 1947, Ruthnaswsmy commented that the provisions of Clause 21 "will break up family life. A minor should be allowed to follow his parents in any change of religion or nationality which they may adopt".

Rajagopalachari questioned the necessity of the provision in Clause 22 when it was covered by the ordinary law of the land, e.g. the Indian Penal Code.[51]

The Sub-Committee of Minorities in its meeting held on April 19, 1947 recommended the redraft of clause 21 as follows:

> No person under the age of 18 shall be made to join or profess religion other than the one in which he was born, except when his parents themselves have been converted, and the child does not choose to adhere to his original faith;
> Nor shall such person be initiated into any religious order involving a loss of civil status.

(b) No conversion shall be recognized unless the change of faith is attested by a Magistrate after due enquiry[52] and communicated this decision to the Advisory Committee on April 19, 1947.[53]

Rajkumari Amrit Kaur in a note dated April 20, 1947 to the Advisory Committee pointed out that "since conversion by force or undue influence only is to be banned, it follows that conversion of an adult to any religion by reason of conviction will be permissible".[54]

The Advisory Committee met for two days on April 21 and 22, 1947. On a proposal by the Chairman of the Advisory Committee, Clause 21, as redrafted by the Minority Sub-Committee, was deleted. He was in favour of deletion of Clause 22 also because this was not a fundamental right. Frank Anthony, M. Ruthnaswamy and Shyama Prasad Mookherjee did not agree and this clause was retained but the last line was omitted.[55] This clause was accordingly redrafted as follows:

> Conversion from one religion to another brought about by coercion or undue influence shall not be recognised by law.[56]

This Clause figured as Clause 17 in the report of the Advisory Committee to the President of the Constituent Assembly sent on April 23, 1947.[57]

Sardar Vallabhbhai Patel, as Chairman of the Advisory Committee on Fundamental Rights, Minority Rights etc, moved a resolution[58] on May 1, 1947 in the Constituent Assembly for inclusion of Clause 17 in the Fundamental Rights. The clause read as follows:

> Conversion from one religion to another brought about by coercion or undue influence shall not be recognised by law.

Sardar Patel did not elaborate it further and instead K.M. Munshi, who was also a member of the aforesaid Advisory Committee, moved an amendment[59] for substitution of Article 17 by the following clause:

> Any conversion from one religion to another of any person brought about by fraud, coercion or undue influence or of a minor under the age of 18 shall not be recognised by law.

Elaborating his amendment Munshi said: "The additions that are made to the clause as it is originally moved are these. First of all, the word 'fraud' is added to the words 'coercion and undue influence'. The second matter is with regard to the conversion of a minor. As a matter of fact, it was proposed by one of the other Committees in some form or other, and it is the general feeling that this clause should be restored in this form—any conversion of a minor under the age of 18 shall not be recognised by law. The only effect of non-recognition by law would mean that even though a person is converted by fraud or coercion or undue influence or be converted during his minority he will still in law be deemed to continue to belong to the old religion and his legal rights will remain unaffected by reason of his conversion. The idea behind this proposal is that very often, if there are conversions by fraud or undue influence or during minority, certain changes in the legal status take place, certain rights are lost. This will have only this effect that the rights will remain exactly the same as at the moment a person was converted by fraud or coercion or undue influence and in the case of a minor at the moment of conversion."[60]

F.R. Anthony opposed this amendment of Munshi with specific reference to "or of a minor under the age of 18". He said: "To this part of the clause I want to add these words: "except when the parents or surviving parents have been converted and the child does not choose to adhere to its original faith". This was more or less the form in which the particular clause was accepted by the Minorities Sub-Committee. We discussed it at length and it was felt that in the form, I have sought to re-introduce, it would best serve the interests that we were considering there.

"I agree that conversion under undue influence, conversion by coercion or conversion by fraud should not be recognised by law. I am only interested in this question, Sir, on principle. My community does not propagate. We do not convert, nor are we converted. But I do appreciate how deeply, how passionately millions of Christians feel on this right to propagate their religion. I want to congratulate the major party for having, in spite of its contentious character, retained the words "right to practise, and propagate their religion". Having done that, I say that after giving with one hand this principal fundamental right, a right which is regarded as perhaps the most fundamental of Christian rights, do not take it away by this proviso, "or of a minor under the age of 18"... You will virtually take away the right to convert...Not a single adult who is a parent, however, deeply he may feel, however deeply he may be convinced, will ever adopt Christianity, because, by this clause you will be cutting off that parent from his children. By this clause you will say, although the parents may be converted to Christianity, the children shall not be brought up by these parents in the faith of the parents. You will be cutting at the root of a family life. I say it is contrary to the ordinary concepts of natural law and justice. This is a right which is conceded in every part of the world, the right of parents to bring up their children in the faith that the parents want them to pursue. You have your safeguards. I have gone further, and unlike the position in other parts of the world, I have even given discretion to the child provided it has attained the age of discretion, to adhere to its original faith... I have also added the word "surviving parent" for this reason... If you do not use the word "surviving parents", if the father who happens to be a widower adopts the Christian faith, and the children wish to be brought up as Christians, it may be said that since both the parents are not alive, the father cannot bring up the children in his faith. He will automatically be cut off from his children.

"I realise how deeply certain sections of this House feel on this question of conversion. But I do ask you, having once conceded the right to propagate, to concede this in consonance with the principles of family law and in consonance with the principles of natural law and justice",[61] he concluded.

Rev. J.J.M. Nichols-Roy was against any amendment to the original clause. "There is a spiritual side in conversion which ought to be taken notice of by this House. Conversion does not mean only that a man changes his form of religion from one religion to another, or adopts a different name of religion, such as, a Hindu becomes a Christian. But there is the spiritual aspect of conversion, that is, the connection of the soul of man with God which must not be overlooked by this House. I know there are those who change their religion being influenced by material considerations, but there are others who are converted being under the influence of spiritual power. When a boy feels that he is called by God to adopt a different faith, no law should prevent him from doing that. The consciences of those youths who want to change their religion and adopt another religion from a spiritual stand-point should not be prevented from allowing those youths to exercise their right to change their legal status and change their religion. We know, Sir, in the history of Christianity, there have been youths....who have been converted to Christianity, who are ready to die for their conviction and who are ready to lose everything. Why should a youth who has such a call of God be prevented by law from changing his religion and calling himself by another name when he feels before God that he is influenced by the Spirit of God to do that and is ready even to sacrifice his life for that? This part of the amendment about minors is absolutely wrong when we consider it from the spiritual standpoint. From the standpoint of conscience I consider that it is altogether wrong not to allow a youth from the age of twelve to eighteen to exercise his own conscience before God. It will oppress that conscience of the youths who want to exercise their religious faiths before God. Why should their consciences be oppressed? That is a very important point, Sir, to be considered by this House. This freedom I consider to be a Fundamental Right of the youths. No law should be made which will work against good spiritual forces. India, especially, is a country of religions, a country where there is religious freedom. If this amendment is carried in this House, it will only mean that in making a law to prevent the evil forces our minds lose sight of the real religious freedom which the youths of this land ought to have. Therefore, I am against this very principle of forcing the youths by not allowing them to exercise their religious conviction according to their conscience",[62] he argued.

Purushottam Das Tandon was very unhappy for this stand of the Christian members. He said: "Some of them have said that in this Assembly, we have admitted the right of everyone to propagate his religion and to convert from one religion to another. We Congressmen deem it very inproper to convert from one to another religion or to take part in such activities and we are not in favour of this. In our opinion it is absolutely futile to be keen on converting others to one's faith. But it is only at the request of some persons, whom we want to keep with us in our national endeavour that we accepted this. Now, it is said that they have a right to convert young children to their faith. What is this? Really this surprises me very much. You can convert a child below eighteen by convincing and persuading him but he is a child of immature sense and legally and morally speaking this conversion can never be considered valid. If a boy of eighteen executes a transfer of deed in favour of a man for his hut worth only Rs. 100, the transaction is considered unlawful. But our brethern come forward and say that the boy has enough sense to change his religion. That the value of religion is even less than that of a hut worth one hundred rupees! It is proper that a boy should be allowed to formally change his religion when he attains maturity.

"One of my brethren has said that we are taking away with the left hand what we gave the Christians with our right hand. What we gave them with our right hand is that they have a right to convert others by an appeal to reason and after honestly changing their views and outlook. The three words, 'coercion', 'fraud' and 'undue influence' are included as provisos and are meant to cover the cases of adult converts. These words are not applicable to converts of immature age. Their conversion is coercion and undue influence under all circumstances. How can the young ones change their religion? They have not the sense to understand the teachings of your scriptures. If they change their religion it is only under some influence and this influence is not fair. If parents are converted why should it be necessary that their children should also change their religion? If they are under the influence of their parents they can change religion on maturity. This is my submission.... I know that most Congressmen are opposed to this idea of propagation. But we agreed to keep the word 'propagate' out of regard for our Christian friends. But now to ask us to agree to minors also being converted is, I think, Sir, going too far",[63] he commented.

Purushottam Das Tandon's contention that "the majority of Congressmen do not like this process of making converts" evoked mixed reactions among the members. While members like Balkrishna Sharma, Jagat Narain Lal fully supported this stand of Tandon, others like C.E. Gibban, Dhirendra Nath Dutta were of the opinion that Tandon was not competent to speak for all Congressmen.

D.N. Dutta suggested that "the whole of this clause 17 should go into the Fundamental Rights Committee and I would be glad if the whole clause could be deleted. I know the reason for enumerating this under the Fundamental Rights, because we are now working under the present setting. But as it is going to be enumerated in the Fundamental Rights, it has to be seen, Sir, whether the amendment of Mr. Munshi is to be accepted or the amendment of Mr. Anthony should be accepted. Mr. Anthony wants that the option of the minors to join the religion they like on attaining majority, should be retained, just as the choice is given to Mohammadan children given in marriage during minority to repudiate the marriage on attaining majority—what we call the option of puberty. A similar right he intends to be given to the children of the parents who have been converted. On attaining majority the child shall have the right of declaring whether he adheres to his original faith or whether he will join the faith of his parents who were converted.... I think this right should not be taken away. It should be given and how it is to be given, it is for the Drafting Committee, or, better still, it should go to the Fundamental Rights Committee to determine whether this clause should remain or how it should remain".[64]

Rev. Jerome D'Souza also supported the suggestion of Dutta of referring the "entire clause back to the Advisory Committee so that the wording of it may be most carefully weighed" because this clause "is bristling with legal and juridical difficulties, quite apart from those other considerations into which, as I said, I regret we have entered with undue warmth".[65]

P.R. Thakur was against conversion of members of Depressed classes. He said: "the victims of these religious conversions are ordinarily from the Depressed classes. The preachers of other religions approach these classes of people, take advantage of their ignorance, extend all sorts of temptations and ultimately convert them. I want to know from Mr. Munshi whether 'fraud' covers all these things. If it does not cover, I should ask Mr. Munshi to re-draft this clause so that fraud of this nature might not be practised on these depressed classes. I should certainly call these 'fraud'."[66]

Algu Rai Shastri, however, supported the amendment of Munshi. He said: "I believe that by accepting the amendment we shall be doing justice to those minors who have perforce to enter the fold of the religion which their parents embrace out of their greed. This practice is like the one prevailing in the transactions of transfer of land and which is that 'trees go with the land'. It is on some such basis that the minor children who do not understand what change of religion or coercion or religious practices mean, have to leave their old faith along with their parents. This evil practice has a very bad effect on the strength of our population. It is proper for us that we, who are framing the charters of Fundamental Rights, should safeguard their interests and save them from such automatic conversion.... Such minors on attaining majority often regret that they were made to change their religion improperly. Wherever, the Europeans... have gone, they (first went) as Missionaries.... The missionary was followed by the batons, the swords and the guns. It was in this way that they employed coercion, for spreading their religions and for extending their Empire. At the same time, they put economic and political pressure on the indigenous tribes and consolidated the foundations of their dominion.... A person who wants to change his religion should be able to do so only after he is convinced through cool deliberation that the new religion is more satisfactory to him than the old one.... But no one should change religion out of greed and temptation. I have a personal experience extending over a period of 24 years as to how elders of the family are induced through prospects of financial gain to change their religion and also with them the children are taken over to the fold of new religion. It appears as if some are taking the land physically in his possession and the helpless trees go with it to the new master.... In his book "Census of India-1911" Mr. S. Kamath has said that the missionaries of one particular religion are reducing the members of another by exploiting the evils of that group. They convert some influential persons by inducement and persuasion. The bitterness of the present is due to such activities.... People of other faiths have intensified and exploited our differences in order to increase their own numbers.... We know that our failure to stop conversion under coercion would result in grave injustice.... This attempt to increase population has increased religious bitterness. The communal proportion has been changed so that the British bureaucracy may retain its hold by a variation in the numbers of the different communities.... The sole interest of the Government in the illusory web of the census lies in seeing a balance in the population of the communities so that these may continue to quarrel among themselves and thereby strengthen its own rule.... The age limit fixed for minors and majors should be adopted in religious matters as well. They say that there would be no incentive for conversion if people have to forego their children. I hear that in Japan the father has one religion and the child another. What does religion mean? Does the mother feed her baby so that the child's religion might change? If the mother's love is true she will surely feed her baby. Does the mother's milk change the religion? We do not wish to snatch away the child from the mother's lap, but we wish to give to the baby a right to record his (natal) religion in the report of the Census and any other Government records, till he attains majority and declares his (new) religion",[67] he concluded.

Jagat Narain Lal was of the view that the acceptance of clause 13 which lays down that "All persons are equally entitled to freedom of conscience, and the right freely to profess, practise and propagate religion, subject to public order, morality or health or to the other provisions of this Chapter was "the farthest limit". None of "the best of the modern world Constitutions", has conceded "this right to propagate". He quoted some provisions of the Constitutions of Swiss Confederation, Irish Free State & USSR in support of his contention. He continued: "The fact is that we desire to make the minorities feel that the rights which they had been enjoying till now shall be allowed to continue within reasonable limits by the majority. We have no desire to curtail them in any way. But we do not concede the right to do propaganda. I want to appeal to those who profess to speak for the minorities not to press for too much. They must be satisfied with this much. It will be too much to press for more. That would be taking undue advantage of the generosity of the majority. That will be very regrettable. It is difficult, rather impossible, for us to go to that limit. I think that the amendment tabled by Mr. Munshi becomes essential if the right to propagate is conceded".[68]

Dr. B.R. Ambedkar in his deliberations supported the original clause moved by Sardar Patel. "The clause, as it stands, probably gives the impression to the House that this question relating to the conversion of minors was not considered by the Fundamental Rights Committee or by the Minorities Sub-Committee or by the Advisory Committee. I should like to assure the House that a good deal of consideration was bestowed on this question and every aspect was examined. It was, after examining the whole question in all its aspects, and seeing the difficulties which came up, that the Advisory Committee came to the conclusion that they should adhere to the clause as it now stands", he stated.

Urging Munshi to drop his amendment he contended, "with regard to the children there are three possible cases which can be visualised. First of all, there is the case of children who are orphans, who have no parents and no guardians in the legal sense of the word… (they) cannot have any kind of religious instructions. I am sure that this is not the result which this House would be happy to contemplate. Therefore, such a class of subjects shall have to be exempted from the operation of the amendment proposed by Mr. Munshi.

"Then I come to the other class viz. children with parents and guardians. They may fall into two categories. the first is this: where children are converted with the knowledge and consent of their guardians and parents. The second case is that of children of parents who have become converts.

"It does seem to me that there ought to be a prohibition upon the conversion of minor children with legal guardians, where the conversion takes place without the consent and knowledge of the legal guardians. That, I think, is a very legitimate proposition. No missionary who wants to convert a child which is under the lawful guardianship of some person, who according to the law of guardianship is entitled to regulate and control the religious faith of the particular child, ought to deprive that person or guardian of the right of having notice and having knowledge that the child is being converted to another faith, That, I think, is a simple proposition to which there can be no objection.

"But when we come to the other case, viz. where parents are converted and we have to consider the case of their children, then I think we come across what I might say a very hard rock. If you are going to say that, although parents may be converted because they are majors and above the age of 18, minors below the age of 18, although they are their children, are not to be converted with the parent, the question that we have to consider is, what arrangement are we going to make with regard to the children?" He wanted to know which religion was to be followed in case of marriage, death etc. of such children. "If you do not want that the children should be converted, you have to make some other kind of law with regard to guardianship in order to prevent the parents from exercising their rights to influence and shape the religious life of their children.... The mere fact that we have made no such reference in clause 17 of the Fundamental Rights does not in my judgement prevent the legislature when it becomes operative from making any law in order to regulate this matter.... The Fundamental Rights Committee, the Minorities Committee and the Advisory Committee.... have given their best attention to the subject... (and) realised that the acceptance of the proposition, namely, that a person shall not be converted below the age of 18, would lead to many disruptions, to so many evil consequences, that we thought it would be better to drop the whole thing altogether.... I have no objection to a provision being made that children who have legal and lawful guardians should not be converted without the knowledge and notice of the parents"[69], he said.

Sardar Vallabhbhai Patel admitted that "it is well known in this country that there are mass conversions, conversions by force, conversions by coercion and undue influence and we cannot disguise the fact that children also have been converted, that children with parents have been converted, and that orphans have been converted. Now, we need not go into all the reasons or the forces that led to these conversions.... There may be different points of view.... This question has been considered in three Committees and yet we have not been able to find a solution acceptable to all. Let us make one more effort.... Let this be therefore referred to the Advisory Committee. We shall give one more chance".[70]

This clause was then referred back to the Advisory Committee.[71]

V

In its Supplementary Report to the Constituent Assembly on August 25, 1947, the Advisory Committee reported that

> "it seems to us on further consideration that this clause enunciates a rather obvious doctrine which it is unnecessary to include in the Constitution and we recommend that it be dropped altogether".[72]

This clause came again for discussion on 30-8-47 when, Sardar Patel observed that "after further consideration of this clause, which enunciates an obvious principle, the Committee came to the conclusion that it is not necessary to include this as a fundamental right. It is illegal under the present law and it can be illegal at any time".[73]

M. Ananthasayanam Ayyanger however did not agree with this proposal of Sardar Patel. His contention was: "It is unfortunate that religion is being utilised not for the purpose of saving one's soul but for disintegrating society. Recently after the announcement by the Cabinet Mission and later on by the British Government, a number of conversions have taken place. It was said that power had been handed over to Provincial Governments who were in-charge of these matters. This is dangerous. What has religion to do with a Secular State? Our minorities are communal minorities for which we have made provision. Do you want an opportunity to be given for numbers to be increased for the purpose of getting more seats in the Legislatures? That is what is happening. All people have come to the same opinion that there should be secular State here; so we should not allow conversion from one community to another. I therefore want that a positive fundamental right must be established that no conversion shall be allowed, and if any occasion does arise like this, let the person concerned appear before a judge and swear before him that he wishes to be converted. This may be an out-of-the-way suggestion but I would appeal to this House to realise the dangerous consequences. Otherwise, later on it may attain enormous propositions. I would like this matter to be considered and the question referred back for a final draft for consideration at a latter sitting".[74]

R.V. Dhulekar was of the opinion "that clause 17 should be retained as it stands. In the present environment, all sorts of efforts are being made to increase the population of a particular section in this country, so that once again efforts may be made to further divide the country. There is ample proof, both within the House and outside that many who live in this country are not prepared to be the citizens of this country. Those who have caused the division of our land desire that India may be further divided. Therefore, in view of the present circumstances, I think that this clause should be retained. It is necessary that full attention should be paid to this. We are being attacked, and we do not want that India's population, the numerical strength of the Hindus and other communities should gradually diminish, and after ten years the other people may again say that "we constitute a separate Nation". These separatist tendencies should be crushed".[75]

Sardar Vallabhbhai Patel summed it up by saying that "much of this debate may be shortened if it be recognised that there is no difference of opinion on the merits of the case that forcible conversion should not be or cannot be recognised by law. On that principle there is no difference of opinion. The question is only whether this clause is necessary in the list of fundamental rights. Now, if it is an objective for the administration to act, it has a place in the Second Part which consists of non-justiciable rights. If you think it is necessary, let us transfer it to the Second Part of the Schedule because it is admitted that in the law of the land forcible conversion is illegal. We have even stopped forcible education, and we do not for a moment suggest that forcible conversion of one by another from one religion to another will be recognised. But suppose one thousand people are converted, that is not recognised. Will you go to a court of law and ask it not to recognise it? It only creates complications, it gives no remedy. But if you want this principle to be enunciated as a seventh clause, coming after clause 6, (i.e., after Article 43) in the Second Schedule, it is unnecessary to carry on any debate; you can do so. There is no difference of opinion on the merits of the case. But at this stage to talk of forcible conversion on merits is absurd, because there cannot be any question about it".[76]

Dhulekar also concurred with this view of Sardar Patel and Sardar Patel said that this clause would be transferred.

At this point Hussain Imam suggested that "this is such a fundamental thing, that there is no need to provide for it. According to the law everything which has been done under coercion is illegal. Anything done by reason of fraud can never stand. Forcible conversion is the highest degree of undesirable thing. But it is not proper, as the Sardar himself has admitted, to provide it in the justiciable fundamental rights. The only place which it can occupy is in the annals of High Court judgements. Any number of judgements exist which have declared that anything done by reason of fraud or coercion is illegal. Therefore, it is not justifiable and cannot be justified by any sensible person in the world. I strongly advocate that it is not necessary to put it in any of the lists of Fundamental Rights."[77]

Then the motion of Sardar Patel "that this should not be put in the Fundamental Rights" was put to vote and was adopted on 30-8-47.[78]

So neither in the Fundamental Rights nor in the Directive Principles we find any safeguard against conversion. The promise of Sardar Patel of making this provision one of the Directive Principles did not materialise.

Sardar Patel was against incorporation of any provision against conversion in the Fundamental Rights chapter. C. Rajagopalachari also questioned the necessity of such a provision which was covered by the ordinary law of the land. At the time of discussion on 1-5-47 the attempt to incorporate such a provision in the Constitution foundered on the rock of conversion of minors mainly due to the opposition of Christian Members who got ample support from Dr. Ambedkar. The second attempt on 30-8-47 ensured its complete banishment from the Constitution.

Prof. K.T. Shah made an unsuccessful bid to put some sort of restriction on conversion when on December 3, 1948 at the time of discussion on clause 19 (since renumbered 25) he moved an amendment for addition of a new provision to clause (1) of Article 19.

"That the following proviso be added to Clause (1) of Article 19:

> "Provided that no propaganda in favour of any one religion, which is calculated to result in change of faith by individuals affected, shall be allowed in any school or college or other educational institution, in any hospital or asylum, or in any other place or institution where persons of a tender age, or of unsound mind or body are liable to be exposed to undue influence from their teachers, nurses or physicians, keepers or guardians or any other person set in authority above them, and which is maintained wholly or partially from public revenues, or is in any way aided or protected by the Government of the Union, or of any State or Public authority therein."

In support of the amendment he argued: "The main article gives the right of freedom of propaganda. I have no quarrel with the right that anybody professing any particular form of belief should be at liberty, in this Liberal State, to place the benefits or beauties of his particular form of worship before others. My only condition—and the amendment tries to incorporate that—is that this freedom should not be abused, as it has been in the past. In places or institutions, where people of tender age or those suffering from any bodily or mental infirmity, are exposed to undue influence, they are liable to be influenced more by the personality of those in authority above them than by the inherent advantages and unquestionable reasoning in favour of a particular religion, and as such result in conversion. That is not a genuine change of opinion, but is the result of undue influence that ought to be stopped.

"I have no quarrel at all with those who would change their opinion after full and mature consideration of such material as may be available to them regarding the beliefs that they inherit from their parents. Most of the religious beliefs in this world are not, may I say without any offence, a matter of reasoned conviction; they are an acquired habit or an inherited prejudice which may not stand the strain of conviction on the opposite side, or reasoning on the controverting side. Accordingly, anybody who desires the mind of the public to be alert free from prejudice and open to conviction, will not object to permitting such freedom of propaganda that may result in conversion.

"I have no objection therefore to anybody speaking, writing, preaching, in any place of public resort, in any open space, in parks, gardens, theatres or any other public place, even to people of tender age or even to people of unsound mind or body; because in those places they are not suffering from any disability, nor are those who are teaching or preaching in those public places in a place of authority, in a place where they can exercise undue influence; and as such it can be presumed that it is rather the force of their argument, the strength of their reasoning that has resulted in proselytising without any undue influence, or unfair authority, upon those people. But when, as in a school or a college, in an hospital or asylum, those who are set in authority as teacher or preacher, physician, guardian or nurse, take advantage of their peculiar position to influence them, to place before them another way of looking at life and its purpose than that they have had from birth, then I think undue influence is exercised and as such objectionable.

"Even that may be permitted so far as that particular institution does not benefit in any way from public revenues, or is not aided, protected, or encouraged by any public authority in the Union or in any part of it. I hope the House realises the extreme moderation of my amendment, and the tightness of the restriction that I have put so far as this proviso is concerned, namely that it will operate only on people in a place or institution where they are suffering from some kind of disability, whether of age or of unsound mind or body, and where, therefore, their changes of belief if it is brought about would be open to suspicion.

"That is one reason. Then again, the preaching or propaganda which may be objected to is by or from people who are set in authority above the young, the helpless, disabled or of unsound mind, that is, as teacher or nurse or guardian. That is also a very substantial limitation.

"Thirdly, the institutions or places carrying on propaganda of this kind resulting in conversion from one religion to another to which we object are places which are maintained wholly or partly by public revenues. They may be receiving financial grant; or they may be receiving recognition, which is perhaps, more valuable than a direct money grant, and charging fees, from the public, so that, they may benefit even though nominally they may not be taking any grants from public revenues, or they may be aided or protected by any public authority.

"With these three very substantial restrictions, I am sure nobody would quarrel or object to my amendment, especially to the idea of propaganda of a kind which is calculated to change the religion or form of belief or worship inherited with one's parentage, if that propaganda is done by people in authority above them; and they in the meantime are suffering from some kind of disability of the type I have illustrated.

"I know, Sir, this is liable to excite strong feeling. There are religions which are professedly proselytising. There are religions which leave the matter of religion to every person's own conscience, and do not indulge in proselytising. Whatever that be; without quarrelling with the freedom of preaching one's religion, I hold that it is the most moderate form of request to the professors or preachers of those religions, which want to proselytise, that they should at least observe this much self-restraint, *viz*. that any institutions maintained by any form of public assistance or receiving any form of public encouragement should not be utilised by them for propaganda or proselytisation, so that, the minds not quite free from other influences, minds suffering from some kind of handicap, shall not be unduly influenced.

"Sir, I have tried to use no expression in the course of these few remarks which might give the slightest occasion for anybody to feel alarmed at the restraint which I am suggesting should be put upon their right to propagate religion. I have not quoted a single instance which may be found in plenty, where undue advantage has been taken to effect conversions in a manner which may be regarded as most reprehensible. Those who are blinded by their faith are welcome to their belief. But I would beg them to realise that in suggesting that those who are suffering from disabilities shall be free from activities of this kind, they will not misunderstand me when I say that I have not the slightest objection to their holding their beliefs and even propagating them but that they should not indulge in this illicit form for carrying on their religious activity.

"Professing no particular religion myself, I can give an assurance to the House that I am not actuated by any feeling of partiality for one or opposition to another. I only wish that this may be left as a matter of purely personal concern. When you meet at a social gathering or congregational union this much decency should be observed that you shall not carry on your influence in an undue manner, but only rely upon the convincing character of your arguments".[79]

There was no further debate on his motion and it was ultimately negatived by the Members at the time of voting.

VI

Freedom of religion is a principle that supports the freedom of an individual or community, in public or private, to manifest religion or belief in teaching, practice, worship and observance; the concept is generally recognized also to include the freedom to change religion or not to follow any religion.[80] The freedom to leave or discontinue membership in a religion or religious group — in religious terms called "apostasy"—is also a fundamental part of religious freedom, covered by article 18 of the Universal Declaration of Human Rights. Historically *freedom of religion* has been used to refer to the tolerance of different theological systems of belief, while *freedom of worship* has been defined as freedom of individual action. Each of these has existed in varying degrees. While many countries have accepted some form of religious freedom, this has also often been limited in practice through punitive taxation, repressive social legislation, and political disenfranchisement. Among the most contentions areas of religious freedom are the right of an individual to change or abandon his or her own religion (apostasy), and the right to evangelize individuals seeking to convince others to make such a change.

Debates have centred round restricting certain kinds of missionary activity by religious denominations. Many Islamic states, and others such as China, severely restrict missionary activities of other religions. Greece, among European countries, has generally looked unfavourably on missionary activities of denominations other than the majority church and proselytizing is constitutionally prohibited.

Conversion to Islam is simple, but Muslims are forbidden to convert from Islam to another religion. In Islam, apostasy is called "*ridda*' ("turning back") and is considered to be a profound insult to God. A person born of Muslim parents that rejects Islam is called a "*murtad fitri*" (natural apostate), and a person that converted to Islam and later rejects the religion is called a *"murtad milli"* (apostate from the community). In Islamic law (*Sharia*) the consensus view is that a male apostate must be put to death unless he suffers from a mental disorder or converted under duress, for example, due to an imminent danger of being killed. Female apostate must be either executed, according to Shafi'i, Maliki, and Hanbali schools of Sunni Islamic jurisprudence (*fiqh*), or imprisoned until she reverts to Islam as advocated by the Sunni Hanafi school and by Shia scholars[81] But M.J. Akbar points out that there is no earthly punishment for apostasy in the *Quran*. Judgement is left to Allah, the ultimate arbiter. As the *Encyclopaedia of Islam* confirms, "In the *Quran*, the apostate is threatened with punishment in the next world". There is no record of any fatwa of beheading of Barack Obama's father at the hands of a cleric for renouncing Islam.[82]

In 2008 Christian Solidarity Worldwide, a Christian human rights non-governmental organization which specializes in religious freedom, launched an in-depth report on the human rights abuses faced by individuals who leave Islam for another religion. The report is the product of a year-long research project in six different countries. It calls on Muslim nations, the international community, the UN and the international media to resolutely address the serious violations of human rights suffered by apostates.[83]

Some orthodox Christians, especially those living in democratic countries, support religious freedom for all as evidenced by the position of the Ecumenical Patriarchate. Many Protestant Christian churches, including some Baptists, Churches of Christ, Seventh-day Adventist Church and main line churches have a commitment to religious freedom. The Church of Jesus Christ of Latter-day Saints also affirms religious freedom. However others, such as African scholar Makau Mutua, have argued that Christian insistence on the propagation of their faith to native cultures as an element of religious freedom has resulted in a corresponding denial of religious freedom to native traditions and led to their destruction. As he states in the book produced by the Oslo Coalition on Freedom of Religion or Belief—"Imperial religions have necessarily violated individual conscience and the communal expressions of Africans and their communities by subverting African religions".[84] Some Indian scholars have similarly argued that the right to propagate religion is not culturally or religiously neutral. Many scholars and intellectuals believe that India's predominant religion, Hinduism, has long been the most tolerant religion.[85] Religious freedom and the right to worship freely were practices that had been appreciated and promoted by most ancient Indian dynasties for over 5,000 years. As a result, people facing religious persecution in other parts of the world including Christians, Jews, Bahai'i Faith and Zoroastrians fled to India as a place of refuge to enjoy religious freedom. This had been the underlying attitude of most rulers of India from time immemorial.

Ancient Jews fleeing from persecution in their homeland 2,500 years ago settled in India and never faced anti-Semitism. Freedom of religion edicts have been found written during Ashoka the Great's reign in the third century BC.

The Dalai Lama, the Tibetan spiritual leader in exile while delivering a discourse on the Four Noble Truths of Buddhism on the occasion of the first anniversary of the Buddha Vihar, Gulbarg, said that religious tolerance of "Aryabhumi", a reference to India found in the *Mahabharata*, has been in existence in this country for thousands of years. "Not only Hinduism, Jainism, Buddhism, Sikhism which are native religions but also Christianity and Islam have flourished here. Religious tolerance is inherent in Indian tradition",[86] the Dalai Lama said.

The 79-year Old Pontiff John Paul II, while visiting India, paid a glowing tribute on November 6, 1999 to the "great" religious freedom that prevails in the country in a greater degree than it does in many other countries. He appreciated the atmosphere of tolerance in India, which he said was part of the country's rich heritage.[87]

Notwithstanding the great geographical expanse of India and the linguistic and cultural specificities of people living in different regions, there prevailed an almost timeless consensus on fundamental civilisational and religious principles. These basic principles of India, which found diverse expressions in sophisticated philosophical discourse as well as in lay beliefs and practices, are collectively known by the name of *Sanatana Dharma*, the timeless discipline that forms the core of all religious doctrines of Indian origin.

All those who entered India from outside soon accepted these basic civilizational and religious principles. Apart from the Greeks, others who made incursions into India included the Shakas and Indo-Parthians, the Kushanas of probably Central Asian origin, and the Hunas. Most of them were convincingly defeated; those who succeeded in establishing significant kingdoms often became great adherents and defenders of the Indian civilization. The Indo-Greeks, Indo-Bactrians, Indo-Parthians, the Kushanas and others thus, instead of disrupting the cultural homogeneity of India, became the carriers of Indian civilizational values and principles far and wide.

Starting from seventh century AD, India faced a new external incursion, this time by the adherents of Islam. Islam, as is known, arrived on the world scene with great expansionary vigour. The initial entry of Islam into South Asia came in the first century after the death of the Prophet Mohammad. Islam could obtain a foothold in India only in 712 AD, with the victory over Sind. Since then Muslims continued to come to India as travellers, traders and mercenaries. Mahmud's frequent raids, altogether fourteen in number (AD 1001-1026) must have given them more knowledge of the country. From the eleventh century onwards Muslim invasions with cold-blooded murders, forcible conversions, looting, devastation of the countryside, breaking up of Hindu idols and desecration of Hindu temples began in India on a large scale and the Indians experienced perpetual insecurity.[88] By the beginning of the thirteenth century AD, the conquest of Northern India was completed from Punjab to Assam and from Kashmir to the Vindhyas and the Muslims had now settled firmly in India.

The Islamic Sultanates who invaded India from the north-west around 1210 AD were subsequently replaced by another Islamic invader in the form of Babur. The Mughal empire was founded by the Mongol leader Babur in 1526, when he defeated Ibrahim Lodi, the last of the Delhi Sultans at the First Battle of Panipat.

The advent of Islam in India resulted in an initial clash between two conflicting, and often incompatible, religions and cultures, which was followed by fusion and synthesis. India had so long assimilated almost all foreign races and cultures that entered the land at different times by broadening her faith and her social structure. Hinduism, for the first time, came face to face with a religion and culture that not only refused to be absorbed into the mainstream but also tried to convert people into its faith.[89]

Islamic rulers, even those who were relatively tolerant of the Indian beliefs and practices and did not attempt to forcibly propagate Islam, were committed to retaining a distinct Islamic identity and presence within the larger and otherwise homogenous civilisation of India. Unlike all those who came into India before them, the Islamic rulers, consciously and perhaps conscientiously, resisted acculturation into the timeless civilisational and religious milieu of India. This thus became the first source of heterogeneity in India, dividing the Indian population mainly into two distinct religious communities, Hindus and Muslims. In time, this demographic heterogeneity led to the Partition of the country into Indian Union and two separate Islamic enclaves.

However, after more than five centuries of Islamic rule and at the pinnacle of Mughal domination during the first half of the seventeenth century, the proportion of Muslims in the population of India had reached no more than one sixth. Emperor Jehangir, who ruled during 1605-1622, records in his memoirs, *Tarikh-i-Salim-Shahi* that "for the whole population of Hindustan, it is notorious that five parts in six are composed of Hindus".[90] This indeed is a measure of the resilience of Indian civilisational values, and the strength of commitment the people of India have in them.

The interaction between Christianity and Hinduism was going on for a long time and the influence of the one on the other was more in evidence where Christianity had been established the longest. While the Christian missionary agencies carried on a relentless war against illiteracy, disease and poverty, they also at the same time carried on their evangelical work. The Christians believe that conversion to their religion is a service to God. So, since the arrival of Europeans in India they took up conversion in right earnest.

In 1881, after about a century of British rule, Christians were just beginning to make their presence felt in India. The Census of 1881 reveals that Muslim constituted 19.969 per cent of the total population while Christians were only 0.711 per cent of the total population of undivided India. However, in the period following 1881, rise in the proportion of Muslims and Christians becomes a continuous phenomenon.

The percentage of Muslims, Christians and Indian Religionists which includes practically all other religionists except Muslims and Christians in the population of the Indian Union in 1901-2001 is given in Table 4.1. The religious demography in the 2011 census is yet to see the light of the day.

Table 4.1: Religious Composition of Indian Union, 1901-2001

Year	*Indian Religionists*	*Muslims*	*Christians*
1901	86.640	12.209	1.151
1911	86.585	12.008	1.407
1921	86.067	12.229	1.704
1931	85.148	12.860	1.992
1941	84.438	13.380	2.182
1951	87.237	10.430	2.334
1961	86.871	10.687	2.442
1971	86.201	11.204	2.595
1981	85.856	11.708	2.436
1991	85.088	12.590	2.322
2001	84.217	13.438	2.345

Source: Tables 2.6 and 2.7a of Religious Demography of India, A.P. Joshi, M.D. Srinivas and J.K. Bajaj, Centre for Policy Studies, Chennai, 2003, p. 25 and p. 27 for the figures of 1901-1991, Statement 1 of Census of India, 2001, The First Report on Religion Data, Statement 1, p. xxvii for 2001.

It will be observed from Table 4.1 that the Muslim population nose-dived in 1951 registering the all time low of 10.430 per cent, possibly due to the cessation of Muslim-dominated areas Pakistan and migration of Muslim population in the wake of Partition. This community has regained its lost glory and even surpassed the highest percentage of 13.380 in 1941 in 2001 itself registering an all-time high of 13.438 per cent. Muslims constitute 67 per cent of the total population of Jammu & Kashmir and 95 per cent in Lakshadweep in the 2001 census. They have a substantial following in the States of Assam (30.9%), West Bengal (25.2%), Kerala (24.7%), Uttar Pradesh (18.5%), Bihar (16.5%), Jharkhand (13.8%), Karnataka (12.2%), Uttarakhand (11.9%) and Delhi (11.7%).[91]

The most significant of the areas where Muslims have registered a high rate of growth is the eastern border belt that begins from Bahraich district of eastern Uttar Pradesh, spreads eastwards along the northern districts of Bihar and West Bengal, and extends up to the western districts of Assam across the intervening northern districts of Bangladesh. In Uttar Pradesh, the belt comprises the districts of Bahraich, Gonda, Sidharthnagar, Mahrajganj and Deoria. In Bihar, the belt consists of Pashchim Champaran, Purbi Champaran, Sitamarhi, Darbhanga, Madhubani, Saharsa, Purnia, Araria, Kishanganj and Katihar. In Jharkhand, the belt camprises the districts of Sahibganj and Godda. In West Bengal, the border belt includes the districts of Birbhum, Murshidabad, Maldah, Dakhin Dinajpur and Uttar Dinajpur. In Assam, the border belt comprises the composite districts of Goalpara, Kamrup, Darrang and Nagaon.[92]

Though the Christian population never crossed the 3 per cent mark—it hovered between 2.595 per cent in 1971 and 2.322 in 1991 in Independent India—they are now in majority in the three States of Nagaland, Mizoram and Meghalaya and have a substantial following in the States of Manipur (34.04%). Christians have a significant presence in undivided Ranchi district of Jharkhand and especially in Gumla component of the reorganised district. In the latter, they form one-third of the population. Christian presence extends to Raigarh district of Madhya Pradesh in the west and Sundargarh district of Orissa in the east. Christians form about 14.5 per cent of the population of these three districts together, spread across three States.[93] The southern States of Kerala (19.00%) and Goa (26.70%) also account for a sizeable Christian population.[94]

Former Home Minister Sushil Kumar Shinde released the Primary Census Abstract-Data Highlights of Census 2011 in a function organised by the Office of the Registrar General and Census Commissioner, in New Delhi on April 30, 2013. But both the Provisional Population Totals and Primary Census Abstract are silent on religious data, though information on religion was duly collected in Column 7 of the Census 2011 Household Schedule. When the results in rarefied categories like number of literates and literacy rate by sex and residence could be arrived at, would it have been difficult to tell how many Hindus, Muslims, Christians, Sikhs and Buddhists are in India. Nor would it have been difficult to determine the decadal population growth rate of respective communities. The hindrance was possibly not technological but political.

The Hindu population pegged at 80.5 per cent in Census 2001 is likely to have fallen below 80 per cent in 2011. In parts of India like West Bengal and Assam, the Muslim population might have increased further. The UPA Government delayed this damning revelation as much as possible, because in an election year the BJP might have taken advantage of the figures. Even after wresting power at the Centre in May 2014, the BJP, also failed to release the figures till now. Apparently all political parties will like to live in denial of a disturbing reality as long as they can.

But one can expect greater Muslim assertiveness as soon as the religious data of Census 2011 is out. It bodes ill for all political parties of India led by Hindus whether they are secular or communal. Some liberal Hindus might advocate abolishing the religious data category in future Census operations. They made a similar plea last time also. But the reality does not disappear if one were to shut one's eyes to it.

The political sensitiveness of the subject can be understood from the huff around the publication of the **First Report on Religion** (Census 2001) in September 2004, which revealed that contrary to overall population trend, growth rate of Muslim population had increased. The decadal growth rate of the Muslims was around 36 per cent which was up from 34.5 per cent between 1981 and 1991 respectively. The Hindu growth rate had fallen to 20.3 per cent from 25.1 per cent in the same corresponding period.

The then Former Home Minister Shivraj Patil compelled the then Census Commissioner Jayant Kumar Banthia to 'adjust' the figures. Patil's argument was that decadal growth could not be determined because there was no Census in Assam in 1981 and J&K in 1991 due to insurgency. Banthia, unwilling to bend, juxtaposed both the adjusted and unadjusted figures on the first page.

VII

By a conscious decision, the Church fanned out to every nook and corner in the wake of colonization and trade. And India was no exception. The heathen was the missionary target, and of all people in India the untouchables and the aboriginals were believed to be the most heathen.

While the colonial rulers since the inception of its rule in the North-eastern region actively pursued a policy of keeping the hills out of any political and ideological influence from the plains through various administrative and regulatory measures, they, at the same time, encouraged the Christian missionaries to move into the tribal areas with two definite objectives—first, to undertake welfare and humanitarian works and second, to convert people to Christianity.

From the very beginning of their rule the British Government activated Christian proselytism among the hill tribes. David Scott, the Governor-

General's Agent for the North-Eastern Frontier, advocated for extending help, even financial help, to the Christian missionaries for proselytisation of the tribal population. He wrote to W.B. Bayley, Secretary to Government on April 27, 1825 thus:

> In reply to a Commission that I sent to my Agent in London for one or more Missionaries of the sort suited to convert the Garos, I have been referred to the Bishop of Calcutta by the person, probably a friend of his, whom my brother consulted. Would Government have any objection to my applying to the Bishop on the subject? I am satisfied that nothing permanently good can be obtained by other means, and that if we do not interfere on behalf of the poor Garos they will soon become Hindus or half-Hindus, retaining and acquiring many of the bad parts of both their resent and improved creeds. I would greatly prefer two or more Moravian Missionaries of the old school who along with religion would teach the useful arts. If Government would ensure them subsistence only in the case of success or of my death, I would willingly take upon myself the expense in the first instance, and 300 pound per annum would suffice. Of success I have no more doubts than that, if allowed, you could make Christians of the Hindu boys; and the great error of the Missionaries appears to me that of directing their attention to polished natives instead of rude tribes who are still in that state of national childhood which enables the stranger priest to enact the schoolmaster and to teach them what he likes. There are many instances of success in cases of the latter description in modern times, but not one by fair means in those of the former since the age of miracles or very near it.

To this the Secretary replied semi-officially, approving generally. "The Government could not however give salary to the people who might be employed in their capacity of Missionaries, but they might call them schoolmasters, and give assistance in that shape".[95] Early British officials in Assam (Assam meant the undivided Assam of 1947) also felt that Assam and its hills inhabited by various tribes, offered the most promising field for Christian faith.[96]

Sensing this, different Christian Missions started their activities in the North-East in a big way. "The American, Norwegian, Welsh, Spanish and Italian Christian missionaries came in quite a few numbers and settled in the inaccessible and dangerous places in the mountains, forests and plains to preach the message of God, to heal the sufferings and to educate the people."[97]

The Christian Missionaries were encouraged by the colonial rulers to set up Churches and take up evangelical work in the hill areas, except the North-East Frontier Tract, so much so that sometimes the missionaries were equated with the colonial rulers. Goswami has stated that Mizos in fact confused the missionaries with administrators during the initial phase of the British rule. "So many people often confused missionaries with administrators and hence acceptance of Christianity meant identification with British administrators."[98]

The spread of Christianity in the hills of North-East India since the middle of the nineteenth century has been spectacular. The success of their missions is best reflected in the census figures during the period 1901-2001, tabulated in Table 4.2. It will be seen from Table 4.2 that while the area now included in Mizoram could achieve the distinction of being an overwhelmingly Christian majority area in the 1951 census, Nagaland and Meghalaya became Christian majority areas in the 1961 and 1981 census respectively.

The Christian population of Manipur registered a three-fold increase during the period 1951-2001. One thing is very peculiar in this State. The outer districts of Senapati, Tamenglong, Churachandpur and Ukhrul have been almost fully Christianised; the share of Christians in population of these districts in 1991 was 83.25, 97.50, 93.36 and 93.69 per cent, respectively. Similarly, Chandel component of the undivided Manipur Central District has also been Christianised to the level of 86.16 per cent.[99] Incidentally, these districts are the playground of secessionist forces.

Hindus and Muslims have been largely restricted to Bishnupur, Imphal and Thoubal components of the undivided Manipur Central district, where they constitute more than 95 per cent of the population.[100]

The Christian population also increased substantially in the remaining States of Arunachal Pradesh, Assam and Tripura. The most spectacular increase was, however, registered by Arunachal Pradesh—a 37-fold increase during the five decades of 1961-2001. The decade of 1971-1981, saw a sudden spurt in the proportion of Christians to 4.32 per cent of the population; in the next decade their population constituted 10.29 per cent of the population and in the next decade of 1991-2001 their population has increased further to 18.72 per cent. Thus, in just three decades Christians have gone from being an insignificant part of the population to become a substantial minority. If this trend continues, Arunachal Pradesh, a tribal-majority State, is likely to be another Christian majority state in another two decades or so. Incidentally, Tirap and Changlang districts, bordering Nagaland and Mynmar, being claimed as a part of Greater Nagaland, have substantial Christian population, 50 per cent and 17.5 per cent, respectively in the 2001 census.

The British government assisted by the Christian missionaries introduced western system of education to bring the tribes in touch with modern civilization and to use the educated class as a link between the ruler and the ruled.

Extensive use of English in school curricula was a decisive contribution to acculturation of the tribal communities. Though vernacular was used for the propagation of the Gospel and primary education, English was the only language for higher education. English served as the *lingua franca* for communication among the educated elements of all tribes and helped the development of pan-tribal solidarity.

The early effects of the missionary work in the tribal societies of North-Eastern India were the weakening of the traditional social sanctions, the general alienation of the newly converted Christians from the community and the inculcation of disrespect for traditional culture. The missionary evangelization created cleavages within the tribal societies by ideologically and institutionally alienating the converts from their traditional communal life. By their physical presence missionaries were important agents in the acculturation process. Their western living standards in the isolated mission stations, their clothes and other gadgets were significant in the acculturation process of the tribal people.[101] The Christian missionaries also whipped up the inveterate prejudices against the Hindus, describing them as inimical to animism and Christianity.[102]

The evil effect of conversion on Indian national life was condemned by our leaders in no uncertain terms. They were more worried about the de-nationalization effect of this new religion. In a paper entitled "The foreign missionary danger", Elwin highlighted "the rapid pace of conversion of tribes and the danger of the conversion within a few years of the entire aboriginal population in to a querulous, anti-national, aggressive" minority community, "with none of the old virtues and few of the new, which will be a thorn in the side of the future Government of India"; and he advocated the prohibition of proselytisation as in many other free countries.[103] He wrote:

> Change of religion is actually harmful to the aborigines. It destroys tribal unity, strips the people of age-long moral sanctions, separates them from the mass of their fellow countrymen and in many cases leads to decadence that is as pathetic as it is deplorable, the methods employed are questionable. There is economic exploitation, exploitation of ignorance and social exploitation. Therefore, missionaries should be withdrawn from tribal areas.[104]

The influence and activities of the Christian missionaries have, no doubt, brought tremendous changes in the life style and consumption pattern of the tribal of the North-East. It was under the inveterate influence and edifice of the church that the Nagas, Mizos, Garos, Khasis and other tribes began to abandon their rude primitive animistic ways of life, giving place, among other things, to political consciousness to achieve the destiny of a modern self-government under the British patronage. But the primary goal of the missionaries was conversion. As Srinivas says:

> The opening of schools, hospitals and other welfare agencies by the missionaries in areas where *Harijans* and tribals live, appear to the

Table 4.2: Christian Population in the North-Eastern States, 1901-2001

Year	Arunachal Pradesh		Assam		Manipur		Meghalaya		Mizoram		Nagaland		Tripura	
	No. of Christian population	% of total population	No. of Christian population	% of total population	No. of Christian population	% of total population	No. of Christian population	% of total population	No. of Christian population	% of total population	No. of Christian population	% of total population	No. of Christian population	% of total population
1901			13,630	0.41	45	.016	20,970	6.16	45	0.05	601	0.59	138	0.08
1911			22,820	0.59	132	.038	36,700	9.31	2,461	2.70	3,308	2.21	138	0.06
1921			41,680	0.90	4,050	1.05	48,730	11.54	27,720	28.17	8,734	5.43	1,860	0.61
1931			79,020	1.42	10,400	2.33	75,520	15.71	59,120	47.52	22,910	12.81	2,596	0.68
1941			37,630	0.56	25,730	5.02	1,060	0.19					316	0.06
1951			160,400	2.00	68,393	11.84	149,378	24.66	177,600	90.52	98,070	46.05	5,266	0.82
1961	1,713	0.51	263,100	2.43	152,043	19.49	270,900	35.21	230,500	86.63	195,588	52.98	10,039	0.88
1971	3,684	0.79	381,010	2.61	279,243	26.03	475,267	46.98	286,141	86.07	344,798	66.77	15,713	1.01
1981	27,306	4.32	NA	NA	421,702	29.68	702,854	52.61	413,840	83.81	621,590	80.22	24,872	1.21
1991	89,013	10.29	744,367	3.32	626,669	34.12	1,146,092	64.58	591,342	85.73	1,057,940	87.47	46,472	1.69
2001	205,548	18.72	986,589	3.70	737,578	34.04	1,628,986	70.25	772,809	86.97	1,790,349	89.97	102,489	3.56

Source: A.P. Joshi, M.D. Srinivas and J.K. Bajaj, *Religious Demography of India,* 2003, Centre for Policy Studies, Chennai, Table D-5, pp. 183-188.

> Hindus as only baits in the trap of conversion. The linking up of humanitarianism with proselytization has made the former suspect. Even very liberal, westernized Hindus feel this way.[105]

Under the influence of the Christian missionaries and education imparted by them, the nascent tribal intelligentsia developed a new culture and a personality sharply different from those of the rest of India. Thus, a section of the newly-educated tribal elites questioned their integration even in 1947 when the insulated hill tribes became a part of Independent India. It is in this context the question of independence and secession of the Nagas, and later of the Mizos emerged. Yonuo points out:

> The Nagas, Kukis, Mizos, Khasis and some other tribes were reluctant to join the Indian Union in the beginning after the partition of the Indian subcontinent took place. The reasons of their apathy towards India were the British policy of exclusion of Naga areas from the mainstream of Indian life, discretionary power given to the Governor regarding applicability of laws, the impact of Christianity, the difference between Hinduised Assamese Manipuri life and Christianized animistic Naga life and their fear of Hindu rule as once apprehended by Winston Churchill. In spite of their own efforts at creating a hill united state called Indo-Burman land, the idea receded quickly into thin air. The Garo-Khasi chose to remain in India whereas the extreme Nagas and Mizos stood swornly for independent states.[106]

The same thing happened in Jaffna of Sri Lanka. Tamil historians in Jaffna once argued that but for the Church and the missionaries, the ethnic strife would not have become so pronounced. It is because of the missionaries who settled down in Jaffna and founded a chain of schools and colleges that the Tamils acquired English education. This gave them a head start both during the British Raj and when Ceylon became independent in 1948, because the bureaucracy required English-educated officers in a multi-ethnic country. The Jaffna Tamils came to occupy important positions in Government and in the judiciary, for instance. This naturally excited the Sinhala majority, which started hating the prominence of the Tamils and thus the ethnic strife between the Sinhala Buddhists and the Sri Lankan Tamils got sharpened.[107]

The involvement of Christian Missionaries in the secessionist movement in the Nagaland was revealed by no less a person than Rev. Michael Scott who was well-known for espousing the Naga cause:

> Many of the missionaries who were allowed there (Nagaland) seem to have conveyed a peculiar form of religion based more on the verbal infallibility of the Bible and a social and political ethics more compatible with a violent form of nationalism than Christ's teaching in the Sermon of the Mount and the New Testament.[108]

The involvement of Christian Missionaries in the movement for the formation of a separate state in the Jharkhand region, or for the creation of small states like Meghalaya is too well known. That the Christian Missionaries selected India as a happy hunting ground for conversion is a historical fact. Organised efforts on the part of the Christian Missionaries to proselytize people since the last decade of the nineteenth century and especially in the 1930s, was the subject matter of controversy raging the country for a long time. The evil effect of conversion brought about by other methods, especially by the money power, on Indian national life was condemned by our leaders in no uncertain terms. Social reformers, from Dayanand Saraswati to Vivekananda to Gandhiji, have questioned the Church's 'real intent' and its methods at one time or another. Gandhiji said, "I believe there is no such thing as conversion from one faith to another in the accepted sense of the term...Christian missions will render true service to India if they can persuade themselves to confine their activities to humanitarian service without the ulterior motive of converting India or at least her unsophisticated villagers to Christianity, and destroying her social superstructure".[109] He was emphatically for an *atma parivartana*, conversion of heart within one's tradition, and against a *dharmantarana*, conversion across religious traditions. He was for reform from within, not for proselytisation. Gandhiji had remarked in 1936 that "Mammon had been sent to serve India and God has remained behind".[110] The Tibetan religious leader Dalai Lama also was of the view that it was advisable for people to stay within their traditional religious fold and not opt for conversions.[111]

VIII

The legislative history relating to the issue of conversion in India underscores the point that the authorities concerned were never favourably disposed towards conversion. While British India had no anti-conversion laws, many Princely States enacted anti-conversion legislations to protect their subjects from being converted. Among these the prominent laws were the Raigarh State Conversion Act, 1936, the Panna Freedom of Religion Act of 1942, the Surguja State Apostasy Act, 1945 and the Udaipur State Anti-Conversion Act, 1946, under which Christianity was banned in those areas. Similar laws were enacted in Bikaner, Jodhpur, Kalahandi and Kota and many more were specifically against conversion to Christianity.

The Raigarh State Conversion Act, 1936 banned the preaching of Christianity and prohibited the entry of Christian missionaries into the kingdom of Raigarh, Jashpur, etc. of Chhotanagpur areas. The Surguja State Apostasy Act, 1945 banned conversion from Hinduism to Islam and Christianity by vesting the power to allow or disallow conversion in the *Darbar* of the Raja under the guise of maintaining law and order and establishing public peace.

The Udaipur State Anti-Conversion Act, 1946 required all conversions from Hindu religion to other faiths to be registered officially. The known purpose of all these laws was to protect Hindus against the "onslaught" of Christian missionaries. It is interesting to note that no parallel laws were enacted in the princely states ruled by the Muslims, e.g. Hyderabad, Rampur, Junagarh etc.[112]

In the post-independence era, Parliament took up for consideration in 1954 the Indian Conversion (Regulation and Registration) Bill providing for compulsory licensing of the missionaries and for registration of conversion with government functionaries. It was opposed mainly by Christians. The Bill was eventually dropped at the behest of Prime Minister J.L. Nehru. In 1960, the Backward Communities (Religious Protection) Bill was introduced. It aimed at checking conversion of Hindus to "non-Indian religions which, as per the Bill included Islam, Christianity, Judaism and Zoroastrianism. This Bill was soon rejected by Parliament for its apparent affront on specific religious faiths. The proposed Freedom of Religion Bill of 1979 was opposed by the Minorities due to the Bill's evident bias."[113]

After the commencement of the Constitution, the Christian Missionaries, taking advantage of 'right to propagate religion' given in Article 25, stepped up their activities in those areas even where activity of the Christian Missionaries was not liked by a section of Hindus who raised a voice of protest. This led to the constitution of a committee popularly known as Niyogi Committee by the Madhya Pradesh Government to enquire into the allegations that "Christian Missionaries, either forcibly or through fraud and temptation of monetary and other gain, convert illiterate aboriginals and other backward people thereby offending the feelings of non-Christians" and that "Missions are utilised directly or indirectly for purposes of political or extra-religious objectives" under Resolution No. 318-716-V-Con dated 14-4-54 of the Political and Military Department of the Government of Madhya Pradesh. The Chairman of the Committee was Dr. M. Bhawani Shankar Niyogi, retired Chief Justice of High Court of Judicature, Nagpur and ex-Chairman, Public Service Commission, Madhya Pradesh. The other members of the Committee were Ghanashyam Singh Gupta, Ex-Speaker Madhya Pradesh Legislative Assembly, Drug, S.K. George, Ratan Lal Malaviya, MP and Bhanu Pratap Singh, MP. B.P. Pathak, Secretary to Public Health Department, Madhya Pradesh was the Member-Secretary of this Committee. The Committee undertook extensive tour in different areas of M.P. between 5-6-54 and 25-11-55 and submitted its report on 18th April, 1956. The Government of M.P. published the Report in two volumes—volume-I & volume-II Part-A & Part-B in 1956 entitled 'Report of the Christian Missionary Activities Enquiry Committee'. I cannot do better than to quote the findings of the Committee.

"On consideration of the material before us we arrive at the following conclusions of fact:

1. Since the Constitution of India came into force there has been an appreciable increase in the American Personnel of the Missionary Organisations operating in India. This increase is obviously due to the deliberate policy of the International Missionary Council to send evangelistic teams to areas of special opportunities opened to the Gospel by the Constitutional provision of religious freedom in some of the newly independent nations, equipped with new resources for mass evangelism through the press, film, radio, and television (Page No. 27 and 31 of the Missionary Obligations of the Church, 1952).
2. Enormous sums of foreign money flow into the country for Missionary work, comprising educational, medical and evangelistic activities. It was out of such funds received from abroad that in Surguja the Lutherans and other proselytizing agencies were able to secure nearly 400 converts.
3. Conversions are mostly brought about by undue influence, misrepresentation, etc. or in other words not by conviction, but by various inducements offered for proselytization in various forms. Educational facilities such as free gifts of books and education are offered to secure the conversion of minors in the primary and secondary schools under the control of the Missions. Money-lending is one of the various forms adopted as a mild form of pressure to induce proselytization. This is found very prominently in the case of Roman Catholic Missions operating in the hill tracts of Surguja, Raigarh, Mandla etc. Cases where coercion was reported to have been used are generally of those converts who wish other members of the family to join their Christian parents or to secure girls in marriage.
4. Missions are in some places used to serve extra-religious ends. In spite of assurances given by foreign and national Missionaries to authorities, instances of indirect political activities were brought to the notice of the Committee.
5. As conversion muddles the converts' sense of unity and solidarity with his society, there is a danger of his loyalty to his country and State being undermined.
6. A vile propaganda against the religion of the majority community is being systematically and deliberately carried on so as to create an apprehension of breach of public peace.
7. Evangelization in India appears to be a part of the uniform world policy to revive Christendom for re-establishing Western supremacy and is not prompted by spiritual motives. The objective is apparently to create Christian minority pockets with a view to disrupt the

solidarity of the non-Christian societies and the mass conversion of a considerable section of *Adivasis* with this ulterior motive is fraught with danger to the security of the State.

8. Schools, hospitals and orphanages are used as a means to facilitate proselytization.
9. Tribals and *Harijans* are the special targets of aggressive evangelisation for the reason that there is no adequate provision of hospitals, schools, orphanages and other social welfare services in the scheduled or specified areas".[114]

The Committee also submitted a set of recommendations. From the point of view of our study the following two recommendations are quite relevant:

(a) To check abuses prevalent regarding conversion from one religion to another it appears desirable to adopt the rule in force in Greece. It is as follows:
"Any attempt by force, or threats of illicit means, or grants of promises of financial or other aid or by fraudulent means of promises, or by moral and material assistance, or by taking advantage of any person's inexperience, or confidence or by exploiting any person's necessity or spiritual (mental) weakness or thoughtlessness, or in general, any attempt or effort (whether successful or not) directly or indirectly to penetrate into the religious conscience of persons (whether of age or under age) of another faith, for the purpose of consciously altering their religious conscience or faith, so as to agree with the ideas or convictions of the proselytising party" should be absolutely prohibited (Page 112, Religious liberty—an inquiry by Bates, 1947).

(b) We have already mentioned that in certain quarters a feeling is entertained that Article 25 of the Constitution gives a right to any person, including foreigners temporarily residing in India, to propagate his religion and that this right includes the right to secure converts. Whether the right to propagate does or does not include a right to convert has been a matter of great controversy. We consider it desirable that the matter should not be left vague or indefinite and recommend that an amendment of the Constitution may be sought, firstly, to clarify that the right of propagation has been given only to the citizens of India and secondly, that it does not include conversion brought about by force, fraud, or illicit means'.[115]

What the Niyogi Committee found in M.P. way back in 1956 was the general picture prevalent in entire India. The condition might even be worse in some areas. However, in 1967-68, Orissa and Madhya Pradesh enacted local laws called the Orissa Freedom of Religion Act, 1967 and the Madhya Pradesh Dharma Swatantrya Adhiniyam, 1968. Along similar lines, the Arunachal Pradesh Freedom of Religion Act, 1978, the Gujarat Freedom of Religion Act, 2003, the Rajasthan Freedom of Religion Act, 2006 and the Himachal Pradesh Freedom of Religion Act, 2006 were enacted. Each of these Freedom of Religion Acts provides definitions of 'Government', 'conversion', 'indigenous faith', 'force', 'fraud', 'inducement' (and in the case of Arunachal Pradesh, that of 'prescribed and religious faith'). Incidentally, Orissa, M.P., Arunachal Pradesh and Himachal Pradesh enacted these laws when these States were ruled by the Congress. Only Gujarat and Rajasthan enacted these laws when the BJP was in power in these States.

So long India was a lovely pasture land for the Christian Missionaries only. With the addition of Petro-Dollar force to this rank the complexion has changed for the worse. The issue of religious conversion raised by the Arya Samaj and now followed by the Sangh Parivar lies in the Hindu fear of numerical decline. The Viswa Hindu Parishad (VHP) took a much more militant stance on the issue of Muslim population growth. Indeed, there were forced conversions, but these were isolated instances; many of these conversions took place due to the preaching of Sufi saints. The conversion issue has assumed a serious dimension since the news of mass-scale conversion of Hindus to Islam at Minakshipuram and other places sometime in 1981 in furtherance of a secret plan of a Muslim organisation to increase the Muslim population in India with the ultimate aim of capturing political power in India received wide publicity. The Viswa Hindu Parishad launched an aggressive movement against the conversion of Hindus to Islam in 1981 when *dalit* families were converted to Islam in Meenakshipuram.

In the aftermath of the Meenakshipuram conversion of February 1981, the Congress-I ruled Central Government through the Ministry of Home Affairs, Government of India, advised the State Governments and the Union Territory Administrations to enact laws to regulate change of religion on the lines of the existing Acts in Madhya Pradesh, Orissa and Arunachal Pradesh,[116] But only Rajasthan, Gujarat and Himachal Pradesh enacted such a law in the first decade of the twenty-first century. The Madhya Pradesh Act was inherited by Chhattisgarh when it was created out of this State in 2000. Tamil Nadu also promulgated the Tamil Nadu Prohibition of Forcible Conversion of Religion Ordinance on October 5, 2002 which was subsequently adopted by the State Assembly on October 31, 2002. But failure to win a single Lok Sabha seat in the 14th Lok Sabha elections held between 20th April and 10th May, 2004, made the Jayalalitha Government to repeal this Act on May 18, 2004.[117]

It may be noted that the Supreme Court in *Rev. Stanislaus* v. *the State of Madhya Pradesh,* AIR 1977 SC 908, 1977 SCR (2) 611 held that the right to propagate conferred by Article 25 did not include the right to convert. The case arose out of appeals from the judgements of the Orissa and Madhya Pradesh High Courts. The Orissa High Court had held that the law passed by the legislature penalising conversions obtained by fraud, coercion and inducement infringed the right to propagate religion under Article 25. The Madhya Pradesh High Court upheld the validity of a similar law.

The five-judge Bench of the Supreme Court, speaking through Chief Justice A.N. Ray, agreed with the Madhya Pradesh High Court judgement and reversed the judgement of the Orissa High Court. The Supreme Court referred to the dictionary meaning of the expression "propagate" and said:

> The expression 'propagate' has been defined in the Shorter Oxford Dictionary to mean "to spread from person to person, or from place to place, to disseminate, diffuse (a statement, belief, practice, etc.)" According to the Century Dictionary (which is an *Encyclopaedic Lexicon of the English Language*) Vol. VI, 'propagate' means as follows:—"To transmit or spread from person to person or from place to place; carry forward or onward; diffuse; extend; as propagate a report; to propagate the Christian religion".
>
> We have no doubt that it is in this sense that the word 'propagate' has been used in Article 25 (1), for what the Article grants is not the right to convert another person to one's own religion, but to transmit or spread one's religion by an exposition of its tenets. It has to be remembered that Article 25 (1) guarantees "freedom of conscience" to every citizen, and not merely to the followers of one particular religion, and that, in turn, postulates that there is no fundamental right to convert another person to one's own religion because if a person purposely undertakes the conversion of another person to his religion, as distinguished from his effort to transmit or spread the tenets of his religion, that would impinge on the "freedom of conscience" guaranteed to all the citizens of the country alike.... It has to be appreciated that the freedom of religion enshrined in the Article is not guaranteed in respect of one religion only, but covers all religions alike, and it can be properly enjoyed by a person if he exercises his right in a manner commensurate with the like freedom of persons following the other religions. What is freedom for one, is freedom for the other, in equal measure, and there can therefore be no such thing as a fundamental right to convert any person to one's own religion.[118]

Commenting on this judgement, K.P. Aleaz has made a distinction between 'conversion' and 'proselytisation'. His point is that what is meant by 'conversion' in the above judgement is 'proselytising'. Propagation and conversion are not opposed to each other; it is propagation and proselytising which are opposed to each other.[119]

This judgement does not whittle down the right under Article 25. However, coupled with the anti-conversion statutes, it has succeeded in putting the issue of conversions within the shroud of illegality. Most importantly, this judicial decision also facilitated the linkage between conversion and propagation ensuring that propagation became an empty shell of a right linked necessarily to a bad word called 'conversion'. As Arvind Narrain, and Clifton D'Rozario very rightly pointed out, "the right of a person to convert from one religion to another has to be viewed against the duality of constitutional rights and historical religious mobility in India".[120]

IX

During the freedom movement, there was a debate on conversions and re-conversions. Muslims had *Tabligh* and *Tanzeem* movements, aiming to win over new followers to the faith, the Hindus under Swami Shraddhananda undertook the *Shuddhi* movement, that is, purifying those people who had converted to Islam and taking them back within the fold of Hinduism. The 1923 Benaras session of the Hindu Mahasabha incorporated the programme in its agenda also.

This is something similar to what is being attempted by the VHP when it talks of re-conversion in the context of tribal groups. "*Operation Ghar Wapsi*" (operation homecoming) had begun in some tribal pockets to reconvert Christian tribals to the Hindu fold. If a low caste Hindu who had converted to another faith or any of his descendants reconverts to Hinduism, he might get back his original caste.[121]

The topic of conversions has come to occupy centre-stage in Indian affairs ever since the visit of Pope John Paul II to this country in November, 1999. His open indictment of India on May 18, 2006 on the ceremonial occasion of presentation of credentials by India's new ambassador Amitava Tripathi on the discriminatory nature of the anti-conversion laws and his call to 'firmly reject' them[122] exposed the true purpose of the evangelical work undertaken by the Christian missionaries. As M.N. Rao, a former Chief Justice of Himachal Pradesh High Court, has rightly pointed out, "when the highest court of this country has upheld the constitutionality of laws prohibiting fraudulent conversions, any criticism that these laws are aimed at depriving the rights of minority religions is absolutely baseless".[123] The controversy over conversion and re-conversion has vitiated the atmosphere.

Organizations like the Viswa Hindu Parishad, the Banabasi Kalyan Parishad, the Bajrang Dal, the Hindu Jagran Vedike, the Hindu Jagran Manch and a host of Hindu organizations have been under pressure for what happened to the Christian community—killings, ransacking and looting of villages, burning of Churches, intimidation and harassment of Christian families and destruction of property including places of worship. There are reports of sporadic incidents of killing of Christian preachers, attacks on Christians and their institutes in many pockets in UP, MP, Haryana, Maharashtra, Punjab, Orissa, Gujarat and Karnataka and even of communal riots that broke out in some pockets of Kandhamal district in Orissa, Dangs district in Gujarat, Chikmagalur, Davangere and other districts in Karnataka and elsewhere resulting in loss of lives and properties. The violence involving the Church and locals in these places has sullied India's image abroad. The incident that attracted world-wide attention was that of Dr. Graham Stuart Staines (58), the Australian Christian missionary who along with his two sons Philip (10) and Timothy (6) was burnt to death by a gang while sleeping in his station wagon at Mohonpur village in Keonjhar district, Orissa on January 22, 1999. In 2003, the Bajrang Dal activist, Dara Singh, was convicted for this offence. Such incidents do not augur well for a secular country like India.

The recent brutal sexual assault on a seventy-year old nun in the convent of Jesus and Mary School in Ranaghat in West Bengal on March 14, 2015 has received world-wide publicity and has brought disgrace to the country. Though the Vice-Chairman of the State Minority Commission, Maria Fernandes, said that the attack on the convent had "communal overtone",[124] subsequent arrest of culprits in this case revealed that there was no communal angle in this incident because criminals perpetrated this offence purely from a criminal motive. However, as Cardinal Baselios Cleemis, head of the Catholic Church in India says, "such attacks disfigure the country's secular fabric. Such attacks cause anxiety within the community. These are bad for India's image globally and bad for the economy".[125] An activist apprehends that there may even be backlash in Western countries, sooner or later, as news spread about the vandalizing of Christian churches, the rape of nuns in Kolkata and Orissa, and the burning down of a Delhi church.[126]

America's watchdog on religious freedom, the United States Commission on International Religious Freedom, in its latest annual report has blamed the Sangh and its affiliates for forcible conversions and attacks on Christian and Muslims and has noted an increase in such incidents after the Narendra Modi government came to power. The report says that Andhra Pradesh, Uttar Pradesh, Bihar, Chhattisgarh, Gujarat, Odisha, Karnataka, Madhya Pradesh, Maharashtra and Rajasthan have witnessed the highest incidence of religiously motivated and communal violence among Indian States. The report has, however, described Modi's reassurance to minorities in February 2015, that his government would not let any religious group incite hatred as a "positive development".[127]

In the wake of raging debate over "conversion and re-conversion", a perceptible analyst has found six different strands to conversion in India. There is first the conversion of lower caste Hindus to Islam or Christianity. The economics element was primary; in fact even among Christians, such groups were called Rice Christians. The Bajrang Dal event where Muslims and Christians reconverted to Hinduism is another variation. The Dal calls this act homecoming (*Ghar Vapsi*). A third type of conversion takes place among Dalit movements. These groups reject caste in Hinduism and opt for new Buddhism. There is a fourth kind of conversion where the individual undergoes a fundamental change of belief and accepts another religion and its tenets. This is a genuine act of belief. There is a fifth act of conversion which is more tactical or instrumental. The individual converts to another religion to evade a legal obstacle. Actor Dharmendra converted to Islam so that he could marry Hema Malini. It is the sixth variant which is becoming most problematic. Here conversion becomes a hustle, an act of enticement, a force or an incentive. It is this act of conversion which is problematic and it is this that the RSS is challenging through large-scale acts of re-conversion. It has opened a Pandora's Box where a conversion becomes an extension of development and elections.[128]

To these another strand may be added, that is, the threat to convert to another religion. Conversion is a question of faith but what seems to surface is that it has become a ransom to demand this or that and it is used as a threat. "If you do not give us land we will convert, we want equality and so we will convert", are some of these threats. Monetary benefits and the hope of poverty alleviation motivated many of the converts. The leaders of the Dhangars—a caste of herders from Agra and nearby regions held a mahapanchayat in Agra on December 28, 2014 and declared that they would convert *en masse* to Christianity if they were not given Scheduled Caste certificates in a month's time.[129]

Of the six strands mentioned above, the fourth is the ideal one. Actually, there can be no objection if the conversion takes place due to real change of heart. It cannot be denied that religious conversion is a matter of individual choice guaranteed as a fundamental right under the Constitution, and not a collective right of any religious community to proselytise. What matters is not whether such conversions are necessary but whether the individual is allowed the freedom of conscience and free profession, practice and propagation of a religion of his or her choice provided under Article 25. Conversion may not be necessary for anyone but the person converting, and there should not be any impediment to such type of conversion.

That every individual is at liberty to convert or reconvert another by argument or persuasion is never questioned or challenged. If conversion is effected for real love of the religion and for no other consideration, it is always welcome. But conversion from one religion to another due to change of heart is a rare thing. Some extraneous factors like inducement, allurement, temptation, undue influence etc. are always at play. Many books on this issue have been written. Causative factors behind the conversion were analysed and ameliorative steps were even suggested. Conversion was found to be a source of potential danger to national unity and stability. Gandhiji had said[130] to the Missionaries that it was not unusual to find Christianity synonymous with denationalisation and Europeanisation.

It may be noted that this 'right to propagate religion' is not confined to citizens of India, but extends to all 'persons' including aliens, and individuals exercising their rights individually or through institutions. While Israel, Korea, China, Sri Lanka and some Latin American nations already have anti-conversion laws in place,[131] India could not even act on the recommendation of the Niyogi Committee to constitutionally restrict the right of propagation only to the citizens of India. If this very sane suggestion was implemented, proselytisation under the cloak of humanitarian work by foreign missionaries could have been prevented. A *Tehelka* investigative report[132] says "a new mood of aggressive evangelism has been emanating from America" and it has India as one of its key targets.

The fifth type of conversion, no doubt, takes place voluntarily. For example, when a Hindu marries a Muslim or a Christian, he may voluntarily get himself converted to Islam or Christianity.[133] But more-often-than-not, there is an open inducement to a Hindu husband who wants to enter into second marriage while the first is subsisting, to become a Muslim. Since monogamy is the law for Hindus and Muslim Law permits as many as four wives in India, errant Hindu husbands embrace Islam to circumvent the provisions of the Hindu law and to escape from penal consequences.[134] While some courts refuse to recognize the rights acquired under the converted law, there have been cases where courts ignored ulterior motive behind the conversions. For instance, a division bench of Justices Pius C. Kuriakose and Babu Mahew P. Joseph of the Kerala High Court has ruled on December 11, 2012 that marriage preceded by conversion—as a means to facilitate marriage—will be deemed invalid before the law.[135] But, Justice Suesh Kait of the Delhi High Court on July 31, 2011 upheld the marriage of cousins born in Hindu community after conversion to Christianity.[136] The Allahabad High Court has ruled on December 16, 2014 that the religious conversion of girls "without their faith and belief in Islam" and "solely for the purpose of marriage" to Muslim boys could not be held valid.[137]

Justices Kuldip Singh and R.M. Sahai of the Supreme Court in *Sarla Mudgal* vs. *Union of India,* AIR 1995 SC 1531 have sealed back-door entries to polygamous marriages by misusing religion. Four writ petitions were disposed in this case. Two petitions related to the same case. A Hindu husband, wanting to marry again while he was still married to his first wife, resorted to the expedient of converting himself and his new bride to Islam. The second petition in the same case was by the "new" wife who alleged that the husband had gone back to his first wife and she had no recourse either under Hindu or Muslim personal law. In the second case, a Hindu husband beat his wife and broke her jaw. Within three years of the marriage he ran away with another Hindu girl and married her after both converted to Islam. In the last case, the Hindu husband told his wife he no longer wanted her and would convert to Islam and marry another Hindu girl. The petitioner sought to restrain the husband from contracting the second marriage. The judges held that the conversions to Islam were undertaken for extraneous purposes and that the marriages in question amounted to bigamy or adultery, having been procured by fraud.

The observation of Justice Sagir Ahmed while nullifying conversion of a non-Muslim to Islam only for the purpose of marriage in *Lily Thomas* merits reproduction. This is what he had said:

> Religion is a matter of faith stemming from the depth of the heart and mind. Religion is a belief which binds the spiritual nature of man to a super-natural being; it is an object of conscientious devotion, faith and pietism. Devotion in its fullest sense is a consecration and denotes an act of worship. Faith in the strict sense constitutes firm reliance on the truth of religious doctrines in every system of religion. Religion, faith or devotion are not easily interchangeable. If the person feigns to have adopted another religion just for some worldly gain or benefit, it would be religious bigotry. Looked at from this angle, a person who mockingly adopts another religion where plurality of marriage is permitted so as to renounce the previous marriage and desert the wife, he cannot be permitted to take advantage of his exploitation as religion is not a commodity to be exploited. The institution of marriage under every personal law is a sacred institution. Under Hindu Law, Marriage is a sacrament. Both have to be preserved.[138]

The third type of conversion, that is conversion to Buddhism, got a stimulus in 1990 when the Neo-Buddhists were treated as Scheduled Castes for the purpose of the affirmative action policies. With the extension of the benefits of affirmative action policies to the Neo-Buddhists, demands have surfaced for according the same benefits to the Dalit Muslims and Dalit Christians.

The first, second and sixth variants, mentioned above, are more or less complimentary to one another. The conversion of poor people by offering them free food and education, the so-called rice Christians, as a practice is going on for several decades, if not centuries, and many true Christians abhor this practice. In November 2011 All Saints pastor C.M. Khanna was arrested by the Jammu & Kashmir police under Sections 153-A and 295-A of the IPC for "deliberately hurting the religious sentiments of the people to disturb peace "by converting young Muslim boys and girls through allurement.[139] Mari

Marcel Thekaekara, a freelance writer, even said that converting people by offering them food and education is technically and theologically not a conversion at all, especially if foreign funds are utilized to accomplish such conversions.[140] Rev. Valson Thampu, however, points out: "Many of the mainline churches in India have in recent times stated publicly that they neither practise nor encourage conversions. But, it continues to be dogmatically assumed, despite paucity of evidence, that conversions are engineered in their thousands, and that they are perforce mercenary in character".[141]

But, Pope John Paul II's open indictment of India on May 18, 2006 on the ceremonial occasion of presentation of credentials by India's new ambassador Amitava Tripathi on the discriminatory nature of the anti-conversion laws and his call to 'firmly reject' them[142] exposed the true purpose of the evangelical work undertaken by the Christian missionaries.

With the wresting of power at the Centre by the BJP in May 2014, there is perceptible rise in the "*Ghar Wapsi*" programme being carried out by the Sangh Parivar in Jharkhand, Bihar, Gujarat and other places by re-converting people from the Christian and Islamic folds. The VHP, however, does not consider *Ghar Wapsi* campaign as an act of religious conversion. "It is no *dharma parivartan* (religious conversion). It's homecoming of those whose forefathers had converted years ago", asserts BJP MP Yogi Adityanath.[143]

It has been alleged that such re-conversions are being undertaken by administering threat to and intimidation of impoverished communities by the Sangh Parivar. For instance, a convenor of the Bajrang Dal for Meerut said on December 23, 2014 that Bangladeshis living in India must either leave the country or convert to Hinduism.[144] There was an allegation that conversion of 57 Muslim families at Madhunagar in Agra on December 8, 2014 (popularly known as Agra conversion) was a forced one. The UP Minority Commission after visiting the area came to the conclusion that the conversion was not forced, but there was an element of cheating involved in it.[145] This Minority Commission in its final report, however, said that no conversion had taken place.[146] Joint General Secretary of VHP Surendra Jain even said that "Muslims are at war across the globe. If they want respect in India, they should become Hindus."[147]

It was the lower castes that Islamic and Christian missionaries focused on, and many changed faith being attracted by the promise of an egalitarian social order. But even after several generations, they still live the same life that their Hindu brethren are condemned to.

Doctrinally, Christianity and Islam may preach egalitarianism, but the fact is that in practice, they observe caste system. Those who converted to Islam and Christianity drawn by the promise of an egalitarian social order have not fared any better than lower caste Hindus. So, while Islam and Christianity did indeed proselytise Hindus, these religions adopted the caste system in all its rigidity. The converts carried the caste with them. So, there are Brahmin Christians, *Dalit* Christians in India. There are separate parishes and even burial grounds for *Dalit* Christians in Kerala and elsewhere. So, the demand to treat the *Dalit* Christians and *Dalit* Muslims at par with the Hindu *Dalits* in the matter of extending affirmative action is gaining ground across India.

Keeping this segment of population in mind, Vyankatesh Abdeo, Vishwa Hindu Parishad (VHP) central secretary told *The Hindu* on December 17, 2014 that "caste matters little for us when the person is back in *Hindu dharma*. But if he or she wants a particular caste, it is made accessible to them".[148]

The Supreme Court judgements are all categorical that the question of caste, which is integral to Hinduism, can be decided neither by the individual concerned nor by those performing any of the rituals of re-conversion. The decision is in the hands of members of the caste that the reconverted person wants to join. Though they have no statutory status, caste associations will determine whether the re-converted person can join their fold. This has far-reaching implications for a *dalit* returning to Hinduism. Such a *dalit* will be entitled to reservations, whether in educational institutions, jobs or elections, only if there is evidence establishing that he has been accepted back into his former caste.

In *Kothapalli Narasayya* vs. *Jammana Jogi,* AIR 1976 SC 937, it is stated:

> These cases show that the consistent view taken in this country from the time Administrator-General of *Madras* vs. *Anandachari* was decided, that is, since 1886, has been that on reconversion to Hinduism, a person can once again become a member of the caste in which he was born and to which he belonged before conversion to another religion, if the members of the caste accept him as a member. There is no reason either on principle or on authority which should compel us to disregard this view which has prevailed for almost a century and lay down a different rule on the subject. If a person who has embraced another religion can be reconverted to Hinduism, there is no rational principle why he should not be able to come back to his caste, if the other members of the caste are prepared to readmit him as a member. It stands to reason that he should be able to come back to the fold to which he once belonged, provided of course the community is willing to take him within the fold. A Mahar or a Koli or a Mala would not be recognised as anything but a Mahar or a Koli or a Mala after reconversion to Hinduism and he would suffer from the same social and economic disabilities from which he suffered before he was converted to another religion. It is, therefore, obvious

> that the object and purpose of the Constitution (Scheduled Castes) Order, 1950 would be advanced rather than retarded by taking the view that on reconversion to Hinduism, a person can once again become a member of the Scheduled Caste to which he belonged prior to his conversion. We accordingly agree with the view taken by the High Court that on reconversion to Hinduism, the first respondent could once again revert to his original Adi Dravida caste if he was accepted as such by the other members of the caste.

In *S. Anbalagan* vs. *Devarajan and others*, (1984) 2 SCC 112, the Supreme Court observed:

> These precedents, particularly those from South India, clearly establish that no particular ceremony is prescribed for reconversion to Hinduism of a person who had earlier embraced another religion. Unless the practice of the caste makes it necessary, no expiatory rites need be performed and, ordinarily, he regains his caste unless the community does not accept him. In fact, it may not be accurate to say that he regains his caste; it may be more accurate to say that he never lost his caste in the first instance when he embraced another religion. The practice of caste however irrational it may appear to our reason and however repugnant it may appear to our moral and social sense, is so deep-rooted in the Indian people that its mark does not seem to disappear on conversion to a different religion. If it disappears, it disappears only to reappear on reconversion. The mark of caste does not seem to really disappear even after some generations after conversion.

In *Kailash Sonkar* vs. *Smt. Maya Devi*, (1984) 2 SCC 91, 25, Justice Fazal Ali made the following observation:

> In our opinion, there is one aspect which does not appear to have been dealt with by any of the cases discussed by us. Suppose, A, a member of the scheduled caste, is converted to Christianity and marries a Christian girl and a daughter is born to him who, according to the tenets of Christian religion, is baptised and educated. After she has attained the age of discretion she decides of her own volition to re-embrace Hinduism, should in such a case revival of the caste depend on the views of the members of the community of the caste concerned or would it automatically revive on her reconversion if the same is genuine and followed by the necessary rites and ceremonies? In other words, is it not open for B (the daughter) to say that because she was born of Christian parents their religion cannot be thrust on her when after attaining the age of discretion and gaining

> some knowledge of the world affairs, she decides to revert to her old religion. It was not her fault that she was born of Christian parents and baptised at a time when she was still a minor and knew nothing about the religion.
>
> Therefore, should the revival of the caste depend on the whim or will of the members of the community of her original caste or she would lose her caste for ever merely because fortunately or unfortunately she was born in a Christian family? With due respect, our confirmed opinion is that although the views of the members of the community would be an important factor, their views should not be allowed to (*sic*) a complete loss of the caste to which B belonged. Indeed, if too much stress is laid on the views of the members of the community the same may lead to dangerous exploitation.
>
> But from that it does not necessarily follow as an invariable rule that whenever a person renounces Hinduism and embraces another religious faith, he automatically ceases to be a member of the caste in which he was born and to which he belonged prior to his conversion. If the structure of the caste is such that its members must necessarily belong to Hindu religion, a member, who ceases to be a Hindu, would go out of the caste, because no non-Hindu can be in the caste according to its rules and regulations. Where, on the other hand, having regard to its structure, as it has evolved over the years, a caste may consist not only of persons professing Hindu religion but also persons professing some other religion as well, conversion from Hinduism to that other religion may not involve loss of caste, because even persons professing such other religion can be members of the caste. This is indeed not an infrequent phenomenon in South India where, in some of the castes, even after conversion to Christianity, a person is regarded as continuing to belong to the caste.

In *C.M. Arumugam* vs. *S. Rajagopal and others*, (1976) 1 SCC 863, the Supreme Court made the following observation:

> These cases show that the consistent view taken in this country from the time *Administrator-General of Madras* vs. *Anandachari* was decided, that is, since 1886, has been that on reconversion to Hinduism, a person can once again, become a member of the caste in which he was born and to which he belonged before conversion to another religion, if the members of the caste accept him as a member. There is no reason either on principle or on authority which should compel us to disregard this view which has prevailed for almost a century and lay down a different rule on the subject. If a person who has embraced another religion can be reconverted to Hinduism, there

> is no rational principle why he should not be able to come back to his caste, if the other members of the caste are prepared to readmit him as a member. It stands to reason that he should be able to come back to the fold to which he once belonged, provided of course the community is willing to take him within the fold. It is the orthodox Hindu society still dominated to a large extent, particularly in rural areas, by medievalistic outlook and status-oriented approach which attaches social and economic disabilities to a person belonging to a scheduled caste and that is why certain favoured treatment is given to him by the Constitution. Once such a person ceases to be a Hindu and becomes a Christian, the social and economic disabilities arising because of Hindu religion cease and hence it is no longer necessary to give him protection and for this reason he is deemed not to belong to a scheduled caste. But when he is reconverted to Hinduism, the social and economic disabilities once again revive and become attached to him because these are disabilities inflicted by Hinduism.

In view of these and other judicial pronouncements, the VHP functionary's statement that people converting to Hinduism could choose their caste is not legally tenable or socially sustainable. The discretion left to caste associations arises from the particular nature of Hinduism, acknowledged by the Supreme Court in several cases. Indeed, if Hinduism is not a proselytising religion, unlike Christianity and Islam, it is because of this caste complexity. If one were to be converted to Hinduism, the question arises which caste is to be assigned to the new convert. This question has become more complicated because the State policy provides for reservations on the basis of caste. "And since most of the conversions from Hinduism had been of oppressed castes, the process of re-conversion is tied up with the reservations policy", points out an analyst.[149]

The affirmative action policy, being caste-based, was a positive impediment for its beneficiaries to convert to another religion other than Hinduism in the post-independence period. This embargo was lifted so far as neo-Buddhists are concerned when the affirmative action policies were extended to them in 1990. But the tribes are not affected by this policy because any tribe, whatever their religion might be, can get this benefit. So in post-independence period, the tribal communities are the targets of conversion as is evidenced by the change in the demographic composition in the North-east in the post-independence period. So, it is no wonder that the primary target of '*ghar wapsi*' programme of the saffron brigade is there conversion of tribals in order to save their original identity as well as culture.[150]

Majority Hindu caste organisations of Kerala remain divided over the Vishwa Hindu Parishad's call that the re-converts could return to any Hindu caste of their choice. V. Ramalingam, State president of the Kerala Brahmana

Sabha said that the organization never encouraged re-conversion. Brahmanism is something that can only be achieved through birth. One has to be born to a Brahmin couple to become a Brahmin. No one can become Brahmin through re-conversion. Vellapally Natesan, General Secretary of the Sree Narayana Dharma Paripalana Yogam, on the other hand, welcomed reconverts to Ezhava community. There has been a drop in the demographic strength of the Ezhava community due to conversions and other factors. If anyone was willing to become an Ezhava by caste, the Yogam would welcome them as the move would help in bolstering the strength of the community. G. Sukumaran of the Nair Service Society, however, refused to comment on the developments and stated that he was yet to study the development.[151]

Conversion is a very emotive issue. It is not simply a matter of God or faith, but a complex web of issues like human relationships, material gain, power, politics and so on. As Anirban Kashyap says:

> Unbridled and unrestricted 'right to propagate religion' has made India a play-ground of money power of those forces, which work for the destabilisation and disintegration of India. So long India was a lovely pasture land for the Christian Missionaries only. With the addition of Petro-Dollar force to this rank the complexion has changed for the worse. India witnessed vivisection of the country on the basis of religion. All efforts should have been directed to contain those forces which might endanger the integrity and stability of the country in later years. But our leaders refused to take lesson from History and decided to turn a deaf ear to those persons who warned them of the likely consequences of their policy.[152]

The likely effect of conversion on the social, communal, religious, and economic condition of the country as well as its impact on the overall law and order situation in the country should have been taken into consideration by our Founding Fathers at the time of Framing of the Constitution. But they failed to insulate the society from the raging 'conversion' and 'anti-conversion' controversy. If some sort of restriction on conversion as suggested by M. Ananthasayanam Ayyanger, R.V. Dhulekar and K.T. Shah in the Constituent Assembly way back in 1947 either as a part of Article 25 or in a separate Article was imposed at that formative stage of nation building it would have contributed immensely to easing the situation in the later years.

In the wake of the controversy generated over "conversion by inducement" of Muslims in Agra, the BJP, at the end of a three-hour discussion in the Lok Sabha on December 11, 2014, tried to turn the tables on the Opposition by calling for a national law to curb conversion.[153] Union Finance Minister Arun Jaitley had offered to the Opposition in the Rajya Sabha on December 15, 2014 two options: A total ban on religious conversions or a ban on forcible religious conversions. But both the CPI(M) and the Congress (I) said that there was no need for a separate anti-conversion law as the Constitution and Indian Penal Code had adequate safeguards against conversion by duress and inducement.[154] Incidentally, in the aftermath of the Meenakshipuram conversion of February 1981 the same Congress (I) while in power at the Centre had advised the State Governments and the Union Territory Administrations to enact laws to regulate change of religion on the lines of the existing Acts in Madhya Pradesh, Orissa and Arunachal Pradesh.[155]

Speaking at a conference of state minorities commissions on March 23, 2015, Union Home Minister Rajnath Singh questioned whether social service could not be performed in India without resorting to conversion.[156] He also called for a national debate on conversion and the need for an anti-conversion law, highlighting Sangh Parivar's concern about demographic change through conversion. He questioned whether any country would allow changes in its demographic character.[157] Stating that the BJP had always been opposed to forcible conversion, BJP president Amit Shah called upon secular bloc to back an anti-conversion law.[158]

The National United Christian Forum (NUCF) — comprising three leading churches of the Catholic Bishops' Conference of India, National Council of Churches in India and Evangelical Fellowship of India—on December 20, 2014 opposed the government's move to ban conversion.[159] Christian missionaries have combined propagation of religion with social service. That it pays off in spite of the existence of an anti-conversion law in Arunachal Pradesh in the shape of the Arunachal Pradesh Freedom of Religion Act, 1978 is proved by the fact that there is a steady increase in the Christian population in this State— a 37-fold increase during the five decades of 1961-2001. If this trend continues, Arunachal Pradesh, a tribal-majority State, is likely to be another Christian majority state in another two or three decades or so. Ms Neelam Taram, former Arunachal Pradesh Home Minister, however, says that in spite of a gradual increase in numbers of Christians in Arunachal Pradesh, there is no confrontation over conversion issue here, although RSS and bodies like Indigenous Faith and Cultural Society of Arunachal Pradesh are trying to encourage locals to preserve their traditional rights and practices.[160]

Senior Supreme Court lawyer Prashant Bhusan even said on December 26, 2014 that an anti-conversion law is unconstitutional as it goes against the fundamental right of citizen to choose or change his/her faith.[161] The Supreme Court has already upheld the constitutional validity of the Freedom of Acts enacted by many State Governments. As M.N. Rao, a former Chief Justice of Himachal Pradesh High Court, has pointed out, "when the highest court of this country has upheld the constitutionality of laws prohibiting fraudulent conversions, any criticism that these laws are aimed at depriving the rights of minority religions is absolutely baseless".[162]

The right to 'propagate' does not confer any right to "convert". It is not the same thing as the right to 'convert'. If in a "secular" democracy every religious outfit taking advantage of the "propagation" clause start propagating the respective religion with the ultimate aim of converting the gullible people it will lead to chaos and violence. This cannot be the ideal situation and no government worth its name can be an idle spectator to such a catastrophe. But, a civilized government must be armed with a law to tackle such a situation.

Religious conversion is a matter of individual choice guaranteed as a fundamental right under the Constitution, and not a collective right of any religious community to proselytize. What matters is not whether such conversions are necessary but whether the individual is allowed the freedom of conscience and free profession, practice and propagation of a religion of his or her choice provided under Article 25.

Why the conversion debate still lingers in free India? Actually, this is inherent in the religions themselves. Islam and Christianity are proselytizing religions. Their tenets not only permit but stand for conversion. Hinduism does not allow conversion. One is born a Hindu and that is that. Hinduism refuses conversion but allows for syncretism. Conversion is exclusive but syncretism allows for combinations. A Hindu will enthusiastically participate in Muharram and Christmas festivals. Hindus may in fact include Christ as an *Ishta Devta.* This clash between two diametrically opposite religious beliefs over the question of conversion is at the root of the troubles continuing for so many years. There may not be any objection if one takes the propagation for the sake of propagation. But, it assumes menacing proportions if it is done with a view to convert and to convert only. None should question the fact of the conversion of an individual if takes place as a result of genuine change of heart, devoid of any coercion, inducement, allurement or incentive. Gandhi stood for an *atma parivartana*, conversion of heart within one's tradition, and was against a *dharmantarana*, conversion across religious traditions. 'Religion' which, strictly speaking, should have been a personal affair, pure and simple, becomes a matter for concern when it crosses the threshold of 'personal' affair and enters the 'public' domain if such conversion/conversions affect public policy, "public order, morality and health".

Constitutional safeguards against conversion/re-conversion brought about by any means other than those taking place due to change of heart or as a result of honest conviction should be explicitly provided as has been done in some States. In other words any conversion brought about by force, fraud or illicit means should be prohibited. Mass evangelization drives and mass conversion can disrupt social harmony. Conversion and re-conversion of people has become a touchy issue leading to communal disharmony and discord. It should not be allowed to deteriorate further. If other countries could enact laws prohibiting conversion and if some of our own State

Governments could enact such laws, what is the harm if a Central Act on that line is enacted. Both the proponents and opponents of 'conversion' should realise that religion is a private affair. It is not meant to be worn on one's sleeves.

Notes and References

1. Rao, B. Shiva, *The Framing of India's Constitution*, Vol. II, 1967, New Delhi, The Indian Institute of Public Administration, p. 76.
2. *Ibid.*, p. 81.
3. *Ibid.*, p. 87.
4. *Ibid.*, pp. 122-23.
5. *Ibid.*, p. 124.
6. *Ibid.*, p. 133.
7. *Ibid.*, p. 140.
8. *Ibid.*, pp. 145-147.
9. *Ibid.*, p. 149.
10. *Ibid.*, p. 160.
11. *Ibid.*, p. 165.
12. *Ibid.*, p. 174.
13. *Ibid.*, pp. 187-188.
14. *Ibid.*, p. 194.
15. *Ibid.*, p. 140.
16. *Ibid.*, p. 201.
17. *Ibid.*, p. 208.
18. *Ibid.*, pp. 212-213.
19. *Ibid.*, pp. 264-269.
20. *Ibid.*, p. 290.
21. *Ibid.*, p. 298.
22. *CAD*, Vol. III dated 1-5-47, p. 477.
23. Rao, B. Shiva, *The Framing of India's Constitution*, Vol. III, 1967, New Delhi, The Indian Institute of Public Administration, p. 10.
24. *Ibid.*, pp. 331-332.
25. *Ibid.*, p. 334.
26. *Ibid.*, p. 409
27. *Ibid.*, p. 524.
28. *Ibid.*, Vol. IV, pp. 41-42.
29. *CAD*, Vol. VII, dated 3-12-48, pp. 817-818.
30. *Ibid.*, p. 822 and dated 6-12-48, pp. 823-824.
31. *Ibid.*, dated 6-12-48, pp. 835-836.
32. *Ibid.*, dated 9-11-48, p. 382.
33. *Ibid.*, dated 6-12-48, p. 831.
34. *Ibid.*, pp. 831-833.
35. *Ibid.*, pp. 833-834.
36. *Ibid.*, pp. 834-835.

37. *Ibid.*, pp. 836-837.
38. *Ibid.*, pp. 837-838.
39. Thomas, Abraham Vazhayil, *Christians in Secular India*, 1974, New Jersey, Associated University Presses, p. 109.
40. *The National Christian Council Review*, December 1945, p. 241.
41. *voice of dharma.org/books/hhce/ch15.htm*
42. *Stainislaus* vs. *State of M.P. A 1977 SC 908.*
43. *Ibid.*
44. Rao, B. Shiva, Vol. II, *op. cit.*, p. 76.
45. *Ibid.*, p. 87.
46. *Ibid.*, p. 126.
47. *Ibid.*, p. 140.
48. *Ibid.*, p. 149.
49. *Ibid.*, p. 166.
50. *Ibid.*, p. 174.
51. *Ibid.*, p. 203.
52. *Ibid.*, p. 206.
53. *Ibid.*, p. 209.
54. *Ibid.*, p. 213.
55. *Ibid.*, pp. 271-272.
56. *Ibid.*, p. 291.
57. *Ibid.*, p. 298.
58. *CAD*, Vol. III, dated 1-5-47, p. 488.
59. *Ibid.*
60. *Ibid.*, pp. 488-489.
61. *Ibid.*, pp. 489-490.
62. *Ibid.*, pp. 491-492.
63. *Ibid.*, pp. 492-493
64. *Ibid.*, p. 495.
65. *Ibid.*, p. 497.
66. *Ibid.*, pp. 490-491.
67. *Ibid.*, pp. 497-499.
68. *Ibid.*, p. 500.
69. *Ibid.*, pp. 501-502.
70. *Ibid.*, pp. 502-503.
71. *Ibid.* p. 503.
72. *CAD*, Vol. V, dated 30-8-47, p. 373.
73. *Ibid.*, p. 363.
74. *Ibid.*, p. 364.
75. *Ibid.*
76. *Ibid.*, pp. 364-365.
77. *Ibid.*, p. 365.
78. *Ibid.*
79. *CAD*, Vol. VII, dated 3-12-48, pp. 820-821.
80. *The Universal Declaration of Human Rights*, the United Nations.
81. en.wikipedia.org/wiki/freedom-of-religion.

82. Akbar, M.J., "The myth of forced Islamic conversions", *The Times of India*, May 25, 2008, p. 15.
83. "No place to call home". *Christian Solidarity Worldwide*, 29 April, 2008.
84. Mutua, Makau, *Facilitating Freedom of Religion or Belief, A Desk book*, 2004, Oslo Coalition on Freedom of Religion or Belief.
85. Ludden, David (ed.), *Contesting the Nation: Religion, Community, and the Politics of Democracy in India*, 1996, University of Pennsylvania Press.
86. "India's religious tolerance lauded", *The Deccan Herald*, December, 19, 2009.
87. *The Hindustan Times*, November 7, 1999, p. 8.
88. Chatterjee, Sarajit Kumar, *The Scheduled Castes in India*, Vol. I, 1996. Gyan Publishing House, New Delhi, pp. 68-69.
89. *Ibid.*, pp. 109-110
90. Price, Major David, *Memoirs of the Emperor Jehangir written by Himself*, (translation), London, Oriental Translation Commttee 1829, p. 15.
91. *Census of India 2001, The First Report on Religion Data*, p. xxix.
92. Joshi, A.P., Srinivas, M.D., Bajaj, J.K., *Religious Demography of India*, 2003, Chennai, Centre for Policy Studies, pp. 104-107.
93. *Ibid.*, pp. 109-110.
94. *Census of India 2001, The First Report on Religion Data*, p. xxix.
95. Mackenzie, Alexander, *The North-East Frontier of India* (originally published entitled *History of the Relations of the Government with the Hill Tribes of the North-East Frontier of Bengal* in1884), 2005, New Delhi, Mittal Publications, pp. 253-64.
96. Bhagbati, A.C., "Social Formation in North-East India" in *People of India, Bio-cultural Dimensions* (ed.), S.B. Roy and A.K. Guha, 1999, New Delhi, Inter-India Publications, p. 179.
97. Yonuo, Asoso, *The Rising Nagas*, 1974, Delhi, Vivek Publishing House, p. 111.
98. Goswami, B.B., *The Mizo Unrest*, 1979, Jaipur, Aalekh Publishers, p. 47.
99. Joshi, A.P., Srinivas, M.D., Bajaj, J.K., *op. cit.*, p. 125.
100. *Ibid.*
101. Chakraborty, Amallendu Kishore, *The Quest for Identity*, 2004, Kolkata, The Asiatic Society, p. 148.
102. Yonuo, *op. cit.*, p. 168.
103. Elwin, V., *The Foreign Missionary Danger*, 1944.
104. *Ibid.*
105. Srinivas, M N., *Caste in Modern India and Other Essays*, 1962, Bombay, Asia Publishing House, p. 107.
106. Yonuo, *op. cit.*, pp. 327-328.
107. Jayanth, V., "The role of the Church", *The Hindu*, January 18, 1999, p. 12.
108. Yonuo, Asoso, *op. cit.*, p. 309.
109. *Harijan*, September 28, 1935.
110. Gandhi, M.K., *Christian Missions and their Plan in India*, *op. cit.*, p. 235.
111. *The Hindu*, January 6, 2013, p. 3.
112. Mustafa, Faizan, "Constitutionality of Anti-Conversion Laws", *The Statesman*, January 8, 2015, p. 16.
113. Anant, Arpita, "Anti-conversion laws", *The Hindu*, December 17, 2002, p. 15.

114. *Report of the Christian Missionary Activities Enquiry Committee, Madhya Pradesh,* Vol. I, 1956, Government of Madhya Pradesh, pp. 136-137.
115. *Ibid.,* pp. 163-164, p. 166.
116. *The Statesman*, November 16, 1982.
117. *The Hindu*, May 22, 2005, p. 6.
118. *Rev. Stanislaus* vs. *the State of Madhya Pradesh*, AIR 1977 SC 908, 1977 SCR (2) 611.
119. Aleaz. K.P., "The essence of believing", *The Statesman,* February 2, 1999, p. 9.
120. Narrain, Arvind and D'Rozario, Clifton, "The bogey of forced conversions", *The Hindu*, October 26, 2008, p. 5.
121. *S. Raja Gopal,* AIR 1969 SC 101. *Kailash Sonkar* (1984) 2 SCC 91.
122. Sirohi, Seema, "Counting Sheep", *Outlook*, June 5, 2006.
123. Rao, M.N. "Religious freedom—legal restrictions on conversions", *The Hindu*, July 8, 2003, p. 16.
124. *The Hindu*, March 18, 2015, p. 9.
125. *Ibid.*, March 18, 2015, p. 8
126. Thekaekara, Mari Marcel, "Being Chrıstian in India", *The Hindu*, March 27, 2015, p. 7.
127. *The Telegraph*, May 1, 2015, p. 10.
128. Visvanathan, Shiv, "Debating the conversion conundrum", *The Hindu*, December 24, 2014, p. 6.
129. *The Times of India*, December 30, 2014, p. 6.
130. Gandhi, M.K., *Christian Missions and their Plan in India*, 1941, Ahmedabad, Navajiban Press, p. 160.
131. *The Telegraph*, February 13, 2006, p. 8.
132. *Tehelka*, February 7, 2004.
133. Kuppuswami, Alladi, "Can conversions be bummed", *The Hindu*, January 30, 1999, p. 12.
134. *Sarla Mudgal* vs. *Union of India* AIR 1995 SC. 1531.
135. *The Times of India*, December 12, 2012, p. 6.
136. *The Statesman*, August 1, 2011, p. 3.
137. *The Times of India*, December 20, 2014, p. 10.
138. *Lily Thomas and others* vs. *Union of India & others*, (2000) 6 SCC 224, para 39.
139. *The Times of India*, November 21, 2011, p. 12.
140. Thekaekara, Mari Marcel, "Being Christian in India", *The Hindu*, March 27, 2015, p. 7.
141. Thampu, Rev. Valson. "Debate, not now…", *The Hindu*, January 26, 1999, p. 25.
142. Sirohi, Seema, "Counting Sheep", *Outlook*, June 5, 2006.
143. *The Hindu*, December 15, 2014, p. 1.
144. *The Times of India*, December 24, 2014, p. 8.
145. *The Times of India*, December 21, 2014, p. 11.
146. *The Times of India*, February 3, 2015, p. 6.
147. *The Hindu*, March 1, 2015, p. 3.
148. *The Hindu*, December 18, 2014, p. 1.

149. Mitta, Manoj, "Ghar wapsi, but conditions apply", *The Times of India*, January 4, 2015, p. 6.
150. *The Times of India*, December 22, 2014, p. 9.
151. *The Hindu*, December 23, 2014, p. 8.
152. Kashyap Anirban, *Communalism and Constitution*, Lancers Books, New Delhi, p. 151.
153. *The Hindu*, December 12, 2014, p. 1.
154. *The Hindu*, December 17, 2014, p. 10.
155. *The Statesman*, November 16, 1982.
156. *The Telegraph*, March 24, 2015, p. 6.
157. *The Times of India*, March 24, 2015, p. 7.
158. *The Times of India*, December 21, 2014, p. 11.
159. *The Hindu*, December 21, 2014, p. 8.
160. *The Statesman*, October 13, 2014, p. 5.
161. *The Hindu*, December 27, 2914, p. 5.
162. Rao, M.N. "Religious freedom—legal restrictions on conversions", *The Hindu*, July 8, 2003, p. 16.

5
Slaughter of Cow

In Indian mythology, the geographical space which the cow occupies becomes as sacred as the holiest pilgrimage and even the dust of that place becomes pure. The chanting of Vedic scriptures, the cow, fire and the mediating agency of the priestly caste of Brahmins constitute the four crucial corners of this holy spectrum. All these sacred elements are compulsory in the performance of the elaborate ritual of the religious *yajna*. Since ghee is essential to this Hindu ritual and symbolizes vitality, good habit and long life, the cow constitutes a crucial cog in this circular logic of divinity and material life.

The cow is revered for other reasons too. The space where the *yajna* is performed is believed to be purified by sprinkling cow urine and cleaned and pasted by cow dung. The last is also presumed to be a disinfectant, a hygienic spiritual reassertion against physical immunity. Fire and cow dung, along with camphor and incense, is integral to the recitation of the *mantras*.

Although these rigorous rituals are often not followed in modern times, according to the normative code of the *yajna*, the host who performs it was traditionally asked to purify himself by drinking *Panchgavya*, a mixture of five cow products: curd, milk, ghee, cow urine and cow dung. According to the cow myth, milk is *sattvaguna* (most pure quality), the cow fulfils all human wants, the Ganga resides in the cow's urine and dung can fight plague and cholera and is an antidote to snake and scorpion bites. Some cow worshippers even believe that wartime houses with cow dung are least damaged by bomb attacks.

Cow has been treated as auspicious and also a symbol of compassion and piousness. Cow is treated as the highest and most pious animal and is given the utmost importance, being at the apex in the Animal world. The belief is that one can attain salvation (*Moksha*) by worshipping the cow and serving her and both Lord Krishna and Balram spearheaded the "Cow worship and preservation" culture. The first Jain *Tirthankara*, Adinatha was also named as Vrishabha meaning 'Oxen Sorub'. Of all beings, the cow is treated, in India, as the most sacred and sanctified. This sense of the unique sacredness of the cow is expressed in the works of ancient Indian Rishis in the *Vedas*, *Smritis*, *Srutis* and the *Puranas*, etc., as well as in later literature and folklore.[1]

Mythological history has it that, during the churning of the oceans (*Sagar Manthan*), as a result of the struggle between Good (represented by *Devas*) and Evil (represented by *Rakshasas*) one of the outcomes was a Cow, named as *Kamdhenu*. The cow was worshipped by the sages and, it is said, that Dhanwantari worshipped *Kamdhenu* and with her blessings, developed a great medicine '*Panchgavya*', comprising five products of the cow (milk, ghee, curd, urine and dung), which even today is used in Ayurveda as a remedy for many diseases.[2]

Rather than from an animal-rights perspective, most Hindus revere the cow for "spiritual reasons" and are guided by a religious heritage argument.[3] So, highly were cows held in esteem by the Society that there were days fixed in the yearly calendar for exclusive worship of the Cow. Three days prior to the festival of *Deepavali* is called "*Bachvaras* (*Vasubaras*), which is a festival when cows are offered "*Puja*". *Dhanteras* is a day when cows are worshipped along with Dhanwantari (the Sage and the deity of medicine). *Balipratipada* or *Padwa* is celebrated the day after *Deepavali* when, in many parts of India, cows are ceremoniously worshipped. Not only cows, but the oxen and the bulls also, were, and still are, the objects of worship. The last day of the month of *Shravan*, called *Pola*, is a day when bulls are decorated and taken in a procession to a public place for collective worship, after which they are then taken from house to house where each family offers '*puja*'. The day after this is celebrated as Children's *Pola*, when the children decorate and worship the wooden idols of bull and take them in a procession to a public place.[4] In the South, Shiva, accompanied by Nandi, the bull, is widely worshipped. During *Mattu Pongal* or '*Gopuja*' in Tamil Nadu, the entire cattle family is worshipped; their horns decorated with flowers and painted, they are given ceremonial baths and *aarti* is performed.[5]

So, holy and auspicious is this gentle creature regarded in our country that it is believed to be able to ward off any evil. Accordingly, if a child is born on an inauspicious day or under an inauspicious sign, it is ceremonially placed beneath the standing cow (*Shantipuja*) and she is asked to save the child from any evil.[6]

Sir Monier-Williams, a great Scholar of Sanskrit, who was Professor of Sanskrit at Oxford University, in his famous '*Sanskrit-English Dictionary*' has given 72 equivalents and meanings of the word "Cow", some of which are reproduced hereunder:[7]

> 1. Gau, 2. Shringne, 3. Tamcha, 4. Maha, 5. Porari, 6. Surabhi, 7. Usara, 8. Arjuni, 9. Agra, 10. Rohini, 11. Dhenudhenuka, 12. Godhenu, 13. Strigavi, 14. Dogdhi, 15. Pinoghani, 16. Pivarrupani, 17. Dhenusha, 18. Govrindarava, 19. Gomutallika, 20. Goprakanda, 21. Vatskama,

22. Vatsala, 23. Vasundhara, 24. Vasudha, 25. Dharitri, 26. Dharini, 27. Medhani, 28. Vatsiya, and 29. Amira.

The role that the cow has played in the Indian traditions and practices has changed over the many centuries and has not remained constant.[8] Interestingly, in addition to the holy image of the animal, it has become an important political tool in the hands of right wing Hindu outfits, challenging the "outsiders"—Muslims and Christians—who are classified as the "beef eaters". While the idea of eating beef is shocking to most Hindus and the call for a ban on this practice has become a political issue, there was a time in India when people had no compunction about slaughtering cattle. Not only was the meat of the animal esteemed as a valuable food, it was as much a mark of generous hospitality—like was the practice among ancient Jews—to slaughter the "fatted calf" in honour of respected guests. Moreover, the offering of beef was deemed an absolute necessity by pious Hindus in their journey from this world to the next.

Rajendra Lal Mitra, the famous Indologist and the first Indian president of the Asiatic Society of Bengal, wrote an article "Beef in Ancient India" in the *Asiatic Society Journal* in 1872. After a thorough study of the ancient Hindu scriptures, he presented passages, which may be deemed incontrovertible, in favour of his thesis that beef was a common item of food among the Hindus.

Henry Colebrook in his article, "The Religious Ceremonies of the Hindus", published in the *Asiatic Researches* in 1801, says that "it seems to have been anciently the custom to slay a cow on the occasion (of the reception of a guest); and a guest was therefore called a *goghna* or cow-killer".[9]

Prof. Dwijendra Narayan Jha in his well researched work, *Holy Cow: Beef in Indian Dietary Traditions,* published in 2001 by the Delhi-based publisher Matrix Books, and later by the London-based Verso Books in 2002 under the title *The Myth of the Holy Cow*, has shown that beef-eating was popular with the Vedic Indians. A survey of ancient Indian scriptures, especially the *Vedas*, shows that amongst the nomadic, pastoral Aryans who settled here, animal sacrifice was a dominant feature till the emergence of settled agriculture. Cattle were the major property during this phase and they offered the same to propitiate the gods. Wealth was equated with the ownership of the cattle. Practically, all the important ceremonies and sacrifices were attended with slaughter of bulls and cows.

Mahadev Chakravarti's article, on "Beef-Eating in Ancient India" appeared at pp. 51-55 of Volume 7, No. 11 of the June 1979 issue of the *Social Scientist*. In support of his assertions he has quoted extensively from the various scriptures and authoritative books. This well-written article merits reproduction:

BEEF-EATING was not peculiar to the people of the Western countries alone, but was popular with the Vedic Indians also. The food items of the Vedic Indians can be gathered from the list of sacrificial victims because what man ate he usually presented to his gods.[10] Practically, all the important ceremonies and sacrifices were attended with slaughter of bulls and cows. The *Gomedha* and *Ashvamedha* sacrifices are important in this respect. The *Sulagava* sacrifice, in which the bull, as the name implies, seems to have been pierced with a spike or lance to appease Rudra, is described in detail in the *Grihyasutras*.

Restrictions in Vedic Literature

In a hymn of the *Rigveda* it is said that "Indra will eat thy bulls".[11] In another hymn of the *Rigveda*[12] Agni is styled *Uksanna* and *Vasanna,* i.e. "eater of bulls and barren cows." Not only for the purpose of sacrifices but for food also, the bovine species were killed in regular slaughter-houses and this is evident from another hymn of the *Rigveda.*[13] Again, it is suggested in the *Rigveda* that the cow was cut up with a sword or axe.[14] It is interesting to note in this context that the modern Hindu practice of *Jhatka-bali*, that is, severing the head of the animal at one stroke, had not yet come into fashion. There are ample evidences how the *Rigvedic* people were fond of beef-eating. Even in funeral ceremony beef-eating was considered an essential part.[15] Interestingly enough in the same *Veda* the cow is sometimes considered inviolable as indicated by her designation *aghnya* ('not to be slain') which occurs sixteen times in the entire *Rigveda,*[16] as opposed to three instances of *aghnya*[17] (masculine). But this fact cannot be regarded as showing that beef-eating was condemned in the *Rigvedic* period. In this connection, we should point out that the Sanskrit word used for the sacrificial cow is Vasa (i.e. 'sterile cow') and a milch cow was seldom sacrificed.[18] It is only in this way that one can explain the lavish praise bestowed on the cow in the *Rigveda* where she is described in a number of hymns as "the mother of Rudras, the daughter of the vasus, the sister of Adityas, and the centre of nectar".[19]

Although we have three references of *aghnya* in the *Rigveda,* still apparently no strict restriction in regard to the slaughter of bulls (as opposed to milch cows) is found. It seems probable that some composers of *Rigvedic* hymns were pre-Aryan (non-Aryan) Indians (who disliked beef-eating) who became Aryanized like the *Asuras* and the *Vratyas* and labelled the whole bovine species inviolable, because outside India this inviolability is utterly unknown.[20]

In the days of *Atharva Veda* beef-eating remained unaltered, although it was censured here and there in that *Veda*. During the *Brahmana* period the habit of beef-eating seems to have increased. Among the *Kamya Ishtis* or minor sacrifices set forth in the *Taittiriya Brahmana* different bovine species were sacrificed to different gods, namely, a dwarf ox to Vishnu, a drooping horned bull with a blaze on the forehead to Indra, a red cow to Rudra, a white barren cow to Surya and so on. The *Aitareya Brahmana* lists the bull as one of the sacrificial animals.[21] From the *Taittiriya* and the *Pancavimsha Brahmanas* we learn that the sage Agastya slaughtered hundred bulls at a sacrifice.[22] The *Shatapatha Brahmana* gives a picture of the inordinate fondness of Yajnavalkya for beef who said: "I for one eat it, provided it is tender (*amsala*)".[23] But, strangely enough, we are to face two exhortations in the same *Brahmana* against eating beef.[24]

Among the *Sutras*, *Kalpasutra* and *Grihyasutra* display less reticence and distinctly suggest beef as an item of food on different occasions of life. According to *Sankhyayana-sutra* a bull or a sterile cow should be killed in the house of the father of the bride on the wedding day and also in the house of the bridegroom when the husband and the wife arrive after marriage.[25] Even at *sraddhas* or periodical oblations to the manes, the sacrifice of a bull or cow is recommended by the *Apastamba* and *Paraskara grihyasutras*.[26] Yajnavalkya indicates how the aroma of beef was thought to be an ailment for the spirits.[27] According to *Vasishtha-sutra* "an ascetic who, invited to dine at a sacrifice, rejects meat shall go to hell for as many years as the slaughtered beast has hairs".[28] The *Khadira* and *Gobhila-Sutras* prescribed the sacrifice of a black cow to the deity of the dwelling-houses when a new house was constructed.[29]

Distinguished guests like one's teachers, priests, kings, bridegrooms and Vedic students on their return home after the completion of their studies are to be honoured with the presentation of a bull or a barren cow to be slaughtered—hence, a guest is denominated in the Vedic literature as *goghna* or cow-killer.[30] The ceremony of *madhuparka* is notable in this context. The *madhuparka* ceremony seems to have been very old because the custom of entertaining a distinguished guest with beef is found both in the *Shatapatha Brahmana*[31] and the *Aitareya Brahmana*[32] and it was in all likelihood known also in the *Rigvedic* period.

Moral Codes and Beef-eating

We now turn to the *Smriti* literature. Manu, like Vasishtha, sanctions the consumption of the flesh of all domestic animals which have but one row of teeth.[33] That this would obviously include beef becomes clear from the comments of even such orthodox pundits like Medhatithi and Raghavananda.[34] Manu also recommends the *madhuparka* with beef for the reception of kings.[35] The *Yajnavalkya-Smriti* distinctly lays down that a *mah-oksa* or 'big bull' is to be slaughtered on such occasions.[36] In fact, both the Manu and *Yajnavalkya Smrti* permit the killing of bovine species on such special occasions, in sacrifices and in rites for manes etc.; otherwise beef-eating was regarded as *upapataka* or minor offence, though not *mahapataka* or mortal sin.[37] In spite of the individual predilections of the author of *Manu Smriti*, who was a staunch upholder of *ahimsa*, who even said that no flesh can be had without killing living beings and killing such beings cannot lead to heaven and so one should give up flesh eating,[38] the general usage was different in his times and centuries were required before the views propounded by Manu became predominant.[39]

From Ancient Science and Literature

The ancient medical works like the *Charaka Samhita* recommend beef for pregnant women, but prohibits it for everyday use for everybody.[40] R.L. Mitra enlightens us that in some medieval Indian works beef soup is especially recommended for people recovering from fainting fits.[41]

The Epics allude to the *gomedha* without any details. In the '*Vanaparva*' of the *Mahabharata*[42] it is stated that animals killed in sacrifices to the accompaniment of Vedic *mantras* went to heaven and it narrates the story of King Rantideva in whose sacrifices two thousand animals, including cows, were killed everyday. In the '*Udyogaparva*' King Nahusha was cursed and hurled down from heaven by the great sage Agastya because he ventured to cast doubts on the Vedic injunctions for the sacrifice of cows and offered insult to a *Brahmana*.[43]

Bhavabhuti in his *Uttara-Rama-Charita* (Act IV) describes how the venerable poet and hermit, Valmiki, when preparing to receive the sage Vasishtha, author of one of the original law books (*Smritis*) slaughtered a number of calves for the entertainment of his guest. From the *Mahaviracharita* of the same author it is evident how Vasishtha, in his turn, likewise entertained Vishvamitra, Janaka, Satananda and other sages with 'fatted calf', and tempted Jamadagnya by saying: "The heifer is ready for sacrifice and the food cooked in ghee".[44]

In Kautilya's *Arthashastra* cattle are classified, where bulls are intended for the slaughter-house, but the killing of the milch cows, and calves, though permitted for sacrificial purposes, is forbidden for butchers' stalls.[45] Ashoka in his Rock Edict I and Pillar Edict I declared how originally thousands of animals were killed in the royal kitchen. Considering the popularity of beef-eating among the people even Ashoka, the great propagator of *ahimsa*, resolved later on to discontinue the slaughter of animals only for some days in the year; for example, he included the breeding bull but, not the cow in the list of animals not to be slaughtered on those days.[46]

Though the custom of slaughtering of cows and bulls prevailed during the Vedic period, nevertheless, even in the Rigvedic times there seems to have grown up a revulsion of feeling against the custom. The cow gradually came to acquire a special sanctity and was called '*Aghnya*" (not to be slain). There was a school of thinkers amongst the *Rishis*, who set their face against the custom of killing such useful animals as the cow and the bull. High praise was bestowed on the cow as will appear from the following verses from *Rigveda*, Book VI, Hymn XXVIII (Cows) attributed to the authorship of Sage Bharadvaja:

1. The kine have come and brought good fortune; let them rest in the cow-pen and be happy near us.
   Here let them stay prolific, many coloured, and yield through many morns their milk for Indra.
6. O Cows, ye fatten e'en the worn and wasted, and make the unlovely beautiful to look on.
   Prosper my house, ye with auspicious voices, your power is glorified in our assemblies.
7. Crop goodly pasturages and be prolific; drink pure sweet water at good drinking places.
   Never be thief or sinful man your master, and may the dart of Rudra still avoid you.

(Translation by Ralph Griffith)

Verse 29 of Hymn 1 in Book X of *Atharva Veda* forbids cow slaughter in the following words:

29. The slaughter of an innocent, O *Kritya*, is an awful deed, slay not cow, horse, or man of ours.
30. The cow is Heaven, the cow is Earth, the cow is Vishnu, Lord of life. The Sadhyas and the Vasus have drunk the outpourings of the cow.
34. Both gods and mortal men depend for life and being on the cow. She hath become this universe, all that the sun surveys is she.[47]

There are several references in our Scriptures regarding the punishment that could be meted out to persons found guilty of killing cows. *Atharva Veda* warns:

> "If you intend to kill our cow, horse or man, we shall pierce you with poisonous arrows so that your evil design does not succeed". (1/16/4)
> *Shloka* 13 of Chapter 9 of *Manu Smriti* commands:
> (He, who is an AATATAYI should be killed at first sight without pondering)—Killer of cow is also an AATATAYI.[48]

P.V. Kane in the *History of Dharmashastras* (Vol. II, Part II) at pp. 772-73 argues that in the times of the *Rigveda* only barren cows, if at all, were killed for sacrifice or meat and cows yielding milk were held to be not fit for being killed. It is only in this way, according to him, that one can explain and reconcile the apparent conflict between the custom of killing cows for food and the high praise bestowed on the cow in *Rigvedic* times. It would appear that the protest raised against the slaughter of cows greatly increased in volume till the custom was totally abolished in a later age. The change of climate perhaps also makes the use of beef as food unnecessary and even injurious to health. Gradually, cows became indicative of the wealth of the owner. The Neolithic Aryans not having been acquainted with metals, there were no coins in current use in the earlier stages of their civilization, but as they were eminently a pastoral people almost every family possessed a sufficient number of cattle and some of them exchanged them for the necessaries of their lives. The value of cattle (*Pashu*) was therefore very great with the early *Rigvedic* Aryans. The ancient Romans also used the word pecus or pecu (*pashu*) in the sense of wealth or money. The English words, 'pecuniary' and 'impecunious', are derived from the Latin root pecus or pecu originally meaning cattle. The possession of cattle in those days denoted wealth and a man was considered rich or poor according to the large or small number of cattle that he owned. In the *Ramayana* King Janaka's wealth was described by reference to the large number of herds that he owned. It appears that the cow was gradually raised to the status of divinity. Kautilya's *Arthashastra* has a special chapter (Ch. XXIX), which deals with "superintendence of cows" and describes the duties of the owner of cows, which are referred to in Ch. XI of the book on *Hindu Law* by Dr. Ganga Nath Jha.[49]

Maharshi Vedavyasa states in the great epic *Mahabharata* in *Anu.* 195 that Bhagvan Brahma, the Creator of the Universe, first created the mother-like cow for all the living creatures.

With the rise of agricultural economy and the massive transformation occurring in society, changes were to be brought in the practice of animal sacrifice also. At that time there were ritualistic practices like animal sacrifices, were sacrifices, which involved 500 oxen, 500 male calves, 500 female calves and 500 sheep to be tied to the sacrificial pole for slaughter. Buddha pointed out that *ashvamedha, purushmedha, vajapeya* sacrifices did not produce good results. According to a story in *Digha Nikaya*, when Buddha was touring Magadha, a Brahmin called Kutadanta was preparing for a sacrifice with 700 bulls, 700 goats, and 700 rams. Buddha intervened and stopped him. His rejection of animal sacrifice and emphasis on non-injury to animals assumed a new significance in the context of new agriculture.

The emphasis on non-violence by Buddha was not blind or rigid. He did taste beef and it is well known that he died due to eating of pork. Emperor Ashoka after converting to Buddhism did not turn to vegetarianism. He only restricted the number of animals to be killed for the royal kitchen.[50]

So, where do matters change and how did the cow become a symbol of faith and reverence to the extent of assuming the status of 'motherhood'? A gradual change in the attitude of the Hindus came about from the time of the *Puranas* (second century A.D. to sixth century A.D.). Rajendra Lal Mitra quotes *Aditya Purana*, which says that in the present Kali age, the *Madhuparka* should be celebrated without slaughtering a cow.

A passage in the *Vrihannaradiya Purana* prohibits the sacrifices of humans, horses and cows and Vedic *yajnas* involving sacrifice of cattle. The author of *Nirnaya Sindhu* argues against the slaughter of large bulls and sheep for Brahmanas as they were detested by the people. The protest against slaughter of animals, Mitra believes, was roused by the influence of Buddhism, which emphatically denounced all sacrifices. The Brahmanas had to contend against Buddhism which preached the doctrine of respect for animal life. Subsequently, more and more prominence was given to such passages from the scriptures, which preached benevolence and mercy for animals.[51]

Over a period of time mainly after the emergence of Buddhism or rather as an accompaniment of the Brahminical attack on Buddhism, the practices started being looked on with different emphasis. The threat posed by Buddhism to the Brahminical value system was too severe. In response to low castes slipping away from the grip of Brahminism, the battle was taken up at all the levels. At philosophical level Shankara reasserted the supremacy of Brahminical values, at political level King Pushyamitra Shung ensured the physical attack on Buddhist monks, at the level of symbols King Shashank got the *Bodhi* tree (where Gautama the Buddha got Enlightenment) destroyed.

One of the appeals to the spread of Buddhism was the protection of cattle wealth, which was needed for the agricultural economy. In a way while Brahminism 'succeeded' in banishing Buddhism from India, it had also to transform itself from the 'animal sacrifice' state to the one which could be in tune with the times. It is here that this ideology took up the cow as a symbol of their ideological march. But unlike Buddha whose pronouncements were based on reason, the counteraction of Brahminical ideology took the form of a blind faith based on assertion. So, while Buddha's non-violence was for the reservation of animal wealth for the social and compassionate reasons the counter was based purely on symbolism. So, while the followers of Brahminical ideology accused Buddha of 'weakening' India due to his doctrine of non-violence, he was not a cow worshipper or vegetarian in the current Brahminical sense. The followers of Buddhism continued to eat flesh including beef.[52]

It was from about the fourth century A.D. that sanctity of the cow became a "firmly fixed dogma" and cow slaughter was strictly prohibited.[53] Cow slaughter became an emotive issue in the over-all Hindu-Muslim relations perhaps since the advent of Islam in India. When Islam, in its transition from Arabia to India, substituted the cow for the sheep as the victim of sacrificial slaughter,[54] cow became a political symbol both of harmony and hatred between the Hindus and the Muslim. The usurper Khusrau, who occupied the throne of Alauddin Khalji with the help of the Hindus, banned cow slaughter to please his retainers. The Muslims were so antagonized by this that he was soon overthrown.[55] Slaughter of the cow was absolutely forbidden wherever Hindu princes retained their independence. Abdul Razzak reports of fifteenth century in Calicut:

> "...everything is procurable in that port, with this sole exception, that you cannot kill cows and eat their flesh. Should anyone be known to have killed a cow, his life would invariably be sacrificed. The cow is held in such respect, that they rub the ashes of its dung upon their forehead—the curse of God upon them".[56]

Afanasy Nikitin's experience during his travels in the Deccan (1466-1472) was the same:

> "...The Indians (Hindus) call the ox 'father' and the cow 'mother': they use the dung as fuel to bake food and cook food and smear their faces, foreheads, and bodies with the ashes".[57]

The fire-worshipping sect of the Parsees having escaped in boats from the Muslim conquerors of Iran, were entertained and allowed to live among the Hindus on the condition that they were not to kill cows. They conformed to "many of the Gentue Ceremonies", and enjoyed the same rights.[58]

Babur (1526-1530), the first Mughal emperor, in his will to his son Humayun (1530-1556), advised him to respect the cow and avoid cow slaughter. Akbar (1556-1605) neither wore a beard nor ate beef.[59] Jahangir and Ahmad Shah prohibited cow slaughter. Nawab Hyder Ali of Mysore made cow slaughter an offence punishable with the cutting of hands of the offenders.[60] But Aurangzeb (1618-1707) disregarded Hindu feeling about cow. Shivaji (1627-1680) was among the first to use cow as a political symbol.

From his time protection of cows became a synonym for the protection of the Hindu community.

One of the triggers for the revolt of 1857 was the bullets lined with beef and pork fat. Mangal Pandey, a god-fearing Brahmin, famously mutinied when he realized he was biting bullets lined with fat of the taboo meat. But the revolt was a Hindu-Muslim effort.

The rebel leaders of the Uprising of 1857 were acutely aware of the problem of Hindu-Muslim conflict and the Muslim chiefs took particularly vigorous action to counteract it. A compact banning cow slaughter, initiated by Emperor Bahadur Shah during Bakr-Id in Delhi when he sacrificed a sheep instead of cow at the Jumma Masjid, was arrived at with the Hindu rajas and sepoys:

> The slaughter of kine is regarded by the Hindus as a great insult to their religion. To prevent thus, a solemn compact and agreement has been entered into by all the Mohammedan chiefs of Hindustan, binding themselves, that if the Hindus will come forward to slay the English, the Mohammedans will, from that very day put a stop to the slaughter of cows, and those of them who will not do so will be considered to have abjured the *Quran*, and such of them as will eat beef will be regarded as though they had eaten pork; but if the Hindus will not gird their loins to kill the English, but will try to save them, they will be as guilty in the sight of God as though they had committed the sins of killing cows...[61]

The true extent of the concession under this national compact can hardly be grasped unless we bear in mind the degree to which Indian Islam had symbolically and emotionally bound to the ceremonial sacrifice of the cow over the centuries.

The imperial order banning cow slaughter at Id was issued in the following form: The creation is God's and the Country is King's: Order of the highest officer of the army that anyone who slaughter a cow, an ox or a calf (male or female), buffalo (male or female) openly or secretly, shall be considered an enemy of His Majesty and shall be punished with death.[62] At Banda, the slaughter of cows and bullocks was prohibited throughout town on the sepoys' own order.[63]

Cow politics came on the centre stage after the Arya Samaj (1875) movement caught on. The first society for the protection of the cow was set up in 1882 by Arya Samaj founder Dayanand Saraswati (1824-1883). Later, innumerable '*gau raksha samitis*' sprouted, sometimes enjoying the patronage of powerful Congressmen and local *maharajas*. The cow became an integral part of the nationalist mobilization even as it was linked with militant assertions of Hindu identity. Nationalism in India developed on communal lines and religion, therefore, was an integral part of it. To the Hindus, the protection of the cow meant protection of their religion, whereas to the Muslims, slaughter of cows was a sacred part of their religion. Both the communities were unwilling to compromise on this issue.

In 1893, for the first time, the whole of eastern UP and large parts of Bihar were in flames over two issues: cow protection and Urdu-Devnagari. In June-July 1893, during Bakr-Id, Muslims in Azamgarh were attacked by mobs from Ghazipur and Ballia districts. The riots spread across the region. The following account of the 1893 riots by M.L. Ferrar, Commissioner of Gorakhpur, is revealing: "The Mohammedans were at the mercy of their enemies, having in most places saved their lives or property by being forced to sign a document (*qraarnama*) that they would not sacrifice cows..." This was the first time India had witnessed communal mayhem on such a large scale.[64]

The cow riots of 1917 were even worse. Once again, UP and Bihar bore the burnt. The worst incidents took place in Bihar's Shahbad district in September-October 1917. A mob of 30,000 went on a rampage, killing Muslims and looting their property. British records show that the rioters in Bihar always belonged to the high-caste Brahmin-Rajput-Bhumihar combination.[65]

During British rule in India, several cases of communal riots were caused due to the slaughter of cows. However, a historical survey of some major communal riots, between 1717 and 1977, reveals that out of 167 incidents of rioting between the two communities, 22 cases were attributable directly to cow slaughter.[66] Even prior to 1717, in 1714, during the reign of Farruksiyar, a riot broke out at Ahmedabad against Muslim cow-slaughter which was quelled with the help of Afghan soldiers brought from outside.[67]

Among the leading figures seeking cow protection were Bal Gangadhar Tilak (1856-1920) and Mahatma Gandhi (1869-1948). Mahatma Gandhi had sought a compromise over cow-slaughtering in order to maintain communal harmony during the Khilafat Movement (1919-1924).[68] He told the Hindus to save Khilafat if they wanted to save cows and he tried to persuade the Muslim leaders to accept the cow-Khilafat formula which meant that in return for Hindu support for the Khilafat Movement, the Muslims would stop killing cows.[69] Looking at the spontaneous support for their demands from the Hindus some of the Muslim leaders of the Khilafat Movement, were so moved that they offered to voluntarily abandon cow slaughter in order to cement the amity. Maulana Abdul Bari and others were prominent in this move.[70]

Although Gandhi himself was a powerful spokesperson for the need to prohibit cow-slaughter, his brief was primarily economic; the utility value of cows in an agrarian economy. This is what was written in the 1938 edition of the *Hind Swaraj*:

> I myself respect the cow, that is, I look upon her with affectionate reverence. The cow is the protector of India because, being an

> agricultural country, she is dependent on the cow. The cow is a most useful animal in hundreds of ways. Our Mohammedan brethren will admit this. But, just as I respect the cow, so do I respect my fellow men. A man is just as useful as a cow no matter whether he be a Mohammedan or a Hindu. Am I, then, to fight with or kill a Mohammedan in order to save a cow? In doing so, I would become an enemy of the Mohammedan as well as of the cow. Therefore, the only method I know of protecting the cow is that I should approach my Mohammedan brother and urge him for the sake of the country to join me in protecting her. If he would not listen to me I should let the cow go for the simple reason that the matter is beyond my ability. If I were overfull of pity for the cow, I should sacrifice my life to save her but not take my brother's. This, I hold, is the law of our religion... What am I to do when a blood brother is on the point of killing a cow? Am I to kill him, or to fall down at his feet and implore him? If you admit that I should adopt the latter course, I must do the same to my Moslem brother.[71]

However, Gandhi's attempt to use the cow symbol for Hindu-Muslim unity backfired; it increased communal separatism. Gandhi needed a more neutral and secular foundation to his approach. Besides, Gandhi had himself sounded uncompromising on the issue of cow-killing.[72] But, he had, no doubt, attempted to soften the conflict over cow-killing. In fact, when a dispute took place over cow killing Gandhi had urged the local leaders to stop public discussion over cow killing.[73] It is interesting to note that in an incident in Bengal, reported in Navayug on April 19, 1921, Gandhi's picture was drawn as Krishna above a Muslim flag.

Gandhi formed the Go Seva Sangh (1924) because he felt that the Gorakshini Sabha (Cow Protection Society) founded in 1882 sounded too aggressive.[74] The Muslims, however, were not prepared to give up cow-slaughtering. They criticized the Gorakshini Sabhas as anti-Muslim and a threat to their religion. Nehru notes in *An Autobiography* that "previously a fruitful source of discord (between Hindus and Muslim) had been the question of cow sacrifice, especially on the Bakr-Id day"; a fresh cause of friction arose on the question of "music before mosques".[75]

Although the cow was not the central issue in Partition's large-scale blood-letting, it was used by Hindu and Muslim miscreants. A cow carcass thrown outside a temple or a pig outside a masjid would inevitably lead to the shedding of human blood.[76] Tragically, Partition did not close the cow chapter in India's history. Incidents over cow slaughter continued to trigger communal riots in many parts of the country.

Now, "beef" has become an instrument of identity politics too. A "beef festival" at the Osmania University of Hyderabad was organized by some *dalits* and left student groups on Ambedkar Jayanti in 2012 to highlight the "non-brahmanical" food traditions in India. This festival is seen as an assertion by those who have remained at the cultural/ideological margins of India that they will not be defined anymore by this so-called mainstream; rather they will define what constitutes this mainstream. However, outside the networks of *dalit* activism there do not seem to be many takers for what these groups call a movement against "Food Fascism".[77]

II

In the Draft Constitution prepared by the Drafting Committee and circulated on February 21, 1948 no mention was made about imposing a ban on slaughter of cow in any of the Articles. When this Draft Constitution was circulated eliciting comments, suggestions etc., Thakurdas Bhargava and Govind Das suggested that the following new article be inserted after Article 38:

> 38A. The State shall endeavour to organize agriculture and animal husbandry on modern and scientific lines and in particular take steps to preserve, protect and improve the useful breeds of cattle and ban the slaughter of cows and other useful cattle, specially milch cattle and of child-bearing age, young stock and draught cattle.

The Drafting Committee considered this amendment and was of the opinion that it involved questions of policy.[78]

At the time of general discussion on the motion for consideration of the Draft Constitution, this issue was first raised on November 5, 1948 by Seth Gobinda Das who pleaded for imposition of total ban on cow slaughter. His argument was: "Ours is an agricultural country. It should have all that is necessary for agriculture. From this point of view the protection of cows is very essential for us. The problem of cow protection is a matter which has been associated with our civilization. To us it is not only a religious or economic, but also a cultural problem. Just as we have declared the practice of untouchability an offence, we can also declare that cow-slaughter in this country would be an offence. We should include some provision in our Constitution for this. We learn from history that only such regimes, whether during Hindu period or Muslim period, as had prohibited cow-slaughter had been popular and successful in our country. History is a witness to the fact that cow-slaughter was abolished here during the rule of many Muslim kings. It may be said that it would entail a heavy financial burden. I submit, however, that even if we impose a tax on the people and ask them to pay it in order to protect the cows, I am of opinion that they would pay it quite willingly. The bogey of financial difficulties used to be raised before us by the British Government. But I would like that in the matter of cow-protection this bogey should not be raised before us".[79]

Ramnarayan Singh's stand was, that "the economy of the country demands that the question of cow protection should form one of the items of the Fundamental Rights".[80]

Pandit Thakur Das Bhargava's stand was for banning slaughter of only useful cattle. He did not plead for total ban on slaughter of cows, but pleaded that "Government shall preserve, protect and improve the useful breeds of cattle, and ban the slaughter of useful cattle, particularly milch cows and young calves. I know that the Congress Party unanimously accepted this proposition when it was put to the House by me at the time of their meeting. But it was my misfortune that this thing could not be debated in the House; and when the occasion came, the House was adjourned." He disclosed that "every Government in India, even the Muslim Kings, the Government of Afghanistan, and even now Burma, have settled this thing by law for all time. In Burma, today, which has got no religion like ours, who do not regard the cow as sacred, they have enacted that slaughter of cows shall be banned. I do not want that. What I want is that slaughter of useful cattle shall be banned. That is my humble submission to this House and I think nobody will disagree. This would, at the same time, give satisfaction to crores of people who regard this question from a different motive, though I do not regard this question from that motive."[81]

Choudhury Ranbir Singh informed the House that he along with Pandit Bhargava, "had jointly moved a resolution on slaughter of cows in the Congress Party and at that time it was unanimously adopted. But unfortunately no mention of it has been made in our Constitution. Though the same was the case in regard to Hindi on which question also the party had come to a decision, yet the mention of Hindi is to be found in the Draft while no mention has been made of the resolution as regards cow protection."[82]

Vishwambar Dayal Tripathi also pleaded that "we should from cultural as well as from economic point of view make provision for cow protection. Our Congress Party had already decided that this should be done. This was probably not known to the Drafting Committee."[83]

On November 24, 1948, a resolution for imposition of ban on slaughter of cow and other useful cattle was formally moved in the Constituent Assembly by Pandit Thakur Das Bhargava. His resolution was for introduction of a new Article 38A in the following form:

> 38A. The State shall endeavour to organize agriculture and animal husbandry on modern and scientific lines and shall in particular take steps for preserving and improving the breeds of cattle and prohibit the slaughter of cow and other useful cattle, specially milch and draught cattle and their young stock.

While moving this resolution for insertion of this new Article Pandit Bhargava informed the House that "this amendment like the other amendment, about which Dr. Ambedkar has stated, is his manufacture. Substantially, there is no difference between the two amendments. In a way this is an agreed amendment. While moving this amendment, I have no hesitation in stating that for people like me and those that do not agree with the point of view of Dr. Ambedkar and others, this entails, in a way a sort of sacrifice. Seth Gobind Das had sent one such amendment to be included in the Fundamental Rights and other members also had sent similar amendments. To my mind it would have been much better if this could have been incorporated in the Fundamental Rights, but some of my Assembly friends differed and it is the desire of Dr. Ambedkar that this matter, instead of being included in Fundamental Rights should be incorporated in the Directive Principles. As a matter of fact, it is the agreed opinion of the Assembly that this problem should be solved in such a manner that the objective is gained without using any coercion. I have purposely adopted this course, as to my mind, the amendment fulfils our object and is midway between the Directive Principles and the Fundamental Rights. I do not want that due to its inclusion in the Fundamental Rights, non-Hindus should complain that they have been forced to accept a certain thing against their will."

Elaborating his resolution he further said that "this amendment is divided into three parts. Firstly, the agriculture should be improved on scientific and modern lines. Secondly, the cattle breed should be improved and thirdly, the cow and other cattle should be protected from slaughter. To grow more food and to improve agriculture and the cattle breed are all inter-dependent and are two sides of the same coin...The best way of increasing the (agricultural) production is to improve the health of human beings and breed of cattle, whose milk and manure and labour are so essential for growing food. Thus the whole agricultural and food problem of this country is nothing but the problem of the improvement of cow and her breed...In 1940, there were 11,56,00,960 oxen in India and in 1945 only 11,19,00,000 were left. That is to say, during these five years, there was a decrease of 37 lacs in the number of oxen. Similarly, the number of buffaloes in 1940, was 3,28,91,300 and in 1945 this figure was reduced to 3,25,44,400. According to these figures, during these five years their number was reduced by four lacs. Thus, during these five years there was decrease of 41 lacs in the sum total of both the above figures taken together.... While there has been no decrease in their slaughter rather, it is on the increase. Therefore, the slaughter of cattle should be banned here", he demanded. He asserted that "our ancient sages and *Rishis*, realising her importance, regarded her as very sacred. Here, Lord Krishna was born, who served cows so devotedly that to this day, in affection he is known as "*Makhan Chor*". I would not relate to you the story of Dalip, how that Raja staked his own life for his cow. But I would like to tell you that even during the Muslim rule, Babur, Humayun, Jahangir and even in the reign of Aurangzeb, cow-slaughter was not practised in India; not because Muslims regarded it to be bad, but because, from the economic point of view, it was unprofitable. Similarly in every country, in China, cow-slaughter is a crime. It is banned in Afghanistan as well. A year ago, a similar law was passed in Burma. Before that, under a certain law cattle only above fourteen years of age could be slaughtered. But the Burma Government realized that this partial ban on cow slaughter was not effective. On the pretext of useless cattle many useful cattle are slaughtered. I have read in newspapers that the Pakistan Government has decided to stop the export of cattle from Western Pakistan, and they too have enforced a partial ban on slaughter of animals. In the present condition in our country, cow-breeding is necessary, not for milk supply alone, but also for the purposes of draught and transport. It is no wonder that people worship cow in this land. But I do not appeal to you in the name of religion. I ask you to consider it in the light of economic requirements of the country. In this connection I would like to tell you the opinion of the greatest leader of our country—the Father of the Nation—on the subject. You know the ideas of revered Mahatmaji on this topic. He never wanted to put any compulsion on Muslims or non-Muslims. He said, "I hold that the question of cow slaughter is of great moment—in certain respects of even greater moment—than that of *Swaraj*. Cow slaughter and man-slaughter are, in my opinion, two sides of the same coin."

Leaving it aside, I want to draw your attention to the speech of our First President, Dr. Rajendra Prasad. After this the Government of India, appointed a committee—an expert representative committee—to find out whether for the benefit of the country the number of cattle can be increased, and whether their slaughter can be stopped. Seth Govind Das was also a member of the committee. The committee unanimously decided that cattle slaughter should be banned. Great minds were associated with the said committee. They examined the question from the economic view-point; they gave thought to the unproductive and unserviceable cattle also. After viewing the problem from all angles they came to the unanimous decision that slaughter of cattle should be stopped. That resolution relates not to cows alone. Slaughtering of buffaloes, which yield 50 per cent of our milk supply, and of the goats which yield 3 per cent of our milk supply, and also bring a profit of several crores, is as sinful as that of cows. Perhaps a cow does not yield that much in other areas. Therefore, I submit that we should consider it from an economic point of view. I also want to state that many of the cattle, which are generally regarded as useless, are not really so. Experts have made an estimate of that. And they came to the conclusion that the cattle which are regarded as useless are not really so, because we are in great need of manure. A cow, whether a milch-cow or not, is a moving manure factory and so, as far as cow is concerned, there can be no question of its being useless or useful. It can never be useless. In the case of cow there can be no dispute on the point."[84]

While Pandit Bhargava's 'agreed amendment' was for prohibiting 'slaughter of cow and other useful cattle', Seth Govind Das's amendment was to 'prohibit the slaughter of any cow', be it useful or useless and in this amendment the word 'cow' includes bulls, bullocks, young stock of genus cow. Elaborating on his amendment Seth Govind Das said: "The amendment moved by Pandit Bhargava prohibits the slaughter of cow and other useful cattle but according to it unfit or useless cows may be slaughtered. But the object of my amendment is, as far as cows are concerned, to prohibit the slaughter of any cow, be it useful or useless and in my amendment word "cow" includes bulls, bullocks and claves all that are born of cows. As Pandit Thakur Das told you, I had submitted this earlier to be included in Fundamental Rights, but I regret that it could not be so included. The reason given is that Fundamental Rights deal only with human beings and not animals. I had then stated that just as the practice of untouchability was going to be declared an offence so also we should declare the slaughter of cows to be an offence. But it was said that while untouchability directly affected human beings the slaughter of cows affected the life of animals only—and that as the Fundamental Rights were for human beings this provision could not be included therein. Well, I did not protest against that view and thought it proper to include this provision in the Directive Principles. It will not be improper, Sir, if I mention here, that it is not for the first time that I am raising the question of cow protection. I have been a member of the Central Legislature for the last twenty-five years and I have always raised this question in the Assembly and in the Council of State. The protection of cow is a question of long standing in this country. Great importance has been attached to this question from the time of Lord Krishna. I belong to a family which worships Lord Krishna as "*Ishtadeva*". I consider myself a religious-minded person, and have no respect for those people of the present day society whose attitude towards religion and religious-minded people is one of contempt. It is my firm belief that *Dharma* had never been uprooted from the world and nor can it be uprooted. There had been unbelievers like *Charvaka* in our country also but the creed of *Charvaka* could never flourish in this country. Now-a-days the Communist leaders of the West also and I may name among them Karl Marx, Lenin, Stalin, declare religion "the opium of the people". Russia recognized neither religion nor God but we have seen that in the last war the Russian people offered prayers to God in Churches to grant them victory. Thus, it is plain from the history of ancient times as also from that of God-denying Russia that religion could not be uprooted.

"Moreover cow protection is not only a matter of religion with us; it is also a cultural and economic question. Culture is a gift of history. India is an ancient country; consequently no new culture can be imposed on it. Whosoever attempts to do so is bound to fail; he can never succeed. Ours is a culture that has gradually developed with our long history. *Swaraj* will have no meaning for our people in the absence of a culture. Great important cultural issues—for instance the question of the name of the country, question of National language, question of National Script, question of the National Anthem and question of prohibition of cow slaughter—are before this Assembly and unless the Constituent Assembly decides these questions according to the wishes of the people of the country. *Swaraj* will have no meaning to the common people of our country. I would like to submit, Sir, that a referendum be taken on these issues and the opinion of the people be ascertained. Again, cow protection is also a matter of great economic importance for us. Pandit Thakur Das Bhargava has shown to you by quoting statistics how the cattle wealth of the country is diminishing. This country is predominantly agricultural in character. I would give some figures here regarding the position of our cattle wealth. In 1935 there were one hundred nineteen million and four hundred ninety one thousand (11,94,91,000) heads of cattle. In 1940 their number came down to one hundred fifteen million and six hundred ten thousand, and in 1945 it further came down to one hundred eleven million and 9 hundred thousand. While on one side our population is increasing our cattle wealth is decreasing. Our Government is carrying on a Grow More Food Campaign. Millions of rupees are being spent on this campaign. This campaign cannot succeed so long as we do not preserve the cows. Pandit Thakur Das has given us some figures to show the number of cows slaughtered in our country. I would like to quote here some figures from the Hide and Skin Report of the Government of India. Fifty two lakhs of cows and thirteen lakhs of buffaloes are slaughtered every year in this country. It shows in what amazing numbers cattle are slaughtered here. Thirty six crores acres of land are under cultivation in India since the secession of Pakistan from our country. We have six crore bullocks for the cultivation of the land. A scientific estimate would show that we need another one and a half crore of bullocks to keep this land under proper cultivation.

"So far as the question of milk supply is concerned I would like to place before you figures of milk supply of other countries as compared to that of our country. In New Zealand milk supply per capita is 56 ounces, in Denmark 40, in Finland 63, in Sweden 61, in Australia 45, in Canada 35, in Switzerland 49, in Netherlands 35, in Norway 43, in U.S.A. 35, in Czechoslovakia 36, in Belgium 35, in Australia 30, in Germany 35, in France 30, in Poland 22, in Great Britain 39, and in India it is only 7 ounces. Just think what will be the state of health of the people of a country where they get only seven ounces of milk per head. There is a huge infantile mortality in his country. Children are dying like dogs and cats. How can they be saved without milk?

"Thus even if we look at this problem from the economic point of view, we come to the conclusion that for the supply of milk and agriculture also, the protection of the cow is necessary.

"I would like to place before the House one thing more. It has been proved by experience that whatever laws we may frame for the prevention of the slaughter of useful cattle, their object is not achieved. In every province there are such laws. There people slaughter cattle and pay some amount towards fines and sometimes escape even that. Thus our cattle wealth is declining day by day.

"Some time back there was a law like that in Burma, but when they saw that cattle could not be saved under it, they banned cow slaughter altogether.

"I would like to emphasize one point to my Muslim friends also. I would like to see my country culturally unified even though we may follow different religions. Just as a Hindu and a Sikh or a Hindu and a Jain can live in the same family, in the same way a Hindu and a Muslim can also live in the same family. The Muslims should come forward to make it clear that their religion does not compulsorily enjoin on them the slaughter of the cow. I have studied a little all the religions. I have read the life of Prophet Mohammad Sahib. The Prophet never took beef in his life. This is an historic fact.

"Pandit Thakur Dass Bhargava pointed out just now that from the time of Akbar to that of Aurangzeb there was a ban on cow-slaughter. I want to tell you what Babur, the first Mughal Emperor told Humayun. He said: Refrain from cow-slaughter to win the hearts of the people of Hindustan".[85]

Ram Sahai wanted "complete prohibition of the slaughter of cows". "But I find here", he said, "that a section of the House does not like this. I also do not like, on my part, to make any proposal that may not receive the unanimous acceptance of the House, nor a proposal that may lead to the curtailment of the freedom of the provinces in this matter. Under the Directive Principles of State Policy, Provinces will have the power to stop cow slaughter totally or partially. Though there is a ban in one form or another on the slaughter of cows, in almost all countries of the world, yet I would not emphasise that fact before you. I hope Honourable Dr. Ambedkar will appreciate and accept the amendment moved by Mr. Bhargava because it is on the basis of the assurance to this effect given by him that the amendment has been moved as a compromise".[86]

Prof. Shibban Lal Saksena in extending his support to the amendment moved by Pandit Bhargava stated that "there are two aspects to this question. One is the religious aspect and the other is the economic aspect. I shall first deal with the religious aspect. I am not one of those men who think that merely because a thing has a religious aspect, it should not be enacted as law. I personally feel that cow protection, if it has become part of the religion of the Hindus, it is because of its economic and other aspects. I believe that the Hindu religion is based mostly on the principles which have been found useful to the people of this country in the course of centuries. Therefore, if thirty crores of our population feel that this thing should be incorporated in the laws of the country, I do not think that we as an Assembly representing 35 crores should leave it out merely because it has a religious aspect. I agree with Seth Govind Das that we should not think that because a thing has religious significance, so, it is bad. I say, religion itself sanctifies what is economically good. I wish to show how important cattle preservation is for us. Mahatma Gandhi in fact, has written in so many of his articles about his belief that cow protection was most essential for our country. From the scientific point of view, I wish to point out that Dr. Wright who is an expert on the subject in his report on our National Income says that out of 22 crores of national income per annum, about eleven crores are derived from the cattle wealth of India, representing the wealth of most of our people who live in the villages.

"Sometimes it is supposed that we have too many cattle and that most of them are useless, and therefore, they must be slaughtered. This is a wrong impression. If you compare the figures, you will find that in India there are only 50 cattle per 100 of the population, whereas in Denmark it is 74, in U.S.A. 71, in Canada 80, in Cape Colony 120, and in New Zealand 150. So in New Zealand, there are about three times the number of cattle per head of population than we have here. So, to say that we have too many cattle is not right. As for useless cattle, scientists say that their excreta have value as manure and its cost is more than the expenditure on the up-keep of such cattle.

"Then again, our agriculture depends mostly on cattle, as it is mostly small holdings where the cultivators cannot make use of tractors and other implements. They depend on bullocks, and if you compare the figure of bullocks, you will find that although we have got an area of 33½ million acres of land to cultivate, we have only six crores of bullocks which works at about 16 bullocks per 100 acres of land which is quite insufficient. Therefore, even from the point of our agricultural economy, we need a very large number of bullocks. It has been estimated that to meet our requirements, we would require about eleven crores more bullocks.

"Then, coming to our requirements of milk and other products, if we compare our milk consumption with that of other countries, we find that it is only 5 oz. per head, and that is very little, compared to the figures of other countries; Therefore I think that we must have this amendment incorporated in our Constitution.

"The other important evils in our country are infant mortality and tuberculosis which have their origin in deficient milk diet. These evils can be remedied only if we preserve our cattle and improve their breed, which is the purpose of this amendment. I therefore think that this amendment should be accepted.

"Then there is the use of Vanaspati ghee, which has become an economic necessity, because there is no pure ghee available anywhere. If we are able to give effect to this amendment we can improve the breed of cattle and then we will be able to do away with the use of Vanaspati, which is so injurious to the health of the nation.

"Also from the point of view of the requirements of our climate this amendment is very necessary. I think the amendment is very well worded. It says that we shall try to "orgnise agriculture and animal husbandry on modern and scientific lines and in particular take steps to preserve, protect and improve the useful breeds of cattle and ban the slaughter of cow and other useful cattle, especially milch cattle and of child-bearing age, young socks and draught cattle", I think the amendment of Seth Givind Das is included in it. I am sure, representatives of people elected on adult suffrage will surely incorporate in their state laws legislation which will give effect to this amendment and we shall then have in our land no cow slaughter. I therefore support this amendment wholeheartedly".[87]

Dr. Raghu Vira emphasized the importance of *Ahimsa* and cow-protection in the Indian civilization where '*Brhama-Hatya* and *go-hatya*'—the killing of the learned man, the scientist, the philosopher or the sage and the killing of a cow are on a par. "Cow is the mother of the individual, she is the mother of the nation", and "the cow shall be saved in the interests of the country and in the interests of our culture",[88] he commented.

R.V. Dhulekar went a step further and pleaded that "India should declare today that the whole human world as well as the whole animal world is free to-day and will be protected. The cow is a representative of the animal kingdom, the *peepal* tree is the representative of the vegetable kingdom, the touchstone or the *Shaligrama* is the representative of the mineral world. All these were worshipped because we wanted to protect the whole humanity...Some people here talked to me and said, "You say that you want to protect the cow and want it to be included in the Fundamental Rights. Is the protection of the cow is a fundamental right of a human being? Or is it the fundamental right of the cow?" I replied to them and tell them suppose it is a question of saving your mother or protecting your mother. Whose fundamental right is it? Is it the fundamental right of the mother? No. It is the fundamental right to protect my mother, to protect my wife, my children and my country. In the Fundamental Rights you have said that you will give justice, equity and all these things. Why? Because you say, "It is your fundamental right to have justice." What does that justice mean? It means that we shall be protected, our families shall be protected. And our Hindu society, or our Indian society, has included cow in our fold. It is just like our mother. In fact it is more than our mother. I can declare from this platform that there are thousands of persons who will not run at a man to kill that man for their mother or wife or children, but they will run at a man if that man does not want to protect the cow or wants to kill her".[89]

Z.H. Lari, a Muslim leader of UP, had no objection if the ban was imposed on religious consideration. He was not happy at the manner in which the problem was projected. He wanted that words should not be minced. He said: "I appreciate the sentiments of those who want protection of the cow—may be on religious grounds or may be in the interests of agriculture in this country. I have come here not to oppose or support any of the amendments but to request the House to make the position quite clear and not to leave the matter in any ambiguity or doubt. The House, at the same time, must appreciate that Mussalmans of India have been, and are, under the impression that they can, without violence to the principles which govern the State, sacrifice cows and other animals on the occasion of Bakr-Id. It is for the majority to decide one way or the other. We are not here to obstruct the attitude that the majority community is going to adopt. But let there not linger an idea in the mind of the Muslim public that they can do one thing, though in fact they are not expected to do that. The result has been, as I know in my own Province on the occasion of the last Bakr-Id, so many orders under Section 144 in various places, districts and cities. The consequence has been the arrests of many, molestation of even more, and imprisonment of some. Therefore, if the House is of the opinion that slaughter of cows would be prohibited, let it be prohibited in clear, definite and unambiguous words. I do not want that there should be a show that you could have this thing although the intention may be otherwise. My own submission to this House is that it is better to come forward and incorporate a clause in Fundamental Rights that cow slaughter is henceforth prohibited rather than it being left vague in the Directive Principles, leaving it open to Provincial Governments to adopt it one way or the other, and even without adopting definite legislation to resort to emergency powers under the Criminal Procedure. In the interests of goodwill in the country and of cordial relations between the different communities I submit that this is the proper occasion when the majority should express itself clearly and definitely.

"I for one can say that this is a matter on which we will not stand in the way of the majority if the majority wants to proceed in a certain way. Whatever may be our inclinations, we feel—we know that our religion does not necessarily say that you must sacrifice cow; it permits it. The question is whether, considering the sentiments that you have, considering the regard which the majority have of certain classes of animals, do they or do they not permit the minority—not a right—but a privilege or a permission which it at present has? I cannot put it higher. I won't class it as interference with my religion. But I do not want that my liberty should be taken away, and especially the peaceful celebration of any festival should be marred by the promulgation of orders under Section 144. I have come to plead that. Therefore, let the leaders of the majority community here and now make it clear and not leave it to the back-benchers to come forward and deliver sermons one way or the other. Let those who guide the destinies of the country, make or mar them, say definitely "this is our view", and we will submit to it. We are not going to violate it. This is the only thing I have come to say. I hope you will not misunderstand me when I say this. It is not due to anger, malice or resentment but it is out of regard for cordial relations between the communities and what is more, due to the necessity of having a clear mind that I say this. Henceforth the Muslim minority must know where they stand, so that, they may act accordingly, and there be no occasion for any misunderstanding between the majority and the Muslims on this point.

"In view of what I have said, I would not oppose nor support any of the amendments, but I would invite a very clear and definite rule instead of the vague phraseology of the clauses which have been put forward. It proceeds to say that we should have modern and scientific agriculture. Modern and scientific agriculture will mean mechanization and so many other things. The preceding portion of the clause speaking about modern and scientific agriculture and the subsequent portion banning slaughter of cattle do not fit in with each other. I appreciate the sentiments of another member who said, "this is our sentiment, and it is out of that sentiment that we want this article". Let that article be there, but for God's sake, postpone the discussion of the article and bring it in clear, definite and unambiguous terms so that we may know where we stand and thereafter there should be no occasion for any misunderstanding between the two communities on this issue which does not affect religion but affects practices which obtain in the country."[90]

Syed Muhammad Sa'adullha, the ex-Premier of Assam and a member of the Constitution Drafting Committee, was also of the same view. He said: "The subject of debate before the House now has two fronts, the religious front and the economic front. Some who want to have a section in our Constitution that cow killing should be stopped for all time probably base it on the religious front. I have every sympathy and appreciation for their feelings; for, I am a student of comparative religions, I know that the vast majority of the Hindu nation regard the cow as their Goddess and therefore they cannot brook the idea of seeing it slaughtered. I am a Muslim as everyone knows. In my religious book, the Holy *Quran*, there is an injunction to the Muslims saying '*La Ikraba Fid Din*', or there ought to be no compulsions in the name of religion. I therefore do not like to use my veto when my Hindu brethren want to place this matter in our Constitution from the religious point of view. I do not also want to obstruct the framers of our Constitution, I mean the Constituent Assembly, if they come out in the open and say directly, "This is part of our religion. The cow should be protected from slaughter and therefore we want its provision either in the Fundamental Rights or in the Directive Principles".

"But those who put it on the economic front do create a suspicion in the minds of many that the ingrained Hindu feeling against cow slaughter is being satisfied by the back-door. If you put it on the economic front, I will place before you certain facts and figures which will show that the slaughter of cows is not as bad as it is sought to be made out from the economic point of view. I have very vast and varied experience of the province of Assam and therefore I will quote you figures from Assam only. In the year 1931, under the orders of the then Central Government, a census of the cattle wealth of the province was undertaken. We found that in 1931, Assam had 70 lakhs of cattle as against a human population of 90 lakhs. It will stagger my friends from the other parts of India when I place before them the fact that the average yield of an Assam cow is but a quarter seer of milk daily and that it is so puny in stature that its draught power is practically nil. Assam is dependant for her draught cattle on the province of Bihar. During the last war when there was tremendous difficulty as regards transport, we could not get any cattle from Bihar, with the result that we were compelled to use our own small cattle for the purpose of ploughing. In order to conserve this cattle, the Government of Assam passed a law prohibiting the slaughter of cattle in milch or cattle which could be used for the purpose of draught. But, wonder of wonders, I personally found that droves of cattle were being taken to the military depots for being slaughtered not by Muslims, but by the Hindus who had big "*sikhas*" on their heads. When I saw this during my tours, I asked those persons why, in spite of their religion and in spite of Government orders, they were taking the cattle to be slaughtered. They said: "Sir, these are all unserviceable cattle. They are all dead-weight on our economy. We want to get cash in exchange for them."

"I know there is a community amongst Hindus themselves who go by the name of '*Rishis*' in our part of the country whose sole occupation in life is to take away the skin from the dead cattle. They have absolutely no objection even to flay the skin of slaughtered cattle. The figures given by Seth Govind Das include the numbers of both the dead and slaughtered cattle. Similarly, the figures given by Pandit Bhargava are not the figures of cattle slaughtered during normal times. They were, as Honourable Members know, war years and, on account of the fact that the Japanese had invaded India through Assam, Assam alone had to accommodate about 5 lakhs of fighting men and an equal number of camp followers. Cattle from all parts of India were then taken to Assam to feed these ten lakhs of people from America and elsewhere, whites as well as blacks. Even the Chinese soldiers were there in Assam, not to speak of soldiers from every part of India. Therefore, those were abnormal years and you cannot base your arguments on the figures of the years 1945 and 1946. [At this point Pandit Bhargava intervened to say that during those years, there was a ban on the slaughter of cattle imposed by the Government of India. They had issued orders banning the slaughter of cattle. It is in spite of that that the figures of slaughter have been so high.]

"We were trying to get cattle from West Punjab just before Partition. The cattle there on an average give half a maund of milk. The Assam Government have been trying to improve the milk yield of their cattle by introducing cattle from England, Australia and Punjab. We have yet touched only the fringe of the problem with our government cattle farms and we have succeeded only in Shillong. The milk yield here has increased but in the plains the milk yield is only quarter seer daily.

"The motion of Pandit Bhargava is that, in order to improve the economic condition of the people, we should try scientific measures. That presupposes that the useless cattle should be done away with and better breeds introduced. Now, I ask you what is to be done with these seventy lakhs cattle that we have got in Assam? Therefore, Sir, if you place it on the economic front, you are met with this proposition that we have got such a big number of uneconomic cattle that must be done away with before you can supplant them with a better breed. [At this point Pandit Bhargava pointed out that many useless cattle have been turned into good cattle by goshalas and other organizations and at least 90 per cent can be salvaged by proper feeding and treatment.]

"Sir, I do not know of goshalas in other parts and I do not want to reply to Pandit Bhargava as I have only ten minutes to speak. I was telling the House that there is a lurking suspicion in the minds of many that it is the Muslim people who are responsible for the slaughter of cows. That is absolutely wrong. There are lakhs of Muslims who do not eat cow's flesh. I am not speaking in any sense of braggadocio when I say that I myself do not take it. Before the partition the Muslims were only one-fourth of the total population. They did not raise sufficient cattle to kill. It is the majority people who sold their cattle to the Muslims to be killed. Now, the Muslims form only one-tenth of the population of the Dominion of India. Do you think that the Mussalmans can raise sufficient cattle to slaughter them? Muslims are poorer than our Hindu brethren. The Muslims are as much agriculturists as the Hindus and the cattle in their farms form their capital asset, the natural source of their power to till the land and produce the food which will maintain them for the entire year. Therefore, it is wrong to say that the Muslims kill the cows either to offend my Hindu friends or for any other purpose. Fortunately or unfortunately, the Muslims are a meat-eating people. The price of mutton is so high that many poor people cannot buy it. Therefore, on rare occasions they have to use the flesh of the cow. From my own knowledge, it is only the barren cows that go to the butcher. Speaking for Assam, it is the hill people who are the worst culprits in this respect. In the town of Shillong, there is only one Muslim butcher against seventy from the hill people, who deal in beef. Sir, in these circumstances, in the name of the economic front, I cannot lend my support to the motion moved by Pandit Bhargava. I am sorry that for the reasons given already, I am compelled to oppose the amendment of Seth Govind Das."[91]

Curiously enough, none of the front ranking leaders participated in the discussion and the motion of Pandit Bharagva having been accepted by Dr. Ambedkar was adopted by the House the same day (24 November, 1948).[92]

At the time of the third reading Article 38A was numbered as 48. But now there was a different version of the Article which read as follows:

> The State shall endeavour to organize agriculture and animal husbandry on modern and scientific lines and shall in particular take steps for *improving the breeds of milch and draught cattle including cows and calves and for prohibiting their slaughter*.

The words in italics were substituted for the words "preserving and improving the breeds of cattle and prohibit the slaughter of cows and other useful cattle specially milch and draught cattle and their young stock" in this Article, as was originally adopted by the Assembly on November 24, 1948. At the time of discussion of this Article on November 11, 1949 Prof. Shibban Lal Saksena pointed out that "this is a very substantial alteration and I do not think the Drafting Committee was authorized to make such an alteration on such a fundamental thing...I appeal that the original should be kept. It is out of order because the Drafting Committee was not permitted to make any such alteration as in this Article.[93]

Pandit Thakur Das Bhargava, mover of original Article 38A, also pleaded for restoration of the article in its original form. "This article has the sanction of the whole House and of the largest party in the Assembly. Moreover, this article...is one which was approved by the Chairman of the Drafting Committee. The original wording was quite different ... Previously it was a much stronger one, but ultimately this was drafted in this form...When a particular article has been passed, after being supported or opposed, there is no reason why the Drafting Committee should tamper with the wording of such a section like this...My submission is that every word in this article is to my mind a sacred one, in this sense that it has got the imprint of the whole House. Secondly, I submit that on the basis of this article, some of the Provincial Governments have taken action. They have gone further and prohibited the slaughter of cows. Therefore when this article has practically been acted upon by some of the provinces, it is not fair now to tamper with it....No doubt it (original Article 38-A) falls far short of the expectations of the general populace but it was a measure on which the House was agreed as a compromise. This compromise ought not to be interfered with."[94]

There was no further discussion on this article. On November 16, 1949 the President of the Assembly asked Prof. Shibban Lal Saksena to withdraw his amendment and we accept this in place of that:

> That in Article 48, for words "for improving the breeds of milch and draught cattle including cows and calves and for prohibiting their slaughter", the words "for preserving and improving the breeds and prohibiting the slaughter of cows and calves and other milch and draught cattle" be substituted.[95]

This amendment was accepted and was adopted on November 16, 1949. Article 48 as it finally emerged after this amendment and now appears in our Constitution is as follows:

> "The State shall endeavour to organize agriculture and animal husbandry on modern and scientific lines and shall, in particular, take steps for preserving and improving the breeds, and prohibiting the slaughter of cows and calves and other milch and draught cattle."

The words "preserving and improving the breeds of cattle and prohibit the slaughter of cows and other useful cattle specially milch and draught cattle and their young stock" of Article 38A were substituted by the words "for preserving and improving the breeds and prohibiting the slaughter of cows and calves and other milch and draught cattle". The words "other useful cattle" do not appear in Article 48.

During the third reading of the Draft Constitution many speakers commented on this Article on prohibition of cow slaughter. Three distinct trends emerged in this discussion—one group criticized for non-imposition of total ban on cow slaughter, another group was happy because at least this provision has been included in the Constitution, while the third group was critical for its inclusion in the Constitution in this form. Seth Gobinda Das,[96] Lakshminarayan Sahu,[97] Ramnarayan Singh,[98] Prof. Shibban Lal Saksena,[99] Algu Rai Shastri,[100] and Jagat Narayain Lal[101] belonged to the first group. Pandit Thakur Das Bhargava,[102] the mover of this Article, came under the second group. The third group included Rev. J.J. Nicholas Ray and Frank Anthony.

Rev. J.J. Nocholas Roy's interpretation of Article 48 was that "this article would only prevent the slaughter of cows which are milch cows and draught cattle, which will be of benefit to people. If it be otherwise, I consider that that would be a blot in this Constitution and an oppression also to people, especially to the Hill people of Assam, who eat beef and who keep cattle for the sake of eating. It would also be an oppression to the people who slaughter cows in sacrifices like the Moslems; even the Hindu Gorkhas of Assam sacrifice buffaloes at the time of the *Durga Puja*. There would be a great deal of disturbance and unrest if this article would be interpreted to mean that all cattle should be prevented from being slaughtered at all times and under all circumstances. This would act against the fundamental rights. I think that is not the meaning of the article...If that be the meaning of this provision...it would place a terrible burden on the State. Think of the millions of cows that will float around the country without any fodder, and sickly, and the amount of money that will be spent on them and the terrible burden it would be on the country. Hundreds of them will die in the fields without being taken care of. It will not be economic at all for any State to prevent the slaughter of cows under all circumstances."[103]

Frank Anthony was very critical for introduction of this article in an indirect way. "What I resent in this Directive Principle is the insidious way in which this provision with regard to the banning of cow slaughter has been brought in. I was not there before. I cannot help saying that those fanatics and extremists who could not bring in this provision through the front door have succeeded in bringing it through the back door. Sir, I am not a beef eater; I am not holding a brief for beef eaters. I say, you may ban cow slaughter, but we should have done it honestly without our tongues in our cheeks, without resorting to methods which may give rise to the accusation of subterfuge...If you had said that (cow slaughter offend the religious susceptibilities of Hindus) I would have sponsored a provision that a ban on cow slaughter should have been introduced in the Fundamental Rights and that cow slaughter should be made a cognizable offence. But, there were not people who were prepared to do that. Why bring in this provision in an indirect way? If it offends your religious susceptibilities, just as much as I expect you to respect my religious susceptibilities, I am prepared to respect yours. As I said, why bring it in, in this indirect way as an after-thought into the Directive Principles? In the way it has been done, it has been attached to a cause purporting to protect the cattle wealth of this country. Any child knows that in this country, in proportion to the population, we have more cattle than in any other country in the world. Any intelligent child also knows that in spite of this huge cattle population, our output for milch and draught purposes is the lowest per capita in the world. The preservation of cattle-wealth and the preservation of the best interests of the country would have required not the banning of cattle slaughtering but the slaughtering of over half of your present cattle population in this country. That is why I say, it should not have been done in this particular way. I only draw your attention to it and leave it at that", he stated.[104]

The tenor, thrust and trend of the discussion in the Constituent Assembly on this emotive subject shows that two Muslim Members, viz. Z.H. Lari and Syed Mohammad Saidulla, as well as Hindu Members like Pandit Thakur Dass Bhargava and Seth Govind Dass, Prof. Shiban Lal Saxena, Dr. Raghuvira and Dhulkar wanted the provision for a total ban on cow slaughter to be included in the Fundamental Rights Chapter of the Constitution. However, the Drafting Committee Report piloted by Dr. Ambedkar having the approval of the then Prime Minister insisted on adopting cow protection only as one of the directive principles. The members mentioned above including Muslim Members wanted it to be in the fundamental right. They also wanted that the protection in directive principles should be for all cattle and its progeny and not for cow and calf only. But Dr. Ambedkar prevailed over them, and what the Constituent Assembly adopted was in the form of Article 48 only.

The manner in which this provision was incorporated suggests some sort of behind-the-scene activity by the Drafting Committee when it was pointed out that there was serious omission on the part of the Drafting Committee in not incorporating the decision of the Congress Party to make provision for cow protection. One Member even alleged that "this was probably not known to the Drafting Committee". The Drafting Committee did not think it necessary even to explain why the demand to "put a complete stop to the slaughter of cows" was not accepted. Instead, the issue was very tactfully diverted to the arena of useful cattle and useless cattle. It was also known to the Drafting Committee that the issue was one of the major irritants to Hindu-Muslim relation. There was no opposition from the Muslim members. On the other hand they urged the government for settlement of this question once for all because they also knew that this issue had been and was going to be a constant irritant to Hindu-Muslim amity.

The two Muslim Members and the Member who represented the Anglo-Indian community in their speeches supported this demand for total ban on cow slaughter, provided it was made out on religious ground. It was admitted by them that "the vast majority of the Hindu nation revere the cow as goddess and therefore they cannot brook the idea of seeing it slaughtered". Everybody felt that it was a religious 'demand' of the Hindus. Since Islam "does no necessarily say that you must sacrifice cow" the Muslims, at least these two representatives of the Muslims, had no objection to concede the 'religious demand' of the Hindus. "It is better to come forward and incorporate a clause in Fundamental Rights that cow slaughter is henceforth prohibited, rather than it being left vague in the Directive Principles leaving it open to the Provincial Governments to adopt it one way or the other", one of them stated. "In the interests of goodwill in the country and of cordial relation between the different communities" and to remove "misunderstanding between the two communities on this issue which does not affect religion but affects practices which obtains in this country", this issue should have been settled once for all, he asserted. Speakers from the minority communities were however critical at the manner at which this provision have been included in the Constitution. They termed it 'backdoor method', 'subterfuge', 'camouflage', 'acts of fanatics and extremists' etc. Their criticism also influenced some of the members who later resented this 'back-door' method.

The considerations, which weighed with the Muslim members to volunteer consent for total ban are still of considerable importance and are a matter of great consequence. Half a century back, it had not been known to Man that cow urine and cow dung have great medicinal value and serious ailments are curable by their use. Bulls and bullocks have great utility to human beings and even if bulls and bullocks cease to be capable of breeding or working they remain useful till death, as yielders of urine and dung.

The king-pin of this Debate was the Muslim members requesting the Hindu Members to be bold and keep the provision as a fundamental right rather than as a directive principle. As an anti-climax, the Hindu Member, Pandit Thakur Dass Bhargava stated that he has accepted the advice of Dr. Ambedkar and would not like to put it in fundamental right, as it may not be agreeable to some of the non-Hindu people in India and, therefore, he did not press for amendment to bring it in fundamental rights. If Pandit Thakur Das Bhargava would have agreed to the suggestion of the Muslim Members referred to above and insisted on the provision being included as a fundamental right, Dr. Ambedkar might have persuaded high-ups and the catastrophe of the "holy, but helpless cow" could have been avoided. It may be noted that the Expert Committee (Datar Singh Committee) of which reference was made by Bhargava in his speech a number of times had recommended that slaughter of cattle is not desirable in India under any circumstances whatsoever, and that its prohibition shall be enforced by law.

The Parliament and Central Government were made powerless and legislatively impotent to make any law for the entire country on this emotive issue by non-inclusion in the fundamental rights and further by making it a State Subject. As the National Commission on Cattle has observed, "for cow and its progeny it was the blackest day".[105]

III

The issue did not die a natural death even after the Constitution was put in place. Soon after the Constitution came into force, most of the States legislated for preservation of the cow and prohibition of its slaughter following the Directive Principle in Article 48. The Assam Cattle Preservation Act came in 1950 itself and is still in the same form. However, the other States have come out with initial laws in the 1950s and, thereafter, the amendments continued to take place repeatedly.

State Acts

The following legislations were brought into the statute books in different States and Union Territories. Some of these Acts have application beyond the present State limits, on account of their being covered by the laws existing before reorganization of the States.

The following States/UTs have no legislation:

1. Arunachal Pradesh
2. Kerala
3. Meghalaya
4. Mizoram

Table 5.1: List of Laws Enacted by States for Cow Protection[106]

Sl. No.	State	Title of Legislation
1.	Andhra Pradesh	The Andhra Pradesh Prohibition of Cow Slaughter and Animal Preservation Act, 1977.
2.	Assam	The Assam Cattle Preservation Act, 1950.
3.	Bihar	The Bihar Preservation and Improvement of Animals Act, 1955.
4.	Chandigarh	The Punjab Prohibition of Cow Slaughter Act, 1955 (Applicable to Chandigarh).
5.	Chhattisgarh	The Madhya Pradesh Agricultural Cattle Preservation Act, 1959 (Applicable to Chhattisgarh).
6.	Daman & Diu	The Goa, Daman & Diu Prevention of Cow Slaughter Act, 1978.
7.	Delhi	The Delhi Agricultural Cattle Preservation Act, 1994.
8.	Goa	The Goa, Daman & Diu Prevention of Cow Slaughter Act, 1978 and The Goa Animal Preservation Act, 1995.
9.	Gujarat	The Bombay Animal Preservation Act, 1954 (Applied to Gujarat).
10.	Haryana	The Punjab Prohibition of Cow Slaughter Act, 1955 (Applicable to Haryana).
11.	Himachal Pradesh	The Punjab Prohibition of Cow Slaughter Act, 1955 (Applicable to the State of Himachal Pradesh).
12.	Jammu & Kashmir	The Ranbir Penal Court, 1932
13.	Jharkhand	The Bihar Preservation and Improvement of Animals Act, 1955 (Applicable to Jharkhand).
14.	Karnataka	The Karnataka Prevention of Cow Slaughter and Cattle Preservation Act, 1964.
15.	Madhya Pradesh	The Madhya Pradesh Agricultural Cattle Preservation Act, 1959.
16.	Maharashtra	The Maharashtra Animal Preservation Act, 1976, The Bombay Animal Preservation Act, 1954.
17.	Manipur	Proclamation by Maharaja Darbar Resolution of 1936.
18.	Orissa	The Orissa Prevention of Cow Slaughter Act, 1960.
19.	Pondicherry	The Pondicherry Prevention of Cow Slaughter Act, 1968.
20.	Punjab	The Punjab Prohibition of Cow Slaughter Act, 1955.
21.	Rajasthan	The Rajasthan Bovine Animal (Prohibition on Slaughter And Regulation of Temporary Migration or Export) Act, 1995.
22.	Tamil Nadu	The Tamil Nadu Animal Preservation Act, 1958 and Government order banning cow slaughter dated 30th August, 1976.
23.	Telengana	The Andhra Pradesh Prohibition of Cow Slaughter and Animal Preservation Act, 1977 (Applicable to Telengana).
24.	Uttar Pradesh	The Uttar Pradesh Prevention of Cow Slaughter Act, 1955.
25.	Uttarakhand	The Uttar Pradesh Prevention of Cow Slaughter Act, 1955 (Applicable to Uttarakhand).
26.	West Bengal	The West Bengal Animal Slaughter Act, 1950.

5. Nagaland
6. Tripura
7. UT of Lakshadweep.

The foundation of all these legislations is the Directive Principle of State Policy contained in Article 48 of our Constitution. Though the theme of the law in these different statutes is more or less the same, the respective legislatures have perceived the problem differently and sought to provide remedies and treatments to the problems, in their own ways and focused the legislations to cover them.

A review of the main features of the legislations enacted by the different States and Union Territories made by the National Commission on Cattle in 2002 indicates that there is a complete lack of uniformity in these State laws. By and large, most of the laws prohibit the slaughter of cows of all ages. However, Assam, Tamil Nadu and West Bengal permit the slaughter of even cows of over 14, 10 and 14 years of age, respectively. Most States prohibit the slaughter of calves, whether male or female. However, except for Bihar and Rajasthan, where age of a calf is given as below 3 years, the other Acts have not defined the age of a calf. In Maharashtra, the definition of calf being followed, by some executive instructions, was 'below the age of one year'.

Delhi, Gujarat, Madhya Pradesh, Punjab and Rajasthan have banned totally the slaughter of cow and its progeny, including bulls and bullocks of all ages. The Uttar Pradesh Act permits the slaughter of bulls and bullocks of over 15 years or who have become permanently incapacitated. However, by an Ordinance issued in 2001, the Uttar Pradesh Government prohibited the slaughter of cow and its progeny.

Most of the legislations specify that offences would be cognizable. However, only Delhi, Goa, Pondicherry, Punjab and Uttar Pradesh have made the offences both cognisable and non-bailable. The maximum term of imprisonment varies from 6 months to 5 years (Delhi and Haryana) and the fine from Rs. 1,000 to Rs. 10,000. Delhi and Madhya Pradesh have fixed minimum term of imprisonment at 6 months.[107]

Very recently, some of these state Acts were amended by the State Legislatures to make them more stringent. For instance, the Karnataka Prevention of Slaughter and Preservation of Cattle Bill, 2010 was passed by both the Houses of the Karnataka legislature in early 2010, amid tremendous furore, to amend the Act of 1964. The 2010 Bill, however, is much more stringent in terms of the way the law is formulated, as well as the punishment spelt out when in violation of the law. The clause on prohibition of cattle slaughter specifies that all cattle slaughter is illegal; anything contained in any other law, custom or usage notwithstanding. The biggest addition in the current Bill is the criminalisation of sale, possession or usage of "beef" (flesh of cattle in any form). With this provision, the definition of the scene of crime becomes a place where beef is consumed or where cattle are slaughtered.[108] The Bill faced intense criticism from the opposition. Former Prime Minister and Janata Dal (Secular) president H.D. Deve Gowda met President Pratibha Patil on August 5, 2010 along with a delegation and urged her to "consider and determine whether it is reasonable and justifiable" to give assent to the Bill.[109] The President returned the Bill to the State Government on February 21, 2012, seeking some clarifications.[110]

Even as the Karnataka Prevention of Slaughter and Preservation of Cattle Bill, 2010, was pending Presidential assent, the State government on December 13, 2012 passed the controversial Karnataka Prevention of Cow Slaughter and Preservation of Cattle (Amendment) Bill, 2012 without debate on the last day of the legislature session in Belgaum. The amendment to the 1964 legislation, now passed, includes several provisions that the State government had proposed as part of the Bill now pending before the President. Among other things, it expands the definition of 'cow' to include bull and bullock in the category.[111] On coming back to power, the Congress withdrew the Karnataka Prevention of Slaughter and Preservation of Cattle Bill, 2010 and the Karnataka Prevention of Cow Slaughter and Preservation (Amendment) Bill, 2012 without any debate in both the Houses of the Karnataka State legislature on December 20, 2014. While the first Bill had been returned by the President, the second Bill was still pending with the Governor.[112]

The Gujarat State Assembly on September 27, 2011 passed the Gujarat Animal Preservation (Amendment) Bill, 2011 unopposed, with the opposition Congress extending support to it. After obtaining the assent of the State Governor on October 14, 2011 the Bill has become an Act. In this Act the six month jail term has been extended to seven years on conviction and the fine has been increased to Rupees 50,000 from Rupees 1,000. Provision to confiscate the vehicle used for carrying beef has also been made in the Act.[113]

The Madhya Pradesh Prohibition of Slaughter of Cow-progeny (Amendment) Bill, 2010 to strengthen the existing law was passed by the State Assembly in 2010 and forwarded to the Union Ministry on September 3, 2010. It received the Presidential assent on December 22, 2011. The amended Act provides that no person "shall slaughter" or "cause to slaughter" or "offer for slaughter" any cow progeny by any means. Besides, no person, including a transporter, shall transport or offer to transport or cause to be transported any cow progeny, either by himself or through an agent, servant or any other person acting on his behalf, within the State or outside it, with the knowledge that the calf would be or was likely to be slaughtered. The Act also provides that any police officer not below the rank of head constable or any person authorized in this behalf by a competent authority shall have the power of entry, inspection, search and seizure and to present the case in the court. Moreover, the amended Act puts the responsibility of proving the prosecution wrong on the accused in a cow slaughter case. A person found guilty of cow slaughter would be liable for 7 years imprisonment, instead of the present 3 years, besides a minimum fine of Rupees 5000.[114] Incidentally, all these three States were ruled by the BJP.

The Maharashtra Animal Preservation Act, 1976 was amended in 1996 by the Shiv Sena-BJP government in its first stint in power. The Bill was pending at the Rashtrapati Bhavan since then. The BJP-SS government on coming back to power in 2014, decided to take up the matter with the President anew. The government wrote a letter to the President on November 13, 2014 followed by a seven-member delegation of MPs to the President on February 26, 2015. Taking immediate cognizance, the President signed it on the same afternoon. The original Act had a loophole that permitted slaughter of cow's progenies provided the meat trader produces a certificate that bull or bullock is fit for killing. The new law not only prohibits sale and purchase of cows, bulls and bullocks for slaughter, but also possession and transport of their meat. It only excludes female buffaloes and their calves which need a fit-for-slaughter certificate before facing the abattoir. It falls on the offender to prove his innocence. If found guilty, the accused can be sentenced to rigorous imprisonment for five years and a fine of Rupees 10,000 or both.[115] The Act came into force on March 4, 2015.[116]

The new law is set to cripple the beef trade on which roughly 1.5 crore people in Maharashtra depend. The trade is mainly controlled by Muslim Quaraishi community. *Dalits* are involved in the hide business and in the transportation of bovines.[117] Beef traders affected by the ban on sale and purchase of beef in Maharashtra have gone on an indefinite strike and boycotted the slaughter of buffaloes, which is permitted under law. Earlier, hundreds of butchers, beef traders, workers at slaughter-houses and employees in the leather and chemical industry, which are closely linked to the supply of cattle, staged a *dharana* at Mumbai's Azad Maidan. Deonar abattoir, the largest slaughter-house in Asia, is among those severally hit. The Bombay High Court which on March 9 refused to grant any relief to the beef traders on the grounds that a law had already been notified, and that the authorities were duty bound to implement it, however, asked the Maharashtra government on March 12, if it could consider giving reasonable time to beef traders to dispose their livestock and animal carcass, the sale of which has been banned.[118]

On March 14, 2015 Haryana government imposed a complete ban on the sale of beef in any form including canned beef in the state. On March 16, 2015 the Haryana Assembly passed by voice vote the "Gau Samrakshan and Gau Samwardhan Bill, 2015". The Bill clamps a complete ban on cow slaughter in the state and provides for a rigorous imprisonment ranging from three years to ten years for killing the animal. The Bill also provides for a fine ranging from Rs. 30,000 to Rs. one lakh and in case of default in payment of the fine rigorous imprisonment for another one year.[119]

Even Kerala, which has not passed any anti-slaughter Act, decided on April 18, 2012 to ban the slaughter of pregnant cows. This decision was taken because of a common view that the slaughter of such cows was a cruel act.[120]

Judicial Pronouncements

Three legislative enactments banning the slaughter of certain animals were passed respectively by the States of Bihar, Uttar Pradesh and Madhya Pradesh. In Bihar, the Bihar Preservation and Improvement of Animals Act, 1956 (Bihar Act 2 of 1956) imposed a total ban on the slaughter of all categories of animals belonging to the species of bovine cattle. In Uttar Pradesh, the Uttar Pradesh Prevention of Cow Slaughter Act, 1955 (U.P. Act 1 of 1956) was enacted which also imposed a total ban on the slaughter of cows and her progeny which included bulls, bullocks, heifers and cows. In the State of Madhya Pradesh, it was the C.P. and Berar Animal Preservation Act (Act 52 of 1949) which was amended and applied. It imposed a total ban on the slaughter of cows and female calf of a cow. The male calf of a cow, bull, bullock, buffalo (male or female, adult or calf) could be slaughtered only on obtaining a certificate. The bans, as imposed by these legislations were challenged before the Supreme Court, mostly by the beef-selling lobby. It was claimed that a ban would interfere with their fundamental right to continue their profession. The underlying and more sensitive ground was that the sacrifice of cows during the Bakr-Id was part of the Muslim religion, and such prohibition would infringe upon the fundamental right of the community to practice their religion. The Constitution Bench of the Supreme Court speaking through the Chief Justice S.R. Das, held that (i) a total ban on the slaughter of cows of all ages and calves of cows and calves of she-buffaloes, male or female, was quite reasonable and valid and is in consonance with the directive principles laid down in Article 48; (ii) a total ban on the slaughter of she-buffaloes or breeding bulls or working bullocks (cattle as well as buffaloes) as long as they are capable of being used as milch or draught cattle was also reasonable and valid; and (iii) a total ban on slaughter of she-buffaloes, bulls and bullock (cattle or buffalo) after they ceased to be capable of yielding milk or of breeding or working as draught animals could not be supported as reasonable in the interests of the general public, and was invalid. Thus, bulls and bullocks can be slaughtered when they ceased to be useful.[121]

This Court also examined whether Article 25 of the Constitution barred the introduction of reasonable provisions for animal husbandry and hygienic slaughter of animals. Chief Justice S.R. Das rightly decided that sub-section (2)(b) clearly provided that freedom of conscience and the profession, practice and propagation of religion did not prevent the State of Bihar, M.P. and U.P. from making such provisions merely because it was also a religious practice of the Muslims to sacrifice animals. Accordingly it rejected the challenge on religious grounds holding that the sacrifice of a cow on Bakr-Id is not an obligatory overt act for a Mussalman to exhibit his religious belief and idea.[123]

In 1961 some States like Bihar, Madhya Pradesh and U.P. wanted to put restriction in age of bulls and bullocks for the purpose of slaughter. For instance, Section 3 of the Bihar Act increased the age limit to 25 in respect of bulls, bullocks and she-buffaloes for the purpose of slaughter. In *Abdul Hamid Quaraishi* vs. *State of Bihar*, (1961) 2 SCR 610; AIR 1961 SC 448 the Supreme Court struck down the benchmark of age restriction imposed by these legislations.

The West Bengal Animal Slaughter Control Act, 1950 was passed ostensibly to prevent slaughter of healthy cows, bullocks, and buffaloes. The Calcutta High Court decided on August 20, 1982 that the power reserved to the State Government under the statute to grant general or special exemption "for any religious, medicinal or research purposes" did not permit of any relaxation for the festival of Bakr-Id. More than twelve years later, on November 16, 1994, the Division Bench of the Supreme Court presided by Mr. Justice Kuldip Singh relying on the earlier ruling of the Supreme Court in 1959 SCR 629 decided the Special Leave petition by agreeing with the High Court and struck down Section 12 of the West Bengal Animal Slaughter Control Act, 1950 which permitted Muslims to slaughter cows on Bakr-Id. In this case the Supreme Court has noted that sacrifice of any animal by Muslims for the religious purpose on Bakr-Id does not include slaughtering of cows as the only way of carrying out that sacrifice. Slaughtering of cows on Bakr-Id is neither essential to nor necessarily required as part of the religious ceremony. An optional religious practice is not covered by Article 25(1).[122]

By the Bombay Animal Preservation (Gujarat Amendment) Act, 1994 (4 of 1994) the restriction that bulls and bullocks below the age of 16 years could be slaughtered, was enlarged to a total prohibition on the slaughter of the progeny of the cow. On October 25, 2005 a seven-judge Constitution Bench of the Supreme Court headed by Chief Justice R.C. Lahoti, after discussing in detail the factual scenario justifying protection of male cow progeny beyond the age of 16 years, and their continuing utility to agrarian economy in particular, and utility of cow and her progeny to the economy in general, especially to agriculture and as a source for non-conventional energy, upheld the constitutional validity of the said amendment and in the process reversed the decision in 1958 in *Mohd. Hanif Quareshi* vs. *State of Bihar*, 1959 SCR 629 on this point.[124] The upholding of the ban by implication means a similar ban by any other state government would be valid, too.

Recommendations of Different Committees/Commissions

The issue of a ban on cow slaughter was agitated over several decades in one form or the other both on the floor of the Parliament as well as outside. The Government set up various Committees and Expert Groups to look into the question as well as related aspects concerning development and preservation of the cattle wealth of the country. Recommendations of some of the more important Committees/Commissions are discussed below.

Cattle Preservation and Development Committee (1947-48)

An Expert Committee under the Chairmanship of Sardar Bahadur Datar Singh was constituted by Government Resolution dated 19th November, 1947. In its Report submitted in November 1948, the Committee recommended that slaughter of cattle is not desirable in India under any circumstances whatsoever, and that its prohibition shall be enforced by law. The Committee suggested that, the first stage, which should be given effect to immediately, should cover the total prohibition of slaughter of all useful cattle other than (a) animals over 14 years of age and unfit for work and breeding, and (b) animals of any age permanently unable to work or breed owing to age, injury or deformity. The committee also suggested that unlicensed and unauthorized slaughter of cattle should be immediately prohibited and made a cognizable offence under law. In the second stage, the Committee envisaged that slaughter of cattle should be prohibited totally. The Committee also made suggestions for arrangements for maintenance and care of serviceable and unproductive cattle and for development of feed and fodder etc.

Committee in U.P. (1948)

A Committee was constituted in Uttar Pradesh in 1948, which included prominent persons from all communities, including the Nawab of Chattari, and Justice Maharaj Singh (a judge of the U.P. High Court and also a Christian). This Committee supported the recommendations of the Sardar Datar Singh Committee.

Expert Committee on the Prevention of Slaughter of Milch Cattle in India (1954-55)

On 10th June, 1954, another Expert Committee was set up under the Chairmanship of the then Animal Husbandry Commissioner, Shri P.N. Nanda, to consider, *inter alia*, what steps should be taken to prevent the killing of milch cows, even when they had gone temporarily dry. In its Report, submitted in January 1955, the Committee stated that a total ban on slaughter of cattle would be undesirable, in view of the shortage of dry and green fodder, and concentrates. The Committee reasoned that, as India had little fodder and cattle feed, it could only maintain 40 per cent of its cattle and, therefore, the remaining 60 per cent should be culled.

Gosamvardhana Seminar (1960)

The problems of salvage from cities and towns of milch stock when they go dry and their calves and ways and means for preserving good-quality cattle in the breeding areas were discussed at the Gosamvardhana Seminar at Mount Abu in June 1960. The Seminar, organized by the Central Council of Gosamvardhana, felt that the only solution was to remove the milch cattle from cities and town to rural areas.

Special Committee on Preserving High-yielding Cattle (1961-62)

A Special Committee on Preserving High-yielding Cattle under the Chairmanship of Shri Shriman Narayan, Member (Agriculture), Planning Commission was constituted on 29th September, 1961. The Committee in its report submitted in July 1962, made several recommendations.

National Commission on Agriculture

In its Report, submitted in 1976, the National Commission on Agriculture made several recommendations in Part VII on Animal Husbandry.[125]

Justice A.K. Sarkar Committee

A Committee under the chairmanship of A.K. Sarkar, former Chief Justice of India was constituted on 29.6.1967 in pursuance of the historical Cow Protection March of Delhi of 7th November, 1966 the firing on which led to the massacre of a number of saints and sages. This Committee had as Members, several stalwarts and renowned Saints, including Jagadguru Sri Shankaracharya Swami Niranjandev Teerth of Puri, R.S.S. Chief M.S. Golwalkar, Charan Singh, D.P. Mishra (both Chief Ministers), Rama Prasad Mukherji, ex-Judge and the Animal Husbandry and Agriculture Ministers of almost all the States. The Parliament was informed on 4.12.1969 that the tenure of the Committee was extended 5 times and that, till date, the Committee had had 12 sittings, had examined 53 persons and had accepted 135 memoranda and had obtained replies to its questionnaires from all the States and the Centre. However, due to withdrawal of its Members by the All-party Goraksha Maha-abhiyan Samiti the Committee could not complete its work. The findings of this most important committee are, however, not known.[126]

National Commission on Cattle

His Holiness Jagadguru Shankaracharyaji of Kancheepuram, who, deeply moved by the tragic plight of sacred cows, the slaughter of thousands having been observed by him during his Kerala visit, announced a fast unto death from 5th August, 2001, unless something was done by the Government to save the cow. Feeling greatly concerned about widespread and persistent demand for protection and preservation of cow and its progeny, as well as about the precious health of the Shankaracharya, the Government constituted the 17-member National Commission on Cattle on 2nd August, 2001 under the chairmanship of Dharampal, a renowned Gandhian and historian of Sevagram. Dharampal, Chairman, was accorded the status of Minister of State in Government of India. In the absence from Delhi of the Chairman, Justice Guman Mal Lodha, Vice Chairman of the Commission functioned as the Acting Chairman and looked after the day-to-day functioning of the Commission.

The Member Secretary, Shri Rajiv Gupta was subsequently replaced by another officer, Smt. Chitra Gouri Lal, in the rank of Joint Secretary to the Government of India. One Member, Shri Laxminarain Modi subsequently resigned from the Membership of the Commission. Another Member, Ms. Ingrid Newkirk was unable to attend any of the meetings of the Commission, due to the fact that she was residing abroad. She, therefore, requested that her name be excluded from the Report. The remaining 15 members of the Commission were as follows:[127]

1. Shri Dharampal, Chairman
2. Justice Guman Mal Lodha, Vice Chairman
3. Smt. Chitra Gouri Lal, Member Secretary and Joint Secretary to the Government of India, Department of A.H. and Dairying
4. Master Munshi Singh, President, Goshala, New Police Post, Railway Road, Khekhda, District Baghpat
5. Justice Ranganath Misra, MP (RS)
6. Shri Manchana Gunde Rao, 1/121-1, Bhageerathi, Sreeniwasa Nagar, Post Jadeherla Town, District Mehboob Nagar-509 302 (AP)
7. H.H. Jagadguru Sri Sri Balagangadharanatha Mahaswamiji, Sri Adi Chunchanagiri Mahasamsthan Mutt, Vijayanagar, Bangalore-560 040
8. Shri Hukum Chand Sawla, H.No. 784, Sudhama Nagar, Indore-9, M.P.
9. Shri C. Udayabhaskar Nair, 5/379 "Divyodayam", Kallepully Road, Puthur, Palakkad-678 001, Kerala.
10. Shri Kesri Chand Mehta, P.B. No. 115, 99, Tilak Road, Malegaon, District Nasik-423 203 (Maharashtra).
11. Shri Sunil B. Mansinghka, Go Vigyan Anusandhan Kendra, Kamdhenu Bhawan, Pandit Bachraj Vyas Chowsk Mahal, Nagpur-440 002

12. Shri Bhawarlal Kothari, Oswal Kothari Mohalla, Bikaner-334 005 (Rajasthan)
13. Shri K.L. Godha, "Prabhu Prasad", 222, Ashok Nagar, Shastri Marg, Udaipur (Rajasthan)
14. Smt. Gohar Aziz, BPMS, 4/321, Anna Salai, Palavakkam, Chennai-600041
15. Shri P. Haridas, Senior Advocate, "Srinath Bagh", 1, Nowroji Road, Chennai-600 031.

The Commission was given the following terms of reference:[128]

(a) To review the relevant laws of the land (Centre as well as States) which relate to protection, preservation, development and well-being of cow and its progeny and suggest measures for their effective implementation,
(b) To study the existing provisions for the maintenance of *Goshalas, Gosadans, Pinjarapoles* and other organizations working for protection and development of cattle and suggest measures for making them economically viable,
(c) To study the contribution of cattle towards the Indian economy and to suggest ways and means of organizing scientific research for maximum utilization of cattle products and draught animal power in the field of nutrition and health, agriculture and energy, and to submit a comprehensive scheme in this regard to the Central Government,
(d) To review and suggest measures to improve the availability of feed and fodder to support the cattle population.

The Commission submitted its report on July 28, 2002, i.e. within a year of its constitution. The Commission after extensive research has given a list of recommendations as follows:

Recommendations of the National Commission on Cattle

1. The prohibition for slaughter of cow and its progeny, which would include bull, bullocks, etc., should be included in Fundamental Rights or as a Constitutional Mandate anywhere else, as an Article of the Constitution. It should not be kept only in the Directive Principles or Fundamental duties as neither of these are enforceable by the courts.
2. The amendment of the Constitution should also be made for empowering the Parliament to make a Central Law for the prohibition of slaughter of cow and its progeny and further for prohibition of their transport from one State to another. This may be done by shifting the

subject and relevant item from the State List to the Central List, or at least to the Concurrent List in the Seventh Schedule of the Constitution.

3. The Parliament should then make a Central Law, applicable to all States, prohibiting slaughter of cow and its progeny. Violation of the Law should be made a nonbailable and cognizable offence. There should be provision for sessions trials for offences committed under the Law, with a punishment of a minimum of three years of rigorous imprisonment and maximum 10 years of rigorous imprisonment with fine. The burden of proof should be on the accused to prove his innocence.
4. The Central Government should constitute a permanent National Cattle Development Commission or Rashtriya Goseva Ayog for preservation and development of cattle all over the country. The Commission should be provided with adequate funds, of say, at least Rs. 100 crores per year
5. There should be a separate Ministry for Cattle Preservation and Development. It should not be under the Department of Animal Husbandry, whose basic mandate is not for cattle preservation but for livestock development and for production of livestock products, including meat products.
6. The Animal Husbandry Department should be reorganized and the subjects allotted to it and the objectives given to it should be for preservation and development of animals and not for animal food by way of meat, etc.
7. No financial aids should be given by Animal Husbandry or Agriculture Departments for construction, renovation or maintenance of slaughter houses.
8. There should be a complete ban on export of beef and veal. Also, steps should be taken to ensure that beef or veal is not allowed to be exported under the guise or pretext of buffalo meat.
9. The Central Government should ensure constitution and functioning of Goseva Ayogs in each of the States and also provide these bodies with adequate funds. These Ayogs should be monitored by the "Rashtriya Go Seva Ayog" to be set up by the Government of India, as proposed above.
10. The implementation of the Cattle Protection Laws should be ensured through the following:
    - Creation of Central Cattle Protection – Rapid Task Police Force with regional offices and branches in all States. It should have a special force deputed on the Bangladesh border to prevent the cattle exodus from the border States and also on the Kerala's borders with Tamil Nadu, Andhra Pradesh and Karnataka.

- In view of Articles 48 and 51(g) of the Constitution of India, appropriate directions may be given under Article 355 or any such provision of the Constitution, to Kerala, Nagaland, Mizoram, Arunachal Pradesh, Tripura, Manipur and other North-Eastern States to enforce the prohibition on slaughter of the cow and its progeny. Special directions may be given to Kerala to stop importing cattle from neighbouring States for slaughter.
- The provision of the existing laws for prevention of cruelty to cattle during transport by rail, truck, road or otherwise, should be effectively enforced. Cruelty to cows during extraction or let-down of milk by giving injections, such as oxytocin, should be prohibited by law and the prohibition should be enforced.
- The Government should issue a Circular banning production of leather of slaughtered cattle and a mechanism for its enforcement should be evolved. Export of goods made of such leather should be banned.
- The penal laws of preventive arrest and detention like POTO, etc., should be amended to detain smugglers and organised *mafia* gangs, who indulge in large-scale smuggling of cattle to Bangladesh, West Bengal and Kerala and also in sale of cattle to illegal slaughter houses, operating all over the country.

11. Cross-breeding of indigenous breeds with imported cattle like Jersey should be prohibited, especially in the breeding tracts of important indigenous breeds. Conservation and preservation of these indigenous breeds should be encouraged. A National Breeding Policy should be evolved and special plans should be developed and implemented, with sizeable financial assistance for developing and preserving indigenous breeds throughout India.
12. Subsidies for purchase of tractors and mechanical appliances for Agriculture should be stopped. Instead, the use of bullocks in ploughing and bullock-driven tractors, generation of power through indigenous electrical equipment and carts should be subsidized, promoted and encouraged.
13. The report of the Organic Manure Task Force Committee 2001 should be accepted and its recommendations implemented in total.
14. The use and production of chemical fertilizers and chemical pesticides should be discouraged, subsidies on these items should be reduced or abolished altogether. The use of organic manure should be subsidised and promoted.
15. The recommendation of the XI Sub-Group (on Meat Sector) set-up by the Planning Commission for the 10th Plan proposals should be rejected outright.

16. *Gaushalas, Gosadans* and Pinjrapoles should be organized through voluntary organizations both by Central and State Governments. The Government should give financial aid for construction and maintenance of such *Gaushalas* on the basis of matching grants for day-to-day expenses; and 70 per cent grant for capital expenses for construction. They must be allowed free land or land at concessional rates, both for construction and for grazing purposes. Sufficient land should also be given for growing fodder for the cattle in these organizations.
17. Pasture lands should be protected, developed and provided for grazing of cattle belonging to farmers at the village level. Forest laws should be amended to provide grazing facilities for cattle within the forest areas or in the outlying lands fringing on the forests.
18. The use of *Gobar* (cow dung) and *Gomutra* (cow urine) of indigenous breeds of cattle should be promoted extensively in agriculture in the form of different manures, composts, Pest-repellents and pesticides.
19. Encouragement should be given to research in cow urine therapy such as that done by the Govigyan Anusandan Kendra, Devalapar, Nagpur and CSIR at Lucknow and other centres, which led to the recent grant of American Patent No. 6410059 for use of cow urine "*Ark*" (Distillate) for enhancing the effect of anti-cancer medicines.
20. The Information and Broadcasting Ministry should undertake propagation for awareness campaign of qualities and virtues of cow milk, cow products, cow urine and cow dung. Acceptance of "*Panchagavya*" by Ayurvedic System of Medicines should be widely propagated and its benefits explained to the people. The medicines from cow products and organic manure utilization should also be given wide publicity by Government media.
21. In the education and awareness campaign, "Farmans" issued by various Mughal emperors, Akbar, Humayun, Jahangir, and Bahadur Shah Zafar prohibiting cow slaughter during their rule should be widely advertised both in electronic media and other media.
22. In the educational curriculum, the subjects should be introduced on *Panchagavya* therapy, cow milk, cow urine and other by-products of cow, the use of cow and bullock in agriculture, organic manure and medicines prepared from cow dung and cow urine.
23. All India University should be established for the above and such subjects should be introduced in all Universities particularly Agricultural Universities and on Animal Sciences and in Veterinary Colleges and Universities and Hospitals.
24. The cultivation of fodder and manufacture of feed for cattle should be encouraged. The States should be asked to ensure production of

fodder and feed in proportion to the size of their cattle population.

25. In some States, such as Punjab and Haryana, standing crop residues which can be used as fodder are burnt. This should be made a penal offence as precious fodder is being wasted, whereas many States are deficient in fodder.
26. On the pattern of Food Corporation of India, a Fodder Corporation of India should be constituted and branches should be established in each State with storage facilities.
27. The Agricultural Universities and Agriculture Ministry with Forest Ministry collaboration should ensure special fodder production drive. The State Governments and the Central Government should subsidise the fodder sale on the pattern of food subsidies given to 'Below Poverty Line' (BPL) Indian citizens from ration shops, through the Public Distribution System.
28. A circular should be sent by the Central Government, directing that the State laws and Municipality laws, prohibiting keeping of cattle in Civil Lines and cities, should be suitably amended to permit the house owner to keep 2 to 4 cows and their progeny in their houses or campus even in the city areas or town areas. At the same time, strict action should be taken against those cattle owners who allow their cattle loose on the streets.
29. A circular should be sent to the State Governments Panchayats and Municipalities to regulate, control, remove and maintain the stray cattle wandering on streets and roadsides without owners. They should be kept in cattle houses or cattle compounds to be maintained by the local Self-Government institutions, Municipalities and Panchayats.
30. The Commission recommends that early steps may be taken for a Parliamentary Legislation applicable to the whole country by repealing various legislations now in force and a resolution as contemplated in Article 249 (i) may be passed by the Rajya Sabha or action under Article 252 could also be initiated, and a central legislation on the subject could be brought about to achieve the desired objects and the common problems in different States could be taken care of by such common legislation.
31. While amending the Fundamental Rights chapter of the Constitution, a proviso to Article 19 may be added after sub-clause 5 "provided, the right to carry on any trade or business shall not in any way extend to the slaughter of the cow and its progeny and /or to conduct business/ trade in Beef."
32. Similar proviso to be added to Article 301 "provided, the right to carry on any trade or business shall not in anyway extend to the slaughter of the cow and its progeny and/or to conduct business/trade in Beef".

33. In the Concurrent List, the following to be added:
    (a) Prohibition of Slaughter of cow and its progeny; and
    (b) Laws relating to the movement of cow and its progeny from State to State.
34. To declare the Indian breeds as the national wealth of India and no slaughter of any native breed of our country shall be permitted at any cost.
35. It is recommended that a Central Cattle Commission be permanently constituted, which shall have as representatives, at least eight Members/Directors, one each in charge of: (i) feed and fodder, (ii) cattle movement, (iii) on enforcement, (iv) grazing lands, (v) breeding, (vi) research, analysis and development, (vii) organic farming, and (viii) veterinary medical services. Such cattle commissions should also be set-up in each State.
36. Grazing lands should compulsorily be set apart, whether Government allotted or temple lands. Use of these lands should be exclusively made available only for cattle grazing and should not be allowed for any other use.
37. If there are any grazing or pasture lands, which have been encroached upon, the encroachment should be immediately removed by the concerned Government authorities.
38. Every State must have a Breed Centre, which should concentrate on the development of the indigenous breeds and not on foreign breeds. These breeding centers should also upgrade and develop the breeds.
39. A Cattle Census should be taken regularly and its results compiled speedily. Breed-wise numbers should be recorded and every indigenous breed must be registered.
40. A Cattle Laws Enforcement Directorate should be constituted, which shall be in charge of the movement of cows, bulls, bullocks and calves from place to place and State to State and also monitor whether the cow/cattle moved out from one State, has been utilized for the purpose for which it was sought to be moved.
41. Centres for promotion of the usage of cow urine, dung and *Panchagavya*, medicines, etc. and also research centres to be constituted for the promotion of production and use of alternative source of energy, such as Gobar gas, alternative methods of farming, through use of draught animal power, organic manure, cow urine pesticides etc.
42. Export and Import of beef to be totally banned.
43. "Save the Indian Breed" campaign to be launched all over the country.
44. There must be a constitutional status of Cow as the National Animal (*Rashtriya Prani*) and killing of cow and its progeny should be made a constitutional offence.

45. All types of manufacture, sale, use and import of Polythene Bags should be banned and prohibited.
46. Throwing eatables or eatable waste in polythene bags on the streets, roads or in dustbins, within the reach of cattle consumption, should be made a penal offence.
47. The Government should encourage and implement breeding policy by which a genetic improvement and upgradation of existing cross-bred cattle should be brought about by further crossing with good indigenous breeds.
48. The auctioning of all the working bullocks in the Municipality Corporations, Panchayats and other places should be stopped. Instead, they should be given retirement and maintained till they die their natural deaths. Their work had been utilized throughout their working life and after that their dung can continue to be used for production of organic manure.
49. Temples and religious places, should be prohibited from selling or auctioning the cattle, which are donated or gifted by worshippers. The trustees of these places should either keep the cattle in their own Goshalas or give them to nearby Goshalas for maintenance.[129]

After discussing in details about the importance of by-products of cattle in the fields of: (1) Agricultural, (2) Medicinal, (3) Cosmetics, (4) Nutritional, (5) Environment, and (6) Energy resources, the National Commission on Cattle recommended that research programmes, should be undertaken, encouraged and supported in national institutions, universities and non-government institutions.[130]

The report of the National Commission on Cattie was submitted on July 28, 2002, i.e. within a year of its constitution. The BJP-led government constituted this commission and was at the helm of affairs when its report was submitted. Its Cabinet cleared a Bill on August 11, 2003 to impose a ban on cow slaughter[131] but failed to push it through the Parliament apparently due to the compulsions of coalition politics. Now, that the BJP has come back to power with a clear majority in the 2014 Lok Sabha elections, it is to be seen whether it implements this National Commission's recommendations.

There is, however, no mention of the National Commission on Cattle's recommendations in the BJP's 2014 election manifesto. It, more or less, reiterated its 2009 Election promises in its 2014 manifesto. It said under the heading Cultural Heritage:

> *Cow and its progeny:* In view of the contribution of cow and its progeny to agriculture, socio-economic and cultural life of our country, the Department of Animal Husbandry will be suitably

strengthened and empowered for the protection and promotion of cow and its progeny.

- Necessary legal framework will be created to protect and promote cow and its progeny.
- A National Cattle Development Board will be set up to implement a Programme for the improvement of indigenous livestock breed.[132]

The Union Home Minister Rajnath Singh, however, assured the seers at a Jain conclave at Indore on March 29, 2015 that the NDA Government would try its level best to bring in a countrywide ban on slaughter of cows by evolving a consensus.[133] Prime Minister Modi also told a well-attended pubic meeting at Bengaluru on April 3, 2015 that cow slaughter ban would benefit the farmers.[134] Since the BJP-led NDA II has not the requisite number in the Rajya Sabha to get the bill passed, it was, therefore, of the view that the bill could be introduced only after a consensus. Already in Kerala both the Congress-led UDF and the CPIM-led LDF have joined hands to protest against such efforts by the BJP-ruled States as a "sign of increasing encroachment of personal liberty and democratic freedom".[135] While Central ministers have ruled out a Central law as livestock is a State subject, clearly, the party will calibrate its position in the long run, not letting it distract attention from its reforms agenda. It will press for stronger anti-cow slaughter laws in all States and actively pursue the legislative route in the States ruled by it. It would not push for central legislation.

In the meantime, under the National Gokul Mission, which has got Rupees 500 crore under the 12th Plan and an additional Rupees 150 crore during 2014-15, the Central Government will set-up a number of Integrated Indigenous Cattle Centres called Gokul Gram. Gokul Gram will function as state-of-the-art training centres for farmers and breeders. Two National Kamdhenu Breeding Centres will be set up—one in the north and another in the south which will work to upgrade non-descript cattle using indigenous breeds like Gir, Shaiwal, Rathi, Deoni, Tharparkar and Red Sindhi. It will not only improve the genetic makeup of *desi* breeds of cows but also increase their stock.[136]

Maneka Gandhi, Union Minister for Women and Child Development and a known animal protection activist, urged her ministerial colleagues to opt for 'gaunyle' a cleaning liquid made from cow urine extracts arguing that it is "environment-friendly" as it does not have a synthetic base like Phenyl, but is not as strong as the latter. The product is being marketed by an NGO, Holy Cow Foundation and Kendriya Bhandar is now stocking the 'gaunyle'. Earlier, Ayush Minister Sripad Naik had voiced for the ayurvedic drug companies that were manufacturing medicinal formulations made from '*panchagavya*', a collective name of five products obtained from cow, including its urine and dung.[137]

IV

At present, preservation, protection and improvement of stock and prevention of animal diseases are presently an item at Entry No. 15 of List II (State List) of the Constitution's Schedule VII. Hence only individual States can legislate on it. This is in tune with the overall scheme of the Constitution under which broad, macro-issues pertaining to governance are with the central government. Issues determining relationships within the communities are left to the States so that appropriate legislations can be brought about after taking into considerations local sensibilities, culture and habits. If Parliament wishes to legislate on it, that would again amount to encroachment on the power of states, and require constitutional amendment.

There are two ways in which Parliament can legislate on the subject. The simple process would be to bring about an amendment of the Constitution and shift entry 15 (relating to preservation, protection and improvement of stock and prevention of animal diseases) of List II of the Seventh Schedule of the Constitution to List III of the same Schedule, which is the Concurrent List, i.e. the list of subjects on which both the Centre and the States are competent to legislate. There have been several such amendments. For example, Education was an item on List II and by the 42nd Amendment in 1976 was shifted to the Concurrent List as item No. 25 of List III. This would require an amendment within Article 368 of the Constitution.

The other course is to take recourse to Article 249 which provides that if the Council of States has declared by resolution supported by not less than two-thirds of the members present and voting that it is necessary or expedient in the national interest that Parliament should make laws with respect to any matter enumerated in the State List specified in the resolution, it shall be lawful for Parliament to make laws for the whole or any part of the territory of India with respect to that matter while the resolution remains in force.

The National Commission on Cattle has recommended[138] that Entry 15 of List II should be shifted to List III to enable Parliament to give proper attention to the matter and bring about proper legislation.

In spite of this constitutional position, Parliament has seen uproarious scene on the vexed question of bringing legislation on cow protection. Agitations against cow slaughter took place sporadically, from time to time in Independent India and, gradually, the movement for a ban on cow slaughter gathered momentum in several parts of the country, mainly in the cities like Mumbai, Allahabad, Ahmedabad, and Delhi. Several organizations took up the cause and a number of demonstrations took place. In 1966, a massive protest march was held, in which people of all faiths, castes and age-groups participated. The peaceful demonstration in Parliament Street, Delhi was fired upon in which around hundred people lost their lives.[139] This led to the constitution of the A.K. Sarkar Committee, referred to earlier.

In the year 1979, Acharya Vinoba Bhave decided to go on an indefinite fast from April 22, 1979 on the question of prevention of cow slaughter. His demand was that the Governments of West Bengal and Kerala should agree to enact legislation banning cow slaughter. On April 12, 1979, a Private Member's Resolution directing the government to ensure total ban on the slaughter of cows of all ages was passed in the Lok Sabha. The Resolution was approved by 42 votes to 8, with 12 absentees. Later, a Constitution Amendment Bill seeking to bring the subject of Prevention of Cow Slaughter on to the concurrent list was introduced in the Lok Sabha on 18-5-1979. The Bill, however, lapsed on account of dissolution of the Sixth Lok Sabha.[140]

In July 1980, Acharya Vinoba Bhave reiterated his demand for a total ban on cow slaughter, while addressing the All India Goseva Sammelan. He requested that cows should not be taken from one State to another.[141]

In 1981, the question of amending the Constitution by introducing a Bill was again examined by the Government, but, in view of the sensitive nature of the issue and owing to political compulsions a 'wait and watch' policy was adopted. However, as a number of complaints were received from time to time that despite the ban on the slaughter of cow and its progeny, healthy bullocks were being slaughtered under one pretext or the other and calves were being maimed, so that, they could be declared useless and ultimately slaughtered, Indira Gandhi, the then Prime Minister, in her letter dated February 24, 1982 wrote to the Chief Ministers of 14 States, viz. Andhra Pradesh, Assam, Bihar, Gujarat, Haryana, Himachal Pradesh, Karnataka, Madhya Pradesh, Maharashtra, Orissa, Punjab, Rajasthan, Uttar Pradesh and Jammu & Kashmir, in which she desired that (i) the ban be enforced in letter and spirit; (ii) the ban on cow slaughter is not allowed to be circumvented by devious methods; and (iii) committees to inspect cattle before they are admitted to slaughter houses be adopted.[142]

A number of Private Member's Bills and Resolutions on Prevention of Cow Slaughter were introduced in Parliament, both in the Lok Sabha, as well as in the Rajya Sabha, from time to time. Some of these attempts are described below:

> In 1985 Private Member's Bill by Dr. A.K. Patel, M.P. was introduced but the Lok Sabha did not approve it[143]. In 1990, a Private Member's Resolution put up by Shri Guman Mal Lodha, regarding suitable legislation to ban slaughter of cow and its progeny throughout the country was introduced. After detailed discussions on August 17, 1990, the Resolution was put to vote in the House and was first passed

> by electronic voting. However, since this would have meant a fall of the Government, the voting was redone by slip-voting, and subsequently the resolution was defeated, although by a narrow margin, due to the fact that several Members were prevailed upon to change their stand to save the V.P. Singh Government.[144]

On February 24, 1994, Shri Kanshi Ram Rana, M.P. introduced in the Lok Sabha a Bill entitled "Ban on Cow Slaughter Bill, 1993", seeking to prohibit the slaughtering of cows in India. An identical Bill was introduced by Shri Kanshi Ram Rana again on November 22, 1996, with the same objects and reasons. In 1999, the Ban on Cow Slaughter Bill, 1999 was introduced in the Lok Sabha by Shri Adityanath, M.P. which provided for complete prohibition on slaughter of cows for all purposes. In 2000, Shri U.V. Krishnam Raju, M.P. moved a motion for introduction of The Prohibition of Cow Slaughter Bill, 2000. On December 22, 2000, Shri S.S. Ahluwalia, M.P. introduced a Private Member's Bill entitled 'Prevention of Cow Slaughter Bill, 2000' in the Rajya Sabha.[145] On April 10, 2003, a Private Member's Resolution moved by Shri Prahlad Singh Patel, M.P. in the Lok Sabha to bring forward a suitable legislation to ban slaughter of cow and its progeny throughout the country was adopted by a voice vote. The move met with stiff resistance from the Opposition parties which walked out in protest.[146]

In 2003 Madhya Pradesh Chief Minister Digvijay Singh wrote to the Prime Minister demanding a national ban on cow slaughter.[147] The BJP Government wanted to introduce a Bill banning cow slaughter in the Lok Sabha on August 21, 2003, but the allies of the ruling NDA forced the government to defer it.[148] Having failed to introduce the Bill due to opposition from its allies, the NDA agenda for governance, released on April 8, 2004, however, made a commitment to bring in legislation for the "protection of the cow and its progeny" if it came back to power in the 2004 general elections.[149]

The entire question of cow slaughter is, however, enmeshed in communal politics. Interestingly, in addition to the holy image of the animal, it has become an important political tool in the hands of right wing Hindu outfits, challenging the "outsiders"—Muslims and Christians—who are classified as the "beef eaters". The BJP is one of those very few political parties wedded to the cause of protection of cow. Cow and its progeny were included in the election manifesto of 1999, and also in the subsequent Lok Sabha elections held in 2004 and 2009. A comparison of the 1999, 2004 and 2009 manifestos of the BJP showcases the differences in the space and classification allotted to this particular item. In the party manifesto of 1999, the subject finds mention under good governance, a sub-section of economy—outlining the economic importance of the cows and its progeny as part of the government's endeavours in animal husbandry and dairying. This measure is deemed important as a necessary step in employment generation and overall reduction in poverty and eradication of hunger. The other mention of the cow in the 1999 manifesto is under agriculture/animal husbandry, where it exemplifies scientific animal husbandry, with an emphasis on upholding the constitutional provision of cow protection and to improve the breed of cow and its progeny. The 2004 election manifesto talks of improvement of livestock breeds with a thrust on the genetic improvement of indigenous cattle. It is here that we find mention of a consensus on a central legislation to protect the cow and progeny. The protection of the cow and its progeny was one of the most important promises made by the BJP for the elections in the Centre as well as the in the States in 2009. In view of the recent judgment by the Constitution Bench of the Supreme Court in *State of Gujarat* vs. *Mirzapur Moti Kureshi Kassab Jamat and others*, (2005) Supreme Court Cases 534 and in keeping with the Directive Principles of State Policy as contained in the Constitution, the manifesto promises to create necessary legal framework to protect and promote cow and its progeny. In the 2009 manifesto, the protection for cow and its progeny falls under the classification "preserving our cultural heritage". The manifesto also lays down the setting up of "A National Cattle Development Board" "to implement a programme for the improvement of indigenous livestock breeds".[150] The same promise was reiterated in its 2014 election manifesto.[151]

Meat of cow and its progeny or beef is cheaper and perhaps is available in greater quantity. A lot of cows and other animals of the species are taken out of India clandestinely. It is generally asserted that for poor people beef is the only low-priced source of protein. It has been given out that "policy makers and economists on food security the world over are recommending that humans shift from being grain consumers to becoming meat eaters".[152] But the fact is that of all the methods of obtaining protein, none is more inefficient than that obtained from beef. Ninety four per cent of the protein fed to cattle is lost as 'production cost'.[153] Sixteen grams of grain go into making one gram of edible beef, translating into 16 times more water, fertilizer and pesticide. Therefore, if the economies of scale are to be the determining factor, the demand to ban beef cannot be faulted, and any criticism on this score is erroneous.[154] However, there is good news for the meat-eaters. The scientists are making efforts to clone meat cells so that people could eat meat without having to kill animals. "Cultured meat"—burgers or sausages grown in laboratory Petri dishes rather than made from slaughtered livestock—could be the answer that feeds the world, saves the environment and spares the lives of millions of animals.[155]

The *Quran* prescribes "*qurbani*" of a quadruped animal like sheep, camel or goat, but never advises people to slaughter cows. The Supreme Court judgement in Bihar, U.P. and M.P. butchers' case (*Md. Hanif Quareshi* vs. *State of Bihar*, AIR 1958 SC 731) maintained that cow slaughter was optional under Muslim Laws. No "Surah" enjoining cow slaughter is to be found in the

Quran. Prophet Mohammed testifies in *Tafseed Dure Mansur*: "Respect the cow because she is the queen of the quadrupeds" and Saint Ali says: "Cow's milk is a medicine and beef is a disease". The famous scripture, Hikmat, also lays down that beef-eating results in rheumatism, leprosy and blood dysentery.[156]

Interestingly, on February 1, 2004 Mufi Habibur Rahman, the head of the *fatwa* bench of the Dar-ul Uloom of Deoband issued a *fatwa* asking for voluntary moratorium on cow killing. The announcement made on the eve of Bakr-Id said: "Though cow slaughter is legitimate under the *Shariat*, it is advised that sheep, goat and camel may be sacrificed in States where there is a ban on cow slaughter. The law of the land should not be violated and peace should be maintained in the States and the country". Mohammad Madani, the Jamiat Ulema-e-Hind general secretary, welcomed the *fatwa* and said that his organization had passed a similar resolution in 2003.[157]

It may be recalled here that the Constitution Bench of the Supreme Court in *Mohd. Hanif Quareshi* vs. *State of Bihar State*, 1959 SCR 629 has observed, *inter alia*:

> It is part of the known history of India that the Mughal Emperor Babur saw the wisdom of prohibiting the slaughter of cows as and by way of religious sacrifice and directed his son Humayun to follow this example. Simiiarly, Emperors Akbar, Jahangir and Ahmad Shah, it is said, prohibited cow slaughter. Nawab Hyder Ali of Mysore made cow slaughter an offence punishable with the cutting of the hands of the offenders. Three of the members of the Gosamvardhan Enquiry Committee set-up by the Uttar Pradesh Government in 1953 were Muslims and concurred in the unanimous recommendation for total ban on slaughter of cows.[158]

According to Dr. Balram Jakhar, former Agriculture Minister and former Speaker of the Lok Sabha, the statistics of 1989 show that the income and production from the Dairy sector was Rs. 4548 per hectare, which was much more than the economic returns per hectare from wheat (Rs. 2443), groundnut-wheat (Rs. 1870), wheat-cotton (Rs. 1798), and maize-wheat (Rs. 1788). Dr. Jakhar also found that cattle-based farming was more profitable than buffalo-based farming. According to figures, an expenditure of Rs. 100 yielded Rs. 117 in cow-based farming and Rs. 114 in buffalo-based farming. He also commended utilization of cow dung and urine for electricity production as it will improve environment also. Dr. Jakhar is very hopeful about the future of agriculture in India, if it is based on organic manure.[159]

The National Commission on Cattle has dealt extensively of the cattle products that are now proved to be of utmost importance in the following fields:[160]

(1) Agricultural
(2) Medicinal
(3) Cosmetics
(4) Nutritional
(5) Environment
(6) Energy resources

The Report of the National Commission on Cattle has analysed the economic viability of cows after they stopped yielding milk and it also came to the conclusion that it shall not be correct to call such cows "useless cattle" as they still continue to have a great deal of utility. Similar is the case with other cattle as well.[161]

V

In 1998, India, hitherto a milk-deficient nation, surpassed the U.S. as the highest milk-producing nation, a position it holds till date. According to the Department of Animal Husbandry, Dairying and Fisheries, the government has invested Rs. 2242 crore to help meet a national demand of 150 million tonnes of milk by 2016-17. Millions of cattle will be produced (mainly through artificial insemination) for this purpose. Today India is home to the world's largest cattle herd, with 324 million head.[162]

India has the world's largest cattle population and a quarter of its cow population. Beef exports was 1,67,291.41 tonnes in 1999-2000 and 2,43,355.58 tonnes in 2000-02, up by 45 per cent. Beef means Buffalo meat.[163] According to M.M. Hashim, chairman of the Council for Leather Exports, India exports leather worth $1.7 billion and the industry provides employment to two million people in the country.[164]

According to the U.S. Department of Agriculture's report on Livestock and Poultry: World Markets and Trade, India became the biggest beef exporter in the world in 2012 (till October) with 16,80,000 tonnes of beef and veal (the meat of a calf no older than three months) exports, followed by Brazil with 13,94,000 tonnes and Australia with 13,80,000 tonnes of exports. In 2013, India's beef exports are forecast 29 per cent higher to a record 2.16 million tonnes, accounting for nearly a quarter of world trade.[165]

A US beef export federation study states India exported $1.24 billion worth of meat in the first half of 2012.[166]

A ban on bovine slaughter can be expected to affect the leather industry, for instance, infringing upon the fundamental right of people engaged in it to make a livelihood. A ban on meat production or export will also cause loss of employment to millions. Right to trade and commerce and pursuit of an occupation is a fundamental right guaranteed by the Constitution in Article

19(g). The seven-judge Constitution Bench of the Supreme Court headed by the Chief Justice R.C. Lahoti held that

> The facts stated in the preamble and the Statement of Objects and Reasons appended to any legislation are evidence of the legislative judgement. They indicate the thought process of the elected representatives of the people and their cognizance of the prevalent state of affairs, impelling them to enact the law. These, therefore, constitute important factors which amongst others will be taken into consideration by the court in judging the reasonableness of any restriction imposed on the fundamental rights of the individuals. The Court would begin with a presumption of reasonability of the restriction, more so when the facts stated in the Statement of Objects and Reasons and the preamble are taken to be correct and they justify the enactment of law for the purpose sought to be achieved.
>
> In the present case, we find that the issue relates to a total prohibition imposed on the slaughter of cow and her progeny. The ban is total with regard to the slaughter of one particular class of cattle. The ban is not on the total activity of butchers (*kasais*); they are left free to slaughter cattle other than those specified in the Act. It is not that the respondent-writ petitioners survive only by slaughtering cow progeny. They can slaughter animals other than cow progeny and carry on their business activity. In so far as trade in hides, skins and other allied things (which are derived from the body of dead animals) is concerned, it is not necessary that the animal must be slaughtered to avail of these things. The animal, whose slaughter has been prohibited, would die a natural death even otherwise and in that case their hides, skins and other parts of body would be available for trade and industrial activity based thereon.
>
> The documentary evidence available on record shows that beef contributes only 1.3 per cent of the total meat consumption pattern of Indian society. Butchers are not prohibited from slaughtering animals other than the cattle belonging to cow progeny. Consequently, only a part of their activity has been prohibited. They can continue with their activity of slaughtering other animals. Even if it results in slight inconvenience, it is liable to be ignored if the prohibition is found to be in the interests of economy and social needs of the country. We hold that though it is permissible to place a total ban amounting to prohibition on any profession, occupation, trade or business subject to satisfying the test of being reasonable in the interest of the general public, yet, in the present case banning slaughter of cow progeny is not a prohibition but only a restriction.[167]

The All India livestock census data of 1992 reveals that out of the total cattle population of 204.58 million, 189.3 million or say 92.7 per cent cattle belong to indigenous breeds. Only 15.2 million (7.3%) cattle are of cross breeds. More than 96 per cent, i.e. 195.8 million cattle are in rural areas as compared to 3.9 per cent, i.e. 8.6 million in urban areas. The main problem stems from the numbers of male cattle that are not used either for breeding or work (0.95 million) and dry cows (24.45 million), together numbering about 25 million. Out of this number, 24 million or say 96 per cent are in the rural areas, while less than 1 million are in the urban areas. Thus, the problem basically lies in the rural areas. It may be noted that the number of 'useless' indigenous male cattle and dry cow is decreasing, the annual growth rate between 1987 and 1992 being of the order of -10.58 per cent and -0.47, respectively.[168]

Cows and buffaloes can be productive until about the age of 14 years. But in the existing set-up, in which cows are kept pregnant for almost 300 days a year, most of them dry up by the age of five or six. And after spending most of her life being milked, enduring hormone injections and the trauma of separation, the cow is sent off to the slaughterhouse.

Twenty-nine States/Union Territories have cow-slaughter protection legislations in place. Unproductive cows, therefore, are routinely trafficked to slaughterhouses in the States where laws are less stringent or non-existent—Arunachal Pradesh, Meghalaya, Mizoram, Nagaland, Tripura, Lakshadweep, and especially Kerala. A large number of cattle is trafficked to Kerala, under inhuman conditions, from the neighbouring states as it is a major consumer of beef and does not have any regulation pertaining to cow slaughter. Cattle are also trafficked to West Bengal, from where they are taken to Bangladesh illegally in connivance with the BSF, local police and local politicians.

According to the Ministry of Food Processing Industries, India has 3,600 slaughterhouses, nine modern abattoirs and 171 meat-processing units licensed under the meat products order. These do not include the numerous and ever-growing number of illegal and unregulated slaughterhouses, estimated to be more than 30,000. According to Tamil Nadu Veterinary and Animals Sciences authorities 1.4 million tonnes of cattle were legally slaughtered in 2012 nationwide.[169]

The affidavits filed by the States to the Supreme Court in response to its directions reveal that illegal slaughter houses are being allowed to function with impunity in different States flouting existing laws. No steps were taken to close down the illegal slaughter houses in Madhya Pradesh, Odisha, Chhattisgarh and Jharkhand. While Jammu and Kashmir, Uttrakhand and the Union Territory of Chandigarh did not at all file any affidavit, Karnataka, Manipur, Puducherry, Andaman and Nicobar, Bihar, Punjab, Nagaland, Tripura and Haryana did not explain the steps taken regarding illegal slaughter houses.

The Supreme Court directed strict implementation of the Prevention of Cruelty to Animals Act, 1960, the Prevention of Cruelty to Animals (Slaughter House) Rules, 2001; and the Transport of Animals Rules, 1978, among other relevant laws.[170]

The BJP-ruled State governments have taken steps mainly in 2014-15 for prohibiting sale of beef. For instance, Maharashtra Government has declared possession and transport of beef as an offence.[171] Madhya Pradesh Chief Minister has announced that besides trading in beef, its transport and its consumption inviting stringent punishment in Madhya Pradesh, the State Government would not give permission to export beef as well.[172] Haryana Agriculture and Animal Husbandry Minister Om Prakash Dhankar had confirmed that stringent punishment would be handed out for cow slaughter and sale and storage of beef in the State.[173] The Rajasthan Assembly has passed a law in March 2015 that bans the slaughter, trading and unauthorized transportation of camels that has been declared as the state animal in 2014.[174] Acceding to the demand of local residents and religious organizations, the Punjab government in March 2015, withdrew the clearance issued for setting up a meat plant at Ghanauri Kalan village in Sangrur district "in the public interest".[175] The UP Animal Husbandry Minister Rajkishore Singh told the Assembly on November 18, 2014 that if the Centre, which is the licensing authority of the slaughter houses, passes an order for their closure, the State Government will ensure its implementation in the state.[176]

Maneka Gandhi has given a horrible account of the functioning of the slaughter houses in Kerala as well as the risk involved in consuming the flesh of such slaughtered animals. She says:

> Thousands of cows and buffalos pour into Kerala illegally every day, smuggled out of Orissa, Tamil Nadu and Karantaka and killed in the most terrible ways possible in 900 slaughter-houses. These are animals that have been overloaded into trucks for days—the law allows six only. These trucks carry more than 80 animls crammed together with chilies in their eyes so that their pain keeps them still, despite broken legs and cramps. Some fall off the trucks and die hanging by their ropes, on the side of truck. Others are trampled on and die. Dead or live, they are bought to these slaughter-houses. Then they are given chemical injections to make their kidneys fail so that they seem heavier when they are weighed by the butchers. They are given injections to freeze the blood so that it doesn't fall everywhere when they are being cut. They are killed in a way that is neither *jhatka* nor *halal*—hammered repeatedly till they fall, then stabbed in the throat with sharpened rods that are twisted till the blood spurts out onto the floor and then hacked with knives still they finally die. None of this will give safe meat to beef-eaters. The animals

> will be full of acid and adrenaline from the stress and pain, the meat is full of gangrene because the limbs have been broken for several days and rot has set in, the chemicals of injections will affect human blood and kidneys, the filth of the hammers and the knives can give tetanus.
>
> But added to all this is another danger: Food and Mouth Disease. Most cattle being shipped to Kerala are being sold because they have FMD.[177]

China is another country which regularly reports outbreaks of FMD, but no one knows what they do to the affected animals. Neither India nor China obey international bans nor do West Asian countries that import the meat.

Ever increasing number of cattle in general and cow and its progeny in particular, roaming on the streets of towns and cities as stray cattle is a serious menace to the environment, transport system and general living of people. It is a serious threat and challenge to society, which needs no elaboration. It is a country-wide problem, spreading from rural areas to metropolitan cities. It is also the crucial issue, generally put forward whenever the question of total ban on cow slaughter arises. Time and again, it has been said that stray cattle are indication of the fact that these are unfit and their rearing is uneconomic. That is why the owners just push them out on the ultimate journey to the slaughter-house.

The Sardar Datar Singh Committee (1947) recommended the establishment of '*Gosadans*' where 'uneconomic' cattle could be housed cheaply and allowed to die a natural death. The scheme could not achieve the projected targets. Only 17 *Gosadans* could be started during the first Five Year Plan period. Established in the States of Bihar, UP, Pepsu, Coorg, Bhopal, Kutch, Vindhya Pradesh, Tripura and Saurashtra these *Gosadans* could have only 5293 cattle against the capacity of 34,000. Lack of funds with the State Governments for meeting their share of expenditure, non-availability of suitable land, absence of legislative measures for the compulsory removal of unproductive cattle from owner's premises, transport difficulties etc. are the reasons generally advanced as to why the '*Gosadan*' scheme could not succeed then.[178]

It has been argued in more than one forum that the present size of cattle population is beyond the carrying capacity of the country. Rearing of dry cows or old and infirm bullocks and oxen will tend to affect the good and useful cattle, as the feed and fodder is inadequate to take care of the total number. Reports of the "Cattle Preservation and Development Committee" (Datar Singh Committee), "Expert Committee on the Prevention of Slaughter of Cattle in India" (P.N. Nanda Committee), Special Committee on Preserving High-Yielding Cattle" (Shriman Narayan Committee) and all other reports on this issue have highlighted this point. The judgement of Hon'ble Supreme Court of India dated 23.4.1958 in the case *Mohd. Hanif Quareshi and others* vs. *The State of Bihar and others*, also gave weightage to this viewpoint. Prof. S.N. Mishra, former director of the Institute of Economic Growth has urged for the elimination of non-productive cattle because that would not only spare the costly cattle feed for milch cattle, but also provide income to farmers through sale of such cattle for meat.[179]

To tackle the problem of stray and 'useless' cattle the National Commission on Cattle proposed the setting of Village Gosadans in the rural areas and Cow Sanctuaries in the urban areas.[180]

Historically speaking, the cow has always had a very special place in the social fabric of the country. Our ancient culture treats all animals as having a soul, in the same manner as human beings have souls. Here, in India, all life including insects, ants, animals and plants, big or small, each and everyone has a sanctity of his or her own. Jain Philosophy of Adinatha and Mahavira recognized "Soul and Life" in animals and plants, trees and vegetables, even before Jagdish Chandra Bose proved it scientifically. It is believed that the soul of each living being migrates from one life-form to another, till the Individual soul, after countless births and rebirths, gets absorbed into the ultimate cosmic or divine form. In India even those, who have over recent centuries been converted to other faiths like Islam or Christianity, often tend to believe in this theory of transmigration of souls from one life to another.

As a columnist puts it, millions of Hindus, especially in the countryside, would not dream of partaking of cow's flesh. They are ignorant of the ancient Hindu sanction for beef. They do not know whether cow protection is a State, Central or Concurrent list subject. They worship *gomata* because that is their folk culture, untouched by the wisdom of the *Brihadaranyaka Upanishad* or the *Mahabharata*. They know nothing of the statecraft and would be content if law and society allowed them to live their own lives without forcing their lifestyle on others.[181]

It may be recalled that Article 51A (g), which was inserted in 1976 by the Forty-second Constitution Amendment Act, provides that every citizen shall have the fundamental duty to protect and improve the natural environment including forests, lakes, rivers, and wild life, and to have compassion for living creatures. Article 48A was also inserted in the Directive Principles of State Policy by the said amendment Act. This Article provides that the State shall endeavour to protect and improve the environment and to safeguard the forests and wild life of the country.

The ban on beef eating may be looked at from another angle, that is, the environmental angle. In 2009 Jairam Ramesh, Union Minister had supported a total ban on beef eating because large cattle population cause methane emissions, deadly for global warming. Speaking at a United Nations Population Fund's function in 2009, he said: "It has been seen that developed countries which eat beef have the maximum amount of emissions... The single-most important cause of emissions is eating beef. My formula is to stop eating beef".[182] His stand in the said meeting was in consonance with the spirit of Article 48A.

The Supreme Court observes:

> By enacting clause(g) in Article 51-A and giving it the status of a fundamental duty, one of the objects sought to be achieved by Parliament is to ensure that the spirit and message of Articles 48 and 48-A are honoured as a fundamental duty of every citizen. While Article 48-A speaks of "environment", Article 51-A (g) employs the expression "the natural environment" and includes therein "forests, lakes, rivers and wildlife". While Article 48 provides for "cows and calves and other milch and draught cattle", Article 51-A (g) enjoins it as a fundamental duty of every citizen "to have compassion for living creatures", which in its wider fold embraces the category of cattle spoken of specifically in Article 48.[183]

The Supreme Court further observes:

> The concept of compassion for living creatures enshrined in Article 51-A(g) is based on the background of the rich cultural heritage of India the land of Mahatma Gandhi, Vinoba Bhave, Mahavira, Buddha, Guru Nanak and others. No religion or holy book in any part of the world teaches or encourages cruelty. Indian society is a pluralistic society. It has unity in diversity. The religions, cultures and people may be diverse, yet all speak in one voice that cruelty to any living creature must be curbed and ceased. A cattle which has served human beings is entitled to compassion in its old age when it has ceased to be milch or draught and becomes so-called "useless". It will be an act of reprehensible ingratitude to condemn a cattle in its old age as useless and send it to a slaughterhouse taking away the little time from its natural life that it would have lived, forgetting its service for the major part of its life, for which it had remained milch or draught. We have to remember: the weak and meek need more protection and compassion.[184]

One hopes that the observations of the highest court of the land are considered by the powers-that-be with all the seriousness that it deserves and the recommendation of the National Commission on Cattle regarding total prohibition of slaughter of cow and its progeny is enshrined in the Fundamental Rights Chapter of the Constitution. In the meantime Village Gosadans for the rural areas and Cow Sanctuaries in the urban areas, as recommended by the National Commission on Cattle, should be established in right earnest throughout the country to take care of all the dry cows and infirm and old bullocks and oxen. The government runs several *gaushalas*, shelters for old cattle, across the country, but these are too few and are not governed by serious norms. Since it has been alleged by no less a person than Maneka Gandhi, the renowned animal welfare activist, that seventy-five per cent of the *gaushalas* across India receive donations and are managed by traders, lawyers and society bigwigs who ill-treat and make money off the animals they are supposed to safeguard,[185] it should be ensured that the *gaushalas/gosadans*/cow sanctuaries, whatever they are called, are run for the purpose for which they have been formed. Transportation of cattle from one state to another in inhuman condition for the purpose of slaughtering in states where the ban on cow slaughter is not in existence or not enforced as well as for smuggling across the border should be prevented by invoking the provisions of the Prevention of Cruelty to Animals Act, 1960 (Act 59 of 1960).

Yet, in recent years, India is witness to a most horrific and systematic rise in animal cruelty. India still allows ritual animal slaughter in religious places and conflict-based animal games are held regularly all over the country. The authorities merely look away while the animals bleed to death in acute agony. And this is in spite of the fact that our Constitution in Article 51A(g) clearly exhorts every citizen of India to have compassion for all living creatures. Possibly this is the only Constitution in the world to have such a provision.

Recently, the Himachal Pradesh High Court on September 1, 2014 banned animal sacrifice throughout Himachal Pradesh. In the order it was directed that "no person throughout Himachal shall sacrifice any animal at any place of public religious worship, including all lands and buildings near such places ordinarily connected with religious purposes, ceremonies, '*yajna*', congregation, or procession connected with any religious worship in a public street hereafter."

The Supreme Court on October 17, 2014 asked the States of Uttrakhand, Uttar Pradesh, Bihar and West Bengal to take appropriate step to stop export of cattle to Nepal during the month of November when Nepal holds the Gadhimai festival in which cattle are slaughtered. The festival, held once in five years, was to be held between November 24 and 29 in Nepal's Bariyarpur area.[186] The royal family of Tonk has decided to do away with the 150-year old tradition of camel sacrifice on Eid-ul-Zuha from 2014.[187]

The proactive judicial pronouncements in respect of animal protection should be equally matched by a proactive administration by enforcing laws that have zero tolerance for any form of cruelty.

Notes and References

1. *Report of the National Commission on Cattle*, 2002, Department of Animal Husbandry and Dairying, Ministry of Agriculture, Government of India (Henceforth *RNCC*), Vol. I, Chapter I, para 7.
2. *RNCC*, Vol. I, Chapter II, para 8.1.
3. Fox, M.W., "India's Sacred Cow: Her Plight and Future", In *The Animal Ethics Reader* (eds.) S.J. Armstrong and R.G Botzler, 2003, London, Routledge, p. 239.
4. *RNCC*, Vol. I, Chapter I, para 11.
5. Kang, Bhavdeep and Bhaumik, Saba Naqvi, The Milky Way, *Outlook*, March 10, 2003, p. 33.
6. *RNCC*, Vol. I, Chapter I, para 12.
7. *Ibid.*, para 6.
8. Jha, D.N., *The Myth of the Holy Cow*, 2002, London, Verso Books, p. 146.
9. *The Asiatic Researches*, Vol.VII, 1801, Essay III, p. 204.
10. A.A. Macdonell and A.B. Keith, *Vedic-Index*, Varanasi, 1958, Vol. II, p. 147.
11. *Rigveda* X. 85, 13-14.
12. *Ibid.*, VIII. 43, 11.
13. *Ibid.*, X. 89, 14.
14. *Ibid.*, X. 79, 6.
15. *Ibid.*, X. 16, 7.
16. *Ibid.*, I. 164, 27 and 40, IV. 16, V. 83, 8, VIII. 69, 21. X. 87, 16 etc.
17. A.A. Macdonell, *Vedic Mythology*, Delhi, 1974, p. 151.
18. D.R. Bhandarkar, *Some Aspects of Ancient Indian Culture*, Madras.
19. *Rigveda* VI. 28, 1-8, VIII. 101. 15-16.
20. D.R. Bhandarkar, *op. cit.*, p. 73.
21. *Aitareya Brahmana* VI. 8.
22. *Taittiriya Brahmana* II. 7, 11/1; *Pancavimsha Brahmana* XXI. 14, 5.
23. *Shatapatha Brahmana* III. 1, 2, 21.
24. *Ibid.*, I 23, 6-9.
25. *Sankhyayana-sutra* I. 12, 10.
26. *Apastamba* II. 7, 16-26, *Paraskara* III. 10, 41-49.
27. *Yajnavalkya* I. 258-60.
28. *Vasistha* XI. 34.
29. *Khadira* IV. 2, 17, *Gobhila* IV. 7, 27. 54.
30. *Asiatic Researches* VII, p. 289; according to Panini (III. 4. 73): *gam hantitasinai goghno*.
31. *Shatapatha*, III. 4 1 2.
32. *Aitareya, Br.* I. 3 4.
33. *Manu Smriti* V. 18.
34. D.R. Bhandarkar, *op. cit.*, p. 77.
35. *Manu Smirti* III. 119-120.
36. *Yajnavalkya Smriti*, I. 109-10.
37. *Manu* V. 27-44, XI. 60; *Yajnavalkya Smriti* I. 109-10.
38. *Manu* V. 48.
39. P.V. Kane, *History of Dharmashastra*, 1941, Poona, pp. 779-80.
40. R.L. Mitra, *Indo-Aryans*, Calcutta, 1881, p. 360.

41. *Loc. cit.*
42. *Mahabharata*, *Van,* 208, 11-12.
43. E.W. Hopkins, *Epic Mythology*, New Delhi, 1968, p. 19.
44. R.L. Mitra, *op. cit.*, pp. 357-358.
45. *Arthashastra*, II. 26, 29.
46. *Journal of the Asiatic Society*, VII, p. 249; R.L. Mitra, *op. cit.*, p. 359.
47. Quoted in *Mohd. Hanif Quareshi* vs. *State of Bihar,* 1959 SCR 629, para 22.
48. *RNCC*, Vol. I, Chapter, para 16.
49. Quoted in *Mohd. Hanif Quareshi* vs. *State of Bihar*, 1959 SCR 629, para 22.
50. Puniyani, Prof. Ram, "Beef eating: Strangulating History", *The Hindu*, August 14, 2010, p. OB-1.
51. Mukherjee, Mihir, *The Statesman*, June 1, 1997, p. 11.
52. Puniyani, Prof. Ram, "Beef eating: Strangulating History", *The Hindu*, August 14, 2010, p. OB-1.
53. Parel, Anthony, "The Political symbolism of Cow in India", *Journal of Commonwealth Political Studies*, Vol. VII, No. 3, Leicester University Press, Leicester, November, 1969, p. 181.
54. Ali, M. Athar, *Elements of Social Justice in Medieval Islamic Thought* (Indian History Congress Symposia Paper No. 14, Delhi, 1997), pp. 12-13 quoted by Rajat Kanta Ray, *The Felt Community, op. cit.*, p. 96.
55. Husain Mahdi (translation), *The Rebla of Ibn Battuta* (India, Maldive Islands and Ceylon), 1953, Baroda, p. 47, quoted by Rajat Kanta Ray, *Ibid.*, p. 96.
56. *Matla-us-Sadain of Abdur Razzak*, (ed.), Vol. iv, p. 103, quoted by Rajat Kanta Ray, *Ibid.*, p. 96.
57. Nikitin, Afanasy, *Voyage Beyond Seas 1466-1472*, translated by Stepan Apresyan, 1985, Moscow, p. 34, quoted by Rajat Kanta Ray, *Ibid.*, p. 90.
58. *Ibid.*, p. 127.
59. Muntakhabu-t-Tawarikh by Abdu-'L-Qadir Ibn-I-Muluk-Shah Known as Al Badaoni, translated by W.H. Lowe, pp. 312-313, quoted by Rajat Kanta Ray, *Ibid.*, p. 96.
60. *Mohd. Hanif Quareshi* vs. *State of Bihar*, 1959 SCR 629, p. 651.
61. Proclamation of Khan Bahadur Khan, *Freedom Struggle in Uttar Pradesh*: Source Material, ed. S.A.A. Razvi, 1957, Publications Bureau, (henceforth *FSUP*) vol. 1, pp. 443-444.
62. Order of the Kotwal of the City, 28 July 1857, *FSUP*, Vol. 1, p. 421
63. Ray, Rajat Kanta, *op. cit.*, p. 422.
64. Kang, Bhavdeep, and Bhaumik, Saba Naqvi, *op. cit.*, p. 38.
65. *Ibid.*
66. Banu, Zenab, *Politics of Communalism*, 1989, Bombay, Popular Prakashan, Appendix IV, pp. 175-193.
67. Bayly, C.A., "The Pre-history of Communalism? Religious Conflict in India, 1700-1860", *Modern Asian Studies*, 1985, 19(2), p. 194.
68. Browne, Judith M., *Gandhi's Rise to Powers: Indian Politics, 1915-1922*, London, 1972, Cambridge University Press, p. 329.
69. *Ibid.*, p. 329.
70. Bhatt, S.C., *The Great Divide: Muslim Separatism and Partition*, 1998, Gyan Books, p. 59.

71. *Hind Swaraj or the Home Rule*, 1938, Navajivan Publishing House, pp. 38-39.
72. Parel, *op. cit.*, p. 186.
73. Browne, *op. cit.*, p. 329.
74. Parel, *op. cit.*, p. 187.
75. Nehru, Jawaharlal, *An Autobiography*, *op. cit.*, pp. 134-135.
76. Kang, Bhavdeep and Bhaumik Saba Naqvi, "The Milky Way', *Outlook*, March 10, 2003, p. 38.
77. "Beef Festival at Osmania", editorial in the *Economic and Political Weekly*, Vol. xlvii, No. 17, April 28, 2012, p. 8.
78. Rao, B. Shiva, *Framing of India's Constitution*, Vol. IV, 1968, New Delhi, The Indian Institute of Public Administration, pp. 55-56.
79. *CAD*, Vol. VII dated 5-11-48, p. 223.
80. *Ibid.*, p. 250.
81. *Ibid.*, dated 6-11-48, p. 278.
82. *Ibid.*, p. 290.
83. *Ibid.*, dated 9-11-48, p. 371.
84. *Ibid.*, dated 24-11-48, pp. 568-570.
85. *Ibid.*, pp. 571-572.
86. *Ibid.*, pp. 573-574.
87. *Ibid.*, pp. 574-575.
88. *Ibid.*, pp. 575-576.
89. *Ibid.*, pp. 576-577.
90. *Ibid.*, pp. 577-578.
91. *Ibid.*, pp. 578-580.
92. *Ibid.*, p. 581.
93. *CAD*, Vol. XI dated 14-11-49, p. 470.
94. *Ibid.*, p. 472.
95. *Ibid.*
96. *Ibid.*, dated 17-11-49, p. 613.
97. *Ibid.*, p. 614.
98. *Ibid.*, dated 18-11-49, p. 641.
99. *Ibid.*, dated 19-11-49, p. 706.
100. *Ibid.*, dated 21-11-49, p. 766.
101. *Ibid.*, dated 25-11-49, p. 948.
102. *Ibid.*, dated 18-11-49, p. 687.
103. *Ibid.*, dated 19-11-49, p. 711.
104. *Ibid.*, dated 25-11-49, pp. 941-942.
105. *RNCC*, Vol. II, Chapter IV-Part II, para 7.
106. *RNCC*, Vol. II, Chapter III, Annexure III(I).
107. *Ibid.*, Vol. I, Chapter II, paras 17.4 to 17.6.
108. Rao, Smitha, "Saffronisation of the Holy Cow, Unearthing Silent Communalism", *Economic and Political Weekly*, Vol. xlvi, no. 15, April 9, 2011, p. 85.
109. *The Hindu*, August 6, 2010, p. 6.
110. *The Times of India*, February 22, 2012, p. 1.
111. *The Hindu*, December 14, 2012, p. 1.
112. *Ibid.*, December 21, 2014, p. 1.

113. *Ibid.*, September 28, 2011, p. 1 and October 15, 2011, p. 1.
114. *Ibid.*, January 3, 2012, p. 8.
115. *The Statesman*, March 4, 2015, p. 2.
116. *The Telegraph*, March 27, 2015, p. 9.
117. *The Times of India*, March 4, 2015, p. 6.
118. *The Hindu*, March 10, 2015, p. 9 and March 13, 2015, p. 9.
119. *The Indian Express*, March 17, 2015.
120. *The Statesman*, April 19, 2012, p. 4.
121. *Mohd. Hanif Quareshi* vs. *State of Bihar,* 1959 SCR 629. (SCR 688); AIR 1958 SC 731.
122. *Ibid., SCR*, p. 651.
123. *State of W.B.* vs. *Ashutosh Lahiri,* (1995) 1 SCC 189.
124. *State of Gujarat* vs. *Mirzapur Moti Kureshi Kassab Jamat and others,* (2005) 8 Supreme Court Cases 534.
125. *RNCC*, Vol. I, Chapter I, Paras 43-49.
126. *Ibid.*, Vol. I, Preface.
127. *Ibid.*, vol. I, Chapter II, Annexture II(2).
128. *Ibid.*, para 2.
129. *RNCC*, Vol. I, Chapter VIII, Recommendations of the Committee on Administration of Cattle Laws.
130. *Ibid.*, Vol. II, Chapter VIII, recommendations of the Committee on by-products, dung, urine, bio-gas, electricity.
131. *The Telegraph*, August 12, 1003, p. 1.
132. *www.bjp.org/images/pdf-2014/full-manifesto-english-07.04.2014.pdf*, p. 41
133. *The Hindu*, March 30, 2015, p. 8.
134. *The Times of India*, April 4, 2015, p. 10.
135. *The Hindu*, March 17, 2015, p. 6.
136. *The Times of India*, September 14, 2014, p. 7.
137. *Ibid.*, March 25, 2015, p. 17.
138. *RNCC*, *op. cit.*, Vol. I, Chapter VII, para 18.
139. *Ibid.*, Vol. I, Chapter II, para 12.1.
140. *Ibid.*, Vol. I, Chapter II, paras 12.2, 12.3, and 12.4.
141. *Ibid.*, para 12.5.
142. *Ibid.*, para 12.6.
143. *Ibid.*, para 13.1.
144. *Ibid.*, para 13.4.
145. *Ibid.*, para 13.7 to 13.13.
146. *The Hindu*, April 11, 2003, p. 1.
147. Kang, Bhavdeep and Bhaumik, Saba Naqvi, The Milky Way, *Outlook*, March 10, 2003, p. 32.
148. *The Hindu*, August 22, 2003, p. 1.
149. *Ibid.*, April 9, 2004, p. 11.
150. Rao, Smitha, "Saffronisation of the Holy Cow: Unearthing Silent Communalism", *Economic and Political Weekly,* Vol. XLVI, No. 15, April 9, 2011, p. 84.
151. *www.bjp.org/images/pdf-2014/full-manifesto-english-07.04.2014.pdf*, p. 41.
152. Mayaram, Shail, "Recreating the politics of genocide", *The Hindu Sunday Magazine*, December 3, 2000, p. II.

153. "The World Food Problem", a *report by the US President's Advisory Committee*, Volume II, May, 1967.
154. Maitra, Ranjan, letters to the editor, *The Statesman*, July 2, 1996, p. 6.
155. Gandhi, Maneka, "When meat isn't murder", *The Sunday Statesman*, 8th Day, June 10, 2012, p. 4.
156. Sen, Samir Kumar, letters to the editor, *The Statesman*. May 10, 1995.
157. *The Telegraph*, February 2, 2004, p. 1.
158. 1959 SCR 629, (SCR p. 651).
159. *Ibid.,* para 23.
160. *Ibid.,* paras 36.1 to 36.6.
161. *Ibid.,* Vol. II, Chapter, V-I.
162. Narain, Anusha, "What's behind that glass of milk?" *The Hindu Magazine*, May 5, 2013, pp. 1-4.
163. Kang, Bhavdeep and Bhaumik, Saba Naqvi, The Milky Way, *Outlook*, March 10, 2003, p. 31.
164. *The Sunday Times of India*, January 7, 2001, p. 12.
165. Narain, Anusha, "What's behind that glass of milk?" *The Hindu Magazine*, May 5, 2013, pp. 1-4.
166. *Ibid.*
167. *State of Gujarat* vs. *Mirzapur Moti Kureshi Kassab Iamat and Others* (2005) 8 SCC 534 (paras 71, 78, 127 and 79).
168. *RNCC*, Vol. II, Chapter VI, paras 43-44.
169. Narain, Anusha, "What's behind that glass of milk?" *The Hindu Magazine*, May 5, 2013, pp. 1-4.
170. *The Statesman*, March 31, 2014, p. 13.
171. *The Times of India*, March 4, 2015, p. 6.
172. *The Hindu*, March 30, 2015, p. 3.
173. *The Hindu*, March 14, 2015, p. 9.
174. *Ibid.*, March 29, 2015, p. 3.
175. *The Statesman*, March 25, 2015, p. 5.
176. *Ibid.*, November 19, 2014, p. 3.
177. Gandhi, Maneka, "Wake-up call for beef-eaters", *The Sunday Statesman*, December 15, 2013, p. 4.
178. *RNCC*, Vol. II, Chapter VI, paras 4 to 6.
179. *The Hindu*, January 13, 1995, p. 15.
180. *RNCC*, Vol. III, Chapter VI, paras 48-50.
181. Datta-Ray, Sunanda K., Beefing it up again, *The Telegraph*, August 30, 2003, p. 12.
182. *The Hindu*, March 31, 2015, p. 9.
183. *State of Gujarat* vs. *Mirzapur Moti Kureshi Kassab Jamat and others* (2005) 8 *Supreme Court Cases* 534 (paras 51, 58).
184. *Ibid.*, para 67.
185. Gandhi, Maneka, "Overcrowded prisons for cows", *The Sunday Statesman*, March 4, 2012, 8th Day, p. 4.
186. *CWP* No. 5076 of 2012, *CWP* No. 9257 of 2011 and *CWP* No. 4499 of 2012.
187. *The Hindu*, November 13, 2014, p. 9.

6
Uniform Civil Code

I

At the first meeting of the Advisory Committee on Fundamental Rights, Minorities, Tribal and Excluded Areas of the Constituent Assembly held on February 27, 1947, Vallabhbhai Patel was unanimously elected chairman and five sub-committees—including one of fundamental rights—were appointed. The Fundamental Rights Sub-Committee held three sittings. At the first sitting which took place on February 27 itself, J.B. Kripalani was elected chairman and the general procedure and order of business for the sub-committee were settled.[1] The next meeting was fixed for March 24 mainly with a view to allow time and opportunity to the members to formulate their own proposals and study those made by others.

Aliadi Krishnaswmi Ayyar submitted a Note on Fundamental Rights on March 14, 1947. K.M. Munshi submitted a Note and Draft Articles on Fundamental Rights on March 17, 1947. Harnam Singh submitted a Draft on Fundamental Rights on March 18, 1947. Ambedkar submitted a Memorandum and Draft Articles on the Rights of States and Minorities on March 24, 1947.[2] None of them did ask for a uniform civil code. Munshi's Draft Articles, however, contained a proposal in Article XI (2) on marriage as follows:

> No marriage valid according to the law of the Union or a State, shall be dissolved unless permitted by the law of the Union or the law of the State concerned and in accordance with the forms and under the conditions of the State concerned.[3]

These drafts and notes were discussed by the Sub-Committee at its second sitting from March 24 to 31. In the meeting held on March 28, 1947, M.R. Masani suggested that a provision should be made for a common civil code applicable to all citizens. It was decided by a majority that this was outside the scope of fundamental rights. The minority consisted of Masani, Rajkumari Amrit Kaur, Ms. Hansa Mehta and Dr. Ambedkar. In this meeting it was also decided that Article XI of Munshi's draft articles should be dropped. Masani proposed that a clause in the following form, based on Article 54 of the Swiss Constitution, be included:

> No impediments to marriages between citizens shall be based merely upon difference of religion.

The proposal was lost by 5 votes to 4. The minority consisted of Masani, Rajkumari Amrit Kaur, Ms. Hansa Mehta and Dr. Ambedkar.

Dr. Ambedkar proposed that there should be no difference between legitimate and illegitimate children as far as the law of inheritance was concerned and that some provisions to this effect should be inserted. This was negatived by 6 votes against 3.

Mrs. Hansa Mehta desired that provision be made prohibiting child marriages. It was decided that the matter be taken up at the stage when non-justiciable rights are considered.[4]

In the meeting held on March 29, 1947 the sub-committee considered that the following, amongst others, should be provided for in the directive principles of social policy:

(6) The Union and every unit thereof shall endeavour to secure for the citizens a uniform civil code.

(7) Marriage shall be based only on the mutual consent of both sexes and it shall be maintained through mutual co-operation with equal rights of husband and wife as a basis. (Japanese Constitution, Article XXIV) Motherhood has a claim upon the protection and care of the State (Weimar, p. 119).[5]

The conclusions arrived at in regard to the different clauses on fundamental rights—both justiciable and non-justiciable—were embodied in the draft report of the Sub-Committee and circulated for comments and suggestions, on April 3. Along with the draft report an explanatory note prepared by the Constitutional Adviser was also sent for the use of the Members. In Chapter II which enumerated the non-justiciable rights were included the following two clauses:

(41) The State shall endeavour to secure for the citizens a uniform civil code.

(42) The State shall endeavour to secure that marriage shall be based only on the mutual consent of both sexes and it shall be maintained through mutual co-operation with equal rights of husband and wife as a basis. Motherhood has a claim upon the protection and care of the State.[6]

B.N. Rau, the Constitutional Adviser's elucidatory notes dated April 8, 1947 on the Draft report mentioned that Clause 41 was taken from Section 94 of the Constitution of Canada. Clause 42 was taken from Article 54, paragraph 2 of the Swiss Constitution and Article 119, paragraph 1 of the Weimer Constitution. The second clause was based on Article 119, paragraph 3 of the Weimer Constitution.[7]

In their minutes of dissent to the draft report recorded on April 14, 1947 M.R. Masani, Hansa Mehta and Amrit Kaur informed that

> We are not satisfied with the acceptance of a uniform civil code as an ultimate social objective set out in clause 41 as determined by the majority of the sub-committee. One of the factors that has kept India back from advancing to nationhood has been the existence of personal laws based on religion which keep the nation divided into watertight compartments in many aspects of life. We are of the view that a uniform civil code should be guaranteed to the Indian people within a period of 5 or 10 years in the same manner as the right to free and compulsory primary education has been guaranteed by clause 24 within 10 years. We, therefore, suggest that the Advisory Committee might transfer the clause regarding a uniform civil code from chapter 2 to chapter 1 after making suitable modifications in it.

With regard to clause 42 on chapter 2 they recorded their dissent as follows:

> We regret that the majority of the sub-committee turned down the proposal to include a clause based on Article 54 of the Swiss Constitution on the following lines:
> No impediments to marriage between citizens shall be based merely upon difference of religion.
> The Special Marriage Act III of 1872, which governs civil marriages between Indians of different religious faiths, demands from both contracting parties at present the following solemn declaration:
>
> > I do not profess the Christian, Jewish, Hindu, Mohammedan, Parsee, Buddhist, Sikh or Jain religion.
>
> Such an impediment to marriage between two Indians is a reflection on our claim to common nationhood. Only as recently as February 26, 1947, Mahatma Gandhi is reported at a prayer meeting to have supported the idea of marriages between persons professing different religious faiths each retaining his or her own religion without abatement. Unfortunately, such marriages cannot be solemnized in India today. Indians who have desired to marry a fellow national of another religious faith have had to leave the borders of India in order to get married, without being forced to perjure themselves. It is only possible. however, for those with more than average means and

> facilities to leave the country for such a purpose and the law has actually prevented several conscientious persons of limited means who were unwilling to comply with its requirements from marrying fellow nationals of their choice. The incorporation in the Constitution of the proposed clause would render such a primitive law as at present prevails *ultra vires* of the Constitution. We strongly urge that this clause be inserted at a suitable place.[8]

During the third and final sitting—April 14 to 16—the draft report was discussed and certain clauses were revised in the light of the members' comments and suggestions. Clause 41 of Chapter was accepted and the last sentence of Clause 42 was decided to be omitted.[9] The Sub-Committee submitted its final report along with the minutes of dissent to the Advisory Committee on April 16. In that report Clauses 41 and 42 of Chapter II appeared as clauses 39 and 40 respectively.[10]

Apart from the minutes of dissent of Masani, Mehta and Kaur, mentioned above, K.T. Shah, in his minute of dissent also drew attention to the drawback of the Special Marriage Act of 1872 as follows:

> While accepting the principle of a common civil code, mentioned in Articles 41 (now 39) and 42 (now 40), I think it necessary to give some indication of the basic principles of that code. For instance, I hold that marriage should, in the eyes of the law, be no more than a civil contract of a monogamous character, i.e. both parties must be of age, free from any coercion or undue influence, and entitled to equal rights and duties under the contract. No impediment should be cast in the way of freedom of choice in marriage on grounds like difference in religious beliefs between the parties. Nor should any special disability or handicap be imposed, such as that under the Special Marriages Act of 1872, under which intending parties to a marriage.—both Indians professing different religions, have to declare that they do not profess any of the named religion. This leads to unnecessary perjury; and comes in the way of a real unification of this country.[11]

The Advisory Committee on Fundamental Rights, Minorities etc. met for two days during April 1947, viz. on April 21 and 22. The Committee discussed the recommendations made by the Sub-Committee on Fundamental Rights together with the interim report of the Minorities Sub-Committee thereon. In their meeting on April 22, 1947 it was decided to postpone consideration of the clauses in Part II of the recommendations of the Fundamental Rights Sub-Committee relating to non-justiciable rights. Finally, the committee authorized the Chairman to submit a report on their behalf to the Constituent Assembly after it was considered by a sub-committee consisting of Pandit Govind Ballabh

Pant, Sir Alladi Krishnaswami Ayyar, Dr. B.R. Ambedkar and K.M. Munshi. (The last three members later became members of the Constitution Drafting Committee).[12]

The Advisory Committee's first report to the Constituent Assembly on April 23, 1947 confined itself to the justiciable rights only. In the supplementary report submitted on August 25, 1947, the Committee stated that "we have come to the conclusion that, in addition to justiciable fundamental rights, the Constitution should include certain directives of State policy which, though not cognizable in any Court of law, should be regarded as fundamental in the governance of the country. The provisions that we recommend are contained in Appendix A." Para 7 of the Fundamental Principles of Governance as contained in Appendix A states that "the State shall endeavour to secure for the citizens a Uniform Civil Code".[13]

This report submitted by Sardar Vallabhbhai J. Patel, Chairman of the Advisory Committee, was placed in the Constituent Assembly on 30-8-47. But no discussion on this subject was held in the Assembly on the date or subsequently, because the Assembly was adjourned on 30-8-47. This report of the Committee on Fundamental Rights, Minorities, etc. together with other reports of the different Committees set-up by the Constituent Assembly was passed on to the Drafting Committee for preparation of the Draft Constitution. Dr. B.R. Ambedkar was the Chairman of the 7-member Drafting Committee. Syed Mohammad Saadulla was one of the members of the Committee.

In pursuance of a recommendation of the Order of the Business Committee, the Constitutional Adviser undertook the preparation of a draft of the Constitution embodying the various decisions of the Assembly on the reports of its committees. Where the Constituent Assembly had not considered any matter, the recommendations of the relevant committees were incorporated. The draft was placed before the Drafting Committee when it met on October 27. In all subsequent deliberations of the Drafting Committee this draft constituted the basic document and the working paper. The Constitutional Adviser's Draft Constitution provided for a uniform civil code in Draft Article 36 as follows:

> The State shall endeavour to secure for the citizens a uniform civil code.[14]

This Article is a verbatim reproduction of clause 7, suggested by the Advisory Committee on Fundamental Rights, Minorities, etc., mentioned above.

The Drafting Committee in its meeting held on November 3, 1947 decided that the words "throughout the territory of India" should be added to this clause.[15]

II

The Draft Constitution prepared by the Drafting Committee was circulated on February 21, 1948. Directive Principles of State Policy in Part-IV of the Draft Constitution contained Article 35 which ran as follows:

> The State shall endeavour to secure for the citizens a uniform civil code throughout the territory of India.[16]

No comment or suggestion was received from any quarter on this provision of the Draft Constitution.

The Draft Constitution was introduced in the Constituent Assembly on November 4, 1948 and this Article was discussed by its Members at several stages, viz.

(1) at the time of discussion on the motion for taking into consideration the Draft Constitution,
(2) during clause-wise discussion,
(3) by bringing amendments to Articles on Fundamental Rights, and
(4) during the third reading of the Constitution.

We will see how the Members of the Constituent Assembly discussed this Article at each of the stages mentioned above.

(l) At the time of discussion on the motion for taking into consideration the Draft Constitution, the question of safeguarding the personal laws was first raised by Mahboob Ali Baig Sahib Bahadur. He said: "One thing with regard to minority rights I am bound to say. There is nowhere any mention of provisions which safeguards the personal law of the people. In India, at least, people of several communities are governed by personal laws based on their religion. It is possible to legislate with regard to personal laws also. That would go against the claims that this Government is going to be secular, which would not interfere with the religious rights of the people".[17] While Mahboob Ali Baig Sahib Bahadur was for safeguarding the personal laws of the people, Hussain Imam was for safeguarding the personal law of the minorities. He stated: "The majority need not have the safeguard, because they are the majority, and nothing can be passed in the legislature without their full consent and concurrence, whereas the minority have not got this privilege and therefore it is necessary that the personal law of the Muslims and other minorities who so desire should be preserved from interference by the legislature without the concurrence of a vast majority of the members thereof".[18] Hussain Imam was the first speaker to mention about the personal law of the Muslims. He was, however, not against the uniform civil code if a 'vast majority of the members' (of the Muslim Community) concurred with that. No other speaker raised this issue at this stage.

(2) During clause-wise discussion, Article 35 was discussed in the Constituent Assembly on November 23, 1948. As many as 8 Members (5 Muslims and 3 Hindus) participated in this discussion. Three amendments were brought forward by the Muslim members. Mohamad Ismail Sahib moved for addition of the following proviso:

> "Provided that any group, section or community of people shall not be obliged to give up its own personal law in case it has such a law."

Naziruddin Ahmad wanted to add the following proviso:

> "Provided that the personal law of any community which has been guaranteed by the statute shall not be changed except with the previous approval of the community ascertained in such manner as the Union Legislature may determine by law."

Mahboob Ali Baig Sahib Bahadur moved the following amendment:

> "Provided that nothing in this article shall affect the personal law of the citizen."

B. Pocker Sahib Bahadur and Hussain Imam did not move any amendment but highlighted the necessity for safeguarding the personal law.

K.M. Munshi, Alladi Krishnaswami Ayer and B.R. Ambedkar, all members of the Drafting Committee, spoke supporting the article.

Now, let us see what were the arguments advanced by the Members of the Constituent Assembly.

Mohamad Ismail Sahib was of the view that "the right of a group or a community of people to follow and adhere to its own personal law is among the fundamental rights and this provision should really be made amongst the statutory and justiciable fundamental rights. It is for this reason that I along with other friends have given amendments to certain other articles going previous to this which I will move at the proper time.

"Now, the right to follow personal law is part of the way of life of those people who are following such laws; it is part of their religion and part of their culture. If anything is done affecting the personal laws, it will be tantamount to interference with the way of life of those people who have been observing these laws for generations and ages. This secular State which we are trying to create should not do anything to interfere with the way of life and religion of the people. The matter of retaining personal law is nothing new; we have precedents in European countries, Yugoslavia, for instance, that is the kingdom of the Serbs, Croats and Slovenes, is obliged under treaty obligations to guarantee the rights of minorities. The clause regarding rights of Mussalmans reads as follows:

> the Serbs, Crot and Slovene State agrees to grant to the Mussalmans in the matter of family law and personal status provisions suitable for regulating these matters in accordance with the Mussalmans usage.

"We find similar clauses in several other European constitutions also. But these refer to minorities while my amendment refers not to the minorities alone, but to all people including the majority community, because it says, "Any group, section or community of people shall not be obliged" etc. Therefore it seeks to secure the rights of all people in regard to their existing personal law.

"Again this amendment does not seek to introduce any innovation or bring in a new set of laws for the people, but only wants the maintenance of the personal law already existing among certain sections of people. Now why do people want a uniform civil code, as in article 35? Their idea evidently is to secure harmony through uniformity. But I maintain that for that purpose it is not necessary to regiment the civil law of the people including the personal law. Such regimentation will bring discontent and harmony will be affected. But if people are allowed to follow their own personal law there will be no discontent or dissatisfaction. Every section of the people being free to follow its own personal law will not really come in conflict with others."[19]

The arguments advanced by Naziruddin Ahmed were as follows: "I do not wish to confine my remarks to the incontinence felt by the Muslim community alone. I would put it on a much broader ground. In fact, each community, each religious community has certain religious laws, certain civil laws inseparably connected with religious beliefs and practices. I believe that in framing a uniform draft code these religious laws or semi-religious laws should be kept out of its way. There are several reasons which underlie this amendment. One of them is that perhaps it clashes with Article 19 of the Draft Constitution. In Article 19 it is provided that "subject to public order, morality and health and to the other provisions of this Part, all persons are equally entitled to freedom of conscience and the right freely to profess, practise and propagate religion". In fact, this is so fundamental that the Drafting Committee has very rightly introduced this in this place. Then in clause (2) of the same article it has been further provided by way of limitation of the right that "Nothing in this article shall affect the operation of any existing law or preclude the State from making any law regulating or restricting any economic, financial, political or other secular activity which may be associated with religious practice." I can quite see that there may be many pernicious practices which may accompany religious practices and they may be controlled. But there are certain religious practices, certain religious laws which do not come within the exception in clause (2), viz. financial, political or other secular activity which may be associated with religious practices. Having guaranteed, and very rightly guaranteed the freedom of religious practice and the freedom to propagate religion, I think the present article tries to undo what has been given in Article 19. We must try to prevent this anomaly. In Article 19 we enacted a positive provision which is justiciable and which any subject of a State irrespective of his caste and community can take to a Court of law and seek enforcement. On the other hand, by the article under reference we are giving the State some amount of latitude which may enable it to ignore the right conceded. And this right is not justiciable. It recommends to the State certain things and therefore it gives a right to the State. But then the subject has not been given any right under this provision. I submit that the present article is likely to encourage the State to break the guarantees given in Article 19.

"I submit, Sir, there are certain aspects of the Civil Procedure Code which have already interfered with other personal laws and very rightly so. But during the 175 years of British Rule, they did not interfere with certain fundamental personal laws. They have enacted the Registration Act, the Limitation Act, the Civil Procedure Code, the Criminal Procedure Code, the Penal Code, the Evidence Act, the Transfer of Property Act, the Sarda Act and various other Acts. They have been imposed gradually as occasion arose and they were intended to make the laws uniform although they clash with the personal laws of a particular community. But take the case of marriage practice and the laws of inheritance. They have never interfered with them. It will be difficult at this stage of our society to ask the people to give up their ideas of marriage, which are associated with religious institutions in many communities. The laws of inheritance are also supposed to be the result of religious injunctions. I submit that the interference with these matters should be gradual and must progress with the advance of time, I have no doubt that a stage would come when the civil law would be uniform. But then that time has not yet come. We believe that the power that has been given to the State to make the Civil Code uniform is in advance of the time. As it is, any State would be justified under Article 35 to interfere with the settled laws of the different communities at once. For instance, there are marriage practices in various communities. If we want to introduce a law that every marriage shall be registered and if not it will not be valid, we can do so under Article 35. But would you invalidate a marriage which is valid under the existing law and under the present religious beliefs and practices on the ground that it has not been registered under any law and thus bastardise the children born?

"This is only one instance of how interference can go too far. As I have already submitted, the goal should be towards a uniform civil code, but it should be gradual and with the consent of the people concerned. I have therefore in my amendment suggested that religious laws relating to particular communities should not be affected except with their consent to be ascertained in such manner as Parliament may decide by law. Parliament may well decide to ascertain the consent of the community through their representatives, and this could be secured by the representatives by their election speeches and pledges. In fact, this may be made an article of faith in an election, and a vote on that could be regarded as consent. These are matters of detail. I have attempted by my amendment to leave it to the Central Legislature to decide how to ascertain this consent. I submit, Sir, this is not a matter of mere idealism. It is a question of stern reality which we must not refuse to face and I believe it will lead to a considerable amount of misunderstanding and resentment amongst the various sections of the country. What the British in 175 years failed to do or was afraid to do, what the Muslims in the course of 500 years refrained from doing, we should not give power to the State to do all at once. I submit, Sir, that we should proceed not in haste but with caution, with experience, with statesmanship and with sympathy".[20]

Mahboob Ali Baig Sahib Bahadur contended that "the words 'Civil Code' do not cover strictly the personal law of a citizen. The Civil Code covers laws of this kind: laws of property, transfer of property, law of contract, law of evidence etc. The law as observed by a particular religious community is not covered by Article 35. That is my view. Anyhow, in order to clarify the position that Article 35 does not affect the personal law of the citizen, I have given notice of this amendment. Now, Sir, if for any reason the framers of this article have got in their minds that the personal law of the citizen is also covered by the expression 'Civil Code', I wish to submit that they are overlooking the very important fact of the personal law being so much dear and near to certain religious communities. As far as the Mussalmans are concerned, their laws of succession, inheritance, marriage and divorce are completely dependent upon their religion. The (Muslim) marriage is interpreted as a contract, while the marriage amongst the Hindus is a *Samskara* and that among Europeans it is a matter of status. I know that very well, but this contract is enjoined on the Mussalmans by the *Quran* and if it is not followed, a marriage is not a legal marriage at all. For 1350 years this law has been practised by Muslims and recognised by all authorities in all States. If some other method of proving the marriage is introduced, we refuse to abide by it because it is not according to our religion. It is not according to the code that is laid down for us for all times in this matter. Therefore, Sir, it is not a matter to be treated so lightly. I know that in the case of some other communities also, their personal law depends entirely upon their religious tenets. If some communities have got their own way of dealing with their religious tenets and practices that cannot be imposed on a community which insists that their religious tenets should be observed. People seem to have very strange ideas about secular state. People seem to think that under a secular State, there must be a common law observed by its citizens in all matters including the matters of their daily life, their language, their culture, their personal laws. That is not the correct way to look at this secular State. In a secular State, citizens belonging to different communities must have the freedom to practice their own religion, observe their own life and their personal law should be applied to them. Therefore, I hope the framers of this article have not in their minds the personal law of the people to cover the words "Civil Code".[21]

B. Pocker Sahib Bahadur, while commending Mohamed Ismail Sahib's amendment for adoption, argued that "I would request the House to consider this amendment not from the point of view of the Mussalman community alone, but from the point of view of the various communities that exist in this country, following various codes of law with reference to inheritance, marriage, succession, divorce, endowments and so many other matters. The House will note that one of the reasons why the Britisher, having conquered this country, has been able to carry on the administration of this country for the last 150 years and over was that he gave a guarantee of following their own personal laws to each of the various communities in the country. This is one of the secrets of success and the basis of the administration of justice on which even the foreign rule was based. I ask, Sir, whether by the freedom we have obtained for this country, are we going to give up freedom of conscience and that freedom of religious practices and that freedom of following one's own personal law and try or aspire to impose upon the whole country one code of civil law, whatever it may mean—which I say, as it is, may include even all branches of civil laws, namely the law of marriage, law of inheritance, law of divorce, and so many other kindred matters?

"In the first place, I would like to know the real intention with which this clause has been introduced. If the words "Civil Code" are intended only to apply to matters of procedure like the Civil Procedure Code and such other laws which are uniform so far as India is concerned at present well, nobody has any objection to that, but the various Civil Courts Acts in the various provinces in this country have secured for each community the right to follow their personal laws as regards marriage, inheritance, divorce, etc. But if it is intended that the aspiration of the State should be to override all these provisions and to have uniformity of law to be imposed upon the whole people on these matters which are dealt with by the Civil Courts Acts in the various provinces, well, I would only say that it is a tyrannous provision which ought not to be tolerated; and let it not be taken that I am only voicing forth the feeling of the Mussalmans. In saying this, I am voicing forth the feeling of over so many sections in the country who feel that it would be really tyrannous to interfere with the religious practices, and with the religious laws, by which they are governed now.

"Now, Sir, just like many of you, I have received ever so many pamphlets which voice forth the feelings of the people in these matters. I am referring to many pamphlets which I have received from organizations of the Hindus, who characterise such interference as most tyrannous. They even question, Sir, the right and the authority of this body to interfere with their rights from the constitutional point of view. They ask: Who are the members of the Constituent Assembly who are contemplating to interfere with the religious rights and practices? Were they returned there on the issue as to whether they have got this right or not? Have they been returned by the various legislatures, the elections to which were fought out on these issues?

"If such a body as this interferes with the religious rights and practices, it will be tyrannous. These organizations have used a much stronger language than I am using. Therefore, I would request the Assembly not to consider what I have said entirely as coming from the point of view of the Muslim community. I know there are great differences in the law of inheritance and various other matters between the various sections of the Hindu community. Is this Assembly going to set aside all these differences and make them uniform? By uniform, I ask, what do you mean and which particular law, of which community are you going to take as the standard? What have you got in your mind in enacting a clause like this? There are the *Mitakshara* and *Dayabaga* systems; there are so many other systems followed by various other communities. What is it that you are making the basis? Is it open to us to do anything of this sort? By this one clause you are revolutionising the whole country and the whole set-up. There is no need for it.

"Sir, as already pointed out by one of my predecessors in speaking on this motion, this is entirely antagonistic to the provision made as regards Fundamental Rights in Article 19. If it is antagonistic, what is the purpose served by a clause like this? Is it open to this Assembly to pass by one stroke of the pen an article by which the whole country is revolutionized? Is it intended? I do not know what the framers of this article mean by this. On a matter of such grave importance, I am very sorry to find that the framers or the draftsmen of this article have not bestowed sufficiently serious attention to that. Whether it is copied from anywhere or not, I do not know. Anyhow, if it is copied from anywhere, I must condemn that provision even in that Constitution. It is very easy to copy sections from other constitutions of countries where circumstances are entirely different. There are ever so many multitudes of communities following various customs for centuries or thousands of years. By one stroke of the pen you want to annul all that and make them uniform. What is the purpose served? What is the purpose served by this uniformity except to murder the consciences of the people and make them feel that they are being trampled upon as regards their religious rights and practices? Such a tyrannous measure ought not to find a place in our Constitution. I submit, Sir, there are ever so many sections of the Hindu community who are rebelling against this and who voice forth their feelings in such stronger language than I am using. If the framers of this article say that even the majority community is uniform in support of this, I would challenge them to say so. It is not so. Even assuming that the majority community is of this view, I say, it has to be condemned and it ought not to be allowed, because, in a democracy, as I take it, it is the duty of the majority to secure the sacred rights of every minority. It is a misnomer to call it a democracy if the majority rides rough-shod over the rights of the minorities. It is not democracy at all; it is tyranny. Therefore, I would submit to you and all the Members of this House to take very serious notice of this article; it is not a light thing to be passed like this."[22]

Hussain Imam said, "India is too big a country with a large population so diversified that it is almost impossible to stamp them with one kind of anything. In the north, we have got extreme cold; in the south we have extreme heat. In Assam we have got more rains than anywhere else in the world, about 400 inches; just near up in the Rajputana desert, we have no rains. In a country so diverse, is it possible to have uniformity in civil law? We have ourselves further on provided for concurrent jurisdiction to the provinces as well as to the Centre in matters of succession, marriage, divorce and other things. How it is possible to have uniformity when there are eleven or twelve legislative bodies ready to legislate on a subject according to the requirements of their own people and their own circumstances. Look at the protection we have given to the backward classes. Their property is safeguarded. In the Scheduled areas—I know of Jharkhand and Santhal Parganas—we have given special protection to the aboriginal population. There are certain circumstances which demand diversity in the civil laws. I, therefore, feel, Sir, that, in addition to the arguments which have been put forward by my friends who spoke before me, in which they feel apprehensive that their personal law will not be safe if the Directive is passed, I suggest that there are other difficulties also which are purely constitutional, depending not so much on the' existence of different communities, as on the existence of different levels in the intelligence and equipment of the people of India. You have to deal not with a uniformly developed country. Parts of the country are very very backward. Look at the Assam tribes; what is their condition? Can you have the same kind of law for them as you have for the advanced people of Bombay? You must have a great deal of difference. Sir, I feel that it is all right and a very desirable thing to have a uniform law, but at a very distant date. For that, we should first await the coming of that event when the whole of India has got educated, when mass illiteracy has been removed, when people have advanced, when their economic conditions are better, when each man is able to stand on his own legs and fight his own battles. Then, you can have uniform laws. Can you have, today, uniform laws as far as a child and young man are concerned?

"Even today under the Criminal law you give juvenile offenders a lighter punishment than you do to adult offenders. The apprehension felt by the members of the minority community is very real. Secular State does not mean that it is anti-religious State. It means that it is not irreligious but non-religious and as such there is a world of difference between irreligious and non-religious. I, therefore suggest that it would be a good policy for the members of the Drafting Committee to come forward with such safeguards in this proviso as will meet the apprehensions genuinely felt and which people are feeling and I have every hope that the ingenuity of Dr. Ambedkar will be able to find a solution for this".[23]

From the above, it may be seen that the following points were highlighted by these members:

1. Marriage is a contract according to Muslim Jurisprudence, but this contract is governed by the *Quran*.
2. The personal law is a part and parcel of the religious laws which cannot be altered.
3. It would be a tyrannous act of the majority community if they want to impose such a law on the minority.
4. Personal laws of the Muslims have been retained in Yugoslavia and other European countries.
5. The Britishers had made certain laws uniform although they clashed with personal laws but they did not interfere with marriage practices and laws of inheritance.
6. Article 35 is antagonistic to Article 19.
7. There may be a uniform civil code but the time has not come.
8. The uniform civil code can be made only with the consent of the members of the community affected.
9. For a vast country like India, it is not desirable to have a uniform code for everybody.

K.M. Munshi, Alladi Krishnaswami Ayer and Dr. B.R. Ambedkar, all members of the Drafting Committee, elaborated the reasons for inclusion of the provision for a Uniform Civil Code in the Constitution. They also had to cover all the points raised by the Muslim Members in their speeches.

K.M. Munshi said: "This particular clause which is now before the House is not brought for discussion for the first time. It has been discussed in several committees and at several places before it came to the House. The ground that is now put forward against it is, firstly, that it infringes the Fundamental Right, mentioned in Article 19 and secondly, it is tyrannous to the minority.

"As regards Article 19, the House accepted it and made it quite clear that— "Nothing in this article shall affect the operation of any existing law or preclude the State from making any law, (a) regulating or restricting"—I am omitting the unnecessary words—"or other secular activity which may be associated with religious practices; (b) for social welfare and reforms". Therefore, the House has already accepted the principle that if a religious practice followed so far covers a secular activity or falls within the field of social reform or social welfare, it would be open to Parliament to make laws about it without infringing this Fundamental Right of a minority.

"It must also be remembered that if this clause is not put in, it does not mean that the Parliament in future would have no right to enact a Civil Code. The only restriction to such a right would be Article 19 and I have already pointed out that Article 19, accepted by the House unanimously, permits legislation covering secular activities. The whole object of this article is that as and when the Parliament thinks proper or rather when the majority in the Parliament thinks proper an attempt may be made to unify the personal law of the country.

"A further argument has been advanced that the enactment of a Civil Code would be tyrannical to minorities. Is it tyrannical? Nowhere in the advanced Muslim countries the personal law of each minority has been recognised as so sacrosanct as to prevent the enactment of a Civil Code. Take for instance, Turkey or Egypt. No minority in these countries is permitted to have such rights. But I go further. When the *Shariat* Act was passed or when certain laws were passed in the Central Legislature in the old regime, the Khojas and Cutchi Memons were highly dissatisfied.

"They then followed certain Hindu customs; for generations since they became converts they had done so. They did not want to conform to the *Shariat*; and yet by a legislation of the Central Legislature certain Muslim members who felt that *Shariat* law should be enforced upon the whole community carried their point. The Khojas and Cutchi Memons most unwillingly had to submit to it. Where were the rights of minority then? When you want to consolidate a community, you have to take into consideration the benefit which may accrue to the whole community and not to the customs of a part of it. It is not, therefore, correct to say that such an act is tyranny of the majority. If you will look at the countries in Europe which have a Civil Code, everyone who goes there from any part of the world and every minority, has to submit to the Civil Code. It is not felt to be tyrannical to the minority. The point however is this, whether we are going to consolidate and unify our personal law in such a way that the way of life of the whole country may in course of time be unified and secular. We want to divorce religion from personal law, from what may be called social relations or from the rights of parties as regards inheritance or succession. What have these things got to do with religion, I really fail to understand. Take for instance the Hindu Law Draft which is before the Legislative Assembly. If one looks at Manu and Yajnavalkya and all the rest of them,

I think most of the provisions of the New Bill will run counter to their injunctions. But after all we are an advancing society. We are in a stage where we must unify and consolidate the nation by every means without interfering with religious practices. If however the religious practices in the past have been so construed as to cover the whole field of life, we have reached a point when we must put our foot down and say that these matters are not religion, they are purely matters for secular legislation. This is what is emphasised by this article.

"Now look at the disadvantages that you will perpetuate, if there is no Civil Code. Take for instance the Hindus. We have the law of *Mayukha* applying in some parts of India; we have *Mitakshara* in others; and we have the law of *Dayabhaga* in Bengal. In this way even the Hindus themselves have separate laws and most of our Provinces and States have started making separate Hindu laws for themselves. Are we going to permit this piecemeal legislation on the ground that it affects the personal law of the country? It is therefore not merely a question for minorities but it also affects the majority.

"I know there are many among Hindus who do not like a Uniform Civil Code, because they take the same view as the honourable Muslim Members who spoke last. They feel that the personal law of inheritance, succession, etc. is really a part of their religion. If that were so you can never give, for instance, equality to women. But you have already passed a Fundamental Right to that effect and yon have an article here which lays down that there should be no discrimination against sex. Look at Hindu law; you get any amount of discrimination against women; and if that is part of Hindu religion or Hindu religious practice, you cannot pass a single law which would elevate the position of Hindu women to that of men. Therefore, there is no reason why there should not be a civil code throughout the territory of India.

"There is one important consideration which we have to bear in mind—and I want my Muslim friends to realise this—that the sooner we forget this isolationist outlook on life, it will be better for the country. Religion must be restricted to spheres which legitimately appertain to religion, and the rest of life must be regulated, unified and modified in such a manner that we may evolve, as early as possible, a strong and consolidated nation. Our first problem and the most important problem is to produce national unity in this country. We think we have got national unity. But there are many factors—and important factors—which still offer serious dangers to our national consolidation, and it is very necessary that the whole of our life, so far as it is restricted to secular spheres, must be unified in such a way that as early as possible, we may be able to say. "Well, we are not merely a nation because we say so, but also in effect, by the way we live, by our personal law, we are a strong and consolidated nation." From that point of view alone, I submit, the opposition is not, if I may say so, very well advised. I hope our friends will not feel that this is an attempt to exercise tyranny over a minority; it is much more tyrannous to the majority.

"This attitude of mind perpetuated under the British Rule, that personal law is part of religion, has been fostered by the British and by British Courts. We must, therefore, outgrow it. If I may remind the honourable Member who spoke last of a particular incident from Fereshta which comes to my mind, Alauddin Khilji made several changes which offended against the *Shariat*, though he was the first ruler to establish Muslim Sultanate here. The Kazi of Delhi objected to some of his reforms, and his reply was—"I am an ignorant man and I am ruling this country on its best interests. I am sure, looking at my ignorance and my good intentions, the Almighty will forgive me, when He finds that I have not acted according to the *Shariat*". If Alauddin could not, much less can a modern Government accept the proposition that religious rights cover personal law or several other matters which we have been unfortunately trained to consider as part of our religion. That is my submission".[24]

Alladi Krishnaswami Ayer mainly dwelt on the question whether personal law was a part and parcel of religion. He said: "After the very full exposition of my friend the Honouable Mr. Munshi, it is not necessary to cover the whole ground. But it is as well to understand whether there can be any real objection to the article as it runs.

> "The State shall endeavour to secure for the citizens a uniform civil code throughout the territory of India."

A Civil Code, as has been pointed out, runs into every department of civil relations, to the law of contracts; to the law of property, to the law of succession, to the law of marriage and similar matters. How can there be any objection to the general statement here that the State shall endeavour to secure a uniform civil code throughout the territory of India?

"The second objection was that religion was in danger, that communities cannot live in amity if there is to be a uniform civil code. The article actually aims at amity. It does not destroy amity. The idea is that differential systems of inheritance and other matters are some of the factors which contribute to the differences among the different peoples of India. What it aims at is to try to arrive at a common measure of agreement in regard to these matters. It is not as if one legal system is not influencing or being influenced by another legal system. In very many matters today the sponsors of the Hindu Code have taken a lead not from Hindu law alone, but from other systems also. Similarly, the Succession Act has drawn upon both the Roman and the English systems. Therefore, no system can be self-contained, if it is to have in it the elements of growth. Our ancients did not think of a unified nation to be welded together into a democratic whole. There is no use clinging always to the past.

We are departing from the past in regard to an important particular, namely, we want the whole of India to be welded and united together into a single nation. Are we helping those factors which help the welding together into a single nation, or is this country to be kept up always as a series of competing communities? That is the question at issue.

"Now, my friend Mr. Pocker levelled an attack against the Drafting Committee on the ground that they did not know their business, I should like to know whether he has carefully read what happened even in the British regime. You must know that the Muslim Law covers the field of contracts, the field of criminal law, the field of divorce law, the field of marriage and every part of law as contained in the Muslim law. When the British occupied this country, they said, we are going to introduce one criminal law in this country which will be applicable to all citizens, be they Englishmen, be they Hindus, be they Muslims. Did the Muslims take exception and did they revolt against the British for introducing a single system of criminal law? Similarly, we have the law of contracts governing transactions between Muslims and Hindus, between Muslims and Muslims. They are governed not by the law of the *Quran* but by the Anglo-Indian Jurisprudence, yet no exception was taken to that. Again, there are various principles in the law of transfer which have been borrowed from the English jurisprudence.

"Therefore, when there is impact between two civilizations or between two cultures, each culture must be influenced and influence the other culture. If there is a determined opposition, if there is strong opposition by any section of the community, it would be unwise on the part of the legislators of this country to attempt to ignore it. Today, even without Article 35, there is nothing to prevent the future Parliament of India from passing such laws. Therefore, the idea is to have a uniform civil code.

"Now, again, there are Muslims and there are Hindus, there are Catholics, there are Christians, there are Jews, in different European countries. I should like to know from Mr Pocker whether different personal laws are perpetuated in France, in Germany, in Italy, and in all the continental countries of Europe, or whether the laws of succession are not coordinated and unified in the various States. He must have made a detailed study of Muslim jurisprudence and found out whether in all those countries, there is a single system of law or different systems of law.

"Leave alone people who are there. Today, even in regard to people in other parts of the country, if they have property in the continent of Europe where the German Civil Code or the French Civil Code obtains, the people are governed by the law of the place in very many respects. Therefore, it is incorrect to say that we are invading the domain of religion.

"Under the Muslim Law, unlike under Hindu law, marriage is purely a civil contract. The idea of a sacrament does not enter into the concept of marriage in Muslim jurisprudence though the incidence of the contract may be governed by what is laid down in the *Quran* and by the later jurists. Therefore, there is no question of religion being in danger. Certainly no Parliament, no Legislature will be so unwise as to attempt it, apart from the power of the Legislature to interfere with religious tenets of peoples. After all the only community that is willing to adopt itself to changing times seems to be the majority community in the country. They are willing to take lessons from the minority and adapt their Hindu laws and take a leaf from the Muslims for the purpose of reforming even the Hindu law. Therefore, there is no force to the objection that is put forward to Article 35. The future Legislatures may attempt a Uniform Civil Code or they may not. The Uniform Civil Code will run into every aspect of Civil Law. In regard to contracts, procedure and property uniformity is sought to be secured by their finding a place in the Concurrent List. In respect of these matters the greatest contribution of British jurisprudence has been to bring about uniformity in these matters. We only go a step further than the British who ruled in this country. Why should you distrust much more a national indigenous Government than a foreign Government which has been ruling? Why should our Muslim friends have greater faith in the British rule than in a democratic rule which will certainly have regard to the religious tenets and beliefs of all people?

"Therefore, for those reasons, I submit that the House may unanimously pass this article which has been placed before the Members after due consideration".[25]

In his reply to the motion, Dr. Ambedkar stated: "Sir, I am afraid I cannot accept the amendments which have been moved to this article. In dealing with this matter, I do not propose to touch on the merits of the question as to whether this country should have a Civil Code or it should not. That is a matter which I think has been dealt with sufficiently for the occasion by my friend, Mr. Munshi as well as by Shri Alladi Krisnhaswami Ayyar. When the amendments to certain fundamental rights are moved, it would be possible for me to make a full statement on this subject, and I therefore do not propose to deal with it here.

"My friend, Mr. Hossain Imam in rising to support the amendments, asked whether it was possible and desirable to have a uniform Code of laws for a country so vast as this. Now I must confess that I was very much surprised at that statement, for the simple reason that we have in this country a uniform code of laws covering almost every aspect of human relationship. We have a uniform and complete Criminal Code operating throughout the country, which is contained in the Penal Code and the Criminal Procedure Code. We have the Law of Transfer of Property, which deals with property relations and which is operative throughout the country. Then there are the Negotiable Instruments Acts and I can cite innumerable enactments which would prove that this country has practically a Civil Code, uniform in its content and applicable to the whole of the country. The only province the Civil Law has not been able to invade so far is Marriage and Succession. It is this little corner which we have not been able to invade so far and it is the intention of those who desire to have Article 35 as part of the Constitution to bring about that change. Therefore, the argument whether we should attempt such a thing seems to me somewhat misplaced for the simple reason that we have, as a matter of fact, covered the whole lot of the field which is covered by a uniform Civil Code in this country. It is, therefore, too late now to ask the question whether we could do it. As I say, we have already done it.

"Coming to the amendments, there are only two observations which I would like to make. My first observation would be to state that members who put forth these amendments say that the Muslim personal law, so far as this country was concerned, was immutable and uniform through the whole of India. Now, I wish to challenge that statement. I think most of my friends who have spoken on this amendment have quite forgotten that up to 1935 the North-West Frontier Province was not subject to the *Shariat* Law. It followed the Hindu Law in the matter of succession and in other matter, so much so that it was in 1939 that the Central Legislature had to come into the field and to abrogate the application of the Hindu Law to the Muslims of the North-West Frontier Province and to apply the *Shariat* Law to them. That is not all.

"My honourable friends have forgotten that, apart from the North-West Frontier Province up till 1937 in the rest of India, in various parts, such as the United Provinces and Bombay, the Muslims to a large extent were governed by the Hindu Law in the matter of succession. In order to bring them on the plane of uniformity with regard to the other Muslims who observed the *Shariat* Law, the Legislature had to intervene in 1937 and to pass an enactment applying the *Shariat* Law to the rest of India.

"I am also informed by my friend, Shri Karunakara Menon, that in North Malabar, the Murumakkathayam Law applied to all—not only to Hindus but also to Muslims. It is to be remembered that the Murumakkathayam Law is a Matriarchal form of law and not a patriarchal form of law.

"The Mussalmans, therefore, in North Malabar were up to now following the Marumakkathayam law. It is, therefore, no use making a categorical statement that the Muslim Law has been an immutable law which they have been following from ancient times. That law as such was not applicable in certain parts and it has been made applicable ten years ago. Therefore if it was found necessary that for the purpose of evolving a single civil code applicable to all citizens irrespective of their religion, certain portions of the Hindu law, not because they were contained in Hindu law but because they were found to be the most suitable, were incorporated into the new civil code projected by Article 35, I am quite certain that it would not be open to any Muslim to say that the framers of the civil code had done great violence to the sentiments of the Muslim community.

"My second observation is to give them an assurance. I quite realise their feelings in the matter, but I think they have read rather too much into Article 35 which merely proposes that the State shall endeavour to secure a civil code for the citizens of the country. It does not say that after the Code is framed the State shall enforce it upon all citizens merely because they are citizens. It is perfectly possible that the future parliament may make a provision by way of making a beginning that the Code shall apply only to those who make a declaration that they are prepared to be bound by it, so that in the initial stage the application of the Code may be purely voluntary. Parliament may feel the ground by some such method. This is not a novel method. It was adopted in the *Shariat* Act of 1937 when it was applied to territories other than the North-West Frontier Province. The law said that there is a *Shariat* Law which should be applied to Mussualmans provided a Mussalman who wanted that he should be bound by the *Shariat* Act should go to an officer of the State, make a declaration that he is willing to be bound by it, and after he has made that declaration the law will bind him and his successors. It would be perfectly possible for Parliament to introduce a provision of that sort; so that the fear which my friends have expressed here will be altogether nullified. I, therefore, submit that there is no substance in these amendments and I oppose them".[26]

These 3 members of the Drafting Committee in their speeches mentioned that—

(1) The Britishers had already abridged many personal laws and made unified acts applicable to all citizens. Marriage and succession were not touched by them. The present Article aims at unifying all these personal laws.
(2) Personal laws are not part of religion. Had it been so, the Britishers would not have been allowed to do it.
(3) In foreign countries unified civil code is applicable to all citizens irrespective of religion.
(4) Personal laws amongst the Muslims also differed from place to place. *Shariat* Act was made applicable to the rest of India only in 1937 and to North-East Frontier Province only in 1939. Some Muslims in some pockets even follow Hindu laws. Some sects of the Muslims also protested when the *Shariat* Act was enforced on them.
(5) Article 35 is not antagonistic to Article 19. Article 19 provides for such enactments.
(6) The Muslims should give up their isolationist policy and help in making India a united nation.
(7) This Article is not tyrannical to minorities.
(8) In no advanced Muslim countries the personal law of each minority has been recognised as sacrosanct.

(9) Equality to women has been accepted as a Fundamental Right. The women will be discriminated if a Uniform Civil Code is not passed.

(10) Even Alauddin Khilji, who established Muslim Sultanate, did not accept that religious rights cover personal laws of the Muslims.

(11) In a vast country like India there are laws like uniform Criminal Procedure Code, Penal Code, the law of Transfer of Property, Negotiable Instruments Act etc. So there is no bar in having a uniform Civil Code.

(12) Above all, an assurance was given that some sort of provision would be made by the parliament to obtain the declaration from individual citizen signifying his willingness to be bound by the uniform Civil Code. On obtaining his declaration the law will bind him and his successors.

(13) There is no legal bar in enacting a uniform Civil Code by the Legislatures even if Article 35 is not adopted in the Constitution.

Article 35 was adopted in the Assembly on November 23, 1948 after this discussion. At the revision stage it was renumbered as Article 44.

III

Even after adoption of Draft Article 35 by the Constituent Assembly on November 23, 1948, efforts were made thrice to keep the personal law outside the purview of this Constitution. Lok Nath Misra brought an amendment to Article 8 and Mohammad Ismail Sahib brought two amendments—one to Article 13 and another to Article 19.

On November 25 1948 at the time of discussion of Article 8, (since numbered 13) Loknath Mishra wanted the following new clause to be inserted after clause (2) of Article 8:

(3) "The Union or the State shall not undertake any legislation or pass any law discriminatory to some community or communities, or applicable to some particular community or communities and no other."

He stated: "In moving this new article I seek nothing more than supplementing Article 35 which we have passed. Article 35 directs the state to do certain things, that is, bring about a uniform civil code. My article simply says that the state should not do, so that it may not frustrate the very purpose for which Article 35 has been enacted. Sir, deliberately we have chosen that our state is a secular state and we have tried to get rid of all the wrangling of religion because of the belief that although religion was made to unite mankind it has been found that it has disunited mankind and has brought various disputes.

Rightly therefore, have we declared that our State would be a secular State and thereby we mean that everybody who inhabits this land, everybody who is a citizen is just a man and his human needs will be fulfilled and his religion, if he has any, will be taken care of by the individual himself.

"If we approve of this purpose, to give mankind that equality, that sense of justice, then when we are here to legislate for a future constitution, we must make it a fundamental right that we will not legislate in a manner and on a matter which will discriminate between one community and another. Our law must be so broad-based, must be so very intrinsically sound that it must apply to every human being, every citizen of this land. When you make any difference between citizens in this land, you can make it only on the lines of community, and community directly means religion and we have deliberately eschewed religion. Therefore, to be frank enough, to be bold enough, to be true enough to our professions, we must make it a point that whenever we bring anything on the anvil of legislation, it must be such that it will apply to one and all of this land and there will be no differentiation. Let people say: We have one fundamental safeguard against equality and injustice. Here is the law. It applies to everybody,—be he a Rajah, be he a Praja, be he a Hindu, be he a Muslim, be he a Parsi, be he a Christian. That itself is enough safeguard, because it will apply to every citizen equally. If the law is bad, it is bad for everybody; if it is good, it is good for everybody. Therefore, I say this must be a fundamental principle. We must accept it here and now that any law that henceforward we may be legislating must be applicable to one and all. To that effect, I candidly place before this House that to avoid all future doubts, all disparity, all discrimination, all distinction, we must make it a law and a fundamental law that the Union or the States shall not undertake any legislation or pass any law discriminatory to some community or communities, or applicable to some particular community or communities and no other. This House has very frankly, openly and boldly accepted the principle in article 35. I simply beg this House to make that article complete and self-sufficient. That gave only a direction; this gives a positive mandate for what we should not do because by not doing all these things, by discriminating between citizens and communities we have divided the country and let it not lead to great divisions. I submit that unless we accept this principle, our idea of a united Nation, of a united mankind and of equality of every citizen in this land will be frustrated. I therefore commend this new article to the consideration of this great House".[27]

This Amendment which was apparently brought to stall the enactment of Hindu Code Bill was, however, not discussed further in the Assembly and it was negatived on November 29, 1948.

On December1, 1948 at the time of clause-wise discussion of Article 13 (since renumbered 19) of the Fundamental Rights, Md. Ismail Sahib, as indicated earlier in his speech on Article 35, wanted to add a new sub-clause, namely sub-clause (h) of clause (I). The wording was as follows: "(h) to follow the personal law of the group or community to which he belongs or professes to belong." His argument was more or less repetition of the earlier one. He again contended that personal law was a part of religion. He said: "Mr. Munshi while speaking on the subject previously said that this had nothing to do with religion and he asked what this had to do with religion. He as an illustrious and eminent lawyer ought to know that this question of personal law is entirely based upon religion. It is nothing if it is not religious. But if he says that a religion should not deal with such thing, then that is another matter. It is a question of difference of opinion as to what a religion should do or should not. People differ and people holding different views on this matter must tolerate the other view. There are religions which omit altogether to deal with the question of personal law and there are other religions like Hinduism and Islam which deal with personal law. Therefore, I say tnat people ought to be given liberty of following their personal law.

"It was also stated by Dr. Ambedkar on the floor of this House that the question of following personal law was not immutable. There were, as a matter of fact, sections of Muslims, who do not follow the personal law prescribed by Islam, but this is a different matter. It is not reasonable to say that simply because a section of people do not want to follow a certain law of a certain religion or a certain part of that religion that other people also should not follow the law and that sections of people should be compelled not to follow that part of the religion which certain other sections of the same community are not following.

"That is not really reasonable and it is really immutable to the people who follow this law and this religion, because people, as they understand it, have not got the right to change their religion as they please. There may be people who contravene their own religion, but that is a different matter and we cannot compel others also to contravene their religion. Here the question of personal law affects only the people who follow this law. There is no compulsion exercised thereby on the general community or the general public. This House will remember that on another question, which is really a religious question—I mean the question of cow-slaughter—an obligation has been placed upon other communities than one which considers the prohibition of cow slaughter as a religious matter. But then, Sir, respecting the views and feelings of our friends, the minority communities who have got the right and privilege of slaughtering and eating the flesh of cows have agreed to the proposal put before the House, though that is going beyond affecting one particular community alone. Here, Sir, observance of personal law is confined only to the particular communities which are following their personal laws. There is no question of compelling any other community at all...There are innumerable number of Hindus who think that interference with the personal law is interference with their religion. I know, Sir, that they have submitted a monster petition to the authorities or to the people who can have any say in the matter. Therefore, it is not only Muslims but also Hindus who think that this is a religious question and that it should not be interfered with. The personal law of one community does not affect the other communities. Therefore, Sir, what I urge is that the freedom of following the personal law ought to be given to each community and it will not interfere with the rights of any other community.

"Again, Mr. Munshi stated that Muslim countries like Egypt or Turkey have not any provision of this sort. I want to remind him that Turkey is under a treaty obligation. Under that treaty it is guaranteed that the non-Muslim Minorities are entitled to have questions of family law and personal status regulated in accordance with their usage. That is the obligation under which Turkey has been placed and that is obtaining in Turkey now.

"Then again with regard to Egypt no such question of personal law arose in that country. But what is to be noted is that whatever the minorities in that country wanted has been granted to them: in fact more than what they wanted has been granted. And if personal law had also been a matter in which they wanted certain privileges that would also have been granted. Then there are other countries. Yugoslavia has agreed to give this privilege to the Muslims in following their family law and personal law. Therefore, what I am asking for is not a matter which is peculiar to myself or to the minority community in this country. It is a thing, Sir, well understood in other parts of the world also."[28]

Kazi Sayed Karimuddin also supported the amendment moved by Md. Ismail. He stated that "the people outside and the Members of the Constituent Assembly must realise that a Muslim regards the personal law as part of the religion and I really assure you that there is not a single Muslim in the country at least, I have not seen one—who wants a change in the mandatory provision of religious rights and personal laws and if there is anyone who wants a change in the mandatory principle, or religion as a matter of personal law, then he cannot be a Muslim. Therefore, if this is the view of the minority Muslims or any other minority that they want to abide by personal law, those laws have to be protected."[29]

Moulana Hasrat Mohani, while extending his support to the amendment moved by Muhammad Ismail delivered a violent speech on December 2, 1948. He said: "Any party political or communal has no right to interfere in the personal law of any group. More particularly, I say this regarding Muslims. There are three fundamentals in their personal law, namely religion, language and culture which have not been ordained by human agency. Their personal law regarding divorce, marriage and inheritance has been derived from the

Quran and its interpretation is recorded therein. If there is anyone, who thinks that he can interfere in the personal law of the Muslims, then I would say to him that the result will be very harmful. I say from the floor of this House that they will come to grief. Mussalmans will not submit to any interference in their personal law, and if anybody has got the courage to say so, then I declare in the House—that Mussalmans will never submit to any interference in their personal law, and they will have to face an iron wall of Muslim determination to oppose them in every way".[30]

His speech, quite naturally, evoked frequent interruptions. From these three speeches no new points emerged except that Moulana Hasrat Mohani more or less threatened of opposing such an enactment tooth and nail because "the personal law of the Muslims has not been ordained by human agency". About the immutability of the personal law and safeguarding the personal law of the minority in foreign countries no new facts other than those already discussed could be marshalled. It was also contended that a Muslim cannot change his religion at his will.

M. Ananthasayanam Ayengar and Dr. B.R. Ambedkar spoke opposing this amendment. Let us see what new grounds they treaded.

Ayengar stated that "amendments have been moved that unless a provision is made in the Fundamental Rights there is no safety and that the majority community may introduce its own personal law or flagrantly violate the personal law of any community. Let us take the communities. There are three main religions. Let us take Mohammedanism. There is absolutely no provision in the Fundamental Rights that you ought to ride roughshod over their personal law. The law of the land as it exists today gives sufficient guarantee so far as that is concerned. But our friends who moved the amendments wanted a double guarantee that their personal law ought not to be interfered with. My submission is that it is impracticable, for, in an advanced society, even the members who belong to a particular community may desire their personal law to be changed. Let us take the Mohammedan Law. I would only refer to two or three amendments that have been made to that law as set out in the *Shariat*. As recently as in 1939 the Central Legislature passed a law for enabling the dissolution of Muslim Marriages under certain circumstances. You will be pleased to note that under the Muslim Law, a man has got the unilateral right to declare a marriage void by pronouncing the word *talaq* and there is another form of divorce called *Kulamp*. Woman normally has no right to dissolve a marriage. She has to go to a Court of law and various matters have to be set out such as impotency and so on. All that has been made easy now. Another consideration is that a woman who cannot lead a family life with the husband in the same household is entitled under certain conditions to separation. These have hitherto not been envisaged nor provided for in the Dissolution of Muslim Marriage Act. As a member of the Assembly I was a member of one of the committees that considered this question. We left the question entirely for the Muslim Members concerned to settle. The *Shariat* Law was introduced in the Assembly and an Act was passed bringing into line with the *Shariat* Law the different pieces of legislation in the provinces of India. This was done four years ago. The Wakf Validation Act was passed in 1930. A time may come when members belonging to the particular community may feel that in the interests of the community progressive legislation has to be enacted. But if we make a provision here that the personal law shall not be interfered with, there will not be any right to the members of that community itself to modify that law. Therefore, it is not necessary that we should introduce it as a fundamental right. There is absolutely nothing in this Constitution which allows the majority to override the minority. This is only an enabling provision. Without the consent of the minority that is affected, no such law will be framed. I, therefore, feel it is unnecessary to include it in the Fundamental Rights."[31]

Dr. B.R. Ambedkar in his reply also contended that "if such a saving clause (with regard to personal law) was introduced into the Constitution, it would disable the legislatures in India from enacting any social measure whatsoever. The religious conceptions in this country are so vast that they cover every aspect of life, from birth to death. There is nothing which is not religion and if personal law is to be saved, I am sure about it that in social matters we will come to a stand-still. I do not think it is possible to accept a position of that sort. There is nothing extraordinary in saying that we ought to strive hereafter to limit the definition of religion in such a manner that we shall not extend beyond beliefs and such rituals as may be connected with ceremonials which are essentially religious. It is not necessary that the sort of laws, for instance, laws relating to tenancy or laws relating to succession should be governed by religion. In Europe there is Christianity, but Christianity does not mean that the Christians all over the world or in any part of Europe where they live shall have a uniform system of law of inheritance. No such thing exists. I personally do not understand why religion should be given this vast, expansive jurisdiction so as to cover the whole of life and to prevent the legislature from encroaching upon that field. After all, what are we having this liberty for? We are having this liberty in order to reform our social system which is so full of inequities, so full of inequalities, discriminations and other things, which conflict with our fundamental rights. It is, therefore, quite impossible for anybody to conceive that the personal law shall be excluded from the jurisdiction of the State. Having said that, I should also like to point out that all that the State is claiming in this matter is a power to legislate. There is no obligation upon the State to do away with personal laws. It is only giving a power."[32]

He also assured the Muslims that "no one need be apprehensive of the fact that if the State has the power, the State will immediately proceed to execute or enforce that power in a manner that may be found to be objectionable by the Muslims or by the Christians or by any other community in India. We must all remember that sovereignty is always limited, no matter even if you assert that it is unlimited, because sovereignty in the exercise of that power must reconcile itself to the sentiments of different communities. No Government can exercise its power in such a manner as to provoke the Muslim community to rise in rebellion. I think it would be a mad Government if it did so. But that is a matter which relates to the exercise of the power and not to the power itself."[33]

They highlighted the necessity of keeping personal law outside religion and again assured that this power would not be executed or enforced immediately without the consent of the minority. This amendment was negative on December 2, 1948.

Mohammad Ismail Sahib again raised the issue of personal law at the time of discussion of Article 19 (since renumbered 25) on December 6, 1948. His contention was that "personal law is part of the religion of the people who are observing the personal law". He wanted some sort of safeguards for the (Muslim) personal Law. After some initial resistance he was allowed by Dr. H.C. Mookherjee, who was the presiding officer then, to move his amendment, which was as follows:

"That after clause (2) of Article 19, the following new clause be added:

> (3) Nothing in clause (2) of this article shall affect the right of any citizen to follow the personal law of the group or the community to which he belongs or professes to belong."

In justification of his amendment he stated: "This provision which I am suggesting would only recognise the age-long right of the people to follow their own personal law, within the limits of their families and communities. This does not affect in any way the members of other communities. This does not encroach upon the rights of the members of other communities to follow their own personal law. It does not mean any sacrifice at all on the part of the members of any other community. Sir, here what we are concerned with is only the practice of the members of certain families coming under the community. It is a family practice and in such cases as succession, inheritance and disposal of properties by way of wakf and will, the personal law operates. It is only with such matters that we are concerned under personal law. In other matters, such as evidence, transfer of property, contracts and in innumerable other questions of this sort, the civil code will operate and will apply to every citizen of the land, to whatever community he may belong. Therefore, this will not in anyway detract from the desirable amount of uniformity which the State may try to bring about in the matter of the civil law.

"This practice of following personal law has been there amongst the people for ages. What I want under this amendment is that that practice should not be disturbed now and I want only the continuance of a practice that has been going on among the people for ages past. On a previous occasion Dr. Ambedkar spoke about certain enactments concerning Muslim personal law, enactments relating to Wakf, *Shariat* Law and Muslim marriage law. Here there was no question of the abrogation of the Muslim personal law at all. There was no revision at all and in all those cases what was done was that the Muslim personal law was elucidated and it was made clear that these laws shall apply to the Muslims. They did not modify them at all. Therefore, those enactments and legislations cannot be cited now as matter of precedents for us to do anything contravening the personal law of the people. Under this amendment what I want the House to accept is that when we speak of the State doing anything with reference to the secular aspect of religion, the question of the personal law shall not be brought in and it shall not be affected."[34]

None however spoke on this amendment of Mohammad Ismail and the same was negatived the same day.

"(4) During the third reading of the Constitution only two members made a passing reference to the provision of the Uniform Civil Code in the Constitution. Jaspat Roy Kapoor thought that "a uniform Civil Code for the whole country is a very good thing. It will be a great unifying factor."[35]

Smt. Hansa Mehta wanted 'a most progressive' personal law. She said: "The other item to which I wish to draw the attention of the House is the Common Civil Code. To my mind this is much more important than even national language. We have too many personal laws in this country and those personal laws are dividing the nation today. It is therefore very essential if we want to build up one nation to have one civil code. It must, however, be remembered that the Civil Code that we wish to have must be on a par with, or in advance of, the most progressive of the personal laws in the country. Otherwise it will be a retrograde step and it will not be acceptable to all".[36]

The speeches delivered in the Constituent Assembly by eminent leaders on a uniform Civil Code in secular India are very much pertinent in the present situation and they need be examined in retrospect. The discussions in the Assembly clearly indicated two opposing trends—the members representing the Muslim League opposing the inclusion of this provision in the Constitution tooth and nail because the Muslim Personal Law, according to them, was immutable, inviolable and ordained by the God and was part and parcel of their religion, whereas the members of the Drafting Committee making efforts to delink Personal Laws from religion. It is one of those very rare occasions when the Muslim members in unison protested so persistently and violently against an Article of the Constitution. Another occasion when the Muslim Members did lodge their protests was when the reservation of seats in the

Legislatures etc. on the basis of communal population was discontinued. But then, there was division amongst them and the majority of the Muslim Members and Muslim intellectuals did support that move of the Constitution-makers. But on this occasion all the Muslim Members including a known socialist like Maulana Hasrat Mohani persisted in their demand to keep the Personal Law outside the ambit of the Constitution. Leaving aside the logical part of it, it must be admitted that the Muslim members were very unhappy and resented its inclusion in the Constitution. Their feelings might have been assuaged to some extent when Dr. Ambedkar assured them of not introducing it without obtaining their concurrence. Whatever it might be, the Muslim Members did register their protests from the very beginning against this Article in no uncertain terms. This provision became a part of the Constitution and there it rested. This sensitive issue was allowed to hang in the balance for more than 65 years or so. No effort was made to translate it into action by enacting a Uniform Civil Code. Though our Governments, both Central and State, have sought to implement most of the directions enumerated in Part IV of the Constitution under the Directive Principles of State Policy, no government has ever sought to formulate a Uniform Civil Code for the people of India as desired by Article 44.

The fact that no action was taken by the Government to enact a uniform civil code did not dispel the apprehension from the minds of the Muslim community of its enactment on a future date. The party in power might have been waiting for the day when the Muslim community on their own would demand for its implementation. That day never came. On the other hand, there is a demand from certain quarters to abrogate this constitutional provision. As pointed out by Anirban Kashyap:

> Either this provision should not have been in the Constitution when there was such a stiff resistance from a section of the Community or this provision in the Directive Principles of State Policy should have been implemented in right earnest much earlier. The moot point for consideration is whether progress in a changing society is compatible with static social laws. Events show that it is not so. A firm decision need therefore be taken by which the country will not only steer clear to the path of progress, but also the assimilation and integration of those divergent forces which are in segregation by that great communal divide will automatically follow. A secular state cannot discriminate on community basis. A uniform civil code for all people living in a secular country like India is a natural corollary to the principle and concept of secularism. A mere decision to make the country secular will not usher in secularism unless such other steps which will really promote secularism are also taken. Otherwise secularism in its real sense will remain a far cry.[37]

IV

The Indian population is like a bunch of flowers in a vase. There is diversity of religious faith, customs, usage, tradition, festivals, food and culture. Before Independence, the foreign rulers, whether in their wisdom or for reasons of expediency, did not interfere in the personal laws of the people and allowed them to be governed by their own laws and customs in matters of marriage, divorce, separation, alimony, maintenance, guardianship, adoption, succession and inheritance which as such concern women intimately.

Our Constitution-makers adopted a safe and pragmatic approach. They conceded the right to religion as a fundamental right, enshrined the principles of justice, equality and liberty to all, irrespective of caste, religion and gender, and set the attainment of a Uniform Civil Code as their goal. The Constitution being the supreme law, all laws made in the country have to pass through the touch-stone of constitutional vires.

While civil and criminal procedural laws are uniform for everybody, there are separate laws for personal family matters. Thus for example, there is the Indian Divorce Act, 1869 and the Indian Christian Marriage Act, 1872 for the Christians, the Parsi Marriage and Divorce Act, 1936 for the Parsis, the Hindu Marriage Act, 1955, the Hindu Succession Act, 1956, the Hindu Minority and Guardianship Act, 1956 and the Hindu Adoption and Maintenance Act, 1956 for the Hindus, Buddhists, Jains and Sikhs, and the Muslim Personal Law (*Shariat*) Application Act, 1937, the Dissolution of Muslim Marriage Act, 1939 and the Muslim Women (Protection of Rights on Divorce) Act, 1986 for the Muslims. The Special Marriage Act, 1954 is a secular legislation. Any one can marry under the provisions of this Act irrespective of caste, creed or religion. Once marriage is registered under this Act, the parties will be governed by the provisions of this Act, their personal laws notwithstanding. It may, however, be noted that the Hindu Marriage Act (HMA) is almost exactly the same as the Special Marriage Act (SMA), so far as the rights and obligations of the spouses are concerned. It differs on the mode of getting married—by registration under SMA, by ritual under HMA. The rituals remain but the rights arising out of that marriage have changed beyond recognition. Inter-caste marriage is in, so is "*sagotra*" marriage. Monogamy is in for men and divorce is possible for both spouses. Then, there is the Foreign Marriage Act, 1969 to deal with marriage taking place outside the country.

The existence of different sets of laws for people belonging to different religious groups often leads to harsh discriminatory situations. Our Constitution is sensitive to the rights of women, Some relevant provisions are: Article 14 which secures to every person, equality before law, and equal protection of law; Article 15(1) which prohibits discrimination on grounds of, *inter alia*, gender or religion and also permits the State to make special laws or provisions for the welfare of women; and Article 26 which provides equal opportunities in matter of public employment. Under Article 51A(e) it is the fundamental duty of every citizen "...to renounce practices derogatory to the dignity of women..."

In this backdrop, women belonging to certain minority religious groups are placed at a disadvantage. Change in the personal laws based on religious beliefs and practices and long-standing customs is not an easy thing, but this is no alibi for non-action or acquiescence. The last few decades have witnessed vociferous debates and controversies over the issue of reform in the personal laws of some minorities and the enactment of a uniform civil code.

In the case of *Jordan Diengdeh* vs. *S.S. Chopra*,[38] the Supreme Court held that the laws relating to judicial separation, divorce and nullity of marriage of different communities are far from uniform. This is why, it observed in 1985: "Surely the time has now come for a complete reform of the law of marriage and make a uniform law applicable to all people irrespective of religion or caste." It carefully examined the provisions contained in the Hindu Marriage Act, 1955, Special Marriage Act, 1954, Parsee Marriage and Divorce Act, 1936, and Dissolution of Muslim Marriage Act, 1939. These Acts are really divergent and, hence, they unduly hamper the growth of a uniform civil code. So, the Apex Court held in this case: "We suggest that the time has come for the intervention of the legislature in these matters to provide for a uniform code of marriage and divorce and to provide by law for a way out of the unhappy situations in which couples like the present have find themselves in. We direct that a copy of this order may be forwarded to the Ministry of Law and Justice for such action as they may deem fit to take." Thus, in its view, the people might have different religions, but they must live under the same legal system.

The Indian controversy is really a controversy over the codification of "personal laws" based on religion or custom. Many personal laws relating to marriage, inheritance, guardianship, divorce, maintenance and property relations in all communities are unjust—especially unjust to women. The 'justice' argument is that religious law and practice (protected under Article 25) must yield to the 'equality', due process and other imperatives (in Article 14 and others). It is precisely this area where the High Courts and even the Supreme Court have fumbled. They could have taken action under Article 13 which makes laws inconsistent with or in derogation of the fundamental rights void. By refusing this 'Article 13' solution, judges avoided controversy and abdicated their role to read equality into doubtful personal laws, argues Rajeev Dhavan.[39]

Religion is definitely not the opium of the people in India, and one of the bases of India's multiculturalism is the existence of different religious communities. The maintenance of personal laws signifies that religion is not only recognized as a practice of the individual but also is established as the basis for a community identity, and is related to state. Hence, the community identity is a political identity too. Religious pluralism is a reality in India and that explains the persistence of personal laws in the otherwise "secular" democratic republic. Any discourse on personal laws thus gravitates into debates over the antagonism between politicized religious identities and their relation with the state and the issue of gender identity is relegated to a secondary position.

From the nineteenth century, the legal purview of religion has narrowed down steadily coming into increasing conflict with the exigencies of capitalism and its legal structures, that seek to promote individualization and class reproduction both. Since the colonial era, there have been attempts to separate religion from most areas of life. Religion ceased to determine the laws on ownership of agricultural land, tenancy, crime, commerce and international relations. It remained confined largely to laws on the family, marriage, and some forms of inheritance, leading to an unreal division between public and private lives. This happened because, in practice, the areas in which personal laws are applicable are interdependent on and related to all other legal spheres and women's lives. The legal compartmentalization of public and private lives is illusory since women's family lives and work capacities are interdependent. The bracketing of laws related to marriage and family as "personal" laws produces a gendered definition of religion, the onus of which is borne mainly by women. This displays the collective interest of men of all religions in maintaining gendered power hierarchies.

Again, the place of religion in the "private" domain has its repercussions. It represents the family as an abode beyond state intervention. It shifts the responsibility of maintaining community identity on women—in marriage and in familial relations. The question that naturally arises is: does this demarcation between the private and public lives reflect the public as the sphere of universalism, nationality, impartiality and equality in the eyes of law built on consent and the private as the sphere of particularism built on the "natural" subjugation of women?

Since, the personal family laws were drafted in a patriarchal social structure, discrimination against women was a foregone conclusion. The issue of women's rights is ridden with various complexities. Set in an adversarial, formidable and expensive court structure, even the limited rights granted by the statutes have become illusory and beyond the reach of most women. Even if India thinks in terms of a Uniform Civil Code, gender justice must be its stated goal. Women's economic rights must be the centerpiece of matrimonial reforms, and they should indicate the attempts towards closing the gap between the private and the public spheres of women. Since patriarchy is reinforced through the economic structure— of feudalism and capitalism—a solution to the oppression and destitution of women will have to be found primarily in the context of the economic structure and state responsibility towards women within these structures. This is possibly what is indicated through the concept of "modernization of the Indian tradition". If the Indian polity decides in favour of a Uniform Civil Code, it has to do it in a tradition-modernity continuum. It is almost impossible to separate the two. Uniform Civil Code has been primarily related to the question of national integration. Rather Uniform Civil Code should address the issue of establishing gender just laws that are rational and scientific, and need not necessarily violate rational traditional practice. For, a combination of tradition and modernity is necessary to address gender identity through a Uniform Civil Code, argues Rukhmini Sen.[40]

Even the Hindu Code had a long and difficult gestation. It is pertinent to note that the Hindu women of the nineteenth century were resigned to their pathetic lot in life; *sati,* polygamy and child marriage, with their attendant horror of early widowhood, all perpetrated in the name of religion, were borne in mute despair. The laws excluded women from all rights of inheritance and treated them with open contempt. In short, a Hindu woman had no legal existence.

Modern education and exposure to Western liberalism opened the eyes of the Hindu intelligentsia of the nineteenth century to the social stagnation of the day. Raja Ram Mohun Roy, horrified at a *sati* performed in the family, went on a spiritual quest. It was largely due to his efforts in mobilizing public opinion that legislation was enacted to ban *sati.* On the strength of the Widow Remarriage Act of 1856, credited to Pandit Ishwarchandra Vidyasagar, eight widows were married between 1864 and 1868 under the auspices of the Brahmo Samaj.

Other movements for social and religious reform sprang up in rest of the country, the Arya Samaj in the North and the Prarthana Samaj in the west. The Arya Samaj sought to revive the purity of the Vedic religion; the Prarthana Samaj patterned itself on the rationalism of the Brahmos. Intellectual giants of the day like M.G. Ranade, R.G. Bhandarkar and others cast about to find ways and means of amelioration. On the whole, legal measures for the suppression of such spectacular and outlandish evils like sati and child sacrifice found ready acceptance, but others seeking to reach into the established pattern of middle class lives gave rise to fierce and prolonged controversies, like the Age of Consent Act. The Civil Marriage Act of 1872, which made child marriage illegal and sanctioned widow and inter-caste marriage, was confined only to the Brahmos and left untouched the Hindu community at large. It was not till 1929 that the Child Marriage Restraint Act (Sharda Act) was passed in British India. Harbilas Sharda had originally fixed the minimum marriageable age for Hindu girls at twelve; the Act was subsequently amended to raise the minimum age to fourteen and cover non-Hindus as well.

By this time there was a palpable change in the social atmosphere of the country. Ramakrishna Paramhansa had already thrilled the Hindus into an awareness of all that was pure, transcendental and everlasting in Hinduism. His veneration of Sharada Devi as the very representation of the mother goddess gave new dignity to Hindu womanhood. Swami Vivekananda gave a new orientation to the Hindu religion. Then Gandhi came and lifted the national movement to unprecedented heights. Women came out of seclusion of their traditional homes to take part in this many-faceted movements; women learnt to organise themselves better. The All India Women's Conference was inaugurated in 1926 and it began discussing issues like marriage and inheritance.

The old Hindu Law permitted polygamy. Under the Hindu law a Hindu male could have any number of wives till recently. Only in the middle of the last century, there were piecemeal legislations to prohibit bigamy—the Bombay Prevention of Hindu Bigamous Act, 1946, and the Madras Hindu (Bigamy Prevention and Divorce) Act, 1949.

In the first few years after Independence, the codification and reform of the Hindu Personal Law was hailed as a sign of the new government's supposed commitment to the principles of gender equality and non-discrimination enshrined in the Constitution. The Parliament enacted the Hindu Marriage Act, 1955, the Hindu Succession Act, 1956, the Hindu Minority and Guardianship Act, 1956 and the Hindu Adoption and Maintenance Act, 1956—which are often referred to as the Hindu Code. The Buddhists, Jains and Sikhs never had any scripture-based personal law of their own and were governed by Hindu law subject to some contrary usages of their own. The codified Hindu laws of 1955-56 were extended to these three communities also.

The Hindu Marriage Act of 1955 codified the laws relating to marriage among the Hindus. It made monogamy the rule for men as much as for women. The minimum age of marriage was fixed at 15 for girls and 18 for men. It legalized divorce. This Act was a great experiment in social legislation and it was challenged in courts many a time. In *Ram Prasad* vs. *State of UP* the service conduct rules and the provisions against polygamy were challenged by a husband whose wife was declared medically incapable of having another child after one female child. He sought permission to remarry, so that, he could have a son, but was denied. He assailed the rule and the law on the ground that under Article 25 of the Constitution, freedom of religion is given to everybody. Article 25(1), according to him, not only guarantees freedom of belief but also protected all religious practices in pursuance of such beliefs and since under Hindu law it is a religious belief that a man without a son cannot attain salvation, a person who marries another woman in order to have a son is protected by the clause. The court dismissed these arguments and held that 'Social Reform' means eradication of practices or dogmas which stand in the way of the country's progress as a whole, but *do not form the essence of religion*. Thus, the State may prohibit bigamy amongst the Hindus because the need of having a natural son by marrying a second wife on the failure of the first wife to get a son was not of the essence of Hindu religious belief, as the purpose might be served by taking an adopted son.[41]

In 1956, the Hindu Succession Act was passed to bring under a single Act the laws of succession among the Hindus, Buddhists, Sikhs and Jains and several matriarchal systems in South India. All the traditional limitations of Hindu women to hold, dispose and transmit property were abolished. The widow, the daughter and the mother were now entitled to an equal share of the property along with the son. The Hindus have come a long way from the days of the Age of Consent Bill.

Even then the Hindu Law Acts of 1955-56 are full of discrimination on grounds of sex. Hindu law does not admit a woman to the position of a *karta*, the head of a household. Section 23 of the Hindu Succession Act, 1956 does not give share to female heirs in the family dwelling house and denies them the right to claim partitions which it gives exclusively to their male co-heirs. The Hindu Minority and Guardianship Act do not allow a mother to act as her children's natural guardian unless their father is dead or otherwise disqualified.[42]

Since the 1950s, successive amendments to different personal laws in the area of marriage and divorce have mainly focused on enlarging the grounds for divorce. In the 1960s and 1970s cruelty and desertion and thereafter mutual consent were added as grounds for divorce in the Hindu Marriage Act and the Special Marriage Act. However, the fact that almost all Indian women and the children with them suffer a steep fall in their standard of living on separation and divorce has been consistently ignored by the policy and lawmakers. Women's organizations and groups have suggested that the amendment to the Marriage Law Amendment Bill, 2012 should be redrafted to make it mandatory for the court to order that both immovable and movable property acquired during the subsistence of marriage be divided equally between the wife and husband. It has also been suggested that the court should take into account any disadvantage suffered by the woman or the children with her and give her a further share of the property.[43]

Following several years of discussion, the UPA government introduced the Marriage Laws (Amendment) Bill, proposing amendments to the Hindu Marriage Act, 1955, and the Special Marriage Act, 1954 in the Rajya Sabha. It was passed by the Rajya Sabha on 26th August, 2013, but could not be taken up for discussion in the Lok Sabha.

Among other things the Marriage Laws (Amendment) Bill empowers the courts to decide the compensation amount for the wife and children from the husband's inherited and inheritable properties once the marriage ends legally.

The Bill allows parties to file for divorce on the ground of "irretrievable breakdown" of marriage. Both parties have to live apart for at least three years before filing such a petition. The Bill also provides for restricting the grant of a decree of divorce if the court is satisfied that adequate provision for maintenance of the children has not been made consistent with the financial capacity of the parties to the marriage. Also, the wife has the right to oppose the grant of divorce on the ground that the dissolution of marriage could result in grave financial hardship, but no such provision has been made for the husband.

Men's rights groups dubbed it as a husband killer law because basically the hard-earned money and property of the man will not belong to him once this Bill becomes law. They have been staging nationwide protests and holding debates on the issue. "Hridaya", a Calcutta-based NGO organized a protest rally in the city on August 25, 2013 against the Bill. Alleging that the Bill, if enacted, will put the institution of marriage in jeopardy and will affect the man's family as well if the man is the provider for his parents, unmarried sisters and brothers, the NGO demanded a gender neutrality law.[44]

Though the present BJP-led government had initially considered tabling the Bill again, Law Minister Sadananda Gowda, in response to a question in the Lok Sabha on December 18, 2014, admitted that the government was having second thoughts about it. He said the government was examining the implications of bringing the Bill as more than 70 representations had been received against it from senior citizen groups and non-governmental organisations such as Save Indian Family and Centre for Reforms. Save Indian Family is an umbrella organisation of various groups which fight for men's rights. "In these representations, grave and far-reaching legal, social and economic implications of the proposed amendments to marriage laws have been raised," Mr. Gowda said. These groups contend that such an amendment will bring down the marriage rate in the country.[45]

The Khap Panchayats in North India enjoy unlimited power in deciding the cases of social relations among the Hindus. In the name of tradition, they have been opposed to inter-caste marriages, inter-village marriages (that is within a radius of 42 villages) as well as same-*gotra* marriages. The rulings by these Khaps, which are almost binding on the families and the society at large, have led to persecution of couples, suicides, honour killings and caste conflicts in rural belts, and even forced bachelors to get brides from other states. The largest number of killings has occurred owing to inter-caste marriages, followed by same village marriages and same-*gotra* marriages. In a significant departure from the age-old traditions, Satrol Khap Panchayat in Hisar only on April 20, 2014 gave a go-ahead to inter-caste marriages as well as weddings between families within the radius of 42 villages. Same-*gotra* marriages, however, remain barred, and the weddings can take place only with parental consent.[46] Pruning the jurisdiction of prohibited areas of marriage will bring revolutionary change in Haryana and elsewhere. This is a right step in the right direction and other Khap Panchayats are expected to follow the example set by the Satrol Khap Panchayat so as to rid the society from the vagaries of their unjust rulings.

In Goa the *Codigo Civil Portugues* or the Portuguese Civil Code (PCC) was introduced in 1870 and has been continuously in force with subsequent modifications. It continued even after Goa's liberation from Portuguese rule in 1961, owing to an assurance by the Jawaharlal Nehru government that the laws prevailing earlier would remain in force. Goa's population comprises approximately 64 per cent Hindus, 31 per cent Christians (mostly Roman Catholics), four per cent Muslims and one per cent representing other communities. All the communities are governed by the PCC.

Registration of all births, deaths and marriages is compulsory and has always been an integral part of the PCC. The procedure of registration of marriages is not entirely uniform. Catholics have the option of solemnizing their marriages in church after obtaining a 'no objection certificate' from the Civil Registrar. The church record of marriage is then transcribed in the civil registry and thus gives the church marriage civil effect. Consequently, a Catholic woman can get a divorce and remarry through the regular civil procedure, though if she wants to remarry in the church it would be necessary for her to get her earlier marriage annulled by the church.

In the case of Hindus, there is no relationship between the civil marriage and the religious marriage; whereas in the case of Muslims the maulvi may ask to see the certificate of civil registration before performing the *nikah*. Most Muslim marriages are registered. Muslim men whose marriages are registered in Goa cannot divorce by pronouncing *talaq* thrice, nor can they have more than one wife.

All wealth or property that is owned or acquired by each spouse during the course of marriage is held in common by the couple under what is known as the 'communion of assets'. In case of divorce, each spouse is entitled to a half share of the property. An ante-nuptial agreement can be drawn up, stating in definite terms what each spouse can claim as his or hers. Such an agreement has to be recorded as a public deed and cannot be changed or revoked. The spouses may opt for a combination of communion and separation of assets, whereby whatever is acquired or earned before marriage is held separately while what is obtained after marriage is held in common.

The inheritance laws are particularly interesting. As both spouses own the property in common, in case of the death of one spouse the other spouse retains ownership over half of the property. According to the Portuguese Law of Succession, half of the remaining property is necessarily shared equally by the male and female offspring. In the absence of descendants, the parents or ascendants are entitled to this share. And in their absence, the brothers and sisters and their descendants are entitled to the said share. It is clearly impossible for parents to disinherit their children entirely, as only half of the property can be disposed of through a will, according to their wishes.

In view of the provisions contained in the PCC with regard to registration of marriage, the common ownership of wealth and property by husband and wife and the equal rights of men and women to inheritance, the PCC in Goa is often upheld as an ideal code. Since, it is non-sectarian and is unlikely to make the minorities feel insecure, many intellectuals feel it should be extended to the rest of India.[47]

The Indian Christians are guided by the Indian Divorce Act, 1869 and the Indian Christian Marriage Act, 1872. Section 10 of the Indian Divorce Act, 1869 quite firmly places Christian women in India at a disadvantage in relation to their husbands. Based on the British Matrimonial Causes Act of 1857, it makes adultery the sole ground of divorce. A husband only has to prove adultery to get a divorce, a wife must prove adultery with desertion or cruelty or—strangely enough—bigamy, in order to ask for a divorce. In other words, it gives the husband the privilege to seek divorce, while the woman is barred from the right as far as is practical. Ironically, the parent law in Britain has been modified more than once, making cruelty, desertion, insanity independent grounds. Divorce laws in India for other communities have been modernized too, though not all of them sufficiently. Christian women in India, fighting for change in the unjust section in the divorce law since Independence, have had a peculiarly rough deal. The issue of allowing Christian women right to seek divorce had been hanging fire for more than 40 years and the Law Commission as well as the High Courts of Bombay, Madras, Andhra Pradesh, Calcutta and Kerala had emphasized the need to bring about gender equality in the matter of divorce available to Christian spouses. Even the Catholic Church in India is amenable, although it does not recognize divorce itself. The Parliament passed the Indian Divorce (Amendment) Act, 2001 to give Christian women right to seek marriage annulment by removing gender bias and to do away with High Court confirmation in divorce cases. The Act also removes the clause of payment of either one-fifth or one-third in alimony ceiling and leaves it to the discretion of the district court to fix quantum of maintenance.

This Act was finalized after a wide-ranging dialogue between the Government, the Parliamentary Standing Committee and Bishops Conference of India and the National Council of Churches. Christian women of any denomination will be allowed to seek divorce under any of the 13 grounds mentioned in the Hindu Marriage Act of 1955 and the Special Marriage Act of 1954, of which the most important are mutual consent and irretrievable breakdown of marriage.[48]

Section 10A(1) of the Indian Divorce Act, 1869 stipulates a minimum two-year separation before couples can file for divorce by mutual consent. The provision for divorce by mutual consent in other statutes such as section 28 of The Special Marriage Act, 1954, Section 13-B of the Hindu Marriage Act, 1955 and Section 32B of The Parsi Marriage and Divorce Act, 1936 prescribes the statutory period of separation as one year. A Bench of Justices Vikramjit Sen and A.M. Sapre of the Supreme Court on March 23, 2015 agreed to examine the validity of this 146-year old provision and issued notice to the Centre on a petition seeking quashing of the said Section.[49]

The Indian Christians are governed by Sections 41 to 48 of the Indian Succession Act of 1925. The Law Commission headed by Justice A.P. Shah in its 247th report submitted to the Ministry of Law and Justice on September 12, 2014 has asked the government to amend Sections 41 to 48 of the said Act as the "scheme envisioned therein incorporates a preferential approach to men and is unfair and unjust to Christian women". The government has been receiving representations from community leaders seeking removal of this anomaly. The government will bring an amendment in Parliament based on the recommendations of the Law Commission.[50]

V

Today each religious denomination has its own personal laws to pursue. Curiously, except the Muslims all religious groups have their personal laws codified and documented, to be utilized in interpretation by the judicial process. Unfortunately Muslims have no codified law, and the same is therefore subject to several interpretations, amendments, alterations or discord by the powers that be. The brunt of such lack of codification is borne by the marginalized illiterate socially backward Muslim women, who deserve by the article enshrined in our Constitution to be brought into the mainstream as an equal partner to share the prosperity of our nation. Moreover, Muslim community is divided in many groups and sects—Shia, Sunni, Ahle-Hadis, Hanafi, Maliki, Shafai, Hanbali, Bohra, Mahdavi, Bareilvi, and Deobandis. The Ahmedias consider themselves as Muslims though some sections of the Muslims do not consider them as such. The personal laws of so many groups and sects need not necessarily be the same. For instance, the Ahle-Hadis consider triple *talaq* invalid while the Hanafis don't, though both of them belong to the same school of Sunni jurisprudence.

Misconception prevails among certain quarters as to the exact scope and content of codification of any personal law and especially the "Muslim Personal Law", because unlike other personal laws, the Muslim personal law derives interpretation from the Holy *Quran*, which Muslims firmly believe to be the revelations of God. The revelations took place during a period of 20 years and they were reduced to writing during the lifetime of the Holy Prophet. The law laid down in the holy Book was supplemented by Hadis or Sunnahs, i.e. precepts and practices of the Messenger of God. But they were not recorded during the lifetime of the Holy Prophet, but were handed down by various persons. Sunnah includes the Arab '*Adat*' (the Arab customary law). *Ijma* and *Qiyas* are two other recognised sources of Muslim law. *Ijma* means the concurrence or consensus of the companions and the disciples of the Holy Prophet; and *Qiyas* is the analogical deduction derived from a comparison of the first three sources, when they did not apply to particular cases.[51]

During the first few centuries after the Holy Prophet, Muslim scholars and jurists notable among whom are Abu Hannifa and his two disciples Abu Yousuf and Iman Mohammed, Malik Iban Anas, Mohammed Shafel and Ahmed Bin Hanibal, put their own gloss on the texts of the *Quran* and the *Hadis*, leading to different schools of Muslim law. Steeped in local traditions and influenced by the values of the times in which they lived, their interpretation of Islamic law was not strictly in accordance with the letter and spirit of the Holy Book or the *Hadis*.

The Islamic law of crimes is very stringent and is enforced in some Muslim countries. The advent of British rule witnessed the imposition of a uniform criminal law—the Indian Penal Code, the Code of Criminal Procedure and other special and local laws which were made applicable to all citizens of the country irrespective of their faith without any protest from any section. Even the Islamic Law of Evidence was supplanted by the Indian Evidence Act. Several common civil codes such as the Indian Contract Act, 1872, the Transfer of Property Act, 1872, the Trust Act, 1882, the Code of Civil Procedure, 1898 (now of 1976), the Evidence Act, 1872, the Negotiable Instruments Act, 1881 and the Companies Act, 1956 were enforced without reference to caste or community. But the British Administrators left untouched the personal or family laws relating to inheritance, marriage, dowry, divorce, guardianship and the like.

The Muslim personal law is based on *Sunnah*. It is very difficult to establish authenticity of those *Hadith* on which certain provisions of the personal law is based. There are serious differences about a particular *Hadith* being true or not. For example, the Shias accept authenticity of the *Hadith* permitting the *muta* marriage (temporary marriage which could even be for a night) whereas the Sunnis reject it.[52] It may be mentioned here that the National Commission for Women has asked the External Affairs Ministry to issue instructions to all embassies and consulates to ensure that visiting foreign nationals do not indulge in "Muta" or short-term marriages or else they would be dealt with strictly as per law.[53]

In pre-Islamic days, there were frequent wars in the Middle East; the male population was considerably reduced and polygamy was in a way necessary. A man was entitled to have as many wives as he desired and they were treated more as chattels. It was a remarkable achievement on the part of the Holy Prophet in restricting polygamy to four wives at a time, in giving social status to women and conferring on them the right to inheritance along with males and the right to own the inherited properties absolutely, which other systems of jurisprudence took so many centuries to do.

Muslim law allows polygamy for men and imposes monogamy on women. Though the Holy *Quran* allows polygamy for men, there is ample evidence to show that Islam favours monogamy. The strict condition laid down in the Holy Book is that the man taking more than one wife should treat them all equally. Part IV, Chapter IV, Verse 3 of the Holy *Quran* reads thus: "And if you are apprehensive that you shall not be able to do justice to the orphans, then marry woman of your choice, two, or three or four; but if you still fear that you cannot do justice, then marry only one, or that which your right hands possess. Thus, it will be more likely that you may not do injustice."

But the ancient jurists conveniently forgot all this in order to cater to the sentiments of the feudal society and freely allowed polygamy. Refreshingly, modern jurists like Syed Amir Ali, Badruddin Tyabji and Syed Mohammed have opined that the *Quran* preferred monogamy to polygamy. An intelligent reading of the holy *Quran* would show that polygamy is an exception and not the rule. It is far from a general licence for men to marry up to four wives, as some non-Muslims and some Muslims, too, think. As a matter of fact bigamous marriages among Muslims are extremely rare in the present social and economic setup.

Jurists are unanimous that in Islamic societies polygamous marriages are permitted but only in certain circumstances, that is, primarily in situations where a man's death has left his widows with no means or support. Polygamy is neither mandatory nor encouraged but merely permitted. The *Quran*'s conditional endorsement stresses that self-interest or sexual desire should not be the reason for entering into a polygamous marriage. This fact was harped upon by the Additional Sessions Judge of Delhi, Ms. Kamini Lau, while dismissing the anticipatory bail plea by a maulvi, accused of forcing a young Muslim girl into a wedding without her consent with a married man who allegedly raped her subsequently.[54] This action of the court received wide support from many Muslim scholars.

While Turkey, Egypt, Sudan, Indonesia, Iraq and Pakistan have put in place strict judicial and administrative regulations on polygamy, the practice is banned in Malaysia and Brunei.[55] It does not stand to reason why the Muslim community in India should resist gender justice, uplift of their women folk and the restructuring and revitalizing of Islamic Law to keep pace with the needs of the time. Organizations such as the Centre for Study of Society and Secularism, Bhartiya Muslim Mahila Andolan, Institute of Islamic Studies and Muslims for Secular Democracy are against polygamy in Muslim society.[56] In a significant move the leading Islamic seminary Darul Uloom Deoband, has appealed to Muslims sometime in April, 2012 not to marry for the second time since it is hard to provide 'equal justice' to two wives in "Indian custom".[57]

In 2008, Khursheed Ahmad Khan employed as an irrigation supervisor of the tube well division of the Uttar Pradesh Government was discharged from service for proved misconduct of contracting another marriage during the existence of the first marriage without the permission of the government. The High Court dismissed his case. He appealed in the Apex Court questioning the validity of the conduct rules saying they violated Article 25 of the Constitution. A bench of Justices T.S. Thakur and A.K. Goel has ruled on February 9, 2015 that government employees cannot have two wives simultaneously if service rules prohibit multiple spouses and a violator is liable to be sacked even if he happens to be a Muslim. Such dismissals cannot be construed as a violation of Article 25 which guarantees every citizen the fundamental right to preach, practice and profess one's religious beliefs.

The Bench quoted approvingly the Apex Court ruling in the *Javed* vs. *State of Haryanam*, (2003) 8SCC 369 in which it was stated: "What was protected under Article 25 was the religious faith and not a practice which may run counter to public order, health or mortality. Polygamy was not an integral part of a religion and monogamy was a reform within the power of the State under Article 25". It was also observed that "a practice does not acquire the sanction of religion simply because it is permitted. Assuming the practice of having more wives than one or procreating more children than one is a practice followed by any community or group of people, the same can be regulated or prohibited by legislation in the interest of public order, morality and health or by any law providing for social welfare and reform which the impugned legislation clearly does."[58]

The concept of widow remarriage though permitted by Islam is rarely practised in Kashmir. Syeda Aasiya Andrabi, a leader of militant women, has called upon and encouraged men to take more than one wife while requesting the women to permit their husbands to opt for polygamy. She even urged her husband, Muhammad Qasim to take a second wife. However, Qasim has spent more than 16 years behind bars. Her call found no response and widow remarriage could never become a norm. The condition of the half widows, that is whose husbands are missing, is even worse as they cannot remarry and are even denied a share in the inheritance. They cannot even think of remarriage as there is no consensus among the religious scholars and theologians as to whether they can be pronounced widows. The Hanafi school of thought says that the half widow must wait for a period of 90 years while the Malliki school of thought holds that the waiting period should be only four years. No religious council or initiative has been undertaken by the ulema to arrive at a consensus.[59]

Divorce in Islam is a vexed question. *Talaq* is the uncontrolled, unbridled and arbitrary exercise of the power of divorce by the husband. According to the *Quran*, the pronouncement of *talaq* must be made during three successive *Tuhars* (period between menstruation) and it becomes irrevocable on the third pronouncement, thus giving time to the husband for reflection and retraction. The *Quran* has also provided for arbitration to effect reconciliation before the final pronouncement of *talaq*. But, later Muslim jurists of "great antiquity and high authority" threw to the winds this salutary procedure and conceived a form under which a husband can bring about dissolution of marriage by unilateral pronouncement of *talaq* thrice in one sitting, called *Talaq-ul-Biddat* (or) *Talaq-I-Badai*, or *Ta!aq al-bida* (the sinful divorce) which is not recognised by the Holy *Quran*. It is this form of divorce which is widely prevalent in this country, despite the dictum of the Prophet of God that of all things allowed in law, the most detestable is divorce. No other system of law has conferred on the husband such a despotic power. Though the practice of divorce by unilateral pronouncement of *talaq* has been done away with-in many Muslim countries, it is still in vogue in this country.

The Shias do no consider the triple *talaq* as valid. The Shia Muslims maintain that one cannot pronounce more than one divorce at a time. The Ismailis also reject the concept of triple *talaq* in one sitting. Among the Sunnis as well, there is no unanimity on this issue. The Hanbalis do not accept it. The Hanbali Imam, Ibn Taymiyyah, wrote a book arguing against it. He vehemently rejected the very concept as un-Islamic and suffered greatly for his views.[60] The *ahle-hadis* sect is against it. The Jamiat *Ahle Hadis* even issued a *fatwa* on May 21, 1993, holding three *talaqs* at one sitting as invalid and ineffective. The four other schools of Sunni jurisprudence—Hanafi, Maliki, Shafai and Hanbali, however, rejected the *Ahle Hadis fatwa.* The Jamait Ulema-e-Hind, a central body of Muslim theologians of the country declared on July 1, 1993 that the pronouncement of *talaq* thrice in a row at one sitting by a Muslim husband is valid and to cohabit with a woman divorced in this manner is illegal and sinful.[61]

There are controversial *hadith* about this form of triple *talaq*. According to one *hadith* which almost all sects agree to, the Prophet's face turned red with anger when someone reported that so and so had given triple *talaq* to his wife in one sitting. Though the Prophet himself denounced it, this form of divorce is being practised widely in India by the Muslims. Apparently, this form of divorce was practiced during the *jahiliyah* (pre-Islamic) period in Arabia and the Prophet tried to abolish it without success. For a man it was a great instrument of control and overlordship over his wife and so, he did not want to give it up even after embracing Islam.

The *Quran* nowhere permits this form of divorce. Since the *Quran* intends to empower all the weaker sections of the society, including women, it prescribed a just and a fair form of divorce. It says the wife should appoint an arbiter who together with the husband would recommend divorce or otherwise. Thus the wife, instead of being thrown out after three *talaqs*, would get a chance to speak before the arbiter and hope for justice. It is not that the *ulamas* are unaware of this significant provision of arbitration in case of divorce in the *Quran*, but they do not wish to practise it. It would go against their male ego.

The *Quran* has dealt with the issue of *talaq* at length in chapters 2, 4 and 65, namely, *Al-Baqara*, *Al-Nisa* and *Al-Talaq*. Four steps before the first *talaq* have been stipulated (4:34-35). When there is marital discord, the *Quran* advises the parties to sort it out (*fa'izu hunna*) among themselves. If differences persist, then as a next step they are asked to undergo temporary physical separation (*wahjuru hunna*) in the hope that this will encourage them to unite. If even this fails, the husband is instructed, as a third step, to once again explain (*wazribu hunna)* to his wife the seriousness and try to bring about a reconciliation.

For instance, in pursuance of *wazribu hunna*, the husband may point out to his wife that if they do not resolve their differences soon enough, their dispute may go beyond the confines of their home and become a subject of gossip, which may not be in the interest of the family. If the dispute still remains unresolved, as a fourth step, the *Quran* requires the matter to be placed before two arbiters, one from the family of each spouse.

It is only after the failure of the four reconciliation attempts that the *Quran* allows the first *talaq* to be pronounced, followed by a waiting period called *iddah* (2:228-232 and 65:1-4). Not more than two divorces can be pronounced within this period, the duration of which is three menstrual cycles (2:228-229). For women who have attained menopause or suffer from amenorrhoea, *iddah* is three months, and in the case of pregnant women it is till the termination of pregnancy (65:4).

If the parties are unable to unite during *iddah*, the final irrevocable *talaq* can be pronounced, but only after the expiry of *iddah* (2:231). Once the *talaq* is invoked, the marital bond stands severed and the spouses cease to be of any relation to each other. However, even after the lapse of *iddah*, the *Quran* offers the disputants a chance to reunite, provided the final *talaq* has not been pronounced. It says, "When you divorce women and they complete their term (*iddah*), do not prevent them from marrying their (former) husbands if they mutually agree on equitable terms" (2:232). In other words, after the expiry of *iddah*, as per 2:231, 232, the parties are given options of re-contracting the marriage on fresh terms, or seek permanent separation—the separation being the third and the final irrevocable *talaq* to be pronounced in the presence of two witnesses (65.2) within a reasonable time.[62]

Asghar Ali Engineer, a crusader and scholar, quotes all the 15 verses in the *Quran* on divorce, in his excellent work *The Rights of Women in Islam*, and rightly stresses that not only is there no sanction for the triple *talaq*, instantly pronounced, but there is an express injunction in the *Quran* for arbitration which would surely be rendered nugatory by the instant pronouncement. It is astonishing that despite the clarity of the *Quran* on the issue of divorce, the Muslim patriarchy has stubbornly refused to adopt the *Quranic* procedure. Since the *Shariat* lacks codification in the form of a legally pursuable document, paragraph, page, line to number, the powers that be render various interpretations arising from the lack of numbered statutes. To prevent such situations, the Muslim personal law needs documentation in the shape of codified numbered statutes, asserts Bader Sayeed, former Chairperson of the Minorities Commission, Tamil Nadu.[63]

Triple *talaq* is not merely un-Islamic; it is also a violation of human rights. Even then it is being practised with impunity. This arbitrary form of divorce reflects the regressive tendency among a section of the Muslim clergy to support the triple *talaq*. The aberrations that have crept in this form of divorce will be better understood by some examples. For instance, in July 2003, Shaikh Sheru from Orissa pronounced *talaq* to his wife Nizama in an inebriated condition. Repenting the next morning, he expressed his desire to continue living with her. But community leaders ordered them to live separately insisting *talaq* uttered under the influence of alcohol being valid. In June 2005, Raza Ali Khan, an Indian vocalist, divorced his German wife of four years by posting her a *talaqnama*. He then remarried. In March, 2006, a couple in Jalpaiguri (West Bengal) Aftab Ansari and Sohela, were ordered by local religious leaders to separate because Aftab had allegedly uttered *talaq* three times in sleep. There have been reports of *talaq* on telephone, e-mail and even *via* SMS. Mufti Salim Akhtar, who runs a *madrasah* in Mumbai, says that such *talaqs* can be considered valid if the husband confirms in person that he had pronounced them.[64]

Many Muslim countries including Turkey, Tunisia, Algeria, Iraq, Iran, Indonesia, Pakistan and Bangladesh[65] follow *talaq-e-ehsan* and have banned tripple *talaq*. In fact Pakistan banned it way back in 1961 when the Muslim Personal Law Ordinance of 1961 was promulgated by the then Pakistan President Muhammad Ayub Khan. It has been widely accepted in Pakistan that not only the provisions of the ordinance are in accordance with the *Quranic* injunctions they have also brought about the much-needed relief to women in Pakistan. No divorce can take place in Pakistan unless the husband has informed the Chairman of the Union Council in writing of his intention to divorce. A copy of that letter has to be provided to the wife. Having adopted this procedure, a three-month period has to elapse before the divorce becomes valid. And, in the meantime, the Chairman will invariably constitute an arbitration council to organize reconciliation. No one can take a second wife unless the arbitration council allows it in writing.[66] A report indicates that there is a distinct upward trend among the Pakistani women to seek divorce from husbands for alleged acts of brutality.[67]

In post-revolution Iran, the Iranian women have won the right of divorce on the following counts: (1) if the husband does not pay maintenance for more than six months and if there is no possibility that he will pay and similarly his inability to fulfil the obligations of married life and ensuring the rights of his wife for that period; (2) misbehaviour and mistreating wife and if she is unable to bear this, she can claim divorce; (3) if the husband suffers from addiction to alcohol or drugs; (4) if the husband neglects wife or family life without any reasonable ground for more than six months continuous; and (5) if the husband takes another wife without the permission of the first wife or unjust behaviour towards her. If the divorce takes place for no fault of the woman, she can claim half the property acquired during the years of the marriage, or equivalent. Not only this, an Iranian woman can also now claim compensation for all the house-keeping she did during the years of marriage if it is proved that she is not to be blamed for divorce. These provisions considerably restrict the privileges of man available to him in other Muslim societies.[68]

Zihar and *Lian* are the two modes which confer on the Muslim wife the right to seek divorce on her own accord that too through the instrumentality of the court. Impotency of the husband has also been recognised as a ground for dissolution by a judicial decree. On no other ground, however, valid or reasonable it may be, does the *Shariat* allow the Muslim women to snap the marital tie on their own accord. In order to save the Muslim women from the miseries of misfit marriages, the Indian Central Legislature passed the Dissolution of Muslim Marriages Act, 1939, which enabled a Muslim wife to seek divorce through the court on grounds laid down in Section 2 of the Act. The Act which has made a deep but beneficial inroad into the Law of the *Shariat* is a landmark social legislation. The enactment has been well received by the community at large and its provisions have benefited many. However, so long as the Muslim husband has the despotic power of unilateral divorce, no Muslim woman can have security of marriage. And as Kader says, "gender-equality is a myth".[69]

In a landmark judgement, Justice H.N. Tilhari of the Allahabad High Court had held in 1994 that mere uttering the word "*talaq*" thrice at one go or during tuhar, without any substantial ground, is *ultra vires* the Constitution and cannot be constitutionally operative under Article 372. Also, it is against Section 2 of the Muslim Personal Law (*Shariat*) Application Act. The judge observed: "*Talaq-e-bidatt* or *Talaq-e-bidai* (the sinful divorce), in which the divorce is pronounced in one go or during one sitting had been regarded by all under the Islam Sunnat as against the mandate of the Holy *Quran*."[70] A full Bench of the Bombay High Court in 2001 had held: "Mere pronouncement of *talaq* by the husband or merely declaring his intentions of his act of having pronounced the *talaq* is not sufficient and does not meet the requirement of law".[71] Justice B.H. Marlapalle of the Bombay High Court held in 2007 that the *talaq* between Dilshad Begum and Ahmadkhan Hanifkhan Pathan was not legal and valid as the husband had not gone through the preconditions of arbitration and reconciliation prescribed by Muslim law.[72] Justice Hasnain Masoodi of Jammu & Kashmir High Court in *Mohammad Naseem Bhat* vs. *Bilquees Akhter and another* held on April 30, 2012 that under the Muslim Shariah law "a husband cannot have unrestricted or unqualified power to pronounce *talaaq*".[73]

The aggrieved Muslim women are now getting relief from the court against triple *talaq* uttered in a single sitting. But how many of them has the wherewithal to approach the High Court? Curiously enough, the Darul Uloom Deoband has issued a *fatwa* on March 13, 2012 holding that if a husband has uttered *talaq* thrice over mobile phone even in a state of drunkenness, that *talaq* is valid.[74] The National Commission for Women once considered of approaching the Supreme Court for a clear ruling on triple *talaq*. It brought out in 2004 a handbook entitled "welfare of Muslim women" which aims at creating awareness among Muslim women in India about their legal and constitutional rights and the changes introduced by various Islamic countries in the *Shariat*.[75]

Muslim women's right to inheritance and maintenance under the personal law is restricted and so also her right of custody and guardianship over her children. The Guardians and Wards Act, 1890 and the maintenance provisions under the Code of Criminal Procedure, 1898 as amended in 1973 are the redeeming factors since these laws are secular and apply to all, irrespective of caste, creed and religion. Before 1949, a wife claiming maintenance under the provisions of the Cr. P.C. had either to put up with a co-wife or forfeit maintenance but, realizing the agony in such cases, the legislature made an amendment in that year which entitles a wife, whose husband remarries, to live separately and seek maintenance. In other words, marrying another woman is a reasonable ground for a wife to live separately, the personal law notwithstanding.

Another aspect is a divorced Muslim wife's right to maintenance beyond the period of *iddat*. The Supreme Court declared in *Mohammed Ahmad Khan* vs. *Shah Bano Begum*, AIR 1985 SC 945 (known as *Shah Bano* case) that a Muslim husband having sufficient means must provide maintenance to his divorced wife, aged 62, who had nothing to support herself and her children beyond the *iddat* period under Section 125 of the Criminal Procedure Code and also asked the Government to implement the directive enunciated in Article 44 of the Constitution. The debate over the Supreme Court verdict in the

Shah Bano case is unprecedented. In the context of this judgement of the Supreme Court, some Muslim leaders are now demanding either for scrapping of Article 44 by amending the Constitution or for keeping the Muslim Personal Laws outside the ambit of this Article. The fundamentalists decried it as interference in their religion and personal law and the liberals hailed it as conforming to the secular provisions meant to prevent destitution and vagrancy.

Following the Shah Bano judgement, the Muslim psyche was exploited by a section of fundamentalist forces to launch an agitation which swept the entire Muslim community. This provision in the Constitution gave an opportunity to the fundamentalists to consolidate their hold over the Muslim masses once again and to unite them raising such touchy issues like 'Islam in danger, Muslim identity in danger' etc. They built up such a movement throughout India that the Government had to enact Muslim Women (Protection of Rights on Divorce) Act in May, 1986. How far this Act protects the rights of the Divorcee Muslim Women is a thing to be pondered over. But it remains a fact that an Act had to be enacted to tide over a situation which was taking the country to a communal outburst. And all these things happened owing to the existence of this provision in the Constitution.

According to Section 3 of this Act, the liability of a Muslim husband to pay maintenance to his divorced wife is limited to the *iddat* period, i.e. three lunar months from the date of formal divorce. The liability to maintain such woman thereafter rests on other relatives or the Wakf Board. Notwithstanding such a provision in Section 3 of this Act, many High Courts have granted maintenance to the divorced wife even after the *iddat* period. For instance, the Allahabad High Court had ordered in 1993 payment of maintenance allowance to a divorced Muslim woman till she remarries.[76] The Punjab and Haryana High Court ruled in 1997 that the husband is bound to pay alimony to his divorced wife even after the expiry of *iddat*.[77] The Bombay High Court also ruled in 2000 that a divorced woman was entitled to alimony even beyond the stipulated *iddat* period.[78] These rulings, based on the provisions of 125 Cr. P.C. should take care of the woman's life-time needs.

A Division Bench of the Supreme Court comprising Justices A.S. Anand and K. Venkataswami ruled in 1997 that the children of Muslim parents are entitled to claim maintenance from their father under Section 125 of the Criminal Procedure Code. They can claim maintenance for the entire period till they attain majority and in the case of females, till they get married. This right cannot be taken away on the basis of the Muslim Women (Protection of Rights on Divorce) Act, 1986. It was held that under Personal Law and the Criminal Procedure Code, a Muslim father's obligation to maintain his children till they attain adulthood is absolute even when the children are living with the divorced wife. Under Section 125 of the Cr. P.C. maintenance of children is obligatory on the father (irrespective of his religion) and as long as he is in a position to do so. Children have no independent means of their own. It remains his absolute obligation to provide for them. The Court held that provisions of the Muslim Women Act which entitles a divorced Muslim woman to claim maintenance from her previous husband for her children for two years from the date of birth of the child concerned does not prevent the minors from claiming separate maintenance from their father under Section 125 Cr. P.C.[79]

A Bench of Justices Dipak Misra and Vikramjit Sen of the Supreme Court on April 16, 2014 quoting an earlier Constitution Bench verdict said: "A Muslim husband is liable to make a reasonable and fair provision for the future of the divorced wife which obviously includes her maintenance as well. Such a reasonable and fair provision extending beyond the *iddat* period must be made by the husband within the *iddat* period. His liability arising from Section 3 of the Muslim Women (Protection of Rights on Divorce) Act to pay maintenance is not confined to the *iddat* period".[80]

VI

Child marriage is another area which requires intervention. This form of marriage is a common practice in many countries around the world. In 2007, two and a half crore girls were married off before they attained the age of 18. Child marriage is especially prevalent in India, Pakistan and Nepal. More than one-third of world's child brides live in India. Child marriage is steeper in rural areas as compared to the urban areas. Rural India witnessed an 'incidence rate' of child marriage that stands at an alarming 58.5 per cent when compared to urban average of 27.9 per cent. It exceeded 50 per cent in eight States of West Bengal, Bihar, Uttar Pradesh, Madhya Pradesh, Rajasthan, Chhattisgarh, Jharkhand and Andhra Pradesh. The phenomenon of child marriage can be attributed to a variety of reasons. The chief amongst these reasons are poverty and culture, tradition and values based on patriarchal norms. Child marriage affects both boys and girls, but statistics show that girls are far more likely to be forced into a child marriage than the boys.

While the mean age for marriage of girls in the country has improved from 19.3 years in 1990 to 21.0 years in 2010 as per the National Family Health Survey 2005-06 (NFHS-3), 47.3 per cent of all young women aged 20-24 were married by age 18, while 16 per cent of men in the age group of 20-49 were married by age 18. The issue is steeped in several multi-dimensional social, economic, cultural, community related aspects which make the prevention of child marriage a challenge to the society.

Many consider child marriage to be a human rights violation, resulting in death, health problems, poverty, violence, child abuse and lack of education. The Prevention of Child Marriage Act (PCMA), 2006 has repealed the Child

Marriage Restraint Act, 1929. The emphasis is on prevention rather than on restraining child marriage. Age of marriage is 21 for boys and 18 for girls. Any marriage of persons below this age is child marriage which is illegal, an offence and punishable under law. The penalty for facilitating child marriage is rigorous imprisonment up to two years and/or a fine up to one lakh rupees. The 205th report of the 18th Law Commission submitted on 5th February, 2008 has recommended certain amendments to this Act.

There is very low registration of cases against child marriage. The National Crime Record Bureau shows that only 60 cases were registered in 2010 for violation of the PCMA Act whereas the average marriage age in sample survey depicts a completely different scenario. The problem of under-reporting of cases was coming up mainly due to the social sanction given to the child marriage; also it was observed that public prosecutors are not keen to take up cases of child marriage, in most cases punishment is not given by the judiciary and the decision to annul marriage lies with the girl after attaining 18 years. Also, due to connivance of family and community, there is lack of strong evidence base in majority of cases, which weakens the case leading to state enforcement officials and non-government organizations facing difficulty in prosecuting families involved in child marriage, according to the Delhi State Legislative Authority (DLSA) member secretary.[81]

Now-a-days, many girls including Muslims girls approach the local administration including police to intervene to prevent such marriages. Due to such interventions many such marriages have been prevented. Muslim girls are, however, at a disadvantage compared to the girls of other communities in this respect. In a recent incident in the district of Perambalur in Tamil Nadu the marriage of a 17-year old Muslim girl was prevented under the instructions of the local District Magistrate Dr. Darez Ahamed. The Federation of Tamil Nadu Muslim Organizations and some political parties protested against such intervention arguing that under the *Shariat* a Muslim girl on attaining puberty can be given in marriage. Generally, 15 years has been taken as the limit. In the instant case the girl was 17 years old. So the district administration cannot interfere in such a marriage.[82]

The Gujarat High Court on December 2, 2014 has upheld the marriage of a minor Muslim girl observing that "according to the personal law of the Muslims, the girl no sooner she attains puberty or completes 15 years of age, whichever is earlier, is competent to get married."[83]

It is a fact that Section 2(vii) of the Dissolution of Muslim Marriages Act, 1939 says that the marriage of a Muslim girl will stand dissolved when "she having been given in marriage by her father or other guardian before she attained the age of 15 years, repudiated the marriage before attaining the age of 18 years, provided that the marriage has not been consummated." In other words, the outdated law presumes that Muslim girls on reaching the age of 15 become legally informed and competent to enter into marital alliances on their own. And Islam is invoked to give legitimacy to such an indefensible supposition. But quoting scriptural evidence A. Faizur Rahman argues that there exists a strong case to delegitimise child marriages and fix 18 as the age of marriage for Muslim girls, thereby bringing Muslim personal law in conformity with the *Quran* and the teachings of the Prophet.[84] When will it happen!

The National Commission for Women and its Delhi Chapter filed a petition before the Supreme Court seeking the formulation of a uniform marriageable age, because different stipulations in as many statutes had created confusion. While hearing this petition, a Division Bench of the Supreme Court comprising Justices Dalveer Bhandari and A.K. Ganguly again pulled up the government for its failure to overhaul the personal laws of minority communities, saying it was a reflection on its secular credentials. The court also said the government's attempts to reform personal laws don't go beyond Hindus, who have been more tolerant of such initiatives. The Bench observed on February 8, 2011: "The Hindu community has been tolerant to these statutory interventions. But there appears a lack of secular commitment as it has not happened for other religions."[85]

In the recent *Mrs. Tahra Begum* vs. *State of Delhi and Ors*[86] the Delhi High Court held that a Muslim minor girl could marry in accordance with the principle of the "Option of Puberty" or *Khiyar-ul-bulugh*. However, in accordance with this very principle, the minor girl may also choose to repudiate the marriage upon attaining majority. In this case, the minor girl clearly expressed her choice to reside with her husband and the court held her agency and choice, over age and minority status. This case has revived the debate about the interplay between the Child Marriage Act, 2006, and the various personal laws.[87]

A Full Bench of the Delhi High Court consisting of acting Chief Justice A.K. Sikri, and Justices Sanjiv Khanna and V.K. Shali held on July 27, 2012:

> The Child Marriage Act is a secular law which specifically deals with the problem of child marriage. Religion of the contracting party does not matter. Being a "special Act" and being a subsequent legislation will override the provisions of the HMA Act (The Hindu Marriage Act, 1955) or for that matter any personal law.[88]

However, inconsistency between different personal laws regarding the legally permissible age at marriage, the option of puberty in personal laws, and judicial computation of the age of discretion, inhibits implementation of the Child Marriage Act, 2006.

On February 14, 2006, the Supreme Court directed the State Governments and the Central Government that marriages of all persons who are citizens of India belonging to various religious denominations should be made compulsorily registerable in their respective States where such marriages are solemnized and *inter alia* directing that as and when the Central Government enacts a comprehensive statute, the same shall be placed before that Court for scrutiny.[89]

A Division Bench of the Kerala High Court consisting of Justices Kurian Joseph and Harun-ul-Rashid asked the Centre in October 2008 to deliberate upon legislation for setting up regulatory bodies at the central and regional levels to control and supervise Muslim marriages and divorces in order to protect Muslim society and women from "indiscrete marriage and divorce".[90]

The Committee on Empowerment of Women (2006-07) in its Twelfth Report (Fourteenth Lok Sabha) on "Plight of Indian Women deserted by Indian husbands" has viewed that all marriages, irrespective of religion should be compulsorily registered and desired that the Government to make registration of all marriages mandatory, making the procedure simpler, affordable and accessible.

The 18th Law Commission of India in its 205th Report titled "Proposal to Amend the Prohibition of Child Marriage Act, 2006 and Other Allied Laws" *vide* paragraph (iv) recommended that "registration of marriages within a stipulated period, of all the communities, *viz*. Hindu, Muslim, Christians, etc. should be made mandatory by the Government".

The 18th Law Commission of India further in its 211th Report titled "Laws on Registration of Marriage and Divorce—A Proposal for Consolidation and Reform", submitted to the Centre in 2008 has recommended the enactment of a "Marriage and Divorce Registration Act" to be made applicable to the whole of India and to all citizens irrespective of their religion and personal law and without any exception or exemption. "The law should deal only with registration of marriages and divorces and not with any substantive aspect now governed by various matrimonial laws—general and community-specific. Accordingly, the Births, Deaths and Marriages Registration Act, 1886 be repealed and Births and Deaths Registration Act, 1969 be re-named as "Births, Deaths and Marriages Registration Act with a provision that officials working and records maintained under the former Act shall be deemed to be working and maintained under the latter Act."

The Commission, which took up this issue *suo motu*, said: "In very few States all marriages, irrespective of the law under which these may have been solemnized, have to be compulsorily registered. The majority of States have not enacted any general law on marriage registration applicable to all communities. In those States where there are laws for compulsory registration of all marriages, such laws are faulty and ineffective. This creates a lot of confusion with registration officials as well as people wanting or required to register their marriages. Under the Constitution, family matters are in the concurrent jurisdiction of the Centre and States. Parliamentary legislation on compulsory registration of marriages is, therefore, not only possible but also highly desirable. This will bring country-wide uniformity in the substantive law relating to marriage registration and will be helpful in effectively achieving the desired goal. Rules under the proposed Act may be made by the State governments, and this will take care of the local social variations. Similarly, for registration of divorces, the laws which provide for any kind of registration of divorce are that of Muslims and Parsis. All other marriage registration laws do not provide for registration of divorces although it is a socially beneficial proposition. Registration of out-of-court divorces among the Hindus, the Buddhists, the Jains and the Sikhs—which the Hindu Marriage Act, 1955 recognises—is extremely desirable. In the Muslim society, there is a system of private registration of marriages by the *kazis*, which needs to be streamlined and linked with registration of marriage with State Registry. Absence of registration of divorces in a community whose personal law allows out-of-court divorce leaves abundant room for misuse of law and often causes great hardship to women."

The Commission also said: "There is a great inhibition against marriage registration which needs to be effectively removed. Advantages of registration of marriage and disadvantages of non-registration are not specified in any law or policy document and therefore there is little clarity in the mind of the people in this respect. The proposed law should also provide that no judicial relief will be granted in a disputed matter if the concerned marriage or divorce is not duly registered under its provisions".[91]

The Union Cabinet in April 2012 approved amendment to the Registration of Births and Deaths Act, 1969 to include registration of marriages under the purview of this law. The Bill defines marriage to include marriage solemnized between a male and female belonging to any caste or religion. It also includes re-marriage. The Bill requires that all marriages (irrespective of religion) shall be registered either under the Act or the Anand Marriage Act, 1909 or any other existing law (including state laws). Marriages registered under the Anand Marriage Act, state laws or any other existing laws are not required to be registered under the Bill. The Bill prescribes a penalty of Rs 50 in case of (a) non-registration of marriage without a reasonable cause; (b) providing false information regarding the registration of marriage; and (c) refusal to furnish certain information such as name and address.

The Registration of Births and Deaths (Amendment) Bill, 2012 was introduced in Rajya Sabha on May 7, 2012 by Salman Khurshid, Minister of Law and Justice. The Bill was referred to the Standing Committee on Personnel, Public Grievances, Law and Justice on May 9, 2012. Rajya Sabha passed the said Bill on August 13, 2013. The Bill could not reach the Lok Sabha for consideration and passage and has lapsed following the dissolution of the lower house on February 21, 2014. In a written reply, Law Minister Ravi Shankar Prasad informed the Lok Sabha on July 21, 2014 that the government was initiating steps to introduce a bill afresh for making registration of marriages compulsory.

As and when such an Act is enacted it will be beneficial to women, protecting them from unnecessary harassment in matrimonial and maintenance cases. It will also provide evidentiary value in matters of custody of children, right of children born from wedlock of two persons whose marriage is registered and the age of the parties to the marriage.[92]

VII

In the courts of law, the story that unfolded after the enactment of the Muslim Personal Law (*Shariat*) Application Act, 1937 and the Dissolution of Muslim Marriages Act, 1939 (DMMA) was a complex one. The gaps and ambiguity left in the 1937 Act were sought to be filled by the courts through an interpretation of the received tradition. This included Anglo-Mohammedan law, rulings of the British Indian courts and a large body of un-codified Muslim law drawing from the holy *Quran*, *Hadith* and *fiqh*. In the early decades, such judge-made law for adjudicating case under these two acts helped define its scope, interpret the provisions and boundaries or criss-crossing that can be made between this law and secular laws regarding marriage.

Tahir Mahmood points out that a similar evolution of these two laws continued after independence when a host of State and Central legislations were enacted from 1948 until 1986. "During the life of 46 years the Supreme Court of India has decided about 50 cases involving questions of Islamic law. The number of various High Court rulings reported since 1947 is about six hundred... The High Court rulings of 1947-1986 have covered the entire gamut of Islamic religious and personal laws. There have been important decisions regarding religious beliefs of particular groups (Ahmadiyas, Bohra, Khojas, Mewatis), religious practices (*namaz*, *pardah*, growing a beard, *dargah* rituals), religious instructions (mosques, shrines, graveyards), religious functionaries (*imams*, *sajjadnashins*, *qazis*), scope of Muslim law (statutory, traditions), matrimonial and family relations, property and succession, pre-emption and *wakf* law and administration."[93] Muslim women litigated not only for their costmary rights over wakf properties, often seeking exemptions from the 1939 DMMA, but also to secure their right to divorce, of maintenance in marriage and, after *talaq*, for child custody, etc. Until 1960, it appears that litigation was mostly around divorce. Muslim women sought divorce under the DMMA, citing lack of maintenance or delay in payment of *mehr* (marriage gift), forcing the courts to adjudicate the claims of those Muslim women who had divorced themselves through customary forms that did not feature in DMMA. In the

1960s, the litigation shifted to maintenance after the *talaq* where the courts debated whether Section 488 in Cr. P.C. applied to Muslim women.[94] The 1970s saw a surge in judicial "activism" around triple *talaq*, maintenance and *mehr* through innovative interpretation.[95] Continuing the received tradition, many judges continued to grant Muslim women maintenance under the ambit of the newly introduced Section 125 of the Cr. P.C.

For instance, in *Bai Tahira*, the Supreme Court unanimously held in 1979 that irrespective of the amount named in the marriage contract as *mehr*, a reasonable amount was due to the woman. Until this amount was discharged, the divorced woman would continue to be entitled to maintenance under Section 125 of the Cr. P.C.[96]

Next year, in 1980, in *Fazlunbi* vs. *Kadher Vali*, the Supreme Court commented: "The liquidated sum paid at the time of divorce must be a reasonable and not an illusory amount and will release the quondam husband from the continuing liability, only if the sum paid is realistically sufficient to maintain the ex-wife and salvage her from destitution which is the anathema of the law."[97]

"Family law is undoubtedly most important among the civil laws. Conscious of its primacy, Islam had prescribed a law based on right principles, and Muslims had received a family code that was useful, complete and comprehensive...but unfortunately this law became victim of 'Mohammedan Law' (Muslim Personal Law) and has become so distorted that now there exists a remote resemblance between the two. The law as applicable in the name of *Shariat* is neither useful nor comprehensive. In fact, no other law has so adversely affected the social life of Muslims. Today, there should be hardly any Muslim family among whose members someone's life has not been ruined by this pernicious law."[98] This scathing attack on the Muslim Personal Law was not penned by any modern, liberal thinker but by Maulana Maudoodi, the founder of Jamaat-e-Islami, whose members in India are ardent votaries of the impugned law.

The All India Muslim Personal Law Board, a body comprising almost all the groups and sects of the Muslims, was formed in December 1972 in response to the government's move to enact a uniform civil code. Its objective is to ensure that the Muslim Personal Laws are not affected due to Article 44 of the Constitution. The Board was so long building up public opinion in this country to create pressure on the Central Government for exemption of the Muslim Personal Laws from the ambit of Article 44. The launching of an agitation to keep the Muslim Personal Laws outside the purview of Article 44 has, of late, attracted the attention of a considerable number of persons to this Article.[99]

Although the AIMPLB has no legal status, it is widely recognized as the body to deal with questions of Muslim personal law. It was thought that the AIMPLB would play a distinct role in ushering in reform in the personal law of the Muslims. It promised to prepare a model *nikaahnama* (marriage contract*)* and drafted one some time in September 2000[100] calling for an abolition of triple *talaq*, but the document ended up by tamely suggesting that men should not resort to '*talaq-e-bidah*' unless inevitable.[101] Its energy is frittered away in balancing the conflicting interests and view points of the groups and interests—Shia, Sunni, Bohra, Mahdavi, Bareilvi, Deobandis, Ahle-Hadis, Hanafi, Shafi, in addition to political outfits, religious organizations and schools of learning—in a board of 201 members. Its failure to bring about any reform has eroded its power base. Its undisputed supremacy is being challenged by the creation in 2005 of two other Muslim personal law boards, one by the Shias and the other by the Bareilvi sect.[102]

The All India Shia Personal Law Board has prepared a model *nikaah-nama* which gives Shia Muslim women the right to divorce their husbands.[103]

The All India Muslim Women's Personal Law Board (AIMWPLB) was also formed in 2005 to focus on Muslim women's issues like marriage, divorce and other legal rights. It released on March 16, 2008 a 12-page model "*Shariat Nikaahnama*" which sought to address the problems being faced by Muslim women in respect of marriage and divorce. Quite predictably, the AIMPLB has questioned the very right of the women to draft such a *nikaahnama.*[104] The Bharatiya Muslim Mahila Andolan (BMMA), a Muslim women advocacy group, has gone one step further. Since the *Shariat* Application Act of 1937, the Dissolution of Muslim Marriage Act of 1939 and the Muslim Women (Protection of Rights on Divorce) Act of 1986—the three Acts forming Sharia law in India—are all men-centric, the BMMA has released in 2014 a draft document for the codification of Muslim Personal Law. Called the Muslim Marriage and Divorce Act, this law, if enacted, will abolish polygamy and unilateral and orally-rendered divorces, make registration of marriages mandatory and fix minimum age for the bride and the groom.[105]

Pandit Jawaharlal Nehru, while defending the introduction of the Hindu Code Bill instead of a uniform civil code, in Parliament in 1954, said, "I do not think that the time is ripe in India for me to try to push it through". It appears that even 60 years thereafter the rulers of the day are not in a mood to retrieve Article 44 from the cold storage where it is lying since 1949. Successive governments have feared that the introduction of a uniform civil code will enrage the minorities, particularly the Muslims whose way of life is wholly regulated by the Muslim Personal Law as enshrined in the *Shariat*. Within the community, marriage, divorce, inheritance, personal relationships etc. are determined by their own laws. It is feared that any attempt to regulate them by a common civil code would be regarded as undue interference in their religious right and "imposing a uniform civil code would exacerbate minority insecurities".[106]

But this is a gross mistake. While religion deals with the relationship between God and man, the legal system determines the relationship between man and man. There may be different religions, but the civil law must be the same and uniform. The *Shariat* can regulate the religious affairs of the Muslims, but marriage, divorce, inheritance, conjugal relations etc., are social factors and, consequently, they must come under a common law.

Moreover, while Turkey, Egypt, Syria, Tunisia, Morocco, Iraq, Malaysia, Indonesia and Jordon have modified their laws through a liberal interpretation of the Personal Law based on the *Shariat*[107], vested interests, certain political leaders and Muslim theologians have brought about a sort of communal crisis in India. Guided by fundamentalism and obscurantism, they have not only opposed Article 44, but the AIMPLB have formally sprung the demand on January 31, 2006[108] for abolition of the provision of the uniform civil code enshrined in Article 44 of the Constitution. In the process, the very task of national integration was thwarted. Way back in 1948, K.M. Munshi had told the Constituent Assembly:

> When you want to consolidate a community, you have to take into consideration the benefit which may accrue to the whole community and not to the customs of a part of it. If you look at the countries in Europe, which have a Civil Code, everyone who goes there from any part of the world and every minority has to submit to the Civil Code It is not felt to be tyrannical to the minority.[109]

The polity is divided on the question of a uniform civil code. The fundamentalist, Muslim clerics and theologians, the Muslim political leaders, the political parties who claim to be secular but pander to the vote-bank politics are, generally, against the uniform civil code. Social activists, women organizations and the right wing political parties like the BJP are in favour of a uniform civil code, though for different reasons. The CPI document indicates need for uniform civil code.[110] Social activist and actress Shabna Azmi, MP called for a Common Civil Code based on gender justice.[111]

The Committee on the Status of Women in India in its report submitted on December 31, 1973 to the Minister for Education and Social Welfare while recommending expeditious implementation of the constitutional directive by the adoption of a Uniform Civil Code, pointed out that "the absence of a Uniform Civil Code in the last quarter of the twentieth century, 27 years after independence, is an incongruity that cannot be justified with all the emphasis that is placed on secularism, science and modernisation. The continuance of various personal laws which accept discrimination between men and women violate the fundamental rights, and the Preamble to the Constitution which promises to secure to all citizens "equality of status and is against the spirit of national integration and secularism."[112] On

September 30, 2014 Press Council of India chief, Justice (Retired) Markandey Katju, while extending his support to the imposition of a uniform civil code described the Muslim personal law as "barbaric, backward and unjust...it is a feudal law. All countries in the world have one law...why shouldn't we? I support the uniform civil code."[113]

The then Kerala Chief Minister, A.K. Antony, was of the view that until and unless the minority communities expressed themselves in favour of a uniform code it was not proper to continue to pursue the matter.[114] According to the Prince of Arcot, Mohammed Abdul Ali, the campaign in favour of a Uniform Civil Code is only an attempt to create a political issue, gather votes for power and browbeat the minorities.[115]

It would, however, be a mistake to think that all Muslims or Muslim leaders are against a uniform civil code. There are many Muslim leaders and thinkers who want a uniform civil code. Take for instance, Arif Mohammad Khan, who resigned from the Rajiv Gandhi cabinet in 1986 in protest against the decision of the government to overturn the Supreme Court's judgement in the *Shah Bano maintenance* case by enacting the Muslim Women (Protection of Rights on Divorce) Act, 1986. M.C. Chagla had lamented:

> Government has refused to do anything about it (a uniform civil code) on the plea that the minorities will resent any attempt at imposition. Unless they are agreeable it would not be fair and proper to make the law applicable to them. I wholly and emphatically disagree with this view. The Constitution is binding on everyone, majority and minority; and if the Constitution contains a directive, that directive must be accepted and implemented. Jawaharlal showed great strength and courage in getting the Hindu Reform Bill passed, but he accepted the policy of *laissez faire* where the Muslims and other minorities were concerned. I am horrified to find that in my country, while monogamy has been made the law for Hindus, Muslims can still indulge in the luxury of polygamy. It is an insult to womanhood; and Muslim women, I know, resent this discrimination between Muslim women and Hindu women.[116]

Unfortunately, Chagla was not the leader of Indian Muslims. Muslim leadership has been occasionally politically progressive but always socially conservative. "And yet Muslims", as Hossainur Rahman says, "are realizing that they need social modernization, not religious fundamentalism. They need managers, teachers, scholars, and technicians, not Mawlanas, Maulvis and *Madrasahs*. Only social mobility and a modern outlook towards marriage, family planning, women and children can save Muslims. Social backwardness and "ghettoisation" are killing the Muslim community. A Uniform Civil Code, if enacted, will give them a breather."[117]

Significantly, Chief Justice Y.V. Chandrachud quoted approvingly a passage from *Muslim Personal Law* authored by Dr. Tahir Mahmood, a famous scholar and an expert on Muslim law: "Instead of wasting their energies in exerting theological pressure in order to secure an immunity for their personal law from the state's legislative jurisdiction, the Muslims will do well to begin exploring how the true Islamic laws, passed off their time-worn interpretations, can enrich the Common Civil Code in India." This is an invaluable piece of advice, which needs wide acceptance.

Tahir Mahmood has suggested an Indian code of Muslim law:

> An Indian code of Muslim law based on an eclectic selection of principles from the various schools of *Shariat* is the ideal solution to all the contemporary problems of Muslim law. Such codes have already been enacted in many Muslim countries. Among the non-Muslim nations while the Philippines enacted a code of Muslim law long ago, South Africa is now preparing one, notably with the help of some Indian scholars. A similar exercise could well be taken up in India too.
>
> In the absence of a proper code Muslim law is suffering from all sorts of ailments. The multiplicity of juristic opinion within Islam, the insistence of various Muslim groups of our age to strictly adhere to particular juristic opinions of ancient times, freedom of every Tom, Dick and Harry today to 'interpret' the religious law and, above all, the self-assumed obligation of people in general to 'enforce' its dictates as understood by them, have altogether turned the Muslim law into a babel.[118]

The Supreme Court of India has time and again turned the spotlight on the issue of evolving a uniform or common civil code. It has regretted that Article 44 of the Constitution has not been given effect to by Parliament.

> In *Mohammmed Ahmad Khan* vs. *Shah Bano Begum*, AIR 1985 SC 945 (known as *Shah Bano case*) Chief Justice Y.V. Chandrachud asserted that "a common civil code will help the cause of national integration by removing disparate loyalties to laws which have conflicting ideologies... There is no justification whatsoever in delaying indefinitely the introduction of a uniform personal law in the country."[119]
>
> In *Ms. Jorden Diengedh* vs. *S.S. Chopra*, AIR 1985 SC 934, Justice O. Chinappa Reddy observed that "surely the time has now come for a complete reform of the law of marriage and make a uniform law applicable to all people irrespective of religion or caste...We suggest the time has come for the intervention of the legislature in these matters to provide for a uniform code of marriage and divorce."[120]

After the judgement of *Shah Bano* case there was some unrest in the Muslim community. So, in consequence of that the Muslim Women (Protection of Rights on Divorce) Act, 1986 was passed which states that the husband is liable to pay maintenance to the wife during *iddat*. But this controversy was resolved by the Hon'ble Supreme Court in *Daniel Latifi*. A Five-Judge Bench of the SC while upholding the validity of the Act held:

> A Muslim husband is liable to make reasonable and fair provision for the future of the divorced wife which obviously includes her maintenance as well. Such a reasonable and fair provision extending beyond the *iddat* period must be made by the husband within the *iddat* period in terms of Section 3(1)(a) of the Act. Liability of Muslim husband to his divorced wife arising under Section 3(1)(a) of the Act to pay maintenance is not confined to iddat period. A divorced Muslim woman who has not remarried and who is not able to maintain herself after iddat period can proceed as provided under Section 4 of the Act against her relatives who are liable to maintain her in proportion to the properties which they inherit on her death according to Muslim law from such divorced woman including her children and parents. If any of the relatives being unable to pay maintenance, the Magistrate may direct the State Wakf Board established under the Act to pay such maintenance.[121]

The *Shah Bano* controversy renewed the debate over personal laws: whether they should be retained or be replaced by a Uniform Civil Code. A decade after *Shah Bano* Justices Kuldip Singh and R.M. Sahai of the Supreme Court in *Sarla Mudgal* vs. *Union of India*, AIR 1995 SC 1531 exhorted the then Government of P.V. Narasimha Rao to take a "fresh look" at Article 44, rebuking in the process "successive governments" for being "wholly remiss in their duty of implementing the constitutional mandate".

In the *Sarala Mudgal* case there were two questions for consideration. First, whether a Hindu husband married under Hindu law could solemnize a second marriage by embracing Islam. Second, whether such a marriage is valid, given that the first marriage was not dissolved under law and the first wife continues to be a Hindu. The Bench held that "the second marriage of a Hindu husband after conversion to Islam without having his first marriage dissolved under law would be invalid." Going beyond the issues, Justice Kuldip Singh added: "Till the time we achieve the goal—a uniform civil code for all the citizens of India—there is an open inducement to a Hindu husband, who wants to enter a second marriage while the first marriage is subsisting, to become a Muslim." He further asserted that implementation of a uniform civil code would not violate the freedom of religion guaranteed under Articles 25 and 26.

Eight years later in *John Vallamattom* a Division Bench of the Supreme Court consisting of Chief Justice of India V.N. Khare, Justice S.B. Sinha and Justice A.R. Lakshmanan said in 2003 that while Article 25 of the Constitution guaranteed freedom of conscience and free profession, practice and propagation of religion, Article 44 divested religion from social relations and the personal law. The Bench observed:

> It is no matter of doubt that marriage, succession and the like matter of a secular character cannot be brought within the guarantee enshrined under Articles 25 and 26 of the Constitution. Any legislation which brings succession and the like matters of secular character within the ambit of Articles 25 and 26 is a suspect legislation, although it is doubtful whether the American doctrine of suspect legislation is followed in this country. In *Sarala Mudgal* vs. *Union of India* [(1995) 3 SCC 635] it was held that marriage, succession and like matters of secular character cannot be brought within the guarantee enshrined under Articles 25 and 26 of the Constitution. It is a matter of regret that Article 44 of the Constitution has not been given effect to. Parliament is still to step in for framing a common civil code in the country. A common civil code will help the cause of national integration by removing the contradictions based on ideologies.[122]

Again, indirectly pushing for the Constitution-suggested Uniform Civil Code, a bench of Chief Justice P. Sathasivam, and Justices Ranjan Gogoi and Shiv Kirti Singh, ruled on February 19, 2014 that Muslim personal law or any other religious code could not prohibit adoption by childless couples as such a right is vested in every Indian under the Juvenile Justice (Care and Protection of Children) Act, 2000. The bench also said that till a Uniform Civil Code, enunciated by Article 44 of the Constitution, was enacted, the JJ Act would apply to all in the country irrespective of religious denominations. "The (JJ) Act is a small step in reaching the goal enshrined by Article 44 of the Constitution. Personal beliefs and faiths, though (they) must be honoured, cannot dictate the operation of the provisions of an enabling statute", the judgment said.[123]

Significantly, though the Supreme Court have stressed on a number of occasions the importance of enacting a uniform civil code as envisaged in the Constitution, it has refused to move beyond its stated stand and did not issue a directive to enact such a law. A Bench of Chief Justice K.G. Balakrishnan and Justice P. Sathasivam of the Supreme Court, while disposing of a PIL which sought a direction on the Centre and the Prime Minister to initiate legislative steps to enact a uniform civil code said on October 17, 2008:

> Neither the Supreme Court nor the Prime Minister can do anything in this matter. We cannot direct Parliament to enact a law. Moreover,

the PM also cannot direct Parliament, which alone will decide which law to enact.[124]

Under the Parsi Matrimonial and Divorce Act, 1936 Parsi chief matrimonial courts were set up by the British in the then presidential towns of Mumbai, Kolkata and Chennai. They could hear matrimonial and divorce cases involving Parsi couples. The courts had a jury system, where five delegates from the community would assist the judge, a high court judge. Many cases have been held up as all the delegates have not been able to meet together even twice a year. The matters at the special court in Bombay had come to a standstill since 2012 as there had been no session with delegates. While directing that evidence can be recorded by a commissioner and it was not mandatory in every case that it should be recorded only before a court with the delegates or a jury present, Justice Gautam Patel of the Bombay High Court said: "A procedural reform is not a matter of faith or religion. Achieving a fair and just result by and within law is no apostasy. No faith could possibly demand that its adherents be made to wait endlessly for their cases to be decided."[125]

The issue of a Uniform Civil Code has given rise to heated debates, controversies and unpleasant reactions several times. It touches the sensitivities of certain groups. This, however, is not to concede that the existing laws should remain untouched, All personal laws have their weak points and good points as well. An endeavour should be made to incorporate the good points under one system and strike down provisions which, on their very face, are harsh, antiquated and discriminatory. For instance, under the Parsi Marriage and Divorce Act, 1936 there is a clear provision against any Parsi contracting another marriage till he or she obtains a legal divorce under the Act, even if he or she changes his or her religion which permits remarriage. Such a provision should be included in all personal laws to stop misuse of religion for entering into bigamous marriages. Likewise grounds for matrimonial relief, divorce by mutual consent, provisions for alimony, equal property rights etc., should be in harmony with the present day social conditions. Personal laws which deny these to women of certain communities need to be reviewed. The Constitution clearly prohibits discrimination on grounds, *inter alia*, of religion. The existence of harsh laws for one set of women and liberal laws for another, conceding of certain rights to some women while denying them to another group simply on grounds of religion, is discriminatory.

What is needed is not an intrusion or invasion into any religious faith or feelings by imposing anything on an unwilling group but a reform within the framework of their already existing system. It is not a question of thrusting a rule of Hindu Law or Parsi Law or any other law on any other religious group but, as Kusum says, "of weeding out provisions which do not fit well in the changed social and legal scenario".[126] As Krishna Iyer says, value-based progressive changes, preserving the separate identity of each religious group, is a feasible project avoiding insult and injury to any minority. This may be a preliminary step to pave the way for a common code.[127]

What is often missed in the bitter polemic is that, as V.R. Krishna Iyer says, a uniform civil code does not mean that the Hindu law would be forced down the throat of other communities. Indeed, a progressive legislation eclectic in character and facultative in operation to begin with, picking the best from every system of family law consistent with the ethos of Indian humanity, may well be different from Hindu law or Christian law or Islamic law and may contain portions of these laws. Moreover, we live in an era where discrimination against women is resisted by people everywhere. One need not violate Islamic law or Hindu scriptures and may even make piecemeal legislation which may be optionally left open for communities to adopt. Human rights are paramount and are accepted in the various instruments emanating from the United Nations. Therefore, we cannot wish them away. At the same time, Indian unity should not be imperiled by rashly inflicting upon an unwilling community a measure unacceptable to them.[128]

We have seen already what was the idea behind a uniform civil code and what the Members of the Constituent Assembly had said on this issue. The idea of a Uniform Civil Code was first mooted by M.R. Masani on March 28, 1947 and he along with Rajkumari Amrit Kaur and Smt. Hansa Mehta had urged that a Uniform Civil Code should be guaranteed to the Indian people within a period of five or 10 years.[129] But that did not happen.

It is not only distinguished Indians who have urged the enactment of a uniform civil code for the country. Even the United Nations has exhorted us to do that. That was made clear to an Indian delegation's presentation to the international body's Convention on Elimination of All Discrimination against Women. The following were dinned into us by CEDAW:

> The tendency to leave reform to communities could become a sanction for keeping things the way they are. This is not only incompatible with the rights of women but represents a breach of principles of the Convention ratified by India in June 1993.
> India should go ahead and enact a secular family law while allowing various communities the choice of whether they wish to be ruled by it or not.
> India should take a cue from Islamic nations like Bangladesh which have introduced wide-ranging reforms in family law.[130]

Shimon Shetreet, director, Sacher Institute of Comparative Law, Hebrew University, Jerusalem and Hiram E. Chodosh, dean, S.J. Quinney College of Law, University of Utah, who had conducted research on the uniform civil code in India, said that the 'polarizing and politicized' issue of drawing up a

Uniform Civil Code, which is essential to guarantee minimum rights to all individuals, can be resolved by a gradual process of mediation.[131]

An idea, however, gained currency that a uniform civil code would come only when the minority communities agree to it. In the *Shah Bano* case cited earlier, Chief Justice Y.V. Chandrachud had stated as follows:

> A belief seems to have gained ground that it is for the Muslims to take a lead in the matter of reforms of their personal law. No community is likely to bell the cat by making gratuitous concessions on this issue. It is the state which is charged with the duty of securing a Uniform Civil Code for the citizens of the country and, unquestionably, it has the legislative competence to do so. A counsel in the case whispered, somewhat audibly, that legislative competence is one thing, the political courage to use that competence is quite another. We understand the difficulties involved in bringing persons of different faiths and persuasions on a common platform. But a beginning has to be made if the Constitution is to have any meaning.
>
> It would have certainly been healthy for all if a uniform secular civil code were formulated for all and made binding on all. But, with communal passions being as they are in this country and tension being a part of the political and social syndrome, an endeavour to secure such a uniform civil code may be fraught with risky consequences. After all, it is not the intention to interfere in ritual matters of any community. What is aimed at is to codify the family laws in such a manner that the best elements from all of them are included in it. It is not the intention to impose the Hindu personal laws or for that matter any other personal laws on any other religious communities.

The Bhartiya Janata Party, a votary of Uniform Civil Code, in its 2014 Lok Sabha election manifesto, under heading Uniform Civil Code has said:

> Article 44 of the Constitution lists Uniform Civil Code as one of the Directive Principles of State Policy. BJP believes that there cannot be gender equality till such time India adopts a Uniform Civil Code which protects the rights of all women and the BJP reiterates its stand to draft a Uniform Civil Code drawing upon the best traditions and harmonizing them with modern times.[132]

Now, that the BJP has wrested power at the centre in the 2014 Lok Sabha elections with an absolute majority, it is to be seen how the BJP translates its election promise in the coming days. But the very propriety of the BJP's demand for a Uniform Civil Code was questioned in an editorial in the *Times of India*, "the biggest flaw in the case for it (Uniform Civil Code) is, well, that the case is being made by BJP and Sangh Parivar affiliates not known otherwise for their secularism. You can't advocate a Uniform Civil Code in one breath and Ram mandir in the next."[133] But if the political parties having secular pretensions are reticent to take up the cause for a Uniform Civil Code lest such a move will hurt its electoral prospects, some other political parties like the BJP will have to take up this cudgel in the interest of the nation as a whole.

It was hoped by the Founding Fathers of the Constitution that a time would come when a uniform law governing civil matters would come into operation without any resistance, little realizing that time would set into motion events that would compromise not just the state but completely vitiate the secular environment of the country. At the moment there is no reasonable prospect of a uniform civil code although literature on the subject is increasing in volume and militancy. There is no near prospect of the common code being enacted by Parliament since no political party or front, which has a chance of coming to power, is likely to take the risk of such a legislative project. The utmost that has been done is to codify the Hindu law in the form of the Hindu Marriage Act, 1955, the Hindu Succession Act, 1956, the Hindu Minority and Guardianship Act, 1956 and the Hindu Adoption and Maintenance Act, 1956 which have replaced traditional Hindu laws based on different schools of thought and scriptural laws into one unified one. As Justice Kuldip Singh of the Supreme Court has observed: "When more than 80 per cent of the citizens have already been brought under the codified personal law, there is no justification whatsoever to keep in abeyance any more, the introduction of uniform civil code for all citizens in the territory of India."[134]

Article 44 is based on the concept that there is no necessary connection between religion and personal law in a civilized society. Article 25 guarantees religious freedom whereas Article 44 seeks to divert religion from social relations and personal law. Muslim personal law was applied to Muslims in British India as a matter of policy. It was not administered as a matter of religion. Moreover days have changed. In India today the judge need not necessarily be a Muslim; apostasy and adultery are not punishable by death; the giving and taking interest by a Muslim is not illegal; the hand of a thief is not cut off; drinking wine and eating pork are not crimes; Muslims and non-Muslims can lawfully marry without changing their religion and their children are legitimate and have right of inheritance under the Special Marriage Act, 1954. The Supreme Court has permitted well known social activist Ms. Shabnam Hashmi to adopt a child even though Muslim Personal Law does not allow it nor the *Quran* explicitly prohibits adoption.[135] As very correctly pointed out by Prof. Hossainur Rahman, "Muslims, however religious in outlook, must realize that a society must be free to reconstruct or it cannot succeed in being secular."[136]

The Muslims, Hindus, Christians, Parsees, are all governed by different set of laws. The Hindu Marriage Act prohibits bigamy but Islamic law doesn't. Nevertheless, men tried to bypass the law and convert to Islam so that they could marry again. The *Sarala Mudgal* case arose because of the said lacuna. All of India's religious personal law systems suffer from "gross sex inequality".

In *Pannalal Bansilal Pitti* vs. *State of Andhra Pradesh*, the Supreme Court has observed:

> In a pluralist society like India in which people have faith in their respective religions, beliefs or tenets propounded by different religions or their offshoots, the founding fathers, while making the Constitution, were confronted with problems to unify and integrate people of India professing different religious faiths, born in different castes, sex or sub-sections in the society speaking different languages and dialects in different regions and provided secular Constitution to integrate all sections of the society as a united Bharat. The directive principles of the Constitution themselves visualize diversity and attempted to foster uniformity among people of different faiths. A uniform law, though is highly desirable, enactment thereof in one go perhaps may be counter-productive to unity and integrity of the nation. In a democracy governed by rule of law, gradual progressive change and order should be brought about. Making law or amendment to a law is a slow process and the legislature attempts to remedy where the need is felt most acute. It would, therefore, be inexpedient and incorrect to think that all laws have to be made uniformly applicable to all people in one go. The mischief or defect which is most acute can be remedied by process of law at stages.[137]

The Directive Principle of enacting a UCC has been urged by the Apex Court repeatedly in a number of judgements as a matter of urgency. They have not only advocated the need, but, as in the *Pannalal* case, even suggested a modality of doing the same.

Way back in 1948 Ambedkar had suggested that "the code shall apply only to those who make a declaration that they are prepared to be bound by it, so that in the initial stages the application of the code may be purely voluntary". The same method was adopted in 1937 in regard to the *Shariat* Act.

Inder Jit, an MP, in a signed article had informed that when on May 17, 1995 in his speech in the Lok Sabha he had recalled the above assurance of Dr. Ambedkar in the Constituent Assembly,

> the reaction of the members was heartening. Speaking immediately after me, Dr. Mumtaz Ansari, a senior Janata Dal leader from Bihar, said that "all Muslims will accept this, whatever has been pointed out...once it is voluntary...There cannot be any sort of arbitrary

imposition of this common civil code. If it is voluntary and if it is up to the Muslims or whoever that community may be...we do not have any objection". Many, including some other Muslim MPs present in the House, nodded approvingly. Later in the lobby some MPs were unanimous that "there can be no objection to a voluntary civil code". Goa already has a Common Civil Code.[138]

So, we have it on the authority of Inder Jit, a former MP, that the Muslims will have no objection to a voluntary common civil code.

The United Nations' Convention on Elimination of All Discrimination Against Women had also suggested way back in 2000 the enactment of an optional secular family code. Iyer, while pleading for moderation, suggests that "to facilitate a national debate, a facultative common code may be drawn up at a non-governmental level".[139] So, what is needed is to formulate a Uniform Civil Code which must be a harmonious blend of the best in all systems of jurisprudence. The difficulty in framing such a code cannot be underestimated. This task can be given either to the Law Commission or to a small committee of jurists who are well versed in the personal laws of all the communities, both written and unwritten, and also the tenets of the various scriptures including the *Quran*. Once such a code is drawn up, it will surely incorporate the salient features of the Muslim Personal Laws, and address, amongst others, the most pressing question of triple *talaq*, registration of marriage and divorce, maintenance and alimony after divorce and inheritance rights of women. This code may be debated nationwide. After that steps may be taken to give it a legal sanctity. An optional common code may be the first step leaving it to the genius of the Indian people to understand, appreciate, assimilate and opt for the benefits of such a code. Such a provision on the line of the Muslim Personal Law (*Shariat*) Adoption Act of 1937 may be incorporated in the Code. What cannot be achieved at one stroke has to be effected step by step and little by little. Let a beginning be made. After all, as pointed out by the noted columnist, B.G. Verghese: "A secular India needs a Uniform Civil Code. To mark time is to march with the communalists".[140]

Notes and References

1. Rao, B. Shiva, *Framing of India's Constitution*, Vol. II, 1967, New Delhi, The Indian Institute of Public Administratio, p. 114.
2. *Ibid.*, pp. 67-114.
3. *Ibid.*, p. 78.
4. *Ibid.*, pp. 128-29.
5. *Ibid.*, p. 136.
6. *Ibid.*, p. 142.
7. *Ibid.*, p. 150.

8. *Ibid.*, pp. 162-163.
9. *Ibid.*, p. 168.
10. *Ibid.*, pp. 176-178.
11. *Ibid.*, p. 195.
12. *Ibid.*, p. 292.
13. *Ibid.*, pp. 304-306.
14. *Ibid.*, Vol. III, p. 13.
15. *Ibid.*, p. 334.
16. *Ibid.*, p. 528.
17. *CAD*, Vol. VII, dated 8-11-48, p. 297.
18. *Ibid.*, pp. 303-304.
19. *Ibid.*, dated 23-11-48, pp. 540-541.
20. *Ibid.*, pp. 541-543.
21. *Ibid.*, pp. 543-544.
22. *Ibid.*, pp. 544-546.
23. *Ibid.*, p. 546.
24. *Ibid.*, pp. 546-548.
25. *Ibid.*, pp. 549-550.
26. *Ibid.*, pp. 550-552.
27. *Ibid.*, dated 25-11-48, p. 612.
28. *Ibid.*, dated 1-12-48, pp. 721-723.
29. *Ibid.*, pp. 756-757.
30. *Ibid.*, dated 2-12-48, pp. 759-760.
31. *Ibid.*, pp. 777-778.
32. *Ibid.*, pp. 781-782.
33. *Ibid.*, p. 782.
34. *CAD,* Vol. VII dated 6-12-48, pp. 830-831.
35. *CAD*, Vol. XI dated 21-11-49, p. 762.
36. *Ibid.*, dated 22-11-49. pp. 796-797.
37. Kashyap, Anirban, *Communalism and Constitution*, New Delhi, Lancers Books, p. 219.
38. *Jordan* vs. *Chopra A*. 1985 SC 945.
39. Dhavan, Rajeev, "Codifying personal laws", *The Hindu*, August 1, 2003, p. 10.
40. Sen, Rukmini, "En-gendering justice", *The Statesman*, June 19, 2003, p. 7.
41. *Ram Prasad* vs. *State of U.P.,* A. 1961 S.C. 853 (864, 874-76).
42. Isa, Mohammad, "*Talaq* for your Constitution", *The Telegraph*, May 22, 1994, p. 6.
43. Singh, Kirti, "Towards Achieving Equal Rights in Marriage", *Economic and Political Weekly*, Vol. XLVII, No. 24, June 16, 2012, pp. 17-19.
44. *The Statesman*, August 26, 2013, p. 14.
45. *The Hindu*, February 19, 2015, p. 1.
46. *The Times of India*, April 21, 2014, pp. 1 & 9.
47. Desai, Nishtha, "Non-sectarian Uniform Civil Code in Goa safeguards women's rights", *The Times of India,* June 28, 1996, p. 15.
48. Editorial entitled "Married to Sense", *The Telegraph*, August 20, 2001, p. 8. *The Statesman*, August 28, 2001, p. 8.
49. *The Times of India*, March 24, 2015, p. 9.

50. *The Times of India*, September 15, 2014, p. 9.
51. Kader, S.A., '*Shariat* and Islamic spirit-I", *The Hindu*, September 13, 1995, p. 12.
52. Engineer, Asghar Ali, "What is so divine about Muslim Personal Law?", *The Telegraph*, May 12, 1994, p. 19.
53. *The Hindu*, July 14, 2004, p. 11.
54. *Ibid.*, January 2, 2013, p. 10.
55. *www.rediff.com/news/2004/dec/12talaq.htm*
56. *The Sunday Times of India*, February 5, 2012, p. 13.
57. *The Statesman*, April 13, 2012, p. 3.
58. *The Telegraph*, February 10, 2015, p. 6.
59. Sikander, Mushtaq Ul Haq Ahmad, "Women in Conflict", *Economic and Political Weekly*, Vol. XLVII No. 9, March 3, 2012, p. 24.
60. Engineer, Asghar Ali, "Un-Islamic triple divorce should be scrapped", *The Times of India*, June 26, 1996, p. 13.
61. *The Statesman*, July 2, 1993, p. 9.
62. Rahman, A. Faizur, "The continuing tyranny of the triple *talaq*", *The Hindu*, April 4, 2012, p. 7.
63. Sayeed, Bader, "Need for Codification", *The Hindu*, July 25, 2000, p. 25.
64. *The Sunday Times of India*, January 21, 2007, p. 5.
65. *www.rediff.com/news/2004/dec/12talaq.htm.*
66. Soz, Sifuddin, "*Shariat* laws and Reform", *The Hindu*, July 13, 1994, p. 12.
67. *Ei Samay, (Ei Duniya)*, January 25, 2013.
68. Engineer, Asghar Ali, "Women and personal law in Iran", *The Hindu*, October 19, 2000, p. 12.
69. Kader, S.A., "*Shariat* and Islamic spirit-I", *The Hindu*, September 13, 1995, p. 12.
70. *The Sunday Statesman*, April 17, 1994, p. 1.
71. *The Sunday Times*, January 21, 2007, p. 1.
72. *Ibid.*
73. *The Hindu*, November 22, 2012, p. 5.
74. *Ibid.*, March 30, 2012, p. 1.
75. *www.rediff.com/news/2004/dec/12talaq.htm*
76. *The Statesman*, February 16, 1993, p. 7.
77. *Ibid.*, October 26, 1997, p. 1.
78. *The Telegraph*, July 13, 2000, p. 5.
79. *Noor Saba Khatoon* vs. *Mohd. Quasim*, AIR 1997 S.C. 3280.
80. *The Hindu*, April 27, 2014, p. 10.
81. *Ibid.*, July 3, 2012, p. 4.
82. *Sambad Pratidin*, July 15, 2012, p. 7.
83. *The Hindu*, December 7, 2014, p. 1.
84. Rahman, A. Faizur, "Islamic law dies not sanction child marriage", *The Hindu*, June 13, 2012, p. 7.
85. *The Times of India*, February 9, 2011, p. 1.
86. *Mrs Tahara Begum* vs. *State of Delhi and Ors*, WP (CRL) 446/2012.
87. Rahman, A. Faizur, "Islamic law dies not sanction child marriage", *The Hindu*, June 13, 2012, p. 7.

88. WP (Crl.) No. 338/2008, Crl. MC No. 1001/2011 & Crl. MA No. 3737/2011, WP (Crl) No. 821/2008 and Crl MA Mo. 8765/2008, WP (Crl) No. 566/2010.
89. *Seema* vs. *Ashwini Kumar,* AIR 2006 S.C. 1158.
90. *The Telegraph*, October 29, 2008, p. 4.
91. *The Hindu*, October 29, 2008, p. 13.
92. *Ibid.*, April 13, 2012, p. 16.
93. Mahmood, Tahir, *Islamic Law in Indian Courts and since Independence: Fifty Years of Judicial Interpretation,* 1997, Delhi, Institute of Objective Studies, pp. 456-457.
94. *Jordan* vs. *Chopra A*. 1985 SC 945.
95. Subramanian, Narendra, "Legal Pluralism, Legal Changes and Gender Inequality: Changes in Muslim Family Law in India", *Law and Social Inquiry,* 33(3), 2008, pp. 631-672.
96. *Bal Tahira A.* vs. *Ali Hussain Fissali Chothia,* AIR 1979 SC 362.
97. *Fazlunbi* vs. *Kadhefr Vali,* AIR 1980 SC 1730.
98. Khan, Arif Mohammed, "For A Common Cause", *The Times of India,* August 19 2009, p. 18.
99. Kashyap, Anirban, *Communalism and Constitution, op.cit.,* p. 196.
100. *The Telegraph*, September 16, 2000, p. 6.
101. Editorial entitled "Divorce in a trice", *The Hindu*, November 1, 2010, p. 12.
102. Ilyas, Syed Qasim Tasool. "Nothing Personal", *The Times of India*, February 4, 2005, p. 12.
103. *The Hindu*, November 6, 2006, p. 5.
104. Ahmed, Shamim, *Anandabazar Patrika*, April 1, 2008, p. 4.
105. *The Times of India*, July 15, 2014, p. 18.
106. Yusuf, Syed, "Code of incivility", *The Telegraph*, August 31, 1995, p. 12.
107. *The Sunday Statesman*, February 14, 1993, p. 12.
108. *The Telegraph*, February 1, 2006, p. 8.
109. *CAD,* Vol. VII, dated 23-11-48, p. 547.
110. *The Sunday Statesman*, February 14, 1993, p. 12.
111. *The Hindustan Times*, March 12, 2000, p. 8.
112. Sharma, Kumud and Sujaya, C.P. (ed.) *Towards Equality: Report of the Committee on the Status of Women in India,* 2012, New Delhi, Pearson Education in South Asia, paras 4,236 and 4,237, p. 108.
113. *The Times of India*, October 1, 2014, p. 14.
114. *The Hindu*, May 13, 1995, p. 6.
115. *Ibid.*, November 27, 1995, p. 4.
116. Chagla, M.C., *Roses in December, An autobiography*, 1974, Bombay, Bharatiya Vidya Bhavan, p. 85.
117. Rahman, Hossainur, "India's Muslim Problem", *The Sunday Statesman*, July 9, 1995, p. 2.
118. Mahmood, Tahir, "Muslim Personal Law: clearing the cobwebs", *The Hindu*, July 30, 2006, p. 14.
119. *Mohammmed Ahmad Khan* vs. *Shah Bano Begum* AIR 1985 SC 945 (p. 954).
120. *Ms Jorden Diengedh* vs. *S S Chopra,* AIR 1985 SC 934 (p. 940).
121. *Daniel Latifi & others* vs. *Union of India,* 2001 SC.

122. *John Vallamattom* vs. *Union of India (2003) 6 Supreme Court Cases 611* (para 44).
123. *The Telegraph*, February 20, 2014, p. 7.
124. *The Times of India*, October 18, 2008, p. 7.
125. *Ibid.*, April 7, 2014, p. 10.
126. Kusum, "A pragmatic approach", *The Hindu Magazine*, July 28, 1996, p. II.
127. Iyer, V.R. Krishna, "Unifying personal laws", *The Hindu*, September 6, 2003, p. 12.
128. Iyer, V.R. Krishna, *The Hindu*, October, 21, 1996, p. 28.
129. Rao, B. Shiva, *Framing of India's Constitution,* Vol. II, *op. cit.*, p. 177.
130. *The Indian Express*, January 28, 2000.
131. *The Hindu*, October 13, 2009, p. 6.
132. www.bjp.org/images/pdf-2014/full-manifesto-english-07.04.2014.pdf, p. 41.
133. Editorial entitled "Drop it for now", *The Times of India*, December 15, 2014, p. 14.
134. Justice Kuldip Singh in the Supreme Court judgement on *Sarla Mudgal* vs. *Union of India*, AIR 1995 SC 1531.
135. *The Telegraph*, February 20, 2014, p. 7.
136. Rahman, Hossainur, "India's Muslim Problem", *The Sunday Statesman*, July 9, 1995, p. 2.
137. *Pannalal Bansilal Pitti* vs. *State of Andhra Pradesh*, AIR 1996 SC 1023; (1996)2 SCC 498.
138. Jit, Inder, "Common Civil Code", *The Times of India*, July 16, 1996, p. 10.
139. Iyer, V.R. Krishna, "Unifying personal laws", *the Hindu*, September 6, 2003, p. 12.
140. Verghese, B.G., "Who's afraid of a Uniform Civil Code?" *The Hindu*, August 13, 2003, p. 10.

7
Retrospect

I

General Trends after 1947

Responsibility of governance of the country and the experience gained in running the administration of the country moulded the stand of the Congress. Idealism yielded place to pragmatism. So long it was dead set against any compromise. Pandit Jawaharlal Nehru as Congress president in 1936 even said: "If we compromise on principles, we shall fall between two stools and deserve our fall. The only right way and the only safe way are to stand four square on our own programme and to compromise with no one who has opposed the national struggle for freedom in the past, or who is in anyway giving support to British imperialism."[1] That was the stand of the Congress in 1936. But the partition changed the outlook and priorities. The Congress Party which claimed to be a secular party championing the cause of all Indians irrespective of caste, creed, religion, language or community—a claim which was consistently rebutted by the Muslim League who branded it as an organization of the Hindus—had to take more than a secular attitude in its policy to uphold its claim of secularity. That the position has substantially altered with the acceptance of partition of the country on the basis of Two Nation Theory, which willy nilly admitted the right of the Muslim League to speak for the Muslims—a claim which was the bone of contention between the Congress and the Muslim League—was not recognised by them. Partition was a direct affront to their policy and ideals. They could never reconcile themselves to the fact of partition. The temporary void caused due to the dissolution of the Muslim League owing to migration of its important leaders and organizers to Pakistan in the wake of partition opened up an opportunity to the Congress to fill up the vacuum in the political arena and to make attempts at endearing itself amongst the Muslims. Its earlier attempts in 1937 of making inroads amongst the Muslims through the 'mass-contact' programme having failed,[2] this time they started to rope in even those elements who had worked for the Muslim League and stood for its policy and programme in the pre-partition days. This policy of making political capital out of a situation had had its impact on this country. Expediency, rather than principle, became the key word with this monolithic all-powerful political party. In the process, the Congress made some significant overtures to woo the feelings of the minorities, specially the Muslims. Dr. Pattabhi Sitaramyya, the then Congress president, even admitted it when he said: "It is a gentleman's agreement that we have entered into, a terrible responsibility that we have taken upon our shoulders, when we asked them (Muslims) to give up their reservations and their separate electorates. We have to find as many representatives from the Muslim community through the medium of the joint electorates as would have been their legitimate share, if they had their separate electorates. Even so (was the case) with the Indian Christians and others".[3] This statement of the then Congress president in the Constituent Assembly on November 25, 1949 clearly indicated a change in the Congress politics. As Anirban Kashyap says:

> Though the system of separate electorate was abolished, the Congress assured all the minorities, based on religion, of continuance of more or less the same benefit so long enjoyed by them under the system of separate electorates. A change was effected only in name but not in practice. The Congress which so assiduously and persistently fought against the Communal Award and the communal electorate, now wanted to perpetuate it, but in a different form and manner. This shift towards communal politics or rather minority politics, in the name of secularism had a baneful effect on the entire gamut of social and political life of the country.[4]

From now on, while fielding candidates for elective posts the Congress started giving more-than-due importance to the religious background of the persons concerned. Muslims for Muslim-dominated areas became the norm. Other political parties started emulating the Congress in this regard. Even the most secular of the political parties, the Communists, select Muslim candidates for Muslim-dominated constituencies. The parties which thrive on casteist policies like Mulayam Singh's Socialist Party, Lalu Prasad Yadav's Raashtriya Janata Dal and the Bahujana Samaj Party, boast of fielding so many Muslim candidates in the Assembly and Lok Sabha elections, as if belonging to the Muslim community is the only qualification for selecting them for contesting the elections. For instance, in the 2012 UP Assembly elections, the Bahujan Samaj Party supremo Ms. Mayawati announced[5] that among the 403 BSP candidates, 88 members belonged to the Scheduled Castes, 113 to the Other Backward Classes and 85 were Muslims. About 21 per cent of candidates of the BSP, a party of the *Dalits*, were Muslims while the percentage of Muslim population in the State according to the 2011 census was 19.3.

Opportunistic politicians have continued with the pre-independence perversion of projecting Muslims as a monolithic 'vote bank', whereas the reality is that the Muslim vote, and for that matter denominational voting, never goes *en masse* to a single party, be it the Congress, the Samajwadi Party or the Rashtriya Janata Dal. Shahid Siddique points out that before Independence even the Muslim League could never get more than 50 per cent of the Muslim votes in U.P. So, analysts deliberately obfuscate the truth when they talk of Muslims voting for this or that party under the sway of one *fatwa* or another. The voting behaviour of Muslims is as varied as that of any other religious group based on their socio-economic, rural-urban and caste-religion divides.[6] This fact will be best revealed if one goes through the figures given in Table 7.1 (see page 431), discussed later.

There is a common tendency to group all Muslims in one monolithic homogeneous category when in actuality it is as diverse as any other religious community in India. Language, caste, ethnicity, culture and economic standing worked together to divide a Muslim from another Muslim no less than a Hindu from another Hindu. Some Muslims were descended from foreign invaders, but many came from families of native Indian converts. The invaders, who were held by popular myth to be a band of brothers, in fact came from different stocks which had settled in different parts of the subcontinent at different times. The converts continued to display much the same variety of languages, races and customs as their Hindu neighbours. At the doctrinal level also there were divisions between the Sunnis and the Shias, Ahmedis, Bohras, Khojas, Memons, Moplas and others. There were furthermore divisions at a social level: town-dwellers and rural-dwellers, landlords and tenants, majority and minority were all divided.[7] Way back in 1882 C.J. Lyall had noted; "In so far as there was a Muslim 'depression' in India, 'religious causes' by themselves had little to do with it. I believe it is almost entirely a question of social position".[8] These ambiguities are no doubt specific to India. In part this was the result of the isolation of the Indian Muslims, in part too of its position as a minority population under foreign rule, but above all it resulted from the differences inside the community itself.

The division of the Muslim society into Sheikh, Sayyed, Moghal, Pathan, Patwegars, Quraishis, Nadafs, Mehadis (Mehadevis), Bohras, Saits, Cutchi Memons, Ahlehadis, etc. has, no doubt, fragmented the Muslim society, whereas Islam ensures a perfect egalitarian society. Traders, landowners, lawyers, religious leaders, men and women of varied groups—Pathans, Rajputs, Bengalis, South Indians and so on and so forth—have multiple identities which to a great extent influence the social behaviour of the Muslims. In the case of Mumbai, besides the general doctrinal classification of Shia and Sunni (which can be further divided by particular schools of theology, such as the Deobandis and Barelvis among the Sunnis. The Barelvis follow a "traditional form of Islam" in which saints and intermediaries have a role to play while the Deobandis emphasize the primacy of Allah, his *tawbid* (unity) and repudiate the agency of saints and such like). There are the Dawoodi Bohras, the Sulaimani Bohras, the Aga Khani Khojas, the Halai Memons, the Kutchie Memons, the Konkani Muslims, the north Indian UP and Bihari Muslims, the moplas, the Deccanis and the Iranis.[9] Despite their diversity and even intra-communal rivalry, which led to Shia-Sunni clashes during Mohurrum, Muslims in India can, however, be looked upon as a single grouping which share certain things in common namely, a religion with a minority status and a collective experience of marginalization by the state.

Marginalization and recurrent programmatic communal violence has meant that Muslims increasingly feel physically and psychologically vulnerable and continually at risk as a community. The implications of this have been the ghettoisation of Muslims in Muslim-specific localities and the rise of neo-fundamentalism within certain quarters of the community.[10] Ghettoisation has very adverse social, psychological and political consequences. Vora and Palshikar maintain that since groups such as Muslims and *dalits* often live in localities that are imprisoned either by spatial or community location, their social existence results in political ineffectiveness.[11] Panikkar suggests that it reinforces tendencies of minoritarianism which promotes a genre of politics based on internal consolidation of the community and also militancy. The impact of these processes on the future peace of the city is also damaging.[12] As Varshney found in his 10-year study of communal violence in post-colonial India, peaceful areas have strong civic institutions—trade unions, professional associations—and neighbourhood organizations that cross the communal divide in addition to active everyday economic relationships between Muslims and Hindus.[13] Thus, when migration takes place from communally heterogeneous to communally homogeneous neighbourhoods, the interaction between communities in everyday social and economic civic settings is minimal, ultimately resulting in their segregation.[14] While homogenous neighbourhoods create the perception of greater safety and security resulting from "being with one's own kind", they also lead to increased isolation and segregation of the community.[15]

Surya Prakash Upadhyay and Rowena Robinson, after a survey of communal literature in post-independence India, note that during the first decade after Independence, there was no large-scale communal violence. Possibly, the migration of Muslim leaders and the ban on Hindu communalists prevented communal violence, but unresolved tensions between communities since the time of Partition began to resurface with the beginning of the 1960s. After the Jabalpur riot of 1961, there were a series of communal riots in different parts of the country. In 1967, in Ranchi, 155 people were butchered. On 9 June, 1968, a communal riot broke out in Nagpur between Hindu scheduled castes, now converts to Buddhism and Muslims. In 1969, after a communal holocaust in

Ahmedabad, the violence spread to other towns—Meerut, Firozabad, Aligarh and Malegaon. North Indian cities were vulnerable to communal violence, particularly Meerut, Moradabad and Aligarh. The 1987 riots in Meerut and the 1989 riots in Bhagalpur sent shock waves throughout India, making Muslims feel terribly insecure. Usually cities with a sizeable Muslim population or with Muslim-owned prosperous businesses were sites of violence. A high incidence of communal violence was also recorded in centres of Islamic learning and those with an Islamic seminary, or with publishing houses bringing out religious books, leaflets and pamphlets, such as Malegaon.

Often a relatively small issue became the spark setting off violence. The Sadar Bazar communal riot in 1974 in Delhi started with the supposed eve-teasing of a Hindu girl by a few Muslim boys. In Malegaon in 1983, fire crackers burst in front of the Jama Masjid were the starting point; on another occasion, there was a controversy around a memorial called the Shahid Smarak on Kidwai Road in Malegaon. In 1978, in Hyderabad, violence erupted over the rape of Rameeza Bee by a Hindu sub-inspector and two Muslim constables and the subsequent murder of her husband. In 1981, in Meenakshipuram, religious conversion provided the spark, while in other cases it was marriage between a Hindu girl and a Muslim boy. These incidents show that communalism draws energy not merely from religious sources, but from every aspect of social living. Any such issue can be communalised and politicised.[16]

The decades that followed Partition saw not only a rise in communal conflicts but also a rise in identity politics. These, according to Saunya Saxena, were based on (1) socio-political factors, Sikh riots, rise of BJP, affirmative action, uneven development; (2) historical legacies (colonial as well as pre-Independence), language, local regional patriotisms (partition of East Pakistan); (3) international developments, 9/11, wars with Pakistan. The decades of the 1980s and 1990s have seen a tremendous politicisation of communal identities, locating them not only in ethnic/cultural differences, but as political constituencies with separate interests.[17] But as Andre Beteille says, the current obsession of identity politics is but an expression of the primacy of the group over the individual. It does not augur well for liberal democracy in India.[18]

In India in the last two/three decades, where communal politics, electoral and otherwise, has intensified and right wing fundamentalist factions have consolidated their hold across religions, not only has there been a visible increase in the incidents of violence against minorities, both Muslims and Christians, but also the violence itself has become more intense and frenzied. This was especially noticeable in the nation-wide violence that broke out after the demolition of the Babri masjid in 1992 and in the specific targeting of Muslim women during the Gujarat riots of 2002.

As a fall-out of the riots, social geography of many of the cities underwent a radical change. Muslims so also Hindus, who lived in mixed areas or housing colonies where they were in substantially smaller numbers consciously chose to move to neighbourhoods dominated by their communities in order to feel more physically secure. This happened not only in Mumbai, Ahmedabad but also in Delhi, Calcutta and its neighbourhoods. Muslims moved into the already dense Muslim dominated areas while Hindus moved into Hindu localities. This is the usual pattern throughout India.

Unfortunately, by seeking refuge in areas where they are in majority, Muslims get increasingly circumscribed in specific identifiable localities. More often than not these Muslim-dominated areas get labelled as "Muslim ghettos". They simultaneously also get branded as "mini-Pakistan" and as areas harbouring so-called criminals and terrorists,[19] though the fact is that the "Muslim ghettos" breeds petty criminals, not because religion and crime overlap but because poverty goes hand in hand with illiteracy, bigotry, a readiness to be roused and anti-social activities. The anti-dote of jobs, schools, hospitals, houses, potable water, sanitation, electricity and above all, equal opportunity is desperately inadequate not only for the Muslims, but for all communities throughout the country.

In places like Gujarat, ghettoization and spatial segregation has taken place so extensively that internal "borders" have come into being, demarcating residential areas of different communities with little or no interaction between them. Edward Sinpson[20] tells us the story of three Muslim men in the Kutch and their changing attitudes towards traditional forms of piety, including saint worship, over a decade. The three men, a businessman, a sailor and the keeper of a shrine, start out more or less as traditionalists, but over time, with the gradual radicalization of Muslim opinion and especially after the Gujarat riots of 2002 become more and more hard-line. The businessman continues to donate money to local shrine, but he also builds a fresh wall around his own house and stops venturing out into Hindu areas. The shrine keeper whose father was a great religious personality of the region sees his own influence decline rapidly after his father's death and after Gujarat 2002 impacts on the religious beliefs of the region's Muslims.

The role of real estate markets in exploiting ghettoisation cannot be ignored. For instance, new building projects in the Mumbai city are increasingly marketing themselves on caste/community lines and as places that you can live in without the troubling presence of the "other". This offers them a niche client base, but the premiums they charge for exclusion more than make up the small clientele. This sort of ghettoisation now has legal sanction. In 2005, the Supreme Court of India upheld the formation of cooperative housing societies where membership is restricted to persons from the same caste or religion.[21] In recent years, there has been an upsurge in exclusive community ghettoes and only vegetarian housing societies. A Times of India report in November 2005 gave examples such as Millat Nagar,

Oshiwara (Andheri West) for Muslims; the Hooseini Coop Housing Society in Kandivali and the upcoming Burhani Park project in Mazagaon only for Dawoodi Bohras; separate enclaves for Jains such as two buildings of Flower Valley complex in Thakur village in Kandivali, Sudha Park in Ghatkopar and Sumer Towers in Mazagaon; the St. Sebastian and Salsette complex in Bandra for Roman Catholics; and the Shreepati Arcade at Nana Chowk only for Gujarati and Marwari vegetarians.[22] The Adarsh Group is promoting apartments in Greater Noida—Gulistan Golf View Heights—as dream homes for elite Muslim brotherhood. The complex will have a mosque, a *madrasah*, and will face *Qibla*—the direction a Muslim faces when offering prayers. Despite the high sales pitch, not all find the idea exciting. For instance, Imtiaz Ahmed, the political scientist, said the idea of India is rooted in inclusion and integration of all communities. Such (ghettoized) apartment complex goes against the constitutional ethos of country. There are others who think that considering the fact that the Muslims are finding it difficult to rent houses in Hindu localities, such a step is in the right direction.[23]

Nida Kirmani in her new book *Questioning the 'Muslim Woman': Space, Identity and Insecurity in an Urban Locality* analyses the general "insecurity" that results in what looks sometimes like an "enclave" (where people choose to go) and other times like a "ghetto" (where people are forced to go), into gendered, class-based and migration-based insecurity, as well as that triggered by housing segregation. Further, she correlates these distinct vectors with historical post-memories of the four "critical events" (1947, 1984, 1992, and 2002) that radically colour the self-perception of the Muslim minority.

Ananya Vajpeyi narrates her experience of how difficult it is for the Muslims to get accommodations in so-called Hindu enclave. She, a Hindu, married to a Muslim from south Kashmir says that they live in what is perhaps the only neighbourhood left in Delhi proper that has a mixed character in terms of both class and community. Most of their middle-class Muslim friends live around Jamia, in Sukhdev Vihar and parts of Okhla, or in Old Delhi, or abutting JNU. This is not because they want to live among other Muslims or Muslims only, but because they cannot find accommodation to rent or buy elsewhere.[24] On the other hand, there are also reports of non-Muslims renting out to Muslims.

II

Caste within Islam

The dominant perception is that Islam is an egalitarian religion and that Indian Muslims on the whole, especially in the post-Sachar scenario, are a marginalized community. The *Pasmanda* Muslim Mahaz, an organization formed in Bihar in 1998, challenges both these formulations. *Pasmanda*, a

Persian term meaning "those who have fallen behind", refers to the Muslims belonging to the *shudra* (backward) and *ati-shudra* (*Dalit*) castes whereas the dominant forward caste Muslims are known as *ashraf* Muslims. The discourse has found resonance elsewhere. In terms of religious interpretation, Masood Falahi's work *Hindustan mein Zaat Paat aur Musalman* (2006) has convincingly demonstrated how the notion of *kufu* (rules about possible marriage relations between groups) was read through the lens of caste by the "manuwadi" ulama and how a parallel system of "graded inequality" was put into place in Indian Islam.

As far as the social sphere is concerned, Ali Anwar's *Masawat ki Jung* (2000) has documented caste-based disenfranchisement of *Dalit* and backward caste Muslims at the hands of self-styled *ashraf* leaders in community organizations like *madrasahs* and personal law boards, representative institutions (Parliament and State Assemblies) and departments, ministries and institutions that claim to work for Muslims (minority affairs, Waqf boards, Urdu academies, AMU, Jamia Millia Islamia etc.). The book also underlines stress of humiliation, disrespect and violence on caste grounds that various *pasmanda* communities have to undergo on a daily basis, at least in northern parts of India. Thus, *pasmanda* commentators contest the two key elements of mainstream 'Muslim' or 'minority' discourse—Islam as an egalitarian religion and Indian Muslims on the whole as an oppressed community. Islam is normatively egalitarian but in Indian conditions it is deeply hierarchical. Similarly, all Muslims are not oppressed, or not to the same degree, at any rate: Muslims are a differentiated community in terms of power, with dominant (*ashraf*) and subordinated (*pasmanda*) sections. Consequently, the so-called 'minority politics', which has been quite content in raising symbolic and emotional issues so far, is really the politics of dominant caste Muslims that secures their interests at the expense of *pasmanda* Muslims. Minority politics has singularly failed to address the bread-and-butter concerns of the *pasmanda* Muslims, who constitute about 85 per cent of the Indian Muslim population and come primarily from occupational and service *biradaris*.

Since, the express object of the *pasmanda* movement has been to raise the issue of caste-based exclusion of subordinate caste Muslims, it has stressed on caste-based solidarity across religions. The counter-hegemonic solidarity on caste lines is effectively encapsulated in the *pasmanda* slogan '*Dalit-Pichda ek saman, Hindu ho ya Musalman*' (All Dalit-backward castes are alike, whether they be Hindu or Muslim).[25]

The *pasmanda* articulation has highlighted the symbiotic nature of majoritarian and minoritarian fundamentalism and has sought to contest the latter from within in order to wage a decisive battle against the former. While opposing the politics of both Hindu and Muslim fanatics, its demands include, amongst others, the deepening of the existing affirmative action policies by conferment of '*Dalit*' status on the *pasmanda* Muslims.

The existence of two broad-based groups 'Sunnis' and 'Shias' and the restrictions imposed on practices by these groups against each other in matters relating to marriages, intimate social interactions and cultural practices definitely lend valuable support to the contention that Muslims are also governed by 'Caste'. As a matter of fact even Christianity is not totally free from this social pathology. For instance, the established differences and consequent restrictions imposed on the Catholics and Protestants in matters relating to places and modes of worship, matrimonial alliances, etc, demolish the very concept of egalitarianism among the Christians. Similarly, the acute difference between the *Dalit* Christians and non-*Dalit* Christians bring disgrace to Christianity. In the Census Report of 1901 the existence of three castes in the Muslim society has been reported. The Census Report of 1911 listed the castes found in the Muslim society. It is seen that there were as many as 55 major and 25 minor castes among the Bengali Muslims.[26]

Whereas in Islam there is no room for such differences between neo-Muslims converted from the low-caste Hindus and those from the high caste Hindus, social inequality prevails. The Muslims are divided into three groups in their social life. (1) *Ashraf* or *Sharif* or noble and high status Muslims. Muslims known as Syed, Sheikh, Mughal, Pathan, Mallick, Meerja and the like belong to this class. They are generally considered the descendants of those who came from abroad. In the Muslim society the position of Syed Muslims is like that of the Brahmins in the Hindu society. The descendants of those who came from abroad or those high caste Hindus who were converted to Islam are known as Sheikh Muslims. At some places the Pathan and Mughal Muslims are treated as *Ajlaf* Muslims. (2) *Ajlaf* or *Atraf* or low-caste Muslims. The Muslims of this group are known as "*Kamina*" or "inferior" or *Razil* as well. *Ajlaf* Muslims are divided into four classes—(i) Sheikh Muslims working as agriculturists—they are accorded high status among the *Ajlaf* Muslims, (ii) Tailors, Jola, Fakir and Rangrez, (iii) Barhi, Bhatiara, Chik, Churihar, Dai, Dhawa, Dhunia, Gaddi, Kalal, Kasai, Kolu, Kunjara, Laheri, Mahifarosh, Mallah, Nalia, Nikari, (iv) Abdal, Bakho, Bedia, Bhat, Chamba, Dafali, Dhobi, Hazzam, Muchi, Nagahi, Nat, Panwaria, Madaria, Tutia. (3) *Arzal* or degraded Muslims—Bhanar, Halalkhor, Hizra, Kasbi, Lalbegi, Mangta, Mehtar etc., are included in this group. In some places Abdal and Bedia Muslims are included in this group. The Muslims of the third group are debarred from entering the Mosque and they are not allowed to cremate dead body in the general cemetery. Muslims of this group are, however, few in number. The moneyed and powerful *Ajlaf* Muslims tried to elevate their position in the social hierarchy by establishing matrimonial relationship with poor *Ashraf* Muslims. It was easier to elevate the social position in such a manner in the urban areas. In the rural areas it was comparatively difficult as the social background of each and every family was known to all. The very fact that the

Muslims also aspire for a higher position in the social hierarchy by climbing up the ladder only points to the existence of caste-like system in the Muslim society.[27]

The division of Muslim society into *ashraf* and *ajlaf* marks the fictional border between immigrants and converts. Muslims who came with the invaders or the local populace that adopted Islam fell into these categories, the respectable section of society were the *ashraf* (plural of *Sharif*) and the commoners were the *ajlaf.* Not only marriage but other close social intercourse was not permissible among them. However, human nature always surmounts such obstacles, as is evident from daily life. The *Ashraf* eventually became the middle class and as such the cream of society—the *Khas* as compared to the *Am,* something that the Mughals earlier commemorated by having a Dewan-e-Khas and a Dewan-e-Am in their Red Forts at Agra and Delhi.

The Mandal Commission has recognised 'backward castes' among the Non-Hindu communities like Muslims, Christians, Sikhs and "has evolved the following rough and ready criteria for identifying non-Hindu OBCs:

(i) All untouchables converted to any non-Hindu religion; and
(ii) Such occupational communities which are known by the name of their traditional hereditary occupation and whose Hindu counterparts have been included in the list of Hindu OBCs. (Examples: Dhobi, Teli, Dheemar, Nai, Gujar, Kumhar, Lohar, Darji, Badhai, etc.)"[28] and estimated their population as 8.40 per cent of the total population.[29]

The Sachar Committee has favoured trifurcating Muslims into *Ashrafs, Ajlafs* and *Arzals*—instead of the conventional-practice of treating the community as a monolithic group—for any affirmative action by the state. Of the three groups, *Arzals,* whose traditional occupation is similar to that of scheduled castes, may be designated as most backward classes (MBCs) and handled separately. While *Ashraf* category includes Muslims of foreign blood and converts from higher castes, *Ajlafs* are those who are loosely equivalent to Hindu OBCs.[30]

Many States have included Muslims in the list of OBCs in right earnest. For instance, at present in West Bengal there are 144 communities in the OBC list. Of them 87 are Muslim communities and their number is 1,91,45,192.[31] Incidentally, the population of the Muslims in the 2001 Census was 2,02,40,543.[32] So, nearly 95 per cent of the Muslim population of the State of West Bengal is treated as OBCs.

If all the States emulate West Bengal, and if the demand of the *Pasmanda* Muslim Mahaz of conferring *Dalit* status on the *pasmanda* Muslims materializes, the notion that caste exists only among the Hindus will lose much of its sting. In the 1990s, Narasimha Rao Government tried in vain to confer Scheduled Castes on *Dalit* Muslims and *Dalit* Christians. In the run-up to the 16th Lok Sabha elections in 2014, the Congress in its supplementary manifesto on "empowerment of minorities" promised 4.5 per cent sub-quota for backward Muslims in the existing other backward caste reservations and Scheduled Caste status to all *Dalit* minorities.[33] Mulayam Singh Yadav's Samajwadi Party in its election manifesto released on April 2, 2014 promised according Scheduled Caste status to *Dalit* Christians and *Dalit* Muslims and reservation for Muslims in jobs in accordance with their population.[34] Though these proposals are being termed as "the most corrupt examples of communalism", it is a fact that Muslims are also being viewed as OBC Muslims and *Dalit* Muslims. Despite the emergence of OBC Muslims and *Dalit* Muslims and the divisions among them on doctrinal differences, the Muslims of all denominations in India, however, unitedly uphold their religion and their minority character.

However, in pre-partition India, Muslims had not thought of themselves as a minority, but claimed to be the 'other community', numerically smaller, but socially more cohesive than the larger, but amorphous Hindu population. The minority status of Indian Muslims was not a cultural or a social fact, but merely numerical. It refers to the proportion of Muslims in the Indian population. But numerical inferiority is no new experience for Indian Muslims. For much of their history it was a factor of no consequence, not only because they enjoyed political ascendancy in the subcontinent but because population proportion were irrelevant to pre-democratic politics.

In Pakistan, the importance of *biradari* (caste) in elections is still reckoned with. In the province of Punjab that accounts for 55 per cent of national assembly seats, Rajputs are dominant in northern Punjab, followed by Jats in central and Balochs in the province's south. The Pakistan People's Party (PPP)—led government had a Rajput PM and a Jat as his deputy before it demitted office in March 2013. The Bhuttos, who founded and have led the party, are of Rajput ancestry. Military ruler Zia-ul-Haq's ban on political parties and the 1985 non-party elections are blamed for re-entrenching the *biradari* system. In an article headlined "Caste plays a surprising role in Muslim Pakistan's elections" Barbara Crossette of the *New York Times* described it as a likely factor that plays a role in a party's choice of candidates ahead of the 1990 elections. Little has changed since then. A Gallup survey ahead of the 2008 elections confirmed the existence of *biradari* as an important civil society institution. The *biradari* link, however, becomes weak in urban centres, although not irrelevant.[35]

III

Religious Identity

Since the 1980s, we have had a strong resurgence of communalism. It has reached out to the middle class in a big way. Communalism has never enjoyed so much respectability and acceptance. It is no longer a dirty word. Today communalism has infected all walks of life. It has charged the atmosphere with distrust and suspicion between Hindus and Muslims and even men of education and culture. Communal politics masks all social identities with the cloak of religion.

So, there is the resurgence of religion. Religion has become much more potent as identity and ideology. Religion was supposed to fade away with spreading globalisation and increasing freedom. Instead, it is booming around the world. If people are wealthier, more educated, and enjoy greater political freedom, one might assume they would also have become more secular. They haven't.

In addition to beliefs and practices, as Andre Beteille argues, there is a third aspect of religion, which may be called religious identity. Religion binds together into a single community, actual or potential, all those who identify with it, no matter how lax or negligent they may be in their actual religious observances. This is the social or political aspect of religion as against its spiritual or mystic aspect. It is the capacity of religion to bind people together, to create a sense of unshakeable loyalty among its adherents and to rally them in the face of real or perceived threats to the community that fascinates the social and political theorist. Identification with the religious community has a life of its own and its ebbs and flows are to some extent independent of the growth and decline of strictly religious beliefs and practices. Moreover, it is well known that those who are most successful in rallying their community in the cause of religion are not themselves always strict in their own religious observance.

Religions create communities of birth. A person acquires his religious identity at birth and generally speaking, retains the same identity until death. His practices may slacken and his beliefs may fade while his identity remains unchanged. In an engaging book, Amartya Sen has pointed out that every individual has a number of different identities. While this is undoubtedly true, some identities, like religious identity, are almost inextinguishable while others may be discarded or adopted with relative ease. A person's religious identity, unlike his other social identities, has important social and political consequences.

Religion has always played a significant part in creating and maintaining order and stability in society. That was indeed one of the main virtues that Gandhi found in religion. While it is undoubtedly true that religion can act as a basis for unity and stability within the community, it is equally true that it can act as a source of division and conflict between communities. Sometimes the religious community as a whole is mobilized by its leaders on the basis of the common identity of its members in opposition to another community whose identity is distinct and separate from its own. Religious leaders who are eloquent in the cause of peace and harmony are not always slow in mobilizing their own flock in the cause of their honour, their dignity and their material interests.

Religion does provide an important basis for creating and maintaining distinct and separate social identities. People learn to live with differences in religious belief and practice even as they learn to live with other differences in belief and practice. A crucial role is played in the elaboration and reinforcement of those differences by what sociologists call religious specialists. The intentions of such specialists as evangelists, *imams* or *mahants* may be peaceful, but their work plays a large part in shaping those identities that are used for mobilising support in political conflicts.[36]

The partition of India had its inevitable impact not only on the Hindus but on the Muslims as well. Those who did not migrate to Pakistan and stayed back had to bear the brunt of the blame for the Partition of India. As a matter of fact, that section of the Muslim community who was more vocal for the partition of India on the basis of the Two-Nation Theory was left behind while their leaders migrated to Pakistan. When asked about the vast majority of Muslims who remained in India, Pandit Nehru is said to have replied: "We never accepted the two nation theory, though we were driven to accept Partition to avoid bloodshed and achieve Independence. We are not a communal state. The Muslims who have decided to stay in India are as much the honourable citizens of the country as are the members of the majority community. We cannot, and must not, live in the past".[37]

But what is the position in the field? In the aftermath of the Gujarat Riot in 2002 Julio Ribeiro, a former Director-General of Police, laments that his most important finding was that there was a widely prevalent perception in the minds of the Hindu upper and middle classes that the revenge that was taken in Ahmedabad was for the good of the city, the state and the country as it would serve as a good lesson to recalcitrant Muslims. They harboured deep misgivings about the Muslim minority, its ethos, its absolutist religious dogma, its perceived penchant for violence and its belief in a brotherhood that extended beyond the borders of the country and was possibly loyal more to this brotherhood than to the land of their birth. They had succumbed to the propaganda that Muslims were a pampered lot and that it was the Congress which had pampered them because of vote bank politics. The communal poison has spread so deep in the hearts and minds of the Hindu middle class that it will have to be extracted by super-human efforts before we can hope to re-establish any semblance of communal unity.[38]

Why communal riots, for that matter any ethnic riot, take place? The most comprehensive study of ethnic riots all over the world by Donald L. Horowitz finds three main factors that lead to deadly ethnic riots. First, there needs to be a hostile ongoing relationship between the groups—tensions of long standing to motivate the killing. Second, there needs to be authoritative social support, potential rioters needs to be assured by public statements from community leaders in their group that the leaders agree killing members of the other group is justified. This support usually extends to the security forces: riots usually become large only if the police are sympathetic, or at least do not make determined efforts to stop the killing. Finally, there needs to be a stimulus, some event—usually implying some sort of threat—that provokes fear, rage, or hatred in the rioting group. For example, a report (true or false) of a violent attack by one of "them" against one of "us" might spark a widespread cry to "teach them a lesson". Alternatively, a political change—even a potential one—might provoke a similar outburst.[39]

Another approach to explaining ethnic riots focuses not on psychology but on social organization. In India, for example, hostile relations between the Hindu and the Muslim communities are common, but most of the riot violence is concentrated in just a few areas. Why is that? The riot-prone areas, as Brass says, it turns out, have "institutionalized" riot systems: community activists and extremist organizations that benefit from keeping tensions high, politicians who benefit from occasional violence, and criminals and thugs who can profit from it.[40]

There is now some acknowledgement of the fact that religious faith is a crucial factor in determining the shape of the Indian psyche and its interaction with the world at large and that the historical evolution of relations between the two major faiths of the Indian subcontinent has left behind a residue of resentment if not outright hostility.[41] Accused and lambasted at every opportunity, the Muslims were pushed into a cocoon. They thought it discreet to remain isolated in their 'ghettos'. Even the psychological trauma of the community was viewed with suspicion and the Muslims were constantly chided for not joining the mainstream. As Robinson says, "Categorised as 'Other', taunted as Pakistani if not vilified as terrorist, the Muslim in India today is an anonymous and frightening figure. Fear and anonymity are, of course, crucial to the maintenance of cultures of hostility and violence."[42] "The pity of partition was not that the country had been divided into two, Independent India and Independent Pakistan, but it was that people had become slaves to bigotry, religious passions and barbarity", says Ayesha Jalal.[43] The biggest loss has been the destruction of a cosmopolitan multi-religious, forward looking pluralist society.

Muslims in India suffer from an identity crisis. The genesis of the crisis lies in the identification of their religion Islam with the Islamic culture of Saudi Arabian and Iranian origin. In Indonesia—the largest Muslim nation—they have a clear demarcation between religion and culture. While an average Indonesian is an avowed follower of Islam, he is proud of his culture. The roots of their culture are in the *Ramayana*. They are proud of Sanskrit. The first name of an Indonesian is Muslim, but the surname is of Indian origin. Sukarno, Suharto and others are of Sanskrit origin. Even the Indonesian national airline is named after Garuda—the vehicle bird of Vishnu. In India, other religious communities like the Parsis have identified with Indian culture. A section of people[44] harbours a feeling that the Muslims in India, by and large, are swayed by blatant bigotry and have contempt for everything sacred to Hindus. As Professor Hossainur Rahman observes, pan-Islamism inflamed their passions, a feeling that, although they had been ground down under the wheels of history, they thought of themselves as a mighty society spread worldwide.[45]

Partition caused incalculable harm to those Muslims who are left behind in India. They became acutely conscious of having to battle it out to prove their credentials in the new dispensation in which they had become "indigestible meat". In the early years after Partition, disturbing comments were often passed by their compatriots, even by some senior political leaders, such as "you got your share of the country". This attitude of the majority community virtually created a "siege mentality" among Muslims, which, till today, is hard to overcome.

The perception of being treated 'unfairly' is still high amongst the Muslim minority of India, more than six decades after independence, states a joint study titled "Education and Employment among Muslims in India" conducted in 2012 by the Indian Institute of Management, Ahmedabad and the Delhi-based think tank Observer Research Foundation (ORF). The Muslims perceive lowest fairness in five core areas of social prestige, economics, education, employment and politics. The perception of being treated unfairly results in a growing sense of insecurity taking root in the psyche of the community, especially in communally sensitive States and particularly among women. The discriminatory attitude of the police and others compounds his feeling; choosing to live in ghettos is a result of the sense of insecurity and discrimination in housing, schools and jobs, states the study.[46]

The Sachar Committee acknowledges that Muslims "carry a double burden of being labelled as "anti-national" and as being "appeased" at the same time.[47] Further, "the perception of being discriminated against is overpowering amongst a wide cross-section of Muslims" and results in "collective alienation".[48]

A feeling of persecution haunts the Muslims in India. In such a situation they take shelter more and more under the protective umbrella of their "religious identity". Their "Indian identity" becomes subservient to their "religious identity". They take recourse to the observance of their religious beliefs and practices more rigidly in order to manifest outwardly their religious identity. As a matter of fact, today's youth is no longer afraid to express his religious self. Compared to the previous generation, they are less inhibited and less embarrassed to appear God-loving. Many educated and urban young are showing signs of a religious bent of mind or a penchant for rituals. According to Swami Ritananda of the Ramakrishna Mission at Golpark in Calcutta, the number of young men choosing the life of renunciation and sacrifice is also on the rise. And this trend is not limited to the Hindus. The Shahi Imam of Tipu Sultan Mosque in Calcutta points out that compared to the past a lot more younger people want to learn about Islam to counter claims by terrorists that theirs is the true version of Islam.[49] Religion, clearly, is in the air. For some, it translates into ritualistic practices, and for others, it is often a way of life.

That is the reason why more and more people from the Muslim community now observe fast during the *Ramdan* days, participate in *Muharram* and *Sabebarat* festivals and go for *Haj* pilgrimage. Now-a-days loudspeakers are used not only for giving *azans*, but for making other announcements as well from the mosques. An equal, if not more, manifestation of religious identity is seen in the observance of religious rituals by the Hindus and even by other religious groups like the Christians and the Sikhs. Aided by the proliferation of religious symbolism in the print and electronic media, Hindu themes and organizations crossed State boundaries and helped diverse sects, castes and classes acquire the consciousness of a popular and more homogeneous Hinduism. Religious performances, celebrations, and demonstrations began to transcend localities and acquire national dimension. As they did, they became more strident, intolerant and militant.

That is also the reason why cow slaughter as well as conversion and re-conversion have become so emotive issues in the Indian politics. The cow emerged as a symbol of Hindu nationalism in the colonial period leading to the formation of organizations like the Gaurakshini Sabha. The Constitution of India in the Directive Principles of State Policies directs the State to "take steps to prohibit cow slaughter". This has led most States in newly independent India to quickly pass laws banning cow slaughter. In the last few years, some States have passed more stringent laws against cow and bovine slaughter, particularly the States ruled by the Bharatiya Janata Party (BJP) such as Chhattisgarh, Gujarat, Madhya Pradesh and Karnataka. In a clear move to promote "Hindutva" ahead of the 2014 Lok Sabha elections, two government agencies—the Gauseva Ayog and the Gauchar Vikas Board—of the BJP-led Gujarat Government organised a Gau Kathamrit Mahotsav for three days on the outskirts of Ahmedabad, a narration of benefits that can be derived from cows. The programme of narrations was undertaken to create awareness about the medicinal properties of many bovine by-products. Apart from the usual milk products, cow urine and cow dung can be of great utility as bio-insecticides and organic manures.[50]

Though Hinduism does not proselytize, some religions, such as Islam and Christianity, allow or even encourage conversion to their own faiths while discouraging and opposing conversion of their own members to other faiths. In medieval Christianity, the apostate was regarded as more reprehensible than the infidel and this is to some extent true of Islam in many countries till this day. Conversion and re-conversion of people has become a touchy issue leading to communal disharmony and discord.

The religious identity presupposes the importance of religious leaders and religious seminaries. The Muslim seminaries control the day-to-day life of its adherents and even issue *fatwas* for them. The Darul Uloom Deoband seminary, founded in 1867 in an old mosque shaded by a pomegranate tree, represented the clerical class' effort to defend the faith after the fall of Mughal power. The seminary's online *fatwa* service runs counter to the new middle-class that is manifesting itself among the Muslims. For example, may a successful private-sector worker shave? No. May a student overseas work at a pork-using Pizza Hut to make pocket money? No. May families attend weddings with "dance, song, mixing of men and women, photography or videography?" No. In one *fatwa*, a believer seeking sanction for visiting a historic church is upbraided: "the good effect of one's Islam is that he gives up nonsense things". Recently, several *fatwas* issued by it made headlines, which included one saying that prayers of those who have tattoo on their bodies or have sprayed perfume with alcohol in it, is not valid.[51] Its *fatwa* against participation of novelist Salman Rushdie in the Jaipur Literature Festival (January 20-24, 2012) led to mass mobilization by Muslim organizations which so much unnerved the State administration that Rushdie could neither personally attend nor even participate in the video-conference on the last day of the Festival.[52]

India's leading Islamic theologian Maulana Wahiddudin Khan described calls for banning Rushdie or his book "alien to our secular constitution" and un-Islamic. "It's against the Islamic spirit", he wrote in his TOI Speaking Tree column.[53] Rushdie in an interview with NDTV said: "...Now I find an India in which religious extremists can prevent free expression of ideas at a literary festival, in which the politicians are too, let's say, in bed with those groups...for narrow electoral reasons."[54] Columnist Praveen Swami even commented that "Salman Rushdie's censoring-out from ongoing literary festival in Jaipur will be remembered as a milestone that marked the slow motion disintegration of India's secular State".[55]

In recent times, '*fatwas*' have been routinely issued by just about anyone in the religious hierarchy—from the Darul Uloom Deoband seminary to any local *masjid* or *maulana* on just about anything—from banning women from wearing lipstick and putting flowers in their hair to blocking cable TV access and music at weddings. Women activists report that increasingly even in

Mumbai and areas around, fatwas and dictats are being routinely issued through pamphlets and Friday sermons by local mosques. Many *fatwas* relate to women, some relate specifically to their movement outside the house—such as visiting restaurants on their own—and others to marriage celebrations, not leaving home and always observing *pardah*.[56]

The Supreme Court, in a significant ruling on February 25, 2014, assured that it would come to the rescue of any citizen who felt harassed by a *fatwa* issued by a Muslim cleric and said *fatwas* and dictates by *muftis* had no sanction in law. "Anything not sanctioned by the law need not be taken cognizance by anyone. The *muftis* can take up any issue and dictate a fatwa. But this will be akin to any common man's view on an issue", it said.[57]

IV

Terrorism and Islam

The term 'fundamentalism' was originally applied to a Protestant movement in the United States of America. The Puritans, who founded New England in the early seventeenth century, were English fundamentalists in their interpretation of the Holy Scriptures and they placed great emphasis on free enquiry. They initiated universal instruction in the western world so that each individual could understand the Bible by means of his own personal criteria. According to Hess,[58] fundamentalism represents a back to basics approach to religion, in the process resisting modernity and seeking to restore an original faith. The emphasis on returning to original sources, described by Hess as new old-time religion, usually arises from disillusionment with prevailing beliefs, practices and interpretations, an approach not usually favoured by mainstream churches. In fact, Hess indicates that in the United States, while the membership of mainstream Protestant denominations declined, that of the independent fundamentalist sects rose sharply, and there was also a fundamentalist revival within Catholicism and Judaism.

Though not a new phenomenon, it is only recently that attention is being given to fundamentalist tendencies among Muslims. It was shortly after the Islamic revolution of 1979 in Iran, culminating in the overthrow of the Shah's regime that the term 'Islamic fundamentalism' came into vogue. In popular usage the term implies a reversion to the original teachings of Islam and carries overtones of fanaticism, intolerance and aggression. It also connotes resistance to the western culture and lifestyle.[59]

Muslims in various parts of the world are today attempting to assert themselves, coming in conflict with the established legal, political and economic systems. Furthermore, controversies are being raised over issues, seemingly trivial in the eyes of the public, such as dress, food and male-female relationships. Islamic fundamentalists are ultraconservative, since they emphasise purity of doctrines and are suspicious of any form of religious innovation.

Periodically, there have been deliberate attempts to reestablish the orthodox version of Islam in India. Generally these efforts advocated a return to the original sources of the religion: the *Quran* and the *Sunnah* (practice and sayings of Muhammad) and the rejection of all forms of religious innovation. Of course, there is no consensus among Muslims as to what constitutes an innovation.

The efforts of Shaikh Ahmad of Sirhind (1563-1624) appear to be one of the earliest attempts at reforming Islamic religious thought in India (the Wahhabi movement started in Arabia around the middle of the eighteenth century). Shaikh Ahmad, born in the early days of Akbar's rule, was noted for his strong resistance to government policies. He criticised the prevailing forms of Sufism and envisaged a return to the fundamentals of Islam. His ideas were said to have later influenced Aurangzeb, Akbar's grandson, born four years after his death. He is referred to in the literature as *Mujaddid Alf-i-Thani,* 'Reformer of the Second Millennium'. Another influential individual was Shah Waliullah of Delhi. His major preoccupation was the reformation of religious thought and his efforts resulted in limited practical reforms. He advocated an independent view of *Fiqh* (Islamic jurisprudence), as opposed to the four established schools of religious thought.

Among the militant and aggressive reformers were Sayyad Ahmad (1786-1831) and Shah Ismail Shahid (1779-1831). These two were actively engaged in reforming social affairs, becoming very influential on the north-western frontier. In the latter part of the nineteenth century, Mirza Ghulam Ahmad of Qadian established another movement with strong modernist tendencies. His declaration of being a *mahdi* (reformer) and a prophet incurred the wrath of mainstream Muslims, who declared him an imposter and an agent of the British. His followers, referred to today as Qadianis and Ahmadis, are regarded as non-believers by orthodox Muslims. Thus, towards the end of the nineteenth century, Islam in India was characterized by marked inter-regional and intra-regional diversity.[60]

Broadly, it is possible to distinguish between two types of reformist efforts in Islam. One is the aggressive and militant type, which is not only involved in proselytising activities, but also attempts to establish the political system of Islam and implement the *Shariah* (Islamic law). The other is the non-militant type which, though basically involved in the spread of Islam, nevertheless confines itself to theological matters. In both cases, the ultimate objective is to return to the original sources of Islam and hence can be described as fundamentalists.

Consequent to the partition of India the Muslim League vanished in north India. All its leaders having migrated to Pakistan, it was left to the Muslims in South India to reorganise politically under the Indian Union Muslim League (IUML) banner in 1948. Following a split in the IUML the Indian National League (INL) was formed after 1972. During the Gulf Oil boom of the 1970s and early 1980s, Muslims from the South, mostly youth, started migrating to the Middle East instead of to the South-East Asia. The South-East Asian countries were multi-religious societies, in contrast to the gulf monarchies. The dominant, purist Wahhabi tradition in the Middle East attracted these youth who began to disdain South Indian syncretic Muslim practices. Islamic reform organisations were formed. Dargah worship, the adulation of saints and their tombs, seen as un-Islamic, came in for sustained condemnation. Social practices such as dowry were derided. The gulf boom, the decline of the moderate IUML/INL and the rise of Wahhabi Islam proved to be a potent cocktail.[61]

The *Shah Bano verdict* on maintenance of Muslim divorced wife was seen as interference in the *Shariah*. Muslim puritan groups capitalised on the weakness of the IUML/INL. What started as an anti-*Dargah* campaign soon entered the town, street and home, and vertically split the community. *Jamaat, namaz, Id* celebrations—everything became two. Youth who returned from the Gulf brought new practices. The gaiety, amity and togetherness that characterised earlier social religious occasions were now lost. The groups championing *Thowheed* (the Oneness of Allah) argued against the Shafi, Hanafi, Maliki and Hanbali schools of jurisprudence and in effect became a fifth school of Islam.[62]

The 1980s and early 90s witnessed the phenomenal rise of the BJP in the Indian politics. The BJP used the militant symbolism of *rath yatras* and *Ram Janmabhoomi* issue for extending its support base. Raychaudhuri says that the *Babri Masjid-Ram Janmabhoomi* controversy is not a symptom of religious revivalism or any spontaneous resurgence of Hindu concern for the honour of the faith. It was in effect the successful end result of a sustained organisational and propaganda campaign launched by the *Sangh Parivar*.[63]

The Ram Janmabhoomi controversy was singularly influential in Muslim politics. The violence following the Babri Masjid demolition—the anti-Muslim riots and bomb blasts in 1993—and the action and inaction of the police, intelligence agencies and courts pushed Muslim youth into the hands of radical groups. Communal tensions and conflicts pervade the atmosphere. Newer areas came under the influence of communal politics.

The Kashmir imbroglio saw the export of terrorism by Pakistan. The Pakistan-based terror outfits like Jaish-e-Mohammed (JeM), Lashkar-e-Taiba (LeT), Harkat-ul-Jihad-al-Islami (Huji), allegedly an offshoot of LeT, with the active help of the Inter-Services Intelligence (ISI) of the Pakistan

Government were involved in many terrorist incidents in many parts of India including Kashmir. Besides, the India-based terrorist organisation of the Students Islamic Movement of India (SIMI) and the "the home-grown *jihadi* militia of Islam", the Indian Mujhadeen (IM) also indulged in such activities in many pockets of the country. New *jihadist* cells have sprung up within India. The recruits include young people, their minds fired by Internet Islamism, as well as veterans once linked to the proscribed SIMI. Many of the Indian recruits are highly educated and economically successful. In 2007, Bangalore-origin, London-based Kafeel Ahmad, a post-doctoral scientist, was killed when he crashed a jeep fitted with improvised explosive devices into Glasgow airport, in the first suicide attack by an Indian national overseas. That summer, north Kashmir resident Aijaz Ahmad Malla was reportedly killed fighting alongside the Taliban in Afghanistan.[64] In Tamil Nadu, volunteers at a Chennai college even signed up to serve with *jihadists* in Syria—recruited by local Islamists, and financed by a Singapore-based executive.[65]

"Each bombing the Indian Mujahideen carries out is a medium for a political message enmeshed with India's dystopic communal landscape: that democratic politics cannot defend India's Muslims", asserts Praveen Swami.[66] And when there is a blast, when one becomes a 'potential victim' it's easy to slip into an anti-Pak, anti-Muslim stance, to disguise communalism in the cloak of nationalism. In the words of Krishna Iyer, suspicion is the upas tree under whose shade reason fails and justice dies.[67] When terror strikes, tolerance takes a hit too. Nationalism can so easily degenerate into communalism.

The 'war on terrorism' has added a new dimension to the fragile 'communal' situation as policemen across the country give free vent to their ignorance and religious prejudice. The Srikrishna Commission as well as numerous other Commissions including fact-finding committees and media reports documented the incriminatory role of the police and its anti-minority attitude. The State Governments have shown no interest in prosecuting the police officials indicated by the Commissions. The calls for sensitisation of the police force towards religious minorities have been many over the years. The tendency of law enforcement agencies to target Muslims for any act of terrorism is well known. All the Muslims rounded up are not necessarily involved in these incidents. Prime Minister Manmohan Singh while addressing the chief ministers' conclave in 2006 asked them to ensure that the campaign against terror did not alienate Muslims, pushing them further towards a radical fringe. He called for the police to be cautious. The remarks came against the backdrop of sharp criticism of Mumbai police's investigation methods by Muslim clerics and MPs as well as the Samajwadi Party and individual Left MPs.[68]

A three-day national conference on the status of Muslims in contemporary India (October 3-5, 2009) has come up with a set of 12 recommendations which included the constitution of a high-power judicial commission headed by a former Chief Justice of the Supreme Court to examine all cases of terror across the country, enactment of a Communal Violence (Prevention, Control and Rehabilitation of Victims) Act, strong action under Section 153A of the Indian Penal Code, a law against communal discrimination on the lines of the SC/ST Act.[69] Syed Ahmed Bukhari, the Shahi Imam of the Jama Masjid in a letter to the Prime Minister in April 2010 has asserted that "99 per cent of Muslims arrested on accusations of terrorism are innocent".[70]

The National Commission for Minorities has drawn the attention of Home Minister P. Chidambaram in July 2012 to a widespread impression in the Muslim community that it is invariably targeted by police after any terrorist strike, and urged the minister to try to dispel this impression among Muslims, which will go a long way in helping build confidence and contribute to developing positive attitudes of mind so necessary in the evolution of India's nationhood.[71] It fell on the next Home Minister, Sushil Kumar Shinde, to announce on May 15, 2013 that the Centre would ask the States to set-up fast track courts to take up cases of Muslim youth who were in jail on terror charges for their quicker trials.[72] On September 30, 2013 he sent an advisory in the form of a letter written to all the Chief Ministers to ensure that innocent Muslim youths are not harassed and illegally detained in the name of terrorism. He asked them to see that the minority community should not have the feeling that Muslim youths are deliberately targeted and deprived of their rights.[73] This move of the Central Government appears to cater to sectional sentiments. Instead of asking for such measures only for a particular community and in the process, being charged of following a policy of communal appeasement, in the fitness of things the Centre should have ensured quicker trial of all under-trial persons languishing in jails, irrespective of religious persuasion. There is no need to communalize the category of innocence.

Many commentators belonging to the ummah have posed the question: "why is it that although Islam is a religion of peace and the ideology of Islam has no place for violence[74], most of the terrorists of today are Muslims?" The answer lies in the Muslim Canon Law which described the geographical territories as *Dar-ul-Harb, Dar-ul-Islam* and *Dar-ul-Aman.* The distinctions have been crucial in Muslim thought and action. *Dar-ul-Harb* literally means "abode of war" or territory that is not under Islamic law. In contrast, *Dar-ul-Islam* (abode of Islam) denotes territory under Islamic law. *Dar-ul-Aman* or "abode of peace" is used to describe territory that is not under Islamic law, but where Muslims can live in peace and harmony without interference in their practice of Islam.

Muslims in a *Dar-ul-Harb* may escape to lands under Muslim rule by way of *Hijrat* (emigration). There is another injunction of Muslim Cannon Law called *Jihad* (crusade) by which it becomes incumbent on a Muslim ruler to extend the rule of Islam until the whole world shall have been brought under its sway, The world being divided into two camps, *Dar-ul-Harb* and *Dar-ul-Islam*, all countries come under one category or the other. Technically, it is the duty of the Muslim ruler, who is capable of doing so, to transform *Dar-ul-Harb* into *Dar-ul-Islam*.

A fourtenth century *fatwa* by the noted Islamic scholar Ibn Taymiyya divided the world into the abode of Islam (*dar-ul-Islam*) and abode of war (*dar-ul-harb*). When General Gerard Lake, as he was known then, captured Delhi in 1803, religious preachers like Shah Abdul Aziz wondered whether the Capital under a Nazrene British Resident was still a *Dar-ul-Islam* or abode of Islam or *Dar-ul-Harb* or abode of war. But his reaction was very circumspect. He offered the argument that only if Friday prayers were no longer held could a country become *Dar-ul Harb*. And since things had not come to such a pass it was evident that the former Mughal domain remained *Dar-ul-Islam*.[75] Sir Syed Ahmed Khan, the founder of the Aligarh movement, urged upon the Muslims to regard India as *Dar-ul-Islam*, because the Muslims were perfectly free to exercise all the essential rites and ceremonies of their religion. The movement for *Hijarat* for the time being died down, but the doctrine that India was *Dar-ul-Harb* had not been given up. It was again preached by Muslim patriots during 1920-21, when the Khilafat agitation was going on.[76]

The Vishwa Hindu Parishad (VHP)'s Dharma Raksha Manch, or Forum to Protect Hinduism, had urged 13 major Muslim organizations on January 28, 2009[77] to issue a *fatwa* that India was not *Dar-ul-Harb* and it was *Dar-ul-Aman*. It was followed up by a letter to the Deoband clergy demanding a *fatwa*, or an edict, to declare India as "friend of Islam to end religion-inspired violence". Islamic seminary Darul Uloom Deoband on February 22, 2009 said it regarded India as *Dar-ul-Aman* or a "Muslim-friendly country". It ceased to be *Dar-ul-Harb* or hostile for Muslims with the end of British rule.[78] A major Muslim body, Jamiat Ulema-i-Hind, has opposed Hindus being dubbed '*kafir*' by Muslims, pointing out that though the term does not have any derogatory connotation, it should be avoided to promote better relations between the two communities. One can call someone non-Muslim, but not '*kafir*' by any means.[79] Al-Qaeda leader Ayman al-Zawahiri has issued his first specific guidelines for jihad, urging restraint in attacking other Muslim sects and non-Muslims and exhorting them to leave alone Christians, Hindus and Sikhs living in Muslim lands.[80]

A *fatwa* against terror, the first of its kind in the country, signed by three muftis was issued by the Darul Uloom Deoband on May 31, 2008. This *fatwa* said: "Islam is a religion of peace and harmony. In Islam, creating social discord, breach of peace, rioting, bloodshed, pillage or plunder and killing of innocent people anywhere in the world are all considered the most inhuman crimes." The *fatwa* concluded saying that "Islam was born to wipe out all kinds of terrorism and spread the message of global peace. Allah knows best".[81] Over three lakh Muslims gathered at Delhi's Ram Lila ground on May 31, 2008 and took a pledge against terrorism.[82] About 6000 muftis gathered in Hyderabad on November 8, 2008 to issue the biggest ever *fatwa* against terror.[83] The Union Home Minister, P. Chidambaram, while attending the 30th annual conference of the Jamiat Ulema-e-Hind on November 3, 2009, sought the support of Deoband ulama in India's war against terror.[84] An organisation "Muslims against Terrorism" has come up to make it clear that the Muslims do not support terrorism anywhere in the world, much less in India. This organisation has denounced the vitriolic speeches of cleric Shaikh Meraj Rabbani of Jamaat Ahl-e-Hadis and appealed to the Government of India to proscribe the organisation to which he belonged.[85]

This effort to marginalise the terrorists is not confined to India only. Minhaj-ul-Quran, a Sufi organisation based in East London has issued a *fatwa* on March 2, 2010, condemning suicide bombings and terrorism—declaring them "un-Islamic".[86] But the most effective of them was the conference held in Mardin in south-eastern Turkey on March 31, 2010 which was attended by 15 leading Islamic scholars from countries like Saudi Arabia, Turkey, India, Senegal, Kuwait, Iran, Morocco, Indonesia, Bosnia, Mauritania and Yemen. The Mardin conference ruled out militant violence and repudiated the *fatwa* issued by the fourteenth century Muslim theologian Iban Taymiyya which proclaimed *jihad* against the Mongols despite their conversion to Islam on the grounds that they could not be true Muslims because they followed the 'man-made' Yasa code instead of the *shariah*. Over the centuries, this *fatwa* had been misused by Muslim extremists to justify violence, even war, against non-Muslims and also other Muslims by declaring them apostates at the slightest difference of opinion.[87]

A quick survey of the communal situation in our neighbouring countries will reveal that China's far-western Muslim-majority Xinjiang region witnesses frequent riots between local Uigurs, an ethnic Turkic Muslim group and Han Chinese migrants. Perhaps drawing lessons from this, the Chinese People's Political Consultative Conference (CPPCC) has decided in its meeting held from March 3 to 12, 2014 to enhance the roles of members from ethnic minorities and religious circles in order to build closer ties with people from minority ethnic and faith groups.[88]

The Buddhist-Rohingya conflict in Myanmar created a widening zone of instability that stretches to Bangladesh, India, Sri Lanka, Malaysia and Indonesia. Bangladesh is vehemently resisting any Rohingya influx. In mid-2012, Lashkar-e-Toiba under its *alias* Jamaat-ud-Dawa created a forum Difa-e-Musalman Arakan (Burma) Conference (Defence of Muslims in Myanmar) in Bangladesh to mobilise support for anti-Myanmar campaign. Other terror outfits, such as Harkat-ul-Jihadi Islami, Jaish-e-Mohammed and Jamaat-ul-

Mujahiden Bangladesh are also trying to exploit the Rohingya's plight to establish new bases in Bangladesh. Jammat-ul-Arakan, a new outfit comprising elements of JMB and Rohingya extremists, is reportedly running militants camps in Bandarban district, along the Bangladesh-Myanmar border.[89] In Myanmar's Rakhine State, which lies northwest of Bangladesh's Chittagong Division, sectarian violence erupted in 2012 between the local Buddhists and the Rohingyas, a Bengali-speaking Muslim minority community. The Buddhists allege that most of the Rohingyas were infiltrators from Bangladesh and therefore have no right to stay in Myanmar. Bangladesh rejects them as Myanmarese, making them nobody's people. Moreover, the huge Western-funded census exercise that started in 2014 since the last British census in the country in 1931 has refused to register the descendants of Bangladeshi Muslims as 'Rohingya'. The implications are serious—unless they can register as Rohingyas, the ethnic category will stand de-recognised with no chance of securing citizenship in the future, written off as 'illegal Bengali migrants' from Bangladesh. That would mean Rohingyas would have to look to Bangladesh and possibly India for shelter.[90] A large number of Rohingyas have already infiltrated into India in search of food and shelter. The presence of the Rohingyas in India worries security forces as they may be exploited by other terrorist outfits. The 'accidental' blast in Khagragarh of Burdwan town in West Bengal on October 2, 2014, the arrest of Bangladeshi nationals from across the state and the arrest of a Rohingya militant from Hyderabad has brought to the fore the nexus between the Jamaat-ul-Mujahideen Bangladesh (JuMB) and the Rohingya militants.

A Malaysian court ruled in October, 2013 that the Arabic word 'Allah' was exclusive to Muslims. Following this ruling an Islamic authority seized 321 Malay-language Bibles from a Christian group in Selangor because they used the word Allah to refer to God. This signals growing intolerance that may inflame ethnic and religious tensions in Malaysia in the near future.[91]

In Indonesia, the world's most populous Muslim country, Islam, Hinduism, Buddhism, Catholicism, Protestantism and Confucianism are the six officially recognized religions. In 2008, the Ahmaddiya community was ordered to stop all its activities that propagated its beliefs. Seven protestant churches in the Bekasi area had been forcibly closed or demolished by local authorities since 2005. It has been alleged that the tendency is towards a creeping Pakistanisation of Indonesia.[92]

Pakistan since its birth has not only systematically driven out the religious minorities from its territory, but also ensured that the religious minorities live under constant physical and mental threats. The Hindu minority of Pakistan not only suffers marginalisation and discrimination, kidnappings also take place under the nose of the government machinery. Many Hindu temples have been desecrated, destroyed, or converted into government offices in Pakistan.

In 1992 alone, hundreds of Hindu temples were destroyed in Pakistan in response to communal riots in India. Despite official promises to rebuild these temples, in many cases, little or no action has been taken to redress the situation. Illegal encroachments on Hindu temples and lands, molestation and abduction of Hindu girls, the demand for huge ransoms in kidnapping cases and frequent arrests of Hindus on false charges have become commonplace in Pakistan.[93]

Pakistan's Christian community is often attacked by the militants. Only on March 15, 2015 at least 15 people were killed and over 80 others injured when Taliban suicide bombers attacked two packed churches during the Sunday mass in Pakistan's biggest Christian colony in the Youhanbad district of Lahore City that is home to more than 10,000 Christians. In 2013 a devastating double suicide bombing in the north-western city of Peshawar killed 82 Christians. Though such attacks are routiningly condemned by the Prime Minister, the whole Christian community in Pakistan is begging the government to provide it security.[94]

Even Ahmedis was declared non-Muslim by the Bhutto government in 1974. It has become a breeding ground of fundamentalist militant organizations like the defunct militant Deobandi Organization, Sipha-e-Sahaba Pakistan (SSP), JeM and LeT. Then there is the United Jihad Council (UJC), a conglomerate of Harkat-ul-Mujahideen (HuM), JeM, LeT, Hizb-ul-Mujahideen, Al Badr, Jamaat-e-Islami and Harkat-ul-Ansar (HuA). This organisation now combines with amalgams of other smaller militant groups, like the Kashmir Freedom Force and the Kashmir Resistance Force. This country is often accused of exporting terrorism to other countries, especially India. Bangladesh has become a hotbed of activities of Pakistan's ISI. It is witnessing a clash between the fundamentalist Islamic organizations and the secular forces.

The "Partition" was swift and vicious in the Punjab and Sindh where religious minorities have practically ceased to exist for all practical purposes. This is not so in the Bengals, where many still live on their ancestral land. More than 25.24 per cent (according to the 2001 census) of Bengal's western half's population is Muslim (the figure was 19.46% in 1951, after the 1947 Partition). In the eastern half, 9.2 per cent of the population in the 2001census is Hindu (it was 22 per cent in 1951). In Bengal, secularism has political currency. It was one of the foundational principles of the 1971 Bangladesh Liberation War.

Overtures to fundamentalist groupings in post-Mujib period gave religion-based politics a fillip in Bangladesh. The rise of militant Islam in Bangladesh is due to the Afghan Jihad and the Taliban Movement. It was the Harkat-ul-Jihad-al-Islami, Bangladesh [HUJI(B)], now banned, which first surfaced as a regular political force. Many of them were Afghan veterans, including one Mufti Hannan who has been sentenced to death for master-minding the plot to kill the then Prime Minister Sheikh Hasina in 2000. The Jagrat Muslim Janata Bangladesh (JMJB) became a formidable organization under the leadership of "Banglabhai", Siddiqur Islam. The JMJB became affiliated with Jamaitul Mujahideen Bangladesh (JMB) under Sheikh Abdur Rahman. During Begum Khaleeda Zia's time, these Islamist outfits gathered enough strength and resources so as to create an organisation that threatened the very fabric of a progressive democratic Muslim country.

Bangladesh was accused of giving shelter to, and allowing its land to be used by, the secessionist groups of the North-east. Only on March 6, 2014, the BSF in its meeting with the Border Guard Bangladesh has handed over a list of 66 camps of Northeast insurgents that exist now in Bangladesh seeking their cooperation in dismantling them.[95]

Hindus in Bangaldesh are the soft target of the fundamentalist forces. In the 1971 Liberation War many of them had to flee to India in search of food and shelter. The same thing had happened after the January 5, 2014 elections. Though barely 4-5 per cent of the Hindus could exercise their franchise, they have become easy targets of anti-election activists, thinking that they voted for the Awami League. Systematic attacks were carried out in the minority-dominated villages. Hundreds of houses were torched and looted. The U.N. Chief expressed his anguish over the continuing post-poll violence terming it "unacceptable". [96]

In earlier decades, the policies of integration and assimilation used to be in place in Western democracies. But the hegemony of national cultures began to be undermined by ghettoisation in housing and social activities. In the US, Canada, Australia, the so-called new nations, the immigrant communities are dispersed over large territories and the problems of ghetto formation are accordingly reduced. However, tiny Denmark (5.4 million people), for instance, suddenly woke up to the pressure of 2,00,000 Muslim residents. France has enormous problems integrating five to six million Muslim immigrants from the former French colonies of North Africa. Islamic militancy in the "zones", the outer suburbs of Paris is an everyday problem because these ghettos are home to the most impoverished of French citizens. The story is the same in Germany, Belgium and so on. The immigrants in the suburbs of Paris are traditional and devout Muslims and live in an ethos very different from the feminist and secular culture of Paris, only a few miles away. In the UK, as immigrants moved into lower or middle class areas, the original inhabitants moved out. Immigrants took over these neighbourhoods, built their own institutions, places of worship and business places. The immigrant/migrant communities are separated from national culture by structural factors such as housing, school education and lack of shared spaces for imbibing the culture of the nation. The 7 July, 2005 suicide bombers were young (in their teens and early 20s) and born of immigrant parents. Among men behind the strike, at least two had fled Africa as children and had found safety in the UK. Safety, yes, but multiculturalism obviously did not create acceptance.[97]

In the Muslim provinces of Chechnya and Dagestan in Russia, insurgency and separatism have been simmering for the last two decades. Now, the involvement of ethnic-Russian converts to Islam is being suspected in the two suicide bombings that killed a total of 34 people in December-January 2014 in Volgograd, a southern Russian city.[98]

A string of events across the world—the murder in Dhaka of US-based writer Avijit Roy, who fought for a more liberal and secular Bangladesh, by Islamic radicals, the attack on a cultural centre in Copenhagen for hosting a debate on Islam and blasphemy, the attack on *Charlie Hebdo* cartoonists for 'insulting the Prophet', the flogging of liberal Saudi blogger Raif Badawi for promoting free thinking and many more—confronts the world at large to the stark reality of the insensitivity and ruthlessness of the religious zealots, masquerading as upholder of "true Islam".

It has been consistently argued, especially by the liberal-Left, that religiously motivated violence is simply a function of racial discrimination, lack of opportunities and poverty, downplaying the role of religion even if the perpetrators explicitly say so. While these factors have to be acknowledged, a perceptive writer has pointed out that tens of thousands of young, educated and middle class Muslims from liberal societies in the West are joining the Islamic State (IS) in Iraq. Jihadi John, who featured in the videos showing beheading of captives by the Islamic State, is an example: he grew up in London and has a degree in Computer Science. Similarly, Umar Abdul Muttalab, the "underwear bomber" who tried to blow up a passenger jet over Detroit on Christmas in 2009, was a son of wealthy Nigerian businessman. Even Osama Bin Laden and the current Al-Qaeda chief Ayman Al-Zawahiri, hail from well-to-do families. It is better not to underestimate the power of religious ideology in inspiriting people to fight for a utopia. With Nigera's Boko Haram pledging allegiance to the IS, we are faced with a translational alliance of dangerous fascist groups seeking to reorganise society in their own vision.[99] There is also the worrying trend of Indian Muslim youth ensnared by fundamentalists like the Islamic State. Mehdi Masroor Biswas, the Twitter handler for ISIS, and Arif Majeed the Kalyan youth who went to Syria, were symptoms of a malaise, points out Kalbe Sadiq, the Shia cleric and scholar of Islam.[100]

It is no doubt a sad commentary that globally Islam and Muslims are increasingly being equated with terrorism and religious hysteria. The debates on them have got more strident, confused and much nastier, especially after 9/11. It devolves on those who profess and practice this religion to find out ways and means for effacing this blot on them. There are already welcome signs of introspection among Muslims in the wake of the *Charlie Hebdo* killings. Most importantly, the traditionally conservative Muslim political and clerical Establishment had broken its silence with Sheikh Ahmed al-Tayeb, the Grand Imam of al-Azhar mosque—the oldest seat of Sunni Islamic learning—proposing a radical overhaul of Islamic teaching; and Egypt's president, Abdel Fattah el-Sisi, calling for a "religious revolution" to purge Islam of extremist tendencies. This is a welcome move because ultimately, as Hasan Suroor says, "the future of Islam as a religion fit for the twentyfirst century hinges on the liberal worldview gaining ground among Muslims."[101]

V

Use of Religion and Caste by Political Parties

In the wake of the ban imposed by the Lucknow Bench of the Allahabad High Court on July 11, 2013 on caste-based rallies[102], the president of the Bahujana Samaj Party Ms. Mayawati has demanded[103] a ban on the religion-based outfits like the Vishwa Hindu Parishad, the Rashtriya Swayam Sevak and the Bajrang Dal. It may be recalled that just after the assassination of Mahatma Gandhi a Resolution regarding elimination of Communal Organizations was adopted in the Constituent Assembly of India (Legislative). This resolution was moved on April 3, 1948 by M. Ananthasayanam Ayyanger and almost all the leaders of all communities including Pandit Jawaharlal Nehru, Prime Minister, and his Cabinet Colleague Dr. Shyama Prasad Mookherjee extended their support to this Resolution. The Resolution ran as follows:

> Whereas it is essential for the proper functioning of democracy and the growth of national unity and solidarity that communalism should be eliminated from Indian life, this Assembly is of opinion that no communal organization which by its constitution or by the exercise of discretionary power vested in any of its officers or organs, admits to or excludes from its membership persons on grounds of religion, race and caste or any of them, should be permitted to engage in any activities other than those essential for the *bona fide* religious, cultural, social and educational needs of the community, and that all steps, legislative and administrative necessary to prevent such activities should be taken.[104]

This resolution was adopted by the Legislative Assembly the same day. When this resolution was moved and discussed in the Legislative Assembly, the Constituent Assembly was not in session, but the Draft Constitution which had already been circulated to all members on February 21, 1948 was being discussed in various forums. Adoption of this resolution by the Legislative Assembly might pave the way for incorporation of such a provision in the Constitution. At least so thought Pandit Nehru when he said:

"now, the future Constitution of India is being hammered out in the Constituent Assembly and no doubt it will give shape to it in the course of the next two or three months and finalise it, and any resolution that we may pass is not going to alter that Constitution as it is finally adopted. But, after all, the Constitution-making body is more or less this body, there is not much difference. And if this House thinks in terms of the Resolution I have no doubt that the Constitution-making body will also think in terms of this Resolution. Further, from such evidence as we have got of the working of that Constitution-making body, it has already gone a long way in terms of this Resolution. It has put aside many of the dangerous features of our old Constitution which led to communalism. Whether other features will remain or not I cannot obviously guarantee. But as far as I am concerned, I think the less we have of any form of communalism the better it is for our Constitution and for the practical working of our Government"[105].

Since no specific proposal in pursuance of this resolution was mooted, Damodar Swarup Seth moved an amendment in the Constituent Assembly on December 7, 1948 for addition of a new article after Article 22. The clause read as follows:

> 22A. The use of religious institutions for political purposes and the existence of political organizations on religious basis is forbidden.

Before he could speak, Dr. Ambedkar interjected that it was covered by Article 19(2)(a) [now Article 25]. H.V. Kamath pointed out that "Article 19(2)(a) regulates or restricts political or other secular activities associated with religion. Seth Damodar Swarup's amendment forbids them altogether. Between a complete ban and mere regulation there is a lot of difference."

Pandit Thakur Das Bhargava commented that an amendment to Article 19(2) seeking to add 'prohibiting' was not accepted by the House. The Vice-President, who was then presiding over the Session disallowed the motion because "it practically means the same thing as Seth Damodar Swarup's amendment. I am afraid this thing has already been covered."[106]

This New Article of Damodar Swarup Seth was for banning of political organization on religious basis. We still find that political organizations are functioning on religious basis. Mention may be made of Akali Dal, Muslim League, Hindu Mahasabha and so on. If this New Article was accepted, functioning of such political organizations championing the cause of communities on religious basis in secular India would have been prohibited. Use of religion by political parties could have been prevented and that would have created a great impact on the social life in India which has been proclaimed a secular State. Exploitation of religion and religious sentiments in furtherance of political objectives of the political parties militates against the basic concept of secularism. The very idea of formation and functioning of political parties on religious basis cuts at the root of secularism. It keeps alive the spirit of separatism amongst different religious communities. It creates, Nehru told the Constituent Assembly, "isolated groups permanently and prevents the groups from coming closer to one another".[107] An artificial barrier is raised which divides the communities on religious lines. It is simply suicidal to pursue this policy in a country which is already ravaged by communalism. Religion and politics should have been separated at any cost. Community should not be made the basis of civic rights. That is a fundamental principle. While it was decided that the State or rather the Government should not side with any religion, it was not thought proper to ensure that the parties which function in a democratic set-up of the country, either as a party in power or in opposition do not function on religious basis. In a secular State the right to representation is only the right to represent the territory in which all communities live and when a Member represents in the legislature, he has the right to speak on behalf of all those living in the territory, of all communities and classes, men and women. That is the idea with which a democracy functions. Pandit Govind Ballabh Pant warned the Constituent Assembly way back in 1947 just after the partition of the country:

> There cannot be any divided loyalty. All loyalties must exclusively be centered round the State. If in a democracy rival loyalties are created or a system is created in which any individual or group instead of suppressing his extravagance cares not for larger or others' interests, then democracy is doomed. For the success of democracy one must train himself in the art of self-discipline. In democracies one should care less for himself and more for others.[108]

As Faizan Mustafa says, a democratic society is rooted in the principle of equal rights for all citizens and gives everyone the right to strive for his betterment. In contrast, communalism and religion-based nationalism divides communities into different religious groups with diverse social interest and varying rights. In the process, the dominant religious group arrogates to itself the right to determine the policies of the nation and set its goals and agenda. In turn, the assertive, dominant section of the community takes over the management of social affairs and its legitimacy goes unquestioned.[109]

The Supreme Court observed that "if a political party espousing a particular religion comes to power, that religion tends to become in practice the official religion. All other religions come to acquire a secondary status, at any rate a less favourable position. This would be plainly antithetical to Articles 14 to 16, 25 and the entire Constitutional scheme."[110] Similarly, as Anirban Kashyap says,

> the parties which are in opposition today and cherish the desire of capturing power tomorrow may exploit religious issues and religious sentiments of the communities they represent and project all sorts of demands, including religious demands, of the communities not only to woo them and to firmly establish their hold over them but also to embarrass the Government in every conceivable way. These parties owe their existence to religious communities and their allegiance is to those religious communities only and not to the country. Their primary and main object is to champion the cause of religious communities and to extract as much concessions and facilities as feasible from the Government, even if required by whipping up communal passions. They live, work and thrive only by exploiting the communal sentiments of a section of people. They have scant regard for the sentiments or for the reactions of other citizens of the country and for the larger interest of the country. They think that they are answerable only to that community which vote for them. In the process, sectarian and communal politics set in. It means introduction by the backdoor of the dangerous principle of communal electorate which the Authors of the Constitution threw out from the front door. The very existence of political parties on religious and communal basis undermines the secular concept of State.[111]

Mahavir Tyagi pointed out in the Constituent Assembly that "a secular State cannot give recognition or weightage to any religious groups of individuals. Beliefs or creeds are a purely individual and private affair."[112] It should not be encouraged or exploited by political parties in furtherance of their political objectives, that too, in a secular State like ours. The only place where it should have a mooring, where it should get a foothold is in a theocratic State.

Use of religion and religious places by political parties cuts at the root of secularism. The very purpose of secularism is defeated if political parties are allowed to thrive on religion and use religious places to their advantages. "In this country we have seen the exploitation, and the prostitution of what we call religion and we have seen to our bitter cost what is done in the name of denominational religion. It has not only led to the dismemberment and division of our country, but it has also led to the worst horrors that could be perpetrated in the name of religion"[113], said Renuka Ray. Once beaten, twice shy, remained only an adage to the Framers. They refused to learn from the past. There might have been opposition, severe opposition from those very political parties and organisations which depend on religion and religious institutions and places for their survival, if the use of religion and religious places in politics was prohibited. It is their umbilical cord. If the cord is cut off, they would feel like fish out of water. They would have either perished or learnt to stand on their own legs without any prop from religion. But this could not be achieved. In a secular State, no organisation, especially political party, can exist on communal and religious basis. Existence of such organisations negates the very concept of secularism. But secularism, as is practised in India, tolerates even such diametrically opposite concepts. Religion dominates. "Religious community and not the nation had now become a factor of identity", bemoaned Tapan Roychoudhury, a historian, in 1992.[114]

This has been possible because of the inability of the Framers to prohibit the functioning of political parties which use religion for political ends. A resolution on banning communal organisations was adopted in the Constituent (Legislative) Assembly in April 1948, but no further action was taken to enforce it. Nehru even in 1961 "considered the banning of communal parties, but found this to be impractical, only because communal parties deny being communal".[115] Once the political parties are allowed to function on communal consideration, the very foundation of secularism is at stake. This was perhaps not properly considered by the Framers otherwise how they could ignore this aspect even after proclaiming a secular State.

Assimilation of different groups of people speaking different languages, practising different religions, following different cultures should have been the prime concern for achieving integration. With that end in view, religion, which is a very strong instrument for whipping up passions and hatred against other religious communities, should have been kept out of reach of those persons who are prone to use it and of those who used it earlier. Since India had already witnessed to what an extent religion could be exploited for the furtherance of political objectives, it was all the more necessary to guard against it. For the protection of the nation and of our hard-won liberty from the peril of communalism adequate safeguards and provisions should have been provided in the Constitution. That was the demand raised in the Constituent Assembly as well by Members like Raj Bahadur, Mahabir Tyagi, L. Krishnaswami Bharati[116] at the time of discussion on motion for consideration of the Draft Constitution. As pointed out by Anirban Kashyap:

> The tendencies, the idiosyncrasies which have been responsible for the vivisection of our motherland should not have been allowed to raise their ugly heads once again. It was absolutely necessary to ensure that the people and the evil forces which might once again try to revive and perpetuate communal politics in the country did not imperil our freedom. Endeavour should have been directed towards wiping out communalism from our body politic for ever. This could have been possible to some extent if all the communities based on religion had merged politically with the rest of the population and not perpetuated communalism by having communal political organizations. Communal politics should have been given a good-

> bye and all communal organizations should have ceased to exist as political organizations and given up their political role.[117]

It may be recalled that with the advent of the Constitution of India in 1950, the consistent policy of law—especially election law—has been to distance politics and political parties from religion. This was first done by the enactment of Clause (3) in Section 123 of the Representation of the People Act, 1951: this clause included in the definition of "corrupt practices"—"the systematic appeal by a candidate or his agent or by any other person, to vote or refrain from voting on grounds of caste, race, community or religion, for the furtherance of the prospects of that candidate's election." Then in 1961, the scope of the R.P. Act was widened by the introduction of another corrupt practice invalidating the election result: Clause (3A) was added "to curb communal and separatist tendencies". This clause defined as corrupt practice the promotion or attempt to promote feelings of enmity or hatred between different classes of citizens on the ground, *inter alia*, of religion by a candidate or his agent or other persons with the consent of the candidate for the furtherance of the prospects of the election of that candidate.

Three years later, the word "systematic" in the expression "systematic appeal" in the original Clause 3 of the Section 123 was deleted; with the result that even a single appeal by a candidate or his agent to electors to vote or refrain from voting for any person on the ground of his religion, has been sufficient to constitute a "corrupt practice".

The Election Commission considered that the elimination of religious overtones in the electoral process should not be left till after the election—it should be tackled even before. Accordingly, the Election Symbols Reservation and Allotment Order, 1968—an order passed by the Election Commission of India under Article 324 of the Constitution—made special provision (for the first time) for registration of "political parties"—they were described as parties based on political principles and with political aim and objects; but distancing of religion (from politics) was not specifically provided for in the 1968 Order.

This was left to Parliament, and in 1988 Parliament amended the R.P. Act adding Section 29A. It provided that every political party had to be registered, and had to subscribe to the principles of "secularism" and that had to be stated in its Memorandum and regulations. The statement of objects and reasons for this amendment said that the purpose was to ensure that political parties would be fully committed to and abide by the principles enshrined in the Preamble to the Constitution.

On the question whether political parties already registered could be deregistered, if it was alleged that they had failed to observe the provisions of their Memorandum—in respect of the matters set out in Clause (5) of Section 29A (including "secularism") there has been no authoritative decision of any Court. But the Election Commission in February 1992 held in a group of petitions filed by Arjun Singh and others seeking deregistration of the BJP as a political party that the provisions of Section 29A do not themselves empower the Commission to deregister a political party on the ground that after registration it has ceased to function in accordance with the provisions of Section 29A(5), where such allegation is disputed.[118]

In *S.R. Bommai and others* vs. *Union of India* decided in March 1994, a Bench of nine Justices of the Supreme Court of India held (seven of them saying so expressly) that in a secular democracy as ours "mingling of religion with politics is unconstitutional" and that "it is imperative that religion and caste should not be introduced into politics by any political party, association or individual, and it is equally imperative to prevent religion and caste polluting politics."

The provision of the amended R.P. Act and the pronouncement of the highest court of the land notwithstanding, political parties championing the cause of religious community/communities as also of communities based on caste are the order of the day. Political parties go on branding this or that political party as "communal" or "casteist" as it suited them, but has not the will, the political will, to incorporate in the "secular" Constitution of ours a provision specifically prohibiting the use of religious institutions for political purposes and the existence of political organizations on religious basis. Is it because they also use religion and religious places in a more sophisticated or subtle form? As a matter of fact if such a provision finds a place in the Constitution there would hardly be a political party worth its name in our "secular" India, because all of them indulge in communalism in this or that form by pandering to the cause of religious communities and caste groups, either directly or indirectly. That is the reason why even those places which never witnessed communal disharmony have become hotbeds of communal strife. Not only the political parties be prevented—constitutionally—from using religion and religious places, they also should not be allowed to use communal organisations in furtherance of their political objectives of capturing or sharing state power. For instance, in Punjab the role of religious sects or '*deras*' assumes importance for the candidates who seek the support of religious leaders to bolster their electoral fortunes during election time. Punjab has nearly 300 major *deras* across the State. Political observers say that most of the deras command a substantial following and any political party or candidate who manages to get the support of a dera stands an excellent chance of securing a good number of votes. Some *deras* are open about their political leanings, while others prefer not to come out directly in support of any particular party or candidate.[119] Syed Abdullah Bukhari, the Shahi Imam of Jama Masjid was the chief architect of the wholesale Muslim support to the Janata Party in 1977 when he had travelled all over the country exhorting Muslims to teach the "cruel murderess" a lesson by voting her out of power. In 1980, Mrs.

Gandhi won over the Imam and, on his appeal, Muslims again voted for the Congress (I). In 1989, it was once again Bukhari who single-handedly brainwashed the Muslims into voting against the Congress (I). In the 1991 elections both V.P. Singh and Rajiv Gandhi tried to obtain a *fatwa* in their favour. He again asked the Muslims to vote for the Trinamul Congress in West Bengal, Lalu Prasad's RJD in Bihar and the Congress in the rest of the country in the 2014 Lok Sabha elections.[120]

Syed Shahabuddin of the Babri Masjid Action Committee fame in his journal, *Muslim India*, asked Muslims to vote *en bloc* in favour of V.P. Singh and, where the situation demands, in favour of Rajiv Ganhdi to defeat the communal forces. This *en bloc* voting is the main bugbear of the BJP.[121] Gujarat saw the Ahmedabad Jama Masjid Imam, Maulana Mohammed Shabir, exhorting the Muslims to vote *en bloc* for the Congress in the 2002 Assembly elections.[122] That, however, did not happen.

Now, the Joint Committee of Muslim Organisations for Empowerment, made up of the likes of the Jamaat-e-Islami, Milli Council and the Imam Sangh, has issued "election guidelines" advising the "aam Musalman" whom to vote for so that the community's votes are not wasted on losing candidates and decided to form consultative bodies at the constituency level to "unite and mobilize the Muslim electorate for the common cause".[123]

The Zakat Foundation of India, the country's largest Muslim charity has threatened in November 2013 to reject candidates of all parties unless a 20-point list of demands is included in the manifestos and followed up with the time-bound written promise. Conferring minority status to Aligarh Muslim University, establishment of an equal opportunity commission, setting up time-bound fast-track courts to try terror cases, implementation of reservation for Muslims under the category of socially and educationally backward classes on the lines of recommendation made by the Ranganath Mishra panel are some of the demands listed in the 20-point. The All-India Muslim Majlis-e-Mushawarat, an umbrella body of Muslim organizations, has agreed with this charter.[124] Since the UPA government did not respond to their overture, the Zakat decided to support the Aam Admi Party of Arvind Kejriwal with the same conditions.[125]

In view of the embargo to ask for vote in the name of religion, no political party could directly exploit the religious sentiments of the voters in the 2014 Lok Sabha elections. Since the BJP, a party branded as a communal party by all the "secular" parties, made an attempt to wrest power from the Congress-led UPA II it was said that "it is a communally charged election". An editorial in *The Statesman* even asserts that "seldom, perhaps never, not even after the demolition of the Babri Masjid has an election been so profoundly influenced by religion".[126] The "secular" parties never miss an opportunity to castigate the BJP as a "communal" party, but they themselves are not shy of using religious leaders for their vote bank politics. In the 2014 Lok Sabha elections, the Jammat-e-Islami-Hind has put out a list of candidates to ensure consolidation of Muslims in favour of those who are in the best position to defeat "communal and fascist forces", thereby meaning the BJP. Another organisation, Jamiat-Ulama-i-Hind, the largest body of Sunni clerics, has appealed for support to 'secular' candidates but has refrained from putting out a list.[127] Perhaps to assert that it is an Islamic institution that has nothing to do with politics, the Darul Uloom of Deoband, the flagship seminary, issued a sort of *fatwa*—"Both Hindus and Muslims should vote in favour of secular parties to save the secular politics of India" and announced that its door would be shut to politicians, irrespective of party lines, till the end of the Lok Sabha elections.[128]

Shekhar Gupta has referred to the '*sants*' and '*moulavis*' and '*gyanis*' who have been wielding steadily stronger influence in the affairs of the nation, all in the guise of protecting the respective religions.[129] Parwez Hafeez has raised the question why an Imam—a prayer leader— should lead the entire Muslim community in mundane matters as well.[130] Even the common Muslims have started questioning as to why they are to follow the *diktat* of the Imams in the matter of casting their votes—it matters little whether they are the Shahi Imam of Jama Masjid of Delhi, Imam Barkati of Tipu Sultan Masjid of Kolkata or Pirzada Thaha Siddiqi of Furfura Sharif.[131] A question may be raised whether we should allow people without responsibility and accountability to decide national issues.[132]

As Arati R. Jerath says, "the British colonialists crafted the divide-and-rule policy to subjugate a feudal society after the 1857 uprising in which Hindus and Muslims fought together to throw the foreigners out. There is absolutely no justification for our political parties to continue the policy in independent India".[133] Sadly enough, the Authors of the Constitution did not ban the existence of communal political organizations. They refused to learn from past experiences and the result is, as we find it today.

VI

Minorities in the Constitution

The term minority is the product of a democratic polity in which numbers count in the acquisition of power. The word "minority" is derived from the Latin word "minor" and the suffix "ity", meaning the smaller in number of two aggregates which constitute a whole. Going by this numeric definition, a minority-group may or may not be politically influential. The Muslims under Mughal rule were numerically small but a politically dominant group. The blacks in pre-Apartheid South Africa were politically subjugated, although they constituted a numerical majority. With the increasing awareness of human rights awareness worldwide, the term minority has come to be associated with a politically dominated and socially discriminated group.

Feagin states that a minority group has five characteristics: (1) suffering discrimination and subordination, (2) physical and/or cultural traits that set them apart, and which are disapproved by the dominant group, (3) a shared sense of collective identity and common burdens, (4) socially shared rules about who belongs and who does not determine minority status, and (5) tendency to marry within the group.[134]

Sociologist Louis Wirth defined a minority group as "a group of people who, because of their physical or cultural characteristics, are singled out from the others in the society in which they live for differential and unequal treatment, and who therefore regard themselves as objects of collective discrimination."[135]

This definition includes both objective and subjective criteria: membership of a minority group is objectively ascribed by society, based on an individual's physical or behavioural characteristics; it is also subjectively applied by its members, who may use their status as the basis of group identity or solidarity. In any case, minority group status is categorical in nature: an individual who exhibits the physical or behavioural characteristics of a given minority group will be accorded the status of that group and be subject to the same treatment as other members of that group.

However, national minority can be theoretically (not legally) defined as a group of people within a given national state:

1. which is numerically smaller than the rest of population of the state or a part of the state;
2. which is not in a dominant position;
3. which has culture, language, religion, race etc. distinct from that of the majority of the population;
4. whose members have a will to preserve their specificity;
5. whose members are citizens of the state where they have the status of a minority; and
6. which have a long-term presence on the territory where it has lived.

A minority group is a sociological category within a demographic. Rather than a relational "social group", as the term would indicate, the term refers to a category that is differentiated and defined by the social majority, that is, those who hold the majority of positions of social power in a society. The differentiation can be based on one or more observable human characteristics, including, for example, ethnicity, race, caste, language, religion, gender, territory, colour, age, wealth, health or sexual orientation.

The Constitution of India is not very specific in its definition of "minority". The Draft Constitution, prepared by the Drafting Committee and circulated on February 21, 1948 contained in Part XIV the "special provisions relating to minorities". The minorities enumerated in this Part were Muslims, Scheduled Castes, Scheduled Tribes, Indian Christians and Anglo-Indian community. The Constitution was criticized by some for the special safeguards that it provides for minorities. In his reply Ambedkar told the Constituent Assembly:[136]

> Speaking for myself, I have no doubt that the Constituent Assembly has done wisely in providing such safeguards for minorities as it has done. In this country both the minorities and the majorities have followed a wrong path. It is wrong for the majority to deny the existence of minorities. It is equally wrong for the minorities to perpetuate themselves. A solution must be found which will serve a double purpose. It must recognise the existence of the minorities to start with. It must also be such that it will enable majorities and minorities to merge some day into one. The solution proposed by the Constituent Assembly is to be welcomed because it is a solution which serves this two-fold purpose. To diehards who have developed a kind of fanaticism against minority protection I would like to say two things. One is that minorities are an explosive force which, if it erupts, can blow up the whole fabric of the State. The history of Europe bears ample and appalling testimony to this fact. The other is that the minorities in India have agreed to place their existence in the hands of the majority. In the history of negotiations for preventing the partition of Ireland, Redmond said to Carson, "ask for any safeguard you like for the Protestant minority but let us have a United Ireland". Carson's reply was: "Damn your safeguards, we don't want to be ruled by you". No minority in India has taken this stand. They have loyally accepted the rule of the majority *which is basically a communal majority and not a political majority*. It is for the majority to realize its duty not to discriminate against minorities. Whether the minorities will continue or will vanish must depend upon this habit of the majority. The moment the majority loses the habit of discriminating against the minority, the minorities can have no ground to exist. They will vanish.
>
> [emphasis added]

It may be recalled that when Ambedkar made this much-quoted exhortations in the Constituent Assembly on November 4, 1948 the vivisection of India on the basis of religion was complete. The religious minority of pre-partition India, the Muslims, had already erupted and blown up the whole fabric of a united India. So, it is not correct to say that "no minority in India had taken this stand" because the Carsons of pre-partition India had already their pound of flesh. So, the relevancy of Redmond-Carson dialogue in the Indian context may be questioned. Moreover, the Draft Constitution had many religion-based provisions as also provisions for reservation of seats in the legislatures on communal basis. Perhaps in justification of such provisions in the Draft Constitution, Ambedkar wanted the majority to discharge "its duty not to discriminate against minorities", and not to put any impediment to such provisions in the Draft Constitution.

Ambedkar's contention that in India the majority *is basically a communal majority and not a political majority* was questioned by many members of the Constituent Assembly who did not like this stand of Ambedkar of dividing the Indians on communal line. The word 'community' is the root of the ugly outlook called 'communalism',[137] remarked Suchet Singh. Maulana Hasrat Mohani, a Socialist, went on to say, "so long as you have this communalism, nothing can be done. Why do you say that Muslims are a Minority? So long as you depict them in communal colours Muslims shall remain a Minority. When we come as members of a political party or as members of the Independent Communist Party or as Socialists and then form a coalition party, then as a whole they will be arrayed against the rest."[138] Maulana Mohani on the same ground advocated for the scrapping of the Minority Report of the Advisory Committee on Minority Rights, Fundamental Rights etc.[139] It may be recalled that when the constitutional document was finished, he declined to sign it. In his view, India's Constitution should have been drafted and approved by a newly-elected group that represented the democratic polity of the new nation and not the communally divided colonial polity of the past.

It may be pointed out when the motion for abolition of separate electorates was debated in the Constituent Assembly Congressmen requested the Muslims to forget about their religious identity. Pant told the Muslim representatives, "your safety lies in making yourselves an integral part of the organic whole which forms the real genuine State".[140] Sardar Patel, who headed the Advisory Committee on Fundamental Rights, Minority Rights, etc., gave an even more scathing reply, indeed what were probably veiled threats, to the Muslims' demand for a separate electorate: "Do you want now peace in this land? If so, do away with it; you can do no harm either to Pakistan or India on anything, but only you will have all over the country what is happening in this country near about us; if you do want it, you can have it".[141]

These words, spoken on 27 August, 1947, probably alluded to the communal riots that took place at that time in India and particularly in Delhi, in which Muslims were the main victims. The debate took off again the next day when the Muslims reiterated their demand for a separate electorate. Patel's rebuttal was:

> Those who want that kind of thing have a place in Pakistan, not here (Applause). Here, we are building a nation and we are laying the foundations of One Nation, and those who choose to divide again and sow the seeds of disruption will have no place, no quarter, here, and I must say that plainly enough (Hear, Hear).[142]

The Advisory Committee had recommended the scrapping of the separate electorate, but not objected to a quota of reserved seats for the religious minorities, including the Muslims. That is the reason why there were provisions in Part XIV of the Draft Constitution for reservation of seats for minorities like Muslims, Scheduled Castes, Scheduled Tribes, Indian Christians and Anglo-Indian community in the House of the People and in the State Legislative Assemblies. Their contrariness, however, had made Patel regret this concession. Therefore, when the Indian Christian leader H.C. Mookherjee and the Shia Muslim leader Tejamul Husain made efforts for abolition of reserved seats for the religious communities, Sardar Patel seized this opportunity. In the meeting of the Advisory Committee held on December 30, 1948 when the chairman of the Committee alluded to the motions given notice of by several members seeking to do away with reservation for minorities,

> The Hon'ble Dr. B.R. Ambedkar raised a point of order to the effect that the political safeguards for the minorities having been accepted by the Constituent Assembly of India they were not within the reach of the Advisory Committee and that if it was the desire of the committee to discuss the matter *de novo* the proper procedure was to move amendments to the provisions contained in the Draft Constitution. The Chairman ruled that there was no bar to a discussion and that the committee also could recommend reconsideration of the whole matter. On merits, however, he thought that unless there was general agreement the conclusions already arrived at should not be disturbed.[143]

On May 25, 1949 Patel introduced in the Constituent Asssembly an amendment cancelling the reservation of seats for religious minorities. During the debate Mohammad Ismail Sahib of the Muslim League strongly objected that this modification did not reflect the general feeling of the Muslim community and argued:

> Unity really means harmony, the adjustment of things which are different with different groups of people not only in this country but also in other parts of the world. Harmony is possible only when all sections of people are satisfied, are contented.[144]

But several Muslim representatives expressed dissonant views. Z.H. Lari, a socialist from Uttar Pradesh, rejected reservation because he did not want to consider the Muslims "as a separate indifferent entity, but as a welcome part of the organic whole".[145] Naziruddin Ahmad from West Bengal considered that the demand for reservations reflected a post-Partition 'fear-complex' which was disappearing now that "the situation has vastly improved and is daily improving".[146] Tejamul Husain spoke along similar lines against any kind of protection, such as separate electorates whose demand amounted to 'asking for charity'. His advice was:

> The majority community will never trust you then. You will never be able to exert yourself. You will be isolated, you will be treated as an alien and your position will be the same as that of the Scheduled Caste. You are not poor. Like the Scheduled Castes, you are not weak, you are not uneducated; you are not uncultured; you can always support yourself. You have produced brilliant men. So do not ask for protection or safeguard. You must have self-confidence in you. You must exert yourself. You must get into the Assembly by open competition. The times have changed. Adjust yourself.[147]

Such a speech exemplifies the responsiveness of minority leaders to the prospect of building a new nation along secular lines. Moreover, Nehru had considered the abolition of reservations for the minority an "historic turn in our destiny"[148] and strongly argued in favour of it.

In view of support coming from the Muslim members, it becames easy for the Iron Man of India, Sardar Patel to scrap the provision for reservation of seats for the Muslim and the Indian Christian communities and the heading of Part XVI was changed to "Special provisions relating to certain classes" in the Constitution at the time of the third reading. However, the other provisions protecting the rights of the religious minorities were retained.

The existence of "religious minorities" as a collective entity is recognized not only in Article 30 but also in Article 26 apropos "every religious denomination" and in Article 27 apropos "any particular religious denomination". The notion that a "collective", especially a religious collective, should be recognized for its separate rights as opposed to individual rights proclaimed in the Fundamental Rights Chapter of the Constitution is fraught with danger, because as Kaufman says, when ethnic groups are differentiated by religion, disputes over the role of religion and the influence of religious values on public policy tend to arise.[149]

The "othering" of a community as a "religious minority" simply because it is identified with a religion different from the "religious majority" community, leads inevitably to communalization of individual identity. Moreover, as Basudeb Chattopadhyaya says, it marks a complete negation of the basic tenets of the plural society, which is espoused since independence. A plural society, by definition, assumes multiplicity of identities, religion being only one of the many markers. Some of these might overlap and even compete with others, but together they constitute what has come to be called Indian identity.[150]

A group may be a minority either by choice or by compulsion. The Muslims in India had no history of political subjugation or social boycott. On the other hand, they never constituted more than one-fourth of the total population of India, yet they ruled the country for nearly seven centuries. The term minority has been associated with them mainly as a political residue of Partition. They enjoy a strong sense of history and culture, which is an essential prerequisite for the progress of any social group. Moreover, various anthropological studies point to the fact that Muslims constitute a national community in Indian society by the single factor of their geographical distribution. They can be found living in the remote areas of the countryside, though they seem to have a sizeable presence in urban areas. Their spatial distribution makes then politically crucial for any political party in quest for power at the Centre. This is realized by the BJP, which is considered to be anti-Muslim because of its pro-Hindu stance, more than any other party in the country. So Rajnath Singh, the BJP president sought to bridge a trust deficit on the eve of the 16th Lok Sabha elections by saying that he was ready to apologise for any mistakes committed by the party in the past and urged the community to give the saffron outfit at least one chance.[151]

"A minority that could force the partition of the country is not a minority at all", was the view of Sardar Vallabhbhai Patel.[152] As an observer points out, the Muslims in India unfortunately constitute a minority more by choice and less by compulsion. Unlike the *Dalits*, they carry no social stigma which could potentially inhibit them from actively participating in the national life. Muslim leaders have encouraged a voluntary process of remaining exclusive among themselves. This alienates them from the socio-economic life of the mainstream.[153] The first order of priority has to be, therefore, to prevent the further alienation of Muslims from the wider public culture by incorporating them into public life as citizens and not as dependent minorities.

But the fact is that Indian politics acknowledged Muslims, in so far as it did, only as a supplicant minority. The resources of the state directed towards them were meant to reinforce their status as minority, not to integrate them more fully into the political process. The more their leadership and the state emphasized their status as minority requiring a distinct ensemble of rights and privileges, the more they put the Muslims in a cocoon of self-defeating isolation.

The Saudi Foreign Minister Prince Saud al-Faisal on a visit to Pakistan had quite rightly advised Islamabad on October 19, 2003 not to consider Indian Muslims as a "minority" who needed "outside help" to resolve their problems.[154] Almost in the same vein 73-year old Congress MP from Karnataka,

K. Rahman Khan said on January 22, 2012 that Muslims in the country should shed their "minority syndrome" and look at themselves as the second-biggest chunk of India's population in order to find solution to their socio-economic problems.[155] Veteran journalist M.J. Akbar asked the Muslims to shed the attitude of minoritism and urged them to unshackle themselves from the "politics of fear" and adopt the "politics of development".[156] It is, however, doubtful if those who are interested in keeping the people divided on religious lines for reaping the obvious mileage will follow this sound advice. As a matter of fact, to some Muslims "minority" and "Muslim" have become synonymous and they even address themselves as minority instead of as Muslim.

But Muzaffar Hussain says:[157]

> According to the Islamic principles, the Muslims don't believe in the word 'minority'. They believe that these principles dictate that they should escape to the other areas if they fail to establish Islamic rule in the place they are residing. Dar-ul-Harb and Dar-ul-Islam are the two terms that have been used in Islam. The place where the Muslims are in minority is called Dar-ul-Harb which means the country of the enemies. It has been said that the Muslims should employ all methods from conversion to *Jihad* to convert the Dar-ul-Harb to Dar-ul-Islam. In today's world it is not easier to leave one's own country as the question remain as to which country one will go and how he will attain the nationality and citizenship of that country? Therefore, it is stressed upon them to increase their population through *Tabligh* (conversion) and establish their own rule there. This is the reason that the fanatics oppose family planning. Islam basically doesn't believe in the term 'minority'. Therefore, the tussle increases with the majorities in the places where Muslims are in minority. The Muslims in the garb of their religious rights always try to acquire more facilities for themselves. Thus, they are involved in creating a new country by encouraging secessionism. The Muslims intend to attain everything in the name of religion in the countries where they are in minority but they never talk of the rights of the minorities living in the Islamic countries. There is a sizeable population of Hindus in the Gulf countries but those countries are not ready to give any facility to them in the name of minority or Human Rights. The Hindus are not allowed there to cremate their kiths and kins as per their belief. They can't construct the places for their worship nor can they celebrate their festivals at public places. During the *Ramzan* the Non-Muslims can't eat anything at day time near the public places. The Muslims expect to get everything as minorities in the countries of Hindus, Buddhists and the Christians, but in the Islamic countries

the minorities don't have such privileges. Due to this nature only, the Muslims as minorities are mostly involved in creating all sorts of feuds and disputes. Every Muslim country has dispute with its neighbouring country because Islam does not believe in nation and nationality. The Muslims follow these principles till they succeed in creating a country for them. Once creation of a new country is over, they establish their rule after accepting all the conditions of the modern nation. So, this principle of Islamic framework is based on double standard. They adopt different criterion till a new country is created and their criterion changes once they occupy a country for themselves. For this duality, Muslims are always looked upon with suspicion.

Muslims while residing in any specific area as minorities increase their population gradually. After coming into sizeable population they expedite a move to create an independent country for them. China is facing such problem at Ziyzng province these days so is the case with Russia at Chechnya. Whenever the governments of those countries become active to deal with them, the Muslims in the guise of terrorists take up arms against the governments. After creation of Pakistan such belief has taken place in the Muslim dominated provinces that they may get a country of their own if they continue to launch movement for the same. Hence, the governments are always concerned over the settlement of the Muslim minorities in any specific area. London is the glaring example of this where Muslims after settling in the suburbs have caused a threat to the British government.

VII

Minority (*continued*)

The minority syndrome amongst the Muslims has been reinforced by several factors—constitutional provisions, legal enactments, judicial pronouncements, administrative measures, socio-economic conditions, and above all, machinations of the political parties.

While the Constitution speaks of religious and linguistic minorities in broad and general terms, it does not specify the groups, which are to be treated as such. One of the consequences of this constitutional silence is that the identification of groups and communities as minorities has been left to the administrative prerogative, at times to court verdicts.

In the *TMA Pai* the majority of the eleven judges Bench of the Supreme Court held that linguistic and religious minorities are covered by the expression "minority" under Article 30 of the Constitution. Since reorganization of the

States in India has been on linguistic lines, therefore, for the purpose of determining the minority, the unit will be the State and not the whole of India. Thus, religious and linguistic minorities, who have been put on a par in Article 30, have to be considered state-wise.[158]

Our Constitution describes the minority groups as "sections of citizens" points out[159] F.S. Nariman, the doyen of the constitutional lawyers. The Constitution has not, however, fixed any numerical strength in order to attract the nomenclature of a minority. According to a judgement of the Kerala High Court, any community—religious or linguistic—which is numerically less than fifty per cent of the population of the State is entitled to claim the protection of the guarantee in Article 30.[160] According to this interpretation, non-Christians have minority status in Nagaland, Mizoram and Meghalaya, the Christian majority States, non-Muslims in Jammu & Kashmir and Lakshadweep, the Muslim majority State/UT, and non-Sikhs in Punjab, the Sikh majority State.

The Central Government constituted the National Commission for Minorities in 1984 and gave it a legal status by an Act of Parliament in 1992. This Act defines "minority" as those communities notified as such by the Government of India. The Central Government has notified in 1993 the five communities of Parsis, Sikhs, Buddhists, Christians and Muslims as national minorities. These five communities are spoken of as minorities because their numerical representation in the overall national population is small. This identification applies at the all-India level. Thus, irrespective of its proportionate share in the population of a State or a particular district of a State, these five communities are treated as minority groups in India. Even here there is no uniformity of nomenclature. For example, Jains, whose representation in the population is miniscule as compared to some of the groups, which are generally seen as constituting minority communities, are not characterised as minority groups. The National Commission for Minorities has recommended in 1997 to include Jains as the sixth national minority community.[161] The Supreme Court in 2005 rejected the appeal of the Jain community for minority status under Section 2(c) of the National Commission for Minorities Act.

The Bench of Chief Justice R.C. Lahoti and Justices D.M. Dharmadhikari and P.K. Balasubramanyan, while rejecting the appeal of the Jain community for minority status under Section 2(c) of the National Commission for Minorities Act, observed on August 8, 2005:

> The constitutional ideal, which can be gathered from the group of articles in the Constitution under Chapters of Fundamental Rights and Fundamental Duties, is to create social conditions where there remains no necessity to shield or protect rights of minority or majority. The above mentioned constitutional goal has to be kept in view by the Minorities Commissions set-up at the Central or State levels.

> Commissions set-up for minorities have to direct their activities to maintain integrity and unity of India by gradually eliminating the minority and majority classes. If, only on the basis of a different religious thought or less numerical strength or lack of health, wealth, education, power or social rights, a claim of a section of Indian society to the status of 'minority' is considered and conceded, there would be no end to such claims in a society as multi-religious and multi-linguistic as India is. The Commission instead of encouraging claims from different communities for being added to a list of notified minorities under the Act should suggest ways and means to help create social conditions where the list of notified minorities is gradually reduced and done away with altogether.[162]

The Supreme Court's remarks can be read as a criticism of the divisive tactics of politicians in the name of social justice. The dispensing of advantages in order to nurture caste-based and religion-based constituencies is the best way to distort the constitutional goal. The Supreme Court has quietly reminded rulers and lawmakers that the way to cohesion and equality lies in exactly the opposite direction.

The five communities which have been notified as national minority groups by the Central Government are all religious communities. This National Commission for Minorities is apparently constituted to look after the welfare and interests of "religious minorities" only. So the title of the commission is rather a misnomer. Its nomenclature should have been the National Commission for Religious Minorities and not the National Commission for Minorities. By constituting a commission for "religious" minorities the Central Government has legally separated the people on the basis of religion.

The second National Commission for Minorities has for the first time submitted a special report in 1999 on religious problems faced by Hindus in general and some specific problems in the States of Jammu & Kashmir, Meghalaya, Mizoram, Nagaland, Punjab and in the Union Territory of Lakshadweep.[163] Earlier, in 1998 it has recommended that the commission's jurisdiction should be extended to the Hindu minority in the militancy-torn State of Jammu & Kashmir.[164] It has recommended in April 1999 state-level minority status for Hindus in Meghalaya.[165]

The Punjab and Haryana High Court on December 17, 2007 struck down a notification issued by the Punjab government on April 13, 2001 permitting the Shiromani Gurdwara Parbandhak Committee (SGPC) to give 50 per cent reservation to Sikh students in colleges run by it on grounds that Sikhs were a minority community.[166] The Supreme Court on November 18, 2010 indicated that it would refer for adjudication by a Constitution Bench the issue whether Sikhs, who form a majority population in Punjab, can claim 'minority' status in that State.[167] The Allahabad High Court on April 5, 2007 ruled that on application of the twin criteria of population and strength, Muslims in Uttar Pradesh could no longer be treated as a religious minority.[168]

Minority Commissions have also been set up at State levels as well to look after the interest and welfare of these five 'national' minorities. Such Commissions are functioning in as many as fifteen States—in Assam, Bihar, Chhattisgarh, Delhi, Jharkhand, Karnataka, Madhya Pradesh, Maharashtra, Manipur, Punjab, Rajasthan, Tamil Nadu, Uttrakhand, West Bengal and Kerala. The State Governments of Chhattisgarh, Maharashtra, Madhya Pradesh, Karnataka, West Bengal, Jharkhand, Delhi, Punjab, Uttar Pradesh and Uttrakhand[169] have already notified Jains as "minority" in accordance with the provisions of the respective State Minority Commissions Act. The Centre decided on January 20, 2014 to treat the Jains as a minority at the national level.[170]

The State's treatment of a community could itself go in defining the word 'minority'. Some numerical minorities like Parsis are a very forward minority community on the basis of their economic and social strength. Sikhs too are forward both educationally and economically. Jains are forward both educationally and economically. A minority, therefore, should be defined not just legislatively, but also educationally, economically, administratively, and above all, territorially.

Besides the National Commission for Minorities, the National Commission for Minority Educational Institutions Act, 2004 (2 of 2005) as amended by the National Commission for Minority Educational Institutions (Amendment) Act, 2006 (18 of 2006) has been constituted to advise the Central or any State Government on any question relating to the education of minorities that may be referred to it. It will also look into specific complaints regarding deprivation or violation of rights of minorities to establish and administer educational institutions of their choice, any dispute regarding affiliation to a scheduled university and report its findings to the Centre for its implementation. It is also empowered to decide all questions of minority status and cancel such recognition if the situation so warrants.

Though this commission is legally empowered to decide the cases of both "linguistic" as well as "religious minority" institutions, it is more concerned with "religious" minority educational institutions. As a matter of fact, since its inception the Commission has accorded minority status to as many as 7727 institutions so far (1180 in 2005-07, 2477 in 2008-2010, 3620 in 2011-12 and 450 up to March 19, 2013).[171]

Then there were the National Commission for Religious and Linguistic Minorities (Justice Ranganath Misra, chairman) and the Committee on Social, Economic and Educational Status of the Muslim Community (Justice R.N. Sachar, chairman). Then there are the National Minorities Development and Finance Corporation, the Central Waqf Council and the Maulana Azad Education Foundation. Both at the Central and State levels, Minority Affairs

Ministry/Department have been created to look after the interests and welfare of the six religious minorities notified by the Central Government.

In some States one minority member is mandatory in the committees that select employees in group C and D posts. The State Public Service Commissions which recruit government employees also have a minority member now. Similar is the case with the School Service Commissions.[172] The Bihar Government has fixed a two-hour period between 12.30 p.m. and 2.30 p.m. for Friday prayers by government employees[173] The Left Front Government in Kerala carved out a separate district with the Muslim-majority areas.

The Central/State Governments often indulge in some measures for the benefit and welfare of the religious minorities. More often than not these measures are declared as unconstitutional and as a result these schemes/policies have got to be shelved. This adversely affects the psyche of the minorities, especially of the Muslims. Take for instance, the decision of the Bench of Justices Aftab Alam and Ranjana Desai of the Supreme Court on July 23, 2012, to reduce the *Haj* discretionary quota to only 500 including 200 for the Haj committee. Earlier on May 8, the Court has directed the Centre to totally phase out the *Haj* subsidy in 10 years, holding that there was no provision in the holy *Quran* for undertaking the visit to Mecca at the expense of the government or others.[174] The Court also pointed out that the annual subsidy of over Rs. 650 crore could be best spent for improving the education and social services available to Muslim groups.

The Calcutta High Court as well as the Karnataka High Court has taken a very serious view of sound pollution due to loudspeakers and firecrackers. A division bench of Justice Bhagabati Prasad Banerjee and Justice A.K. Chakraborty of the Calcutta High Court on November 21, 1996 banned the use of loudspeakers at all places of worship, irrespective of religion. It was stated that as India is a secular state the ban would cover all religions and steps to control noise pollution should cover all religious communities. The High Court has given strict directions to the West Bengal Pollution Control Board and Calcutta Police to be very vigilant against noise pollution.

The Karnataka High Court in 1996 asked the Bangalore Police Commissioner to act against commercial establishments, social and religious bodies, shops and the likes, which cause noise pollution thus infringing upon the rights of citizens, particularly sick persons, students and old people.

Earlier in 1953 the Commissioner of Police Calcutta banned the use of a loudspeaker for giving azan and Justice J. Sinha of the Calcutta High Court upheld that action of the Commissioner.[175]

The Supreme Court has held that in the name of religion nobody can be permitted to add to noise pollution or violate noise pollution norms. Religious practice to use voice amplifiers should not adversely affect rights of others, of being not disturbed in their activities.[176]

Though the PA system was not in vogue at the time of the Prophet Mohammad, pious members of the Muslim community believe that *Azaan* through PA system carries the message of Allah to a large number of people as well as calls them for prayers. If it is prohibited, the objective of the *Azaan* will be defeated. Since the order on enforcing ban on sound pollution touches the religious sensibilities of the largest religious minority community, the order could not be enforced anywhere in the country. The PA systems in the mosques are now being used for purposes other than giving *Azaans* as well.

The Trinamool Congress Government in West Bengal declared a monthly honorarium of Rupees 2,500 for the Imams and Rupees 1000 for the Muezzins on April 9, 2012 and May 2, 2012, respectively. A division bench of Justice Pranab Kumar Chattopadhyay and Justice Murari Prasad Shrivastva struck down this decision on September 2, 2013 calling it "arbitrary" and "offending to the Constitution". The court observed that the honorarium has "unnecessarily created tension among different religious communities which should be avoided in a secular state".[177]

It may be recalled that a large number of Hindu priests under the banner of Bangiya Purohit Sabha (BPS) served a 5-point memorandum to the Chief Minister through the District Magistrate of Malda on October 5, 2012 urging for grant of similar wages to the purohits, amongst others. Interestingly, the priests got support from the Congress MP Abu Hasem Khan Choudhury.[178] On August 23, 2012, priests in Kolkata had marched with a similar demand.[179]

VIII

Developmental Programme for the Minorities

In 1975, Prime Minister Indira Gandhi launched the 15 Point Programme for the welfare of minorities. It was restructured in 1982 and again in 1986. After the Congress-led UPA came to power in 2004 Prime Minister's New 15 Point Programme was introduced. The programme aims at enhancing opportunities for education; ensuring an equitable share for minorities in economic activities etc. Prime Minister's New 15-Point Programme for Welfare of Minorities is as follows:

(A) Enhancing Opportunities for Education

(1) Equitable Availability of ICDS Services

The Integrated Child Development Services (ICDS) Scheme is aimed at holistic development of children and pregnant/lactating mothers from disadvantaged section, by providing services through Anganwadi Centres such as supplementary nutrition, immunization, health check-up, referral services, pre-school and non-formal education. A certain percentage of the ICDS projects and Anganwadi Centres will be located in blocks/villages with a substantial population of minority communities to ensure that he benefits of the scheme are equitably available to such communities also.

(2) Improving Access to School Education

Under the Sarva Shiksha Abhiyan, the Kasturba Gandhi Balika Vidyalaya Scheme, and other similar Government schemes, it will be ensured that a certain percentage of such schools are located in villages/localities having a substantial population of minority communities.

(3) Greater Resources for Teaching Urdu

Central assistance will be provided for recruitment and posting of Urdu language teachers in primary and upper primary schools that serve a population in which at least one-fourth belong to that language group.

(4) Modernizing Madrasahs Education

The Central Plan Scheme of Area Intensive and Madrasahs Modernization Programme provides basic educational infrastructure in areas of concentration of educationally backward minorities and resources for the modernization of Madrasahs education. Keeping in view the importance of addressing this need, this programme will be substantially strengthened and implemented effectively.

(5) Scholarships for Meritorious Students from Minority Communities

Schemes for pre-matric and post-matric scholarships for students from minority communities will be formulated and implemented.

(6) Improving Educational Infrastructure through the Maulana Azad Education Foundation

The Government shall provide all possible assistance to Maulana Azad Education Foundation (MAEF) to strengthen and enable it to expand its activities more effectively.

(B) Equitable Share in Economic Activities and Employment

(7) Self-Employment and Wage Employment for the Poor

The Swarnjayanti Gram Swarojgar Yojana (SGSY), the primary self-employment programme for rural areas, has the objective of bringing assisted poor rural families above the poverty line by providing them income generating assets through a mix of bank credit and Governmental subsidy. A certain percentage of the physical and financial targets under the SGSY will be earmarked for beneficiaries belonging to the minority communities living below the poverty line in rural areas.

The Swarnjayanti Shahary Rozgar Yojana (SSRY) consists of two major components, namely the Urban Self-Employment Programme (USEP) and the Urban Wage Employment Programme (UWEP). A certain percentage of the physical and financial targets under USEP and UWEP will be earmarked to benefit people below the poverty line from the minority communities.

The Sampurna Grameen Rozgar Yojana (SGRY) is aimed at providing additional wage employment in rural areas alongside the creation of durable community, social and economic infrastructure. Since the National Rural Employment Guarantee Programme (NREGP) has been launched in 200 districts, and SGRY has been merged with NREGP in these districts, in the remaining districts, a certain percentage of the allocation under SGRY will be earmarked for beneficiaries belonging to the minority communities living below the poverty line till these districts are taken up under NREGP.

Simultaneously, a certain percentage of the allocation will be earmarked for the creation of infrastructure in such villages, which have a substantial population of minorities.

(8) Upgradation of Skill through Technical Training

A very large proportion of the population of minority communities is engaged in low-level technical work or earns its living as handicraftsmen. Provision of technical training to such people would upgrade their skills and earning capability. Therefore, a certain proportion of all new ITIs will be located in areas predominantly inhabited by minority communities and a proportion of existing ones to be upgraded to 'Centres of Excellence' will be selected on the same basis.

(9) Enhanced Credit Support for Economic Activities

The National Minorities Development and Finance Corporation (NMDFC) was set up in 1994 with the objective of promoting economic development activities among the minority communities. The Government is committed to strengthen the NMDFC by providing it greater equity support to enable it to fully achieve its objective.

Bank credit is essential for creation and sustenance of self-employment initiative. A target of 40 per cent of net bank credit for priority sector lending has been fixed for domestic banks. The priority sector includes, *inter alia*, agricultural loans, loan to small-scale industries and small business, loans to retail trade, professional and self-employed persons, educational loans, housing loans and micro-credit. It will be ensured that an appropriate percentage of the priority sector lending in all categories is targeted for the minority communities.

(10) Recruitment to State and Central Services

In the recruitment of police personnel, State Governments will be advised to give special consideration to minorities. For this purpose, the composition of selection committees should be representative.

The Central Government will take similar action in the recruitment of personnel to the Central police forces.

Large scale employment opportunities are provided by the Railways, nationalized banks and public sector enterprises. In these cases also, the concerned departments will ensure that special consideration is given to recruitment from minority communities.

An exclusive scheme will be launched for candidates belonging to minority communities to provide coaching in Government institutions as well as private coaching institutes with credibility.

(C) Improving the Conditions of Living of Minorities

(11) Equitable Share in Rural Housing Scheme

The Indira Awaas Yojana (IAY) provides financial assistance for shelter to the rural poor living below the poverty line. A certain percentage of the physical and financial targets under IAY will be earmarked for poor beneficiaries from minority communities living in rural areas.

(12) Improvement in Condition of Slums Inhabited by Minority Communities

Under the schemes of Integrated Housing and Slum Development Programme (IHSDP) and Jawaharlal Nehru Urban Renewal Mission (JNURM), the Central Government provides assistance to States/UTs for development of urban slums through provision of physical amenities and basic services. It would be ensured that the benefits of these programmes flow equitably to members of the minority communities and to cities/slums, predominantly inhabited by minority communities.

(D) Prevention and Control of Communal Riots

(13) Prevention of Communal Incidents

In the areas, which have been identified as communally sensitive and riot prone districts, police officials of the highest known efficiency, impartiality and secular record must be posted. In such areas and even elsewhere, the prevention of communal tension should be one of the primary duties of the district magistrate and superintendent of police. Their performance in this regard should be an important factor in determining their promotion prospects.

(14) Prosecution for Communal Offences

Severe action should be taken against all those who incite communal tension or take part in violence. Special court or courts specifically earmarked to try communal offences should be set up so that offenders are brought to book speedily.

(15) Rehabilitation of Victims of Communal Riots

Victims of communal riots should be given immediate relief and provided prompt and adequate financial assistance for their rehabilitation.

The Prime Ministers 15-point programme which aims at enhancing opportunities for education, ensuring an equitable share for minorities in economic activities etc. is in operation in one form or another for more than 35 years. Has the programme achieved its desired objective? The Sachar Committee tells a different story.

In June 2005, one year after the Congress-led coalition, UPA I, took over from the BJP-led NDA, Prime Minister Manmohan Singh appointed a seven-member High Level Committee—that Committee is called "the Sachar Committee" after its chairman—to report on the condition of the Muslim minority and suggest remedies for its deteriorating condition. That Muslims across India face inequities at all levels and in all spheres has long been known. The Sachar Committee only confirmed this notion. The report submitted by the Committee on November 17, 2006 showed that only 8 per cent of urban Muslims were part of the formal sector whereas the national average was 21 per cent for India's city dwellers and that Muslims were also poorer than average Indians. According to a survey conducted by the NSSO, the average monthly expenditure of urban Muslims were rupees 800 a month, that is, the same as that of the *Dalits* and adivasis and much less than that of the upper caste Hindus (Rupees 1469). Its micro-level finding is that the community ranks somewhat above the Scheduled Castes and Scheduled Tribes, but below other minorities, Other Backward Classes, and upper castes in all indicators examined: educational attainment, access to health and infrastructural facilities, representation in salaried jobs in the public and private sectors, managerial positions, and presence in the civil services and in the police.

The Sachar Committee Report made seventeen-page long recommendations. The panel did not propose reservation for the community as a whole. It recommended "multifarious measures including reservation" only for Muslims with traditional occupations comparable to those of SCs and STs. Specific policy initiatives and practical steps recommended include improved access to bank credits and government programmes, focus on free education, setting up quality government schools in Muslim-dominated areas, linking *madrasah* education to a higher secondary education board, directing a portion of college and university funding to ensuring student diversity, and sensitizing teachers to the issues of pluralism and diversity. The report proposed an Equal Opportunity Commission, modelled on the United Kingdom's Race Relations Act, 1976, a redressal mechanism for "aggrieved minorities".[180]

An idea has gained currency that special economic and other developmental programmes have got to be earmarked for a particular community in order to uplift that particular community economically, educationally and politically. The Government of India initiated the concept of Tribal Sub-Plan (TSP) in 1972 on the recommendations of an Expert Committee set up by the then Ministry of Education and Social Welfare and the Special Component Plan (SCP), now called Scheduled Caste Sub-plan (SCSP) in 1978. SCSP and TSP are seen as a critical initiative in closing the development gap between the Scheduled Castes/Scheduled Tribes when compared to others by eradicating poverty and health problems and developing communication for removal of isolation of their habitats. Further the Central Government also extends Special Central Assistance (SCA) to States as an additive to SCP and SCSP.

Since such affirmative action programme for the minorities could not be launched, the device of Prime Minister's 15 Point Programme for Welfare of Minorities was resorted to. In view of the findings of the Sachar Committee about the pitiable socio-economic conditions of the Muslims, the CPI(M) Polit Bureau member and Rajya Sabha MP Brinda Karat sought a special economic package for Muslims.[181] The Prime Minister also wanted that minorities must have first claim on resources and said so in the National Development Council meeting on December 9, 2006.[182] The BJP lost no time in denouncing the Prime Minister's remarks as one more example of Muslim appeasement.[183] It is to be noted that the minority leadership did not protest against this assertion of the Prime Minister and did not say that the Prime Minister instead should have stated that every Indian, irrespective of faith has the first claim. This mindset explains, as an observer puts it, "the inability of a secular democratic India to move towards a modern version of cooperative federalism from asymmetric federalism, and to change the very idiom of Indian politics from identity and group politics to issue-based politics."[184]

Dr. Abusaleh Sharif, a leading Indian economist and the man who actually authored the most comprehensive Sachar Committee Report as its member secretary, presented a paper on "Six Years After Sachar: A Review of Inclusive Polices in India", in a seminar organised in January 2013 to review the progress made in Muslim welfare programmes since 2006. The paper noted that the rate of growth of education at all levels had remained the lowest for Muslims between 2004-05 and 2009-2010, and said that the level of Muslim exclusion could only be addressed through institutional reforms and not *via* "pro-Muslim policy statements and even Muslim-focused programmes". The paper was critical of the functioning of the Ministry of Minority Affairs and recommended the establishment of a coordinating body under the Prime Minister's Office. Dr. Sharif also argued that socially inclusive development efforts needed to move away from special purpose vehicles—such as the National Commission for Minorities and the National Minorities Financial Development Corporation—so that they could be integrated into mainstream ministries.[185] He also strongly opposed reservation, as it is nothing more than a political gimmick. Besides the primacy of education, Sharif says access to credit is the key to Muslim development as the community is largely self-employed.[186] It may be noted that as per government data, more than Rupees 1,95,000 crore bank loan has been disbursed among the members of the minority communities.[187]

The 'Social Development Report 2012: Minorities at the Margins' prepared by Zoya Hasan, Mushirul Hasan, Tanweer Fazal, Javed Alam Khan and Abusaleh Sharif, among others, says the UPA government has failed to implement the recommendations of the Sachar Committee, with its response to Muslim deprivation at best being "cautious and minimalist". Most of the benefits intended for minorities are being cornered by either the majority population or non-Muslim minorities, claims the report. The report lists misplaced focus of minority-oriented programmes, lack of funds and fear of 'minority appeasement' taunts as the reasons for the government's failure to fulfil its promises.[188]

West Bengal claimed the top spot in awarding scholarships to students belonging to minority communities. Since May 2011, nearly Rupees 1,456 crore scholarships to around 82 lakh minority students have been sanctioned for their higher studies. Term loan and micro credit amounting to more than Rupees 600 crore have so far been provided to nearly 3.5 lakh minority community person. And the State budget for Minorities and Madrasah

Education Department was raised by almost four times from Rupees 472 crore in 2010-11 to Rupees 2,383 crore in 2015-16 Chief Minister Mamata Banerjee wrote on a social networking website on March 12, 2015.[189]

Renowned journalist Sumer Kaul holds that the policy of taking affirmative action on the basis of caste and religion not only has proved ineffective in bringing about mass uplift in the communities concerned, but it is also inherently crafty and divisive.[190] Tanweer Alam, a Delhi-based activist has noted that in the 12th Plan a focused strategy has been adopted, making blocks instead of the districts the basic unit for planning and implementing of the minority welfare schemes. Now, that area-specific approach had been adopted, benefits should go directly to minority concentrated villages where a substantial number of Muslims live. Bottlenecks are now being streamlined. Amid all this, nobody can honestly claim that benefits of economic development have bypassed Muslims.[191]

It is high time the powers-that-be should realize that community-specific developmental programmes can never raise the socio-economic status of the target group. Had it been so, the conditions of the Scheduled Tribes and the Scheduled Castes would have been much above the national average by this time, considering the plethora of schemes undertaken for their uplift. Sixty years of affirmative action have led to the emergence of elite groups among them who have cornered all the benefits earmarked for the Scheduled Tribes/ Scheduled Castes. Only the holistic approach of planned development can achieve a lasting solution. Sectarian approach may at best give a boost to the 'vote-bank' politics.

The Supreme Court warned in 2005:[192]

> Differential treatment to linguistic minorities based on language within the state is understandable but if the same concept for minorities on the basis of religion is encouraged, the whole country, which is already under class and social conflicts due to various divisive forces, will further face division on the basis of religious diversities. Such claims to minority status based on religion would increase in the fond hope of various sections of people getting special protections, privileges and treatment as part of constitutional guarantee. Encouragement to such fissiparous tendencies would be a serious jolt to the secular structure of constitutional democracy. We should guard against making our country akin to a theocratic state based on multi-nationalism.... If each minority group feels afraid of the other group, an atmosphere of mutual fear and distrust would be created posing serious threat to the integrity of our Nation. That would sow seeds of multi-nationalism in India.

The advantages or concessions given to religious minorities are perceived as desirable enough by themselves. Occasionally, these are combined with concessions given to the reserved group with which the community may overlap. The whole exercise becomes self-defeating; the constitutional ideal aiming ultimately at the creation of similar socio-economic conditions, and equal opportunities for everybody is reduced to a race for various types of special status in competition with other groups. Instead of encouraging division in a country torn by class and economic disparities, the aim should be to narrow the gap in socio-economic standards between the privileged and the underprivileged. As a matter of fact, socio-economic standards are not uniformly low among all religious groups and also within the group itself.

In this context it is worthwhile to ponder over the following:

> [In] a full-blooded democracy, if you seek to give safeguards to a minority, you isolate it. May be you protect it to a slight extent, but at what cost? At the cost of isolating it and keeping it away from the main current in which the majority is going—I am talking on the political plane of course—at the cost of forfeiting that inner sympathy and fellow-feeling with the majority.[193]

This was said not by any RSS *Sarsanghsamchalak,* but by a towering Congressman and a secularist by the name of Jawaharlal Nehru.

IX

Political Marginalization of Muslims

In addition to socio-economic decline, the Muslims in India also suffer from political marginalization. A survey indicates that Muslims voters constitute more than 30 per cent in as many as 35 seats, between 21 and 30 per cent in 38 seats and between 11 and 20 per cent in 135 seats. Overall, Muslims voters can determine the fates of candidates in as many as 220 out of 543 Lok Sabha seats.[194] Muslims would have been more politically dominant had there been no partition in 1947.

A *Times of India* survey says that in Assam Muslim electorate plays a decisive role in at least six out of 14 LS sets. In West Bengal, Muslims play a key role in 26 out of 42 constituencies. Out of a total of 80 seats in UP, Muslims' role is decisive in 34 LS seats. In Bihar, 14 constituencies hinge on Muslim votes and in Maharashtra, Muslims are key factors in 17 constituencies.[195]

But as Table 7.1 reveals, in the Lok Sabha, their under-representation is more and more in evidence. In 1980, the percentage of Muslim MPs in the Lok Sabha was almost proportional to their share in the population (9% compared to 11.4% according to the 1981 census). Then they experienced steady erosions which accelerated from the late 1980s till the late 1990s, when the BJP-led NDA (which did not field many Muslim candidates) came

Table 7.1: Representation of the Muslim MPs in the Lok Sabha (1980 to 2009)

Year	*Seats*	*Muslim candidates*	*Muslim MPs*	*Percentage of the MPs*	*Success rate*
1980	542	131	49	9.0	37
1984	542	123	46	8.4	37
1989	543	133	33	6.0	25
1991	543	149	28	5.1	19
1996	543	140	28	5.1	20
1998	543	146	28	5.1	19
1999	543	175	32	5.8	18
2004	543	168	35	6.4	21
2009	543	832	30	5.5	3.6

Source: Zoya Hasan, *Politics of Inclusion: Castes, Minorities and Affirmative Action*, New Delhi, OUP, 2008, p. 257 for 1980 to 2004, and Election Commission for 2009.

to power. They started to improve significantly in 2004 with the electoral defeat of the BJP. But in 2009 the percentage of Muslim MPs decreased again in spite of the electoral victory of the Congress-led UPA II. The situation, in fact, is as bad as it was in the late 1990s when Muslim MPs represented only 5.1 per cent of the house members, whereas the Muslims constituted 12.1 per cent of the Indian population according to the 1991 census. The 16th Parliament has returned just 23 MPs from the Muslim community, the worst ever since 1980. The near-dismal performance of most political parties which have thrived on tapping the minority vote bank in the past is more significant than the representation of Muslims in the Lok Sabha. In the 16th Lok Sabha Muslim MPs constitute only 4.24 per cent of Lok Sabha MPs whereas Muslims comprise 13.4 per cent of the population according to the 2001 census. Such under-representation of the Muslims in the Lok Sabha perhaps prompted the National Minority Commission Chairman Prof. Tahir Mahmood to appeal in July, 1999 to all political parties to ensure at least 100 seats for minorities in the next Lok Sabha.[196]

The communal question has been a bleeding cancer for more than seven decades, yet no major political party has initiated the self-critical heart-searching. The CPI did at least acknowledge its blunder in lending support to the two-nation theory through the Adhikari Resolution of 1942. Has the Congress explored and made known its own contribution to the growth of communalism? Do the inheritors of the Hindu Rashtra tradition recall that the concept of Hindu Rashtra and the Aryan theory of race were being propagated decades before the fateful Pakistan Resolution of March 23, 1940? Have prominent leaders of Muslim communal groups refuted and debunked that false concept? How many Akali leaders are prepared to disown the communal sentences in the Anandpur Sahib Resolution? Such self-criticism is faint, if not inaudible.

The *Sangh Parivar* and its political branch, the BJP, have been accused for being responsible for creating a fanatic political atmosphere since the 1980s. But, as Desai asserts, "the danger of Hindu communalism is far broader than the influence of the RSS, which no doubt is the arch villain of the piece".[197]

It is not only the *Sangh Parivar* that exploits religious sentiments for political gain and the establishment of cultural hegemony. If the parivar has made its slogan *garv se kaho hum Hindu hain* (say with pride we are Hindu), Islamic groups have asserted their cultural purity and have appealed to people to go "Back to Islam", the original Islam followed by the Prophet, and in Mecca. Religious sentiments are exploited and the appeal to follow Muslim Personal Law is always made. *Madrasahs* are seen as sources of growing Islamisation. There may be formal schooling in religious texts, and often the maulana and mulla socialise students into Islamic traditions. Islamisation and political communalism is engineered by the religious groups and exploited by the political elites.

Within the Muslim community, various orthodox groups such as the Jama'at-e-Islami and the Tablighi Jama'at and terrorist outfits such as the Lashkar-e-Taiba and Hizbul Mujahideen invoke different religious interpretations that may or may not have direct political aims. Similarly, for groups such as the Student Islamic Movement of India (SIMI), Islam is a complete world view and ideology that governs every aspect of a Muslim's personal as well as collective life. For it, it is not the Constitution of India but Islam that lays down a complete code of conduct. Unfortunately, its activities stereotype the entire Muslim population of India. As scholars point out, they have also established close links with various Islamist groups in several other countries. For them, democracy and secularism are un-Islamic.[198] "In SIMI discourse, Hinduism is painted in the most lurid colours and as an inveterate foe of Islam and its followers. The only way to salvation, then, is by converting to Islam."[199]

In independent India the political parties are primarily responsible for the growth of communalism in the country. They chant secularism as a *mantra* as if it is a new religion more potent than Buddhism, Christianity, Marxism and Gandhism but actually use it as a stepping stone for capturing power. The craze for power and the means adopted by political parties were in a way responsible for the current threat to secularism faced by the nation. Measures which gave credibility to communal forces had been adopted by them. The most secular of the political parties, the Marxists, had supplied "in the 1930s and '40s the intellectual arguments that Jinnah needed for the creation of Pakistan, which left the subcontinent soaked in blood."[200] Sixty years after independence, the CPM, a party named after the man who said religion is the opium of the masses, has set up a group that will deal exclusively with issues concerning minorities, especially Muslims.[201]

Jawaharlal Nehru said in *An Autobiography* that "many a Congressman was a communalist under his national cloak. But the Congress leadership stood firm and, on the whole, refused to side with either communal party or rather with any communal group".[202] It was possible for someone of Nehru's stature to grasp the different dimensions of communalism and the dangers it posed to the Indian polity. Since, according to Nehru, "the want of clear ideals and objectives in our struggle for freedom undoubtedly helped the spread of communalism",[203] it was all the more incumbent on him to ensure that all vestiges of communalism were wiped out from our body politic for ever at that nascent stage of nation-building immediately after independence. He was the unquestioned supreme leader of the nation then. But he had neither the courage nor the desire to tackle this menace by taking it by its forelock. He frittered away his energy in the controversy over "majority communalism" and eventually failed to take concrete steps to combat communalism as a whole, be it majority communalism or minority communalism. As a result the poisonous tree of communalism has grown to a monstrous one spreading its tentacles in almost all branches of human behaviour.

Some of the most blatant communal campaigns and instances of violence are known to have had the acquiescence if not the connivance of the Congress in power. As pointed out by Madhu Purnima Kishwar, "the overall track record of the Congress in this matter is no better, if not much worse, than that of the BJP. In addition to the 1984 massacre of Sikhs in north India, it masterminded numerous riots through the 1970s, 1980s and 1990s. None of the killers of politically engineered riots in Meerut, Malliana, Bhiwandi, Bhagalpur, Hyderabad, Mumbai, Ahmedabad, Surat and scores of others were ever punished. The Congress also injected terrorism into Punjab by its covert support of Bhindranwale's *Khalistani* brigades in order to wrest control of the SGPC that presides over well-endowed gurdwaras." [204]

It has often been said that the BJP and the Congress are opposite side of the same coin. One is insidiously communal, the other overtly secular in a pseudo sort of way. Essentially, both pander to voter blocs defined by religious identities, quite oblivious of the fact that there are human beings on both sides of the divide with similar hopes, aspirations and dreams. Ordinary Muslims surely want the same things as common Hindus: education, jobs, houses, security and opportunities to go ahead. They also want to lead a normal life shorn of the sigma of "pro-Pakistani" or being "communal". Yet, both the Congress and the BJP dabble in emotive politics with impunity. They won't allow them to forget their religious identity. It is much easier to whip up communal passions in the hope of polarizing votes than it is to win elections by delivering on promises. And this is true for all political parties. All indulge in either "soft" or "hard" communalism by pandering to this or that section of religious community, though they scream from the rooftops to prove their secular credentials.

Firoz Bakht Ahmed, grandnephew of Maulana Abdul Kalam Azad has made a worthwhile suggestion:

> The responsibility of stopping communalists and pseudo-secularists, who are present in equal measures in the majority and minority communities, lies with all of us. Muslims should take care of their rabble-rousing elements, shake up their leadership and substitute it with devoted, pragmatic and sincere leaders willing to solve the real problems of the community without mobilizing them along emotional and religious lines. And balanced, secular Hindus should realise that their overwhelming advantage in the power structure—an 80 per cent majority in the electoral base—has ensured that their cultural interests are never to be threatened by any combination of forces or so-called *jihad*.[205]

But can it be implemented? All the political parties, big or small, have a stake in stoking the communal fire. Sri Jayendra Saraswathi, Shankaracharya of the Kanchi Kamakoti Peetham has very correctly hit the nail on the head when at a function organized by the All-India Tanzeem-i-Imam Masjid on June 20, 2010 in Bhopal to emphasise communal harmony among the Hindus and Muslims he said that "all problems faced by this country are political and not communal".[206]

In his book *My Eleven Years with Fakhruddin Ahmad*, Fazle Ahmed Rehmany quotes an incident which throws interesting light on the psychology of secularism and its need to keep Muslims in isolation and in a sort of protective custody. During the Emergency period, some followers of the Jamaat-e-Islami found themselves in the same jail as the members of the RSS; here they began to discover that the later were no monsters as described by the 'nationalist' and secularist propaganda. Therefore, they began to think better of the Hindus. This alarmed the secularists and the interested Maulavis. Some Maulavis belonging to the Jamaat-ul-Ulema-i-Hind met President Fakhruddin Ahmad, and reported to him about the growing rapport between the members of the two communities. This "stunned" the President and he said that this boded an "ominous future for Congress Muslim leaders". And he promised that he would speak to Indiraji about this dangerous development and ensure that Muslims remain Muslims".[207]

British novelist Martin Amis in a two-part essay in *The Observer* (September 10-11, 2006) to mark the fifth anniversary of 9/11, lays emphasis on the Islamic ethos where *umma* takes precedence over the individual. "Indeed there is no individual; there is only the *umma*—the community of believers", he says arguing that the "totalitarian" nature of Islam demands of its followers total "surrender of independence of mind". An independent-minded Muslim is a contradiction, according to him.

The impediments to the emergence of a robust Muslim politics lay in Partition itself. Labouring under the shadow of Partition, the Congress set itself up as a benefactor of Muslims. In doing so, it defined which Muslim interests and vestments in identity were important and required protection. As a result, as N.J. Nanporia, former editor of the *Times of India* and *The Statesman*, in an article in the *Sunday Mail* on the 'Appeasement Syndrome' says, the minorities have been conditioned into believing that appeasement is their unqualified right and exclusive privilege.[208]

"Religious fundamentalism is a potent incubator of terrorism and that is something which is going to stay in India. The hope that religious fundamentalism would mellow over a period of time had been proven wrong. The spread of education and liberalism had failed to stem the tide of religious fundamentalism. It will not go in a hurry. It will not go away even if there is more employment or there is high level of education—some terrorists are highly educated." This is what was said by the Union Home Secretary, R.K. Singh to a gathering of senior security officials from paramilitary and police forces on May 6, 2013[209] who, after retirement joined the BJP and won the 1914 Lok Sabha elections as a BJP candidate from Arrah constituency. So what is the alternative? The alternative lies in finding an identity where the role of religion will be minimal and that identity could be the political identity. Political identity is determined by the combination of geographical location, language, ethnicity, culture, economic interest and religion. By itself, religion does not denote political identity. Nor do economic interests. Pure and simple political identity is likely to accelerate the process of the ultimate disappearance of the unifying element of religion. More or less the same sentiment was expressed by Hasrat Mohani in the Constituent Assembly way back in 1948.[210] Rajinder Puri also suggests that the alternative can be found in the constitution of political identity.[211] Pratap Bhanu Mehta's prescription is that the only way in which all our interests will be secure is if we write a new social contract that liberates religion from entanglement in the state.[212]

What is required is the emergence of a strong, forward looking leadership amongst the Muslims. An editorial in *The Statesman* has put the position in the proper perspective thus:

> Perhaps the biggest failure of secularism is the absence of a strong, enlightened Muslim leadership capable of giving the community a modern perspective, restoring self-confidence and accepting that the Indian system is relatively open and, in spite of corruption and decay, recognizes ability when it sees it. Unfortunately, politicians in power took to placating the likes of Imam Bukhari, rather than work towards giving the Muslim a truly republican identity—as an individual and a citizen.[213]

But as Hasan Suroor says, India's "secular" political establishment, barring the Left, has relied on a class of Muslim "leaders", whose own political interest lies in keeping the community backward-looking.[214]

X

Secularism

Though the word "secular" did not figure anywhere in the Draft Constitution, many members of the Constituent Assembly always thought that they were framing a "secular" Constitution for free India. There was, however, divergence of opinion as to what this term "secular" actually connoted, whether it stood for no-religion or anti-religion or irreligion or neutrality in matters of religion. They had actually a difference of opinion amongst them about the actual significance and purport of the term "secular". Tejamul Husain thought that "a secular state should not have anything to do with religion"[215] and "in a secular state, there is no such thing as minority".[216] The same view was held by Lok Nath Misra, Prof. K.T. Shah, Damodar Swarup Seth, Chaudhuri Ranbir Singh, and Mahabir Tyagi. "Our State shall remain unconcerned with religion"[217], said Lok Nath Misra whereas Prof. K.T. Shah felt that "the state in India being secular shall have no concern with any religion, creed or profession of faith and shall observe an attitude of absolute neutrality in all matters relating to the religion of any class of its citizens or other persons in the Union".[218] Damodar Swarup Seth observed that "in a secular state minorities based on religion or community should not be recognised. Recognition of minorities based on religion or community is the very negation of secularism".[219] Chaudhury Ranbir Singh apprehended that "our object of establishing a secular state, in this country would merely remain an unrealised dream if we decide to provide safeguards on grounds of religion".[220] Mahabir Tyagi contended that "we are a secular state. We cannot give any recognition or weightage to any religious group of individuals".[221] There were other views as well. Kazi Syed Karimuddin felt that "because this is a secular state, it does not mean that people should have no religion".[222] M. Thirumala Rao thought that "a secular state may not allow religion to play a very important part to the exclusion of other activities of the state".[223] L. Krishnaswami Bharati observed that a secular "state does not interfere with it. Religion will be there. It is a personal affair and the state as such does not side with one religion or another. It tolerates all religions".[224] S.V. Krishnamurthy Rao however thought that "in a secular state, the provision for freedom to propagate religion is out of place in our Constitution and should be omitted".[225] Mahboob Ali Baig Sahib Bahadur's view was however different. "In a secular state citizens belonging to different communities must have the freedom to practise their own religion, observe their own life and their personal laws should be applied to them",[226] he pleaded. Mohammad Ismail Sahib had almost the same view. "This secular state should not do anything or interfere with the way of life and religion of the people"[227] and it should maintain the "neutrality which it has avowedly taken in the matter of religion",[228] he said. V.S. Sarwate's opinion was that "a secular state does not either ban religion or despise it. Its attitude is perfectly neutral".[229] To Pandit Lakshmi Kanta Moitra, "by secular state is meant that the State is not going to make any discrimination whatsoever on the ground of religion or community against any person professing any particular form of religious faith. This means in essence that no particular religion in the state will receive any state patronage whatsoever".[230] M. Ananthasayanam Ayangar defined a secular state as a state "where the state is expected to view all denominations in the same light, and not give encouragement to any particular denomination at the expense of others".[231] "It only means that the state or the government cannot aid one religion or give preference to one religion as against another. It has not lost faith in all religions",[232] he said. Hussain Imam contended that a "secular state does not mean that it is anti-religious and as such, there is a world of difference between irreligious and non-religious".[233] H.V. Kamath also more or less echoed the same idea when he stated that "a secular state is neither a God-less state nor an irreligious nor an anti-religious state".[234] This divergent opinion on the character of a secular state prompted Lok Nath Misra to comment that "gradually it seems to me that our secular state is a slippery phrase, a device to by-pass the ancient culture of the land. If religion is beyond the ken of our state, let us say so and delete all references to rights relating to religion".[235]

Nehru, while intervening in the debates on citizenship on August 12, 1949, however, cautioned against giving too much importance on the word secular. He said:

> Another word is thrown up a good deal, this secular State business. May I beg with all humility those gentlemen who use this word often to consult some dictionary before they use it? It is brought in at every conceivable step and at every conceivable stage. I just do not understand it. It has a great deal of importance, no doubt. But, it is brought in all contexts, as if by saying that we are a secular State we have done something amazingly generous, given something out of our pocket to the rest of the world, something which we ought not to have done, so on and so forth. We have only done something which every country does except a very few misguided and backward countries in the world. Let us not refer to that word in the sense that we have done something very mighty.[236]

The Constitution-makers thought that the problem of religious minority would cease to exist, if the concept of secularism was brought in. The Framers "refused to yield to the communal passion which was raging throughout the whole country"[237] in the wake of the partition of the country and did not abandon the policy of secularism. It was assumed that the partition of the country had completely wiped out the virus of communalism from our society for ever and would no longer divide the country on communal line, since Nehru and many of his contemporaries assumed that harmony between different religious communities was the normal state of affairs and that conflicts were an aberration.[238]

The Framers thought that the problem of communalism would no longer be a source of constant trouble and danger to the integrity and stability of India. They thought that "the question of minorities which had been a headache and which thwarted all efforts for the solution of national problems has ceased to be a live issue. Much of the old rancour had disappeared and the country was on the path of achieving a real national unity."[239] They thought that their idea of secularism would transform the independent India into a truly secular India where "whatever religion an individual may belong to, it is only his talents and spirit of service that will count and not his community".[240] But in reality it has become a very handy weapon in the hands of those forces which have not even an iota of faith in secularism and do not practise it in their daily activities to denigrate others who oppose and expose their policies and are considered to be stumbling blocks in the furtherance of their objectives. As pointed out by Anirban Kashyap,

> While an ideal has been accepted, it might be that our hearts had not the courage and our mind had not the vision which alone could have placed it in the real perspective. A policy is framed, but not implemented or even if implemented, is done in a manner as to completely nullify the purpose for which it was framed. This lopsided manner of implementation is corroding the entire fabric of the nation which is torn asunder between pulls and counter-pulls of forces working at cross purposes.[241]

In their eagerness to do something spectacular, something novel or extraordinary, quite out of the normal way, our national leaders wanted India to be a secular state. So far so good. But the religiosity ingrained in them made their approach towards secularism somewhat ambivalent. They could neither be strictly secular in their approach towards religion nor carve out that place of honour for the religion as they would have liked it. They faltered, prevaricated and proved utterly incapable whenever they were required to come to grips with the most fundamental fact of Indian life—religion. As a result, they introduced the Indian variety of secularism in this Constitution, which evidently was devoid of clarity of purpose and practical vision.

The Constitution promises that the state shall have no religion of its own. However, in practice, many of the elements of national culture are highly Brahminical. One can find that most of the time the nomenclature of tanks and missiles in India has been derived from Hindu gods and symbols—*agni*, *nag*, *trishul*, and so on. This has been in vogue for very long time in Indian defence policy. Hence, it does not appeal to Muslims. For Ahmad "the choice of secularism as a principle of a state policy constituted a radical breach from India's past historical traditions".[242] Dixit questions Ahmad's approach to secularism and calls Muslim non-adherence to secular norms as "Communal Secularism" or "Compartmentalised Secularism".[243]

Moreover, the "assimilative", "tolerant" nature of Hinduism creates dilemmas for other communities. *Saraswati vandana*, lightening of the lamp, classical music, and festivals and celebrations with Hindu elements marginalise the cultural elements of other religious groups. "An emphasis on the adoption of symbols such as *Dharma Chakra*, popularisation of festivals at *Ramlila*, broadcasting of Bhajans and devotional songs in the early morning programme of All India Radio, extension of the governmental patronage to the Sadhu Samaj, etc., betray a strong Hindu bias in the approach of the new rulers".[244]

In Madhya Pradesh, the BJP government sought to make *yoga* and *Surya namaskar*—compulsory in schools. The *Surya namaskar* carries with it a suggestion of sun worship, which is anathema to orthodox Muslims. The pressure eased only after the Madhya Pradesh High Court ruled against compulsory enlisting for *yoga*.[245] The Nitish Kumar government's move to hold *Surya Namaskar* in all secondary schools in the State of Bihar had drawn strong protests from the Muslim groups which term the idea as "un-Islamic" and "anti-secular".[246] The National Fatwa Council in Malaysia has gone one step further by asking Muslims on November 22, 2008 to avoid *yoga* because it uses Hindu prayers and encourages a union with God that is blasphemous.[247] Earlier, the orthodox Muslims objected to the singing of the *Vande Mataram* because, according to Maulana Abdul Hameed Noumani of the Jamiat-Ulema-i-Hind, "any Muslim who believes in Allah cannot endorse a song written in praise of a goddess."[248] For praising Narendra Modi's developmental policies, Maulana Ghulam Mohammed Vastanvi, Vice Chancellor of Deoband seminary was sacked on July 24, 2011.[249]

In India, no government is sworn in without consulting astrologers. Leaders who thunder about secularism on public platforms make an equal show of their own personal religious piety by visiting shrines and temples, seeking blessings of sundry godmen and women of dubious antecedents, and observing rituals to the extreme even while performing their official duties. India should have banned state patronage or participation of all religious functions, but it did not. Holi, Diwali, Id and many other festivals continue to be patronized by the State and the electronic media gloats over them. It is a lopsided view of secularism which allows State participation in the religious functions of all communities. In all truly secular countries, as in the West, this is scrupulously avoided. India should have banned the mention of a person's religion in all official documents and court papers, but it did not, though the Bombay High Court has held on September 24, 2014, that the government cannot compel any person to declare his religion in any document, form or declaration.[250] Shreekant Sambranti has very rightly questioned:

> Why can we not qualify the fundamental right of freedom of worship by saying that in your home or place of worship only, not the road, not parks and playgrounds and certainly not public buildings and conveyances? Why must religious piety be exemplified through competitive prayers on loudspeakers, and secularism through competitive *iftaar* parties? Why denunciation of obscurantism of any kind must always be tempered by 'politically correct' considerations, i.e. do not antagonise the obscurantists, especially if they happen to be from minorities? Why does the government have to run temple trusts and waqf boards and subsidise *haj*? And yes, if we are all equal in the eyes of the law, why not a common civil law? [251]

And why inculcate the politics of "separate identity" on whatever basis it might be? Why the constitutional privileges and safeguards be provided on group/community basis when the fundamental rights as enshrined in the Constitution are to be enjoyed by individuals and the fundamental duties are to be discharged by individuals? Why inculcate this "group" and "community" feelings? Why this segmentation of people on the basis of religion, caste, race, creed, language, region and so on and so forth? Why the predominance of sectarian politics? Why moot a proposal for establishment of Minority universities when it is not sanctioned by the Constitution and circumvent it by proposing to establish them in minority-dominated areas?[252] How could Muslim MPs ask the Central Government to create exclusive schools for minority children in predominantly Muslim areas in a secular set up?[253] Why use the prefix "Muslim", "Christian", "Hindu", "Sikh" to a legislator to denote his religion? Why a legislator should champion the cause of sectarian and segmental groups? Why succumb to the *fatwas* issued by religious institutions and persons? Why be worried for a communal conflagration if the festivals of the two major communities coincide? Why 128 communal incidents in 21 days resulting in the death of 62 persons should take place in UP in August-September, 2013[254] and for that matter why any communal riot should at all take place in secular India? Why there should be repercussions in India of any "hurt feelings" in far off countries? Why religious instructions be imparted at state cost? Why nullify the Supreme Court verdict in *Shah Bano* case? Can India be part theocratic and part secular?[255] Why treat the different segments of Indians as "vote banks" and not as Indians? Why unabashedly follow the pernicious British policy of creating divisions in our ranks? Many such unpalatable and uncomfortable questions confront the "secular" policies of the State and by extension the "secular" political parties.

As if the existing communal divisions are not enough, the UPA II Government was toying with the idea to enact a legislation titled, "Prevention of Communal and Targeted Violence (Access to Justice and Reparations) Bill, 2011, popularly known as Communal Violence Bill. The Bill's original draft had divided the Indian populace into two broadly defined categories: the "Group" and "Others". Members of minority communities, SC and ST formed the "Group" and the rest were categorised into "Others". The Bill presumed that any sort of riot mongering in the country was the handiwork of the majority community, by putting the onus solely on "Others". A seven-member authority for communal harmony, justice and reparations, at the national as well as at state level, should be constituted whose at least four members, including Chairman and Vice-Chairman shall belong to the minority community "Group". The authority will have overwhelming control over the police forces, armed forces and other investigative agencies and will be vested with enormous powers. Simple legal principles such as the presumption of innocence have been given the go-by in this Bill. Many provisions of the Bill militate against Constitutional provisions.[256] The UPA II Government was desperate to enact such a blatant communal and flawed law but ultimately failed to get it through in the 15th Lok Sabha.

The problem of secularism and announcements such as "Secularism is dead"[257] refer both to the philosophy of secularism as well as the gap between its theory and practice. Theoretically for some, secularism is non-partisan and non-religious, but in actual practice its alignment with communities creates a problem. According to Professor Sanjay Subrahmanyam, Indian secularism is about mediating between different communities and groups[258], while for Fatima Bhutto, grand daughter of Zulfikar Bhutto, secularism in this part of the world means tolerance.[259] Manmohan Singh, India's Prime Minister, however, thinks that religious harmony, not mere tolerance, is the bedrock of India's secularism.

In India, secularism is not viewed as a separation of religion and politics but as giving equal status (*sarva dharma samabhava*) and acting in a non-partisan way (*dharma-nirapeksha*) towards all religions. In the wake of the Gujarat riot in 2002, both K. Subrahmaniam[260] and Swapan Dasgupta[261] have argued that our interpretation of secularism as *sarva dharma samabhava* (equal respect for all religions) is not entirely correct and may have been a political expedient for creating vote banks.

The predicament of a secular India was manifest when due to protest by the Milli Ittehad Parishad, a minority outfit, Tasleema Nasreen's *Nirbasan* was not released from the auditorium of the 36th Kolkata International Book Fair on February 1, 2012, but was released from the stall of the publisher of the book, the People's Book Society. But the said book was launched at the Amar Ekushey Book Fair in Dhaka, organised by the Bangla Academy, an organisation of the Bangladesh government, without any hitch on February 2, 2012.[262]

In early 2013, in the face of protests, Kamal Haasan's *Vishwaroopam* was first taken off the screen and exhibited only after cuts were made.[263] A scheduled lecture organised by the JBAS Centre for Islamic Studies at the University of Madras on July 29, 2013 on the topic "Islam, Gender and Reform" by the Islamic scholar, Prof. Amina Wadud was cancelled in the face of threats to disrupt the meeting.[264] Abeedheen, P.K. Abdul Rahiman and others expressed their anguish and shock at the cancellation of the lecture by Amina Wadud, an African-American convert to Islam who has been in the forefront of what has been referred to as "Islamic feminism" in the USA.[265]

The situation is so surcharged that even the Right to Education Bill which makes schooling compulsory for every child between six and 14, was opposed by the All India Muslim Personal Law Board, because it thought that it would make the functioning of madrasas difficult and infringe on the rights of minorities to run educational institutions. Maulana Rabey Nadvi, rector of the noted Islamic seminary Dar-ul-Uloom, Nawda, Lucknow and the AIMPLB chief said that this Bill recognized only one type of school and education and voiced apprehension that it could be used to outlaw *madrasahs* imparting religious education.[266]

Wendy Doniger, author of the controversial book, *The Hindus: An Alternative History*, observes in an interview that "Hindus have generally been very tolerant about ideas; they did not persecute people whose beliefs about the gods were different from their own. But Hindus have not always been tolerant about behaviour—about what people ate, touched, or wore—and this, of course, makes for trouble with Muslims and Sikhs. What worries me most about the *Hindutva* brigade is that they are just as intolerant of behaviour but also intolerant of ideas, censorship of a fundamentalist nature."[267] The renowned painter M.F. Hussain, took citizenship of a foreign country in the wake of the tirade against him for painting nude picture of goddess Saraswati.

As pointed out by Anirban Kashyap wayback in 1988,

> In a secular State there cannot possibly be any classification of community on the basis of religion. The term 'religious minority' is an anathema in a secular State. If one recognizes religious minority, then one recognizes the existence of religious majority as well. And that is a very dangerous concept. As viewed by Nehru, "minorities could be dealt with in a hundred ways but a majority in a democratic

> system could become dangerous if it functioned as a religious majority". But that was not the purpose of ushering secularism. In a secular State there may be ethnic minority, linguistic minority, racial minority but not religious minority. If the State recognizes religious minority, it accepts religion as well. Then willingly it gets involved with religion. Instead of non-involvement in religious matter, it becomes very much bogged down in religious matters. The energy of the State is frittered away on matters purely religious in nature. The question of equality of religion comes in the picture, as if, the State instead of recognizing only one religion, as is done in a theocratic state, recognizes all religions and protects them. Instead of keeping the State outside the purview of religion, the State now is very much entangled in it. In spite of secularism introduced in the Constitution, it became ineffective in containing communalism because of this conception. Secularism in India, as is practised today, has done more harm than good to the cause of secularism.[268]

There is not an iota of doubt that in India secularism has miserably failed because, as Luthra says, "instead of forging it as an instrument of tolerance, enlightenment and breaking away from superstition and rigid dogma, the political leaders have succumbed to the temptation of exploiting the caste, communal and religious ties for use as vote banks. Thus, the leadership has not worked for a secular democratic India but for the promotion of partisan communal interests."[269]

What is needed is a more thorough analysis of the secular paradigm as it applies to India than has so far been attempted and corrective actions that follow from it. As long as the State continues to act on the premise that it is its business to be involved in the religious affairs of its citizens, secularism in its true sense will be a distant dream.

Delving into the causes of the 2002 Gujarat riot Shreekant Sambranti has noted:

> The fundamental grievance the Hindu harbours against the Muslim is the primacy the latter supposedly accords to his religion. This, the Hindu believes, transcends the nation-state. That the Hindu fanatic also accords his own religion primacy above everything else does not appear unpatriotic, because the nation and the religion are assumed to be coterminous. Hindus point to the Muslims' presumed dogmatic adherence to the *Quran* and their allegiance to religious leaders beyond the pale of India. More specifically, a Muslim is assumed to be a Pakistani supporter, if not a loyalist, and to a true-blue Hindu, Pakistan is the proverbial red rag before the bull. The second fundamental Hindu grievance is that Muslims (and all other

> religious minorities) have been given privileges not accorded to the Hindus. Again citing chapter and verse to prove or disprove whether this is indeed the case is pointless, because frequent repetitions have convinced even the moderate Hindu majority of this, leave alone the hardliners. Separate marriage and inheritance laws, provisions of running schools, management of places of worship, are all quoted as examples. This discrimination is not considered positive but rather a gross distortion of it.[270]

Praveen Swami, a columnist has argued that "this spurious secularism has served in the main to institutionalise and sharpen communal boundaries. It has also allowed clerics to exercise influence over state policy—insulating themselves from a secularising world."[271] Bal Raj Madhok even observed that India is a communal state pandering to Muslim interests.[272]

Why this distortion in the nature of secularism? Anirban Kashyap gives a plausible reason for the emergence of the Indian variety of secularism in the Indian polity thus:

> Secularism as practised in India is conditioned by the Communal Award of 1932. The Communal Award of 1932 which divided India on communal line and on community basis had a legal seal in the 1935 Act. That Award continued to haunt the Framers of the Constitution even after independence. Though they could not accept its logic, they could not leave it either. The communal division formally legalised in the 1935 Act persisted in free India as well, some with constitutional sanction and some without it...Though the provision for separate electorate on communal basis did not find any place in the Constitution, for all practical purposes, it is followed in principle and practice. Dr. Pattabhi Sitaramayya, the then Congress President admitted that in the Constituent Assembly on November 25, 1949. Apparently, this was done with an eye to the Muslim bloc votes. It was the Congress which started it and other political parties have taken up the cue from it. While selecting constituencies and the candidates, communal consideration is always uppermost in their mind. Not only they are selected on communal consideration but other considerations like adequate representation to different sections, interests and groups are also duly taken note of. The Communal Award divided the population basically on communal line. Then representation was earmarked for various sections and interests like Landowners, Planters and Miners, Commerce and Industry, Labour, University, etc. In free India the same considerations are at work. The political parties not only select candidates from amongst intellectuals, educationists, teachers, labourers, agriculturists, women,

> youth, religious communities, linguistic and ethnic groups, scheduled castes and tribes and so on, but also give publicity that they have selected candidates in such a manner that various interests and groups get representations in the legislatures. None represents the general masses. Only sectional, group or communal interests are represented. The same principle of the Communal Award is followed, but with a difference. There was statutory obligation under the 1935 Act whereas there is no such obligation in the Constitution, except with regard to SCs/STs. The impact of the Communal Award is still felt and all the political parties emulate the underlying principle. As the political parties could not shake off the yoke of the Communal Award, similarly the Framers of the Constitution could not get rid of the communal approach or bias. While they wanted India to be secular, might be truly secular, they conditioned secularism with a communal tinge. It is not secularism in the true sense but secularism of Indian variety where it got mixed up with communal interest. The umbilical cord of the Communal Award could not be severed. As a result, the Framers, though intended to frame a secular Constitution, could not incorporate those provisions which are really secular in character.[273]

The Preamble of the Constitution did not contain at the time of its commencement on January 26, 1950 the much-hyped word "secular" in it. It became a part of the written Constitution only from January 3, 1977 after this word was incorporated in the Preamble of the Constitution by the 42nd Amendment. The secular character of the Constitution is reflected in Articles 15(1), 16(2) and 29(2) which prohibit discrimination of citizens, *inter alia*, on the ground only of religion, race or caste. These are the common factors. The fundamental duties set out in clauses (a), (c) and (e) of Article 51A, inserted by the above amendment, also highlight the need for unity, integrity of India and to promote harmony and spirit of common brotherhood amongst the people transcending the sectional diversities like religion, language, and region. The Directive Principles of State Policy adumbrated in Part IV of the Constitution embody the concept of a welfare State. The Supreme Court has invoked the basic structure doctrine to clarify the following features of the Constitution—(a) the integrity of the judiciary, judicial review and the separation of powers; (b) Federalism; (c) Secularism; and (e) Equality.

But at the same time, the secular Constitution contains provisions for (a) imparting of religious instruction in educational institutions in Article 28(2); (b) establishment of educational institutions by religious minorities in Article 30; (c) propagation of religion in Article 25(1) and by implication the right to convert and reconvert; (d) separate laws by not enforcing a uniform civil code, and did not contain provisions for; (e) imposing a total ban on slaughter of cow; and (f) prohibiting the use of religious institutions for political purposes and the existence of political organizations on religious basis.

Tahir Mahmood, a former chairman of the National Minorities Commission and an ex-member of the Law Commission of India has emphasized the fact that,

> At the time of its adoption, the Constitution neither declared any state religion nor proclaimed India a secular state. By pronouncing "equality before law and equal protection of law" as fundamental rights, it mandated the state not to discriminate between the two "on grounds only of religion, race, caste, sex, place of birth or any of them" in respect of public places and employment or appointment under the state. This was considered enough to make the country 'secular' without a formal declaration to that effect. The principle of undeclared secularism was, however, countered by several community-specific provisions either initially incorporated into the Constitution or inserted by some early amendments to it. In the years to come, the state applied, and the courts interpreted, some general constitutional provisions in ways that benefited particular religious communities. Even after inclusion of the word "secular" in the Preamble, all the religion-based provisions survived and remain in force to this day. The custodians of state authority have also continued to apply, and the courts of justice interpret, the general constitutional provisions the same way as before. Successive governments and the judiciary have consistently believed that these special constitutional provisions, administrative measures and judicial decisions detract nothing from the secularity of the state.[274]

That is the crux of the problem. The state has applied these religion-based provisions because these are part of the Constitution and the Judiciary in their wisdom thought that these provisions are not "unconstitutional". In the fitness of things the Judiciary should have struck down these religion-based provisions as "unconstitutional" at least after the word "secular" was incorporated in the Constitution. Why that did not happen is a million dollar question. But the question is not about the existence of certain religion-specific provisions in our secular Constitution but why those were at all included by the Framers of the Constitution which they thought was "secular" in nature and why these provisions were retained in the Constitution even after declaring the Constitution as "secular" and why the Framers did not include in the Constitution certain provisions which even in pre-independent India had played a direct role in communal polarisation and in vitiating communal atmosphere. The Framers of the Constitution were charged with a sacred duty of framing a Constitution which will no longer put the country into the labyrinth of communalism which engulfed the country resulting in its vivisection on religious basis. They not only failed in their assigned duty but performed their duty in such a lopsided manner as to put the nation on perpetual disharmony and conflict. They were under the hypnotic spell of 'divide and rule' policy which coloured their vision and deeds. They could not rise above the divisive politics of the British-era.

The presence or absence of the provisions mentioned in earlier chapters, amongst others, in our Constitution gave a new lease of life to communalism and communal politics. When the opportunity came to the Indians to wipe out communalism, root and branch, from the body politic, as Anirban Kashyap says, "the Framers prevaricated, vacillated and even evaded the stark naked truth of life. They brought in the concept of secularism, but had not the courage to follow it in letter and spirit. They had the eagerness to make India secular—the word itself was no doubt ideal in the framework of the then Indian society—but not the capability to follow it. They were afraid to take such measures which would actually promote secularism. In the process, an Indian variety of secularism has grown up"[275] which is touted by some as pseudo-secularism. Without going into the debate whether the "*burqa* of secularism" is preferable to "naked communalism",[276] it can be said that when the opportunity came to the Indians to wipe out communalism from the body politic, the Framers compromised on every issue, on principles, with everybody and with secularism as well. The resultant effect is manifest in every nook and corner of the country. In the words of M.R.A. Baig, "India can only have the humanism it deserves. Those who preach humanism but do not practise it, who condemn communalism but do not combat it, who are anxious to reform but afraid to be radical, and who treat the symptoms, but not the disease might tell their rosary every morning. It could run like this—Jabalpur, Jamshedpur, Ranchi, Hazaribagh, Meerut, Bhiwandi, Delhi, Aligarh, Ahmedabad, Poona and on and on and on".[277]

An in-depth introspection of the causes of this malady will lead us to believe that the old Congress-led secularism does not serve our needs any more than religious pride, which is but thinly disguised religious bigotry. All dictionaries define secular as "not pertaining to religion". This definition must prevail literally in all the doings of our State, and not an equally deferential treatment of all religions. One is prone to agree with Syed Shahabuddin's diagnosis that the ideal of secularism had failed in India because of the break between precept and practice.[278] Bharucha rightly says, "It is now widely accepted that there can be no secularism without a process of secularisation, but the challenge of actualising it through concrete social, political, economic and educational measures is an enormous task".[279]

Is it then possible to move beyond today's ghettoising denominational secularism? An editorial in *The Times of India* gives the answer:

> Today's secularism is mostly a coded appeal to minorities, but a genuinely non-denominational secularism would cut across majority—minority divides and have broad appeal to today's aspirational sections as well as young Indians who want to get ahead on the basis of equality and merit.[280]

Communalism in whatever form it might be should have no place in a free secular India. If India is to be strong and viable, then its polity must be secular, its politicians must believe in secularism and its policies must aim at nation-building. Secularism must promote a flat model in which it treats everyone as a citizen of the Indian republic with whom it has a direct relationship, breaking away from the hierarchical colonial model of the state mediating between communities and cultivating intermediary layers who claim to represent a particular group, community or collective. If India is to survive then the "politics of religion and caste" will have to be terminated.

Notes and References

1. Nehru, Jawaharlal, Congress President in 1936, *Indian Annual Register*, 1936-I, p. 272.
2. Majumdar, R.C., *History of the Freedom Movement in India*, Vol. III, 1977, Firma KLM, Calcutta, pp. 468-77.
3. *CAD*, Vol. XI, dated 25-11-49, p. 946.
4. Kashyap, Anirban, *Communalism and Constitution*, 1988, Lancers Books, New Delhi, pp. 79-80.
5. *The Hindu*, January 16, 2012, p. 1.
6. Siddiqui, Shahid, "Believe me, Muslims are not a herd", *The Hindu*, February 6, 2012.
7. Seal, Anil, *The Emergence of Indian Nationalism*, 1968, Cambridge, pp. 299-300.
8. Note, 24 September, 1882, *Muslim Selections*, part 3, p. 337, quoted by Anil Seal, *op. cit.*, p. 306.
9. Khan, Sameera, "Negotiating the Mahalla Exclusion, Identity and Muslim Women in Mumbai", *Economic and Political Weekly*, April 28, 2007, p. 1528.
10. *Ibid.*, p. 1531.
11. Vora, Rajendra and Suhas Palshikar, "Politics of Locality, Community and Marginalization" in Sujata Patel and Jim Masselos (eds.), *Bombay and Mumbai: The City in Transition*, 2003, Oxford University Press, New Delhi.
12. Panikkar, K.N., *An Agenda fir Cultural Action and Other Essays*, 2006, Three Essays Collective, Gurgaon.
13. Varshney, Ashutosh, *Ethnic Conflict and Civic Life: Hindus and Muslims in India,* 2002, Oxford University Press, New Delhi.
14. Khan, Sameera, *op. cit.*, p. 1529.
15. *Ibid.*, p. 1531.

16. Upadhyaya, Surya Prakash, and Robinson, Rowena, "Revisiting Communalism and Fundamentalism in India", *Economic and Political Weekly*, Vol. XLVII, No. 36, September 8, 2013, pp. 41-42.
17. Saxena, Saumya, "Reinvention of Communal Identities and Implications for Democracy, *Economic and Political Weekly*, Vol. XLVIII, No. 34, August 2013, pp. 47-48.
18. Beteille, Andre, "Pluralism and liberalism", *The Hindu*, January 4, 2002, p. 10.
19. Khan, Sameera, *op. cit.*, p. 1529.
20. Osella, Filippo and Osella, Caroline (ed), *Islamic Reform in South Asia*, 2013, Cambridge University Press.
21. *Zaroastrian Cooperative Housing Society Limited* vs. *District Registrar of Cooperative Societies (Urban) decided on April 15, 2005 in Appeal (Civil) 1551 of 2000.*
22. Khan, Sameera, *op. cit.*, p. 1532.
23. *The Times of India*, September 7, 2014, p. 7.
24. Vajpeyi, Ananya, "States of insecurity", *The Telegraph*, September 1, 2013, p. 10.
25. Ansari, Khalid Anis, "Muslims that 'minority politics' left behind", *The Hindu*, June 17, 2013, p. 6.
26. Census of India, 1911, Table XIII, Part B-Musalmans and Appendix to Table XIII Part B-Musalmans, pp. 191-192.
27. De, Amalendu, *Bengali Buddhijibi O Bichchinnatabad (Bengali Intelligential and Separatism),* 1974, Calcutta, Ratna Prakashan, pp. 169-171.
28. *Report of the Backward Classes Commission (Mandal Commission),* First Part, Volumes I and II, 1980, Para 12.18, p. 56
29. *Ibid.,* Para 12.22, p. 56.
30. *Report of the Prime Minister's High Level Committee, November 2006*, Chapter ten, pp. 192-193, para 3.
31. *Bartaman*, January 18, 2013, p. 11.
32. *Census of India, The First Report on Religion Data*, p. xxxii.
33. *The Times of India*, April 25, 2014, p. 1.
34. *The Statesman*, April 3, 2014, p. 3.
35. *The Times of India*, May 7, 2013, p. 11.
36. Beteille, Andre, "Religious identities", *The Telegraph*, January 19, 2011, p. 14.
37. Quoted by Muhammad, Mahmood Bin, "In search of a leader", *The Hindu*, September 7, 1999, p. 25.
38. Ribeiro, Julio, "Lost middle ground", quoted in *Communalism Condemned Gujarat Genocide 2002* (edited), 2002, Kolkata, Progressive Publishers, pp. 46-47.
39. Horowitz, L. Donald, *Ethnic Groups in Conflict*, 2000, University of California Press.
40. Brass, R. Paul, *Theft of an Idol—Text and context in the Representation of Collective Violence*, 1997, Princeton N.J., Princeton University Press.
41. Das, Soumitro, "How relevant is Nehru's vision?" *The Statesman*, September 24, 1997, p. 8.
42. Robinson, Rowena, *Tremors of Violence: Muslim Survivors of Ethnic Strife in Western India*, 2005, Sage, New Delhi.

43. *The Hindu*, July 23, 2013, p. 12.
44. Churiwal, Paramanand, "Muslims' identity crisis", letters to the editor, *Ibid.*, July 30, 1995, p. 12.
45. Hasan, Mushirul, "The Great Akbar of Independence struggle", *The Hindu*, November 8, 2013, p. 6.
46. *The Hindu*, November 9, 2012, p. 4.
47. *Report of the Prime Minister's High Level Committee, November, 2006*, Chapter two, p. 11, para 2.
48. *Ibid.*, p. 15, para 4.
49. Mitra, Dola, 'Turning to God", *The Telegraph*, June 4, 2006, p. 9.
50. *The Statesman*, December 14, 2013, p. 1.
51. *Ibid.*, December 10, 2012, p. 3.
52. *The Hindu*, January 14, 2012, p. 3 and January 25, 2012, p. 1.
53. *The Times of India*, January 25, 2012, p. 13.
54. *Ibid.*
55. Swami, Praveen, "Salman Rushdie and India's new theocracy", *The Hindu*, January 21, 2013, p. 6.
56. Khan, Sameera, *op. cit.*, p. 1530.
57. *The Times of India*, February 26, 2014, p. 1.
58. Hess, B., Markson, E. and Stein, P., *Sociology*, 1991, New York, Macmillan, p. 408.
59. Hiro, D., *Holy Wars: The Rise of Islamic Fundamentalism*, 1989, New York, Routledge, pp. 3-20.
60. Mustapha, Nasser, "The Influence of Indian Islam on Fundamentalist Trends in Trinidad and Tobago", in *The Indian Diaspora: Dynamics of Migration*, (ed.) N. Jayram, 2004, Sage Publications, pp. 130-131.
61. Kalanthai Peer Mohammed, Tamil writer, commentator and observer of Muslim politics in an interview, *The Hindu*, August 5, 2013, p. 7.
62. *Ibid.*
63. Raychaudhuri, Tapan, "Shadows of the *Swastika*: Historical Perspectives on the Politics of Hindu Communalism". *Modern Asian Studies*, 2000, 34(2), p. 260.
64. *The Hindu*, March 25, 2014, p. 2.
65. Swami, Praveen, "Second sunrise of Indian *jihad*", *The Hindu*, April 1, 2014, p. 6.
66. *Ibid.*
67. Iyer, V.R. Krishna, "Bridging the communal divide", *The Hindu*, February 11, 2003, p. 17.
68. *The Times of India*, September 24, 2006, p. 5.
69. *The Hindu*, October 6, 2009, p. 4.
70. *Ibid.*, April 21, 2010, p. 11.
71. *The Telegraph*, July 29, 2012, p. 4.
72. *The Times of India*, May 16, 2013, p. 7.
73. *The Statesman*, October 1, 2013, p. 2.
74. Khan, Maulana Wahiduddin, "A Religion of Peace", *The Times of India*, December 12, 2008, p. 16.
75. Smith, R.V., *The Sunday Statesman*, July 7, 2013, p. 2.

76. Dr. Babasaheb Ambedkar, Writings and Speeches, Vol 8, "*Pakistan or The Partition of India*", 1990, Government of Maharashtra, pp. 294-95.
77. *The Hindu*, January 29, 2009, p. 11.
78. *The Hindustan Times*, February 23, 2009, p. 1.
79. *The Times of India*, February 24, 2009, p. 14.
80. *Ibid.*, September 18, 2013, p. 15.
81. Bhaumik, Saba Naqvi, "Islam", *Outlook*, June 16, 2008, p. 14.
82. *Ibid.*
83. *The Telegraph*, November 4, 2008, p. 4.
84. *The Times of India*, November 4, 2009, p. 6.
85. *The Hindu*, April 7, 2010, p. 3.
86. *The Telegraph*, March 3, 2010, p. 2.
87. *The Times of India*, April 1, 2010, p. 15.
88. *The Statesman*, March 9, 2014, p. 7.
89. *The Times of India*, April 22, 2014, p. 5.
90. Bhaumik, Subir, "Counting on trust", *The Telegraph*, April 26, 2014, p. 12.
91. *The Times of India*, January 3, 2014, p. 14.
92. Aiyar, Pallavi, "The Pakistaniation of Indonesia", *The Hindu*, June 15, 2013, p. 7.
93. Suri, Kavita, "By fair means or foul", *The Statesman*, January 5, 2006, p. 7.
94. *The Hindu*, March 16, 2015, p. 10.
95. *Ibid.*, March 10, 2014, p. 5.
96. *Ibid.*, January 8, 2014, p. 2.
97. Naidu, Ratna, "Whither Secularism: Is It a Problem of Definition?", *Economic and Political Weekly*, Vol. xlviii no. 3, January 19, 2013, p. 59.
98. *The Times of India*, January 2, 2014, p. 11.
99. Naig, Udhav, "Terror, Islam and the liberal-Left response", *The Hindu*, March 17, 2015, p. 7.
100. *The Times of India*, December 23, 2014, p. 6.
101. Suroor, Hasan, "Towards the birth of a 'new' Islam?" *The Hindu*, March 23, 2015, p. 7.
102. *The Statesman*, July 12, 2013, p. 1.
103. *The Hindu*, July 15, 2013, p. 1.
104. *Constituent Assembly of India (Legislative Assembly) Debates*, Vol. IV, dated 2-4-48, p. 3151.
105. *Ibid.*, p. 3121.
106. *CAD*, Vol. VII, dated 7-12-48, p. 890.
107. Nehru, *Ibid.*, dated 8-11-48, p. 323.
108. Pant, Pandit Gobind Ballabh, *CAD*, Vol. V, dated 27-8-47, p. 244.
109. Mustafa, Faizan, "Communal Virus", *The Statesman*, November 15, 2004, p. 8.
110. *S.R. Bommai* vs. *Union of India*, AIR 1994 SC 1918.
111. Kashyap, Anirban, *Communalism and Constitution*, 1988, *op. cit.*, pp. 175-76.
112. Tyagi, Mahabir, *CAD*, Vol. VII, dated 9-11-48, p. 362.
113. Renuka Ray, *CAD*, Vol. VII, dated 7-12-48, p. 878.
114. Dr. Tapan Roychoudhuri, *The Sunday Statesman*, April 12, 1992.

115. Sarvapalli, Gopal, *Jawaharlal Nehru—A Biography*, Volume III, Delhi, Oxford University Press, p. 173.
116. *CAD*, Vol. VII dated 9-11-48, p. 348, pp. 361-2, p. 365.
117. Kashyap, Anirban, *Communalism and Constitution, op cit.*, p. 176.
118. Nariman, F.S., "Secular Norms-I", *The Statesman*, January 15, 1996, p. 10.
119. *The Hindu*, January 19, 2012, p. 10.
120. *The Telegraph*, April 5, 2014, p. 6.
121. Hafeez, Parwez, "The dilemma before the Muslim voters", *The Telegraph*, April 25, 1991, p. 6.
122. Punj, Balbir, "Results from the Lab", *Outlook*, December 30, 2002, p. 14.
123. *The Telegraph*, April 3, 2009, p. 4.
124. *Ibid.*, November 21, 2013, p. 4.
125. *Ibid.*, December 31, 2013, p. 8.
126. Editorial titled "Message from Deoband", *The Statesman*, April 14, 2014, p. 6.
127. *The Times of India*, April 24, 2014, p. 9.
128. Editorial titled "Message from Deoband", *The Statesman*, April 14, 2014, p. 6.
129. Gupta, Shekhar, "The Bhindrawala effect", *The Indian Express*, March 16, 2002.
130. Hafeez, Parwez, "The dilemma before the Muslim voters", *The Telegraph*, April 25, 1991, p. 6.
131. *Ei Samay*, April 17, 2014, p. 2.
132. Sambrani, Shreekant, "Gujarat's Burning Train: India's Inferno?" *Economic and Political Weekly*, April 6, 2002, p. 1310.
133. Jerath, Arati R., "Binocular Disorder", *Outlook*, December 24, 2012, p. 16.
134. Feagin, Joe R., *Racial and Ethnic Relations*, 1984, (2nd edition), Prentice-Hall, p. 10.
135. Wirth, Louis, "The Problem of Minority Groups.", in Ralph Linton (ed.), *The Science of Man in the World Crisis*,1945, New York, Columbia University Press, p. 347.
136. *CAD*, Vol. VII, dated 4-11-48, p. 39.
137. *Ibid.*, Vol. IX; dated 23-11-49, p. 853.
138. *Ibid.*, Vol. VII dated 4-11-48, p. 46.
139. *Ibid.*, Vol. V dated 28-8-47, p. 277.
140. *Ibid.*, Vol. V, dated 27-8-47, p. 223.
141. *Ibid.*, p. 226.
142. *Ibid.*, dated 28-8-47, p. 271.
143. Rao, B. Shiva (ed.) *Framing of India's Constitution*, Vol. IV, 1966-1968, New Delhi, The Indian Institute of Public Administration, p. 598.
144. Mohamed Ismail Sahib, *CAD*, Vol. VIII, dated 25-5-49, p. 278.
145. *Ibid.*, Vol. VIII, dated 25-5-49, p. 283.
146. *Ibid.*, p. 296.
147. *Ibid.*, dated 26-5-49, p. 334.
148. *Ibid.*, p. 329.
149. Kaufman, Stuart J., "Ethnicity as a generator of conflict", In *Routledge Handbook of Ethnic Conflict* edited by Karl Cordell and Stefan Wolff, 2011, New York, Routledge, p. 100.

150. Chattopadhyaya, Basudeb, Introduction, *Communalism Condemned Gujarat Genocide 2002* (edited), 2002, Kolkata, Progressive Publishers, p. ix.
151. *The Times of India*, February 26, 2014, p. 1.
152. *CAD*, Vol. VIII, dated 26-5-49, p. 351.
153. Ahmad, Tufail, "Defining Minority", *The Statesman*, November 16, 1995, p. 6.
154. *The Hindu*, October 21, 2003, p. 11.
155. *Ibid.,* January 23, 2012, p. 3.
156. *Ibid.,* February 19, 2013, p. 8.
157. Hussain, Muzaffar, *Insight into Minoritism*, 2004, New Delhi, India First Foundation, pp. 41-42.
158. 2002 (8) SCC 481.
159. Nariman, F.S., "Minorities at the Crossroads", *Economic and Political Weekly,* Vol. XLIX, No. 46, November 15, 2014, p. 41.
160. *Patroni* vs. *Kesavan A. 1965 Ker. 75.*
161. *The Hindu*, January 10, 1997, p. 15.
162. *Bali Patil & another* vs. *Union of India & others Appeal (civil)* 4730 of 1999 decided on August 8, 2005.
163. *The Statesman*, November 19, 1999, p. 8.
164. *The Times of India*, March 3, 1998. p. 11.
165. *The Statesman*, April 2, 1999, p. 2.
166. *The Hindu*, December 18, 2007, p. 5.
167. *Ibid.,* November 19, 2010, p. 1.
168. *Ibid.,* April 6, 2007, p. 17.
169. Rashkow, Ezra D., "The Jain Endangerment: Discourse", *Economic and Political Weekly*, Vol. XLVII, no. 49, December 7, 2013, pp. 25-26.
170. *The Times of India*, January 21, 2014, p. 1.
171. *http://ncmei.gov.in/writereaddata/filelinks/cbb33e58_MSC-2013.pdf*
172. *The Telegraph*, 13 December, 1997, p. 7.
173. *The Hindu*, July 26, 2012, p. 3.
174. *Ibid.*, July 24, 2012, p. 9.
175. *Maaud Alam* vs. *Police Commissioner,* AIR 1956 Cal 9.
176. *Church of God (Full Gospel) in India* vs. *K.K.R.M.C. Welfare Association,* AIR 2000 SC 2773.
177. *The Times of India,* September 3, 2013, p. 1.
178. *Ibid.,* October 6, 2012, p. 7.
179. *Bartaman*, August 25, 2012, p. 14.
180. *Report of the Prime Minister's High Level Committee, November, 2006,* Chapter 12, pp. 237-254.
181. *The Hindu*, November 6, 2006, p. 12.
182. *Ibid.,* December 10, 2006, p. 1.
183. *Ibid.*
184. Mukherjee, Subrata, "Basis of nationhood", *The Statesman*, April 22, 2013, p. 6.
185. *The Hindu*, January 14, 2013, p. 8.
186. *Outlook*, December 4, 2006, pp. 36-38.
187. *Dainik Statesman*, February 15, 2014, p. 3.

189. *The Hindu*, March 13, 2015, p. 2.
190. Kaul, Sumer, "Indian identity", *The Statesman*, December 9, 2006, p. 6.
191. Alam, Tanweer, "Top Myths About Muslims", *The Times of India*, March 21, 2014, p. 14.
192. *Bali Patil & another* vs. *Union of India & others Appeal (civil)* 4730 of 1999 decided on August 8, 2005.
193. *CAD*, Vol. VIII, dated 26-5-49, p. 330.
194. *Dainik Statesman*, February 27, 2014, p. 1.
195. *The Times of India*, April 27, 2014, p. 6.
196. *The Statesman*, July 3, 1999, p. 1.
197. Desai, R.R., "Congress(I), Communist Parties and Communalism", *Economic and Political Weekly*, 19(20), 1984, p. 1196.
198. Upadhyaya, Surya Prakash, and Robinson, Rowena, "Revisiting Communalism and Fundamentalism in India", *Economic and Political Weekly*, Vol. XLVII, No. 36, September 8, 20123, p. 43.
199. Sikand, Y., "Countering Fundamentalism Beyond the Ban on SIMI", *Economic and Political Weekly*, 2001, 36(40), p. 3804.
200. Punj, Balbir, "Results from the Lab", *Outlook*, December 30, 2002, p. 14.
201. *The Telegraph*, November 1, 2006, p. 8.
202. Nehru, Jawaharlal, *An Autobiography*, 1962, New Delhi, Allied Publishers, p. 136.
203. *Ibid.*, p. 137.
204. Kishwar, Nadhu Purnima, "On Secular Fatwas', *The Times of India*, April 22, 2011, p. 18.
205. Ahmed, Firoz Bakht, "The Clutches of communal frenzy", *The Sunday Statesman*, 8th Day, September 15, 2013, p. 1.
206. *The Hindu*, June 21, 2010, p. 22.
207. Quoted by Ram Swarup, "Indian Secularism X-rayed", *The Indian Express*, January 2, 1991.
208. Reproduced in *The Organiser*, January 18, 1987.
209. *The Telegraph*, May 7, 2013, p. 6.
210. *CAD*, Vol. VII dated 4-11-48, p. 46.
211. Puri, Rajinder, "Message from Deoband", *The Statesman*, February 1, 2011, p. 7.
212. Mehta, Pratap Bhanu, "The Dilemmas of Muslim Politics-II", *The Hindu*, May 18, 2002, p. 10.
213. Editorial entitled "Republican Minorities" in *The Statesman*, June 15, 1995, p. 6.
214. Suroor, Hasan, "Mumbai attacks and the Muslim question", *The Hindu*, December 2, 2008, p. 9.
215. *CAD*, Vol. VII, dated 3-12-48, p. 818.
216. *Ibid.*, dated 7-12-48, p. 863.
217. *Ibid.*, dated 6-12-48, p. 823.
218. *Ibid.*, dated 3-12-48, p. 815.
219. *Ibid.*, dated 8-12-48, p. 899.
220. *Ibid.*, dated 6-11-48, p. 289.
221. *Ibid.*, dated 9-11-48, p. 362.

222. *Ibid.*, dated 2-12-48, p. 757.
223. *Ibid.*, dated 9-11-48, p. 348.
224. *Ibid.*, dated 6-12-48, p. 834.
225. *Ibid.*, dated 9-11-48, p. 382.
226. *Ibid.*, dated 23-11-48, p. 544.
227. *Ibid.*, dated 23-11-48, p. 540.
228. *Ibid.*, dated 7-12-48, p. 867.
229. *Ibid.*, dated 7-12-48, p. 879.
230. *Ibid.*, dated 6-12-48, p. 831.
231. *Ibid.*, dated 7-12-48, p. 866.
232. *Ibid.*, dated 7-12-48, p. 882.
233. *Ibid.*, dated 23-11-48, p. 546.
234. *Ibid.*, dated 6-12-48, p. 825.
235. *Ibid.*, dated 6-12-48, p. 823.
236. *CAD*, Vol. IX, dated 12-8-49, p. 401.
237. Arun Chandra Guha, *Ibid.*, Vol. XI, dated 21-11-49, p. 727.
238. Das, Soumitro, "How relevant is Nehru's vision?" *The Statesman*, September 24, 1997, p. 8.
239. Ajit Prasad Jain, *CAD*, Vol. XI, dated 22-11-49, p. 805.
240. M. Ananthasayanam Ayangar, *Ibid.*, dated 18-11-49, p. 662.
241. Kshyap, Anirban, *Communalism and Constitution*, *op. cit.*, p. 241.
242. Ahmad, Imtiaz, "Secularism and Communalism", *Economic and Political Weekly*, 1969, No. 4 (28/30), p. 1137.
243. Dixit, Prabha, "Secularism and Communalism: A Comment", *Economic and Political Weekly*, 1969, No. 4(44), p. 1752.
244. Shakir, Moin, "Religion and Politics: Role of Islam in Modern India", *Economic and Political Weekly*, 1979, No. 14 (7/8), p. 471.
245. Editorial in *The Hindu* entitled "Plying the communal card", January 19, 2002, p. 6.
246. *The Sunday Statesman*, February 17, 2013, p. 4.
247. *The Sunday Times of India*, November 23, 2008, p. 11.
248. Bhaumik, Saba Naqvi, "*Vande Mataram*", *Outlook*, September 11, 2006, p. 46.
249. *The Times of India*, July 31, 2011, p. 9.
250. *The Statesman*, September 25, 2014, p. 4.
251. Sambrani, Shreekant, "Gujarat's Burning Train: India's Inferno?" *Economic and Political Weekly*, April 6, 2002, p. 1310.
252. *The Telegraph*, May 23, 2013, p. 4.
253. *Ibid.*, December 21, 2006, p. 8.
254. *The Times of India*, October 18, 2013, p. 12.
255. Dang, Satyapal, "India cannot be part theocratic and part secular", *The Telegraph*, May 6, 1988, p. 6.
256. Basu, Arnab and Sibasish, Samyak, "Inherently flawed legislation", *The Statesman*, January 23, 2014, p. 16.
257. Nandy, Asish, "Closing the Debate on Secularism: A Personal Statement", in Anuradha Dimgwaneu Needham and Rajeswari Sunder Rajan (ed.) *The Crisis of Secularism in India*, Durham, Duke University Press, pp. 107-117.
258. *The Hindu*, November 30, 2013, p. 9.

259. *Ibid.,* November 5, 2013, p. 7.
260. Subramaniam, K., "Securing Secularism", *The Times of India*, Mach 26, 2002, p. 6.
261. Dasgupta, Swapan, Secular nemesis, *India Today*, April 8, 2002.
262. *The Hindu*, February 3, 2012, p. 16.
263. *Ibid.*
264. *The Hindu*, August 5, 2013, p. 7.
265. Open letter in the *Economic and Political Weekly*, Vol. xlviii no. 34, dated August 24, 2013, p. 5.
266. *The Telegraph*, April 26, 2011, p. 5.
267. *The Times of India*, February 12, 2014, p. 10.
268. Kashyap, Anirban, Communalism and Constitution, *op. cit.,* p. 236.
269. Luthra. P.N., "Towards Ayodhya", *The Statesman*, March 16, 1993, p. 8.
270. Sambrani, Shreekant, *op. cit.*, p. 1309.
271. Swami, Praveen, "Salman Rushdie & India's new theocracy", *The Hindu*, January 21, 2012, p. 6.
272. Madhok, Bal Raj, "Secular State?", *The Statesman*, September 2,1993, p. 8.
273. Kashyap, Anirban, *Communalism and Constitution*, *op. cit.*, pp. 236-238.
274. Mohamood, Tahir, "Appeasing the Majority?" *The Times of India*, July 18, 2013, p. 14.
275. Kashyap, Anirban Communalism and Constitution, *op. cit.*, p. 242.
276. *The Hindu*, July 17, 2013, p. 4.
277. Baig, M.R.A., *The Muslim Dilemma, in India*, 1974, Delhi, Vikas Publishing House, p. 98.
278. *The Statesman*, April 24, 1989, p. 3.
279. Bharucha, Rustom, "In the Name of the Secular: Cultural Interactions and Interventions", *Economic and Political Weekly,* No. 29(45/46), 1994, p. 2925.
280. Editorial in *The Times of India* titled "Secular Alternative", April 10, 2014, p. 14.

Bibliography

Published Government Documents

Constituent Assembly Debates, 1946-50, Vol. I to Vol. XII.

Census of India, 1911, Vol. I, India, Report by E.A., Gait Calcutta, Superintendent, Government Printing Press, (reprinted by Usha, Delhi, 1987).

Census of India, 1931, Vol. I, India, Report (with complete survey of tribal life and system) by J.H. Hutton, (reprinted by Gian Publishing House, Delhi, 1989).

Census of India 2001, The First Report on Religion Data.

Report of the Christian Missionary Activities Enquiry Committee, Madhya Pradesh, Vol. I, 1956, Government of Madhya Pradesh.

Report of the Backward Classes Commission (Mandal Commission), First Part, Volumes I and II, 1980.

Report of the National Commission on Cattle, 2002, Department of Animal Husbandry and Dairying, Ministry of Agriculture, Government of India.

Report of the Prime Minister's High Level Committee, November, 2006.

Rao, B. Shiva (ed.), *Framing of India's Constitution,* Vol. I to Vol. V, 1966-1968, New Delhi, The Indian Institute of Public Administration.

Books

Abrar, Dr. Rahat and Ishaque, Dr. M. Qamar, 2002, "Introduction," in *Directory of Muslim Educational Institutions in India,* New Delhi, Institute of Objective Studies.

Agarwal, R.C., 1988, *Constitutional Development and National Movement of India*, New Delhi, S. Chand & Company (Pvt.) Ltd.

Ahmad, A., 1964, *Studies in Islamic Culture in the Indian Environment*, London, Claredon Press.

Dr. Babasaheb Ambedkar Writings and Speeches, 1990, Vol. 8, "*Pakistan or the Partition of India*", Government of Maharashtra.

Amin, Shahid, 2005, "Representing the Musalman: Then and Now, Now and Then", in Shail Mayaram, MSS Pandian and Ajay Skaria (ed.), *Muslims, Dalits and Fabrications of History*, Subaltern Studies, Vol. 12, New Delhi, Permanent Black and Ravi Dayal.

Anjum, Dr. Ghulam Yahya, 2001, *Nisab-e Taleem*, Jamia Hamdard, New Delhi.

Armstrong, S.J. and Botzler, R.G., (ed.), 2003, *The Animal Ethics Reader,* London, Routledge.

Baig, M.R.A., 1974, *The Muslim Dilemma in India*, Delhi, Vikas Publishing House.

Bamford, P.C., 1974, *Histories of the Non-Co-operation and Khilafat Movements*, Delhi, Deep Publications (originally published by the Government of India Press in 1925).

Banu, Zenab, 1989, *Politics of Communalism*, Bombay, Popular Prakashan.

Basu, D.D., 1988, *Shorter Constitution of India,* New Delhi, Prentice Hall of India.

Bayly, Susan, Saints, 1992, *Goddesses and Kings: Muslims and Christians in South Indian Society 1700-1900*, Cambridge University Press, pp. 79-80.

Bhagbati, A.C., 1999, "Social Formation in North East India" in *People of India, Bio-cultural Dimensions* (ed.), S.B. Roy and A.K. Guha, New Delhi, Inter-India Publications.

Bhatt, S.C., 1998, *The Great Divide: Muslim Separatism and Partition*, Gyan Books.

Biswas, Kalipada, 1966, *Yukta Banglar shesh adhaya* [the last phase of United Bengal], Calcutta, Orient Book Company.

Bose, Subhas Chandra, *The Indian Struggle (1920-1942)*, 2005, Kolkata, Revised second edition, Natyachinta Foundation.

Brass, R. Paul, 1997, *Theft of an Idol—Text and context in the Representation of Collective Violence*, Princeton N.J., Princeton University Press.

Browne, Judith M., 1972, *Gandhi's Rise to Powers: Indian Politics, 1915-1922*, London, Cambridge University Press.

Chagla, M.C., 1974, *Roses in December: An Autobiography*, Bombay, Bharatiya Vidya Bhavan.

Chakraborty, Amalendu Kishore, 2004, *The Quest for Identity*, Kolkata, The Asiatic Society.

Chandra, Bipan, 1984, *Communalism in Modern India*, New Delhi, Vikas.

Chandra, Bipan, Mukherjee Mridula, Mukherjee Aditya, Panikkar, K.N., and Mahajan, Sucheta, 1989, *India's Struggle for Independence*, 1989, New Delhi, Penguin Books.

Chatterjee, A., 1958. *Constitutional Development of India, 1937-47,* Calcutta, Firma K.L. Mukhopadhyay.

Chatterji, Prashanto K., 1975, *The Making of India Policy 1853-65*, Calcutta, Orient Longman Limited.

Chatterjee, Sarajit Kumar, 1996, *The Scheduled Castes in India*, Vol. I, New Delhi, Gyan Publishing House.

Chatterji, Suniti Kumar, Preface, 1983, *The Cultural Heritage of India*, Volume IV, reprint, Calcutta, The Ramakrishna Mission Institute of Culture.

Chattopadhyaya, B.D., 2005, *Studying Early India: Archaeology, Texts and Historical Issues*, Delhi, Permanent Black.

Chattopadhyaya, Basudeb, 2002, Introduction, *Communalism Condemned Gujarat Genocide* (edited), Kolkata, Progressive Publishers.

Cordell, Karl and Wolff, Stefan, (ed.), 2011, *Routledge Handbook of Ethnic Conflict*, New York, Routledge.

Dale, Stephen Frederic, 1980, *The Mappilas of Malabar, 1498-1922: Islamic Society in the South Asian Frontier*, Oxford University Press.

Das, Arvind, N., 1994, *India Invented: A Nation in the Making*, New Delhi, Manohar.

Das, Durga, 1974, *India From Curzon to Nehru and After*, Calcutta, Rupa & Co.

De, Amalendu, 1974, *Bengali Buddhijibi O Bichchinnatabad (Bengali Intelligentia and Separatism)*, 1974, Calcutta, Ratna Prakashan, pp. 169-171.

Elwin, V., 1944, *The Foreign Missionary Danger*, 1944.

Embree, A., 1992, *Utopias in Conflict: Religion and Nationalism in Modern India*, Delhi, Oxford University Press.

Evaluation Report on Madrassa Education Scheme, 2003, Hamdard Education Society, New Delhi.

Evans, Walter Bennett, 2013, *The Genesis of the Pakistan Idea*, New Delhi, Oxford University Press.

Feagin, Joe R., 1984, *Racial and Ethnic Relations*, 1984, Prentice-Hall.

Fox, M.W., 2003, "India's Sacred Cow: Her Plight and Future". In *The Animal Ethics Reader* (eds.) S.J. Armstrong and R.G. Botzler, London, Routledge.

Galanter, Marc, 1984, *Competing Equalities*, Delhi, Oxford University Press.

Gandhi, M.K., 1941, *Christian Missions and their Plan in India*, Ahmedabad, Navajiban Press.

Goswami, B.B., 1979, *The Mizo Unrest*, Jaipur, Aalekh Publishers.

Guha, Ranajit, (ed.), 1989, In *Subaltern Studies VI: Writings on South Asian History and Society*, Delhi, Oxford University Press.

Harklots, G.A., 1921, *Islam in India*, London, Kurzon Press.

Hasan, Mushirul, 1979, *Nationalism and Communal Violence in India*, Delhi, Manohar.

Hess, B., Markson, E. and Stein, P., 1991, *Sociology*, New York, Macmillan.

Hind Swaraj or the Home Rule, 1938, Ahmedabad, Navajiban Publishing House.

Hiro, D., 1989, *Holy Wars: The Rise of Islamic Fundamentalism*, New York, Routledge.

Horowitz, L. Donald, 2000, *Ethnic Groups in Conflict*, University of California Press.

Husain Mahdi, 1953, *The Rebla of Ibn Battuta* (India, Maldive Islands and Ceylon) (translation), Baroda.

Hussain, Muzaffar, 2004, *Insight into Minoriytism*, New Delhi, India First Foundation.

Jalal, Ayesha, 1985, *The Sole Spokesman: Jinnah, the Muslim League and the Demand for Pakistan*, Cambridge, Cambridge University.

Jha, D.N., 2002, *The Myth of the Holy Cow*, second edition, London, Verso Books.

Joshi, A.P., Srinivas, M.D., Bajaj, J.K., 2003, *Religious Demography of India*, Chennai, Centre for Policy Studies.

Joshi, Sashi and Josh, Bhagwan, 1994, *Struggle for Hegemony in India, 1920-1947*, 1994, Delhi, Sage Publications.

Kakar, Sudhir, *The Colours of Violence: Cultural Identities, Religion and Conflict*, 1996, Chicago, University of Chicago Press.

Kashyap, Anirban, 1988, *Communalism and Constitution*, New Delhi, Lancers Books.

________, 1990, *Disintegration and Constitution*, New Delhi, Lancers Books.

Kaufman, Stuart J., 2011, "Ethnicity as a generator of conflict", In *Routledge Handbook of Ethnic Conflict* edited by Karl Cordell and Stefan Wolff, New York, Routledge.

Khilani, Sunil, 1997, *The Idea of India*, Delhi, Penguin.

Linton, Ralph (ed.), 1945, *The Science of Man in the World Crisis*, New York, Columbia University Press.

Lowe, W.H., *Muntakhabu-t-Tawarikh by Abdu-'L-Qadir Ibn-I-Muluk-Shah Known as Al Badaoni*, translation)

Ludden, David (ed.), 1996, *Contesting the Nation: Religion, Community, and the Politics of Democracy in India*, University of Pennsylvania Press.

Mackenzie, Alexander, 2005, *The North-East Frontier of India* (originally published entitled *History of the Relations of the Government with the Hill Tribes of the North-East Frontier of Bengal in 1884*), New Delhi, Mittal Publications.

Mahmood, Tahir, 1997, *Islamic Law in Indian Courts and since Independence: Fifty Years of Judicial Interpretation,* Delhi, Institute of Objective Studies.

Mahmud Ali, S., 1993, *The Fearful State: Power, People And Internal War in South Asia*, London, Zed.

Majumdar, Dr. R.C., 1977, *History of the Freedom Movement in India*, Vol. III, Calcutta, Firma KLM.

Majumdar, R.C., 1978, *Struggle for Freedom*, 1978, second edition, Bombay, Bharatiya Vidya Bhavan.

Majumdar, R.C., Majumdar A.K., and Ghose, D.K. (ed.), 1965, *British Paramountcy and India, Renaissance*, Part II, Bombay. Bharatiya Vidya Bhavan.

Mill, James, 1826, *The History of British India*, 1826, London. Since then the work has been reprinted several times.

Monier, Williams, 1883, *Religious Thought and Life in India*, London, J. Murray.

Mustapha, Nasser, 2004, "The Influence of Indian Islam on Fundamentalist Trends in Trinidad and Tobago", in *The Indian Diaspora: Dynamics of Migration*, (ed.) N. Jayram, Sage Publications.

Mutua, Makau, 2004, *Facilitating Freedom of Religion or Belief, A Deskbook* Oslo Coalition on Freedom of Religion or Belief.

Mujahid, Sharif al, 1981, *Quaid-I-Azzam Jinnah: Studies in Interpretation*, Karachi, South Asia Books.

Namboodiripad, E.M.S., 1981, *The Mahatma and the Ism*, Calcutta, National Book Agency (P) Ltd.

Nandy, Asish, 2007, "Closing the Debate on Secularism: A Personal Statement", in Anuradha Dingwaney Needham and Rajeswari Sunder Rajan (ed) *The Crisis of Secularism in India*, Durham, Duke University Press.

Naqvi, Mushtaq, 2006, *Partition: The Real Story*, Renaissance Publishing House.

Nehru, Jawarharlal, 1962, *An Autobiography*, New Delhi, Allied Publishers, (first published in 1936 by John Lane, the Bodley Head Limited, London).

Niemeijer, A.C., 1972, *The Khilafat Movement in India 1919–1924*, The Hague, Martinus Nijhoff.

Nikitin, Afanasy, *Voyage Beyond Seas 1466-1472*, translated by Stepan Apresyan, 1985, Moscow.

Nilekani, Nandan, 2008, *Imagining India*, Penguin, Allen Lane.

Osella, Filippo and Osella, Caroline (ed.), 2013, *Islamic Reform in South Asia*, Cambridge University Press.

Padgaonkar, Dileep, 2002, "India Injured", in *Communalism Condemned Gujarat Genocide 2002* (ed.), Kolkata, Progressive Publishers.

Page, D.J.H., 1973, "Prelude to Partition: All India Muslim Politics, 1909-1930, unpublished D.Phil. Thesis, Oxford.

Pandey, G., 1989, "The Colonial Construction of Communalism: British Writings on Banaras in the nineteenth Century", In *Subaltern Studies VI: Writings on South Asian History and Society* (ed.) Ranjit Guha, 1989, Delhi, Oxford University Press, p. 132.

Pandey, Gyanendra, 1990, *The Construction of Communalism in Colonial North India*, Delhi, Oxford University Press.

Panikkar, K.N., 2006, *An Agenda for Cultural Action and Other Essays*, Gurgaon, Three Essays collective.

Patel, Sujata and Masselos, Jim (eds.), 2003, *Bombay and Mumbai: The City in Transition*, New Delhi, Oxford University Press.

Pirzada, S.S., 1986, The Collected Works of Quaid-E-Azam Mohammad Ali Jinnah: 1921–1926, Volume 2, Karachi, East-West.

Price, Major David, 1829, *Memoirs of the Emperor Jehangir written by Himself*, (translation), London, Oriental Translation Committee.

Radhakrishnan, Dr. S., 1926, *The Hindu View of Life*, Oxford University Press.

Raghupathy, V., Mohan, Vasundara (ed.), 2013, *Secularism and Pluralistic. Democracy in India*, New Delhi, Concept Publishing Company Pvt. Ltd.

Rahaman, A., 1983, Foreword to *Aligarh and Jamia fight for national Education System* by S.M. Tonki, New Delhi, People's Publishing House.

Ramachandran, V.G., 1982, *Fundamental Rights and Constitutional Remedies*, Volume II, Lucknow.

Ray, Rajat Kanta, 2003, *The Felt Community*, New Delhi, Oxford University Press.

Razvi, S.A.A. (ed.), 1957, *Freedom Struggle in Uttar Pradesh: Source Material*, Vol. I, Publications Bureau.

Ribeiro, Julio, 2002, "Lost middle ground", in *Communalism Condemned Gujarat Genocide 2002* (edited), Kolkata, Progressive Publishers, pp. 46-47.

Robinson, Rowena, 2005, *Tremors of Violence: Muslim Survivors of Ethnic Strife in Western India*, New Delhi, Sage.

Roy, S.B. and Guha, A.K. (ed.) 1999, *People of India, Bio-cultural Dimensions*, New Delhi, Inter-India Publications.

Sachau, Edward C., (ed.), 1983, *Alberuni's India*, New Delhi.

Salamatullah, Dr., 1990, *Hindustan me Musalman ki Taleem*, Maktaba Jamia, New Delhi.

Samaroo, B., 1988, "Early African and East Indian Muslims in Trinidad and Tobago", paper presented at a conference on Indo-Caribbean History and Culture, University of Warwick, May 1988.

Sarvapalli, Gopal, *Jawaharlal Nehru—A Biography*, Volume III, Delhi, Oxford University Press, p. 173.

Sarvepalli, Gopal, (ed.), *Selected Works of Jawaharlal Nehru*, Vol. 7, New Delhi, Oxford University Press.

Sarkar, Sumit, 1973, *The Swadeshi Movement in Bengal 1903-1908*, New Delhi, Peoples Publishing House.

Sarkar, Sumit, 1983, *Modern India 1885-1947*, New Delhi, Macmillan India.

Seal, Anil, 1968, *The Emergence of Indian Nationalism*, Cambridge, Cambridge University Press.

Shail Mayaram, MSS Pandian and Ajay Skaria (ed.), 2005, *Muslims, Dalits and Fabrications of History*, Subaltern Studies, Vol. 12, New Delhi, Permanent Black.

Sharma, Kumud and Sujaya, C.P. (ed.), 2012, *Towards Equality: Report of the Committee on the Status of Women in India,* New Delhi, Pearson Education in South Asia.

Sikand, Yoginder, 2006, *Bastion of Believers*, Delhi, Penguin.

Srinivas, M.N., 1962, *Caste in Modern India and Other Essays*, Bombay, Asia Publishing House.

Subramanian, Lakshmi, 1996, *Indigenous Capital and Imperial Expansion: Bombay, Surat and the West Coast*, Delhi, Oxford University Press.

Syed Hamid, 1988, "Deeni Madaris aur Asri Uloom," in *Deeni Madaris aur unke masayal*, Seminar papers, Azamgarh. Idara-e Ilmia, Jamiat ul Falah.

Tablot, Cynthia, 1995, "Inscribing the Other, Inscribing the Self: Hindu-Muslim Identities in Pre-Colonial India", *Comparative Studies in Society and History*, Vol. 37.

Tagore, Saumyendranath, 1975, *Rammohun Roy: His Role in Indian Renaissance*, Calcutta, The Asiatic Society.

Tonki, S.M., 1983, *Aligarh and Jamia Fight for National Education System*, New Delhi, People's Publishing House.

Thomas, Abraham Vazhayil, 1974, *Christians in Secular India*, New Jersey, Associated University Press.

Thurston, M., 1989, *Castes and Tribes of Southern India*, Madras, Christian Literature Society.

Titmus, M.T., 1930, *Islam in India and Pakistan*, Madras, Christian Literature Society.

Varshney, Ashutosh, 2002, *Ethnic Conflict and Civic Life: Hindus and Muslims in India,* Oxford University Press, New Delhi.

Vora, Rajendra and Suhas Palshikar, 2003, "Politics of Locality, Community and Marginalization" in Sujata Patel and Jim Masselos (eds.), *Bombay and Mumbai: The City in Transition*, New Delhi, Oxford University Press.

Wirth, Louis, 1945, "The Problem of Minority Groups", in Ralph Linton (ed.), *The Science of Man in the World Crisis*, New York, Columbia University Press.

Yonuo, Asoso, 1974, *The Rising Nagas*, Delhi, Vivek Publishing House.

Zelliot, Eleanor, 1969, *Dr. Ambedkar and the Mahar Movement*, Ph.D. dissertation, 1969, University of Pennsylvania.

Articles

Ahmad, Imtiaz, 1969, "Secularism and Communalism", *Economic and Political Weekly*, No. 4 (28/30), pp. 1137-58.

_______, 1984, "Political Economy of Communalism in Contemporary India", *Economic and Political Weekly*, No, 19 (22/23), pp. 903-06.

Ahmad, Tufail, 1995, "Defining Minority", *The Statesman*, November 16.

Ahmed, Samim, 2008, "Secular dilemma", *The Telegraph*, May 6.

_______, 2008, *Anandabazar Patrika*, April 1.

Akbar, M.J., 2008, "The myth of forced conversion", *The Times of India*, May 25.

Alam, Muzaffar, 2002, "Modernisation of madrasas in India", *The Hindu*, April 23.

Alam, Tanweer, 2014, "Top Myths About Muslims", *The Times of India*, March 14.

Aleaz. K.P., 1999, "The essence of believing", *The Statesman,* February 2.

Anant, Arpita, 2002, "Anti-conversion laws", *The Hindu*, December 17.

Ansari, Khalid Anis, 2013, "Muslims that 'minority politics' left behind", *The Hindu*, June 17.

Aiyar, Pallavi, 2013, "The Pakistanisation of Indonesia", *The Hindu*, June 15.

Bakshi, Rajni, 1984, "Changing Dimensions of Communalism", *Economic and Political Weekly*, 19(51/52), pp. 2152-53.

Basu, Arnab and Sibasish, Samyak, "Inherently flawed legislation", *The Statesman*, January 23, 2014.

Bayly, C.A., 1985, "The Pre-History of Communalism Religious Conflict in India, 1700-1860", *Modern Asian Studies*, 19(2), pp. 192-193.

Beteille, Andre, 2002, "Pluralism and liberalism", *The Hindu,* January 4.

Beteille, Andre, 2011, "Religious identities", *The Telegraph*, January 19.

Bhagat, R.B., 2001, "Census and the Construction of Communalism in India", *Economic and Political Weekly*, November 24, pp. 4352-56.

Bharadwaj, Krishna, 1990, "Economic Development and Commualism: A Note", *Social Scientist*, 18(8/9), pp. 66-70.

Bharucha, Rustom, 1994, "In the Name of the Secular: Cultural Interactions and Interventions", *Economic and Political Weekly,* No. 29(45/46), pp. 2925-34.

Bhaumik, Saba Naqvi, 2001, "Old-school ties", *Outlook*, December 31.

_______, 2004, "Madrasah kids need zero-terror seal", *Outlook*, October 25.

_______, 2006, "*Vande Mataram*", *Outlook*, September 11.

_______, 2008, "Islam", *Outlook*, June 16.

Bhaumik, Subir, 2014, "Counting on trust", *The Telegraph*, April 26.

Chakrabarti, D., 1994, "Modernity and Ethnicity in India", *South Asia*, No. 17, pp. 143-155.

Chhachhi, Amrita *et. al.*, 1993, "Concern on Communalism", *Economic and Political Weekly,* No. 28(17).

Chowdhury, Prasenjit, 2005, "Jinnah's Secularism-I", *The Statesman*, July 11.

Churiwal, Parmanand, 1995, "Muslims' identity crisis", letters to the editor, *The Statesman,* July 30.

Dang, Satyapal, 1988, "India cannot be pat theocratic and part secular", *The Telegraph*, May 6.

Das, Soumitro, 1997, "How relevant is Nehru's vision?" *The Statesman*, September 24.

Dasgupta, Swapan, 2002, Secular nemesis, *India Today*, April 8.

Datar, Abhay, 2012, "The Lucknow Pact of 1916", *Economic and Political Weekly*, vol. xlvii no. 10, March 10, pp. 65-69.

Datta, P.K., 1993, "Dying Hindus: Production of Hindu Communal Common Sense in early Twentieth Century of Bengal", *Economic and Political Weekly*, June 19, pp. 1305-19.

Datta-Ray, Sunanda K., 2003, Beefing it up again, *The Telegraph*, August 30.

Desai, Nishtha, 1996, "Nonsectarian uniform civil code in Goa safeguards women's rights", *The Times of India*, June 28.

Desai, A.R., 1984, "Congress (I), Communist Parties and Communalism", *Economic and Political Weekly*, 19(20), pp. 1196-97.

Dhavan, Rajeev, 2003, "Codifying personal laws", *The Hindu*, August 1.

Dixit, Prabha, 1969, "Secularism and Communalism: A Comment", *Economic and Political Weekly*, No. 4(44), pp. 1751-54.

Dutta, Ratna, 1972, "Social and Economic Compulsions behind Communalism", *Economic and Political Weekly*, No. 7(5/7), pp. 255-57, 261, 263-264.

Engineer, Asghar Ali, 1994, "What is so divine about Muslim Personal Law?" *The Telegraph*, May 12.

_______, 1996, "Un-Islamic triple divorce should be scrapped", *The Times of India*, June 26.

_______, 2000, "Women and personal law in Iran", *The Hindu*, October 19.

Gandhi, Maneka, 2012, "Overcrowded prisons for cows", *The Sunday Statesman*, 8th Day, March 4.

_______, 2012, "When meat isn't murder", *The Sunday Statesman*, 8th Day, June 10.

_______, 2013, "Wake-up call to beef-eaters", *The Sunday Statesman*, December 15.

Gupta, Shekhar, 2002, "The Bhindrawala effect", *The Indian Express*, March 16.

Hafeez, Parwez, 1991, "The dilemma before the Muslim voters", *The Telegraph*, April 25.

Hamid, Saiyid, 1988, "The Court and the Community", *The Times of India*, February 29.

Haider, Syed Najaf, 1988, "AMU Affairs", Letters to the editor, *The Times of India*, March 23.

Hasan, Mushirul, 1980, "Communalism in the Provinces: A Case Study of Bengal and the Punjab 1922-26", *Economic and Political Weekly*, August 16, pp. 1395-1406.

_______, 2003, "The *Madrasahs* in India", *The Hindu*, May 21.

_______, 2013, "The Great Akbar of Independence struggle", *The Hindu*, November 8.

Heehs, Peter, 1997, "Indian Communalism: A Survey of Historical and Social Scientific Approaches", *Journal of South Asian Studies*, No. 20(1), p. 101.

Ilyas, Syed Qasim Tasool. 2005, "Nothing Personal", *The Times of India*, February 4.

Isa, Mohammad, 1994, "*Talaq* for your Constitution", *The Telegraph*, May 22.

Iyer, V.R. Krishna, 1996, *The Hindu*, October, 21.

_______, 2003, "Bridging the communal divide", *The Hindu*, February 11.

_______, 2003, "Unifying personal laws", *The Hindu*, September 6.

Jamal, Arif, 2001, "Clotted Streams", *Outlook*, July 23.

Jayanth, V., 1999, "The role of the Church", *The Hindu*, January 18.

Jerath, Arati R., 2012, "Binocular Disorder", *Outlook*, December 24.

Jit, Inder, 1996, "Common Civil Code", *The Times of India*, July 16.

Kader, S.A., 1995, "*Shariat* and Islamic spirit-I", *The Hindu*, September 13.

Kalanthai Peer Mohamed, 2013, *The Hindu*, August 5.

Kang, Bhavdeep and Bhaumik, Saba Naqvi, 2003, "The Minky Way," *Outlook*, March 10.

Kaul, Sumer, 2006, "Indian identity", *The Statesman*, December 9.

Kharkhate, Deena, 1990, "Congress (I) and Communalism", *Economic and Political Weekly*, No. 25(2).

Khan, Maulana Wahiduddin, 2008, "A Religion of Peace", *The Times of India*, December 12.

Khan, Sameera, 2007, "Negotiating the Mahalla Exclusion, Identity and Muslim Women in Mumbai", *Economic and Political Weekly*, April 28, pp. 1527-1533.

Khan, Arif, Mohammed, 2009, "For A Common Cause", *The Times of India*, August 19.

Kishwar, Nadhu Purnima, 2011, "On Secular Fatwas", *The Times of India*, April 22, 2011.

Kooiman, Dick, 1995, "Communalism and Indian Princely States: A Comparison with British India", *Economic and Political Weekly*, No. 30(34), pp. 2123-33.

Krishna, Gopal, 1985, "Communal Violence in India: A Study of Communal Disturbance on Delhi", *Economic and Political Weekly*, 20(3), pp. 117-131.

Kuppuswami, Alladi, 1999, "Can conversions be bummed", *The Hindu*, January 30.

Kusum, 1996, "A pragmatic approach", *The Hindu Magazine*, July 28.

Lieten, G.K. 1994, "On Caste and Communalism in Uttar Pradesh", *Economic and Political Weekly*, No. 29(14), pp. 777-781.

Luthra, P.N., 1993, "Towards Ayodhya", *The Statesman*, March 16.

Madhok, Bal Raj, 1993, "Secular State?", *The Statesman*, September 2.

Mahmood, Tahir, 2006, "Muslim Personal Law: clearing the cobwebs", *The Hindu*, July 30.

Maitra, Ranjan, 1996, Letters to the editor, *The Statesman*, July 2.

Mazumdar, Jaideep, 2006, "The Bengal Alifate", *Outlook*, January 30.

Mayaram, Shail, 2000, "Recreating the politics of genocide", *The Hindu Sunday Magazine*, December 3.

Mehta, Pratap Bhanu, 2002, "The dilemmas of Muslim Politics—II", *The Hindu*, May 18.

_______, 2002, "Minority institutions and the state", *The Hindu*, August 10.

Mitra, Dola, 2006, "Turning to God", *The Telegraph*, June 4.

Mitta, Manoj, 2015, "Ghar wapsi, but conditions apply", *The Times of India*, January 4.

Mahmood, Tahir, 2013, "Appeasing the Majority?" *The Times of India*, July 18.

Mukherjee, Mihir, 1997, *The Statesman*, June 1.

Muhammad, Mahmood Bin, 1999, "In search of a leader", *The Hindu*, September 7.

Mustafa, Faizan, 2004, "Communal Virus", *The Statesman*, November 15.

_______, 2009, "Religious policing—I", *The Statesman*, June 12.

Naidu, Ratna, 2013, "Whither Secularism: Is it a Problem of Definition?", *Economic and Political Weekly*, Vol. xlviii no. 3, January 19, pp. 53-61.

Naig, Udhav, "Terror, Islam and the Liberal-Left response", *The Hindu*, March 17, 2015.

Narain, Anusha, 2013, "What's behind that glass of milk?" *The Hindu Magazine*, May 5.

Nariman, F.S., 1996, "Secular Norms-I", *The Statesman*, January 15.

_______, 2014, "Minorities at the Crossroads", *Economic and Political Weekly*, Vol. XLIX, No. 46, November 15, pp. 40-45.

Narrain, Arvind and D'Rozario, Clifton, 2008, "The bogey of forced conversions", *The Hindu*, October 26.

Nayar, Kuldip, 2013, "Communalism legitimized", *The Statesman*, January 10.

Oomen, John, 1995, "Politics of Communalism in Kerala", *Economic and Political Weekly*, No. 30(11), pp. 544-47.

Pandey, Geetanjali, 1984, "North Indian Intelligentsia and Hindu-Muslim Question: A Study of Premchand's Writings", *Economic and Political Weekly*, 19(38), pp. 1664-70.

Parel, Anthony, 1969, "The Political symbolism of Cow in India", *Journal of Commonwealth Political Studies*, Vol. VII, No. 3, Leicester University Press, Leicester, November.

Puri, Rajinder, 2011, "Message from Deoband", *The Statesman*, February 1.

Punj, Balbir, 2002, "Results from the Lab", *Outlook*, December 30.

Puniyani, Ram, 2010, "Beef eating: Strangulating history", *The Hindu*, August 14.

Rahman, A. Faizur, 2012, "The continuing tyranny of the triple *talaq*", *The Hindu*, April 4, 2012.

_______, 2012, "Islamic law dies not sanction child marriage", *The Hindu*, June 13.

Rahman, Hossainur, 1991, "The two faces of Islam", *The Statesman*, April 17.

Rahman, Hossainur, 1995, "India's Muslim Problem", *The Sunday Statesman*, July 9.

Raja, Hilda, 2002, "Minority institutions", *The Hindu*, August 27.

Rao, M.N., 2003, "Religious freedom—legal restrictions on conversions", *The Hindu*, July 8.

Rao, Smitha, 2011, "Saffronisation of the Holy Cow: Unearthing Silent Communalism", *Economic and Political Weekly*, Vol. XLVI, no. 15, April 9, pp. 80-87.

Rashkow, Ezra D., "The Jain Endangerment: Discourse", *Economic and Political Weekly*, Vol. XLVII, no. 49, December 7, 2013, pp. 24-27.

Rauf, Taha Abdul, 2011, "Violence Inflated on Muslims: Direct, Cultural and Structural", *Economic and Political Weekly*, Vol. xlvi, no. 23, June 4, pp. 69-76.

Raychaudhuri, Tapan, 2000, "Shadows of the *Swastika*: Historical Perspectives on the Politics of Hindu Communalism". *Modern Asian Studies*, 34(2).

Sambrani, Shreekant, 2002, "Gujarat's Burning Train: India's Inferno?" *Economic and Political Weekly*, April 6, pp. 1305-1310.

Sahaya, S. 1986, *The Statesman*, May 15.

Saxena, Saumya, 2013, "Reinvention of Communal Identities and Implications for Democracy", *Economic and Political Weekly*, Vol. XLVIII, No. 34, August, pp. 47-53.

Sayeed, Bader, 2000, "Need for Codification", *The Hindu*, July 25.

Sayyid, S. and Tyrer, L.D., 2002, "Ancestor worship and the irony of the "Islamic Republic' of Pakistan", *Contemporary South Asia* II (1), p. 63.

Sen, Samir Kumar, 1995, Letters to the editor, *The Statesman*. May 10.

Sen, Rukmini, 2003, "En-gendering justice", *The Statesman*, June 19.

Shakir, Moin, 1979, "Religion and Politics: Role of Islam in Modern India", *Economic and Political Weekly*, No. 14 (7/8), pp. 469-474.

Sikand, Y., 2001, "Countering Fundamentalism Beyond the Ban on SIMI", *Economic and Political Weekly*, 36(40), pp. 3803-04.

Sikander, Mushtaq Ul Haq Ahmad, 2012, "Women in Conflict", *Economic and Political Weekly*, Vol. XLVII, No. 9, March 3, p. 24.

Singh, Kirti, "Towards Achieving Equal Rights in Marriage", *Economic and Political Weekly*, Vol. XLVII, No. 24, June 16, 2012, pp. 17-19.

Sirohi, Seema, 2006, "Counting Sheep", *Outlook*, June 5.

Siddiqui, Shahid, 2012, "Believe me, Muslims are not a herd", *The Hindu*, February 6.

Smith, R.V., 2013, *The Sunday Statesman*, July 7.

Soz, Sifuddin, 1994, "*Shariat* laws and reform", *The Hindu*, July 13.

Subramaniam, K., 2002, "Securing Seculaism", *The Times of India*, March 26.

Subramanian, Narendra, 2008, "Legal Pluralism, Legal Changes and Gender Inequality: Changes in Muslim Family Law in India", *Law and Social Inquiry*, 33(3), pp. 631-672.

Suri, Sanjay, 2005, "ILM by rote", *Outlook*, August 15.

Suroor, Hasan, 2008, "Mumbai attacks and the Muslim question", *The Hindu*, December 2.

________, 2015, "Towards the birth of a 'new' Islam?", *The Hindu*, March 23.

Swarup, Ram, 1991, "Indian secularism X-rayed", *The Indian Express*, January 2.

Swami, Praveen, 2013, "Salman Rushdie and India's new theocracy", *The Hindu*, January 21.

________, 2014, Second sunrise of Indian *jihad*", *The Hindu*, April 1.

Syed, Shahabuddin, 1988, "AMU seems to have developed a siege mentality", *The Times of India*, May 13.

Thampu, Rev. Valson, 1999, "Debate, not now…", *The Hindu*, January 26.

Thapar, Romesh, 1980, "Muslim Communalism", *Economic and Political Weekly*, 15(35), p. 1463.

Thapar, Romila, 1990, "Communalism and the Historical Legacy: Some Facets", 1990, *Social Scientist*, 18(6/7), pp. 4-20.

Thekaekara, Mari Marcel, 2015, "Being Christian in India", *The Hindu*, March 27.

Upadhyaya, Surya Prakash, and Robinson, Rowena, 2012, "Revisiting Communalism and Fundamentalism in India", *Economic and Political Weekly*, Vol. XLVII, No. 36, September 8, pp. 35-57.

Verghese, B.G., 2003, "Who's afraid of a uniform civil code?" *The Hindu*, August 13.

Vajpeyi, Ananya, 2013, "States of insecurity", *The Telegraph*, September 1.

Visvanathan, Shiv, 2014, "Debating the conversion conundrum", *The Hindu*, December 24.

Vyas, Neena, 1988, "Communalist lobby targets AMU admission", *The Statesman*, March 2.

Wantoo, Pran *et al.*, 2002, "Separate Religion from Politics", *Economic and Political Weekly,* No. 37(20).

Wilkinson, Steven, 2002, "Putting Gujarat in Perspective", *Economic and Political Weekly,* No. 38(17). pp. 1579-83.

Yusuf, Syed, 1995, "Code of incivility", *The Telegraph*, August 31.

Web-Sites Consulted

en-wikepedia.org/wiki/gurukul
ops.amu.org/reorient.htm
en.wikipedia.org/wiki/freedom-of-religiom.
middleeast.about.com/od/glossary/g/me071201b.htm
v.education.mapsofindia.com/universities/national commission for minority educational institutions
voice of dharma.org/books/hhce/ch15.htm
Khan, Amir Ullah, Saqib, Mohammad and Anjum, Zafar H, To Kill the Mockingbird, Madarsah System in India: Past, Present, and Future, www.idfresearch.org/ipnservice/pdfs/madarsas.pdf.
www.rediff.com/news/2004/dec/12talaq.htm
www.amaidi.org/pdf/History of Indian Education.pdf
www.merriam-webster.com/dictionary/madrasa
www.bjp.org/images/pdf-2014/full-manifeso-english-07.04.2014.pdf
www.merriam-webster.com/dictionary/madrasa
"Throttling the Madrasha in the name of security", Milli Gazette, New Delhi, http.//www.milligzette.com./archives/01072001/ib.htm
Dr. Fahimuddin, Globalization and Growth of Madrasahs in India, seminar paper,
http://www.bsos.umd.edu/socy/conference/newpapers/uddin.txt
http://www.pakistan.gov.pk/Quaid/politician6.htm
http://ncmei.gov.in/writereaddata/filelinks/c296efcb_Guidelines.pdf
http://ncmei.gov.in/writereaddata/filelinks/cbb33e58_MSC-2013.pdf

Newspapers

The Hindu, March 31, 2015.
_______March 30, 2015.
_______March 29, 2015.
_______March 18, 2015.
_______March 17, 2015.
_______March 16, 2015.
_______March 14, 2015.
_______March 13, 2015.
_______March 10, 2015.
_______March 1, 2015.
_______December 27, 2014.
_______December 23, 2014.
_______December 21, 2014.
_______December 18, 2014.
_______December 17, 2014.
_______December 15, 2014.
_______December 12, 2914.
_______December 7, 2014.

________November 13, 2014.
________ October 6, 2014.
________April 27, 2014.
________March 25, 2014.
________January 2, 2013.
________January 6, 2013.
________January 14, 2013.
________February 19, 2013.
________July 15, 2013.
________July 17, 2013.
________July 23, 2013
________August 5, 2013.
________September 3, 2013.
________November 5, 2013.
________November 30, 2013.
________January 3, 2012.
________January 14, 2012.
________January 16, 2012.
________January 19, 2012.
________January 23, 2012.
________January 25, 2012.
________January 28, 2012.
________February 3, 2012.
________March 30, 2012.
________April 13, 2012.
________July 3, 2012.
________July 24, 2012.
________July 26, 2012.
________November 9, 2012.
________November 22, 2012.
________December 14, 2012.
________February 23, 2011.
________April 19, 2011.
________September 28, 2011.
________October 15, 2011.
________April 7, 2010.
________April 21, 2010.
________June 16, 2010.
________June 21, 2010.
________July 11, 2010.
________July 14, 2010.
________August 6, 2010.
________November 1, 2010, editorial "Divorce in a trice".
________November 19, 2010.

_______January 29, 2009.
_______October 6, 2009.
_______October 13, 2009.
_______October 29, 2008.
_______April 6, 2007.
_______December 18, 2007.
_______January 7, 2006.
_______January 9, 2006, editorial "Religious reservation and AMU".
_______April 27, 2006.
_______November 6, 2006.
_______December 10, 2006.
_______August 5, 2005, editoral "Pakistan's *madrasahs* in perspective".
_______May 22, 2005.
_______December 3, 2005.
_______April 9, 2004.
_______July 14, 2004.
_______April 11, 2003.
_______August 22, 2003.
_______October 21, 2003.
_______January 19, 2002 editorial "Plying the communal card".
_______June 21, 2002.
_______January 10, 1997.
_______January 13, 1995.
_______May 13, 1995.
_______August 6, 1995.
_______November 27, 19.
The Statesman, March 25, 2015.
_______ March 4, 2015.
_______ January 8, 2015.
_______ November 19, 2014.
_______ October 13, 2014.
_______ September 25, 2014.
_______ April 25, 2014.
_______ April 14, 2014, editorial "Message from Deoband".
_______ April 3, 2014.
_______ March 31, 2014.
_______ March 9, 2014.
_______ January 29, 2013.
_______ February 17, 2013.
_______ July 12, 2013.
_______August 26, 2013.
_______ September 15, 2013.
_______ October 11, 2013.
_______ December 14, 2013.

_______ January 24, 2012.
_______ April 13, 2012.
_______ April 19, 2012.
_______ December 10, 2012.
_______May 9, 2002.
_______ August 1, 2011.
_______ August 28, 2001.
_______ April 2, 1999.
_______ July 3, 1999.
_______ November 19, 1999.
_______ October 26, 1997.
_______ June 15, 1995, editorial "Republican Minorities".
_______ April 17, 1994.
_______ February 14, 1993.
_______ February 16, 1993.
_______ July 2, 1993.
_______ April 24, 1989.
The Times of India, April 4, 2015.
_______ March 25, 2015
_______ March 24, 2015.
_______ March 4, 2015.
_______ February 3, 2015.
_______ December 30, 2014.
_______ December 24, 2014.
_______ December 23, 2014.
_______ December 22, 2014.
_______ December 21, 2014.
_______ December 20, 2014.
_______ December 15, 2014 Editorial entitled "Drop it for now".
_______ October 1, 2014.
_______ January 2, 2014.
_______ January 3, 2014.
_______ January 21, 2014.
_______ February 12, 2014.
_______ February 23, 2014.
_______ February 26, 2014.
_______ April 5, 2014.
_______ April 10, 2014 editorial "Secular Alternatives".
_______ April 14, 2014.
_______ April 22, 2014.
_______ April 27, 2014.
_______ July 16, 2014.
_______ September 7, 2014.
_______ September 14, 2014.

_______ September 15, 2014.
_______ May 7, 2013.
_______ May 16, 2013.
_______ August 7, 2013.
_______ September 3, 2013.
_______ September 16, 2013.
_______ September 18, 2013.
_______ October 18, 2013.
_______ January 25, 2012.
_______ February 5, 2012.
_______ February 22, 2012.
_______ October 6, 2012.
_______ December 12, 2012.
_______ February 9, 2011.
_______ July 31, 2011.
_______ November 21, 2011.
_______ February 9, 2010.
_______ April 1, 2010.
_______ February 24, 2009.
_______ November 4, 2009.
_______ October 18, 2008.
_______ November 23, 2008.
_______ January 21, 2007.
_______ September 24, 2006.
_______ June 12, 2005.
_______ January 7, 2001.
_______ March 3, 1998.
The Telegraph, May 1, 2015
_______ March 27, 2015.
_______ March 24, 2015
_______ February 10, 2015
_______ February 20, 2014.
_______ May 7, 2013,
_______ May 23, 2013.
_______ November 21, 2013.
_______ December 31, 2013.
_______ July 29, 2012.
_______ March 17, 2011.
_______ April 26, 2011.
_______ October 17, 2011.
_______ March 3, 2010.
_______ March 25, 2010.
_______ April 8, 2010.
_______ April, 29, 2010.

_______ April 3, 2009.
_______ October 29, 2008.
_______ November 4, 2008.
_______ January 6, 2006.
_______ February 13, 2006.
_______ November 1, 2006.
_______ December 21, 2006.
_______ February 2, 2004.
_______ June 16, 2003.
_______ August 12, 2003.
_______ February 14, 2002.
_______ March 20, 2002.
_______ August 20, 2001, editorial "Married to Sense".
_______ July 13, 2000.
_______ September 16, 2000.
_______ December 13, 1997.
The Hindustan Times, February 23, 2009.
_______, March 12, 2000.
_______, November 7, 1999.
The Indian Express, March 17, 2015.
_______ May 10, 2013.
_______ July 7, 2010.
_______ January 28, 2000.
The Deccan Herald, December, 19, 2009.
Muslim India, October 21, 2001.
Outlook, December 4, 2006.
The Organiser, January 18, 1987.
Bartaman, January 18, 2013.
_______ , August 25, 2012
Dainik Statesman, February 27, 2014.
_______ , March 22, 2013.
_______ , January 8, 2013.
Ei Samay, (Ei Duniya), January 25, 2013
Ei Samay, April 17, 2014.
Sambad Pratidin, July 15, 2012.

List of Case Laws

Abdul Hakeem Qureshi vs. *State of Bihar*, AIR 1961 SC 448.
Acharya Jagdishwaranand Avadhuta etc. vs. *Commissioner of Police*, Calcutta & Anr. (1984) 1 SCR 447.
Andhra Pradesh Christian Medical Association vs. *Government of Andhra Pradesh*, AIR 1986 SC 1490.

Associated Managements of Primary and Secondary Schools in Karnataka vs. *State of Karnataka and Ors.*, 2008 K.L.J 1.

Azeez vs. *Union of India, A.* 1968 SC 662.

Bali Patil & another vs. *Union of India & others Appeal,* (civil) 4730 of 1999 decided on August 8, 2005.

Brahmchari Sidheswar Shai vs. *State of West Bengal,* (1995) 4 SCC 646, AIR 1995 SC 2089.

C.M. Arumugam vs. *S. Rajagopal and others,* (1976) 1 SCC 863.

Church of God (Full Gospel) in India vs. *K.K.R.M.C. Welfare Association*, AIR 2000 SC 2773.

Commissioner, Hindu Religious Endowments, Madras vs. *Sri Lakshmindra Thirtha Swamiar of Sri Shirur Mutt*, (1954) SCR 1005.

D.A.V. College vs. *State of Punjab* (I) A 1971 SC 1731.

D.A.V. College vs. *State of Punjab* (II) A 1971 SC 1737.

Daniel Latifi & others vs. *Union of India*, 2001 SC.

Fazlunbi vs. *Kadhefr Vali*, AIR 1980 SC 1730.

Jordan vs. *Chopra A.*, 1985 SC 945.

Jiwan Khan vs. *Habid*, I.L.R. 14 Lah. 518 [1933].

John Vallamattom vs. *Union of India*, (2003) 6 Supreme Court Cases 611.

Kailash Sonkar vs. *Smt. Maya Devi*, (1984) 2 SCC 91.

Kerala Education Bill, A. 1958 SC 956.

Kothapalli Narasayya vs. *Jammana Jogi*, AIR 1976 SC 937.

Maaud Alam vs. *Police Commissioner,* AIR 1956 Cal 9.

Mittal vs. *Union of India*, A. 1983 SC 1.

Mohammmed Ahmad Khan vs. *Shah Bano Begum*, AIR 1985 SC 945 (p. 954).

Mohd. Hanif Quareshi vs. *State of Bihar*, 1959 SCR 629. (SCR 688); AIR 1958 SC 731.

Mohinder Singh Gill & Another vs. *The Chief Election Commissioner*, AIR 1978 S.C. 851.

Ms Jorden Diengedh vs. *S.S. Chopra*, AIR 1985 SC 934 (p. 940).

N. Ammad vs. *Emjay High School*, (1998) 6 SCC 674.

Noor Saba Khatoon vs. *Mohd. Quasim*, AIR 1997 S.C. 3280.

Pannalal Bansilal Pitti vs. *State of Andhra Pradesh*, AIR 1996 SC 1023; (1996)2 SCC 498.

Patroni vs. *Kesavan*, A. 1965 Ker. 75.

Ram Prasad vs. *State of U.P.*, A. 1961 S.C. 853 (864, 874-76.

Resham Bibi vs. *Khuda Bakhsh*, I.L.R. 19 Lah. 277 [1938].

Rev. Stanislaus vs. *The State of Madhya Pradesh*, AIR 1977 SC 908, 1977 SCR (2) 611.

Rev. Father vs. *State of Bihar*, A 1969 SC 465.

S. Anbalagan vs. *Devarajan and others*, (1984) 2 SCC 112.

S.R. Bommai vs. *Union of India*, AIR 1994 SC 1918.

Sarıa Mudgal vs. *Union of India*, AIR 1995 SC 1531.

S. Raja Gopal, AIR 1969 SC 101.

Seema vs. *Ashwini Kumar*, AIR 2006 S.C. 1158.
St. Xavier's College, Ahmedabad vs. *State of Gujarat*, 1974(1) SCC 717.
St. Stephen's College vs. *University of Delhi*, (1992) SCC 55.
State of Bombay vs. *Education Society*, (1955) 1 SCR 568.
State of Gujarat vs. *Mirzapur Moti Kureshi Kassab Jamat and others*, (2005) 8 Supreme Court Cases 534.
State of Kerala vs. *Mother Provincial*, AIR 1970 SC 2079.
State of W.B. vs. *Ashutosh Lahiri*, (1995) 1 SCC 189.
T.K.V.T.S.S. Medical Educational and Charitable Trust vs. *State of Tamil Nadu*, AIR 2002 Madras 4.
T.M. Pai Foundation vs. *State of Karnataka*, 2002 (8) SCC 481.
Zaroastrian Cooperative Housing Society Limited vs. *Deitrit Registrar of Cooperative Societies (Urban)* decided on April 15, 2005 in Appeal (Civil) 1551 of 2000.

Index